Managing Data Integrity for Finance

Discover practical data quality management strategies for finance analysts and data professionals

Jane Sarah Lat

<packt>

BIRMINGHAM—MUMBAI

Managing Data Integrity for Finance

Group Product Manager: Kaustubh Manglurkar

Publishing Product Manager: Arindam Majumdar

Book Project Manager: Farheen Fathima

Senior Editor: Rohit Singh

Technical Editor: Rahul Limbachiya

Copy Editor: Safis Editing

Proofreader: Safis Editing

Indexer: Manju Arasan

Production Designer: Joshua Misquitta

DevRel Marketing Executive: Nivedita Singh

First published: January 2024

Production reference: 1160124

Published by Packt Publishing Ltd.

Grosvenor House

11 St Paul's Square

Birmingham

B3 1RB, UK.

ISBN 978-1-83763-014-1

www.packtpub.com

Contributors

About the author

Jane Sarah Lat is a finance professional with over 14 years of experience in financial management and analysis for multiple blue-chip multinational organizations. In addition to being a **Certified Management Accountant** (**CMA U.S.**) and having a **Graduate Diploma in Chartered Accounting** (**GradDipCA**), she also holds various technical certifications, including Microsoft Certified Data Analyst Associate and Advanced Proficiency in KNIME Analytics Platform. Over the past few years, she has been sharing her experience and expertise at international conferences to discuss practical strategies on finance, data analysis, and management accounting. She is also the President of the **Institute of Management Accountants** (**IMA**) Australia and New Zealand chapter.

About the reviewers

Joshua Arvin Lat is the **Chief Technology Officer** (**CTO**) of NuWorks Interactive Labs, Inc. He is also a globally recognized AWS Machine Learning Hero. He previously served as the CTO of three Australian-owned companies and also served as the Director for Software Development and Engineering for multiple e-commerce start-ups. He is the author of the books *Machine Learning with Amazon SageMaker Cookbook*, *Machine Learning Engineering on AWS*, and *Building and Automating Penetration Testing Labs in the Cloud*. Due to his proven track record in leading digital transformation within organizations, he has been recognized as one of the prestigious **Orange Boomerang: Digital Leader of the Year 2023** award winners.

Nathania Wijanto is a senior financial analyst with over seven years of experience in financial management and data analytics. She currently works at a large financial services firm in Sydney, combining technical expertise in data analysis and financial acumen to drive actionable insights. Prior to that, she worked at a Big Four firm and an American telecommunications company to streamline reporting processes and improve data quality, as well as drive valuable insights to support financial and operational decisions.

William Bowrey is an experienced Finance Leader with over 30 years of experience working for multinational corporations in financial planning, analysis, reporting, and accounting roles. He currently works for a large customer experience BPO and technology company where business insight has been driven through the implementation of key integrated management reporting systems that marry financial data with operations, sales, and human capital data, producing reliable, actionable, and timely business analysis. Prior to that, he worked in manufacturing and sales support roles, delivering financial analysis for turnkey projects.

Table of Contents

2

Avoiding Common Data Integrity Issues and Challenges in Finance Teams 27

3

Measuring the Impact of Data Integrity Issues 51

Part 2: Pragmatic Solutions to Manage Financial Data Quality and Data Integrity

5

Using Business Intelligence Tools to Fix Data Integrity Issues 119

6

Implementing Best Practices When Using Business Intelligence Tools 171

7

Detecting Fraudulent Transactions Affecting Financial Report Integrity 227

Part 3: Modern Strategies to Manage the Data Integrity of Finance Systems

8

Using Database Locking Techniques for Financial Transaction Integrity 255

9

Using Managed Ledger Databases for Finance Data Integrity 291

10

Using Artificial Intelligence for Finance Data Quality Management 355

Index 405

Other Books You May Enjoy 414

Preface

Maintaining the integrity and reliability of financial data is key to the success of any organization as more companies around the world have been using financial and operational data to make business decisions. If you've been working in the industry for a long time, you probably know by now that data integrity management plays a critical role in helping ensure compliance and avoiding significant financial penalties as well. Unfortunately, there is a big gap when it comes to the proper analysis and management of financial data in organizations globally. In addition to this, companies building their own internal applications and systems are not equipped with the knowledge and experience to guarantee the integrity of the financial data in the databases used to store transactions and generate reports.

I've written this hands-on book to help finance, data, and technical professionals learn various concepts and practical solutions to manage the integrity of the financial data used by various types of organizations. This will be equally useful to those planning to build their own internal systems and processes for handling financial transactions, records, and reports. Whether you are a beginner or a seasoned professional, this book is for you!

Who this book is for

This book is intended for financial analysts, technical leaders, and data analysts interested in learning practical strategies for managing data integrity and data quality using relevant solutions, tools, and strategies.

What this book covers

Chapter 1, Recognizing the Importance of Data Integrity in Finance, gives a quick overview of the concepts relevant to the succeeding chapters in the book.

Chapter 2, Avoiding Common Data Integrity Issues and Challenges in Finance Teams, dives deep into the data integrity issues and challenges faced by different finance teams.

Chapter 3, Measuring the Impact of Data Integrity Issues, teaches you how to develop and generate data quality scorecards using a framework.

Chapter 4, Understanding the Data Integrity Management Capabilities of Business Intelligence Tools, focuses on the common data quality capabilities of business intelligence tools and more popular tools online.

Chapter 5, Using Business Intelligence Tools to Fix Data Integrity Issues, teaches you how to use business intelligence tools in order to solve data integrity issues.

Chapter 6, Implementing Best Practices When Using Business Intelligence Tools, guides you on how to implement various best practices when using business intelligence tools.

Chapter 7, Detecting Fraudulent Transactions Affecting Financial Report Integrity, focuses on processes and strategies to detect fraudulent transactions that affect financial report integrity.

Chapter 8, Using Database Locking Techniques for Financial Transaction Integrity, dives deep into how specific SQL and database techniques prevent transaction data integrity issues.

Chapter 9, Using Managed Ledger Databases for Finance Data Integrity, teaches you how to use managed ledger databases to enforce data integrity in financial systems and applications.

Chapter 10, Using Artificial Intelligence for Finance Data Quality Management, exposes you to artificial intelligence solutions relevant to data quality and data integrity management.

To get the most out of this book

You are expected to have a basic understanding of concepts relating to finance, accounting, and data analysis. Basic knowledge of finance management is not required but will help with grasping the intermediate topics of the book.

Software/hardware covered in the book	**Operating system requirements**
Microsoft Power BI Desktop	Windows (preferred)
Tableau, Tableau Prep Builder, and Tableau Cloud	
Alteryx Designer	

If you are using the digital version of this book, we advise you to type the code yourself or access the code from the book's GitHub repository (a link is available in the next section). Doing so will help you avoid any potential errors related to the copying and pasting of code.

Download the example code files

You can download the example code files for this book from GitHub at `https://github.com/PacktPublishing/Managing-Data-Integrity-for-Finance`. If there's an update to the code, it will be updated in the GitHub repository.

We also have other code bundles from our rich catalog of books and videos available at `https://github.com/PacktPublishing/`. Check them out!

Accessing high-resolution images

The high-resolution version of images used in this book are accessible on GitHub at `https://github.com/PacktPublishing/Managing-Data-Integrity-for-Finance/tree/main/images`.

Conventions used

There are a number of text conventions used throughout this book.

`Code in text`: Indicates code words in text, database table names, folder names, filenames, file extensions, pathnames, dummy URLs, user input, and Twitter handles. Here is an example: "Using the `SELECT FOR UPDATE` statement applies a row-level lock on that row and waits for the previous instance to complete before going to the next."

A block of code is set as follows:

```
INSERT INTO Accounts (AccountID, Balance)
VALUES (1, 100.00);
```

When we wish to draw your attention to a particular part of a code block, the relevant lines or items are set in bold:

```
CREATE TABLE Accounts (
    AccountID int,
    CustomerName varchar(100),
    Balance decimal(10, 2) CHECK (Balance >= 0)
);
```

Bold: Indicates a new term, an important word, or words that you see onscreen. For instance, words in menus or dialog boxes appear in **bold**. Here is an example: "To access the **Data Analysis** GPT, click on **Explore** in the sidebar and select **Data Analysis** from the list of GPTs available."

> **Tips or important notes**
> Appear like this.

Get in touch

Feedback from our readers is always welcome.

General feedback: If you have questions about any aspect of this book, email us at `customercare@packtpub.com` and mention the book title in the subject of your message.

Errata: Although we have taken every care to ensure the accuracy of our content, mistakes do happen. If you have found a mistake in this book, we would be grateful if you would report this to us. Please visit `www.packtpub.com/support/errata` and fill in the form.

Piracy: If you come across any illegal copies of our works in any form on the internet, we would be grateful if you would provide us with the location address or website name. Please contact us at `copyright@packt.com` with a link to the material.

If you are interested in becoming an author: If there is a topic that you have expertise in and you are interested in either writing or contributing to a book, please visit `authors.packtpub.com`.

Share your thoughts

Once you've read *Managing Data Integrity for Finance*, we'd love to hear your thoughts! Scan the QR code below to go straight to the Amazon review page for this book and share your feedback.

`https://packt.link/r/1-837-63014-3`

Your review is important to us and the tech community and will help us make sure we're delivering excellent quality content.

Download a free PDF copy of this book

Thanks for purchasing this book!

Do you like to read on the go but are unable to carry your print books everywhere?

Is your eBook purchase not compatible with the device of your choice?

Don't worry, now with every Packt book you get a DRM-free PDF version of that book at no cost.

Read anywhere, any place, on any device. Search, copy, and paste code from your favorite technical books directly into your application.

The perks don't stop there, you can get exclusive access to discounts, newsletters, and great free content in your inbox daily

Follow these simple steps to get the benefits:

1. Scan the QR code or visit the link below

`https://packt.link/free-ebook/9781837630141`

2. Submit your proof of purchase
3. That's it! We'll send your free PDF and other benefits to your email directly

Part 1: Foundational Concepts for Data Quality and Data Integrity for Finance

This part covers important concepts relating to data quality and data integrity relevant to finance, data, and tech professionals.

This part has the following chapters:

- *Chapter 1, Recognizing the Importance of Data Integrity in Finance*
- *Chapter 2, Avoiding Common Data Integrity Issues and Challenges in Finance Teams*
- *Chapter 3, Measuring the Impact of Data Integrity Issues*

1

Recognizing the Importance of Data Integrity in Finance

Imagine if everyone online suddenly started complaining on social media that their bank savings accounts had unauthorized deductions. This is exactly what happened when thousands of customers of one of the major banks in Southeast Asia discovered that their account balances ended up negative due to duplicate transactions! This led to customers feeling anxious while reports of this data integrity issue went viral online. *How would you feel if your hard-earned money suddenly disappeared overnight due to a data integrity issue?*

Maintaining the integrity, accuracy, and reliability of financial data is key to the success of any organization. Data integrity plays a crucial role in finance, as business owners and decision-makers utilize financial and operational data in making long-term business decisions. If you've been working as a finance professional for a long time, you probably know by now that data integrity management plays a significant role in helping ensure compliance and avoiding significant financial penalties. Understanding the relevant concepts and strategies is the first step for every professional trying to master the art of financial data integrity management. In this introductory chapter, we will examine the importance of data integrity in finance and demystify various key concepts relevant to the succeeding chapters of this book.

That said, we will cover the following:

- Understanding the impact of data integrity issues in finance
- A quick tour of concepts relevant to data integrity management
- Debunking the myths and misconceptions surrounding finance data integrity management

With these in mind, let's get started!

Understanding the impact of data integrity issues in finance

Can you spot the wolf hiding among the sheep in *Figure 1.1*? In finance, the presence of data integrity issues can be compared to a wolf hiding among a flock of sheep. Much like the wolf presents a hidden threat to the sheep, a single data integrity issue can negatively impact the entire financial system's reputation and stability.

Figure 1.1 – A wolf hidden among sheep

The wolf symbolizes the subtle yet potentially catastrophic effects of a data integrity breach. While data integrity issues such as corrupted financial records, inaccurate reporting, and duplicated transactions due to software bugs might initially go unnoticed, they might cause serious financial losses in the long term. That said, the inability to manage data integrity issues properly can lead to a wide range of implications on the integrity of financial transactions and systems. Let's look at these in the following subsections.

Lack of trust in systems

In order to properly make informed business decisions based on reports and numbers, the financial data used for the reports needs to be as accurate as possible. When decision-makers encounter discrepancies in the reports generated using the data stored in an organization's internal systems, they lose their trust and confidence in these systems and databases.

At the same time, when customers encounter inconsistencies in their financial statements, accounts, or transactions, they lose trust in the financial institution's ability to manage their accounts and personal data effectively. This not only damages the institution's reputation, but it also leads to the loss of customers. That said, taking care of the integrity of financial data is essential not only for internal decision-making but also for securing customers' trust as well.

Damage to reputation

If not addressed, data integrity issues can significantly harm an organization's reputation after an incident. Continuing the story where the bank's customers were affected by erroneous duplicate transactions, even if the data integrity issue was resolved after a few days, there were a lot of social media posts from customers wanting to move their accounts to another bank.

> **Important note**
>
> Unfortunately, all it takes is a single incident to negatively impact the trust and confidence customers have in a company that it has worked hard to build over a long time.

Financial impact

Data integrity issues can lead to errors and discrepancies in financial reports and documents that detail an organization's financial performance and position. This in turn could negatively impact the organization's revenue and income.

> **Note**
>
> In *Chapter 2, Avoiding Common Data Integrity Issues and Challenges in Finance Teams*, we will discuss how a transaction coding error in one of the world's biggest banks failed to capture the complete threshold transaction reports from its **intelligent deposit machines** (**IDMs**), which led to significant financial penalties for the company.

Compliance issues with laws and regulations

In addition to what has been discussed already, data integrity issues can lead to compliance issues with global laws and regulations that have been established to counter fraud and improve the reliability of financial reporting. Included in this list are the **Sarbanes-Oxley Act** (**SOX**), **Basel III**, and even the **General Data Protection Regulation** (**GDPR**), all of which mandate strict data management and protection standards to ensure integrity, transparency, and accountability in financial practices. Non-compliance with these regulations can result in significant financial penalties that can negatively impact an organization's financial health and public image.

At this point, you should have a better appreciation of why financial data integrity management is important. In the next section, we'll discuss various concepts relevant to data integrity management to prepare us for the succeeding chapters in this book.

A quick tour of concepts relevant to data integrity management

Making better business decisions relies on having accurate and trustworthy financial data. To help us get started, we'll begin with several foundational concepts, which will be essential in understanding the topics in later chapters.

Levenshtein distance

With companies often dealing with transactions and records from multiple sources, utilizing string similarity algorithms such as the **Levenshtein distance** can help reconcile these datasets by matching similar entries especially when there are issues finding the exact match due to typos or minor discrepancies.

The Levenshtein distance, invented by Vladimir Levenshtein, measures the similarity between two strings by counting the number of edits needed to transform one word into another. It quantifies this similarity in terms of inserting, deleting, or substituting characters required for the conversion. Let us take a simple example between `health` and `wealth`. The computed distance is one (`1`) since it will take a single edit operation to substitute `h` with `w`.

To help demonstrate how this metric works, here are a few more examples:

- From `rat` to `cat`: `1`
- From `book` to `back`: `2`
- From `saturday` to `sunday`: `3`
- From `apple` to `apricot`: `5`

This can be used for identifying and managing data integrity issues, as it can help detect potential duplicate entries as well as any typographic errors in the data. The Levenshtein distance can be used to check whether an account already exists in the database by looking for similar names in the database (with the search results sorted with the smallest computed distance presented first).

> **Note**
>
> For example, searching `Sara Lat` in a database should return results including `Sarah Lat` since the Levenshtein distance is very small (just a one-letter difference). Here, even if there are encoding issues, the algorithm can still identify and match similar entries despite not having an exact match. Imagine the possibilities this opens up for enhancing data retrieval accuracy, particularly in large databases where typos, abbreviations, or minor discrepancies are common! For more information on this topic, feel free to check `https://en.wikipedia.org/wiki/Levenshtein_distance`.

Machine learning

Machine learning (**ML**) is a subset of **artificial intelligence** (**AI**) that enables computers to learn from data and mimic human intelligence. One of the practical applications of machine learning is **anomaly detection**, which involves identifying unusual patterns or outliers in the datasets. This is particularly useful for detecting unusual transactions that may indicate fraudulent activity *automatically*. Now, instead of looking for unusual transactions manually, machine learning-powered automated systems can efficiently process and analyze large amounts of transactional data in real-time to flag discrepancies and issues. *Awesome, right?*

> **Note**
>
> Recently, powerful AI-powered solutions such as **ChatGPT** and **Google Bard** became available for a wide range of applications including data quality management. We'll cover this in more detail in *Chapter 10, Using Artificial Intelligence for Finance Data Quality Management*.

Orphaned records

Orphaned records are database records whose corresponding parent or related record(s) supposedly stored in another database table no longer exists. This situation may occur due to various reasons such as a record being deleted or modified without the related record(s) being updated as well.

Let's say we have two related tables called `Product Details` and `Transactions`, as seen in *Figure 1.2*. We can see that the `Product_ID` column in the `Product Details` table contains additional details about the product (for example, the product name, price, and cost). The `Transactions` table, on the other hand, contains information on when a product was sold and how many were sold.

Product Details table

Product_ID	Product_Name	Product_Price	Product_Cost	Product_Gross_Profit	Product_Gross_Profit_%
151001	Car insurance	995	350	645	64.8%
151002	Life insurance	1,250	475	775	62.0%
151003	Income protection insurance	775	380	395	51.0%
151004	Home contents insurance	295	150	145	49.2%

Transactions table

Transaction ID	Transaction Date	Product_ID	Sales_Manager	Quantity
2020008	08-Jan-20	151001	Shane Hurstley	35
2020009	09-Jan-20	151001	Shane Hurstley	60
2020010	10-Jan-20	151004	Shane Hurstley	20
2020011	11-Jan-20	151002	Shane Hurstley	200
2020012	12-Jan-20	151002	Shane Hurstley	400
2020013	13-Jan-20	151002	Shane Hurstley	250
2020014	14-Jan-20	151002	Shane Hurstley	380
2020015	15-Jan-20	151002	Shane Hurstley	500
2020016	16-Jan-20	151002	Shane Hurstley	200
2020017	17-Jan-20	151002	Shane Hurstley	15
2020018	18-Jan-20	151002	Shane Hurstley	10
2020019	19-Jan-20	151002	Shane Hurstley	12
2020020	20-Jan-20	151002	Shane Hurstley	10
2020021	21-Jan-20	151003	Shane Hurstley	70
2020022	22-Jan-20	151003	Shane Hurstley	80
2020023	23-Jan-20	151003	Shane Hurstley	90
2020024	24-Jan-20	151003	Shane Hurstley	100
2020025	25-Jan-20	151003	Shane Hurstley	120

Figure 1.2 – Related tables being connected by the Product_ID column

Here, the `Product_ID` column serves as the bridge connecting these two tables. We can see that there are four unique `Product_ID` values under the `Transactions` table, which have matching records in the `Product Details` table.

Product Details table

Product_ID	Product_Name	Product_Price	Product_Cost	Product_Gross_Profit	Product_Gross_Profit_%
151001	Car insurance	995	350	645	64.8%
151003	Income protection insurance	775	380	395	51.0%
151004	Home contents insurance	295	150	145	49.2%

Transactions table

Transaction ID	Transaction Date	Product_ID	Sales_Manager	Quantity
2020008	08-Jan-20	151001	Shane Hurstley	35
2020009	09-Jan-20	151001	Shane Hurstley	60
2020010	10-Jan-20	151004	Shane Hurstley	20
2020011	11-Jan-20	151002	Shane Hurstley	200
2020012	12-Jan-20	151002	Shane Hurstley	400
2020013	13-Jan-20	151002	Shane Hurstley	250
2020014	14-Jan-20	151002	Shane Hurstley	380
2020015	15-Jan-20	151002	Shane Hurstley	500
2020016	16-Jan-20	151002	Shane Hurstley	200
2020017	17-Jan-20	151002	Shane Hurstley	15
2020018	18-Jan-20	151002	Shane Hurstley	10
2020019	19-Jan-20	151002	Shane Hurstley	12
2020020	20-Jan-20	151002	Shane Hurstley	10
2020021	21-Jan-20	151003	Shane Hurstley	70
2020022	22-Jan-20	151003	Shane Hurstley	80
2020023	23-Jan-20	151003	Shane Hurstley	90
2020024	24-Jan-20	151003	Shane Hurstley	100
2020025	25-Jan-20	151003	Shane Hurstley	120

Figure 1.3 – Orphaned records in the Transactions table

If, for example, the record with `Product_ID = 151002` was inadvertently deleted from the `Product Details` table (similar to what we have in *Figure 1.3*), we would have several *orphaned records* in the `Transactions` table not having the corresponding `Product Details` record in the first table. This could cause reconciliation errors that can become discrepancies in financial reports.

> **Note**
>
> We will cover how to detect orphaned records and manage data integrity in our hands-on examples in *Chapter 6, Implementing Best Practices When Using Business Intelligence Tools*, and *Chapter 10, Using Artificial Intelligence for Finance Data Quality Management.*

Financial reporting

Distributing financial data to interested parties, such as creditors, investors, and regulatory agencies, is the process of **financial reporting**. Since they form the basis for the financial statements that provide a snapshot of an organization's financial status, taking care of data integrity is essential for accurate financial reporting.

One of the ways that an organization can ensure the integrity of financial reports is by setting up internal controls. These processes are set up by the company to provide a level of reasonable assurance as to the reliability of the financial statements, prevent fraud, and ensure compliance with regulations. It is important to note that if there are errors or discrepancies relating to inaccurate or misleading reporting, the company is at risk of penalties and fines.

> **Note**
>
> Being data-rich and information-poor is a common challenge. This emphasizes the importance of data integrity in transforming raw data into usable information, as exemplified in the creation and analysis of financial reports.

Balance sheet

The company's financial position and state can be understood by referring to the **balance sheet**. At a specific point in time, it discloses information regarding its assets, liabilities, and shareholders' equity. The balance sheet, together with the statement of profit and loss, and the statement of cash flows are the most common financial statements prepared by businesses. We will discuss the balance sheet here and the other two in the later part of this section.

These financial statements can be prepared by different individuals depending on the size of the company. If it is a small business, the owner can prepare it. Alternatively, external accountants can be hired to assist in the preparation of these reports. A balance sheet is usually prepared on a monthly basis or depending on the needs of the business.

> **Note**
>
> In order to make sure that the numbers add up, accounts reconciliation procedures are done as part of the internal controls. After the balance sheet has been prepared and if the company is publicly held, public accounting firms can be hired to review the balance sheet and conduct external audits.

Nowadays, companies may utilize software to speed up the preparation of financial reports. However, despite this, data integrity issues can still be present since the process of accounts reconciliation and recording may still be manual.

XYZ Company
Balance Sheet
As of December 31, 2022 and December 31, 2021 (in USD)

Assets				
Current Assets		**Dec 31, 2022**		**Dec 31, 2021**
Cash and cash equivalents	$	53,174	$	10,000
Accounts receivable		14,000		12,000
Inventory		12,500		18,000
Prepaid expense		2,500		2,000
Total current assets		**82,174**		**42,000**
Property, plant, and equipment - net				
Equipment		52,000		52,000
Less: accumulated depreciation		(9,750)		(3,250)
Land		60,000		60,000
Building		260,000		-
Less: accumulated depreciation		(3,900)		-
Property, plant, and equipment - net		**358,350**		**108,750**
Intangible assets - net				
Intangible assets		18,000		18,000
Less: accumulated amortization		(6,500)		(2,500)
Intangible assets - net		**11,500**		**15,500**
Total non-current assets		**369,850**		**124,250**
Total assets	**$**	**452,024**	**$**	**166,250**
Liabilities and Shareholders' Equity				
Current Liabilities				
Accounts payable	$	28,012	$	25,000
Accrued interest		3,900		-
Notes payable		15,000		15,000
Accrued expenses		4,476		6,000
Total current liabilities		**51,388**		**46,000**
Loans Payable		119,000		25,000
Long-term debt		**119,000**		**25,000**
Total liabilities		**170,388**		**71,000**
Shareholders' Equity				
Common stock		75,000		23,000
Additional paid-in capital		45,000		16,000
Retained earnings		161,636		56,250
Shareholders' Equity		**281,636**		**95,250**
Total liabilities and shareholders' equity	**$**	**452,024**	**$**	**166,250**

Figure 1.4 – Sample balance sheet

Let's have a quick look at an example of a balance sheet. In *Figure 1.4*, we have a sample report for a hypothetical business detailing the company's assets, liabilities, and shareholders' equity. To help us understand the balance sheet better, we need to familiarize ourselves with the following key concepts:

- **Asset**: An asset is a resource that a company owns or controls, which is expected to provide future financial benefits. In the balance sheet example provided in *Figure 1.4*, assets include those that contribute to the value of the business. These include current assets, property, plant and equipment, and intangible assets. The assets of a company generally depend on the business type, and the components can change as necessary.
- **Liability**: This is a debt that a business is obligated to settle in the future. It represents a future outflow of resources. In simple terms, liabilities (and equity, which we will discuss next) are the sources of funding used to acquire assets.
- **Equity**: This is what remains from the assets after all liabilities are paid. Types of equity include common stock, preferred stock, and retained earnings. Simply put, this is the portion that the owners have claim to once the liabilities are settled. When money is invested in a company, it can be in the form of common stock or preferred stock. Then, when the business starts generating profits, the earnings are kept in the business and placed under the retained earnings account. A portion of the earnings are sometimes paid to the stockholders in the form of dividends.

A balance sheet needs to be always balanced. The reason it is called a balance sheet is that the assets should equal the sum of the liabilities and shareholders' equity. The liabilities and equity fund the acquisition of business assets, which is why they need to be equal. Insufficient data, erroneous transactions, mistakes in inventory, or errors in equity calculations could likely be the causes of an unbalanced balance sheet.

> **Important note**
> If errors in the balance sheet go undetected and the balance sheet is publicly reported, this can potentially negatively impact the company's reputation as well as its stock price.

Profit and loss statement

Business owners and accountants utilize the **profit and loss** (**P&L**) report as an essential financial statement. Based on the company's revenues and expenses, the report details its net profit or loss. It describes how a company can generate revenue and earn income after deducting the expenses.

Now, let's look at a quick example of a P&L report. *Figure 1.5* shows an example P&L statement for our fictional company where we break down its sales, cost of goods sold, expenses, and net income.

XYZ Company
Statement of Profit and Loss
For the Year Ended December 31, 2022 (in USD)

Comparative financial statement		
Gross Sales	**Dec 31, 2022**	**Dec 31, 2021**
Product A	$ 525,000	$ 475,000
Product B	85,000	85,000
Total Sales	**610,000**	**560,000**
Total Cost of Goods Sold		
Beginning Inventory	18,000	5,000
Purchases	230,000	200,000
Less: Ending Inventory	12,500	18,000
Total Cost of Goods Sold	**235,500**	**187,000**
Gross Profit	**374,500**	**373,000**
Expenses		
Franchise Fee	50,000	50,000
Insurance	15,000	5,000
Maintenance and Repairs	8,000	3,500
Office Supplies	5,000	3,000
Office Rent	25,000	26,750
Depreciation Expense	10,400	3,250
Amortization Expense	4,000	2,500
Utilities	16,750	8,000
Wages	30,000	30,000
Total Operating Expenses	**164,150**	**132,000**
Operating Income	**210,350**	**241,000**
Interest expense	3,900	-
Net Income Before Taxes	**206,450**	**241,000**
Taxes on Income	66,064	77,120
Net Income After Taxes	**$ 140,386**	**$ 163,880**

Figure 1.5 – Statement of Profit and Loss

Here, we can see that the business earns its revenue from selling products. Then, the cost of goods sold is deducted from the sales to get the gross profit. Afterward, the expenses needed to run the business—such as the franchise fee, insurance, maintenance, and taxes—are deducted to get the net income after taxes. The P&L report also enables the company to look at net income and overall profitability to determine how to best manage its resources.

> **Note**
>
> Imagine we have a P&L report where the cost of goods sold account increased significantly without the corresponding increase in revenue. This could flag the presence of potential data integrity issues, which affect the accuracy of the profitability of the business. As mentioned earlier, one way to ensure the integrity of financial statements in general—and the profit and loss statement in particular—is to set up internal controls. Take, for example, internal controls for payroll in order to minimize the risk of fraud. Some examples of this are the segregation of duties between the timesheet approver, payroll processor, and payroll issuer, having a different bank account for payroll, and comparing the actual payroll expense with the budget. This will be discussed in more detail in *Chapter 7, Detecting Fraudulent Transactions Affecting Financial Report Integrity*.

Cash flow statement

Another major financial report in addition to the balance sheet and the P&L statement is the **cash flow statement**. This report connects the balance sheet and income statement because it shows how money flows in and out of the company. The beginning and ending balances of this account, as well as the change in the cash level over the course of the period, are shown in the cash flow statement.

Figure 1.6 shows the statement of cash flows for an imaginary company. The cash flow statement can be prepared in two ways, either through the *direct method* or *indirect method*. The direct method details the incoming and outgoing cash flows from operations, while the indirect method presents cash flows using the net income as a starting point.

XYZ Company
Statement of Cash Flows
For the Year Ended December 31, 2022 (in USD)

	Amount
Cash flows from operating activities	
Net income	$ 140,386
Adjustments to reconcile net income to net cash provided by operating activities:	
Depreciation and amortization	14,400
Changes in current assets and liabilities:	
Increase in accounts receivable	(2,000)
Increase in prepaid expenses	(500)
Decrease in inventory	5,500
Increase in accounts payable	3,012
Increase in accrued interest	3,900
Decrease in accrued expenses	(1,524)
Net cash provided by operating activities	**163,174**
Cash flows from investing activities	
Capital expenditures	(260,000)
Net cash used from investing activities	**(260,000)**
Cash flows from financing activities	
Proceeds from issuance of long-term debt	94,000
Issuance of common stock	81,000
Dividends paid	(35,000)
Net cash provided by financing activities	**140,000**
Net increase in cash during the year	43,174
Cash at the beginning of the year	10,000
Cash at the end of the year	$ **53,174**

Figure 1.6 – Statement of Cash Flows

In our example, we are using the indirect method where we calculated the **Net cash provided by operating activities** by starting with the net income and adjusting it based on changes in cash provided by operating activities.

The statement also shows the **Cash flows from investing activities**, such as funding capital expenditures or selling equipment, and **Cash flows from financing activities**, such as proceeds from issuing debt or paying dividends to stockholders.

> **Important note**
>
> The financial reports that we have discussed are external reports and there are various internal reports that are generated and processed by internal teams to address a company's specific needs and ensure that reviews, integrity checks, and analysis are done properly.

Budgeting

Budgeting is the process of creating a plan or estimate regarding the expected revenue and expenses in the future. This may also involve establishing financial objectives and allocating the required resources to meet these objectives. In order to plan effectively for the future and allocate resources properly, it is essential to make sure that the budgeting data is accurate.

> **Note**
>
> For example, a payroll employee creates a ghost employee in the payroll system and is able to pocket these payments. Having a budgeting process would help flag data integrity issues and potentially fraudulent transactions. That being said, we can estimate how much the expected payroll cost each month would be. Having a different payroll employee compare the budget with the actual payouts will assist in identifying a ghost employee.

Forecasting

Making projections about potential financial outcomes based on past performance and other relevant information is known as **forecasting**. Ensuring data integrity is critical to the forecasting process since accurate and reliable data is needed as a basis for the projections. One of the key activities done by companies while facing the challenges during COVID-19 was cash flow forecasting. Gaining visibility over cash flows allows a company to manage and run its operations effectively and have a buffer, especially when things do not go necessarily as planned. For the cash flow forecast to be effective and useful, the underlying data needs to be reliable and accurate. Thus, there is a need for data quality and integrity.

Say, for example, the business owners wanted to invest USD 200,000 to install building improvements that would make the business more profitable in the long run. However, they want to make sure that this is feasible and would not put the business in a dire situation in terms of cash flow. Assuming that the management expects to have the same level of operations for next year and pay the same level of dividends as 2023, we can create a simple statement of cash flow forecast, as seen in *Figure 1.7*:

XYZ Company
Statement of Cash Flows
For the Year Ended December 31, 2022 (in USD)

	Actuals 2022	Forecast 2023
Cash flows from operating activities		
Net income	$ 140,386	$ 140,386
Adjustments to reconcile net income to net cash provided by operating activities:		
Depreciation and amortization	14,400	14,400
Changes in current assets and liabilities:		
Increase in accounts receivable	(2,000)	(2,000)
Increase in prepaid expenses	(500)	(500)
Decrease in inventory	5,500	5,500
Increase in accounts payable	3,012	3,012
Increase in accrued interest	3,900	3,900
Decrease in accrued expenses	(1,524)	(1,524)
Net cash provided by operating activities	**163,174**	**163,174**
Cash flows from investing activities		
Capital expenditures	(260,000)	(200,000)
Net cash used from investing activities	**(260,000)**	**(200,000)**
Cash flows from financing activities		
Proceeds from issuance of long-term debt	94,000	-
Issuance of common stock	81,000	-
Dividends paid	(35,000)	(35,000)
Net cash provided by financing activities	**140,000**	**(35,000)**
Net increase in cash during the year	43,174	(71,826)
Cash at the beginning of the year	10,000	53,174
Cash at the end of the year	$ **53,174**	$ **(18,652)**

Figure 1.7 – A simple cash flow statement forecast

We can see that holding other assumptions constant, by investing USD 200,000 into improvements will lead to a negative cash flow of USD 71, 826 for the business. This means that the cash flow from operations will not be sufficient to fund the expenditure, and the business needs to take on a loan from a bank or issue additional stock to finance the spending.

But what if there was an error in the calculation of the USD 140,386 income caused by an oversight in recording the revenue for Product B? Suppose in 2022, we have a revenue of USD 85,000 for this product (as seen in *Figure 1.5*), but we should have USD 65,000 instead. This mistake will cause a ripple effect in the calculation of the gross profit as well as the net income before taxes and taxes on income. Given that we assumed that for 2023 we will have the same level of operations as 2022 for simplicity in our example, this will have an effect on how much cash needs to be borrowed or raised to fund the investment in the building improvements.

Note

With advancements in technology and artificial intelligence, companies have started using machine learning in forecasting. Similar to the cash flow forecast just seen, for the machine learning forecast to be useful, the training data needs to be reliable and accurate.

Depreciation

Companies can recognize and report the decline in the value of fixed assets over time on their financial statements through **depreciation**. It is computed using the asset's cost, expected useful life, and any residual value. This way, depreciation allows businesses to more precisely reflect the true cost of utilizing an asset over its useful life rather than being expensed in full on a one-time basis. At the same time, it helps reflect the cost of utilizing the asset in the same period when revenue was generated. Depreciation is shown as an expense on the income statement and as a decrease in the asset's value on the balance sheet:

XYZ Company
Building Depreciation Schedule

Cost: USD 260,000 *Useful life: 10 years*

Year	Book Value Period Start	Depreciation Expense	Accumulated Depreciation	Book Value Period End
2021	260,000	3,900	3,900	256,100
2022	256,100	26,000	29,900	230,100
2023	230,100	26,000	55,900	204,100
2024	204,100	26,000	81,900	178,100
2025	178,100	26,000	107,900	152,100
2026	152,100	26,000	133,900	126,100
2027	126,100	26,000	159,900	100,100
2028	100,100	26,000	185,900	74,100
2029	74,100	26,000	211,900	48,100
2030	48,100	26,000	237,900	22,100
2031	22,100	22,100	260,000	0

Figure 1.8 – Building depreciation schedule

Figure 1.8 details the building depreciation schedule allocating the cost of the asset over its useful life of 10 years. It can be gathered from the details that the building was acquired in 2021 at a value of USD 260,000 and expected to have a resale value of zero by 2031, when it will be fully utilized.

Newly constructed buildings usually last 40 years. Given that it will be used for 10 years, we can conclude that it is not a new one. The initial cost of the asset can differ depending on whether the business is following **Generally Accepted Accounting Principles** (**GAAP**) or **International Financial Reporting Standards** (**IFRS**). However, in this example, we will assume that there is no difference for simplicity. Also, estimates regarding how long an asset can be used, the depreciation method, and how much it can be sold for are approximations that could change depending on expectations.

> **Important note**
>
> It is critical to ensure the integrity and correctness of depreciation estimates. If, for example, there was an error in the useful life or depreciation method used to calculate the depreciation expense, this will have a *flow-on effect* (that is, a ripple effect) on the P&L statement values and calculations. Once these data integrity issues are detected, they could lead to restatements of prior periods' financial statements, particularly when they contain *material* inaccuracies.
>
> For more information on this topic, feel free to check the following link: `https://www.investopedia.com/terms/r/restatement.asp`.

Variable cost

While fixed costs stay the same regardless of the amount of production or sales, **variable costs** fluctuate based on the quantity of goods or services produced or sold. Materials, direct labor costs, and packaging costs are examples of variable costs, sometimes referred to as direct expenses, which are directly associated with the production or sale of a certain good or service. Office rent, administrative staff pay, and real estate taxes are examples of fixed costs.

> **Important note**
>
> Understanding the difference between variable and fixed costs is critical for financial management since it enables a business to determine pricing and profitability while also understanding the entire cost of production or sales at various output levels. Knowing the trend of the variable cost for a product helps identify any irregularities early in the process. If, for example, the variable costs significantly increased, it can mean that the cost of producing the product has increased, or it could indicate errors, inconsistencies, or potentially even fraud.

Risk management

Risk management is the process of identifying, assessing, and minimizing the different risks and threats (including data integrity issues) that could potentially impact an organization's business operations and financial performance. It is necessary that accurate and reliable data is available in order to identify and evaluate these threats. You can also use this data in the development of effective risk mitigation strategies. In *Chapter 2, Avoiding Common Data Integrity Issues and Challenges in Finance Teams*, we will discuss how one of the biggest banks globally failed to perform the appropriate risk assessments of possible data corruption for their **intelligent deposit machines** (**IDMs**), which led to significant financial penalties.

Insurance

Insurance is a legal contract between two parties where the insurer provides financial coverage for any loss that the insured may suffer from an unforeseen loss. In addition to this, filing for an insurance claim causes business interruptions and requires that the data is current, comprehensive, and accurate.

Fraud in the insurance industry costs billions of dollars per year. One way to address this risk is to improve and manage data integrity by ensuring that the data can be trusted and that the records are up to date and correct.

> Note
>
> We will cover how fraud can negatively affect the integrity of financial reports under *Chapter 7, Detecting Fraudulent Transactions Affecting Financial Report Integrity.*

Transaction

A **transaction** is an exchange between two parties representing a transfer of resources. Each transaction is recorded as an entry in its financial records. Some examples are selling a product to customers, paying the rent on the company office, paying the wages and salaries of employees, or buying equipment needed for production. One way to help ensure data integrity at a transaction level is by using **database locking techniques** and features available in database applications. These techniques would make sure that updates performed during transactions are correctly reflected (that is, the numbers are adding up correctly!). We'll cover these techniques in more detail in *Chapter 8, Using Database Locking Techniques for Financial Transaction Integrity.*

In addition to this, database transactions can be stored and audited using various solutions including ledger databases such as **Amazon Quantum Ledger Database** (**QLDB**). Using these special types of databases, even if transactions are deleted, they can still be validated and audited using the features provided by the ledger database. We will discuss this further in *Chapter 9, Using Managed Ledger Databases for Finance Data Integrity.*

Mutual exclusion

Another technique to help ensure data integrity in system transactions is to utilize a **mutual exclusion** lock (or **mutex** lock), which prevents simultaneous access to a common entity or resource. Imagine having a bank account that contains a total of `$200`. Suppose two separate deposits are initiated at the same time—one deposit of `$50` and another of `$100`. In this scenario, a mutex would lock the account for one deposit transaction, preventing the other from accessing the account simultaneously. This ensures accurate updating of the account balance, as each deposit is processed in isolation. Once the first deposit (`$50`) is completed and the account balance is updated, the mutex unlocks, allowing the second deposit (`$100`) to proceed, thereby maintaining the integrity of the transaction process as well as the final account balance (which should be `$350`). Without a lock, you might end up having an incorrect final account balance of `$250`!

To help demonstrate how effective these types of locks are when building financial systems, let's have a quick example where multiple running processes or threads are updating a shared resource (*first without a mutex*) using the **Python** programming language:

```
import threading
counter = 0

def increment_counter():
    global counter
    for _ in range(100000):
        counter += 1

threads = []
for i in range(10):
    thread = threading.Thread(target=increment_counter)
    threads.append(thread)
    thread.start()

for thread in threads:
    thread.join()

print(f"Final counter value without mutex: {counter}")
```

Here, we have a shared `counter` variable as well as multiple threads updating the counter at the same time. *What happens if we run this code? Without a mutex lock, the concurrent threads will try to update the counter at the same time and accidentally overwrite the updates performed by other threads!*

> **Note**
>
> The expected final value of the counter is 1,000,000. However, without a mutex lock, you will most likely get a value *less than* 1,000,000 (which is incorrect). You would be surprised that running the code multiple times may yield different results as well! In case you want to run this example yourself, make sure to (1) install `Python 3.7.X` on your laptop/local machine, (2) create a file named `no_mutex.py`, and (3) run `python3 no_mutex.py` in your terminal application. Alternatively, you can run the code on websites such as `https://www.online-python.com/`.

Now, let's update the previous example and have it use a mutex lock:

```
import threading
counter = 0
counter_lock = threading.Lock()

def increment_counter():
    global counter
    for _ in range(100000):
        with counter_lock:
            counter += 1

threads = []
for i in range(10):
    thread = threading.Thread(target=increment_counter)
    threads.append(thread)
    thread.start()

for thread in threads:
    thread.join()

print(f"Final counter value with mutex: {counter}")
```

This time, we will get the correct final value of the `counter` variable (1,000,000) since the usage of a mutex lock helped ensure that an update to the same resource is completed first before the next update operation is performed. Feel free to run the code multiple times and you should see that the result should always be the same (that is, 1,000,000). *Awesome, right?*

> **Note**
> For more information about this topic, feel free to check the following page: `https://en.wikipedia.org/wiki/Lock_(computer_science)`.

Now that we've established a good foundation with these concepts, let's move on to the final section of this chapter.

Debunking the myths and misconceptions surrounding finance data integrity management

There are several myths and misconceptions that can negatively influence the financial practices and processes of various departments in an organization. In this section, we will cover the different beliefs within an organization that can lead to data quality issues and noncompliance, which could in turn lead to major financial consequences. Once we are able to debunk these myths and misconceptions, we can establish more effective strategies and practices that ensure the integrity and reliability of financial data in our own organizations.

Myth 1 – only large financial organizations are concerned about data integrity

Data integrity issues affect organizations of varying sizes, from start-ups and small businesses to large organizations. As mentioned earlier in this chapter, poor financial data integrity management can result in serious financial consequences or regulatory offenses. For example, start-ups may end up deprioritizing financial data integrity management and avoid strict processes that could slow down progress. This could lead to inconsistencies in their financial reporting, budget forecasts, and internal audits, potentially resulting in significant long-term financial and reputational damage.

Though small businesses can have less complexity and less regulation compared to bigger organizations, there is still a need to maintain data integrity throughout the data lifecycle. This enables business owners and management to confidently rely on the data and make informed business decisions.

Myth 2 – only finance professionals should be concerned about data integrity

While finance professionals play a crucial role in data integrity management, this responsibility needs to be shared across the entire organization. This involves promoting a culture of quality within the organization, increasing data literacy through training, and having an environment of openness.

For one thing, software engineers need to be mindful of data integrity issues and risks when building financial applications. Junior software engineers are *probably not aware* that adding `0.1` and `0.2` using languages such as **Python** or **JavaScript** without converting these floating-point values to decimal would yield a result of `0.30000000000000004` instead of `0.3`! Where did that extra `0.00000000000000004` come from?! To help solve this mystery, developers should be aware that a **floating-point number** (often referred to simply as **float**) is stored in a format that cannot accurately represent all decimal numbers. Using float instead of **decimal** when developing financial applications is a bad idea, as this would have several significant implications including approximation errors and rounding errors.

This is best demonstrated with a simple code example using the **Python** programming language:

```
principal = 1000
rate = 0.001 # 0.1%
time = 1/365
interest_float = principal * rate * time
interest_float
```

Running this block of code would result in `0.0027397260273972603`, similar to what we have in *Figure 1.9*:

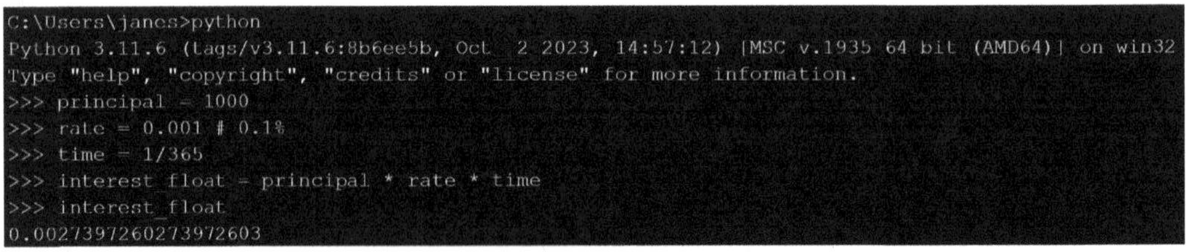
C:\Users\janes>python
Python 3.11.6 (tags/v3.11.6:8b6ee5b, Oct 2 2023, 14:57:12) [MSC v.1935 64 bit (AMD64)] on win32
Type "help", "copyright", "credits" or "license" for more information.
>>> principal = 1000
>>> rate = 0.001 # 0.1%
>>> time = 1/365
>>> interest_float = principal * rate * time
>>> interest_float
0.0027397260273972603

Figure 1.9 – Getting the results for interest_float

Let's try performing the same calculation, but this time we'll use the decimal data type:

```
from decimal import Decimal
principal = Decimal('1000')
rate = Decimal('0.001') # 0.1%
time = Decimal('1') / Decimal('365')
interest_decimal = principal * rate * time
interest_decimal
```

This will result in `Decimal('0.0027397260273972602739726027397260274 0')`, as can be seen in *Figure 1.10*:

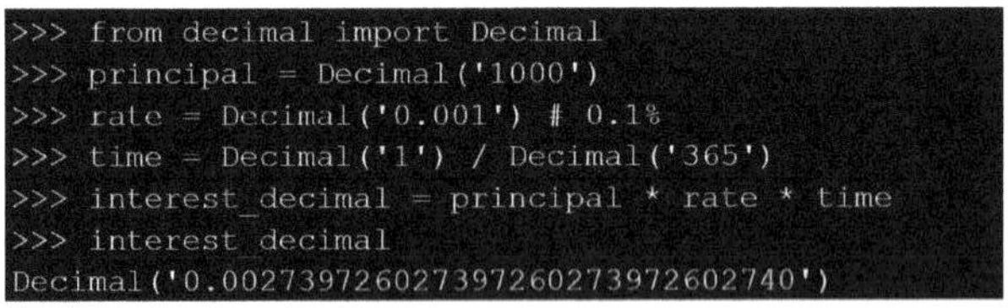
>>> from decimal import Decimal
>>> principal = Decimal('1000')
>>> rate = Decimal('0.001') # 0.1%
>>> time = Decimal('1') / Decimal('365')
>>> interest_decimal = principal * rate * time
>>> interest_decimal
Decimal('0.002739726027397260273972602740')

Figure 1.10 – Getting the results for interest_decimal

Once we subtract the interest values (one stored as a floating-point number and the other stored in decimal form), we will get a difference similar to what we have in *Figure 1.11*:

>>> interest_decimal - Decimal(interest_float)
Decimal('-2.138700175834419705439358950E-20')

Figure 1.11 – Getting the difference between the interest calculations

This difference may seem small, however, *what if the interest calculations are needed, for example, on overnight deposits worth hundreds of millions of dollars?*

> **Note**
>
> For more information about this topic, feel free to check the following link: `https://en.wikipedia.org/wiki/Floating-point_arithmetic`.

Myth 3 – only internal financial reporting systems are affected by data integrity issues

Any type of financial system with a database can be affected by data integrity issues. This includes banking systems, accounting software, investment management platforms, and even payroll systems.

Note that data integrity issues can negatively impact machine learning-powered financial systems as well. ML-powered financial applications make use of **machine learning models**, which learn from data to identify patterns, make decisions, or predict outcomes. *What if the data used to train these models have data integrity issues?* In such cases, these models may produce inaccurate or biased results, as they rely on the quality of the training data to make predictions. This could lead to significant challenges in application performance and even potentially yield harmful results, especially in finance. As the saying goes: garbage in, garbage out.

As more organizations around the world build ML-powered financial applications, taking care of the integrity of data and addressing the phenomenon called **machine learning drift** is critical. While we won't discuss machine learning drift in detail, it's important that we are aware that this drift leads to a decline in model accuracy, which impacts the effectiveness of a machine learning system. It is essential that we know that data integrity issues, such as inconsistencies, missing values, or biases, significantly contribute to this drift.

Myth 4 – processes that improve data integrity are expensive and difficult to implement

Contrary to popular belief, improving the quality and integrity of data used by organizations doesn't have to be expensive. There are practical ways and processes that can be implemented using the most commonly used tools available, such as Microsoft Excel, Google Sheets, and Power BI. These tools offer functionalities such as data validation, conditional formatting, and pivot tables, which can be leveraged to maintain accurate and consistent data. In addition to this, integrating basic data checks and regular audits into routine processes can go a long way to preserving the integrity of financial data. Training staff in effective data management and the use of these tools can also be done with minimal expense.

> **Note**
>
> Using various solutions and features for data integrity management will be covered further in *Chapter 4, Understanding the Data Integrity Management Capabilities of Business Intelligence Tools*.

Myth 5 – only electronic data is affected by data integrity issues

All types of data are affected by data integrity, whether stored digitally or on paper. It is important to be able to accurately store and retrieve data whether from an electronic database or hardcopy documents. One way of minimizing risks in the data collection process is anticipating and managing potential human errors ahead of time. This can be addressed by doing data validation checks, double-checking the work, having a standardized process, or enabling automation.

> **Note**
>
> While there are machine learning-powered tools to help automate the encoding process, it is crucial to remember that these tools also require regular monitoring and validation to ensure that they are functioning correctly and adapting to any changes in data formats or structures.

That's pretty much it! At this point, we should have a better understanding of the myths and misconceptions and a deeper appreciation of the right mindset and approach toward ensuring the integrity of financial data.

Summary

We started this chapter by talking about the impact of financial data integrity issues if these are not addressed and managed properly. We then discussed various concepts relevant to data integrity management, as these will help us better understand the topics in the upcoming chapters. These include a few foundational financial concepts, as well as a few advanced topics such as mutual exclusion locks and orphaned records. Toward the end of this chapter, we covered the myths and misconceptions that surround finance data integrity, which gave us a deeper appreciation of the right mindset and attitude toward data integrity.

If there are topics that are new to you or that you have not yet grasped fully, feel free to go back and review the concepts discussed in this chapter. In the next chapter, we will dive deeper into how to avoid common data integrity issues and challenges in financial services.

Further reading

For more information on the topics covered in this chapter, feel free to check out the following resources:

- Flynn, Shannon. *A Guide to Data Integrity for Business Reliability and Trust* (May 2022) on *Big Ideas for Small Businesses*: `https://bigideasforsmallbusiness.com/a-guide-to-data-integrity-for-business-reliability-and-trust/`
- Wagner, Stephen, and Dittmar, Lee. *The Unexpected Benefits of Sarbanes-Oxley* (April 2006) in *Harvard Business Review*: `https://hbr.org/2006/04/the-unexpected-benefits-of-sarbanes-oxley`

2

Avoiding Common Data Integrity Issues and Challenges in Finance Teams

In the previous chapter, we learned that financial data integrity management is critical for every organization trying to make data-driven financial decisions and avoid regulatory issues and penalties. That being said, for a finance and data professional, it is important to have the skills to be able to detect and address data integrity issues before they become critical—and even to prevent these issues in the future.

In this chapter, we will build on top of the concepts discussed in the first chapter and cover the following topics to help us avoid common data integrity issues and challenges in finance teams:

- Detecting manual data encoding issues in financial teams
- Avoiding common reconciliation errors and mistakes in finance teams
- Preventing balance sheet data integrity issues
- Handling data corruption and financial transaction data integrity issues in internal systems and databases

This is an exciting chapter where you will be introduced to topics that are crucial for finance and data professionals striving to uphold the highest standards of data integrity in their operations. With these in mind, let's begin!

Detecting manual data encoding issues in finance teams

Despite the advancement of automation tools and systems in these past few years, manual encoding errors and mistakes are still prevalent in finance teams and industries globally. Encoding issues and errors affect the reliability and trustworthiness of the data, making the reports generated using this data unfit for use in business decisions. Thus, it is important that these issues are detected early on to prevent this from happening. Here are some of the suggestions and recommendations to help solve these issues.

Utilizing available tools to check for data integrity issues in encoded data

To manage manual encoding data integrity issues, it is important that the collected data is checked and validated using available tools before it is used. This will ensure the accuracy and completeness of the data before it is analyzed or processed. These checks confirm that the data entries use the correct data type or format. At the same time, these checks can assist in finding mistakes made during (and after) entering the data in order to reduce data entry errors.

For scenarios in which finance professionals manually encode data to an Excel spreadsheet, here's an example of how we can use the built-in **data validation** function in Microsoft Excel to set up a rule that helps ensure that a cell or group of cells in the spreadsheet) contains only dates and not a different data type. To use this feature, we simply locate it under the **Data** tab, similar to what we have in *Figure 2.1*:

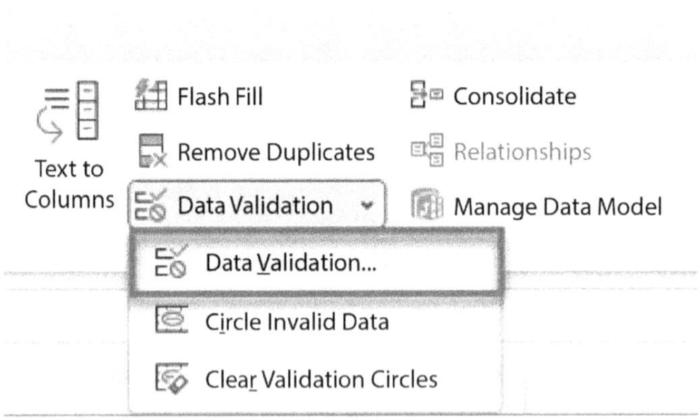

Figure 2.1 – Data Validation on the Data tab

As highlighted in *Figure 2.1*, we select **Data Validation** and then specify a few configuration parameters to limit what type of data can be entered in the cells:

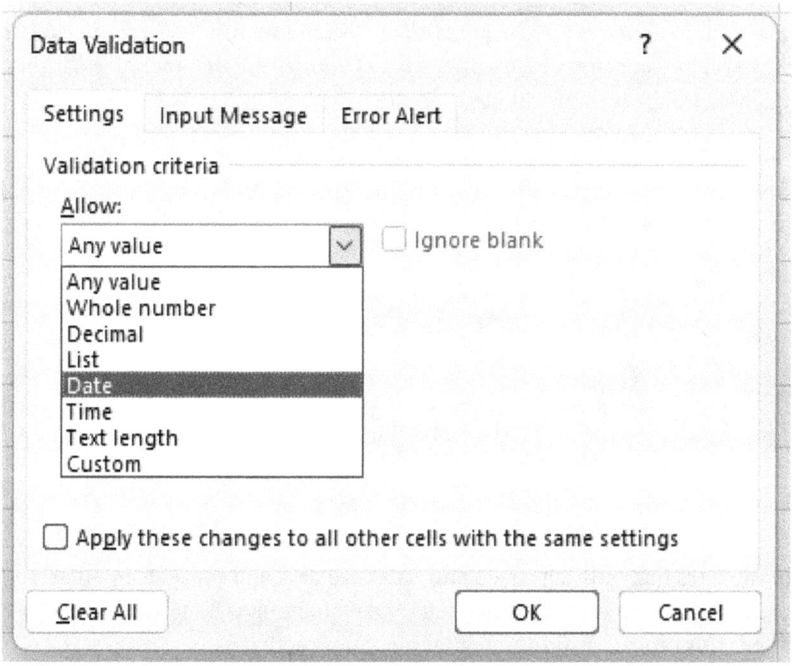

Figure 2.2 – Options for data types to be used

Having this setup ensures that the data type of what's entered in the cells is consistent from the start, and it prevents issues along the way. If you think about it, this simple tweak makes it less error-prone to work with data in the long run! For example, if a business is collecting personal information such as its employees' birthdays using Excel, we can format the cells as **Date** to make sure that only date values are entered in the field.

Regularly audit encoded data

In order to find data integrity issues in the manually encoded data, it is important to review and audit the financial data and transaction records *frequently*. Having a regular process for auditing the data quality can assist in finding any issues that manual and automated checks might have overlooked.

> **Note**
>
> At the same time, regular audit work helps you comply with regulations such as the **Sarbanes-Oxley Act** (**SOX**) and **Basel III** framework mentioned in *Chapter 1, Recognizing the Importance of Data Integrity in Finance*.

One way to mitigate various risks (including the risk of asset misappropriation schemes) is to establish anti-fraud controls such as **accounts reconciliation** by making sure that the information is true and consistent through verification using different sources.

Let's say you want to make sure that payments are made only to legitimate vendors and suppliers who delivered goods and services to your company. This can be accomplished by doing a three-way match between the **purchase order** (**PO**), **supplier invoice**, and the **receipt report** (as seen in *Figure 2.3*):

Figure 2.3 – Three-way matching for accounts payable

This procedure validates that only approved purchases are paid and prevents financial losses due to fraud or negligence. In addition to this, conducting regular audits on vendor lists and payment histories further strengthens this process against potential fraudulent activities.

Monitoring and recording changes

You can speed up the detection of data integrity issues in encoded data through the usage of tools or systems that track and monitor data changes. When documents are shared and collaboration tools such as Google Sheets are used (during and after the manual encoding steps and processes), it is essential that there is a process for identifying *what modifications are made* and *by whom*.

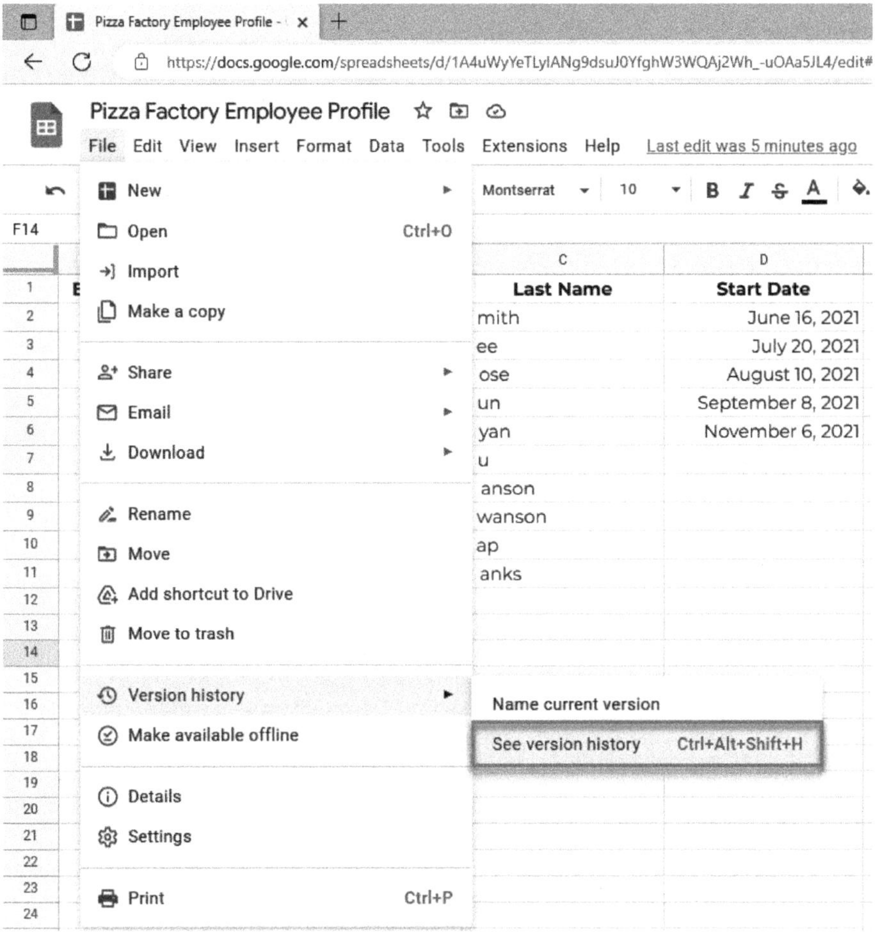

Figure 2.4 – Version history in Google Sheets

For example, we can easily track changes using **Google Sheets** by opening the **File** menu and then selecting **See version history** (under **Version history**). This will then show the previous versions of the file, who made changes, and when these changes were made. *Convenient, right?*

Having the right team structure and composition

Dealing with data integrity issues and concerns is not the job of a single person. It involves hiring the right team of professionals assigned with the right set of roles and responsibilities. In reality, each individual in the team would have their own set of strengths and weaknesses. This means that there are specific members in your team who may be more prone to causing data encoding and data integrity issues when working on a specific set of tasks. This also means that others may be more equipped for detecting and auditing work completed by others. That said, assigning these professionals to supervisory roles is recommended.

Important note

Of course, it is essential for professionals to undergo thorough training and demonstrate a clear understanding of data integrity principles (and even management principles in general) before they are assigned or promoted to a specific role. This ensures that they are well prepared to oversee, identify, and correct any issues effectively.

Putting robust data governance and compliance policies and procedures in place

In addition to what's been discussed already, it's essential to ensure that robust data governance, compliance policies, and procedures are in place. This involves defining precise roles and responsibilities for data management, developing protocols for data access and change, and routinely evaluating and updating these rules to make sure these rules comply with practical best practices in the industry.

With the increase in fraud and cyberattacks resulting in irreversible data integrity issues (along with major financial and reputational damage to the business), there is a growing need for awareness and strong measures against various types of threats.

Note

Imagine making a huge payment to your supplier and then receiving a call from them a week later saying that they have not yet received it yet! This is exactly what happened to one of the Australasian investment firms just before Christmas in 2018. One of their portfolio companies made a payment after receiving an invoice from a legitimate e-mail address of the supplier. Though the bank account had changed, nothing else seemed unusual since the language of the email was the same. It was only then that they realized that they had suffered from a **business e-mail compromise** (**BEC**) attack, which is when scammers trick employees and organizations into sending money (or providing confidential information). This type of attack is growing, particularly in Australia, due to a gap in Australian banks' abilities to verify if the **account name** matches the **bank-state-branch** (**BSB**) and the **account number** being used. If more effort or more focus on checking the correctness and integrity of the bank account had been exerted, this issue would have not happened. Another way that this could have been prevented is by having a procedure in place where whenever the bank details change, there is a need to confirm the bank details verbally (that is, by calling the supplier or by adopting solutions to assist in identifying and blocking questionable payments).

Now, let's dive deeper into how we can avoid common reconciliation errors and mistakes in finance teams.

Avoiding common reconciliation errors and mistakes in finance teams

A number of problems could arise throughout the account reconciliation and accounting process that would influence the integrity of financial data. Let's dive deeper into the common reconciliation errors.

Understanding common reconciliation errors

Some of the most prevalent problems in the area of reconciliation include those discussed in the following subsections. Afterward, we'll discuss how to avoid and prevent these issues.

Unrecorded transactions

Transactions that are not documented in the financial records may cause discrepancies between the financial records and the supporting documents. Simply put, it is essential to ensure that all transactions are appropriately recorded and documented to prevent this type of issue.

For example, a cash sale in a restaurant might not be recorded due to the rush of evening sales when the store is about to close for the day. Another example would be receiving an invoice from a supplier and failing to record it on a *timely basis*.

Transposition errors

Transposition errors are mistakes that happen when numbers are inverted or flipped during input, causing the balances to change—sometimes significantly.

For example, a cash accountant could record the receipt of cash as `USD 15,629` instead of `USD 15,692`. Or, an invoice for equipment might be recorded as `USD 175,886` instead of `USD 157,688`. While these errors might seem easy to spot, once a team is working on numerous transactions simultaneously, detecting such discrepancies can become significantly more challenging, especially if these errors are buried within large volumes of data.

Duplicate payments

A **duplicate payment** is a payment that is made twice to the same provider by an organization. This can be caused by various issues, such as human data entry errors, the volume of invoices an accounts payable team handles, a lack of proper procedures in handling purchases, or receipts for duplicate invoices sent by the vendor. *Imagine losing thousands or even millions of dollars because of a duplicate payment!*

Errors in classification or errors in recording transactions

Errors in classification or errors in recording transactions happen when a transaction is incorrectly classified due to a lack of understanding or confusion as to the nature of the activity. For example, a fixed asset accountant records the depreciation of the equipment directly against the equipment account instead of using the accumulated depreciation account.

At this point, we have covered the most prevalent problems in the accounting and account reconciliation process, so we can now proceed to the recommended practices that finance teams and data professionals can employ to prevent them.

Preventing reconciliation errors

Internal controls have the power to stop mistakes and problems such as fraud and oversight. Here are recommended practices to prevent common reconciliation errors and mistakes made by finance teams regarding data integrity.

Establishing an accurate and well-documented account reconciliation process

A well-documented reconciliation process that explains the stages required, who is in charge of each phase, and the desired outcome is important in preventing issues. Documentation helps the business retain knowledge inside the organization whenever an employee leaves or transitions to another role. This can also help with onboarding new employees who need to get a better understanding of the process.

> Note
>
> Moreover, documentation plays a vital role in maintaining control under regulatory frameworks and laws. Companies must maintain accurate financial records and have strong internal controls in place to prevent fraud along with various types of issues.

Reviewing and updating the account reconciliation process regularly

The account reconciliation process needs to be reviewed and updated *regularly* in order for the process to remain effective and reliable. There are cases when weaknesses and limitations in the internal controls enable malicious actors to find a way to exploit these protocols. Thus, it is necessary to review the procedures more frequently to prevent this from happening.

Perform timely account reconciliation

Carrying out timely and regular account reconciliation enables the business to have accurate and dependable financial information on which to base financial decisions. Performing periodic account reconciliation helps you spot errors in recording transactions, identifying potentially unrecorded transactions or even discovering fraud along the way.

Use automated tools

There are various automated tools and software applications available for performing account reconciliation procedures. If you've used one or more of these tools before, you're aware that properly using these would help improve efficiency and minimize errors.

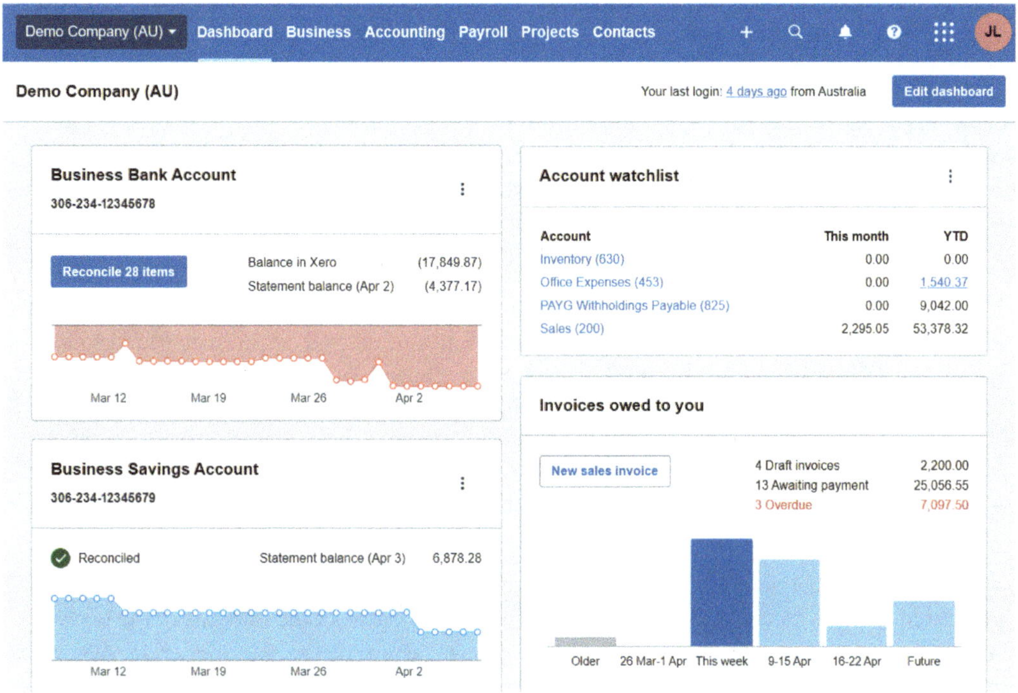

Figure 2.5 – Xero accounting software

One example is **Xero**, which is an online accounting software popularly used by small businesses. It offers a more efficient way of doing bank reconciliation. This solution enables the reconciliation of transactions daily, streamlining the process by checking and automating account reconciliation using suggested matches, as well as facilitating bulk reconciliation of transactions.

> **Note**
>
> It is important to note that the usage of automated tools does NOT guarantee the absence of data integrity issues. Unfortunately, a significant number of professionals using these tools have that incorrect assumption.

Reconciliation procedures and internal controls play an important role in an organization. By ensuring that these are in place, they serve as foundations to reinforce the accuracy of financial statements, prevent fraudulent activities, and enable informed financial decisions.

Preventing balance sheet data integrity issues

In *Chapter 1, Recognizing the Importance of Data Integrity in Finance*, we learned that the **balance sheet** is one of the major financial reports that businesses and organizations prepare in addition to the **statement of profit and loss** and the **statement of cash flows**. These provide information that stakeholders and decision-makers need to understand the company's financial position, how a company generates revenues and earns income, and the way the company utilizes its cash in operating its business.

By going through these financial statements, you will be able to familiarize yourself with the business and how it is doing. These reports provide a certain level of information needed to understand the numbers, generate the ratios, and review the indicators that convey how the business is operating. Moreover, this will help you make decisions on which financial and operational levers to pull to improve various aspects of the business, such as efficiency or profitability.

> **Note**
>
> Picture yourself in the driver's seat of your car. To reach your desired destination, you need to look at the dashboard in front of you that displays your speed, gas level, and warning signals that let you know if there's something wrong. Building and operating a successful business is the same. By recognizing and being aware of the information these reports provide, and by understanding what they mean, you gain a clearer picture of how the company is performing, which allows you to make more insightful business decisions to *drive* success.

If a company is publicly traded and is open to investment from the general public, it is usually covered by a higher level of compliance and reporting requirements to protect the interests of the investors and the public. This could be in the form of preparing financial reports based on **Generally Accepted Accounting Principles** (**GAAP**) or establishing strong internal controls to comply with SOX.

The most common financial reports are detailed as follows, and additional reports are required depending on the level of reporting needed for the company:

- **Balance sheet**: A balance sheet shows the company's financial position and discloses information regarding its assets, liabilities, and shareholders' equity at a given point in time
- **Profit and loss statement** (**P&L**): A profit and loss statement details the company's revenues, expenses, net profit or loss, and how it generates revenue and earns income
- **Cash flow statement**: A cash flow statement connects the balance sheet and income statement by showing how money flows in and out of the company

Given that there are different parties who rely on the financial statements in general and on the balance sheet in particular, to make insightful decisions, it is important that focus is put on ensuring data integrity to provide that level of trust and reliability in the reports.

Now that we have covered the importance of why balance sheet data integrity is important, we can now discuss specific ways to prevent these issues from happening. We'll look at each of these in turn.

Implementing strong internal controls

The goal of a business is to translate the efforts and investments into generating cash. Unfortunately, this can be jeopardized by weak internal controls, especially when handling cash transactions. Let's go back to our example of cash sales not being recorded due to the rush in evening sales in a restaurant (which we discussed in the *Unrecorded transactions* section earlier in this chapter). This scenario highlights how easily revenue can slip through the cracks when proper tracking mechanisms are not in place.

Given that digital cash is relatively easier to safeguard than physical cash, there is a need for strong internal controls to be put in place to address the risk of having physical cash. Procedures include establishing a process for the segregation of duties, setting up physical access controls such as a cash register, and considering moving away from cash transactions and toward electronic payments.

Establishing a process for the segregation of duties

The segregation of duties is the separation of potentially conflicting tasks to different team members so that not a single person is in control of an entire business process:

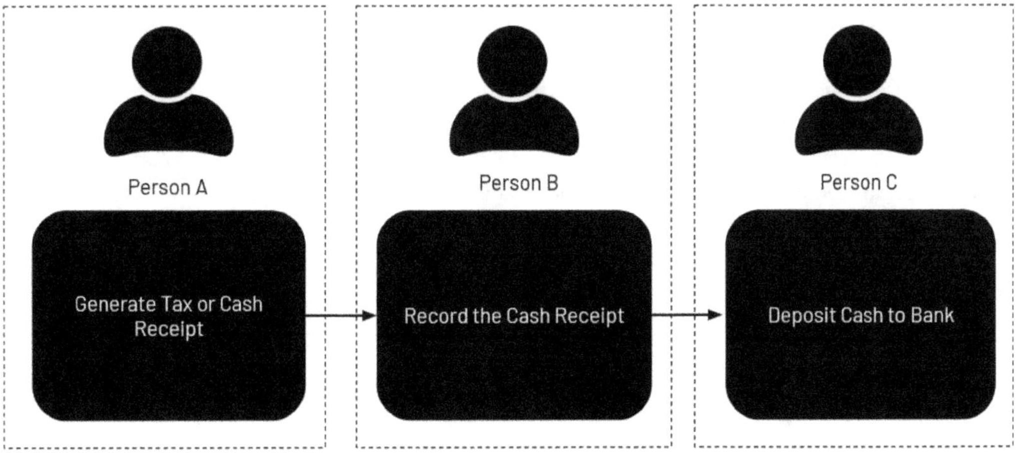

Figure 2.6 – The segregation of duties for cash sales

Figure 2.6 demonstrates an example of how to handle the segregation of duties for cash sales. To address the risk of a restaurant not recording a cash sale due to a rush in evening sales, there needs to be a process in place where the person doing the sale generates a tax or cash receipt. A different employee should record the cash receipt and a third employee should deposit the cash to the bank. Making different individuals carry out these tasks reduces the risk of data integrity issues, fraud, or theft in handling cash on hand.

Setting up access controls

Access controls are checks and controls that are put in place to govern and limit access to important assets or storage devices to ensure that they are protected from illegal access, modification, or theft. These can be physical or digital access controls that help protect the data and the records from being modified or tampered with by unauthorized users.

> **Note**
>
> Ensuring data integrity requires protection against unauthorized access, modification, or destruction, which is achieved by implementing security measures such as access controls, authentication, encryption, and firewalls. Security breaches can compromise data integrity, leading to severe consequences. That being said, a strong security procedure is essential to maintaining the overall data integrity of records, systems, and databases.

In our example of protecting cash on hand, physical access controls need to be set up to deter inappropriate access or theft. Setting up a cash register for customer transactions, doing daily bank deposits, and having the cash moved from the cash register to a safe at the end of the day can address this risk. Without these guardrails in place, there would be a higher risk of financial loss due to theft, fraud, or errors, which could harm the financial stability and reputation of the organization.

Physical access controls can also be set up to protect computer information systems and storage devices to prevent unauthorized access. These can help organizations guard important assets and maintain their dependability and accuracy. On the other hand, digital access controls are those that allow access to financial information and information systems only to authorized individuals through passwords or other security techniques. By setting up access controls for financial information systems, organizations can maintain the integrity of their data and prevent malicious actors from making unauthorized modifications.

Utilizing trustworthy data sources

In order to safeguard the data integrity of a balance sheet, it is important to establish the accuracy and validity of relevant data sources and continuously monitor the quality of the data used.

Determining the sources in creating the balance sheet

In preparing the balance sheet, the accounting department needs to determine what sources are to be used. Some of the most common examples are the general ledger, financial records (such as bank statements, sales, and purchase orders), payroll records, and tax records. Depending on the type of business and accounting system employed, certain sources of data may be more important than others in maintaining data integrity.

> **Note**
>
> For example, a retail business may rely heavily on sales and purchase orders, while a service-based company may place more emphasis on payroll records.

Establishing the accuracy and validity of data sources

It is important to determine where the data originated, how it was processed, and who/which entity provided the information.

Let's take, for example, establishing the validity of the cash balance in a balance sheet. One way of substantiating this is by comparing it with the cash balance in the bank statement since the bank statement is a document coming from a financial institution that is reliable, objective, and can be verified with other sources of information. Though there may be differences between the company's cash balance and the bank statement, these are common as a result of reconciling items and can be addressed and resolved.

Continuously monitoring data quality

Monitoring data quality on a continuous basis is critical since inaccurate data can lead to poor business decisions or potential legal problems. Having standards and processes to follow and adhere to can help you address issues early on and avoid problems down the line.

In the world of finance and data management, two companies can take vastly different approaches to maintaining data integrity. Let's take *Company A* and *Company B* as examples. *Company A* is a *reactive* company that only addresses data integrity issues as they arise. They have no set protocol or system in place to proactively monitor their data for accuracy and consistency. For instance, when a customer complains about an error on their invoice, *Company A* will investigate the issue and fix the problem. However, this reactive approach can be time-consuming and costly, and it can also harm their reputation if errors go unaddressed for too long. On the other hand, *Company B* is a relatively more *proactive* company that actively monitors their data to prevent issues from occurring. They have a robust system in place that continuously monitors their data, alerts them to any discrepancies, and provides them with real-time insights into their data's accuracy and consistency. For instance, they use data analytics tools to monitor their financial transactions and detect any suspicious activities that could compromise data integrity. This approach helps *Company B* to quickly identify and address data integrity issues, thereby minimizing the risk of financial losses and reputational damage.

In summary, while *Company A*'s reactive approach may be sufficient for some businesses, *Company B*'s proactive approach to maintaining data integrity is more effective in detecting and preventing issues before they arise. By using data analytics tools to monitor and analyze their data, *Company B* can detect any issues early on and take action to address them promptly.

> **Note**
>
> Another way is to develop a system to measure data quality through data quality metrics, which will be covered in further detail in *Chapter 3, Measuring the Impact of Data Integrity Issues*.

By constantly reviewing the standards and processes, measuring the data quality, and identifying and resolving issues, you can ensure the data integrity of the balance sheet.

Well-documented policies and procedures

Documenting the policies and procedures that are being done for balance sheet preparation is essential for ensuring that the processes are followed consistently and that industry regulations and standards (such as SOX) are observed. For example, SOX compliance requires you to keep documentation of internal controls and is crucial in demonstrating their effectiveness and compliance during audits. Creating documentation is vital in upholding accountability and openness in the process of balance sheet preparation. Having a written record of the procedures helps you identify areas that need improvement and quickly address issues.

> **Note**
>
> This documentation (along with other documents and resources) can also be used as evidence in legal disputes or investigations. The policies and procedures recorded can be utilized to train new employees on how to prepare balance sheets in accordance with industry regulations and company standards. Additionally, documenting these policies and procedures guarantees consistency in the preparation of balance sheets, even when there are changes in the workforce or employees shift positions within the company.

Having well-documented policies and procedures would be useful for training employees and improving their data literacy and data integrity management skills. Given the evolving landscape and complexities of managing the technologies available, it is important to educate the employees with the right skill set and mindset to ensure that the company is better able to manage the risks involved.

> **Note**
>
> As the pandemic continues to impact economies globally, companies have been forced to adjust their budgets and cut back on spending on non-revenue generating activities and initiatives. One of the areas that has been negatively affected is employee training, with many companies choosing to limit their training budgets to conserve resources. This has resulted in a reduction in the number of training sessions, as well as a shift toward virtual training methods that are less expensive than in-person training. While limiting training budgets may help companies save money in the short term, it can have long-term implications for the development and growth of employees. Without proper training along with well-documented processes, employees may struggle to adapt to changes in the industry, which can lead to decreased productivity and an increase in mistakes in the workplace. That being said, it is crucial for organizations to find a balance between conserving resources and investing in their employees' professional development, especially during these challenging times.

Employing technology and automation

Leveraging technology and automation allows organizations to save time during balance sheet preparation and improve accuracy if they are set up correctly. Using online platforms and solutions to integrate directly with various data sources, using applications that automate (or semi-automate) the reconciliation process, and employing tools to address data quality are some of the ways to improve data integrity and reduce manual work as well.

> **Note**
>
> The common data quality management capabilities of business intelligence tools will be covered in more detail in *Chapter 4, Understanding the Data Integrity Management Capabilities of Business Intelligence Tools.*

Now, let's dive deeper into handling data integrity issues in systems and databases.

Handling data corruption and financial transaction data integrity issues in internal systems and databases

System-level data integrity and data corruption bugs can result in a wide range of issues, both minor and severe. A system failure or corrupted file may cause operational delays, decreased productivity, and missed deadlines. Additionally, such incidents may result in violations of data privacy laws and regulations, leading to costly fines and harm to a company's reputation. Furthermore, errors in application development, such as improper data validation or input, may lead to unnoticed data integrity issues, which may cause inaccurate financial reporting, compromised decision-making, and potential legal consequences. Therefore, safeguarding data integrity must be a top priority for businesses, and strategies should be established to prevent and mitigate the risks of data corruption and related issues.

> **Note**
>
> Let's talk about a popular example of how system-level data integrity and data corruption bugs (application development mistakes) can cause a myriad of other problems. In 2018, one of the biggest banks globally was fined about USD 470 million as a result of system data corruption and data integrity issues involving the bank's **intelligent deposit machines** (**IDMs**) and various compliance infractions against the **Anti-Money Laundering and Counter-Terrorism Financing Act** (**AML/CTF**). The IDMs, which were introduced in 2012, allow for deposits to the bank account to be made immediately available for both local and international transfers. This system data integrity issue made the IDMs susceptible for use by criminals and syndicates since there were no limits on the amount that could be deposited and the funds could be transferred overseas right away. Thus, criminals were able to exploit and use them for laundering money from drug sales, which assisted the syndicates in their operations. The lion's share of the fine mainly related to the late filing of the 53,506 **threshold transaction reports** (**TTRs**) that were not captured and went unreported due to a coding error that did not take into account the transaction code related to the cash deposit for IDMs. This incident calls attention to the fact that when data corruption occurs, it affects the data integrity of the information and can lead to horrendous financial implications and reputational damage to the business.

In order to handle data corruption and data integrity issues in systems and databases, it is essential to do a risk assessment of possible data corruption, establish detection systems, do a root cause analysis of the problem, and implement preventative measures.

Risk assessment of possible data corruption

It is crucial that risk assessment procedures are defined and implemented consistently for the different business units and different types of risks, especially when a change is introduced. Maintaining data integrity is crucial for businesses, especially when it comes to data security and privacy. Risk assessment procedures are an effective way of achieving this. They help businesses identify vulnerabilities and potential risks that may affect the integrity of their data. By analyzing data quality and the likelihood of risks, businesses can put in place effective measures to prevent data breaches, cyberattacks, and other security incidents that could jeopardize data integrity. These measures could include secure data handling procedures, implementing encryption protocols, and enforcing access controls. With consistent risk assessment procedures, businesses can maintain data integrity and avoid data quality issues that could negatively affect their operations.

> **Note**
>
> In the bank's case, the IDMs constituted a new channel to make deposits and have the funds transferred immediately to recipients outside the country. The bank did not perform adequate risk assessments before rolling out the machines and did not do subsequent regular reviews either. Carrying out these checks would have helped identify these concerns early on and would have allowed the bank to create controls to mitigate and address these risks. It was only five years later, in 2017, that the company established a daily limit of about USD 13,600 on its ATMs when making deposits to a personal bank account, and in 2018, it placed a limit of about USD 6,600 on cash deposits to the bank's personal or business account.

Establishing detection systems

Detection systems need to be established so that activities are monitored, potential suspicious activities are flagged, and transactions are reviewed and actioned on. Establishing effective detection systems is crucial for maintaining data quality and integrity, particularly in areas such as fraud detection and prevention. By monitoring activities and flagging potential suspicious behaviors, businesses can detect and respond to data breaches and other security incidents that can compromise data quality and integrity. In addition, reviewing transactions and taking prompt action can help to prevent financial losses and legal issues that may arise from data breaches and other security incidents. Furthermore, detection systems can help to identify potential data quality issues, such as duplicate records, incorrect data inputs, and missing data. By addressing these issues promptly, businesses can maintain the accuracy and consistency of their data, ensuring that critical business decisions are based on reliable and trustworthy information. In summary, implementing effective detection systems is essential for maintaining data quality and integrity, as well as protecting businesses from potential financial and legal risks.

> **Note**
>
> Going back to our example earlier, the bank had an existing process of generating a TTR that captured transactions above a certain amount, which was estimated to be USD 6,600. At the time it launched the intelligent ATMs, two transaction codes, **5022** and **4013**, were being used and searched for by the system generating the TTR. However, the cash deposits from the IDMs used the reference code **5000**, which caused the **53,506** TTRs that were not reported. These could all have been prevented much earlier if proper detection systems had been established. The roll out of the IDMs and the bank's failure to address the issues early on resulted in an investigation by a government regulatory body for breaching the Anti-Money Laundering and Counter-Terrorism Act. It has been concluded that the IDMs became a convenient way for customers to transfer money immediately; however, the lack of risk-based controls and appropriate limits made it vulnerable to exploitation for money laundering purposes by syndicates. That said, the bank was fined about USD 470 million as a civil penalty as a result. Eventually, the bank acknowledged the deficiencies in its processes and agreed to improve its risk assessment procedures and implement new policies to address them. The updates included manual reviews of automated reporting and improved communication between the business units to help them share information when changes were made. This could have addressed the spike in cash deposits using the IDMs and the creation of the new transaction code to identify the deposits. If preventative measures were in place, this risk could have been mitigated and addressed.

Implementing preventative measures

In *Chapter 1, Recognizing the Importance of Data Integrity in Finance*, we discussed what orphaned records are and how the existence of these orphaned records can cause reconciliation errors as well as discrepancies in financial reports. *If we are able to prevent this type of issue, would this mean that our database is free from data integrity issues? Unfortunately, no!* That's because there are various data integrity issues beyond just orphaned records that can affect a database where records are stored.

With this in mind, it's essential that we have a good awareness of what prevention measures options and constraints are available when using databases (especially when using relational database management systems such as PostgreSQL).

NOT NULL constraint

The NOT NULL constraint is used to ensure that a column in a database table cannot contain a NULL value. With this, we are able to guarantee **data completeness** since every record in the table has a valid value for that column. To show how this constraint works, let's look at a simplified example with a single table called Accounts where we ensure that CustomerName must always have a value:

```
CREATE TABLE Accounts (
    AccountID int,
    CustomerName varchar(100) NOT NULL,
    Balance decimal(10, 2)
);
```

Here, we have defined the CustomerName column with a NOT NULL constraint. This means that every record in the Accounts table must have a value for CustomerName. Now, let's see what happens if we try to insert a record without specifying a CustomerName:

```
INSERT INTO Accounts (AccountID, Balance)
VALUES (1, 100.00);
```

This would produce an error as the operation doesn't have a value for CustomerName, which is required to be non-null when we define the table.

> **Note**
>
> That said, the transaction (that is, the INSERT operation) would not push through because of the error.

UNIQUE constraint

The UNIQUE constraint is used to ensure that all values in a specific column (or a combination of columns) in a database table are dissimilar from each other. This constraint guarantees that no duplicate values are present in the specified column(s). With this, we're able to maintain the uniqueness of each record in the table. For instance, in a table of user accounts, a UNIQUE constraint on an email address column ensures that no two users can register with the same email address.

To show how this constraint works, let's have a simplified example where we have a table named `Customers` where each customer has a unique email address. We can enforce this uniqueness with a `UNIQUE` constraint on the `Email` column:

```
CREATE TABLE Customers (
    CustomerID int,
    Name varchar(100),
    Email varchar(100) UNIQUE
);
```

In this example, the `Email` column is defined with a `UNIQUE` constraint. This means that no two rows in the `Customers` table can have the same email address. Now, let's say you tried inserting two records with the same email address:

```
INSERT INTO Customers (CustomerID, Name, Email)
VALUES (1, 'Jane Lat', 'jane@example.com');

INSERT INTO Customers (CustomerID, Name, Email)
VALUES (2, 'Jane Sarah', 'jane@example.com');
```

The first `INSERT` statement will succeed, but the second will fail with a unique constraint violation because `'jane@example.com'` is already used for another customer. This ensures that each email address in the `Customers` table is unique, as required in many applications for customer identification.

FOREIGN KEY constraint

The `FOREIGN KEY` constraint is used to establish a link between two tables in a database in order to ensure **referential integrity**. This constraint is applied to a column in one table, which points to a primary key column in another table. With this setup, we are able to ensure that the value in the foreign key column matches one of the values in the referenced primary key column. With this, we are able to guarantee that relationships between data in different tables are maintained correctly. This prevents orphaned records and preserves the logical connections within the database.

To show how this constraint works, let's have a simplified example where we have two tables: `Accounts` and `Transactions`. Each transaction is linked to an account in the `Accounts` table. We enforce this relationship using a `FOREIGN KEY` constraint. That said, let's create the `Accounts` table that will hold account information:

```
CREATE TABLE Accounts (
    AccountID int PRIMARY KEY,
    CustomerName varchar(100),
    Balance decimal(10, 2)
);
```

Next, let's create the `Transactions` table. Here, `AccountID` will be a foreign key that references the `AccountID` in the `Accounts` table:

```
CREATE TABLE Transactions (
    TransactionID int PRIMARY KEY,
    AccountID int,
    TransactionDate date,
    Amount decimal(10, 2),
    FOREIGN KEY (AccountID) REFERENCES Accounts(AccountID)
);
```

In this example, the `Transactions` table has an `AccountID` column that references the `AccountID` in the `Accounts` table. With the constraint we set up, we are able to ensure that every transaction recorded in the `Transactions` table is associated with a valid `Accounts` record. When we try to insert a transaction, the `AccountID` in the `Transactions` table must correspond to an existing `AccountID` in the `Accounts` table. Consider the following, for instance:

```
INSERT INTO Transactions (TransactionID, AccountID, TransactionDate,
Amount)
VALUES (101, 1, '2023-01-01', 500.00);
```

This `INSERT` operation will only succeed if there is an account with `AccountID = 1` in the `Accounts` table. If there's no such record, the `INSERT` operation will fail due to the `FOREIGN KEY` constraint we defined earlier.

CHECK constraint

The `CHECK` constraint is used to specify a condition that each row in a database table must satisfy. This constraint ensures that the data in a particular column (or a combination of columns) adheres to a specified rule. For example, we can use this constraint to ensure that a `'salary'` column contains only values above a certain minimum amount. Another example of this involves having a `'birthdate'` column containing dates that fall only within a particular range.

To show how this constraint works, let's look at a simplified example where we have a single table called `Accounts`:

```
CREATE TABLE Accounts (
    AccountID int,
    CustomerName varchar(100),
    Balance decimal(10, 2) CHECK (Balance >= 0)
);
```

Here, we define a table structure with a constraint on the Balance column. Now, if we insert or update a record that sets the Balance to a negative value:

```
INSERT INTO Accounts (AccountID, CustomerName, Balance)
VALUES (1, 'Jane Doe', -100.00);
```

This would result in an error since our insert operation attempts to insert a negative balance, which is prevented and blocked by the CHECK constraint.

> **Note**
>
> Note that CHECK constraints can be used to guarantee the correctness of a formula between two columns in a database table. For example, if you have a table with columns for 'Price', 'Quantity', and 'TotalCost', you could set up a constraint that ensures that 'TotalCost' is always equal to the product of 'Price' and 'Quantity' field values.

Domain constraint

A domain constraint helps ensure that values in a database column fall within a specified range, type, or format. To show how this constraint works, let's see a simplified example where we have a single table called Accounts:

```
CREATE TABLE Accounts (
    AccountID int,
    CustomerName varchar(100),
    Balance decimal(10, 2),
    Type varchar(20) CHECK (Type IN ('Savings', 'Checking', 'Credit',
'Loan'))
);
```

The Type column is constrained to only allow four possible values: 'Savings', 'Checking', 'Credit', or 'Loan'. Here, we have a domain constraint by limiting the domain of acceptable values for the Type column. Let's try inserting a record with a Type value outside of the allowed values:

```
INSERT INTO Accounts (AccountID, CustomerName, Balance, Type)
VALUES (1, 'Jane Doe', 1000.00, 'Investment');
```

This would yield a constraint violation error because 'Investment' is not an allowed value for the Type column (since we have a domain constraint defined).

Failure to implement preventative measures against data integrity issues can result in serious consequences such as compliance issues and financial implications. It is a fundamental principle in data management that prevention is better than cure, especially in the context of maintaining data integrity. That being said, any transactions that could potentially lead to data integrity issues should be designed not to push through. This will ensure that the system proactively safeguards against the risks of data corruption.

> **Note**
>
> In addition to what has been discussed already, there are other techniques that can be used to guarantee and manage the integrity of the data. These include using atomic increments and decrements along with various types of locking techniques (**mutex locks**, **table locks**, and **row-level locks**), implementing **write-ahead logging**, utilizing the **event sourcing** pattern, and enforcing strict application deployment and testing protocols. Using one or more of these would help prevent a variety of data integrity issues in financial systems and applications.

Performing regular security audits

Lastly, performing regular security audits is critical for identifying vulnerabilities in the system, especially those that could compromise the integrity of financial data. Imagine a hacker (that is, an attacker) compromising a system and *directly* updating financial database records. Such an incident *could* lead to inaccuracies in financial reporting and serious legal and regulatory consequences. By proactively addressing security issues, businesses would be able to minimize the likelihood of a data breach and safeguard the accuracy and reliability of their financial data. In some cases, these incidents may result in *undetected* unauthorized transactions and can lead to financial reporting inaccuracies or financial loss. In unfortunate situations, organizations may fail to detect such breaches entirely.

> **Note**
>
> In other cases, direct financial record updates *may* be performed by attackers, which are masked by data integrity issues (*also caused by attackers*). These issues can potentially affect millions of records to hide their tracks or the true extent of the breach.

At this point, we should have a few more tricks up our sleeve to avoid common financial data integrity issues and challenges. Feel free to go back and review the concepts discussed in this chapter before moving on to the next chapter.

Summary

In this chapter, we discussed the importance of data integrity as a critical foundation for every organization making financial data-driven decisions. We learned how to detect manual data encoding errors by implementing data validation, conducting data audits, and performing timely account reconciliations. Next, we covered the most common account reconciliation problems and how to avoid them using known procedures and available tools. We also discussed how to prevent balance sheet data integrity issues since the balance sheet is one of the major financial reports that businesses prepare and that stakeholders use when making decisions. Toward the last half of the chapter, we covered how to handle data corruption and data integrity issues in systems and databases using various strategies and solutions.

This chapter gave a comprehensive overview of the complex challenges and issues of various companies and how to address and mitigate them. In the next chapter, we will dive deeper and explore how to measure the impact of data integrity issues. We will cover why it is critical to understand the financial impact of these measures, learn the relevant data quality metrics for data and transactions, learn the importance of data profiling and establishing data quality frameworks, and dive deeper by performing hands-on exercises in preparing a sample data quality scorecard using spreadsheets.

Further reading

For more information on the topics covered in this chapter, feel free to check out the following resources:

- *Cybersecurity: Another hat for the modern CFO to wear?*: `https://cfomagazine.com.au/cybersecurity-another-hat-for-the-modern-cfo-to-wear/`
- *BDO and AusCERT Cyber Security Survey Report 2021*: `https://www.bdo.com.au/en-au/services/advisory/risk-advisory-services/cyber-security/cyber-security-survey-reports`

3

Measuring the Impact of Data Integrity Issues

Data is considered one of the most important assets for any organization in this digital era. It serves as a foundation for decision-making, business strategy, and reporting, as well as long-term planning. However, given the increasing amount of data being generated, the risk of data integrity issues has also increased significantly. Thus, it is crucial that organizations measure the impact of data integrity issues and ensure that proactive measures are in place to prevent these issues from occurring. *Imagine that a company needs information about its inventory purchases to ensure that its production is supported, but finds out that the inventory data has mistakes and errors, making its forecasts inaccurate.* This is the reason why there is a need for metrics measured by data quality scorecards.

In this chapter, we will cover the following:

- Why measure the impact of data integrity issues?
- Reviewing the relevant data quality metrics for financial data and transactions
- Data profiling using a data quality framework
- Preparing a sample data quality scorecard in Microsoft Excel
- Preparing a sample data quality scorecard in Google Sheets
- Microsoft Excel and Google Sheets functionalities to improve data quality and integrity

By the end of this chapter, you will have a deeper understanding of the various metrics to measure data quality, as well as be able to make use of these metrics to create sample data quality scorecards in both Microsoft Excel and Google Sheets.

Technical requirements

Before we dive into our discussion, we must have the following in place:

- **Microsoft Excel** 2016 or later (in case you do not have this installed on your machine, you may access **Microsoft 365** for free on the web through this link: `https://www.microsoft.com/en-au/microsoft-365/free-office-online-for-the-web`)
- A web browser to access **Google Sheets**
- A **Google** account to access **Sheets** (free version)

The sample data quality scorecard in Microsoft Excel is saved in the Packt **GitHub** repository and can be accessed at this link: `https://github.com/PacktPublishing/Managing-Data-Integrity-for-Finance/tree/main/ch03`.

> **Note**
> The scorecard for Google Sheets can be accessed here: `https://docs.google.com/spreadsheets/d/1wD759gINukpu9VJOJWECdG0PwcrWX_C-2DfsASZBxAc/edit?usp=drive_link`.

Once these are ready, you can proceed to the following steps.

Why measure the impact of data integrity issues?

The impact of data integrity issues can have direct cost implications, indirect costs, and even lost opportunities for the business. Data integrity issues, especially in transaction data, may lead to direct costs to the business such as the cost of correcting errors, reworking processes, and potential regulatory penalties. These expenses need to be accounted for since they could be quite significant.

Costs can also be indirect, such as a decrease in productivity, lower customer satisfaction, and harm to a company's reputation. These can be quite difficult to estimate; however, they can still have a substantial impact on the bottom line. Problems with data integrity may also lead to lost opportunities, such as declines in sales or missed investment opportunities. Though these are quite challenging to quantify, they can still have a notable impact on the business's financial performance.

Now that we have covered the different types of costs resulting from data integrity issues, let's discuss the reasons why there is a need to measure them.

To manage the risk of basing decisions on bad data

Management, decision-makers, and stakeholders base their decisions on insights gleaned from financial reports and transaction data. If there are underlying issues related to the integrity and quality of the data, then this could potentially lead to wrong decisions or those that could have an adverse impact on the business.

To manage the risk of not complying with regulations

If a company's systems and reports have data integrity issues, this could potentially result in issues with noncompliance with regulations. The scenario we discussed in the previous chapter is a good example, where the bank was fined USD 470 million for breaching the **Anti-Money Laundering and Counter-Terrorism Financing Act** (**AML-CTF**). This was the result of data integrity issues with its **intelligent deposit machines** (**IDMs**).

> Note
>
> Please refer to *Chapter 2, Avoiding Common Data Integrity Issues and Challenges in Finance Teams*, for more information on this topic.

To manage the risk of damage to reputation

A company facing data integrity issues with its systems and processes also runs the risk of damage to its reputation, which would lead to reduced trust from its customers and lost revenue. Continuing with our example of the bank, given the high media attention where the data integrity issue led to a money laundering scandal, the company faced a high risk of damage to its reputation. It was a good thing that the company agreed and followed a remediation plan to create new processes and procedures to restore trust in the business.

> Note
>
> In addition to what has been discussed, data integrity issues would lead to increased costs associated with cleaning and fixing various types of issues, increased employee workload while correcting issues, and even system downtime to accommodate data cleaning and correction activities (which may impact online sales and employee productivity).

Data integrity issues definitely have a significant impact on the business, whether they are considered direct costs, indirect costs, or lost opportunities.

Now that we have discussed these, let's now review the relevant data quality metrics for financial data and transactions.

Reviewing the relevant data quality metrics for financial data and transactions

In the previous section, we discussed the importance of understanding the impact of data integrity. In this section, we will cover the different data quality metrics that we will use later in our scorecards.

While data quality and data integrity are closely related concepts in the field of data management, they each focus on different aspects of how data is maintained and utilized within an organization.

> **Note**
>
> To help explain the *difference* between data integrity and data quality, imagine a shipping company that needs to deliver packages to a particular address. To get the package where it needs to be, the company has to ensure that the parcel is sealed properly and remains intact during transit. Not only that, it also has to guarantee that it is delivered in a timely manner to the correct address and that it fits the customer's expectations. Connecting this with the concepts of data integrity and data quality, data integrity resembles the shipping company's procedures to ensure that packages are secured, handled properly, and protected from theft or damage during transit. The company makes sure that the product is received by the customer in the same condition that it was sent. Meanwhile, data quality is similar to the shipping company's focus on *context-specific* attributes such as timeliness, accuracy, and relevance to the customer's needs.

It is crucial to examine various data quality indicators for financial data and transactions to guarantee the data's accuracy, completeness, consistency, timeliness, and validity. *Figure 3.1* shows the important measures that can be used to evaluate the quality of financial data:

Figure 3.1 – Dimensions of data quality

Let's examine each of these in turn.

Accuracy

This metric assesses how accurate financial data is and how closely it reflects reality. A known source of truth, such as a bank statement or invoice, might be used to compare the data against actual records in order to make a determination. When data is accurate, business decision-makers are able to rely on the information and make informed decisions.

Completeness

This metric assesses the presence and existence of all necessary financial data values. Completeness can be determined, for instance, in an **accounts payable** system, by ensuring that all invoices have been entered. Another example is when querying data from a database, it is important that the records loaded from the database (including all relevant field values of each record) are complete prior to making any analysis.

> **Note**
>
> When using relational database systems such as PostgreSQL, the **NOT NULL constraint** as well as the **foreign key constraint** can help in ensuring the completeness of data and financial transactions. For more information about this topic, feel free to check *Chapter 2, Avoiding Common Data Integrity Issues and Challenges in Finance Teams.*

Consistency

This metric assesses the consistency of financial data from various sources (for example, multiple systems and databases). Consistency needs to be checked by comparing the data in various accounting systems used by an organization. This would also refer to consistency in terms of formatting for zip codes, rounding decimals in a worksheet, or how names are entered into the database. As we will discuss in the last section of this chapter, consistency can be enhanced through the use of data validation. For example, typographical errors or formatting issues can lead to mismatches for records stored in different systems and databases.

> **Note**
>
> The **Levenshtein distance**, discussed in *Chapter 1, Recognizing the Importance of Data Integrity in Finance*, can be used to address various types of consistency issues in data. For example, let's say we have a database of bank customer names where minor spelling discrepancies exist (for example, "`Jane Sarah Lat`" versus "`Jane Sarahh Lat`"). Using the Levenshtein distance, we are able to quantify the similarity between these names and potentially identify them as referring to the same individual. This allows for more effective data cleansing and standardization, as well as improved matching and deduplication processes. It is important to note that the Levenshtein distance should be part of a broader toolkit to ensure the integrity of data. That being said, it should be used with care and in combination with other data integrity and quality assurance measures.

Another good example of a data consistency issue occurs when various systems adopt different currency formats. This can lead to discrepancies in financial reporting and analysis. For example, one system might represent a monetary value as `$1,000`, another as `1000 USD`, and yet another as `1,000 dollars`.

Timeliness

This score assesses how current and relevant the data is. Collecting and updating financial data on which to base financial reports, on a timely basis, is important because more recent information must be relied upon to make decisions. A report such as the balance sheet showing the previous year's financial performance may not be relevant in making decisions compared to the latest balance sheet prepared the previous week. Thus, the element of timeliness is crucial in decision-making, though it needs to be balanced with the effort and accuracy of such information.

Validity

This metric assesses the degree to which financial data complies with a certain set of guidelines or criteria. One way to determine authenticity in an accounts receivable system is to see whether all client invoices adhere to the organization's billing rules.

> **Note**
>
> You can begin by determining which financial information and transactions are most important to your company before reviewing these indicators. After that, you can construct a procedure for routinely monitoring and assessing data quality and create a checklist of metrics to review. Manual data checks, automated data quality techniques, or a combination of the two may be used for this.

Now that we have covered the relevant data quality metrics, we can go into data profiling.

Data profiling using a data quality framework

A crucial step in determining the quality of your data is **data profiling**. This entails examining your data to comprehend its composition and linkages. We will be discussing the data profiling features of business intelligence tools in the next two chapters. In this section, we will be using a data quality framework to accomplish data profiling by performing the general steps seen in *Figure 3.2*:

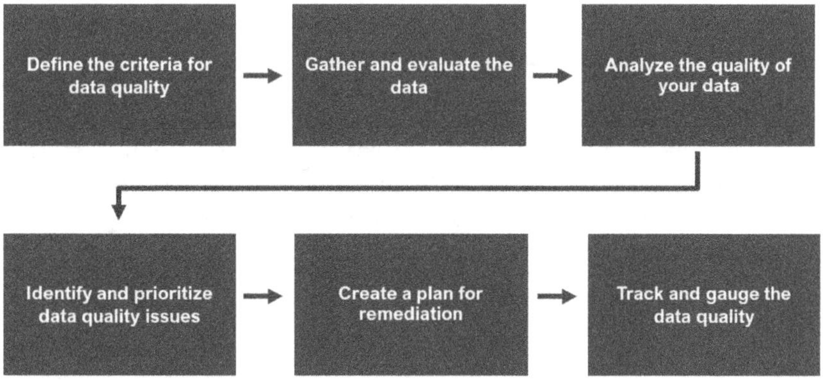

Figure 3.2 – General steps for data profiling

Let's go through this, step by step.

Define the criteria for data quality

Determine the relevant data quality metrics that are important to the business. These are the indicators of accuracy, completeness, consistency, timeliness, and validity that we covered earlier in the chapter. To which metrics we will give more importance will be context-specific and depend on what the company aims to achieve.

Continuing our scenario at the start of this chapter on the company needing information about its inventory purchases, but being unable to rely on its records because of the errors found, it will give more weight to accuracy and validity compared to other metrics.

Gather and evaluate the data

Get a representative sample of the data and analyze this using data profiling tools. These tools can help identify patterns, connections, or any irregularities in the data. For example, data profiling features are available in **Microsoft Excel** (*2016 and later versions*) through **Power Query Editor**. Power Query Editor is available not just in Excel but also in Power BI and other Microsoft products. Though there are some differences between the various editor versions, we will be covering the data profiling features of Power Query for **Power BI** in *Chapter 5, Using Business Intelligence Tools to Fix Data Integrity Issues*.

Analyze the quality of your data

Utilize the data quality metrics from our first step to assess the quality of the data. Evaluate whether there are any problems or areas where the data does not satisfy the standards for quality. We will have a better grasp of the state of our data when we review each metric and indicate a score for each one, as we will see under *Scoring the KPIs* in the *Preparing a sample data quality scorecard in Microsoft Excel* section.

Identify and prioritize data quality issues

After evaluating the potential problem areas, they should be clearly identified and assessed based on their impact on business operations. The issues that will be focused on as well as the resources that will be invested into addressing the problems will be dependent on what the business deems important. Resources are not limitless; therefore, proper care and consideration need to be given to make sure that these resources are deployed properly.

Create a plan for remediation

Create an actionable plan to deal with data quality problems. Manual data cleaning, utilizing automated technologies for data quality, and standardizing data management procedures within the team may all be necessary.

Track and gauge the data quality

To ensure that the data is accurate, complete, and trustworthy over time, constantly monitor and measure its quality. We will be covering this further under *Update the scorecard regularly* in the next section.

> **Important note**
>
> It's important to note that a data quality framework is not a *one-size-fits-all* solution and should be customized to fit various contexts and requirements. Depending on the specific needs and characteristics of the organization or industry, the framework should be tailored to address the unique aspects. For instance, what works for a specific business in terms of data quality might differ significantly from the needs of another business. In addition to this, the framework should be flexible enough to accommodate various types of data being managed, as well as regulatory requirements and business goals.

Let's now put what we've learned into action and prepare sample data quality scorecards using common work tools, such as Microsoft Excel and Google Sheets.

Preparing a sample data quality scorecard in Microsoft Excel

In the previous section, we discussed using data quality frameworks to get a better understanding of the quality of the data we are working with. In this section, we will discuss how to decide which metrics to use and create a sample template in Excel, then apply it to a fictional scenario for a company encountering issues with its data.

Establish the data quality metrics to be used

To prepare a data quality scorecard in Excel, we must first establish the data quality metrics that we will use. We covered them earlier in the chapter and we will create a sample scorecard that includes KPIs for completeness, accuracy, consistency, timeliness, and validity.

Define the scale for scoring KPIs

There are two options we can use when scoring the KPIs. It can either be **qualitative** or **quantitative**.

Scoring the KPIs qualitatively involves using the high, medium, and low criteria as follows:

- **High**: The data receives a high score if it is able to satisfy the predetermined quality standards. For example, the data receives a high score if it is accurate, complete, consistent, timely, and valid.
- **Medium**: The data receives a medium score when it only partially meets the predetermined data quality standards. For example, the data receives a medium score if it has a few errors, omissions, or inconsistencies, but does not significantly impact the analysis.
- **Low**: A low score is given to the data if it does not satisfy the predetermined quality standards. For example, the data receives a low score if it contains significant errors and inconsistencies that have a critical impact on the analysis.

Using these criteria is a simple technique that makes it easier to evaluate data quality and pinpoint areas where improvement is needed. To maintain consistency in scoring, it is important that guidelines and definitions are set within the team as to what constitutes high, medium, and low data quality.

Another useful visual aid when using this option is through color coding, as can be seen in *Figure 3.3*. One of the benefits of using color is that it makes it easier to identify the score of the KPI by associating a score with a particular color.

Score	Description
High	Satisifies the predetermined quality standards
Medium	Partially satisfies the predetermined quality standards
Low	Does not satisfy the predetermined quality standards

Figure 3.3 – Color coding as a visual tool

This can be set up using the **Styles** group under the **Home** tab in Excel, as can be seen in *Figure 3.4*:

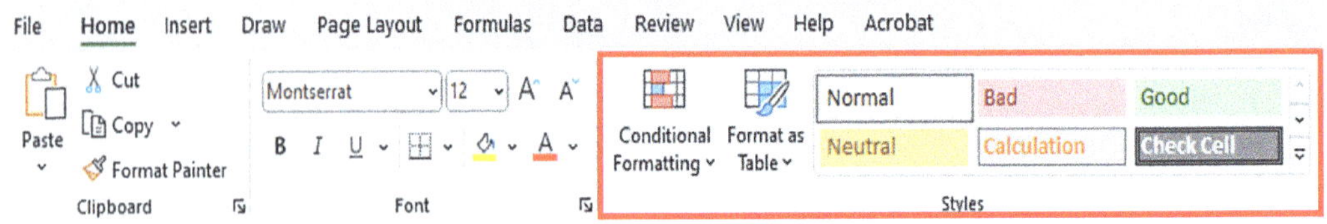

Figure 3.4 – Styles under the Home tab

In this screenshot, the ribbon has been customized to move the **Styles** tray beside the **Font** tray to show that it is under the **Home** tab. In the default settings, it is further to the right, after **Alignment** and **Number**.

> **Note**
>
> It should be noted that scoring KPIs qualitatively can be subjective. This is one of the ways of measuring them and, as an alternative, quantitative measures can be used instead or in combination.

Now that we have covered how we can measure the KPIs qualitatively, we can dive into how we can measure them quantitatively. **Quantitative scoring** is done by evaluating each criterion and assigning it a numerical value or percentage based on the assessment. Having a description for each KPI provides more detail as to how each score is evaluated, and provides more context with the assessment. For example, if 80% of the data points are complete, it can be assigned a score of 80% or 8 out of 10, as can be seen in *Figure 3.5*:

Key Performance Indicator (KPI)	Description	Score
Completeness	How comprehensive is the data? Are there any missing data points?	80%

Figure 3.5 – Measuring the KPI quantitatively

This method provides an objective assessment of data quality based on predefined criteria, and can result in judgments that are more uniform and standardized. At the same time, they can be used for easier benchmarking and trend analysis if assessing data quality over time.

Deciding which one to use will depend on the needs and requirements of the business, as well as the type of data being assessed. For our discussion, we will use the quantitative KPIs and assign a weight for ease of calculation.

Assign a weight for the KPI

The **weight** column is an indicator of how important each KPI is to the overall scorecard. The weights will vary depending on which KPI is essential to the business. For our example, we will weigh completeness at 30%, since this is an important part of our analysis, as illustrated in *Figure 3.6*:

Key Performance Indicator (KPI)	Description	Weight	Score	Overall Score
Completeness	How comprehensive is the data? Are there any missing data points?	30%	80%	

Figure 3.6 – Placing weight on a KPI

Get the overall score for the KPI

The overall score can be calculated by multiplying the weight of 30% and the score of 80% to give us 24%, as can be seen in *Figure 3.7*:

Key Performance Indicator (KPI)	Description	Weight	Score	Overall Score
Completeness	How comprehensive is the data? Are there any missing data points?	30%	80%	24%

Figure 3.7 – Overall score for the KPI

If, later on, it is noted that the other metrics are deemed more important than completeness, this weight can be updated to reflect the change in expectations.

Create the template in Excel

Now that we have the basic format, we can build the template in Excel with the KPI, description, weight, score, and overall score columns and add the KPIs of completeness, accuracy, consistency, timeliness, and validity.

Figure 3.8 shows an example of a template created in Microsoft Excel where the KPIs are listed and weighted to get the overall score:

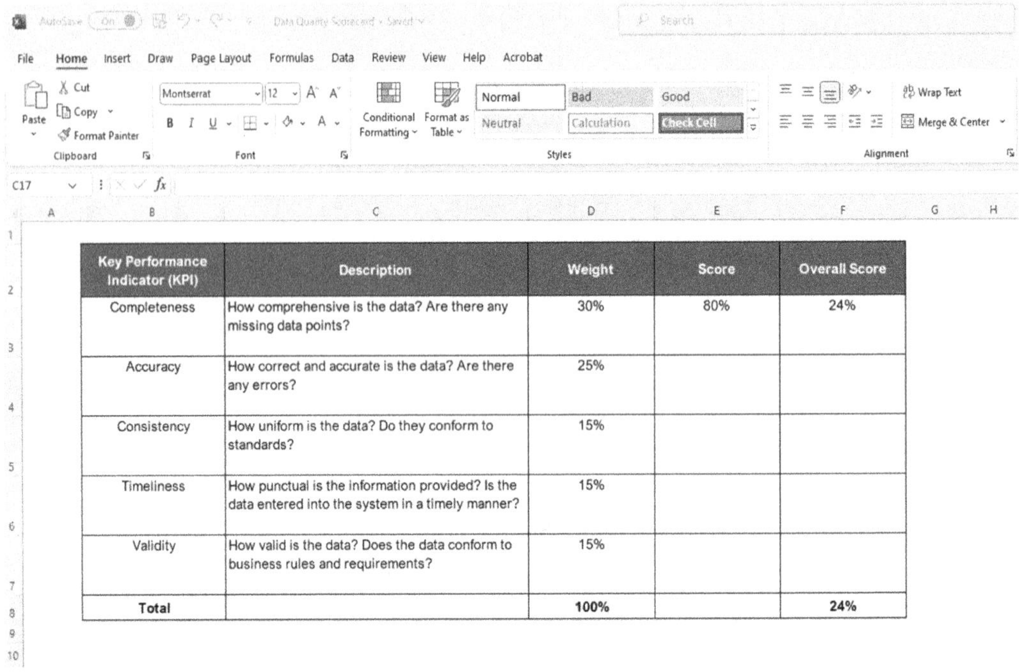

Key Performance Indicator (KPI)	Description	Weight	Score	Overall Score
Completeness	How comprehensive is the data? Are there any missing data points?	30%	80%	24%
Accuracy	How correct and accurate is the data? Are there any errors?	25%		
Consistency	How uniform is the data? Do they conform to standards?	15%		
Timeliness	How punctual is the information provided? Is the data entered into the system in a timely manner?	15%		
Validity	How valid is the data? Does the data conform to business rules and requirements?	15%		
Total		**100%**		**24%**

Figure 3.8 – Create the template in Excel

Once we have plotted the needed information in Excel, as can be seen in the preceding figure, we can assess each metric and assign a score, which we will discuss next.

Scoring the KPIs

Accuracy measures how correct and accurate the information is, as well as whether there are any errors in the data. If, based on the review, errors are found in 30% of the data, we can give it an accuracy score of 70%. The overall score is calculated by multiplying the weight and the score to give us 18%, as can be seen in *Figure 3.9*:

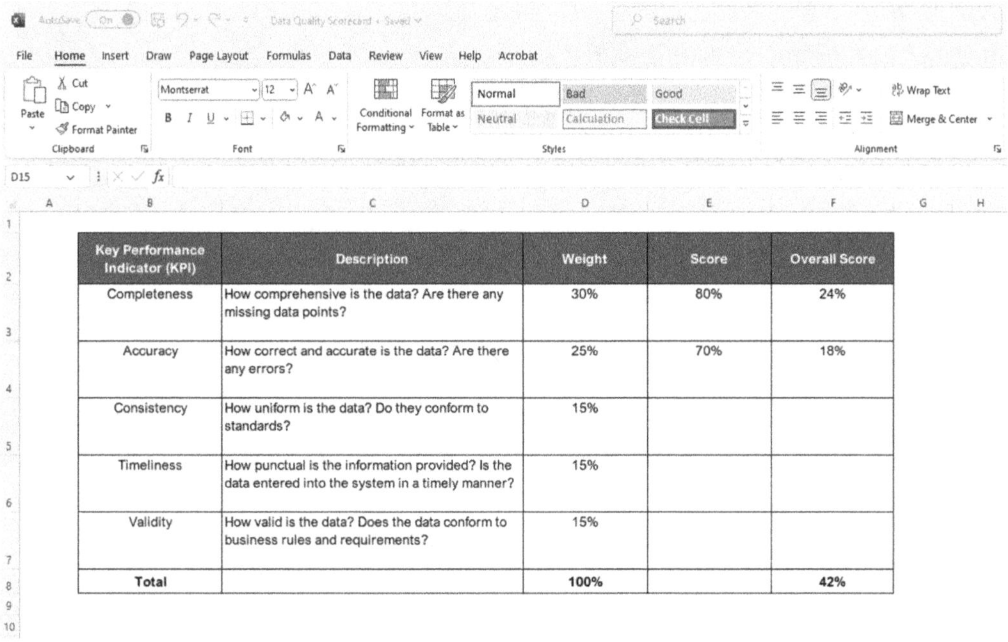

Key Performance Indicator (KPI)	Description	Weight	Score	Overall Score
Completeness	How comprehensive is the data? Are there any missing data points?	30%	80%	24%
Accuracy	How correct and accurate is the data? Are there any errors?	25%	70%	18%
Consistency	How uniform is the data? Do they conform to standards?	15%		
Timeliness	How punctual is the information provided? Is the data entered into the system in a timely manner?	15%		
Validity	How valid is the data? Does the data conform to business rules and requirements?	15%		
Total		**100%**		**42%**

Figure 3.9 – Reviewing the accuracy of the data

By reviewing the KPI and assigning a score, the finance team can ask critical questions such as the following:

- How can we improve the accuracy of the data?
- How can we take corrective action to address the errors?
- What steps can we implement to ensure that the data entered into the system is accurate?

The next steps will be reviewing each KPI and assessing them as to their consistency, timeliness, and validity. *Figure 3.10* shows the completed scorecard after this assessment:

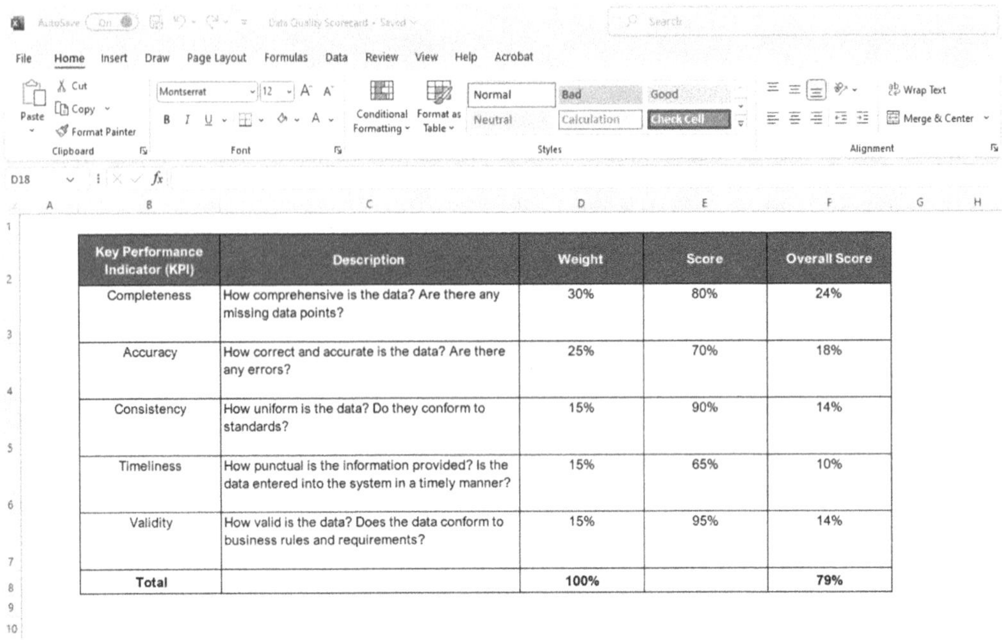

Key Performance Indicator (KPI)	Description	Weight	Score	Overall Score
Completeness	How comprehensive is the data? Are there any missing data points?	30%	80%	24%
Accuracy	How correct and accurate is the data? Are there any errors?	25%	70%	18%
Consistency	How uniform is the data? Do they conform to standards?	15%	90%	14%
Timeliness	How punctual is the information provided? Is the data entered into the system in a timely manner?	15%	65%	10%
Validity	How valid is the data? Does the data conform to business rules and requirements?	15%	95%	14%
Total		**100%**		**79%**

Figure 3.10 – Completed scorecard

Looking at the scorecard, we can see that it has an overall score of 79%, suggesting that the data quality can be relied on, though there are areas that need to be improved on as well. Having a higher percentage would entail that the data can be trusted and business decisions can be made with more confidence.

Update the scorecard regularly

Reviewing and updating the scorecard regularly enables the business to identify issues early on and prevent them from developing into major problems. This also improves performance, as it allows the organization to monitor progress and course-correct as needed. Moreover, it promotes greater accountability and provides an avenue for improvement in order for the organization to achieve its goals.

Now that we have covered the steps to creating a data quality scorecard, let's dive into an example!

The finance team of the Pizza Factory has been struggling with data quality issues in its **inventory** data. It noticed some discrepancies in the inventory reports and missing data points in the spreadsheets. The team knew that this was having an impact on its ability to make informed decisions in terms of purchasing the needed inventory and taking the necessary actions when required.

To measure the data quality and integrity level of the inventory data, the finance team agreed that it needed to develop a data quality scorecard that included the KPIs for completeness, accuracy, consistency, timeliness, and validity.

The team added weights for all metrics after assessing their importance, as can be seen in *Figure 3.11*. Completeness, accuracy, and timeliness were rated high for the business, giving these metrics a higher weight compared to consistency and validity.

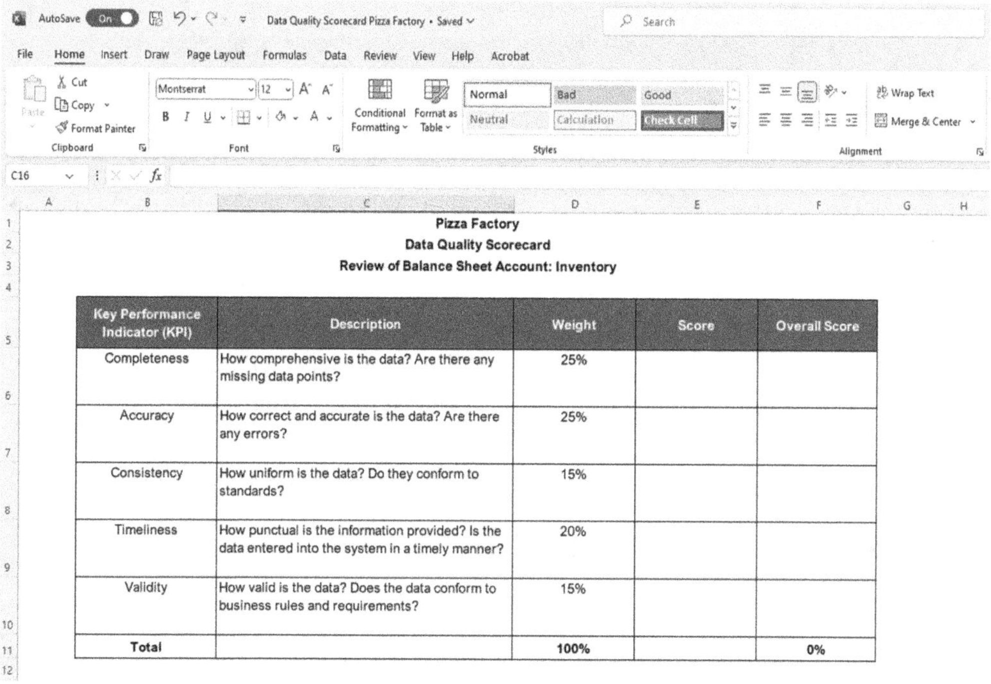

Key Performance Indicator (KPI)	Description	Weight	Score	Overall Score
Completeness	How comprehensive is the data? Are there any missing data points?	25%		
Accuracy	How correct and accurate is the data? Are there any errors?	25%		
Consistency	How uniform is the data? Do they conform to standards?	15%		
Timeliness	How punctual is the information provided? Is the data entered into the system in a timely manner?	20%		
Validity	How valid is the data? Does the data conform to business rules and requirements?	15%		
Total		**100%**		**0%**

Figure 3.11 – Scorecard template for reviewing the Pizza Factory inventory data

Next, the team looked at the data and reviewed each KPI to provide the score. During the review, it was noted that the inventory reports contained discrepancies and missing data around 30% of the time, which affected the completeness of the report. It also noted errors and based on its estimate, these errors had an impact of 25%, thus affecting accuracy.

Given that the discrepancies and missing data occurred around 30% of the time, the team scored completeness at 70% to get an overall score of 18% for this metric. As the errors were impacting 25% of the data, accuracy was scored at 75% to get an overall score of 19%. This is illustrated in *Figure 3.12*:

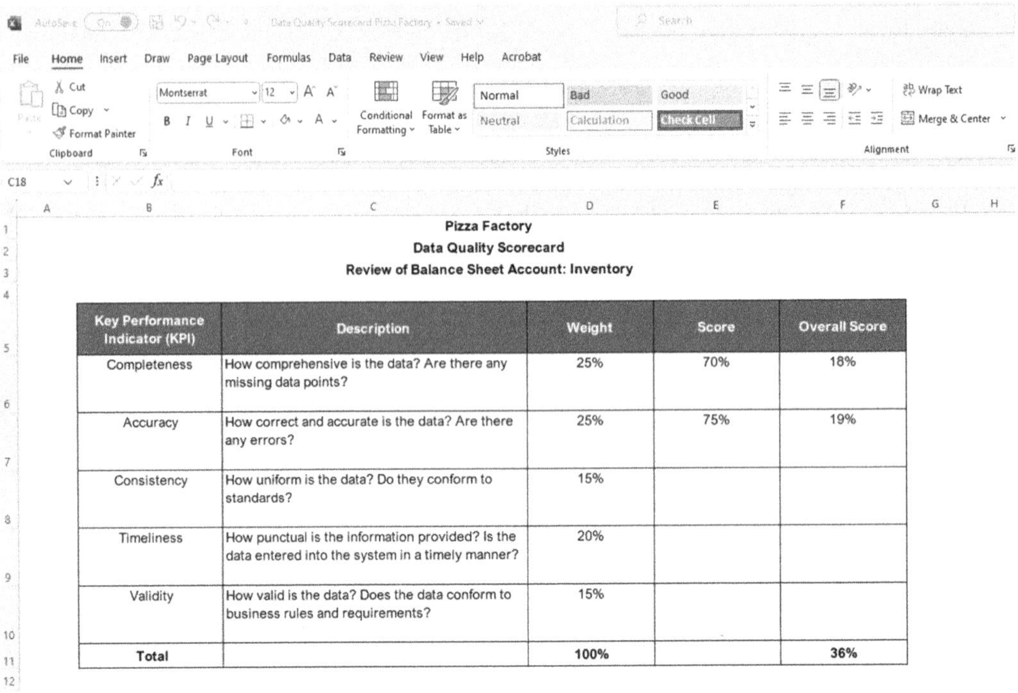

Pizza Factory
Data Quality Scorecard
Review of Balance Sheet Account: Inventory

Key Performance Indicator (KPI)	Description	Weight	Score	Overall Score
Completeness	How comprehensive is the data? Are there any missing data points?	25%	70%	18%
Accuracy	How correct and accurate is the data? Are there any errors?	25%	75%	19%
Consistency	How uniform is the data? Do they conform to standards?	15%		
Timeliness	How punctual is the information provided? Is the data entered into the system in a timely manner?	20%		
Validity	How valid is the data? Does the data conform to business rules and requirements?	15%		
Total		**100%**		**36%**

Figure 3.12 – Reviewing the completeness and accuracy of the inventory account

By reviewing the completeness and assigning a score, the finance team had the following questions:

- How can we improve the completeness of the data?
- How can we take corrective action to address the discrepancies and missing information?
- What steps can we implement to ensure that the data entered into the system is complete and that discrepancies are minimized?

The finance team then continued reviewing each metric and assigning a score to each one. The completed scorecard can be seen in *Figure 3.13*:

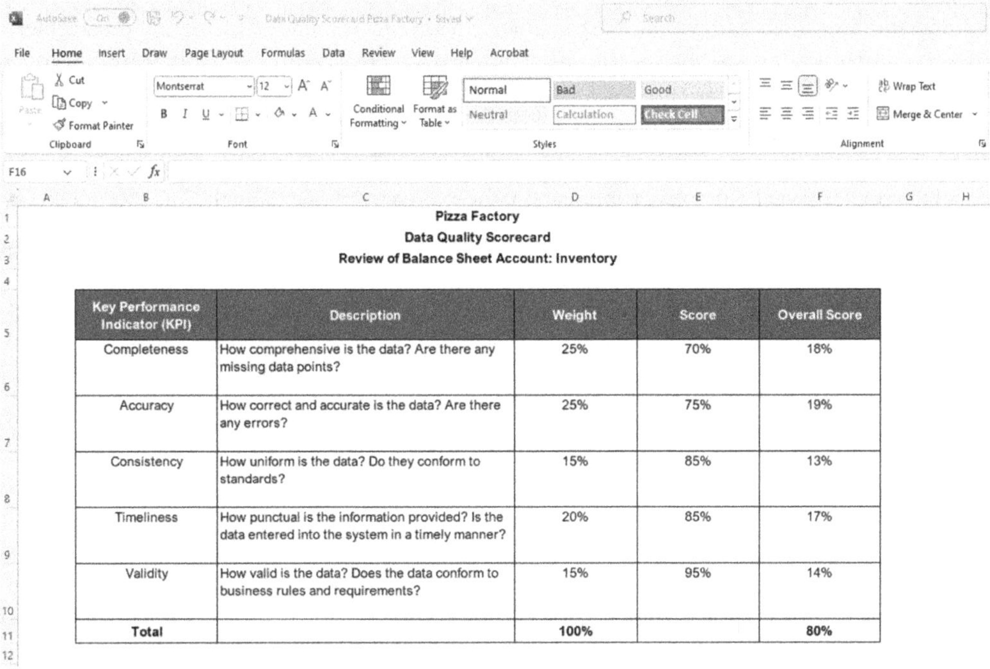

Pizza Factory
Data Quality Scorecard
Review of Balance Sheet Account: Inventory

Key Performance Indicator (KPI)	Description	Weight	Score	Overall Score
Completeness	How comprehensive is the data? Are there any missing data points?	25%	70%	18%
Accuracy	How correct and accurate is the data? Are there any errors?	25%	75%	19%
Consistency	How uniform is the data? Do they conform to standards?	15%	85%	13%
Timeliness	How punctual is the information provided? Is the data entered into the system in a timely manner?	20%	85%	17%
Validity	How valid is the data? Does the data conform to business rules and requirements?	15%	95%	14%
Total		**100%**		**80%**

Figure 3.13 – Completed scorecard after reviewing the Pizza Factory inventory account

During the review, the team noted that the data was relatively consistent and that it was conforming to standards, with a score of 85%. In most cases, the information was entered into the system in a timely manner, giving it a score of 85%. The information was valid as well, based on the available business information, getting a score of 95%. After getting the score for each metric and weighting them, the team calculated that the inventory account had an overall score of 80%.

The finance team pinpointed that the areas that needed attention were completeness and accuracy, and that these were the areas that if addressed, would significantly impact the business positively. The team then moved into diving deeper into what was causing the issues. It found out that the previous person entering the information in the system had resigned and that another person had taken over the role of recording the information without proper handover. At the same time, there was no proper documentation as to what information was required for the system. A replacement person had not been found since the operations manager had not managed to find the time to interview the new person for the role. During this discussion, the finance team highlighted that because of what happened, it was impacting the management's ability to make decisions in terms of purchasing the inventory to run operations properly.

Now understanding what had happened, the finance team recommended hiring the replacement as a priority and went into further discussions with management to ensure that procedures were in place to properly capture the inventory records. They also worked together to identify which critical aspects of inventory were necessary, such as the type of product, price, date of purchase, and expiry date. Another review was done two months after implementing the changes. Reviewing the scorecard can be done more frequently; however, in this case, the team agreed that enough time was needed to hire the replacement, document the procedures, and implement the changes.

After this period, improvements could be seen in both completeness and accuracy, as seen in *Figure 3.14*:

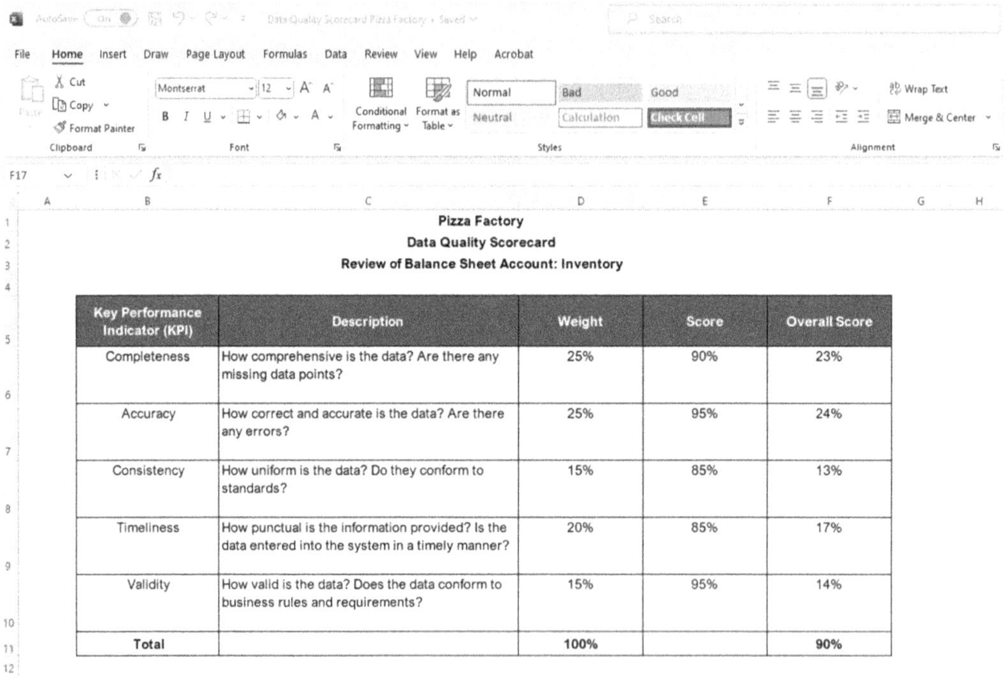

Pizza Factory
Data Quality Scorecard
Review of Balance Sheet Account: Inventory

Key Performance Indicator (KPI)	Description	Weight	Score	Overall Score
Completeness	How comprehensive is the data? Are there any missing data points?	25%	90%	23%
Accuracy	How correct and accurate is the data? Are there any errors?	25%	95%	24%
Consistency	How uniform is the data? Do they conform to standards?	15%	85%	13%
Timeliness	How punctual is the information provided? Is the data entered into the system in a timely manner?	20%	85%	17%
Validity	How valid is the data? Does the data conform to business rules and requirements?	15%	95%	14%
Total		**100%**		**90%**

Figure 3.14 – Completed scorecard after reviewing the Pizza Factory inventory account, two months after the previous review

During discussions with management, the team noted that the information in the reports was more complete and accurate, which increased its trust in the data. Since the information was now more reliable, it allowed the business to make purchases of inventory in a more timely manner and make more informed decisions. Overall, performing the exercise to create a data quality scorecard to monitor inventory proved beneficial to the business.

At this point, now that we have covered a sample data quality scorecard in Microsoft Excel, we can discuss creating a scorecard using Google Sheets. The steps to preparing this scorecard are quite similar and we will modify them using the functions in Google Sheets.

Preparing a sample data quality scorecard in Google Sheets

Continuing with our example of the Pizza Factory, management noticed that it was receiving a lot of follow-up inquiries from its suppliers as to when the invoices they sent would be paid. Upon discussion with the finance team and looking at the **accounts payable** account, it noticed that some of the transactions had missing data, such as payment terms and due dates, and also noted that some invoices were duplicated in the system.

Management was worried that the late payments would affect its relationship with its suppliers and increase the risk of duplicate payments. In addition to this, management wanted to take advantage of potential discounts if it paid the invoices before their due dates. Apparently, the person who had resigned after handling the recording of the inventory had also been the one responsible for recording the accounts payable, which affected the quality and integrity of the data in the system. Given the success of the data quality scorecard during the review of inventory, management requested that the same procedure be done for the accounts payable account. It also inquired whether it would be possible to use Google Sheets instead of Microsoft Excel for ease of sharing and collaboration.

With this in mind, the finance team set out to create the data quality scorecard using Google Sheets.

Establish the data quality metrics to be used

When preparing the data quality scorecard in Google Sheets, the data quality metrics to be used must first be established.

The finance team initially laid out the main KPIs of completeness, accuracy, consistency, timeliness, and validity, as well as their descriptions, as seen in *Figure 3.15*:

Key Performance Indicator (KPI)	Description
Completeness	How comprehensive is the data? Are all invoices, receipts, and other relevant documents being entered into the system?
Accuracy	How correct and accurate is the data? Are there any discrepancies or errors in the data?
Consistency	How uniform is the data? Are all data fields being consistently and accurately filled out?
Timeliness	Is the data entered into the system in a timely manner?
Validity	Are the accounts payable data entries valid and authorized? Are there any discrepancies or inconsistencies that could indicate fraud or other financial irregularities?

Figure 3.15 – Initial data quality metrics for reviewing the Pizza Factory accounts payable account

However, they wanted to ensure that relevant and meaningful details, such as payment terms and due dates, were captured in the accounts payable data, as well as to measure whether there were potential duplicates in the transactions. Thus, they decided to add relevance and uniqueness to the data quality scorecard, as can be seen in *Figure 3.16*:

Key Performance Indicator (KPI)	Description
Completeness	How comprehensive is the data? Are all invoices, receipts, and other relevant documents being entered into the system?
Accuracy	How correct and accurate is the data? Are there any discrepancies or errors in the data?
Consistency	How uniform is the data? Are all data fields being consistently and accurately filled out?
Timeliness	Is the data entered into the system in a timely manner?
Validity	Are the accounts payable data entries valid and authorized? Are there any discrepancies or inconsistencies that could indicate fraud or other financial irregularities?
Relevance	Are the accounts payable data captured relevant to the organization's objectives? Are the data fields correctly labeled and categorized?
Uniqueness	How unique are the transactions in the system? Are the invoices free of duplicates or redundancies?

Figure 3.16 – Updated data quality metrics for reviewing the Pizza Factory accounts payable account

Define the scale for scoring the KPIs

The next step is to define the scale for scoring the KPIs. In the previous section, we discussed the two options, which are qualitative and quantitative. The finance team decided that quantitative metrics worked previously and that assigning a numerical value allows for easier weighting of the components.

Assign a weight for the KPI

After that, the team assigned weights to each of the KPIs depending on how important they were to the business needs. *Figure 3.17* shows the weights that have been placed for each of the KPIs. It can be noticed that completeness has the highest weight at 20%, followed by accuracy, validity, relevance, and uniqueness at 15%, then consistency and timeliness at 10%:

Key Performance Indicator (KPI)	Description	Weight
Completeness	How comprehensive is the data? Are all invoices, receipts, and other relevant documents being entered into the system?	20%
Accuracy	How correct and accurate is the data? Are there any discrepancies or errors in the data?	15%
Consistency	How uniform is the data? Are all data fields being consistently and accurately filled out?	10%
Timeliness	Is the data entered into the system in a timely manner?	10%
Validity	Are the accounts payable data entries valid and authorized? Are there any discrepancies or inconsistencies that could indicate fraud or other financial irregularities?	15%
Relevance	Are the accounts payable data captured relevant to the organization's objectives? Are the data fields correctly labeled and categorized?	15%
Uniqueness	How unique are the transactions in the system? Are the invoices free of duplicates or redundancies?	15%
Total		**100%**

Figure 3.17 – Assigning weights to the KPIs

The finance team feels more confident that by establishing the criteria and weights for each KPI, it will be able to measure the data quality of the accounts payable account to address management's concerns.

Get the overall score for the KPI

To calculate the overall score for the KPI, multiply the weight of the KPI by the score after the review has been done.

In checking the completeness of the accounts payable information in the system, the finance team noted that not all invoices were recorded and that there were some missing transactions covering about 15% of the data. Thus, they set 85% as the score and used the weight of 20% to get an overall score of 17% for this metric, as shown in *Figure 3.18*:

Key Performance Indicator (KPI)	Description	Weight	Score	Overall Score
Completeness	How comprehensive is the data? Are all invoices, receipts, and other relevant documents being entered into the system?	20%	85%	17%

Figure 3.18 – Calculating the overall score

This format is similar to what we discussed in the previous section for Microsoft Excel, but we will be adding additional KPIs that are relevant to this scenario.

Create the template in Google Sheets

Since we have the basic format, we can now build the template in Google Sheets containing the KPI, description, weight, score, and overall score columns, as can be seen in *Figure 3.19*:

Data Quality Scorecard: Accounts Payable

Pizza Factory
Data Quality Scorecard
Review of Balance Sheet Account: Accounts Payable

Key Performance Indicator (KPI)	Description	Weight	Score	Overall Score
Completeness	How comprehensive is the data? Are all invoices, receipts, and other relevant documents being entered into the system?	20%	85%	17%
Accuracy	How correct and accurate is the data? Are there any discrepancies or errors in the data?	15%		
Consistency	How uniform is the data? Are all data fields being consistently and accurately filled out?	10%		
Timeliness	Is the data entered into the system in a timely manner?	10%		
Validity	Are the accounts payable data entries valid and authorized? Are there any discrepancies or inconsistencies that could indicate fraud or other financial irregularities?	15%		
Relevance	Are the accounts payable data captured relevant to the organization's objectives? Are the data fields correctly labeled and categorized?	15%		
Uniqueness	How unique are the transactions in the system? Are the invoices free of duplicates or redundancies?	15%		
Total		**100%**		**17%**

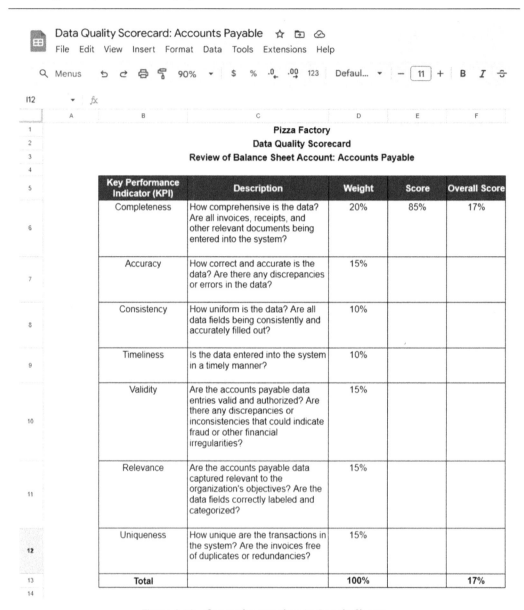

Figure 3.19 – Create the template in Google Sheets

Scoring the KPIs

Once the information is plotted in Google Sheets, assessing each metric and assigning a score can now be done.

The finance team reviewed each of the metrics and assigned them a score, as can be seen in *Figure 3.20*:

Pizza Factory
Data Quality Scorecard
Review of Balance Sheet Account: Accounts Payable

Key Performance Indicator (KPI)	Description	Weight	Score	Overall Score
Completeness	How comprehensive is the data? Are all invoices, receipts, and other relevant documents being entered into the system?	20%	85%	17%
Accuracy	How correct and accurate is the data? Are there any discrepancies or errors in the data?	15%	90%	14%
Consistency	How uniform is the data? Are all data fields being consistently and accurately filled out?	10%	80%	8%
Timeliness	Is the data entered into the system in a timely manner?	10%	80%	8%
Validity	Are the accounts payable data entries valid and authorized? Are there any discrepancies or inconsistencies that could indicate fraud or other financial irregularities?	15%	95%	14%
Relevance	Are the accounts payable data captured relevant to the organization's objectives? Are the data fields correctly labeled and categorized?	15%	60%	9%
Uniqueness	How unique are the transactions in the system? Are the invoices free of duplicates or redundancies?	15%	70%	11%
Total		**100%**		**80%**

Figure 3.20 – Completed scorecard after reviewing the Pizza Factory accounts payable

While the team was checking, it noted that invoices were being entered into the system most of the time, but that about 15% of invoices were not being entered, thus giving *completeness* a score of 85%. In terms of errors and discrepancies, it was noted that these occurred about 10% of the time, giving a score of 90% for *accuracy*.

In terms of *consistency*, the fields were filled out consistently about 80% of the time, and invoices were entered into the system in a timely manner about 80% of the time as well. For *validity*, the team found that the invoices were valid and authorized with no indications of fraud or irregularities, giving it a high score of 95%.

The team identified issues while reviewing *relevance* and *uniqueness*. It was noted that the payment terms, due dates, and potential discounts were not being properly captured in the records, thus giving *relevance* a score of 60%. At the same time, there were invoices captured multiple times in the system, leading to *uniqueness* having a score of 70%.

Upon reviewing these KPIs, the finance team started to ask these questions to improve the relevance of the data:

- How can we improve the relevance of the data?
- Which fields need to be captured to ensure that this data is relevant to the business objectives?
- What steps can we implement to ensure that the data entered into the system is relevant?

Questions to improve the uniqueness of the information were also top of the agenda, such as the following:

- How can we improve the uniqueness of the data and avoid duplications?
- How can we take corrective action to address the duplicates found in the report?
- What steps can we implement to ensure that the data entered into the system is free of duplications?

By addressing these questions, the finance team can work together with management to improve the data quality and integrity of the accounts payable account. It understands that by addressing these questions and creating an action plan, it will be able to ensure that payment is made to the suppliers on time, reduce the risk of duplicate payments, and take advantage of any potential discounts if invoices are paid before their due dates.

Now that we have covered both Microsoft Excel and Google Sheets, we can dive deeper into certain functionalities to improve data quality and integrity.

Microsoft Excel and Google Sheets functionalities to improve data quality and integrity

In the previous sections, we covered how to create sample data quality scorecards in both Microsoft Excel and Google Sheets. In this section, we will discuss the built-in capabilities these tools have to enhance the quality and integrity of data. We will begin our discussion with **version control**, which is a way to monitor changes made to files. Next, we will talk about **collaboration tools** to enable multiple users to make changes to the same file and give read-write permissions. After that, we will cover the **data validation** functionality in Google Sheets, as we discussed this for Microsoft Excel in the previous chapter. Lastly, we will touch on **conditional formatting**, which is a very useful tool to help in reviewing movements and trends.

Version control

Users can make changes to a file and keep track of changes over time in both Microsoft Excel and Google Sheets. This gives a history of file revisions and ensures that everyone is using the same version of the scorecard or a shared file they are using.

> **Note**
>
> We covered monitoring and tracking changes for Google Sheets in *Chapter 2, Avoiding Common Data Integrity Issues and Challenges in Finance Teams.*

In this section, we will cover how to track changes in Microsoft Excel. These instructions refer to Excel for **Microsoft 365**, but this feature is available for earlier versions as well:

1. Select **File | Options** and click on **Quick Access Toolbar**. A window will pop up to show **Excel Options**.
2. Select **Quick Access Toolbar** and, under **Choose commands from:**, select **All Commands**, as can be seen in *Figure 3.21:*

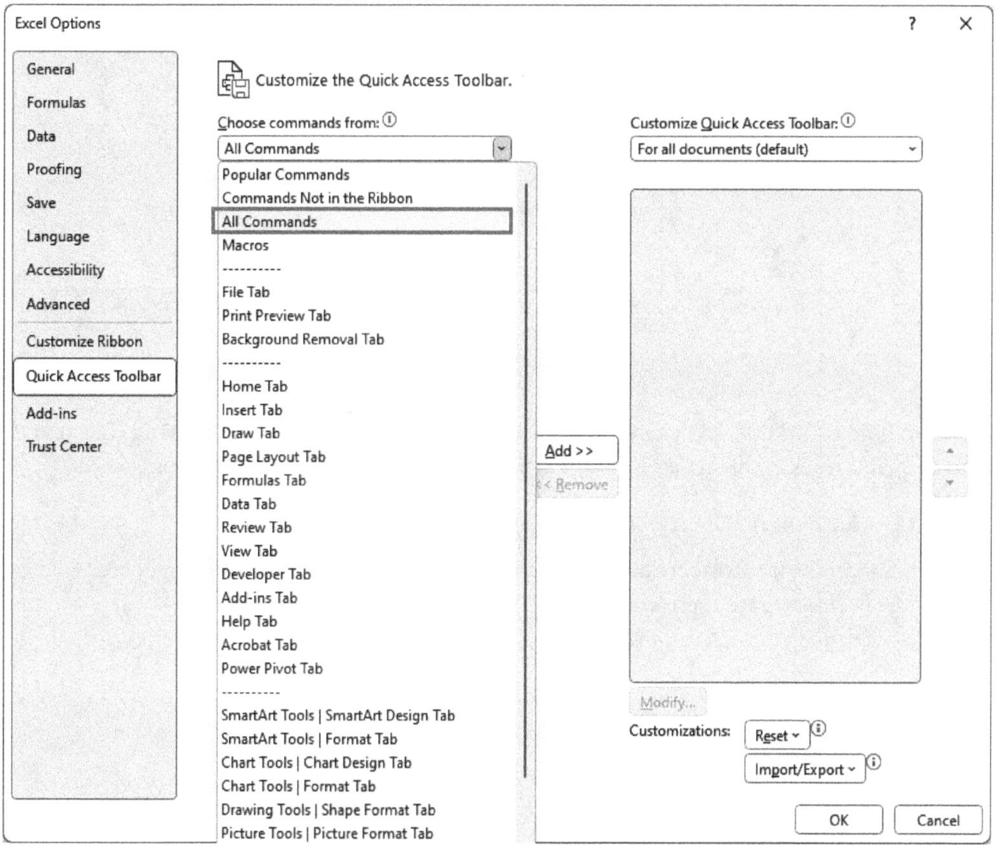

Figure 3.21 – Select All Commands under Choose commands from

3. From the list, find **Share Workbook (Legacy)**, select it, and click on **Add**. It will be added to the list on the right side, as shown in *Figure 3.22*:

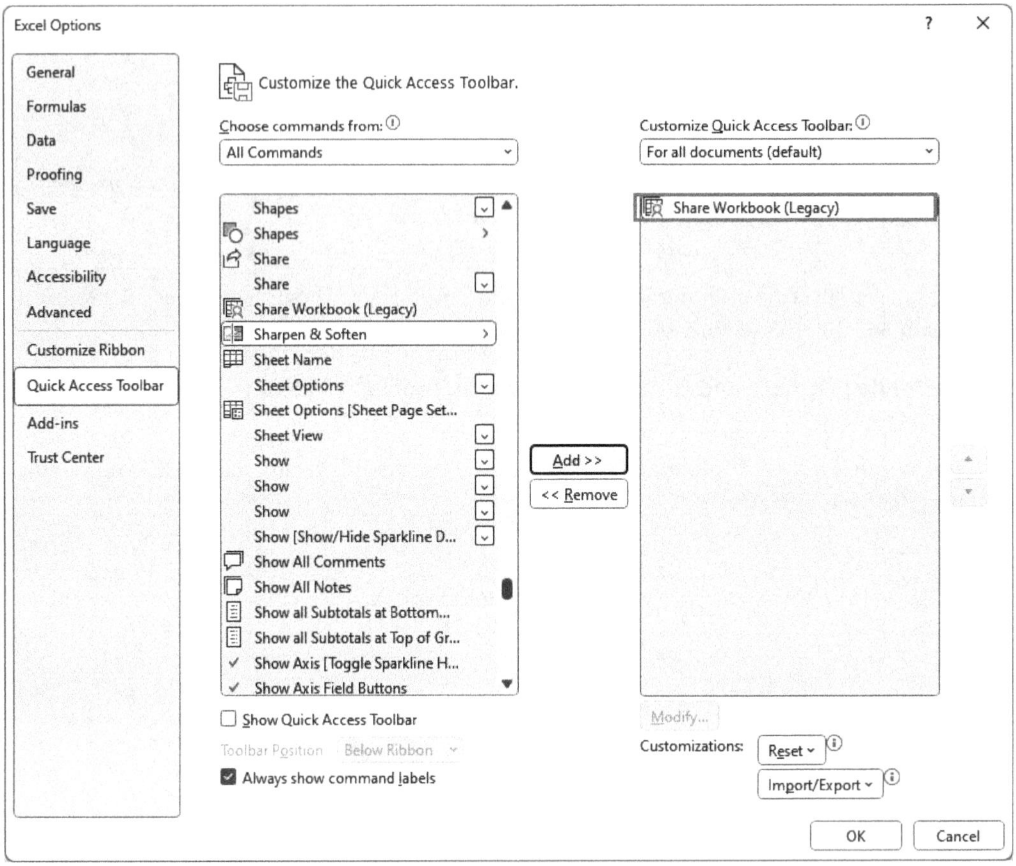

Figure 3.22 – Adding Share Workbook (Legacy) to the Quick Access Toolbar

Now that we have added this, let's enable **Track Changes (Legacy)** and **Protect Sharing (Legacy)** to allow us to enable tracking of changes, as well as protect the shared tracking with a password:

1. Find **Track Changes (Legacy)** in the list, select it, and click on **Add**.
2. Next, find in the list **Protect Sharing (Legacy)**, select it, and click on **Add**. *Figure 3.23* shows how the list looks once these are added:

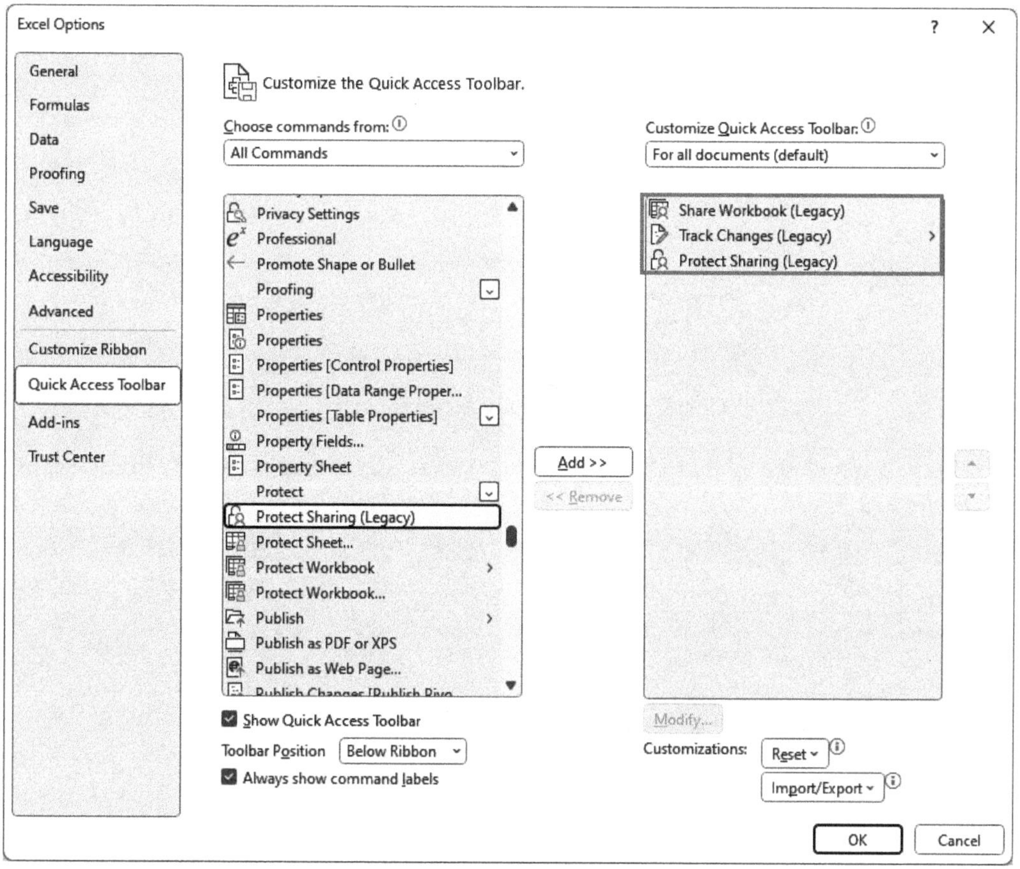

Figure 3.23 – Adding Track Changes (Legacy) and Protect Sharing (Legacy)

3. Click on **OK**. Completing this step will add these commands to the **Quick Access Toolbar**. Next, we will unhide the **Quick Access Toolbar** so that they are easily accessible.
4. Go to the lower-right corner of the ribbon to find a drop-down button. Click on it and select **Show Quick Access Toolbar**, as can be seen in *Figure 3.24*:

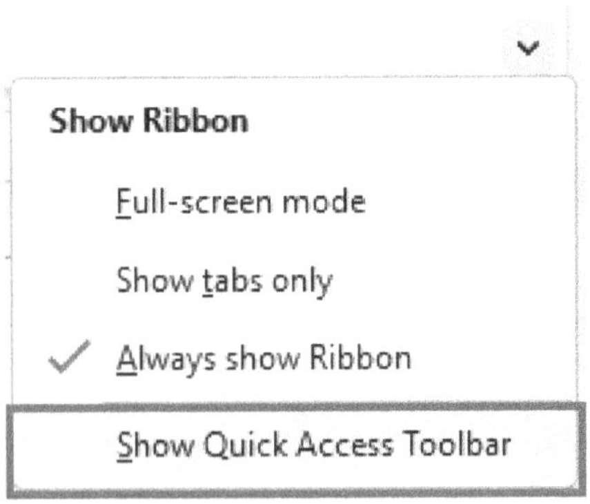

Figure 3.24 – Show Quick Access Toolbar

This will unhide the toolbar and show the three items we selected earlier, as can be seen in *Figure 3.25*:

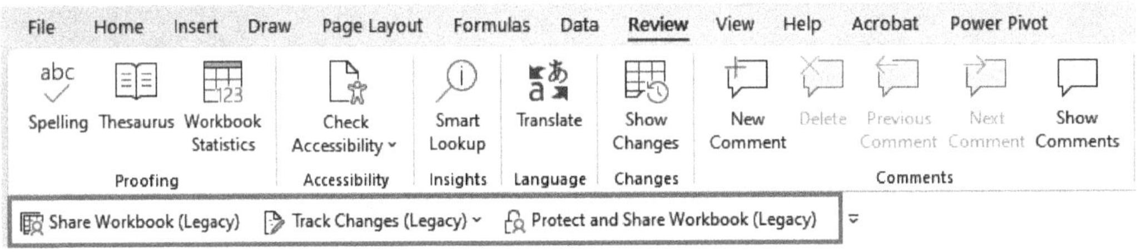

Figure 3.25 – Quick Access Toolbar

Enabling these will allow the user to share the workbook and track changes in the file for version control.

Now that we know how to activate version control in Excel for Microsoft 365, let us check out how to improve collaboration by sharing the files we are working on and setting permissions.

Collaboration tools

Both Microsoft Excel and Google Sheets improve collaboration as well as set permissions to view or edit the file we are working on.

To do this in Microsoft Excel, go to the upper-right corner of the window and click on **Share**, as shown in *Figure 3.26*:

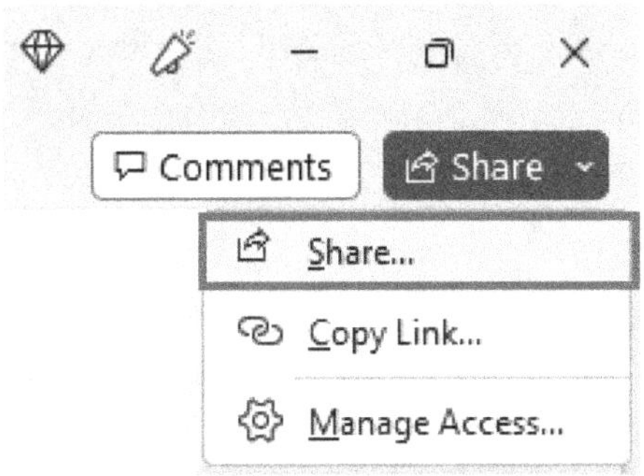

Figure 3.26 – Sharing a file in Microsoft Excel

A window will pop up, as can be seen in *Figure 3.27*, which provides the option to share the link to the file with anyone or with specific people, as well as set the settings for that person to be able to edit or view the file:

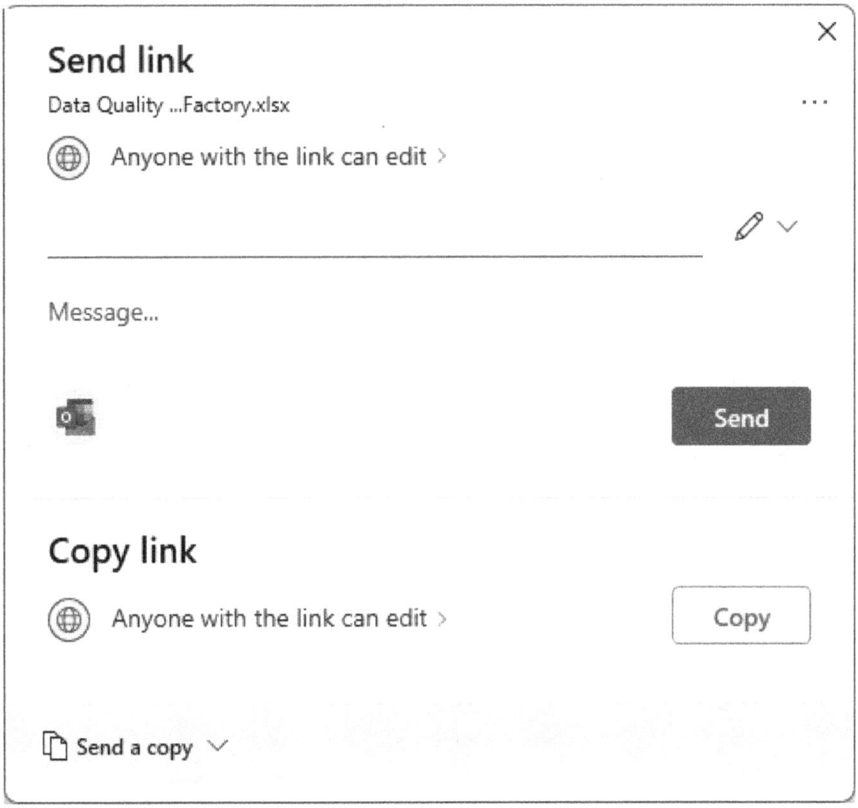

Figure 3.27 – Sending the link to the file and editing the settings in Microsoft Excel

In order to share the file, you need it to be on OneDrive. If it is not yet saved there, you will get a prompt to do so.

> **Note**
>
> You might be asking *"Why are we doing this in the first place?"* There is an increased need for collaboration in the workplace, and this makes it easier for multiple people to make changes to the same file.

Google Sheets also allows files to be shared and settings to be specified for editing or viewing. To do this, go to the upper-right corner of the window and click on **Share**, as seen in *Figure 3.28*:

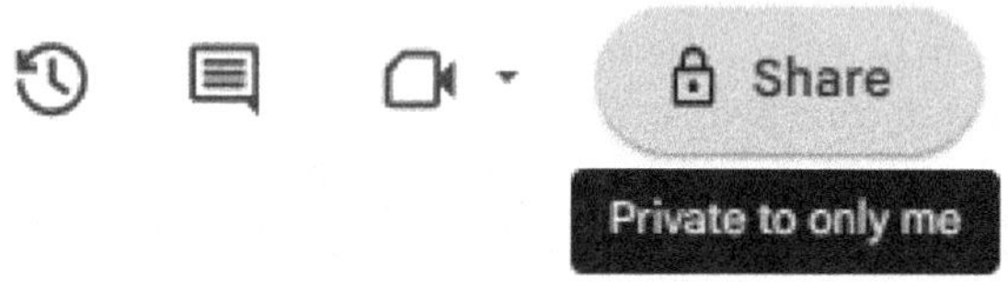

Figure 3.28 – Share a file in Google Sheets

A pop-up window that enables the file to be shared with a person or a group will appear, and specify whether the file should be restricted or can be opened by anyone with the link, as shown in *Figure 3.29*:

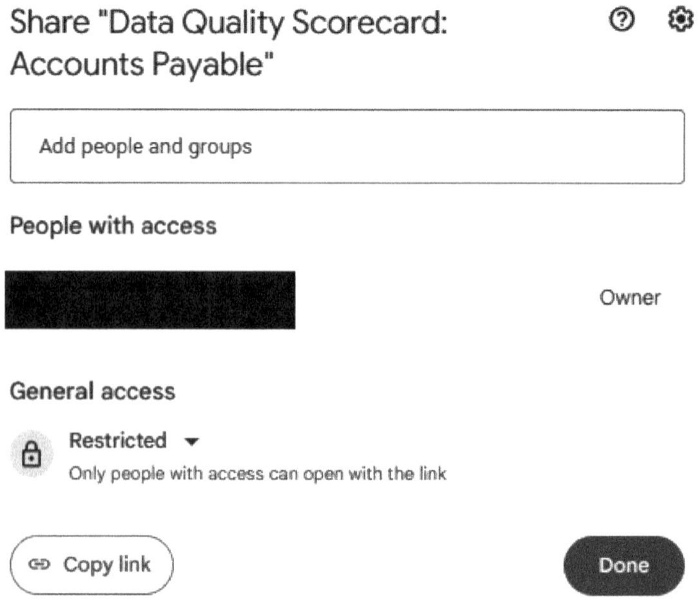

Figure 3.29 – Sending the link to the file and editing the settings in Google Sheets

> **Important note**
>
> When giving permissions or access, it is advised that the *principle of least privilege* is followed. This means that a user is granted access or privileges only up to the point that is necessary for them to carry out their tasks. Doing so ensures that risks such as unintended access to information (as well as unauthorized modifications) are minimized. For more information, feel free to check out `https://en.wikipedia.org/wiki/Principle_of_least_privilege`.

Another feature that can be used is **Comments**. This allows notes for users to provide explanations for calculations or more context about the data. In Microsoft Excel, it can be found under the **Review** tab, as can be seen in *Figure 3.30*:

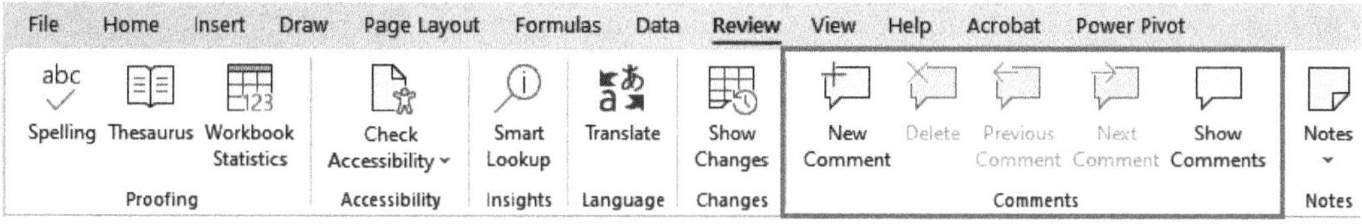

Figure 3.30 – Comments under the Review tab in Microsoft Excel

In Google Sheets, it can be found by selecting **Insert** and finding **Comment**, as illustrated in *Figure 3.31*:

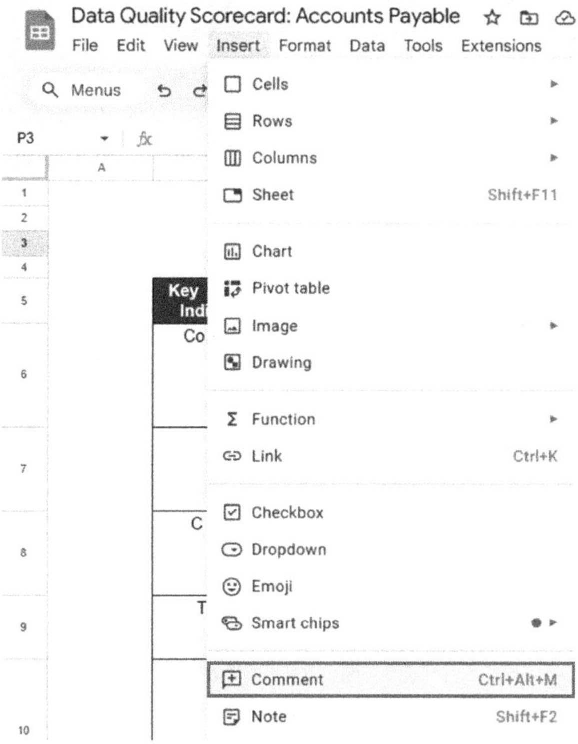

Figure 3.31 – Comments under Insert in Google Sheets

Granting permissions to access Google Sheets and adding comments are useful tools for collaboration.

In Google Sheets, is there a way to ensure that the data added to a cell has a particular type or is covered by rules? This is what we will cover next.

Data validation

Data validation assists in checking that the data uses the correct data type or format, as well as reducing data entry errors. We briefly covered this topic for Microsoft Excel in *Chapter 2, Avoiding Common Data Integrity Issues and Challenges in Finance Teams*, under the *Detecting manual data encoding issues in financial teams* section. Here, we will cover it for Google Sheets.

To find this feature, go to **Data** and select **Data validation**, as shown in *Figure 3.32*:

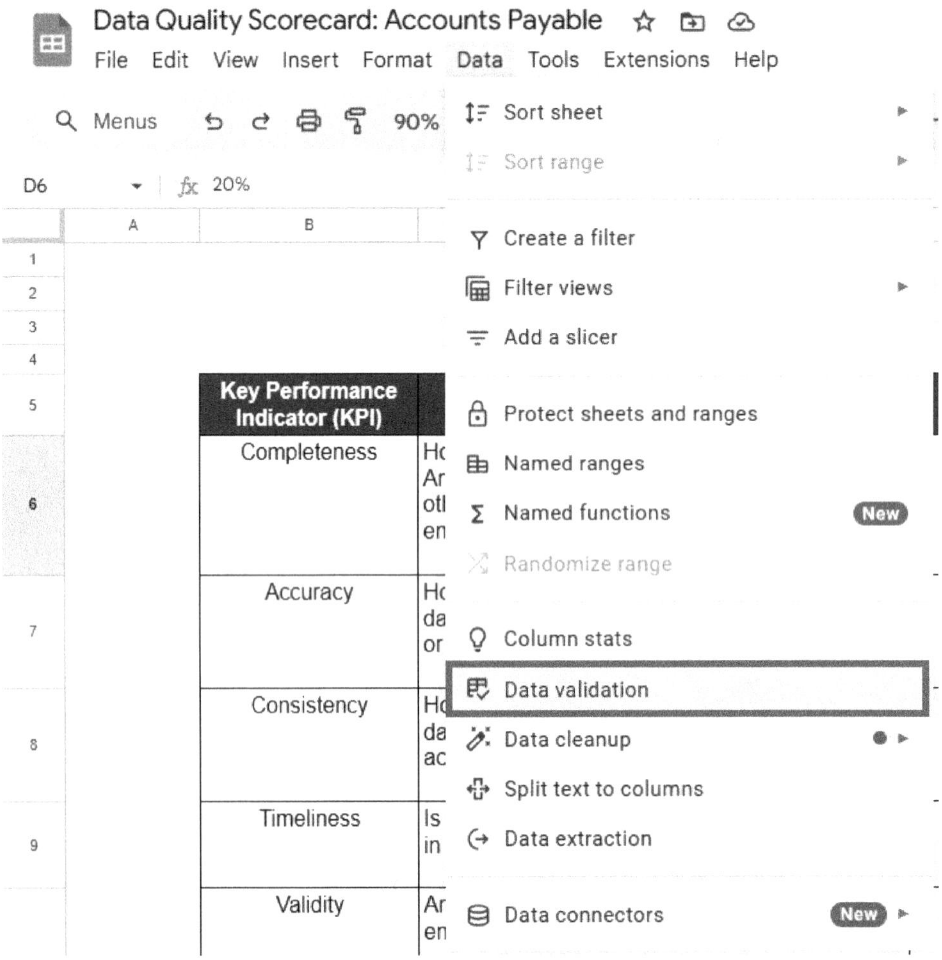

Figure 3.32 – Data validation in Google Sheets

A pop-up window will appear where you can set rules on what information can be entered into the highlighted cell, which minimizes the risk of data entry or formatting errors.

Now that we know how to create rules that will impact the data entered into our spreadsheet, the last feature we will cover is conditional formatting, which can make it easier to see certain values.

Conditional formatting

Conditional formatting enables users to apply formatting to cells or ranges of cells based on specific criteria or a set of rules or conditions. This feature enables you to quickly identify any errors or inconsistencies in your data or data quality scorecard.

To find this in Microsoft Excel, select **Conditional Formatting** in the **Home** tab, as illustrated in *Figure 3.33*:

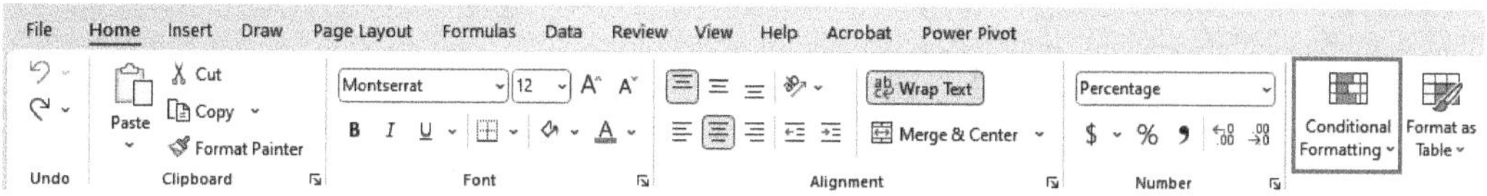

Figure 3.33 – Conditional Formatting in Microsoft Excel

This feature enables you to format cells or a range of cells, apply rules to highlight and format values meeting a threshold, and add data bars, color scales, and icon sets to make it easier to understand the data.

To set this up in Google Sheets, go to **Format** and select **Conditional formatting**, as can be seen in *Figure 3.34*:

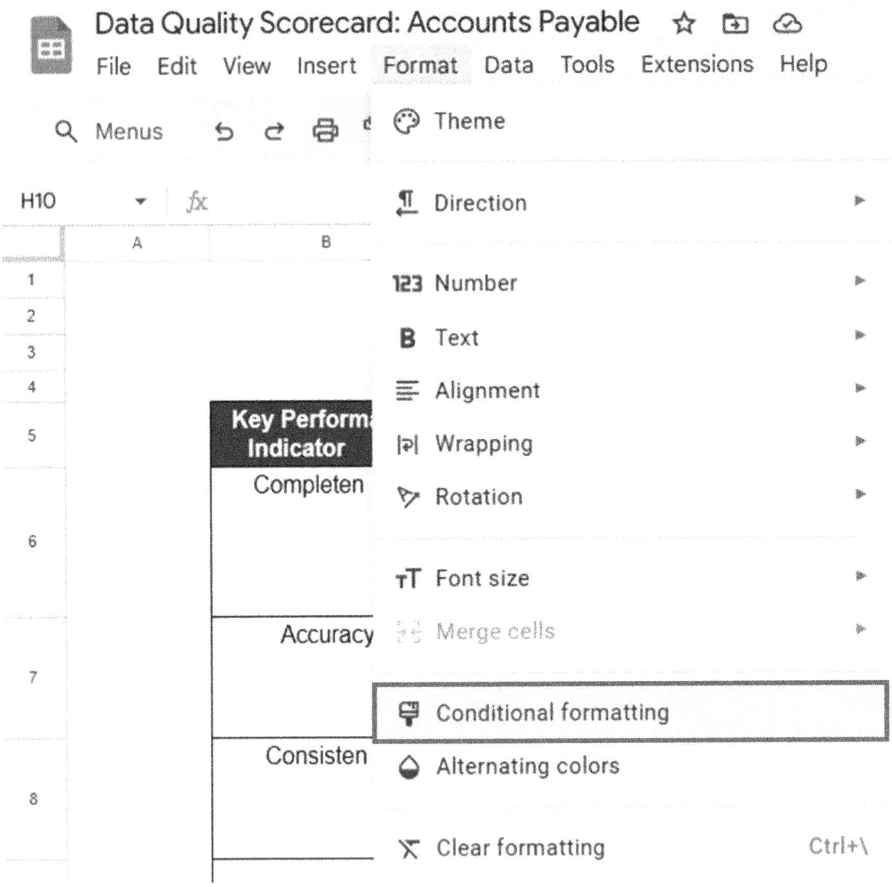

Figure 3.34 – Conditional Formatting in Google Sheets

By using these features of version control, comments, data validation, and conditional formatting, your finance teams and spreadsheet users can effectively manage changes and versions in the worksheets and data quality scorecards you are using, as well as mitigate risks and errors.

Summary

In this chapter, we discussed why we need to measure the impact of data integrity issues and learned that these can have direct costs, indirect costs, and even lead to lost opportunities for the business. We then reviewed the relevant data quality metrics for financial data and transactions. We covered the KPIs of completeness, accuracy, consistency, timeliness, and validity, which serve as the criteria for measuring data quality. We then discussed data profiling using a data quality framework, which is a crucial step in determining the quality of data. After that, we prepared sample data quality scorecards using Microsoft Excel and Google Sheets, and discussed functionalities to improve data quality and integrity. Both these tools offer a range of features to address data quality and data integrity.

In the next chapter, we will cover the common data quality management capabilities of business intelligence tools, as well as learn how these tools can be used to manage data integrity issues.

Further reading

For additional information on the topics covered in this chapter, you may find the following resources helpful:

- Redman, Thomas C. *Bad Data Costs the US $3 Trillion per Year*:
  `https://hbr.org/2016/09/bad-data-costs-the-u-s-3-trillion-per-year`
- Nagle, Tadhg, Redman, Thomas C, and Sammon, David. *Only 3% of Companies' Data Meets Basic Quality Standards*:
  `https://hbr.org/2017/09/only-3-of-companies-data-meets-basic-quality-standards`
- Segner, Michael. *5 Helpful Data Quality Frameworks You Need to Know*:
  `https://www.montecarlodata.com/blog-data-quality-framework/`
- *Switch from Excel to Sheets > Collaborate in Sheets*:
  `https://support.google.com/docs/answer/9331169?hl=en`
- *Highlight Patterns and Trends with Conditional Formatting*:
  `https://support.microsoft.com/en-us/office/highlight-patterns-and-trends-with-conditional-formatting-eea152f5-2a7d-4c1a-a2da-c5f893adb621`

Part 2: Pragmatic Solutions to Manage Financial Data Quality and Data Integrity

In this part, you will learn about a variety of practical solutions to detect, manage, and mitigate data integrity issues in finance.

This part has the following chapters:

4

Understanding the Data Integrity Management Capabilities of Business Intelligence Tools

Imagine that you are the Chief Financial Officer (CFO) of a multinational corporation. It's the end of the fiscal quarter and your team is working tirelessly to finalize the quarterly financial reports. Just when you think you are ready to present the numbers to the board, an internal audit unfortunately reveals discrepancies in the financial data reported! The consequences are distressing as incorrect financial statements could mislead investors, result in regulatory penalties, and severely damage your company's reputation. In today's data-driven business landscape, scenarios like this underline the importance of ensuring the quality and integrity of financial data for decision-making and compliance. Poor data quality can indeed lead to erroneous financial statements, misinformed business decisions, and regulatory violations, among other costly issues. This is where the role of **business intelligence** (**BI**) tools becomes invaluable for finance professionals as these tools enable them to identify data inconsistencies, validate data against predefined rules, and detect anomalies and errors in real time. In this chapter, we will explore various BI tools available for managing data quality and data integrity in finance.

That said, we will cover the following:

- Recognizing the importance of BI tools
- Exploring common data quality management capabilities of BI tools
- Reviewing the most popular BI tools and how to get started with them

By the end of this chapter, you will have a better idea of what these BI tools are capable of. Without further ado, let's begin!

Technical requirements

Before we start, we must have the following ready:

- **Power BI Desktop**, April 2023 or later (no licenses required)
- **Tableau Desktop**, 2023.1 or later (free trial version)
- **Tableau Prep Builder**, 2023.1.0 or later (free trial version)
- **Tableau Cloud** (free trial version)
- **Alteryx Designer**, 2022.3 version or later (free trial version)

It's okay if you have not installed these applications yet—we will cover the installation when we discuss these tools in the *Reviewing the most popular BI tools and how to get started with them* section.

> Note
>
> This chapter will serve as the foundation for the hands-on examples that we will be working on in *Chapter 5, Using Business Intelligence Tools to Fix Data Integrity Issues*, and *Chapter 6, Implementing Best Practices When Using Business Intelligence Tools.*

Recognizing the importance of BI tools

In the past, finance professionals relied heavily on manual processes to collect, analyze, and validate data. For a long time, spreadsheets were the go-to tools for financial modeling. In addition to this, internal audits were conducted through labor-intensive, manual reviews of financial statements and records. As you can see, this approach was not only time-consuming but also prone to human error. Ensuring data integrity and quality was a constant challenge, as even a single oversight could lead to inaccurate financial reporting and compliance issues. If data inconsistencies were identified late in the process, it became difficult to correct them and increased the risk of delaying critical business decisions.

The advent of BI tools has revolutionized the way finance professionals manage data quality and integrity. These tools employ various algorithms and even machine learning techniques to automatically identify data inconsistencies, validate data against predefined rules, and detect anomalies in real time. They also offer capabilities such as **data profiling**, **data lineage**, and **data governance**, which provide a comprehensive view of the data landscape within an organization. This not only speeds up the data validation and analysis processes but also significantly reduces the risk of errors. With real-time insights and automated checks, finance teams can now make more informed decisions faster, while also ensuring the highest levels of data quality and compliance.

Let's say that you are a financial controller at a manufacturing company that deals with hundreds of vendors. In the past, managing payments was a very time-consuming task. Your team would *manually* reconcile invoices with purchase orders and delivery notes—a process that took several days each month. Unfortunately, there were a lot of recurring mistakes, including double payments, missed discounts, and late fees. Suppose during one audit, it was discovered that a significant sum had been overpaid to a vendor due to discrepancies in the manual reconciliation process. This led to a complicated and time-consuming recovery effort. *What if the entire vendor payment process could be transformed and accelerated with the use of BI tools?* For one thing, these tools could *automatically* pull data from various sources, including procurement, accounts payable, and inventory management systems. In addition to these, built-in automated features and formulas can be used to cross-reference invoices with purchase orders and delivery notes — flagging any inconsistencies for immediate (manual) review.

> **Note**
>
> In this scenario, we can use BI tools to automatically detect data integrity issues and discrepancies between purchase orders and their associated invoice amounts. This will allow the team to quickly spot and correct the issues before proceeding with the payments. This will not only save time but also prevent any overpayments that would have been difficult to recover later.

If you are not yet convinced, it's worth noting that organizations and professionals globally have recognized the pivotal role of BI tools and the value they bring. These past few years, an increasing number of professionals globally have been pursuing various certifications to showcase their expertise in leveraging BI tools!

Exploring common data quality management capabilities of BI tools

In the previous section, we discussed how important BI tools are to finance professionals and organizations. Now, in this section, we will focus on various data quality management capabilities available in most BI tools. Understanding these features in depth will help us choose the right tool when dealing with finance data integrity issues.

Data profiling

Data profiling involves examining, analyzing, and producing insightful summaries of data. We covered the general steps for data profiling in *Chapter 3, Measuring the Impact of Data Integrity Issues*, in the *Data profiling using a data quality framework* section.

This typically involves the following steps:

1. Defining the criteria for data quality
2. Gathering and evaluating the data
3. Analyzing data quality
4. Identifying and prioritizing data quality issues
5. Creating a remediation plan
6. Tracking and gauging data quality

> **Note**
> We will cover the data profiling features for Microsoft Power BI during our hands-on example in *Chapter 5, Using Business Intelligence Tools to Fix Data Integrity Issues*. By helping us to examine the datasets to determine whether there are null values, duplicate entries, as well as errors or anomalies, these features enable us to understand and diagnose the data to improve its integrity and quality. This step is usually carried out prior to data cleansing during the initial stages of data analysis.

Data cleansing

Data cleansing is the process of correcting or deleting inaccurate, damaged, improperly formatted, duplicate, or incomplete data after we have identified it during the data profiling step.

> **Note**
> We will cover how to do this when we discuss managing data integrity issues in Power BI and best practices when using BI tools in *Chapter 5, Using Business Intelligence Tools to Fix Data Integrity Issues*, and *Chapter 6, Implementing Best Practices When Using Business Intelligence Tools*.

Cleaning the data is an important step in improving data integrity, as well as to ensure that the reports we generate and the insights we develop are accurate and reliable. For example, we can use the **Data Cleansing tool** in Alteryx Designer to remove null values in rows and columns, remove leading and trailing spaces in text, as well as filter out unwanted characters. We will further discuss Alteryx in the *Reviewing the most popular BI tools and how to get started with them* section in a later part of this chapter.

Data validation

Data validation involves verifying the source data's quality and accuracy before using, importing, or processing it. This is a form of data cleansing. If you remember, we discussed data validation in *Chapter 2, Avoiding Common Data Integrity Issues and Challenges in Finance Teams*, in the *Detecting manual data encoding issues in financial teams* section, and in *Chapter 3, Measuring the Impact of Data Integrity Issues*, in the *Microsoft Excel and Google Sheets functionalities to improve data quality and integrity* section.

Ensuring that data validation is performed enhances the accuracy, consistency, and reliability of the data before we perform additional analysis and reporting. For example, we can use the **data roles** feature in **Tableau Prep** to validate the data. This is a useful tool when working with large sets of information. We will cover this more in the *Dealing with large financial datasets using data validation* section in *Chapter 5, Using Business Intelligence Tools to Fix Data Integrity Issues*.

Data lineage

Data lineage is the process of following the flow of data across time, giving insight into the data's origin, changes over time, and its destination in the data pipeline. This improves the transparency and trust in the reports given that you know where they came from. It can also enhance the data quality and integrity, making it easier to pinpoint where any errors or inconsistencies may have been introduced.

For example, we can use the **data lineage** feature in the **Power BI service**. This is very useful in understanding the flow of data from where it originated up to its destination, as well as knowing what the impact could be if a change is initiated in the workflow.

> **Note**
>
> Although the Power BI service is outside the scope of this book, feel free to check out this feature here: `https://learn.microsoft.com/en-us/power-bi/collaborate-share/service-data-lineage`.

Data governance

Data governance is the process of handling data throughout its life cycle, from collection to use and eventual disposal. This is necessary for all organizations since data has evolved into one of the most important assets for businesses across all industries as they continue their digital transformation journeys. Without it, organizations may struggle to ensure data accuracy, security, and compliance, which may lead to potential data breaches, misinformation, and legal issues.

Both data governance and data integrity are closely linked concepts of data management and are important in making sure that the data is reliable, consistent, and fit to serve its purpose. For example, we can use the **Data Management** feature in Tableau for this.

> **Note**
>
> The **Data Management** feature is outside the scope of this book; you can learn more about this by checking out `https://help.tableau.com/current/server/en-us/dm_overview.htm`.

Now that we have covered the common data quality management capabilities of BI tools, let's review the most popular BI tools and get started by exploring them in the next section!

Reviewing the most popular BI tools and how to get started with them

In the previous section, we explored the common data quality management capabilities of BI tools. In this section, we will discuss some of the most popular BI tools at the moment and how to set them up on your local machine or personal computer/laptop. We will also cover the relevant features of these tools to improve data integrity.

Microsoft Power BI

Microsoft Power BI is a powerful BI tool that allows users to visualize, analyze, and share data insights across an organization. The tool offers a broad spectrum of features, ranging from basic data visualizations to advanced analytics capabilities.

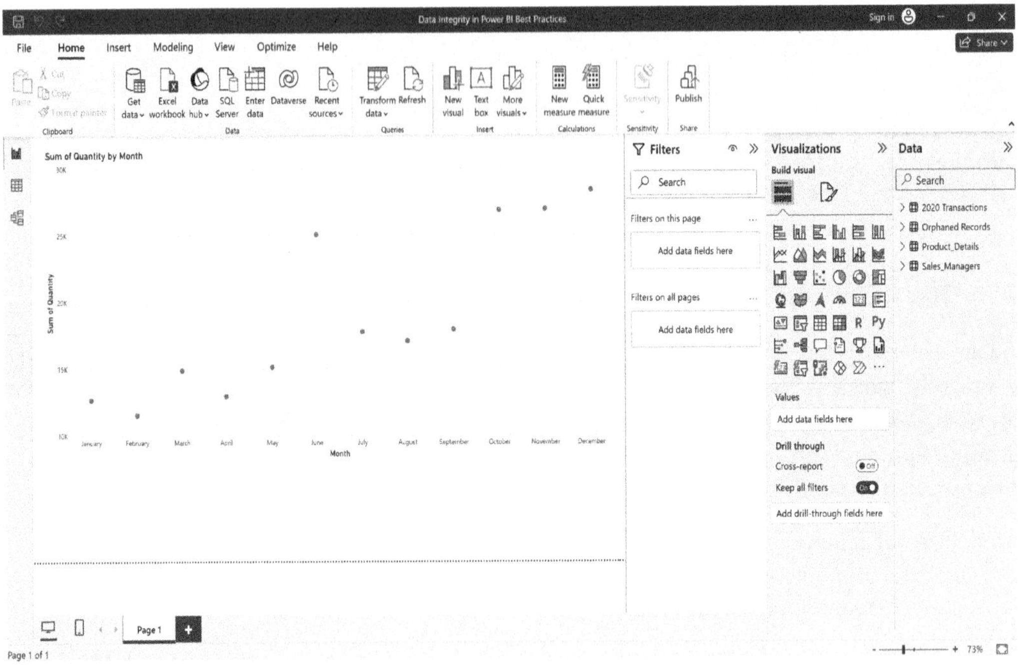

Figure 4.1 – Sample visualization in Microsoft Power BI

Figure 4.1 shows a sample visualization in **Power BI Desktop**. Here, we make use of a scatter chart to visualize the data to more easily identify any potential outliers.

Given that we will use Power BI in the following chapter to profile and cleanse the data, let's quickly discuss how to set this up on your local machine or laptop.

Getting started

In this book, we will be using **Power BI Desktop**. The setup steps are as follows:

1. Open a new browser tab and visit `https://powerbi.microsoft.com/en-us/getting-started-with-power-bi/`:

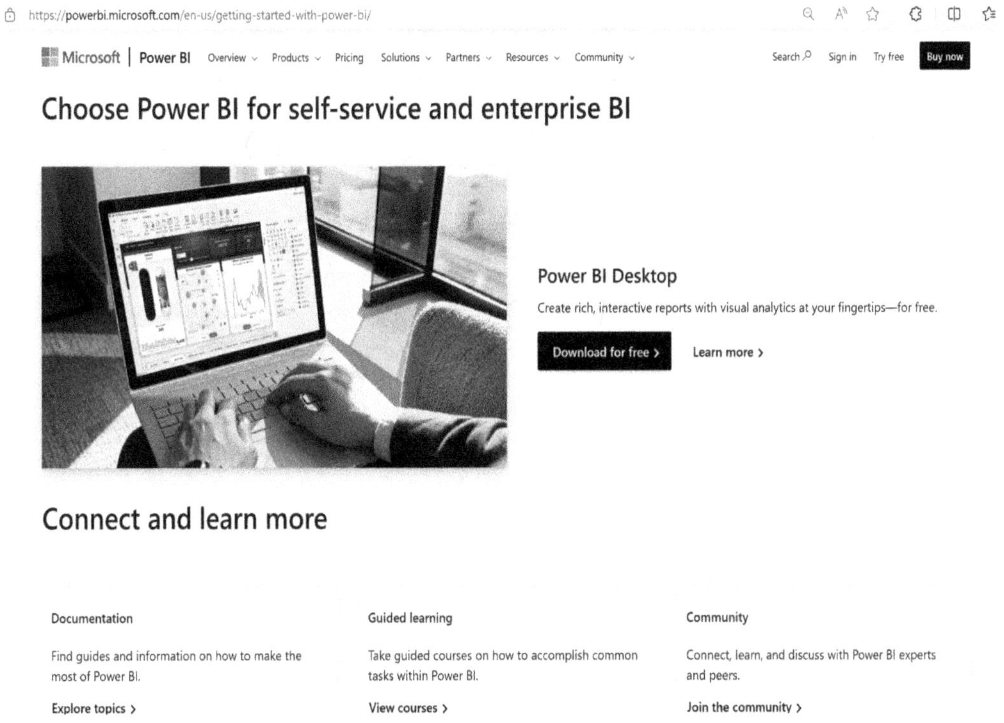

Figure 4.2 – Downloading Power BI Desktop

Click on **Download for free**, as seen in *Figure 4.2*.

2. The Microsoft Store window will pop up, as shown in *Figure 4.3*:

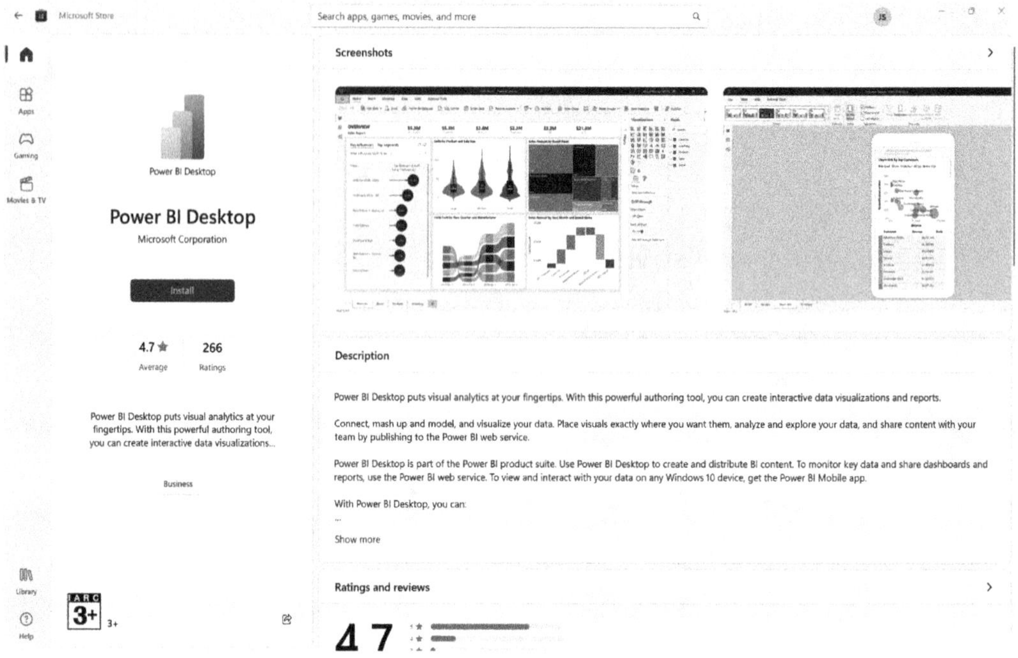

Figure 4.3 – Installing Power BI Desktop from the Microsoft Store

Click on **Install**.

> **Note**
>
> The **Microsoft Store** is a platform managed by Microsoft as a means to distribute Windows applications.

3. Once you have installed Power BI Desktop, click on **Open**.

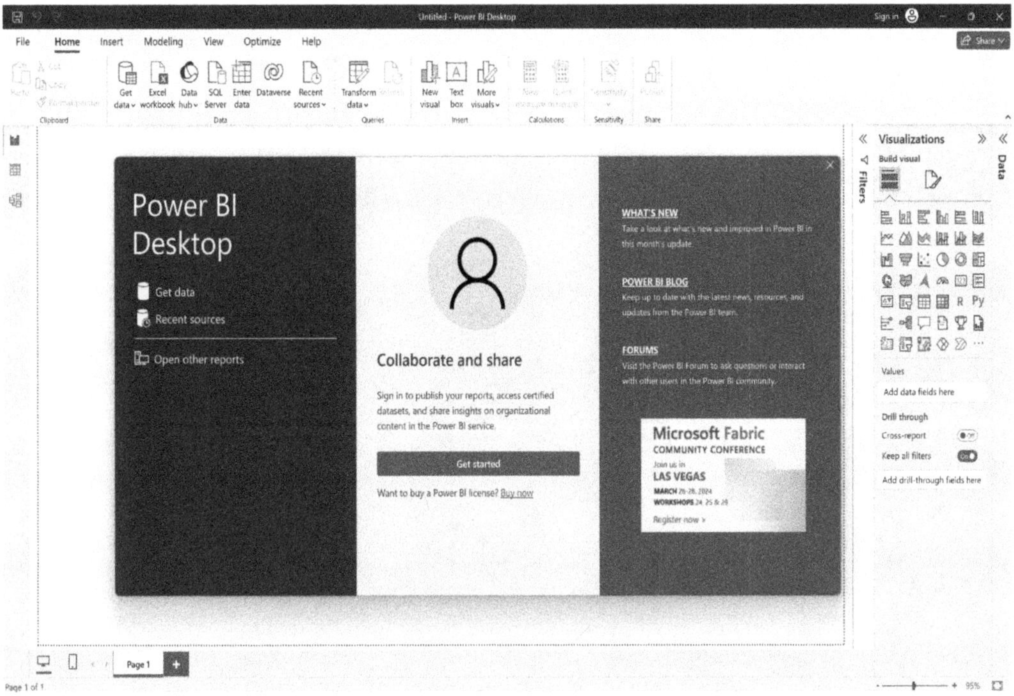

Figure 4.4 – The Microsoft Power BI Desktop window

This will launch Power BI Desktop, as seen in *Figure 4.4*.

Wasn't that surprisingly easy? Overall, Microsoft Power BI is a versatile tool that offers a range of features to manage and analyze data. Its intuitive interface and powerful capabilities make it an incredible tool for businesses of all sizes, allowing users to gain insights and make informed decisions based on their data.

Now that we have installed Power BI, let's go over the different elements of this tool to improve the quality and integrity of data in the next section.

Features related to data integrity

Here are some of the key capabilities available in Power BI Desktop for data integrity:

- **Power Query**: Power Query is a tool for transforming and preparing data. With this feature, users can clean and transform data from various sources, ensuring consistency and accuracy. This is where the data profiling features are located, as well as the ways to shape your data prior to doing any visualizations. We will cover data profiling and other features related to data integrity during our hands-on exercises in the next two chapters.

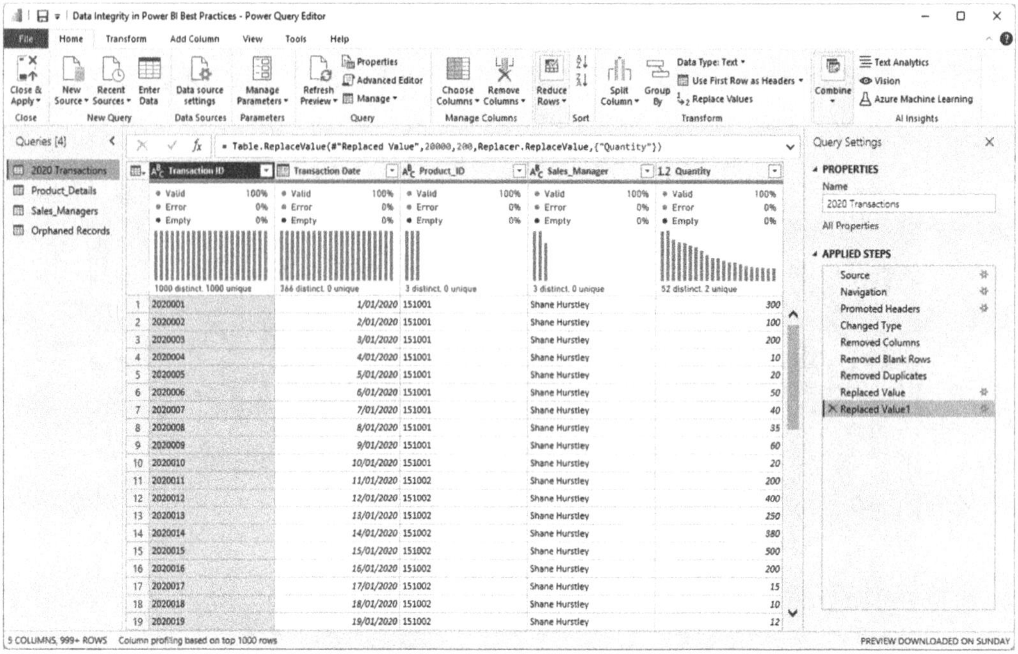

Figure 4.5 – The Power Query Editor

- **Visualizations**: Visualizations are powerful ways to present insights from the data after it has been cleaned and validated. Power BI offers a range of visualization and reporting options, including charts, graphs, and maps. Users can create interactive dashboards and reports that can be shared with others, allowing for collaboration and data-driven decision-making. At the same time, data integrity issues and anomalies can be discovered through visualizations as well. We will be covering this in the *Using data visualization to identify data outliers* section in *Chapter 6, Implementing Best Practices When Using Business Intelligence Tools*.
- **Managing relationships in data models**: In Power BI, managing relationships between tables is a crucial aspect of data modeling. It involves establishing relationships between tables, specifying their cardinality, and selecting the appropriate join type. We will dive deeper into this topic in the *Managing relationships in data models* section in the next chapter.

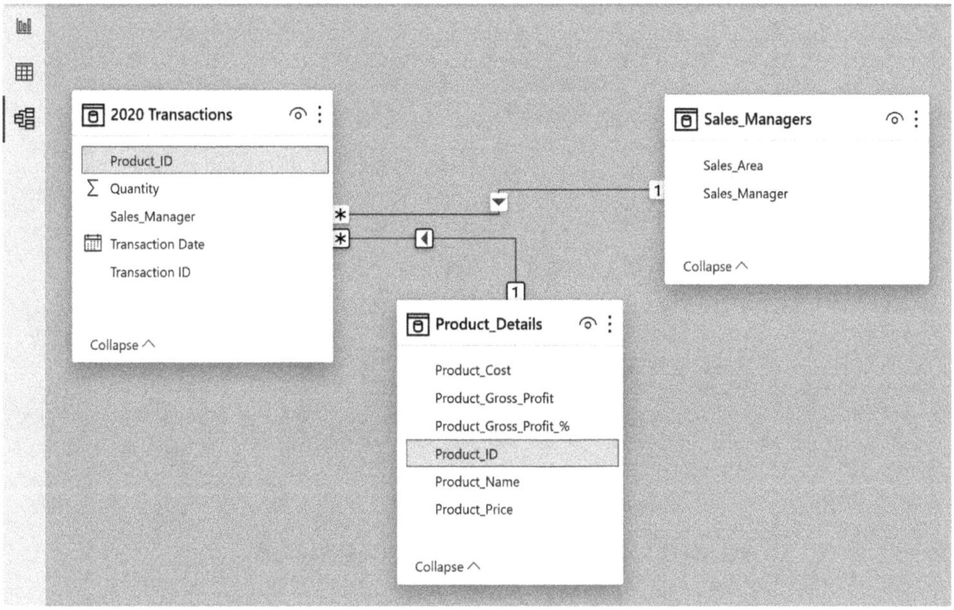

Figure 4.6 – Managing relationships in Power BI

Figure 4.6 shows a sample data model to view the relationships between the different tables. We will discuss the properties and how to edit relationships during our hands-on example.

- **Data governance**: Power BI provides *several* data governance features that help organizations ensure their data is secure, compliant, and properly managed. These features include **data classification**, **data protection**, **auditing** and **compliance**, **data lineage**, and **collaboration** and **sharing**. With these features, users can classify data based on sensitivity levels, control access to specific data rows and columns, track user activity and data usage, monitor data refresh activity, and collaborate on data analysis securely. By leveraging these data governance features, organizations can gain insights from their data while minimizing the risk of data breaches, regulatory violations, and other data-related issues.

Now that we have discussed the various features of Power BI to help us improve data quality and integrity, let's cover another popular tool used by finance professionals and organizations—the **Tableau** platform. In the next section, we will learn what makes this tool useful for managing data integrity issues and requirements.

Tableau by Salesforce

Tableau is a widely used data visualization and BI tool that enables users to create interactive and visually appealing dashboards and reports. With Tableau, users can connect to different data sources (for example, **spreadsheets**, **databases**, and **cloud-based platforms**) and create interactive data visualizations that can be easily shared across an organization.

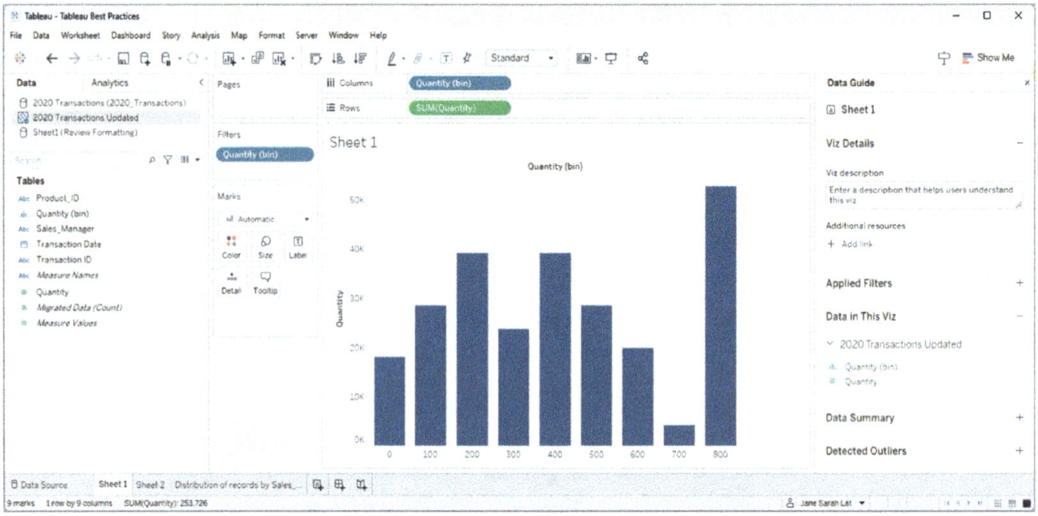

Figure 4.7 – Sample visualization in Tableau Desktop

Figure 4.7 shows a sample visualization in Tableau Desktop to show the frequency of transactions, which we will cover in *Chapter 6*, *Implementing Best Practices When Using Business Intelligence Tools*.

In this book, since we will be working with products from the Tableau platform such as **Tableau Desktop**, **Tableau Prep Builder**, and **Tableau Cloud** for our hands-on exercises, let's take some time to set them up on your computer or laptop.

Getting started

The installation steps are as follows:

1. To download both Tableau Desktop and Tableau Prep Builder, go to `https://www.tableau.com/` and click on **TRY NOW**, as seen in *Figure 4.8*:

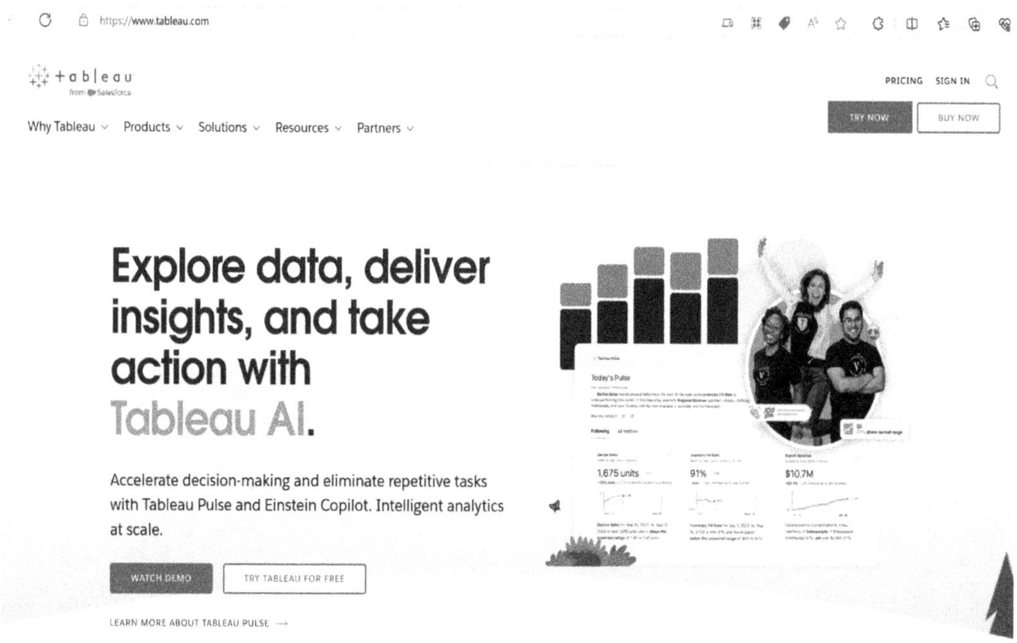

Figure 4.8 – Click on TRY NOW on the Tableau website

We will be using the free trial version in our hands-on exercises.

2. This will lead you to the window to start the free trial; scroll down until you see the ways to explore the platform, as seen in *Figure 4.9*:

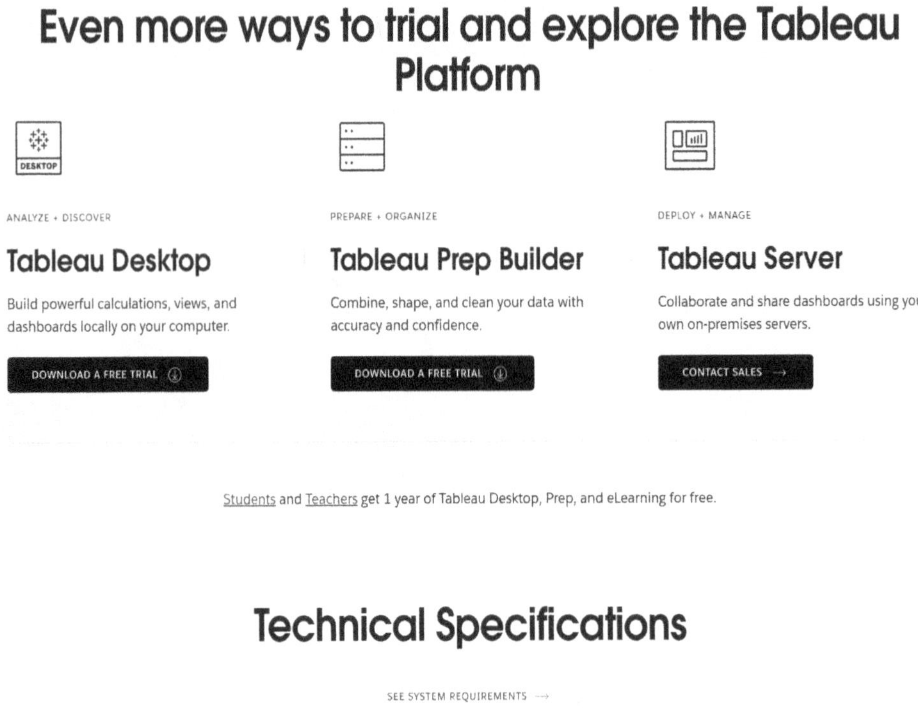

Figure 4.9 – Ways to explore the Tableau Platform

Make sure that you read the technical specifications and check the system requirements before proceeding.

3. Click on **DOWNLOAD A FREE TRIAL** for Tableau Desktop.

Tableau Desktop: Start your free 14-day trial
Almost there!
It only takes 15 seconds to fill out. If you're already registered, sign in.
First Name
Last Name
Business E-mail
Organization
- Company Size -
- Department -
- Job Role -
- Country/Region -
Phone (e.g. (201) 555-0123)
By registering, you confirm that you agree to the processing of your personal data by Salesforce as described in the Privacy Statement.
DOWNLOAD FREE TRIAL

Figure 4.10 – Registration page for the free trial

This will lead to a window where you need to input your details, as shown in *Figure 4.10*. Type your details in there and click on **DOWNLOAD FREE TRIAL**.

> **Note**
>
> Tableau provides students with a one-year academic license and gives access to Tableau Desktop, Tableau Prep Builder, and learning resources. Instructors, however, can request a renewable license for the software, learning resources, and curricula as part of the **Tableau for Teaching (TfT)** program.

4. Upon clicking, the installer will download automatically and the file will be saved in the `Downloads` folder. Once the download is complete, click on the application to start the installation.

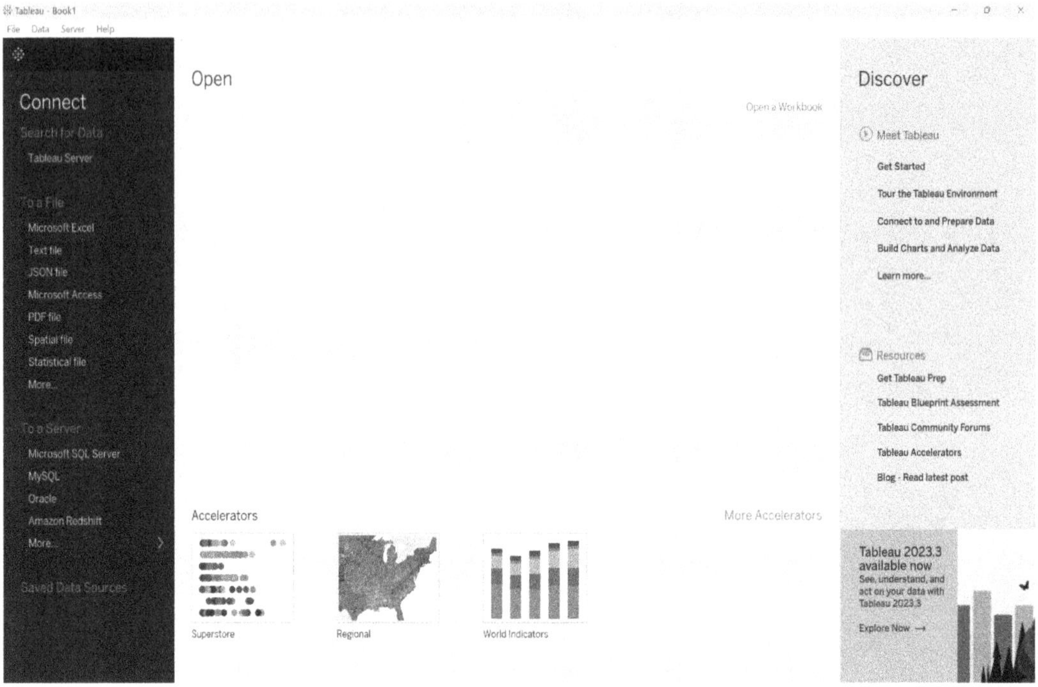

Figure 4.11 – After installing Tableau Desktop

After the installation is complete, Tableau Desktop will load, as shown in *Figure 4.11*

5. Do the same steps for **Tableau Prep Builder** that we did for Tableau Desktop. Once both are installed, you may now move on to the next steps, relating to Tableau Cloud.

6. For Tableau Cloud, we will be creating an account with the following link: `https://www.tableau.com/products/online/request-trial`.

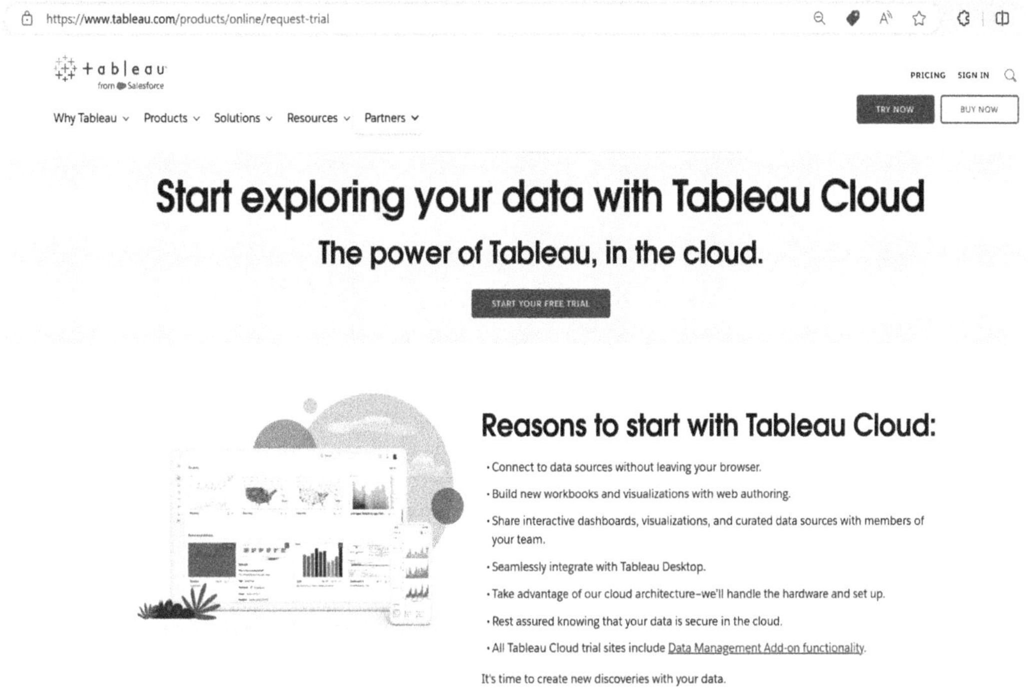

Figure 4.12 – Tableau Cloud website

When the website loads, click on **START YOUR FREE TRIAL**. It will lead you to the window to enter your details. Once you complete the form and submit it, you will get a message informing you that you will receive an email to activate your trial.

Once you receive the email, click on **LET'S GET STARTED** to activate your account and start the free trial. This will take you to the page to create a password. Once that is done, it will confirm that your account has been activated.

7. When you sign in to your account, you will be taken to a window to create a site name, as shown in *Figure 4.13*:

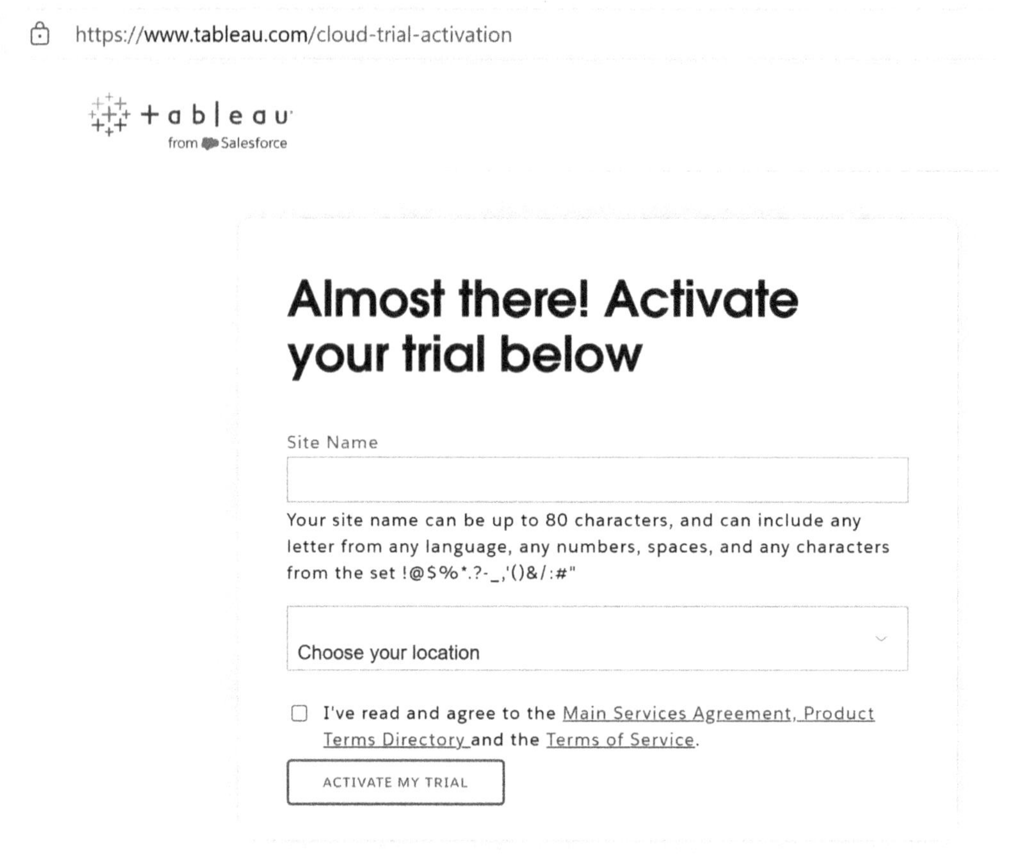

Figure 4.13 – Creating a site name

Type `Managing Data Integrity for Finance` or another name you deem fit for our hands-on exercise. Once you have entered this and have chosen your location, tick the checkbox for the agreement and terms of service, and click on **ACTIVATE MY TRIAL**.

You will be taken to a window showing that your Tableau trial is being activated. Once this is complete, it will load the website.

8. Next, we will create a project that we will use in our hands-on exercise for the next chapter. Click on **New**, then select **Project**, as shown in *Figure 4.14*:

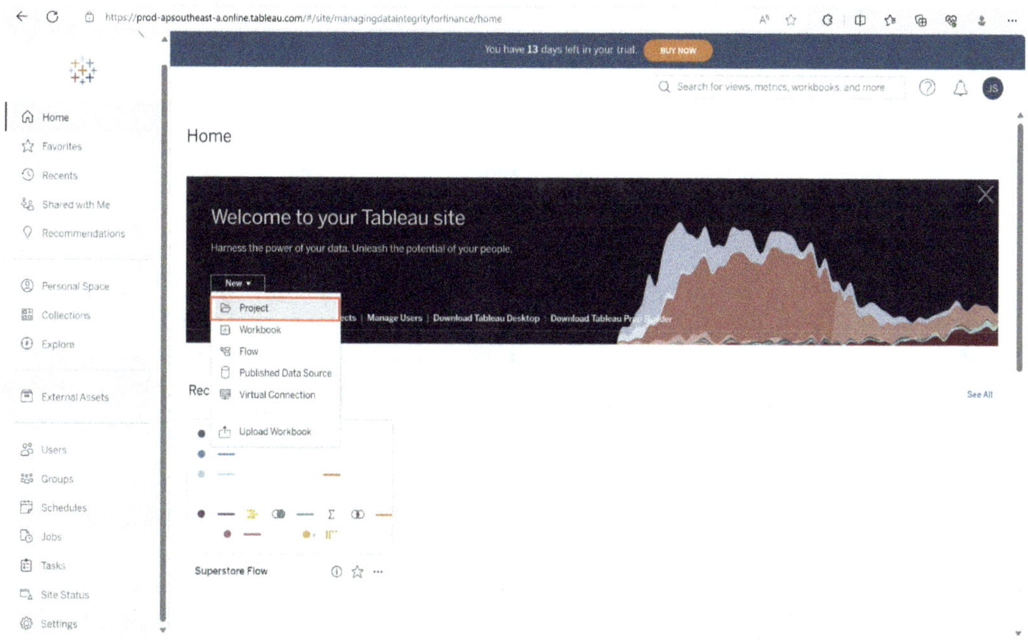

Figure 4.14 – Creating a project in Tableau Cloud

In the **Enter a name for the new project** text box, input `Managing Data Integrity for Finance` and then click on **Create**. Once this is complete, a message will pop up saying that the project has been created.

> **Note**
>
> **Tableau Public** is also available and provides similar features to Tableau Desktop, though there are limitations and some differences in the application. Here is the website to check it out further: `https://public.tableau.com/app/discover`.

Now that we have set up the applications needed for Tableau, let's touch on its various attributes that help improve data quality.

Features related to data integrity

Here are some of the key capabilities available in Tableau to address data quality issues:

- **Data profiling, data cleaning, and data shaping in Tableau Prep**: One of the key features of Tableau is its ability to provide advanced analytics capabilities to users of all skill levels. With Tableau Prep, users can easily clean, shape, and transform data before analyzing it in Tableau Desktop. We will be covering these features further in the next two chapters.

- **Visualizations**: Visualizations are powerful ways to present insights from the data after it has been cleaned and validated. Similar to Power BI, Tableau also offers a range of visualizations, including charts, graphs, and maps, which can be customized to meet specific business needs. Tableau also provides a range of sharing and collaboration options, allowing users to share dashboards and reports with others, and collaborate on data-driven decision-making. We will be covering how to use data visualization to identify data outliers with Tableau in *Chapter 6, Implementing Best Practices When Using Business Intelligence Tools*.
- **Data lineage**: Understanding the origin of your data is crucial in ensuring its reliability. Moreover, being aware of the other users of the reports you are making enables you to assess the impact of the updates you make. With a **Data Management** license and the activation of **Tableau Catalog**, you can access the lineage details for your information. We will see where we can find the lineage feature in the *Using data visualization to identify data outliers* section in *Chapter 6, Implementing Best Practices When Using Business Intelligence Tools*, as well.

Overall, the Tableau products are powerful tools that provide a range of features for managing and analyzing data. Their intuitive interfaces, advanced analytics capabilities, and visualization options make them valuable assets for businesses of all sizes, enabling users to gain insights and make informed decisions. We will cover these in the next two chapters during our hands-on examples.

> **Note**
>
> Please note that the installation instructions and steps outlined in this chapter may vary depending on your operating system, so be sure to follow the specific guidelines relevant to your system for a successful setup.

Alteryx analytics cloud platform

In the previous sections, we discussed Microsoft Power BI and Tableau by Salesforce, which are two relevant tools used by finance professionals and organizations around the world. In this section, we will cover a *low-code/no-code* analytics platform called **Alteryx**.

Alteryx is a data analytics and data preparation tool that enables users to *blend*, *cleanse*, and *analyze* data from multiple sources. With Alteryx, users can connect to various data sources, including cloud-based platforms, databases, and spreadsheets, and create automated workflows to prepare data for analysis. *Figure 4.15* shows a sample workflow in Alteryx:

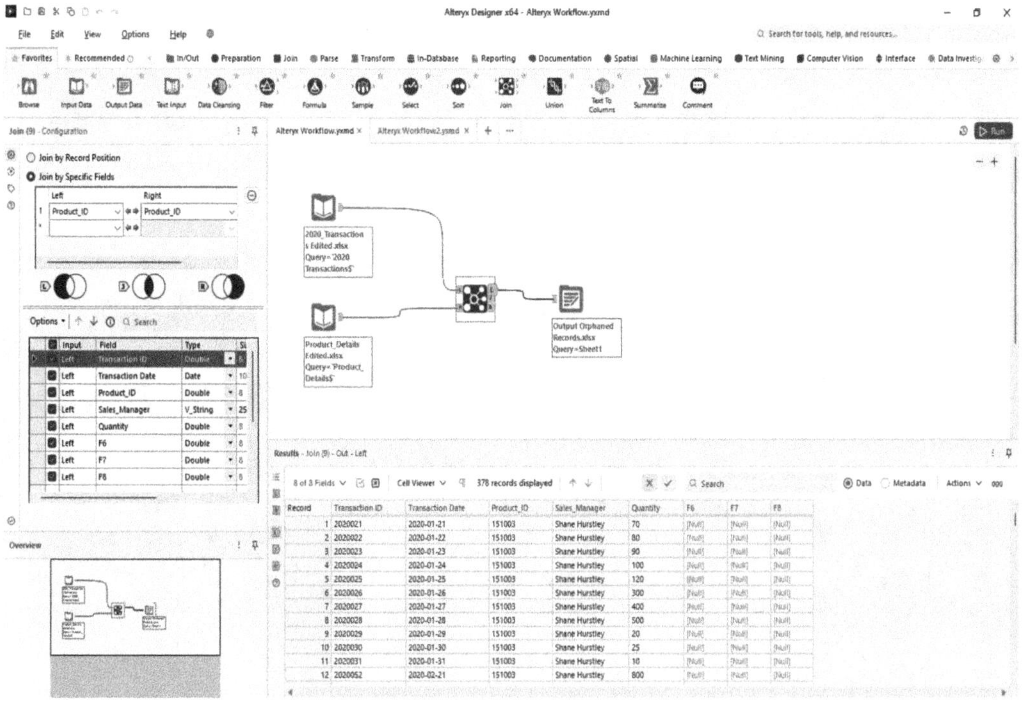

Figure 4.15 – Workflow in Alteryx

I know you are excited to know how this works! We will discuss this further in our hands-on example in *Chapter 6, Implementing Best Practices When Using Business Intelligence Tools*.

Getting started

The steps to install Alteryx are as follows:

1. To install Alteryx Designer, go to `https://www.alteryx.com/` and click on **Start Free Trial**, as seen in *Figure 4.16*:

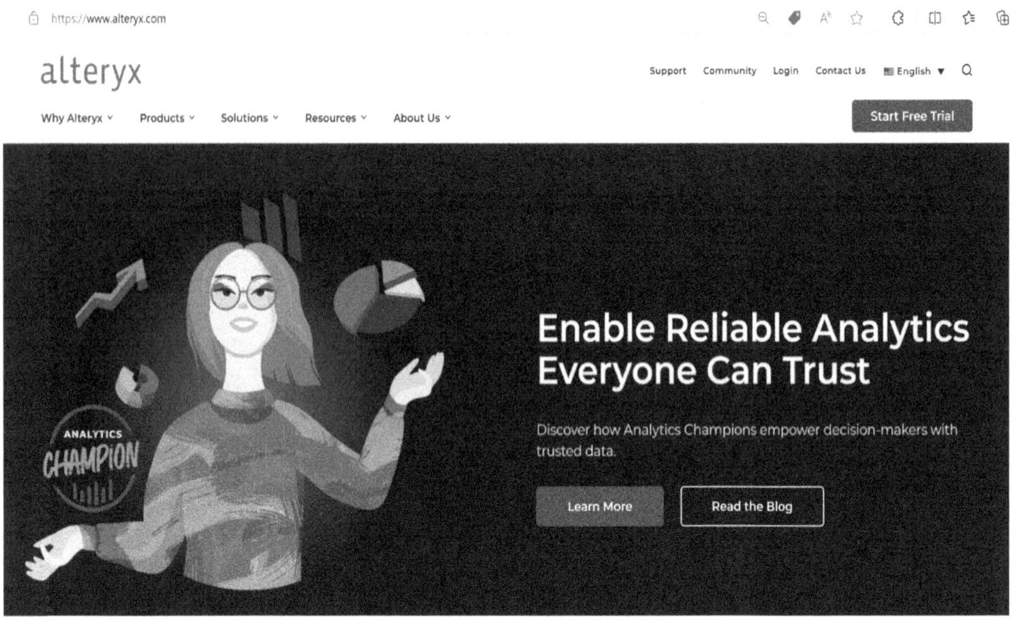

Figure 4.16 – The Alteryx website

You will also be able to explore the products and solutions offered on this website.

2. This will lead you to the window to either start the trial for Designer Desktop or Designer Cloud. Since we will be using Designer Desktop in this book, select that option, as seen in *Figure 4.17*:

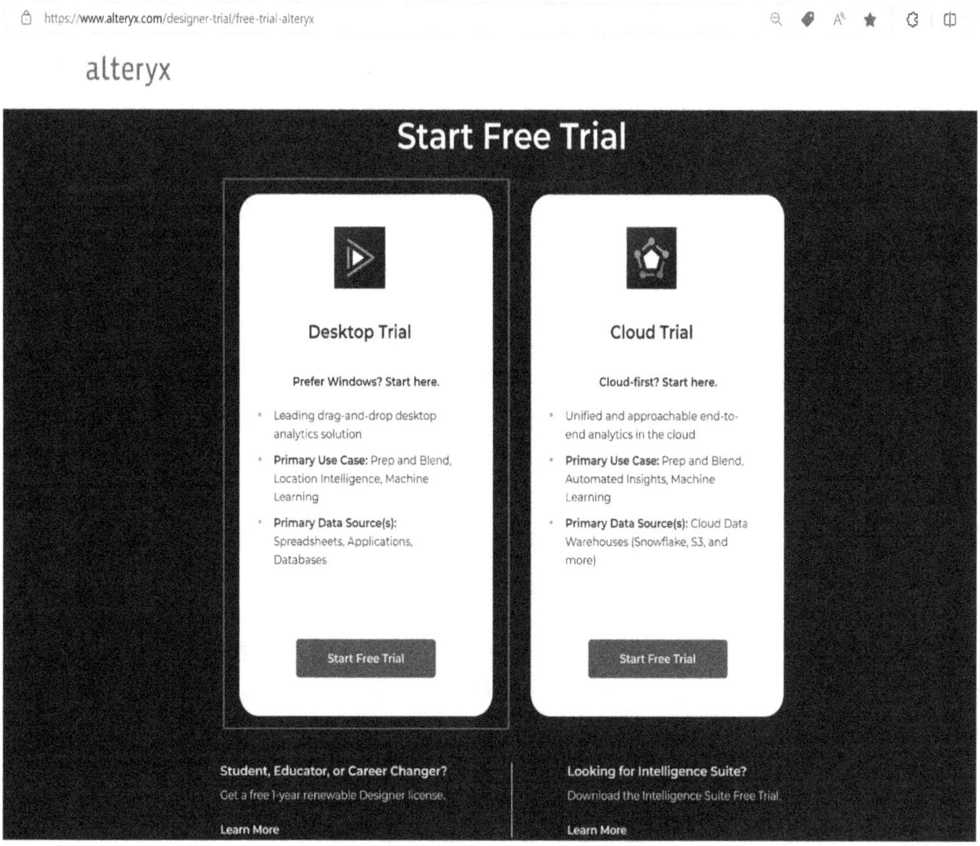
https://www.alteryx.com/designer-trial/free-trial-alteryx
alteryx
Start Free Trial
Desktop Trial
Prefer Windows? Start here.
Leading drag-and-drop desktop analytics solution
Primary Use Case: Prep and Blend, Location Intelligence, Machine Learning
Primary Data Source(s): Spreadsheets, Applications, Databases
Start Free Trial
Cloud Trial
Cloud-first? Start here.
Unified and approachable end-to-end analytics in the cloud
Primary Use Case: Prep and Blend, Automated Insights, Machine Learning
Primary Data Source(s): Cloud Data Warehouses (Snowflake, S3, and more)
Start Free Trial
Student, Educator, or Career Changer?
Get a free 1-year renewable Designer license.
Learn More
Looking for Intelligence Suite?
Download the Intelligence Suite Free Trial.
Learn More

Figure 4.17 – Selecting Designer Desktop

At the time of writing, new users can trial the desktop version for 30 days.

> **Note**
>
> Alteryx provides an education license for students and instructors with the **Alteryx SparkED program**. Students are given a one-year renewable license for Alteryx Designer at no cost, along with e-learning materials, while educators are given a complimentary, fully-enabled license for Alteryx Designer and resources to integrate the SparkED program into their teaching curricula. For more information, visit `https://www.alteryx.com/sparked`.

3. This will lead you to the window where you need to submit your details to be able to download the installer, as seen in *Figure 4.18*:

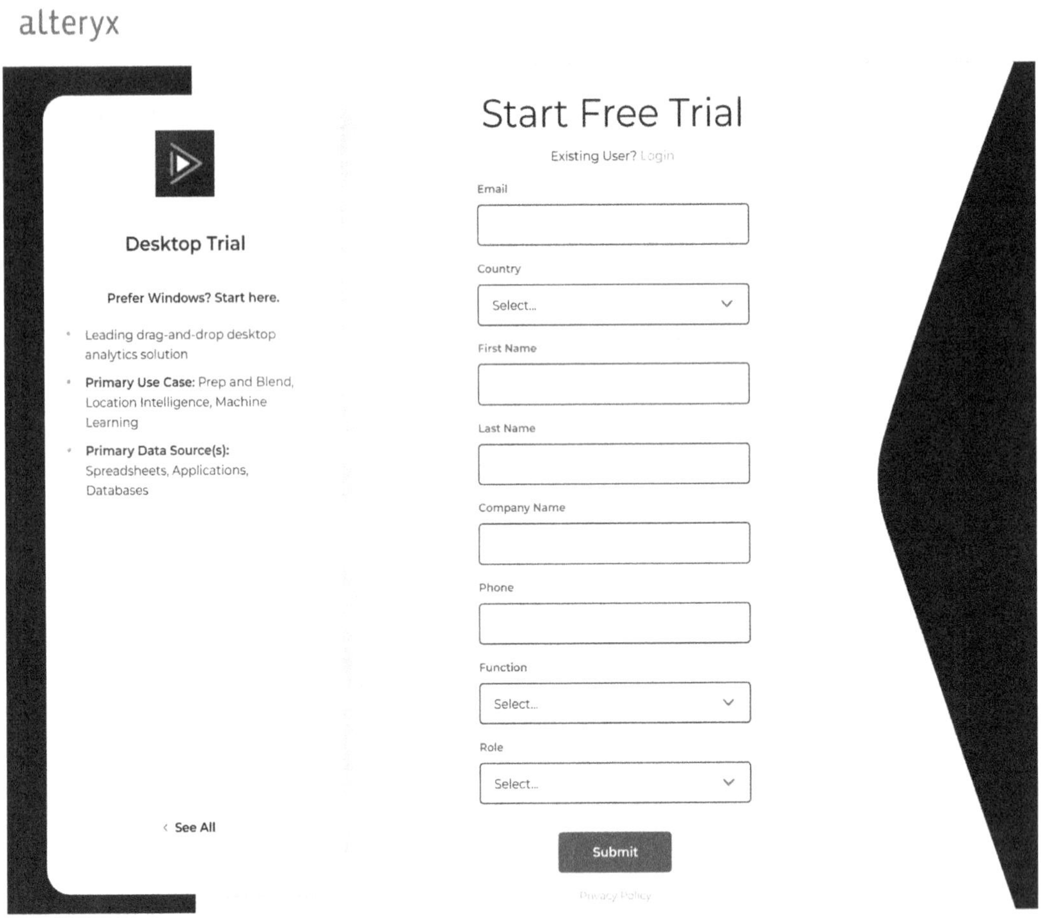
alteryx
Desktop Trial
Prefer Windows? Start here.
Leading drag-and-drop desktop analytics solution
Primary Use Case: Prep and Blend, Location Intelligence, Machine Learning
Primary Data Source(s): Spreadsheets, Applications, Databases
See All
Start Free Trial
Existing User? Login
Email
Country
Select...
First Name
Last Name
Company Name
Phone
Function
Select...
Role
Select...
Submit

Figure 4.18 – Inputting details to register for the trial

> **Note**
>
> Visit `https://www.alteryx.com/products/alteryx-designer` for more information about the application. It is important that you are familiar with the system requirements as well, which you can find on this website.

4. Once you submit your details, the installer will automatically download to your `Downloads` folder. Once that is complete, double-click on it and start the installation.

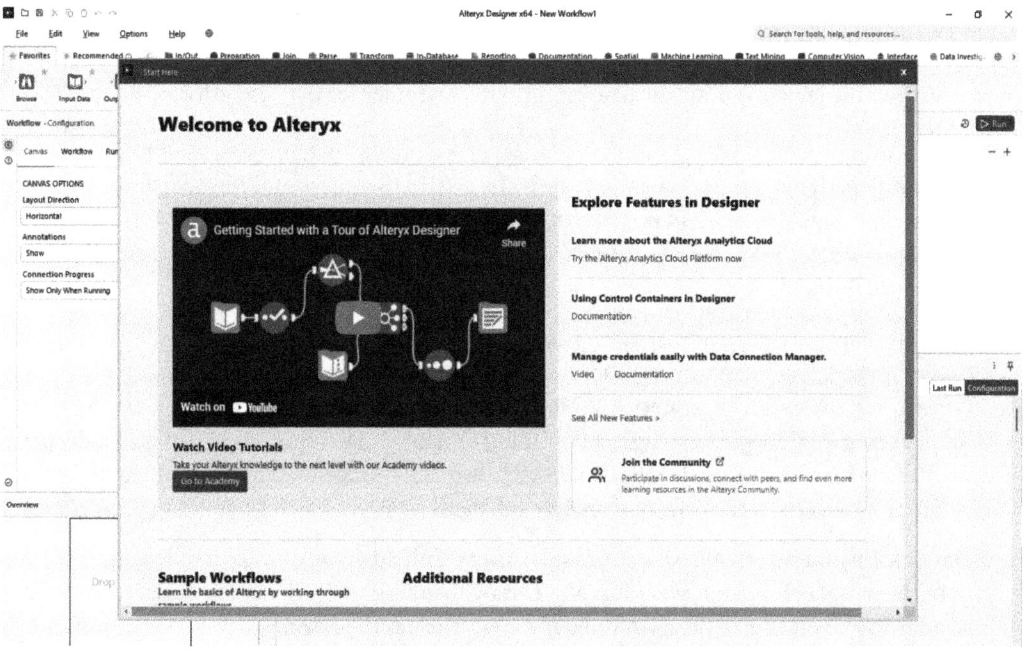

Figure 4.19 – Welcome screen after installation

Once installation is complete, Alteryx Designer will load, as shown in *Figure 4.19*.

> **Note**
>
> Please note that the installation instructions and steps outlined in this chapter may vary depending on your operating system, so ensure to follow the specific guidelines relevant to your system for a successful setup.

Overall, Alteryx is a powerful tool that provides a range of features for managing and analyzing data. Its intuitive interface, advanced analytics capabilities, and data preparation features make it a valuable asset for businesses of all sizes, enabling users to gain insights and make informed decisions based on their data.

Now that we have installed the application on our local machine, let's discuss how we can use this tool to improve the quality of our data.

Features related to data integrity

Here are some of the key capabilities available in Alteryx Designer for data integrity:

- **Data profiling**: Data profiling in Alteryx Designer is a process that involves analyzing a dataset to identify patterns, trends, and anomalies. The goal is to understand the data and assess its quality and completeness. Alteryx Designer provides several tools and functionalities for data profiling, including the **Data Profiling** tool, which generates a summary of statistics for each column in the dataset.

  This summary includes information such as the data type, the number of null values, the minimum and maximum values, the average and median values, and the distribution of values. Other tools, such as the **Frequency Table** tool and the **Field Summary** tool, can also be used for data profiling. By performing data profiling in Alteryx Designer, users can gain a deeper understanding of their data, identify potential data quality issues, and make informed decisions about how to clean, transform, and analyze the data.

- **Data cleansing**: Alteryx Designer provides users with an array of tools and functionalities to perform data cleansing, including the **Data Cleansing** tool, which allows users to clean, standardize, and validate data. Additionally, tools such as the **Formula** tool and the **Join** tool can also be leveraged for data cleansing.

  By performing data cleansing in Alteryx Designer, users can ensure that their data is accurate, consistent, and reliable, enabling them to make informed business decisions and enhance the efficiency of data-driven processes.

- **Data blending**: Alteryx Designer offers a range of tools and functionalities to enable data blending. One such tool is the **Join** tool, which enables users to merge data from two or more datasets based on a common field. Another tool is the **Union** tool, which combines data from multiple datasets with the same structure into a single dataset.

In addition to these tools, Alteryx Designer also provides several data preparation tools, such as the **Filter** tool and the **Sort** tool, which can be used to refine data for blending. By utilizing data blending in Alteryx Designer, users can create a coherent and consolidated dataset that provides insights into business operations and supports informed decision-making.

We will cover the Join tool in *Chapter 6, Implementing Best Practices When Using Business Intelligence Tools*, when we discuss how to manage **orphaned records**.

If this is your first time using Alteryx Designer, one way to easily find the tools and learn more about them is by using the **search bar**, as shown in *Figure 4.20*:

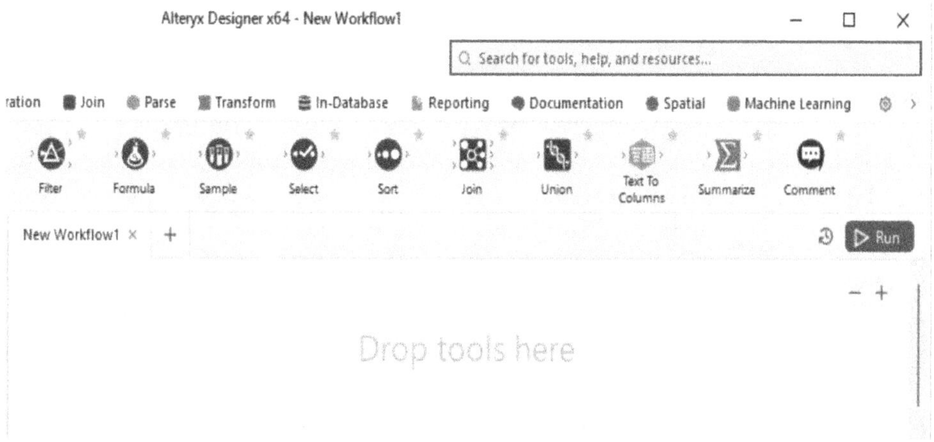

Figure 4.20 – Search bar function

It is located in the top-right corner of the screen and is very useful when searching for tools and understanding what help results and resources are available in the community.

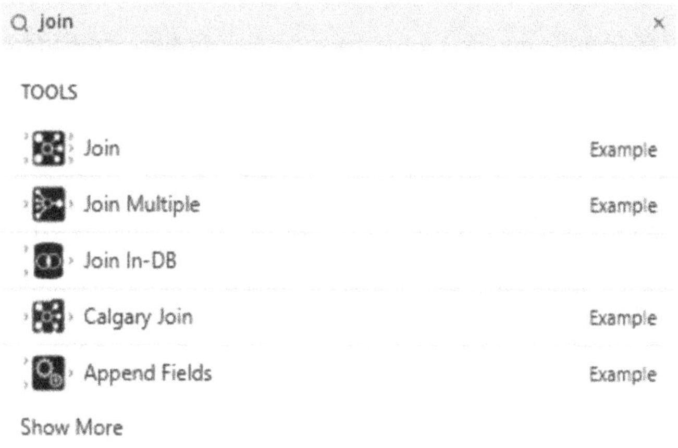

Figure 4.21 – Using the search bar function

As an example, you can search for the **Join** tool by typing it in the search bar, as can be seen in *Figure 4.21*.

Now that you have installed the applications on your laptop or computer, feel free to explore the various capabilities to make yourself more familiar with them, and see how you can use them to address the challenges you are facing when working with data. I hope that you now have a better appreciation of these tools and how they can improve the quality of your data and reporting. In the following chapters, we will work on some hands-on exercises and dive deeper into the topics.

Summary

In this chapter, we started with a quick discussion on how BI tools could help finance professionals and organizations in today's data-driven landscape. We then focused on several data integrity management capabilities of these tools, including relevant features such as **data profiling**, **data cleansing**, **data validation**, **data lineage**, and **data governance**. After that, we introduced some of the most popular BI tools used globally—including **Microsoft Power BI**, **Alteryx**, and **Tableau**.

With what we have covered in this chapter, you have learned about why BI tools are helpful for professionals as well as the capabilities and features these tools have to enhance and improve the integrity of the data. In the next chapter, we will continue our discussion on BI tools! We will build on top of what we learned here in this chapter, and dive deeper into how to use various BI tools to solve common data integrity issues for finance.

Further reading

For additional information on the topics covered in this chapter, you may find the following resources helpful:

- *2023 Gartner Magic Quadrant for Analytics and Business Intelligence Platforms*: `https://www.gartner.com/doc/reprints?id=1-2D773G95&ct=230411&st=sb`
- *Microsoft named a Leader in the 2023 Gartner Magic Quadrant for Analytics and BI Platforms*: `https://powerbi.microsoft.com/en-in/blog/microsoft-named-a-leader-in-the-2023-gartner-magic-quadrant-for-analytics-and-bi-platforms`
- *Salesforce Tableau named a Leader in the 2023 Gartner Magic Quadrant for Analytics and BI Platforms*: `https://www.tableau.com/blog/tableau-leader-gartner-magic-quadrant-analytics-business`
- *Alteryx—Data Profiling*: `https://www.alteryx.com/glossary/data-profiling`
- *Tableau Prep—Use Data Roles to Validate your Data*: `https://help.tableau.com/current/prep/en-us/prep_validate_data.htm`
- *Tableau—The Benefits and Challenges of Data Governance*: `https://www.tableau.com/learn/articles/what-is-data-governance`

5

Using Business Intelligence Tools to Fix Data Integrity Issues

In the previous chapter, we discussed the data integrity features available in the most common **business intelligence** (**BI**) tools. We also covered how to get started with using them. In this chapter, we will delve into how to manage data integrity issues when using **Microsoft Power BI**, **Tableau from Salesforce**, and **Alteryx**. We will, we'll build on top of what we've learned already and explore various features to ensure the integrity of financial data.

That said, these are the topics that we will explore in this chapter:

- Managing data integrity issues with BI tools
- Data profiling features
- Data cleansing methods
- Managing relationships in data models
- Dealing with large financial datasets using data validation

By the end of this chapter, you will have gained a deeper understanding of what these BI tools are capable of, particularly in terms of fixing data integrity issues.

Technical requirements

This chapter is a continuation of our discussion from *Chapter 4, Understanding the Data Integrity Management Capabilities of Business Intelligence Tools*. Thus, we will be using the software we used in the previous chapter:

- **Power BI Desktop**, April 2023 or later (no licenses required)
- **Tableau Desktop**, 2023.1 or later (free trial version)
- **Tableau Prep Builder**, 2023.1.0 or later (free trial version)
- **Tableau Cloud** (free trial version)
- **Alteryx Designer**, 2022.3 version or later (free trial version)

Our sample datasets are saved in the official GitHub repo: `https://github.com/PacktPublishing/Managing-Data-Integrity-for-Finance/tree/main/ch05`.

We will be using the datasets created about a fictional company in our hands-on exercises throughout this chapter and *Chapter 6, Implementing Best Practices When Using Business Intelligence Tools*. Save the files on your computer, and then work on the hands-on solutions as you read along.

> **Note**
>
> You can also access the *PBIX*, *YXZP*, *TFLX*, and *TWBX* files for the final reports. At this point, you might be wondering what these files are. Files with a *PBIX* extension are those that are produced by **Power BI Desktop**. They contain information such as the data, models, formulas, and visualizations that were added or created by the user. The equivalent of that for **Alteryx Designer** is the *YXZP* file, where the workflow's inputs, outputs, and configurations are saved. *TFLX* and *TWBX* files are file formats for **Tableau from Salesforce**. *TFLX* is a **Tableau Prep** flow file that contains the packaged workflow from Tableau Prep, while *TWBX* is a Tableau workbook file from **Tableau Desktop** containing the packaged worksheets, models, and visualizations created. Click on each of the files and download them to your working folder. You are now ready to import the data. You may proceed with the next steps once these are ready.

Managing data integrity issues with BI tools

BI tools have a powerful suite of capabilities, one of which is the ability to **extract, transform, and load** (**ETL**) data from multiple sources. We will discuss first the ETL capabilities of Microsoft Power BI Desktop in reviewing the data type format used for an Excel file prior to loading the information for further analysis, and then we will cover how to do this in Tableau Desktop. Let's dive into the topics!

First, we load the data into Power BI by clicking on **Get data** under the **Home** tab and selecting **Excel workbook**, as highlighted in *Figure 5.1*:

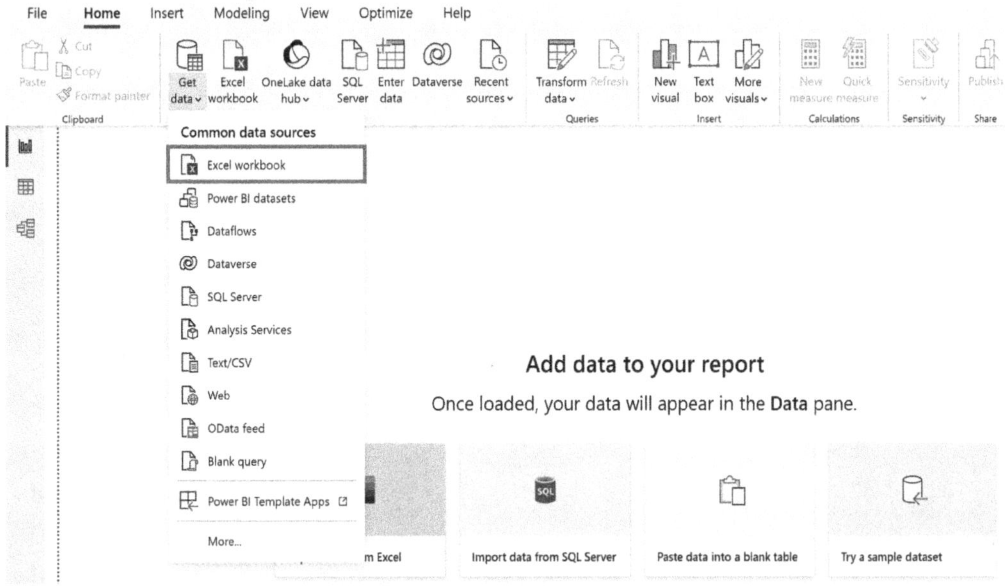

Figure 5.1 – Getting data from Excel workbook

We can see from this figure that from **Get data**, we can load various common data sources, such as an Excel workbook, Power BI datasets, SQL Server, or even data from the web. You can also click on **More…** to extract the data from other sources, such as a PDF file, a SharePoint folder, and online services such as Google Analytics and Salesforce Reports. For the purposes of this book, we will use the Excel workbook as the source.

This will open a pop-up window. Locate where the files are saved, select `2020_Transactions.xlsx`, and then click on **Open**.

Now that we have extracted this dataset, we can start transforming it for our use. The **Navigator** window will open something similar to what we have in *Figure 5.2*:

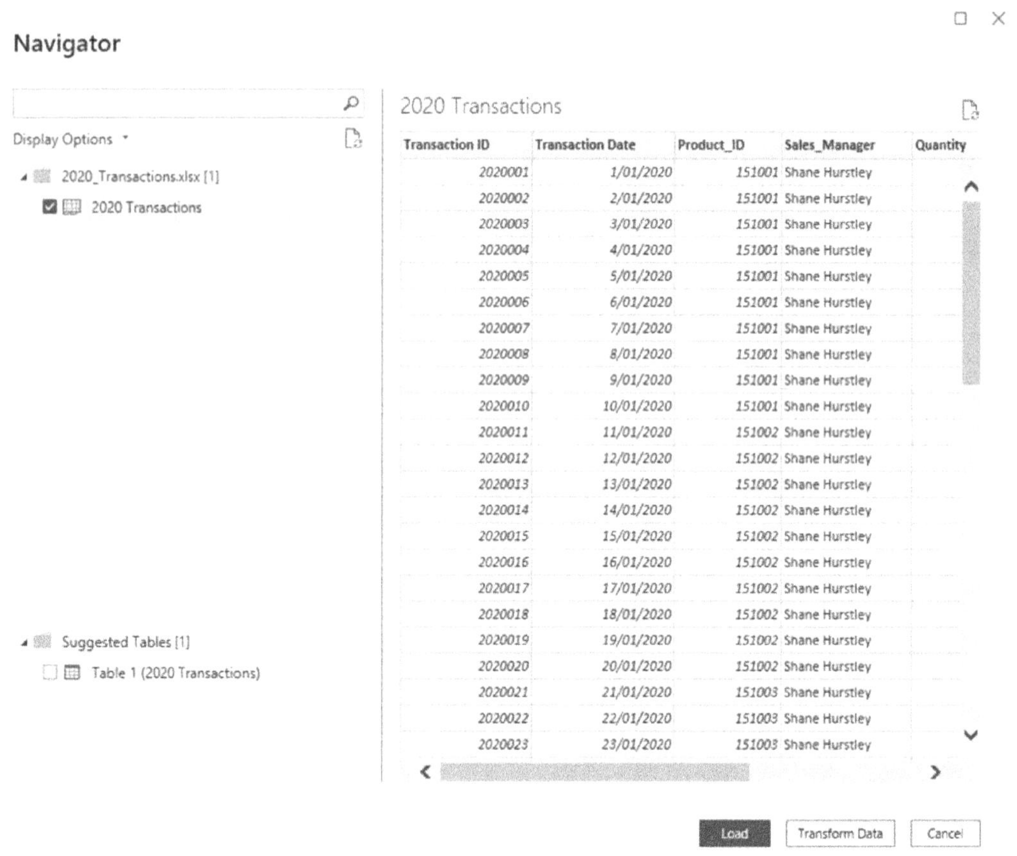

Figure 5.2 – The Navigator window

The **Navigator** window shows the data being loaded to Power BI. When you tick the box in front of **2020 Transactions**, this will generate a preview of what is in the file. You have the option to either load, transform the data before loading, or cancel the action. Since we want to review whether there are any data integrity issues in the file, click on **Transform Data**.

The **Power Query Editor** will appear, as seen in *Figure 5.3*:

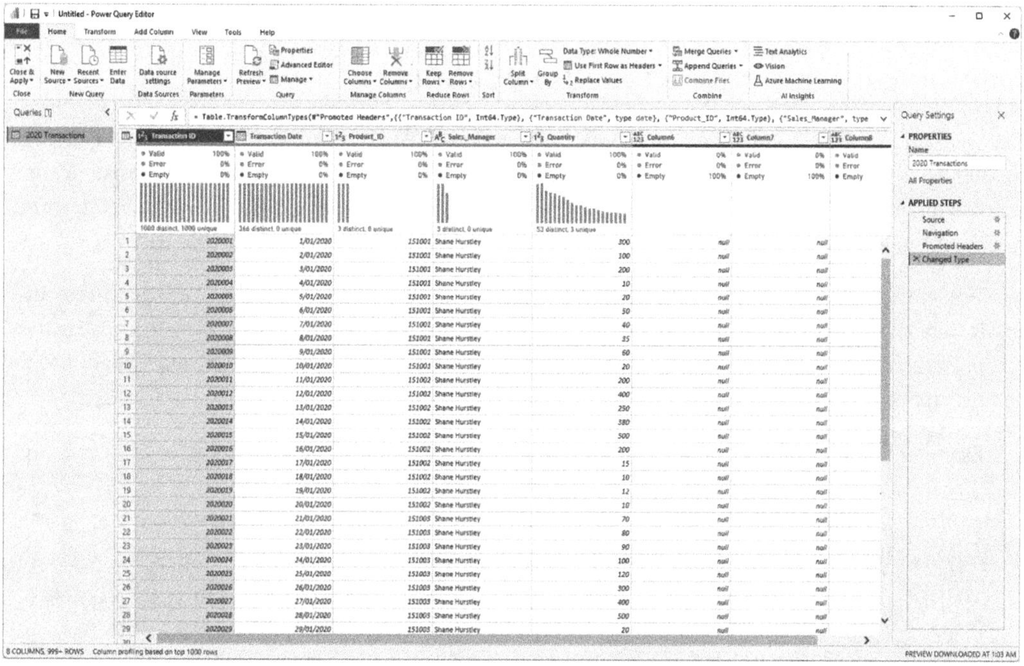

Figure 5.3 – The Power Query Editor

You can connect to new data sources using the Power Query Editor, as well as modify and transform the data. As we briefly covered in the *Features related to data integrity* subsection under *Microsoft Power BI* in *Chapter 4, Understanding the Data Integrity Management Capabilities of Business Intelligence Tools*, this is where we can shape, cleanse, and prepare the data before performing further analysis and visualizations.

The Power Query Editor is a powerful ETL tool that is available not only in Power BI but also in **Microsoft Excel**, **Microsoft Power Platform** dataflows, and **Microsoft Azure Data Factory** wrangling dataflows. At the time of writing, there are two experiences available for Power Query, offering almost the same experience for the user. The first one is when using the *online* version of the Microsoft applications mentioned earlier, and the second one is using the *desktop* version of Excel and Power BI Desktop. Learning Power Query is a skill that can be used in a number of applications—so it is quite valuable to have!

> **Note**
>
> To learn more about Power Query, check out `https://learn.microsoft.com/en-us/power-query/power-query-what-is-power-query`.

Now that we know what Power Query is, let's dive deeper into various data cleansing features of this tool to prepare our data!

Ensuring consistent data type formatting

After we load the dataset into the Power Query Editor, we need to review the data types to ensure consistency as this will form the foundation for what we will be doing going forward. Consistency in data type formatting is necessary in order to perform accurate data analysis and helps prevent errors when working with functions and formulas.

If we look at the icons beside the column names, as illustrated in *Figure 5.4*, we can see that there are already data types used when the data was loaded into the model. Power Query aims to convert the source columns of the data types into that which support efficient storage, calculation, and visualization. The next step is reviewing whether these are correct.

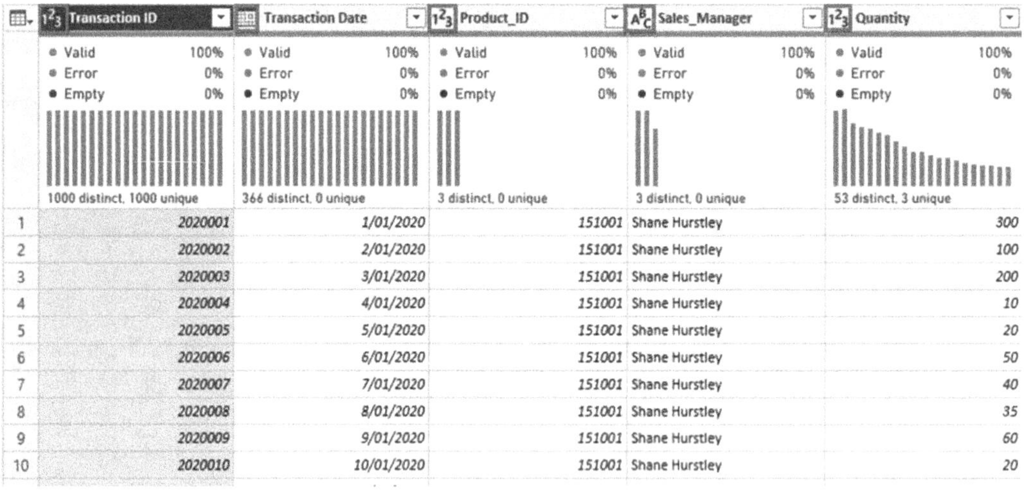

Figure 5.4 – Data types for each column

We can see that the **Transaction ID** and **Product_ID** columns are formatted as whole numbers. The **Transaction Date**, **Sales_Manager**, and **Quantity** columns are formatted correctly.

Given that the **Transaction ID** and **Product_ID** columns are not whole numbers, and we are not going to perform any calculations for these fields, we will change them to text.

We can do this in several ways. First, we can click on the icon on the left side of the column name and select the correct data type, as shown in *Figure 5.5*:

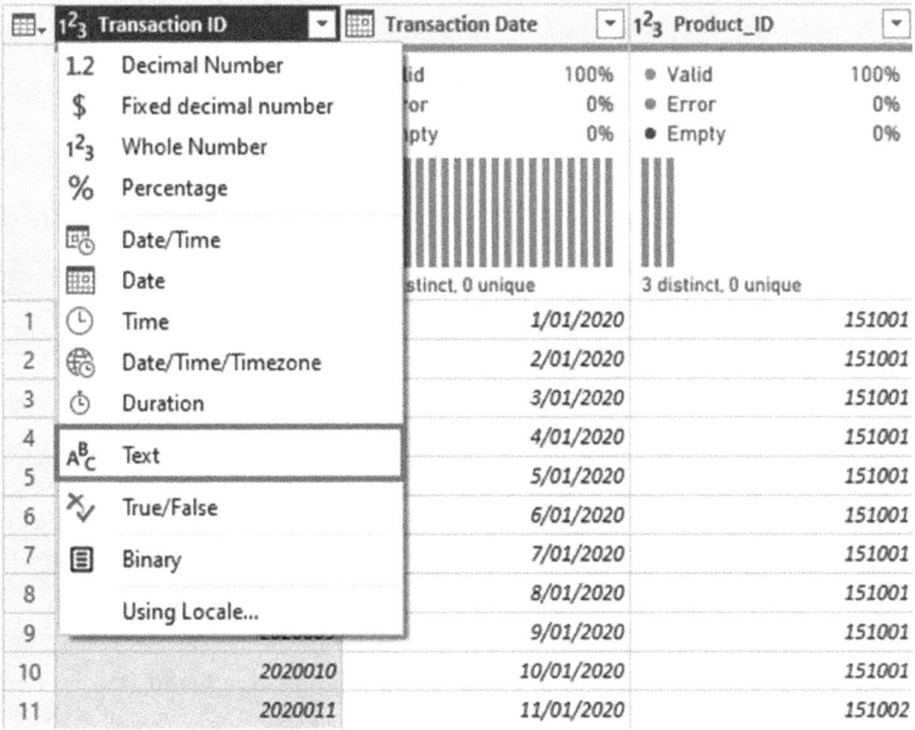

Figure 5.5 – Clicking on the icon at the left side of the column to show the different data types

Second, we can right-click on the related columns to display the shortcut menu, select **Change Type**, and then select **Text**.

The third way is clicking on the column to be changed, going to the **Home** tab, choosing **Date Type: Whole Number**, and selecting **Text**, which is the correct format, as seen in *Figure 5.6*:

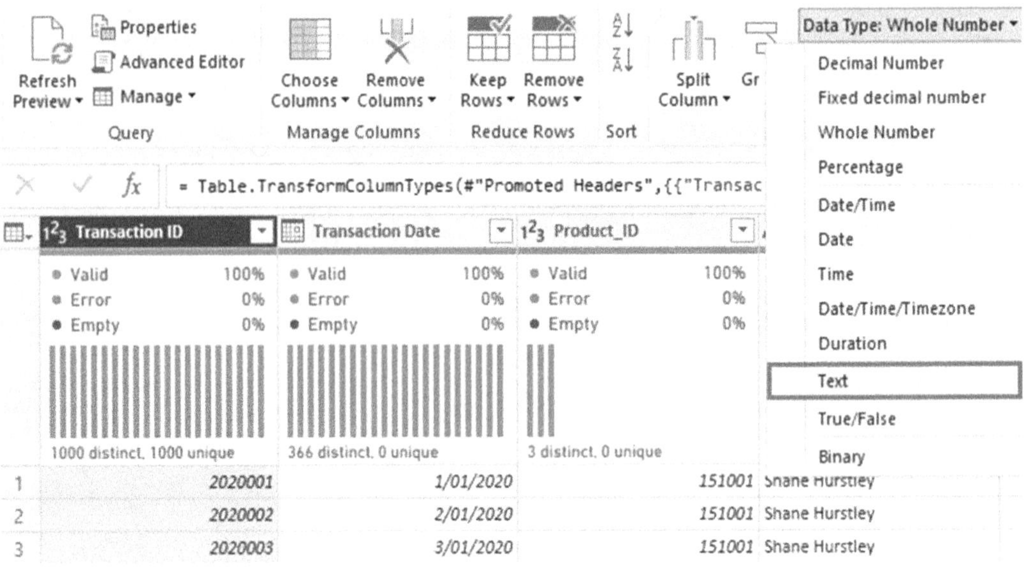

Figure 5.6 – Locating the Data Type selection under the Home tab

As we can see, there are a few ways to update the data type of a column. Ensuring that the data type used is consistent is a key quality metric, as we covered in *Chapter 3, Measuring the Impact of Data Integrity Issues*. This makes the data easier to analyze and more reliable.

Let's use one of these options and update the data type from **Whole Number** to **Text**. If a pop-up window relating to **Change Column Type** appears, as shown in *Figure 5.7*, you may select either **Replace current** or **Add new step** since the outcome will be the same for both. The difference would be that it will add another step for the latter, which will be reflected under the **Applied Steps** list.

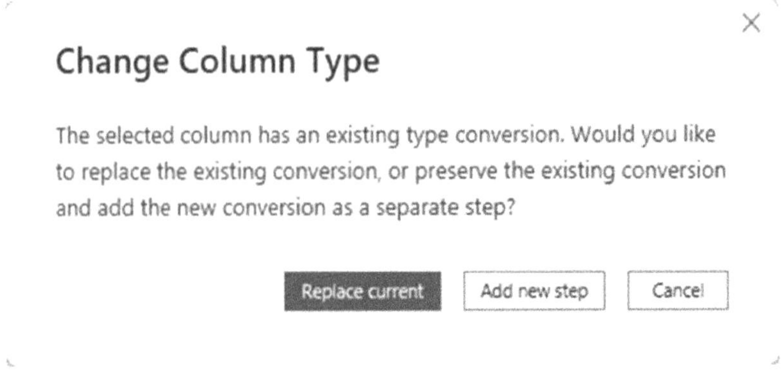

Figure 5.7 – Replace the current step when changing the column data type

When the data is loaded in Power Query, it tries to automatically detect the correct data type, as we saw in *Figure 5.4*, which is why there is already an existing one. As analysts and business professionals, we have more insight as to what the appropriate type is as well as what context we are using it for, which is why we are updating it.

Once the changes are done, the icons will update and will be shown, as seen in *Figure 5.8*:

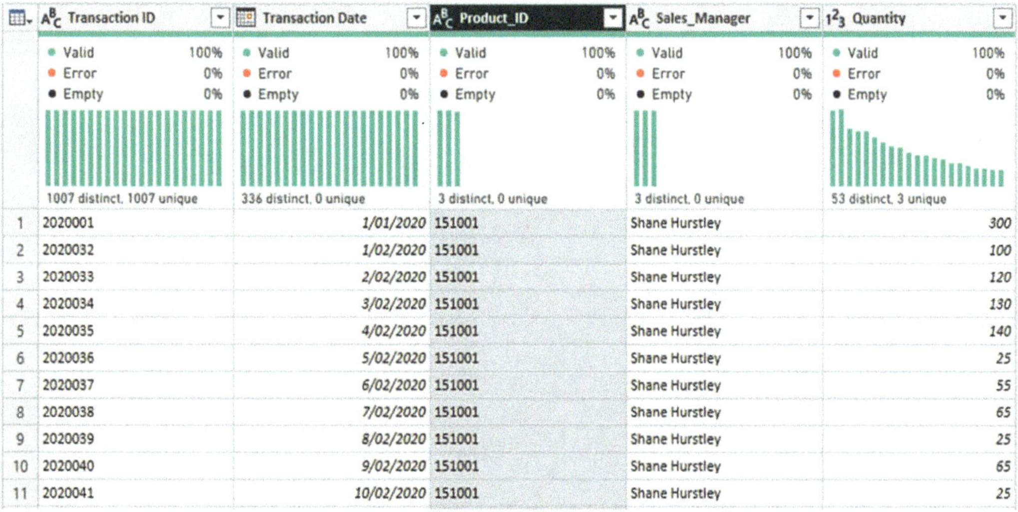

	Transaction ID	Transaction Date	Product_ID	Sales_Manager	Quantity
	Valid 100% / Error 0% / Empty 0%	Valid 100% / Error 0% / Empty 0%	Valid 100% / Error 0% / Empty 0%	Valid 100% / Error 0% / Empty 0%	Valid 100% / Error 0% / Empty 0%
	1007 distinct, 1007 unique	336 distinct, 0 unique	3 distinct, 0 unique	3 distinct, 0 unique	53 distinct, 3 unique
1	2020001	1/01/2020	151001	Shane Hurstley	300
2	2020032	1/02/2020	151001	Shane Hurstley	100
3	2020033	2/02/2020	151001	Shane Hurstley	120
4	2020034	3/02/2020	151001	Shane Hurstley	130
5	2020035	4/02/2020	151001	Shane Hurstley	140
6	2020036	5/02/2020	151001	Shane Hurstley	25
7	2020037	6/02/2020	151001	Shane Hurstley	55
8	2020038	7/02/2020	151001	Shane Hurstley	65
9	2020039	8/02/2020	151001	Shane Hurstley	25
10	2020040	9/02/2020	151001	Shane Hurstley	65
11	2020041	10/02/2020	151001	Shane Hurstley	25

Figure 5.8 – Transaction ID and Product_ID formatted as Text

Now, all our columns have the appropriate data types.

Let's load the other two files, named `Product_Details.xlsx` and `Sales_Managers.xlsx`. The `Product_Details.xslx` file contains the price, cost, and gross profit for each project, while the `Sales_Managers.xslx` file contains the region that the sales managers support.

To do this, click on **New Source** under the **Home** tab and select **Excel Workbook**, as illustrated in *Figure 5.9*:

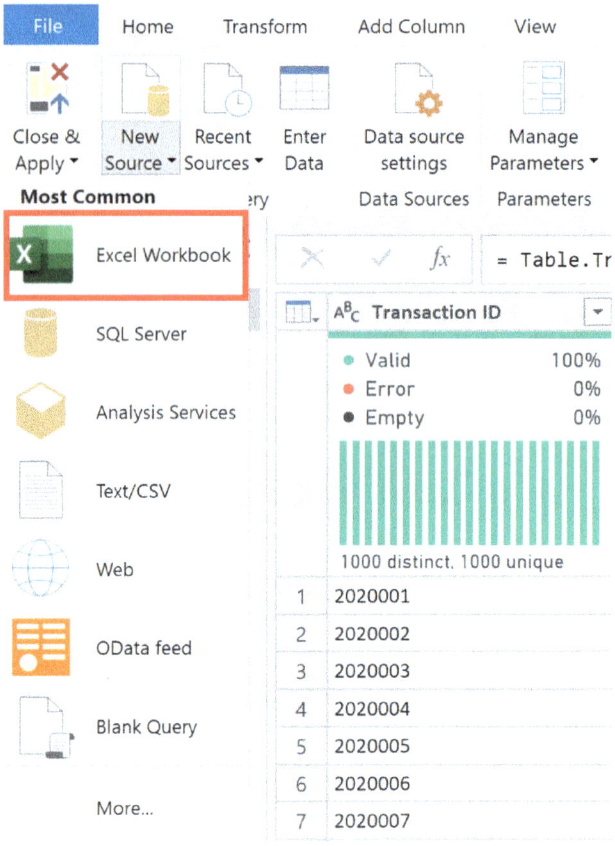

Figure 5.9 – Adding a new source in the Power Query Editor

Locate where the two files mentioned earlier are saved. Once they are selected, the **Navigator** window, similar to *Figure 5.2*, will appear.

> **Note**
>
> The **Power Query Editor** enables us to *connect* and *combine* data from different sources—this is an important feature given that valuable information resides in a number of places from traditional databases to cloud-based solutions, and various online services. This ability is a must-have.

Once they are loaded into the editor, check the data types of the columns. For the **Product_Details** table, make sure that the **Product_ID** column is formatted as text; **Product_Price**, **Product_Cost**, and **Product_Gross_Profit** as a fixed decimal number; and **Product_Gross_Profit_%** as a percentage.

After making these changes, the updated **Product_Details** table with the data type formats will be visible, as seen in *Figure 5.10*:

Product_ID
Product_Name
Product_Price
Product_Cost
Product_Gross_Profit
Product_Gross_Profit_%
Valid 100%
Error 0%
Empty 0%
3 distinct, 3 unique
1 151001 Car insurance 995.00 350.00 645.00 64.82%
2 151002 Life insurance 1,250.00 475.00 775.00 62.00%
3 151003 Income protection insurance 775.00 380.00 395.00 50.97%

Figure 5.10 – Updated Product_Details table

Although the **Product_Price**, **Product_Cost**, **Product_Gross_Profit**, and **Product_Gross_Profit_%** values are given in a simple table in our example, in practice, this information is not usually provided in a straightforward manner and needs to be calculated from the company's underlying data.

For the **Sales_Managers** table, ensure that the first rows are used as headers. We can see in the editor that after loading the data, the headers are in the first row, as illustrated in *Figure 5.11*:

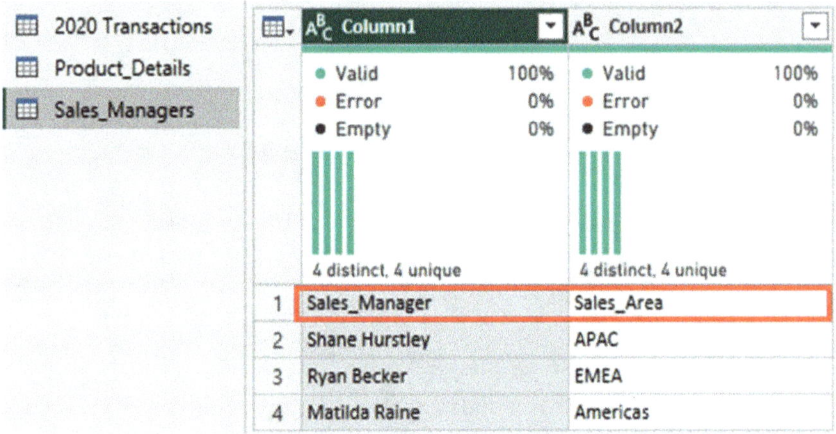
2020 Transactions
Product_Details
Sales_Managers
Column1
Column2
Valid 100%
Error 0%
Empty 0%
4 distinct, 4 unique
1 Sales_Manager Sales_Area
2 Shane Hurstley APAC
3 Ryan Becker EMEA
4 Matilda Raine Americas

Figure 5.11 – The Sales_Manager table after loading

To solve this, go to the **Home** tab, and select **Use First Row as Headers**, as shown in *Figure 5.12*:

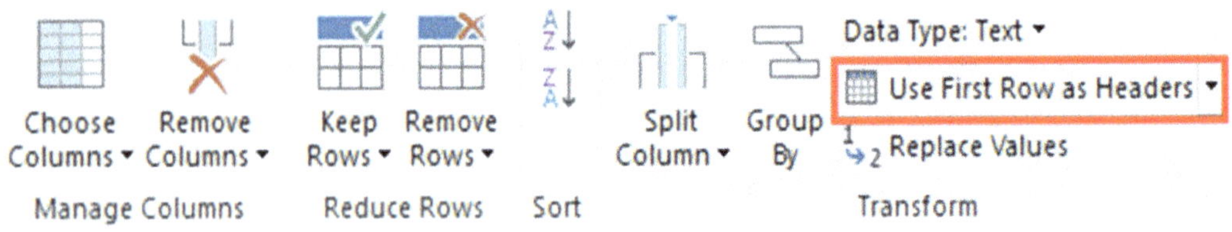
Choose Columns
Remove Columns
Keep Rows
Remove Rows
Split Column
Group By
Data Type: Text
Use First Row as Headers
Replace Values
Manage Columns
Reduce Rows
Sort
Transform

Figure 5.12 – Use First Row as Headers

When Power Query loads the information, it automatically detects the column headers, as we saw when we loaded the `2020_Transactions.xlsx` and `Product_Details.xlsx` files. Sometimes, it is not able to, and when that happens, we can promote the first row as headers.

After the change is made, the updated table will look like *Figure 5.13*:

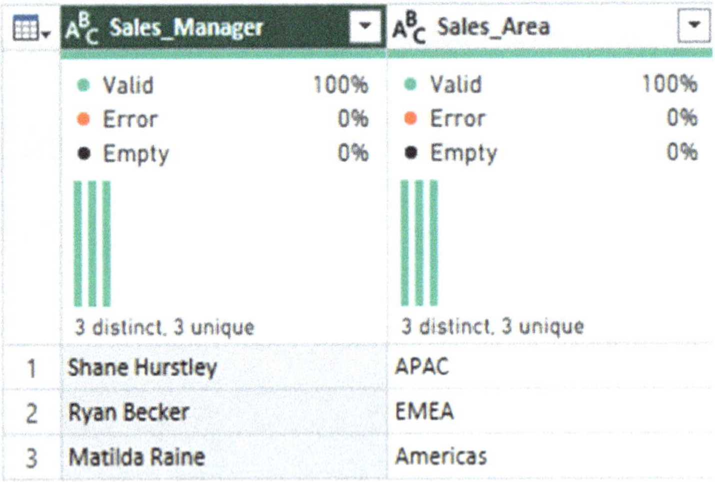
Sales_Manager
Sales_Area
Valid 100%
Error 0%
Empty 0%
Valid 100%
Error 0%
Empty 0%
3 distinct, 3 unique
3 distinct, 3 unique
1 Shane Hurstley APAC
2 Ryan Becker EMEA
3 Matilda Raine Americas

Figure 5.13 – Updated column headers

As we will cover later in the chapter, under the *Managing relationships in data models* section, ensuring that our tables are labeled with appropriate headers makes it easier to create and manage relationships, as well as perform joins, which we will discuss in the *Identifying orphaned records in Power BI* section in the next chapter.

Everything else looks good, so we can now go to the **Home** tab and select **Close & Apply**, as shown in *Figure 5.14*. This action closes the Power Query Editor and implements the changes.

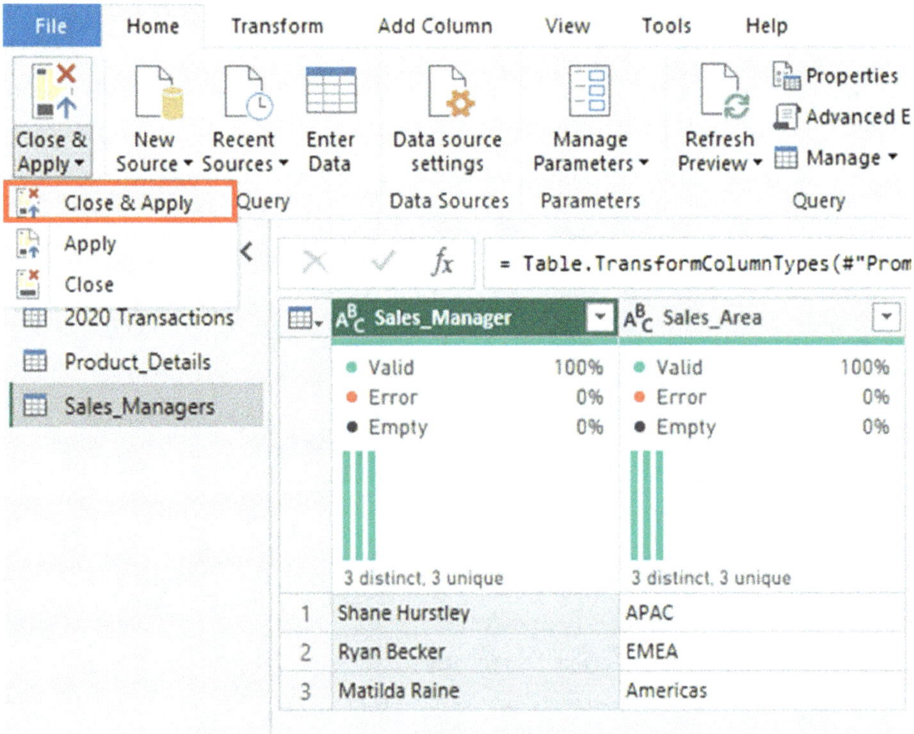

Figure 5.14 – Close & Apply under the Home tab

After that, a pop-up window will appear loading the data, which will disappear after the loading is complete, and lead to the blank **report canvas**. The information we loaded in this step will be integrated into the data model and used in later sections of this chapter.

> **Note**
>
> To learn more about the different data types in Power Query, check out `https://learn.microsoft.com/en-us/power-query/data-types`.

Making sure that the data types we use are consistent is critical for data integrity. Now that we have discussed this through Microsoft Power BI Desktop, let's see how we can do this through another common tool used by businesses—**Tableau Desktop**. We will explore this in the next section.

Data type consistency techniques

For this example, we will use the `Review Formatting.xlsx` file downloaded from the GitHub repository.

First, let's open **Tableau Desktop** and click on **Data** | **New Data Source**, as illustrated in *Figure 5.15*:

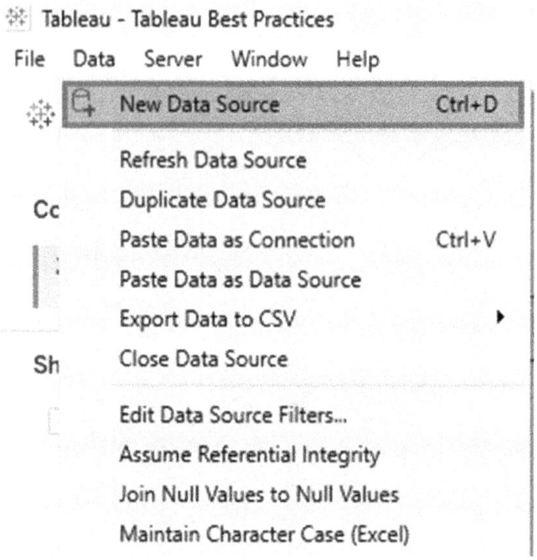

Figure 5.15 – Selecting New Data Source under the Data tab

This will lead you to the **Connect** window, where you can access various data sources, as shown in *Figure 5.16*:

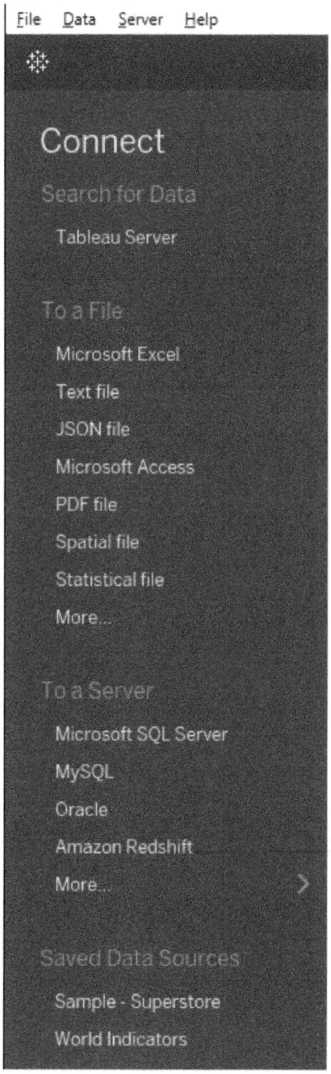

Figure 5.16 – Connecting to different sources

We can see that we are able to interface with various sources of data to files, such as Microsoft Excel, text, or PDF, or to servers, such as **Microsoft SQL Server**, **Oracle**, or **Google Analytics**, as well as searching for data on **Tableau Server** or **Tableau Cloud**.

The dataset we will use is in Microsoft Excel; therefore, under **To a File**, select **Microsoft Excel**. A pop-up window to connect to the file will appear. Locate where the `Review Formatting.xlsx` file is saved and select it.

Once this is loaded, we can see the **Data Source** page, as seen in *Figure 5.17*:

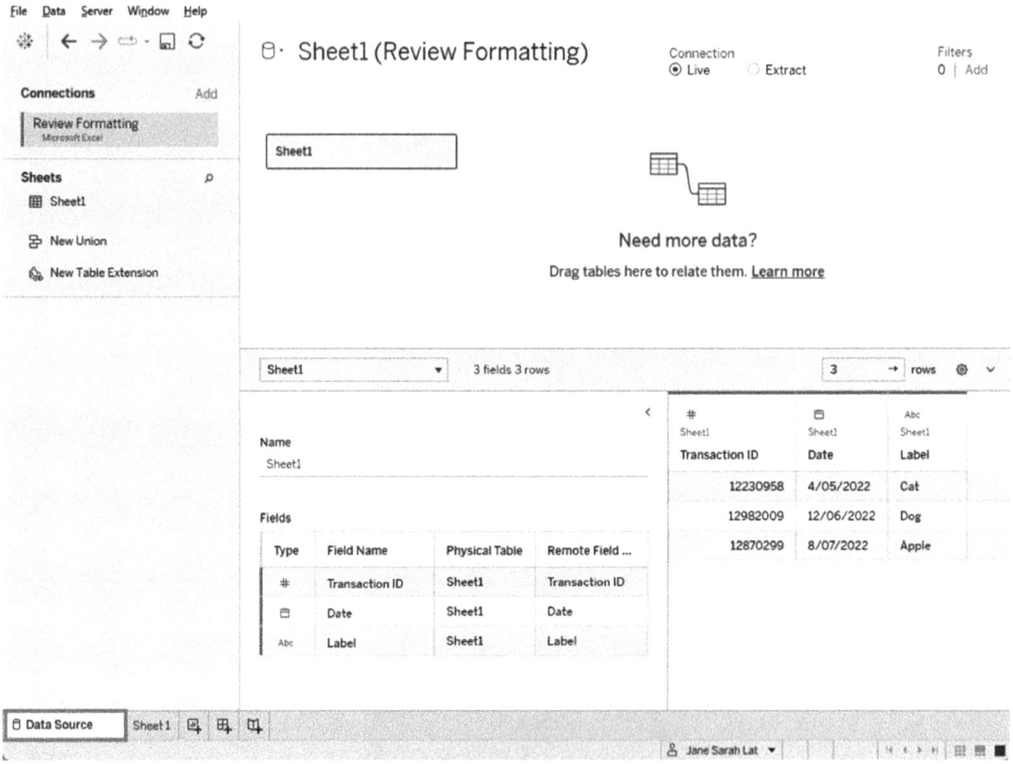

Figure 5.17 – Data Source page

This will create a live connection to the source, and any changes that we will make are reflected in Tableau but not the data source file.

> **Note**
>
> There are cases when it will be much more efficient to use data extracts because live connections can become slower with more complex workbooks. To learn more about this, feel free to check out `https://www.tableau.com/blog/tableau-cloud-tips-extracts-live-connections-cloud-data`.

If we examine the information further in the **metadata grid**, we can see that the **Transaction ID** column is set as a **Number (whole)** data type, the **Date** column is set as **Date**, and the **Label** column is set as **String**, as seen in *Figure 5.18*:

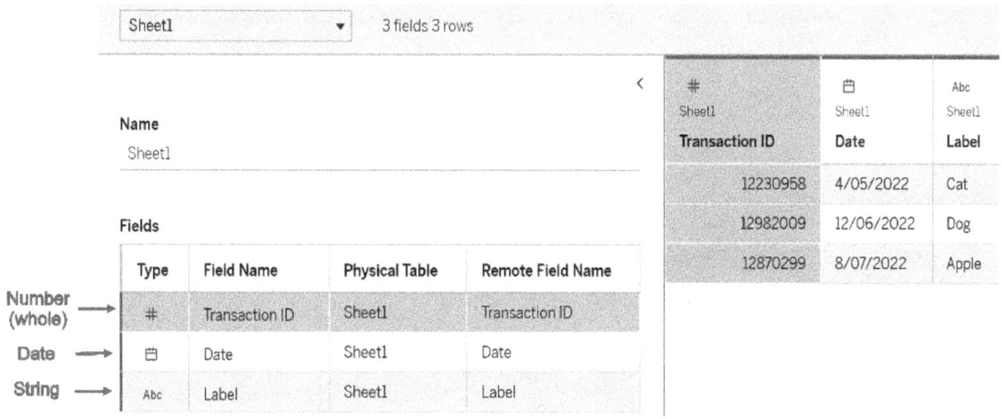

Figure 5.18 – Information loaded to Tableau Desktop

From this, we can see that the **Transaction ID** column needs to be updated.

> **Note**
>
> The metadata grid shows the different fields of your data source as rows, making it easier to examine and manage.

For **Transaction ID**, since we will not be doing any calculations for this field, we can change this to **String**. We can do this in two ways. The first is by clicking on # under **Type** to show the selection, and then clicking on **String**. The second way is by going to the **Data** pane found in **Sheet1** beside the **Data Source** page, clicking on the dropdown for **Transaction ID**, selecting **Change Data Type**, and choosing **String**, as illustrated in *Figure 5.19*:

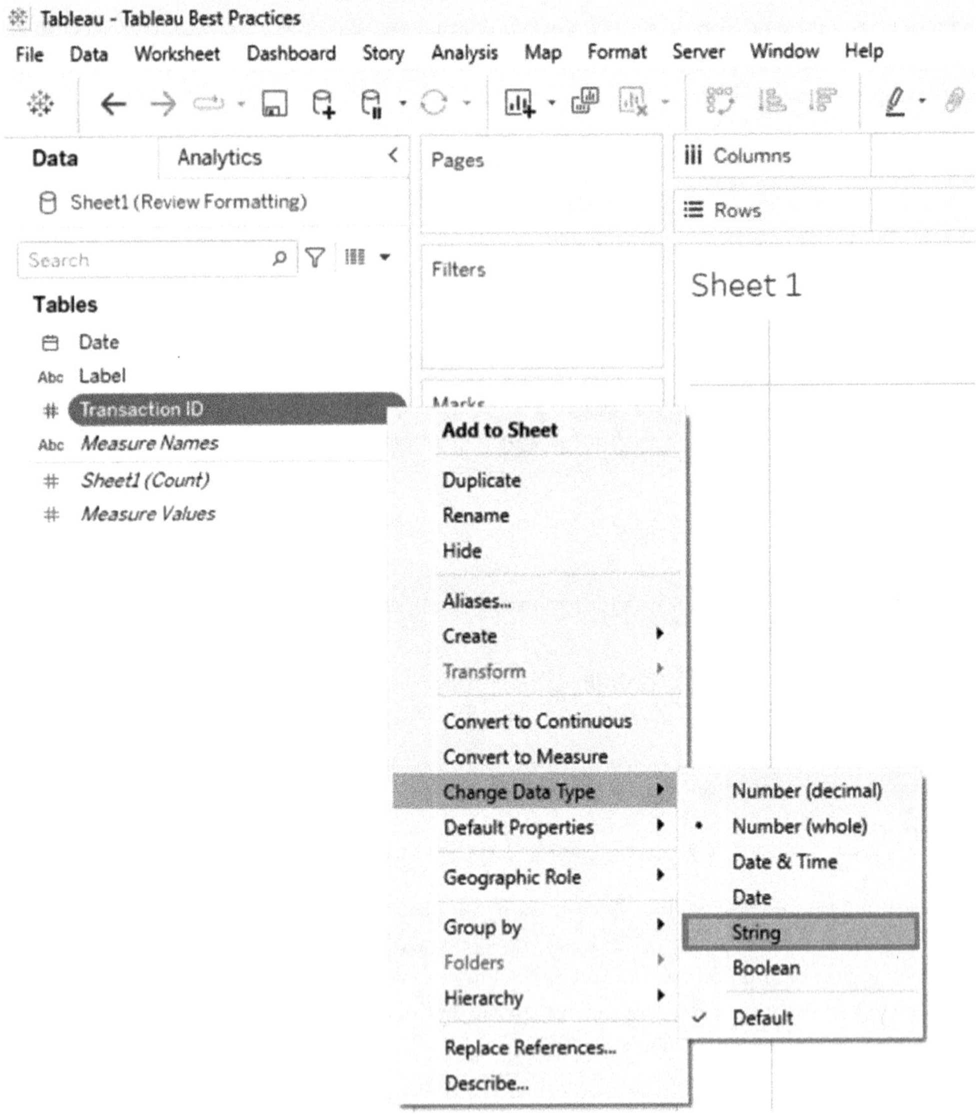

Figure 5.19 – Updating the data type for Transaction ID

The **Date** and **Label** columns are correct, hence we do not need to make any changes. Now that we have covered reviewing data types and how to update them, let's load the dataset we will be using for our hands-on exercise, which is the `2020_Transactions.xlsx` file that we worked on in Power BI earlier.

Follow the same steps we did earlier in *Figures 5.15* and *5.16* to add this file as a new data source. Once this is loaded, the connection will be established, as can be seen in *Figure 5.20*:

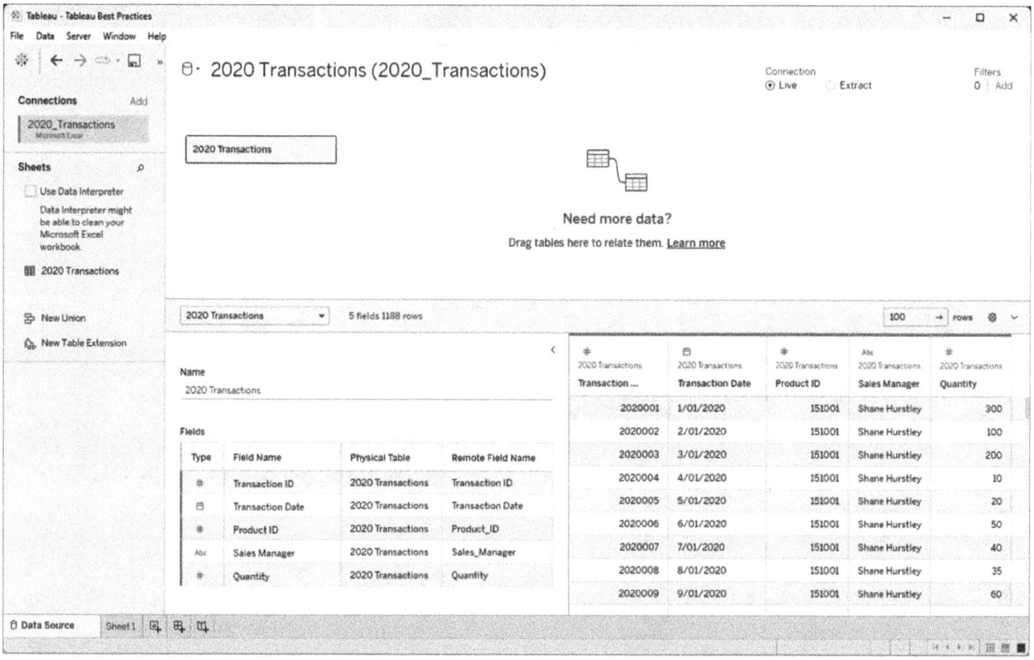

Figure 5.20 – 2020_Transactions.xlsx loaded in Tableau Desktop

A live connection to the data source has been created, showing the five fields of the table in the metadata grid, as well as a *preview* of the 100 rows under the **data grid**. You will also notice, on the left-hand side under **Sheets**, that the **Use Data Interpreter** option is available. It was not showing earlier when we were working on the `Review Formatting.xlsx` file. This was because it was already formatted in a way that Tableau understands.

If we check the box beside **Use Data Interpreter**, it will clean the data, and you can check the results by clicking on **Review the results**. An Excel file will be generated to show how the file has been interpreted.

> **Note**
>
> To learn more about Data Interpreter, check out `https://help.tableau.com/current/pro/desktop/en-us/data_interpreter.htm`.

Our next steps are to review the **Fields** type of the columns and to update **Transaction ID** and **Product ID** from **Number (whole)** to **String** since we will not be doing any calculations for these fields. *Figure 5.21* shows the updated fields once the changes are made:

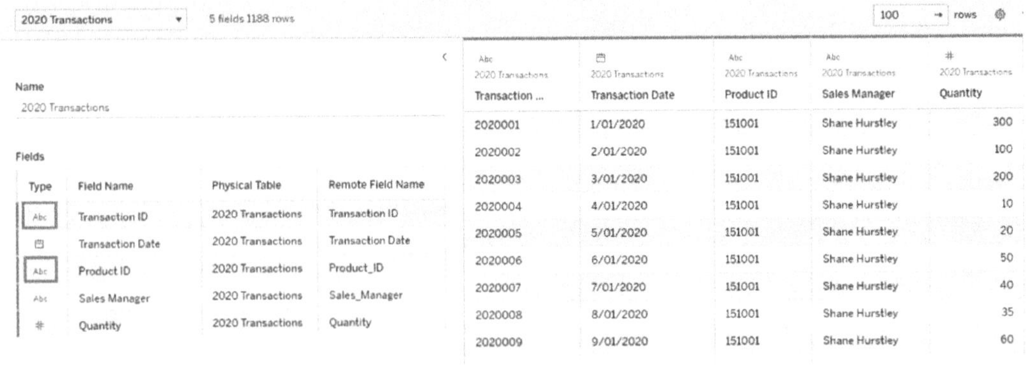

Figure 5.21 – Field types updated to String

We do not need to make any revisions to **Transaction Date**, **Sales Manager**, and **Quantity** since they are already correct.

> **Note**
>
> As we covered in this section, preparing the data and ensuring that the data types are consistent after loading to our BI tools is important. This is not only for aesthetic purposes but also to enhance the reliability and quality of the data we are working on.

Now that we have covered this topic, we can dive deeper into the data set and discuss another key feature available in BI tools, which is **data profiling**! Save and close the file for now, and we will work on it again in the next chapter, in the *Creating the histogram* section.

Data profiling features

Microsoft Power BI has data profiling features that offer simple ways to examine and analyze the data in the Power Query Editor. These are found under the **View** tab on the ribbon, as shown in *Figure 5.22*:

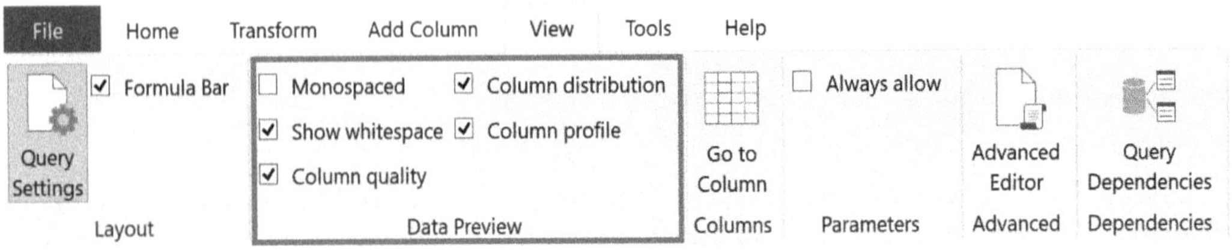

Figure 5.22 – Data profiling tools in the View tab

In the next subsections, we will cover the **data profiling** features of **column quality**, **column distribution**, and **column profile**.

Column quality

This feature indicates what the column quality of the data is in five categories as shown in *Figure 5.23*:

Category	Indicator
Valid	Green
Error	Red
Empty	Dark grey
Unknown	Dashed green
Unexpected error	Dashed red

Figure 5.23 – Column quality indicators

The colors reflect the quality of the data in the columns and make it easier to analyze and examine.

Figure 5.24 shows where the column quality is found in the Power Query Editor:

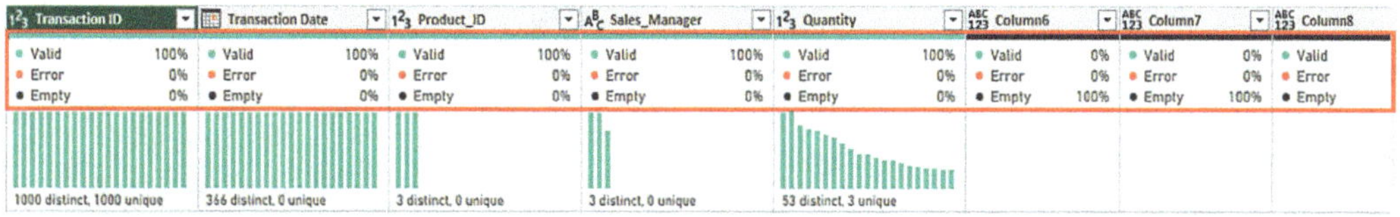

Figure 5.24 – Column quality

We can see from the indicators that the first five columns are valid, while the last three are empty. This means that there are excess columns that can be removed. Select these empty columns by using *Ctrl* + click or *Shift* + click. The selected columns will appear as shown in *Figure 5.25*:

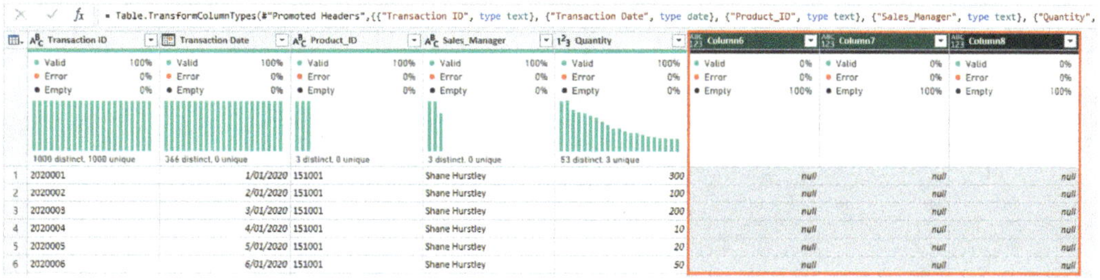

Figure 5.25 – Selecting the columns to be removed

There are two ways that these excess columns can be removed. First, go to the **Home** tab, then to **Manage Columns**, and select **Remove Columns** as seen in *Figure 5.26*:

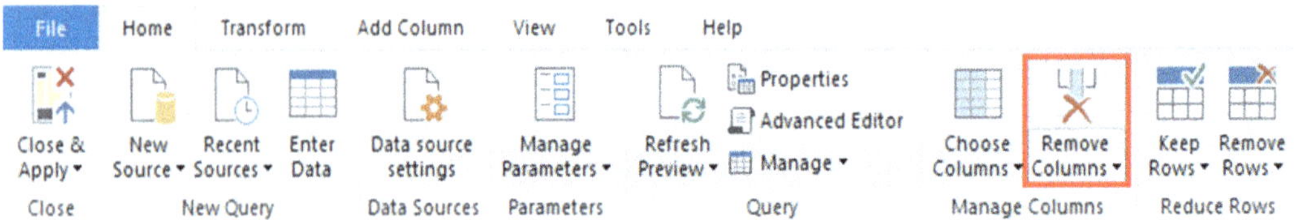

Figure 5.26 – The Remove Columns option under the Home tab

The other way is to right-click on the table and select **Remove Columns**.

Once these columns are deleted, they will disappear and the **Removed Columns** step will be added to the **APPLIED STEPS** window, as seen in *Figure 5.27*:

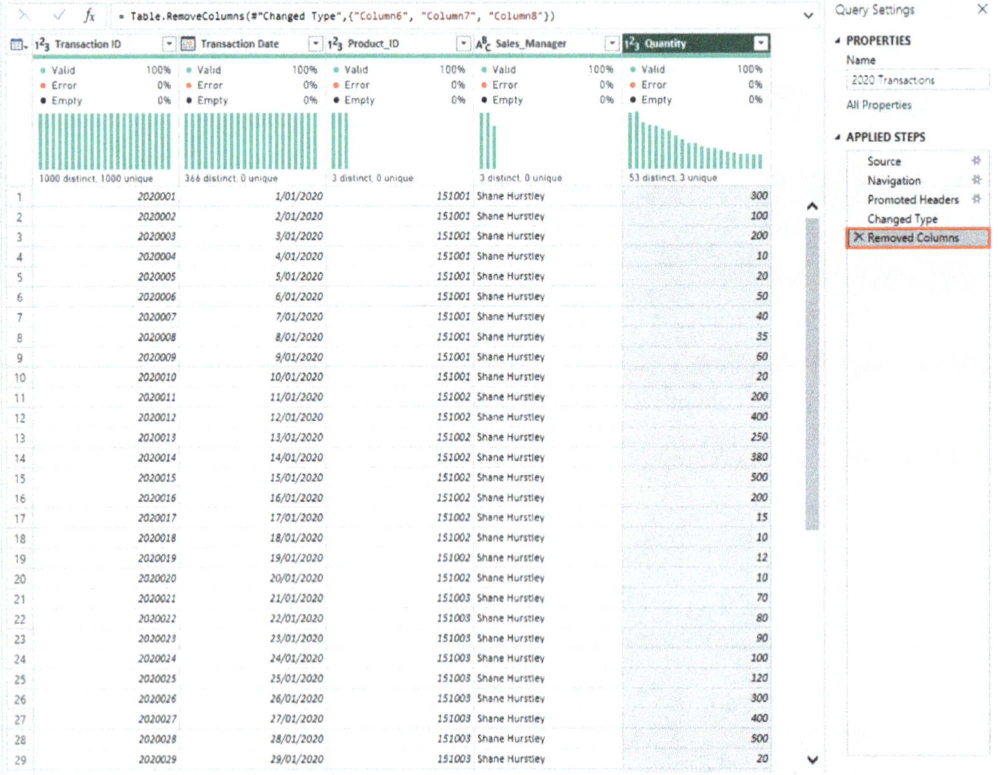

Figure 5.27 – Removed Columns under APPLIED STEPS

APPLIED STEPS is very useful in tracking the transformations done to the data and allows you to go back to the data's previous state prior to the transformation by deleting the step.

You might be wondering, *What are the green bars underneath the column quality indicators?* We will discuss just that in the next section!

Column distribution

The column distribution can be found under the column names beneath the column quality, as highlighted in *Figure 5.28*:

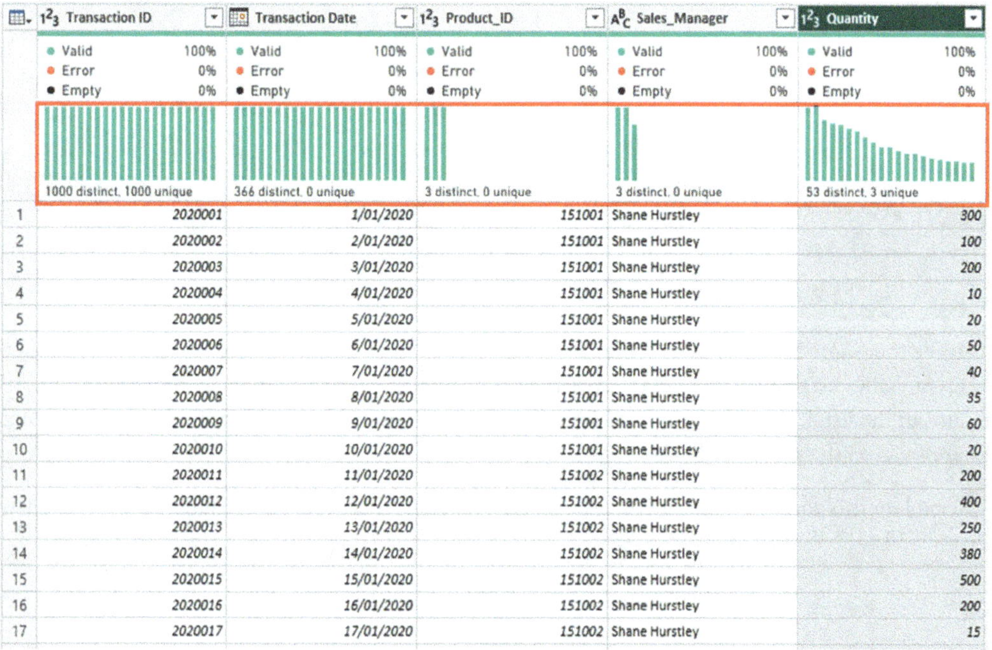

Figure 5.28 – Column distribution

This feature shows the frequency and distribution of the values in the columns and is arranged in descending order, starting with the value that appears most frequently.

If we hover our cursor above this feature for the **Quantity** column, we get the information about the data, as shown in *Figure 5.29*:

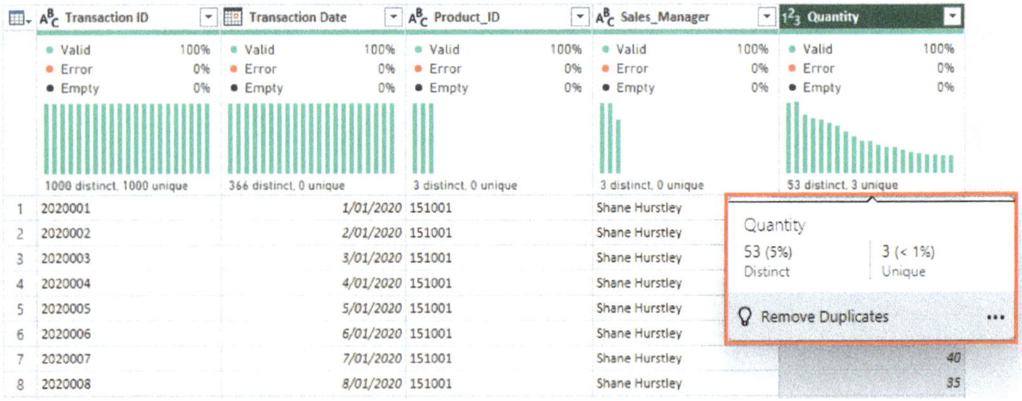

Figure 5.29 – Column distribution information

We can see that there are 53 *distinct* types, 3 of which are *unique*. **Distinct** refers to the total number of different values no matter how many times they appear in the dataset. When an item appears more than once in the list, it counts as one distinct count. The **unique** value, on the other hand, is the total number of values that occur only once.

We can explain this concept better by creating a **pivot table** in Microsoft Excel using the layout shown in *Figure 5.30*:

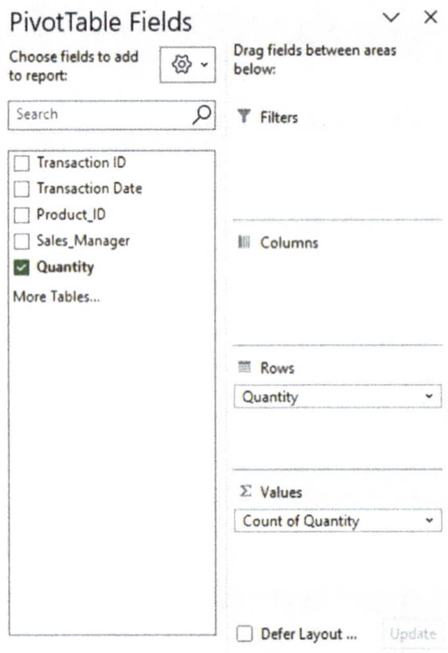

Figure 5.30 – PivotTable Fields

To create this layout, drag the **Quantity** field under **Rows**, and **Quantity** under **Values** making sure that **Count of Quantity** is shown.

If we select the items under the row labels, we can see that the total count is 53, which is the total **distinct** type we saw earlier. Next, let's sort **Count of Quantity** in the pivot table so we can easily see the frequency. We can do this by clicking on **Sort** under the **Data** tab, as can be seen in *Figure 5.31*:

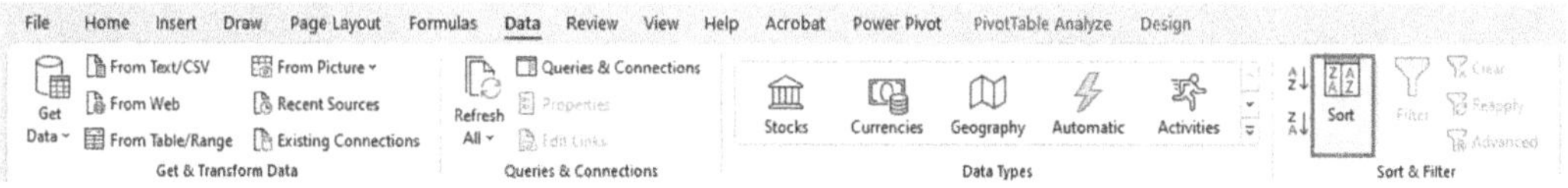

Figure 5.31 – Sorting the data in the pivot table

In the option under **Sort**, select **Smallest to Largest**. This will sort the pivot table as shown in *Figure 5.32* and help us easily identify the unique values:

	A	B
1		
2		
3	**Row Labels**	**Count of Quantity**
4	7	1
5	20,000	1
6	8	1
7	77	2
8	44	2
9	66	2
10	125	2
11	101	2
12	16	3
13	130	3
14	140	3
15	85	4
16	110	4
17	88	5
18	35	5

Figure 5.32 – Unique values on the Pivot table

If we examine this, we can see the quantity sold per transaction and that three items are not that common and should be checked and reviewed further, particularly the transaction with 20,000 items. We will dive deeper into this in the *Using data visualization to identify data outliers* section in the next chapter.

Now that we have covered what column quality and column distribution are, let's discuss what column profiling is and how understanding this feature can help improve data integrity.

Column profile

This function offers a more thorough examination of the information for the selected column. It also includes a **Column statistics** chart in addition to the **Value distribution** chart, as illustrated in *Figure 5.33*:

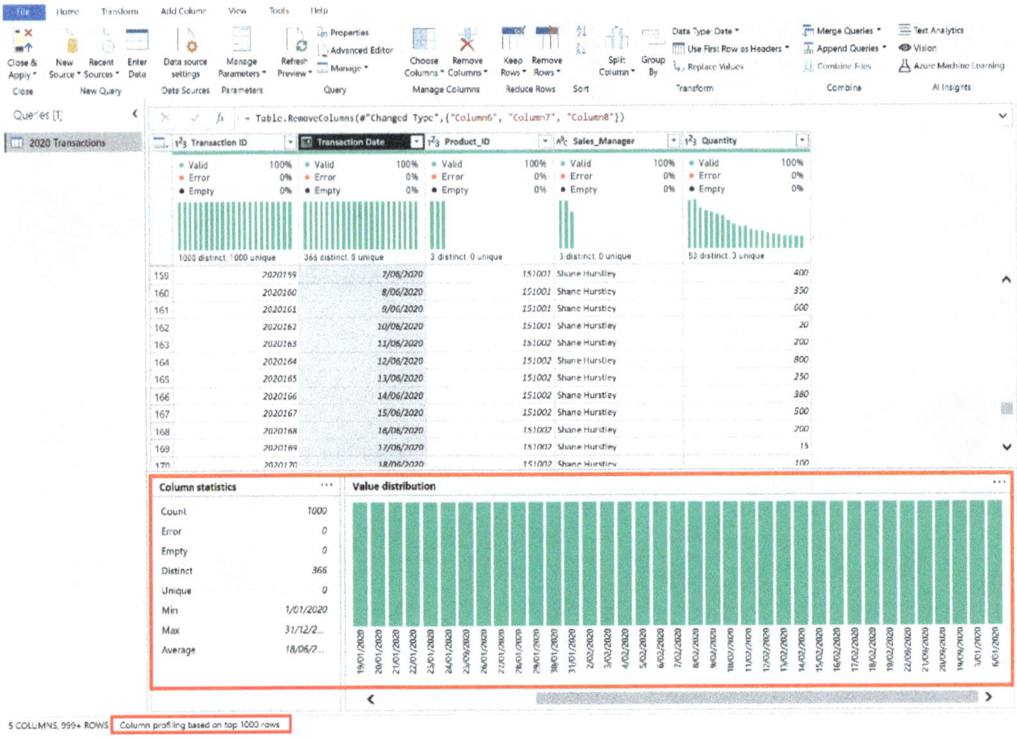

Figure 5.33 – Column profile

As seen in the screenshot, these are is shown underneath the data preview section.

You can also see, in the bottom far-left corner of the Power Query Editor window, that column profiling has been done based on the top 1,000 rows.

This is done by default and can be changed by clicking on this part and selecting **Column profiling based on entire data set**, as illustrated in *Figure 5.34*:

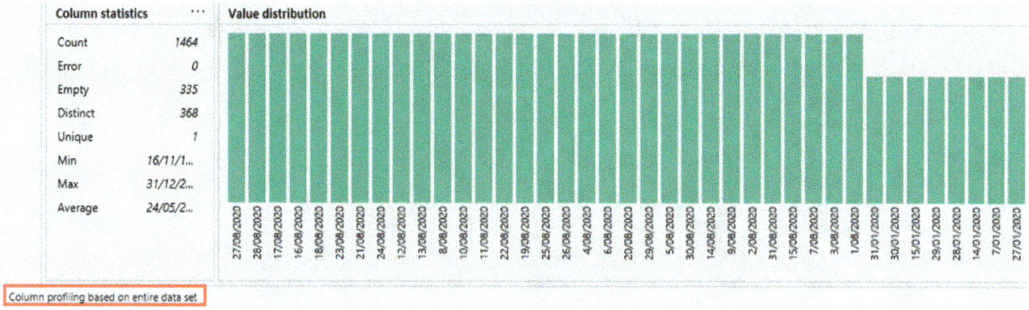

Figure 5.34 – Column profiling based on entire data set

Getting the column profile for the entire dataset provides an overall view and a better understanding of our underlying data.

Now that we have covered the major data profiling features in Power BI, let's act on the insights we gained from examining the data by doing data cleansing. Performing these steps will enhance the quality and integrity of the data we are working on. We will be covering how to do this in the next section.

Data cleansing methods

As we mentioned in the previous chapter, in the *Exploring common data quality management capabilities of BI tools* section, data cleansing is a key step in improving the integrity of the data. In this section, we will continue our hands-on examples to cleanse the dataset using Power BI Desktop.

Removing empty cells

If we examine the column statistics in *Figure 5.34*, our total transaction count is 1,464, no errors have been found, and there are 335 empty cells. If we scroll to the bottom of the table, we can find that rows 1,130 up to 1,464 have null values or empty cells. We can remove these by going to the **Home** tab, clicking on **Remove Rows**, and selecting **Remove Blank Rows**, as shown in *Figure 5.35*:

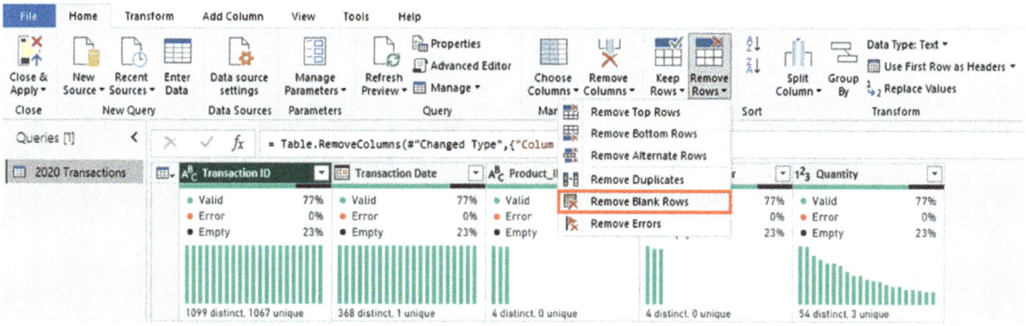

Figure 5.35 – Removing empty cells

If we scroll down the data table after this step, we can see that the table now ends on row 1,129 and the empty cells have been removed, as illustrated in *Figure 5.36*:

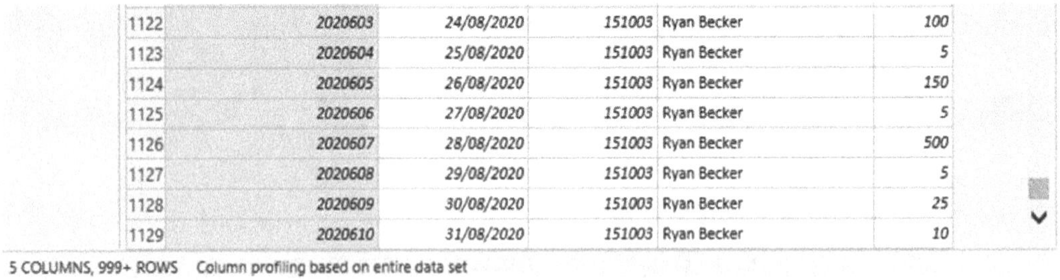

1122	2020603	24/08/2020	151003	Ryan Becker	100
1123	2020604	25/08/2020	151003	Ryan Becker	5
1124	2020605	26/08/2020	151003	Ryan Becker	150
1125	2020606	27/08/2020	151003	Ryan Becker	5
1126	2020607	28/08/2020	151003	Ryan Becker	500
1127	2020608	29/08/2020	151003	Ryan Becker	5
1128	2020609	30/08/2020	151003	Ryan Becker	25
1129	2020610	31/08/2020	151003	Ryan Becker	10

5 COLUMNS, 999+ ROWS Column profiling based on entire data set

Figure 5.36 – After removing empty cells

The **Column** statistics will update and reflect that there are zero empty cells. The **Column** statistics also show the unique and distinct values for the columns. In the next section, we will dive deeper into how to use these fields in determining the existence of duplicate values in our dataset.

Removing duplicates

Imagine analyzing a report about the increase in revenue month over month, only to find out that the change was not due to an increase in sales, but rather because of a duplication in the data! This is why it is critical that the data is prepared, reviewed, and cleansed prior to generating reports and performing further analysis.

In this section, we will continue with our hands-on example, determine whether there are duplicate values, and remove them.

Our next step is to examine the **Value distribution** chart for the transactions. When we click on **Transaction ID** and analyze the column profile, we can see in the **Column statistics** field that there are 1,098 distinct values and 1,067 are unique, as illustrated in *Figure 5.37*:

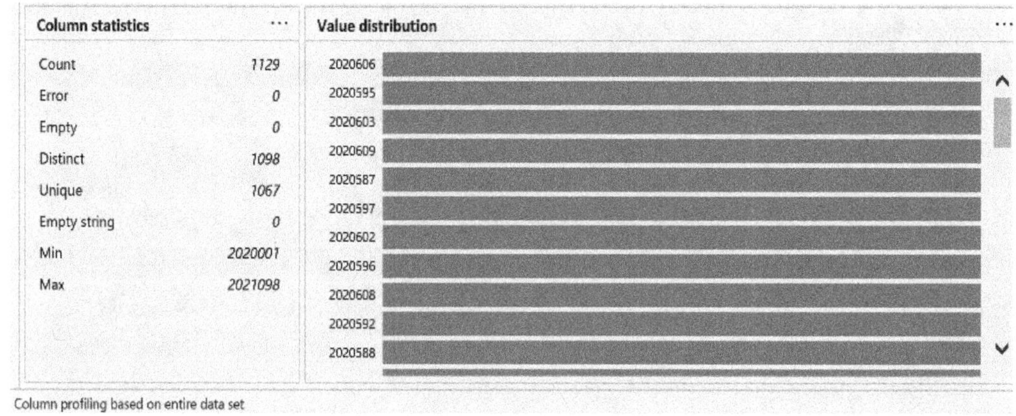

Figure 5.37 – Column profile for Transaction ID

As we covered earlier, in the *Column distribution* section, the **Unique** statistic means the total count of values appearing just once. Given that this is showing **1067**, while **Distinct** is showing **1098**, there are indications that we have duplicate transactions in our dataset.

Go to **Value distribution**, scroll down, and hover over the bar for transaction ID **2020580**, as seen in *Figure 5.38*:

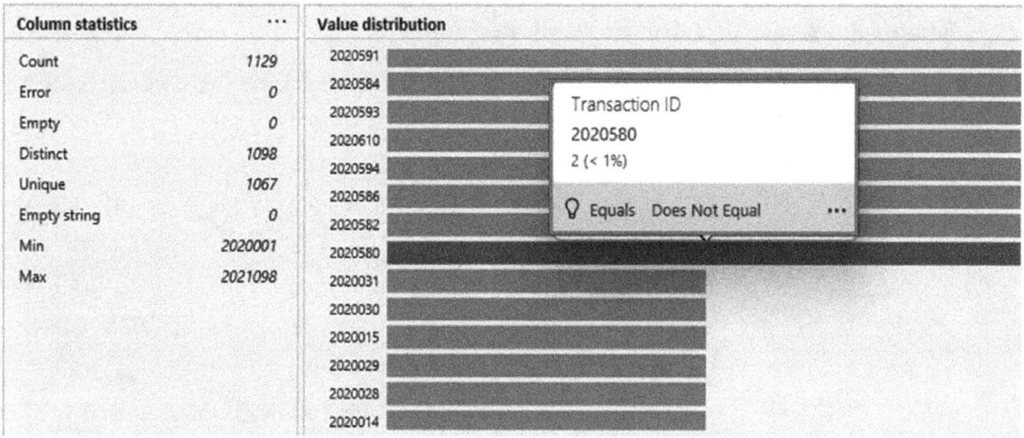

Figure 5.38 – Selecting transaction ID 2020580

You will note that the count for this transaction ID is **2**, as well as those above it.

If we select transaction ID **2020028** on the lower part of the chart, we can see that the count of the **Transaction ID** field is **1**, as highlighted in *Figure 5.39*:

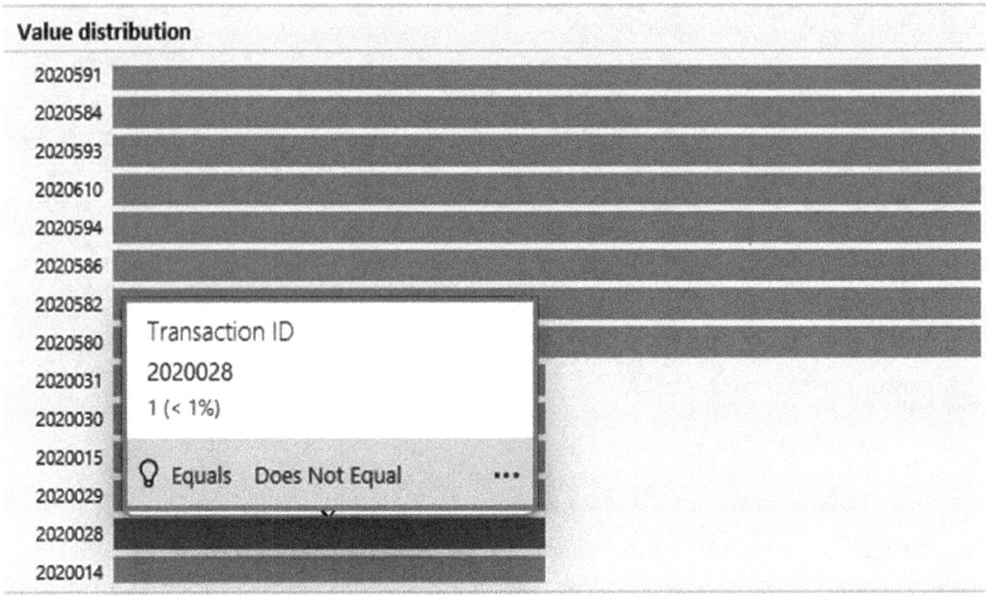

Figure 5.39 – Selecting transaction ID 2020028

From the information we have available, we can confirm that we do have duplicate values. To remove these items, select the column with the duplicates, which in this case is **Transaction ID**. Go to **Home**, click on **Remove Rows**, and select **Remove Duplicates**.

If we examine **Column statistics** and **Value distribution** after performing these steps, we can see that the **Distinct** and **Unique** values are now **1098**, as illustrated in *Figure 5.40*:

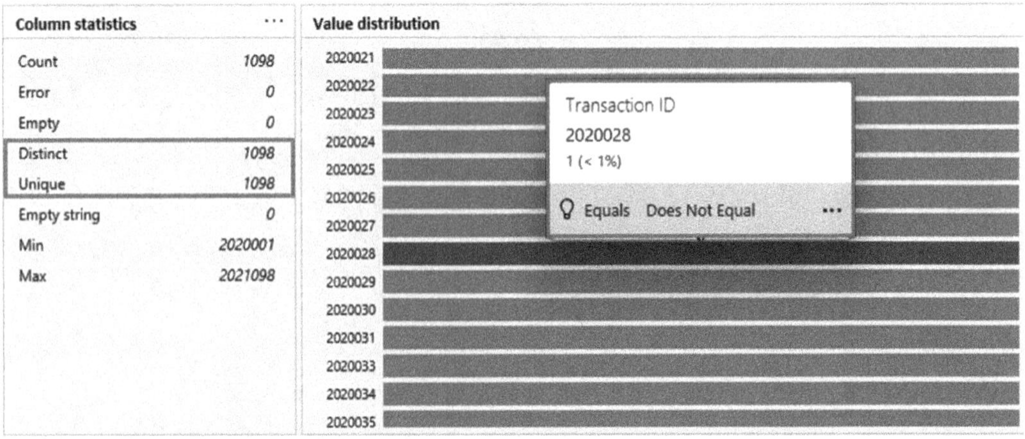

Figure 5.40 – Column profile after duplicate rows are removed

The **Value distribution** value for the transaction ID is now **1** across the items.

> **Note**
>
> The **Column profile** is very helpful in examining the data. Other useful fields to check the data are **Min** and **Max**. We will cover this further in the next section.

Identifying data outliers

Let's continue with our example in the Power Query Editor, and look at the **Transaction Date** column. When we click on this column and examine the **Column statistics** field, we will notice that the **Min** value is showing **16/11/1900**, as seen in *Figure 5.41*:

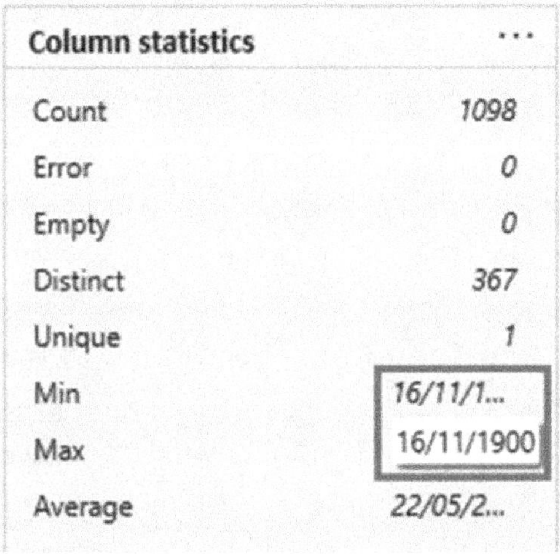
Column statistics
Count 1098
Error 0
Empty 0
Distinct 367
Unique 1
Min 16/11/1...
Max
16/11/1900
Average 22/05/2...

Figure 5.41 – Min showing an outlier

From this information, we can see that the **Min** value is an outlier and needs to be corrected. The **Max** value is correct since our data is for **2020**.

To review the data in the **Transaction Date** column, click on the dropdown and select **Custom Filter...**, as shown in *Figure 5.42*:

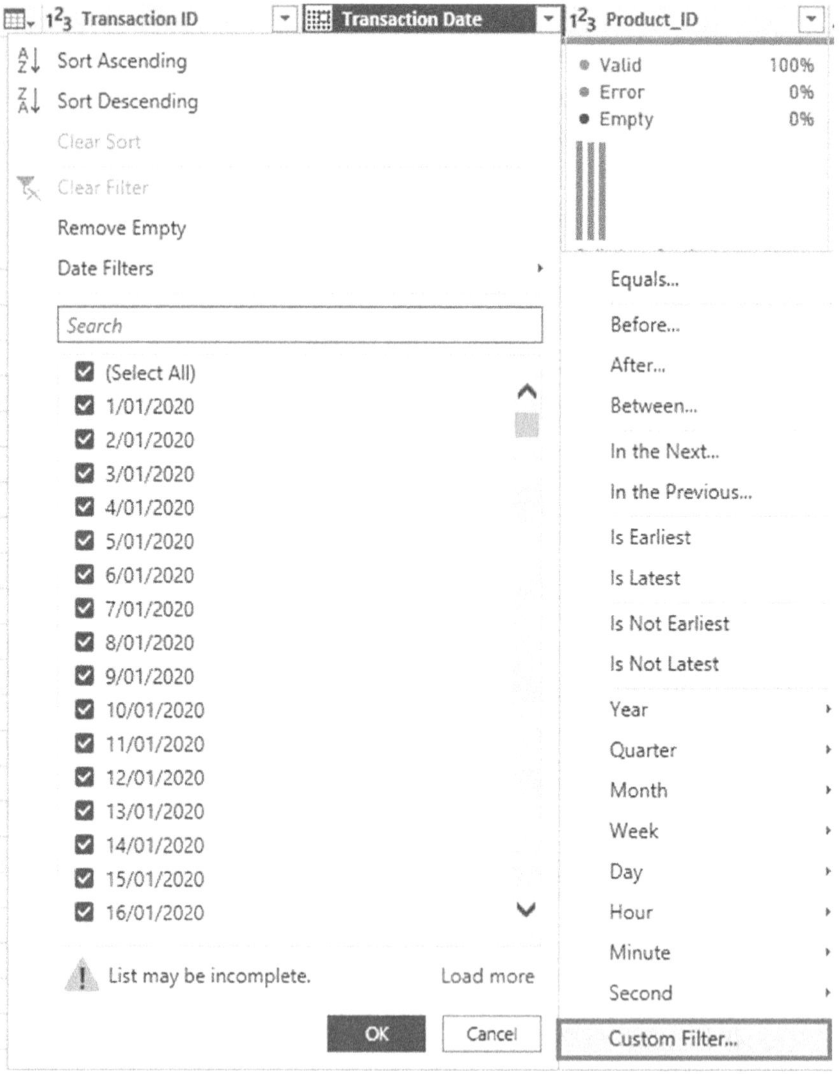

Figure 5.42 – The Custom Filter… option to add conditions

We can try looking for this value by using **Search**. However, given that there is a **List may be incomplete** message, it will be more efficient to use **Custom Filter…**.

Select **is before** and enter `1/01/2020` to filter the transactions before 2020, then choose **Or**, select **is after**, and enter `31/12/2020` to filter the transactions after 2020, as can be seen in *Figure 5.43*:

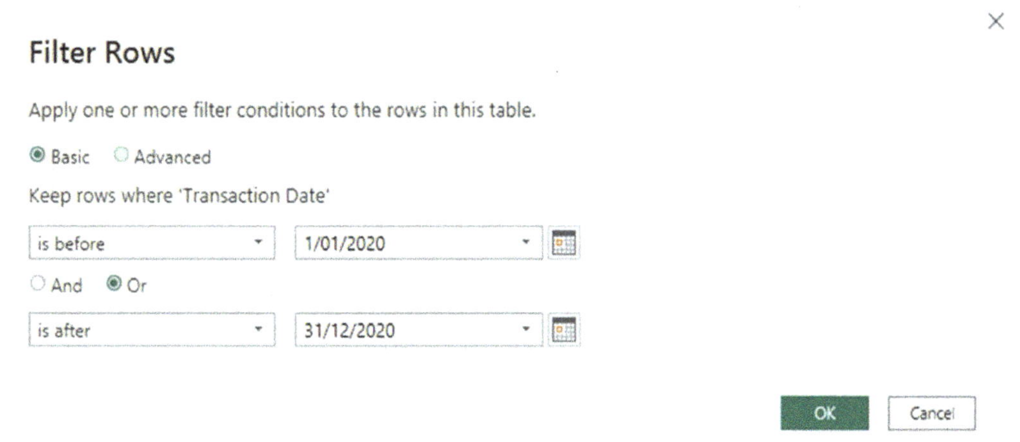
Filter Rows
Apply one or more filter conditions to the rows in this table.
Basic
Advanced
Keep rows where 'Transaction Date'
is before
1/01/2020
And
Or
is after
31/12/2020
OK
Cancel

Figure 5.43 – Filtering transactions before and after 2020

Doing this step will filter transactions before and after 2020. Since we have only one transaction outside this range, this is being displayed and filtered out, as seen in *Figure 5.44*:

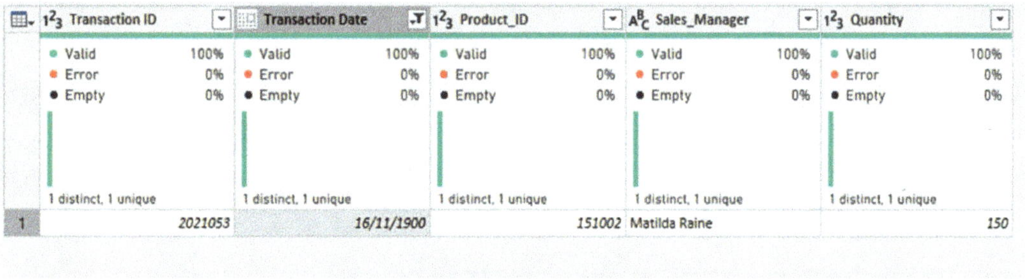
Transaction ID
Transaction Date
Product_ID
Sales_Manager
Quantity
Valid 100%
Error 0%
Empty 0%
1 distinct, 1 unique
1
2021053
16/11/1900
151002
Matilda Raine
150

Figure 5.44 – After filtering the rows

Make sure you undo the filter by clicking on the **X** mark beside **Filtered Rows** under **APPLIED STEPS**, as seen in *Figure 5.45*:

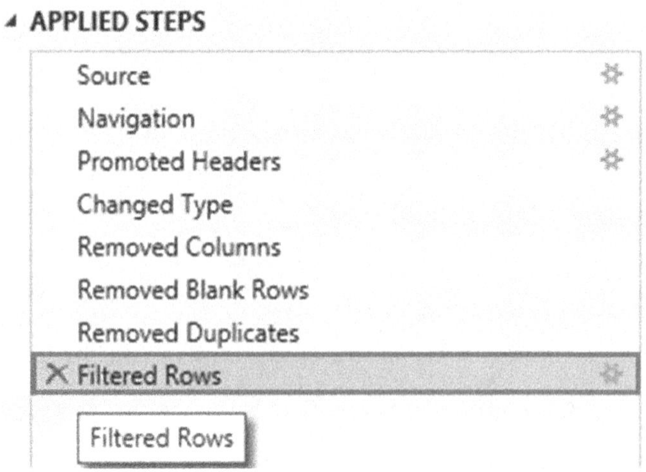

Figure 5.45 – Removing the filter

The previous steps we executed were to check whether there were any dates that were not for 2020. We are undoing the last step to show the entire dataset before we perform the filter.

The next part will cover how to correct the outlier to 2020. Under the **Home** tab, select **Replace Values**.

The **Replace Values** pop-up window will appear. Under **Value To Find**, place `16/11/1900`, and under **Replace With**, put `16/11/2020`, as shown in *Figure 5.46*. Click on **OK**.

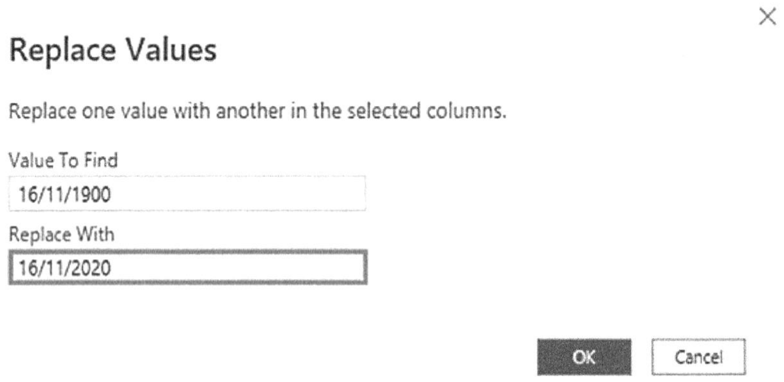

Figure 5.46 – Replacing the value and updating the year

This will update the item and we can now see that we no longer have any unique values for the **Transaction Date** column, as seen in *Figure 5.47*. The **Min** row is now correctly reflecting **1/01/2020**.

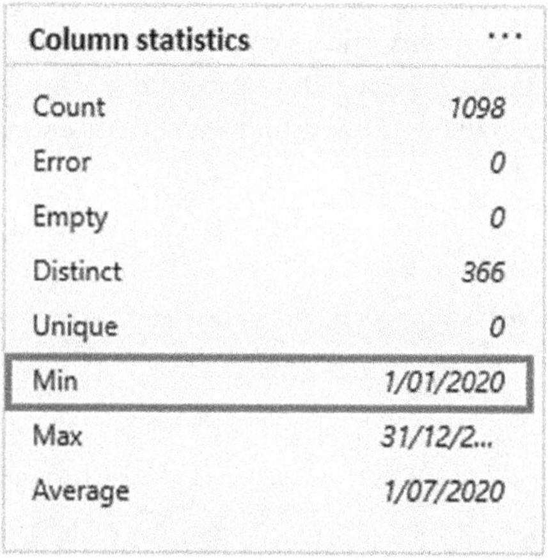
Column statistics
Count 1098
Error 0
Empty 0
Distinct 366
Unique 0
Min 1/01/2020
Max 31/12/2...
Average 1/07/2020

Figure 5.47 – Updated Column statistics field for the Transaction Date column

> **Note**
>
> You can see that the date convention being used is day, month, year—for example, `1/01/2020`, which is the sequence used in Australia and the United Kingdom. In the United States and other countries, however, the sequence is month, day, year—for example, `01/1/2020`.

To check the locale being used, go to **File**, then select **Options and settings**, and click on **Options**, as shown in *Figure 5.48*:

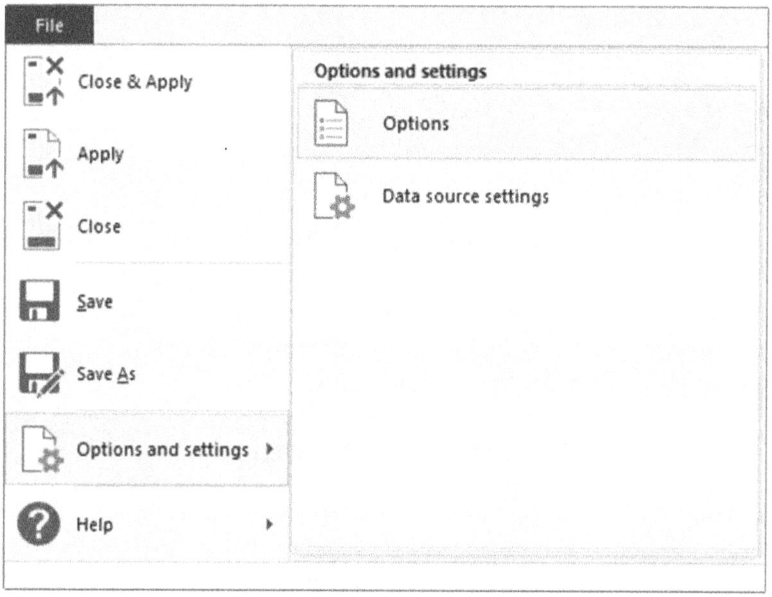

Figure 5.48 – Options and settings

Go to **Regional Settings** (under **Current File**), which will show the **Locale for import** page, as illustrated in *Figure 5.49*. We can see that **English (Australia)** is being used in this example. If you need to change the setting, click on the dropdown and select the appropriate locale.

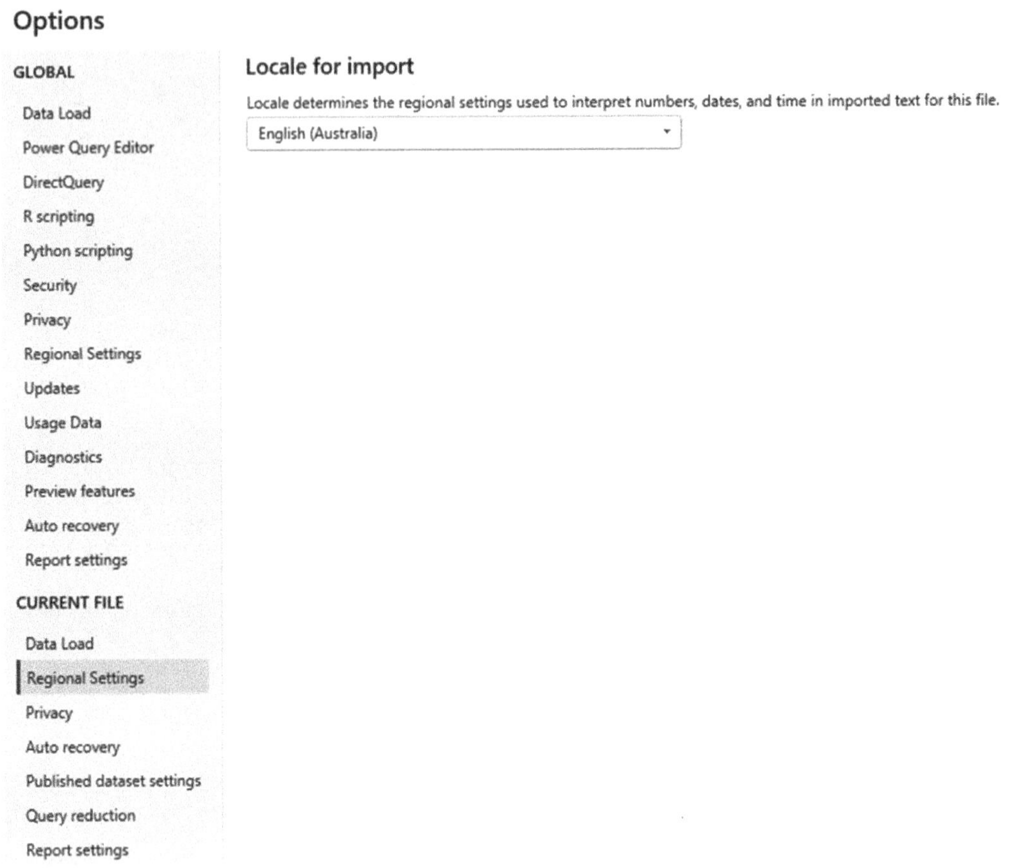

Figure 5.49 – Regional setting used is English (Australia)

Now that we have covered common data cleansing methods and checked the locale settings, let's cover another important concept, which is how to manage relationships in data models. We will learn how to deal with this using Power BI in the next section.

Managing relationships in data models

Ensuring that the relationships in our data models and tables are well defined enhances the reliability and accuracy of the reports we generate. When data is loaded in Power BI Desktop, it tries to automatically identify the relationships in the table similar to detecting the data types when loading data to Power Query. We can manage the relationships by going to **Model view**, as we will discuss in this section.

Continuing with our hands-on example, let's close the Power Query Editor by selecting **Close & Apply**. This will lead us to the report canvas. Next, click on the **Model view** icon, as seen on the left-side panel in *Figure 5.50*, to show the data model:

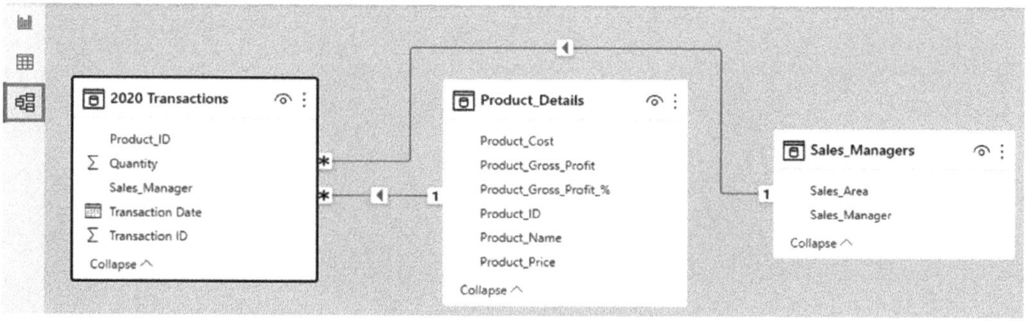

Figure 5.50 – Model view to view and edit the relationships

When we do this, we see the relationships that Power BI has automatically created. If we click on the relationship lines, as shown in *Figure 5.51*, we can see that **Product_ID** under **2020 Transactions** is connected to **Product_ID** under **Product_Details** in a **many-to-one (*:1) relationship**—where * means *many*.

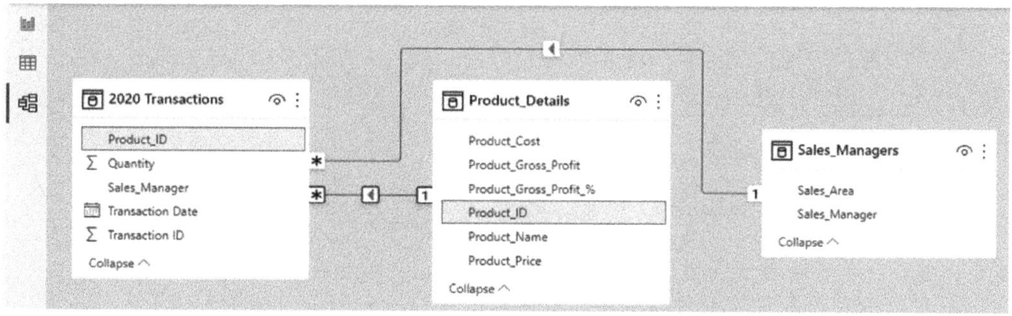

Figure 5.51 – Product_ID relationship for the data

The same goes with **Sales_Manager**: there are multiple transactions identifying the sales transaction to a particular sales manager. **Many-to-one** (*:1) or **one-to-many** (1:*) is the most common cardinality type.

Note

To learn more about different cardinality types in Power BI, check this link out: `https://learn.microsoft.com/en-us/power-bi/transform-model/desktop-relationships-understand#relationship-properties`.

If you want to edit or delete a relationship, such as when a relationship is created incorrectly, simply right-click on the line for **Sales_Manager**, which will show both **Delete** and **Properties**. Let's select **Properties**, as illustrated in *Figure 5.52*:

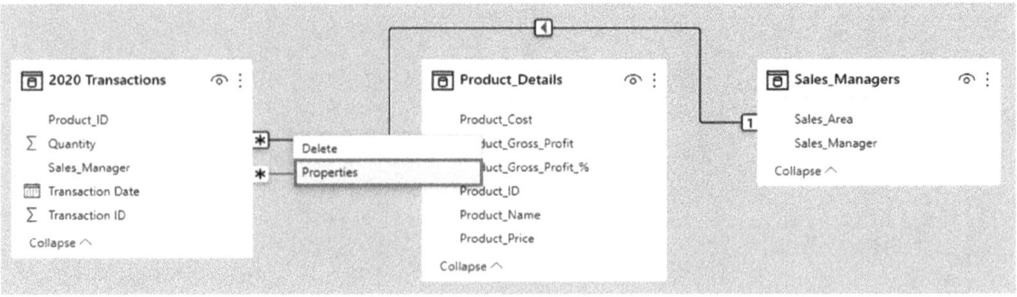

Figure 5.52 – Relationship properties

When you click on the relationship, its properties will appear in the **Properties** pane on the right side of the window. The difference with doing the step in *Figure 5.52* is that it will open the **relationship editor**, which shows a preview of the tables being connected.

A pop-up window will appear showing **Edit relationship**, as in *Figure 5.53*:

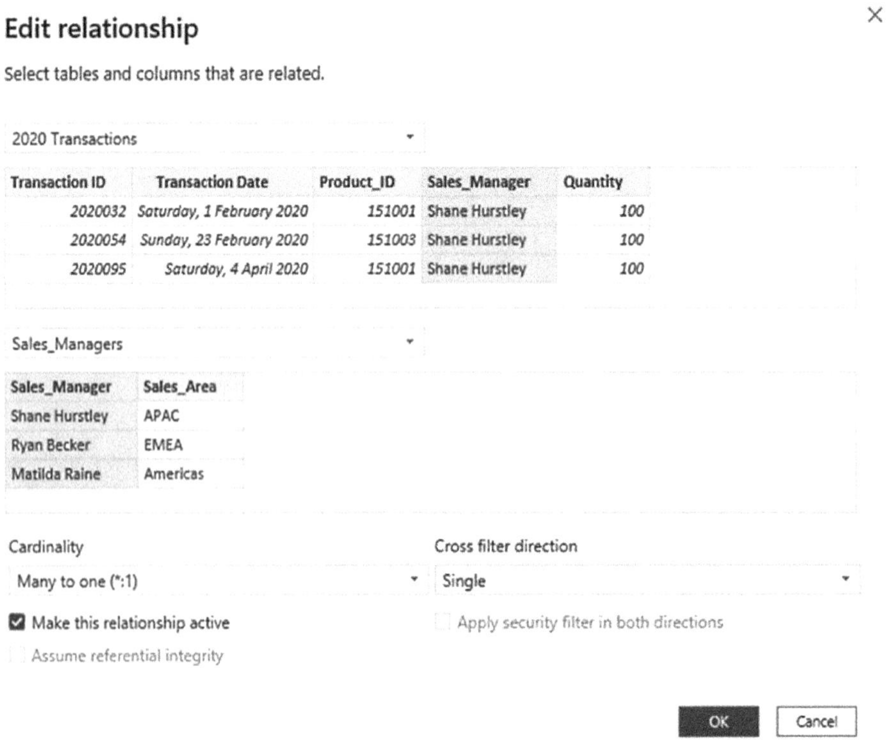

Figure 5.53 – The Edit relationship window

We can see here that the common column between the two tables is the **Sales_Manager** column, and that Power BI has automatically correctly connected these tables using the **many-to-one relationship**. This is the reason why it is important to properly label the column names in the tables and use consistent data types.

> **Note**
>
> If later we would like to visualize or create calculations using the total quantity sold for each of the regions, we can use this link between these tables.

Let's look at the properties for **Product_ID** as well, as shown in *Figure 5.54*, by doing the same steps.

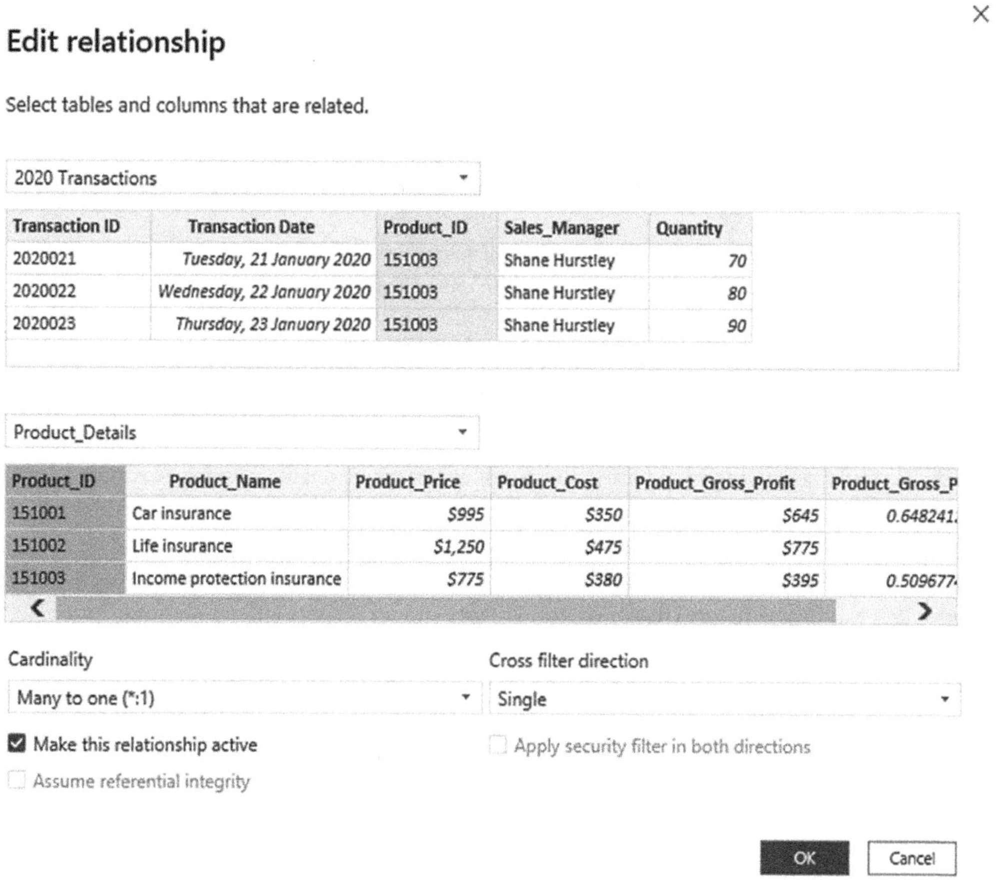

Figure 5.54 – Relationship properties for Product_ID

We can see that the common column between these two tables is **Product_ID**, which is highlighted in gray in both. If later we need to create visualizations or calculations to get the total revenue, total cost, gross profit, and gross profit percentage, we can use this connection between the tables.

> **Important note**
>
> Setting up the relationships properly in the data model serves as a foundation to improve data integrity. We will be able to generate reliable and in-depth analyses and calculations because the relationships in the tables are well defined. As we will cover in the *Managing orphaned records* section in the next chapter, we can perform consistent data retrieval operations such as joins because of this.

Up to this point, you have gained an appreciation of the different important features of Power BI that enhance the quality of your data. In the next section of this chapter, we will dive deeper into another common data quality management feature available in BI tools, which is data validation. This time, we will use Tableau, so close the Power BI file for now; we will continue to work on it in the next chapter.

Dealing with large financial datasets using data validation

When dealing with large financial datasets, the tendency is to allow a certain percentage of incorrectness or inaccuracy due to the effort needed to clean the data. However, outliers in the data will affect analysis and report generation, especially if these outliers and errors aren't cleaned due to time-saving methods in the overall process. That said, guidelines should be created on what the thresholds are in advance for each column and set of records. These guidelines then need to be converted into automated processes available in the BI tool.

An example would be a guideline where column values cannot be negative, cannot exceed a certain threshold, or should be a particular set of values. This guideline would then be converted into a rule that can then be used to automatically detect data issues. Once the incorrect records have been tagged accordingly, these records can be analyzed and corrected manually. In some cases, this is doable. However, for relatively large datasets, it might be more practical to be able to identify the affected records automatically.

One way to do this is through validating data using **data roles** in Tableau Prep. These serve as a tool for data cleansing and ETL processes to prepare the data for subsequent analysis. As we will see in this section, data roles enable data validation for **email addresses**, **URLs**, and **geographic fields**, and at the same time, allow us to create a **reference list** to help validate the data and enable us to quickly identify the outliers and errors.

To follow along with this example, download the `NSW_Post_Code.xlsx` and `Sales_Transactions.xlsx` files from the GitHub repository mentioned earlier. We will be using the list of suburbs in **New South Wales** (**NSW**) from `NSW_Post_Code.xlsx` as the reference to validate the suburbs in the `Sales_Transactions.xlsx` file.

Open Tableau Prep and connect to the `NSW_Post_Code.xlsx` data source. This will add the file under **Connections** and add the sheet as the first step in the workflow. After that, click on the + sign beside the sheet and select **Clean Step**, as shown in *Figure 5.55*:

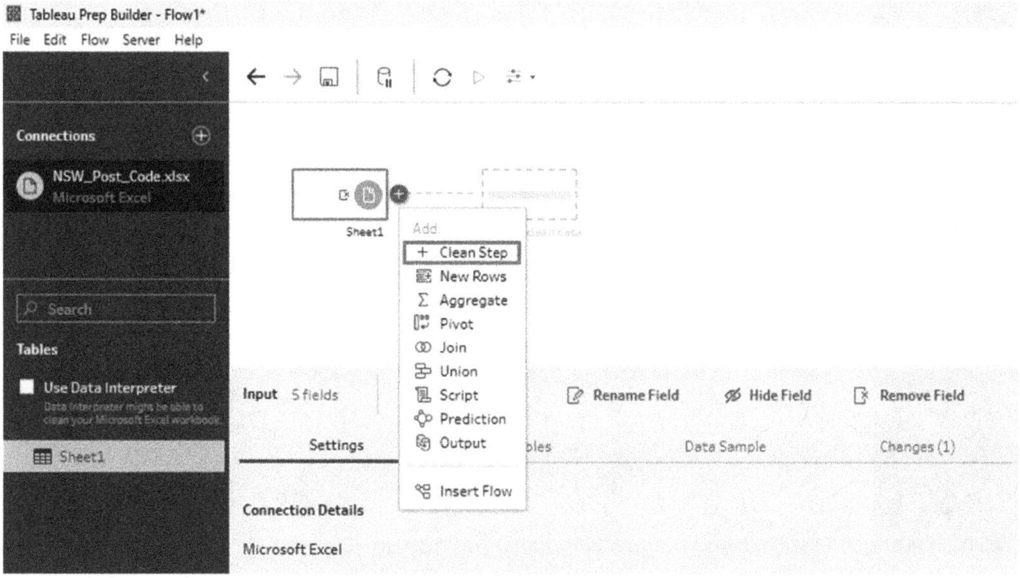

Figure 5.55 – Add clean step

By adding this step, you will be able to perform data cleansing operations such as filtering, renaming, grouping, or removing fields. Since the file we are loading will serve as a reference list, in the profile pane, data grid, or list view, click on the **...**, or ellipsis, beside **Suburb**. Then select **Publish as Data Role...**, as illustrated in *Figure 5.56*:

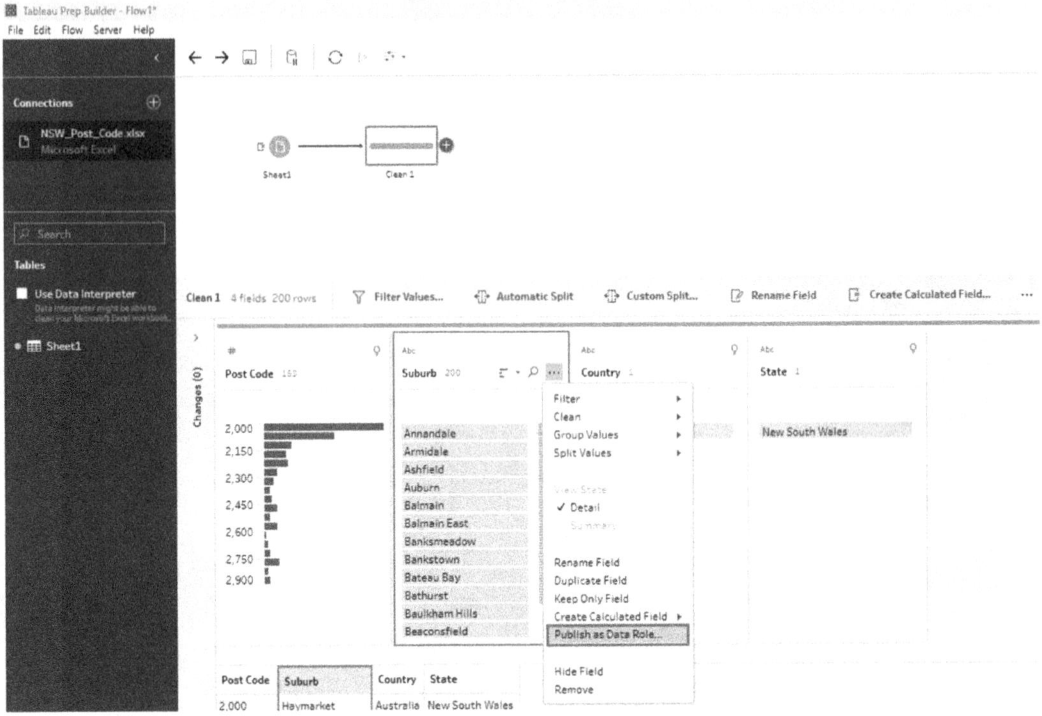

Figure 5.56 – Publish as Data Role…

Once this list is published as a data role, it will become the guide against which Tableau Prep will match the data with during validation.

To do this step, you need to be connected to Tableau Cloud. Click on **Run Flow**, as seen in *Figure 5.57*:

Figure 5.57 – Publish output as a data role

Once this is complete, a pop-up message saying **Finished Running Flow** will appear.

Check the Tableau Cloud website to confirm that the role has indeed been created, as shown in *Figure 5.58*:

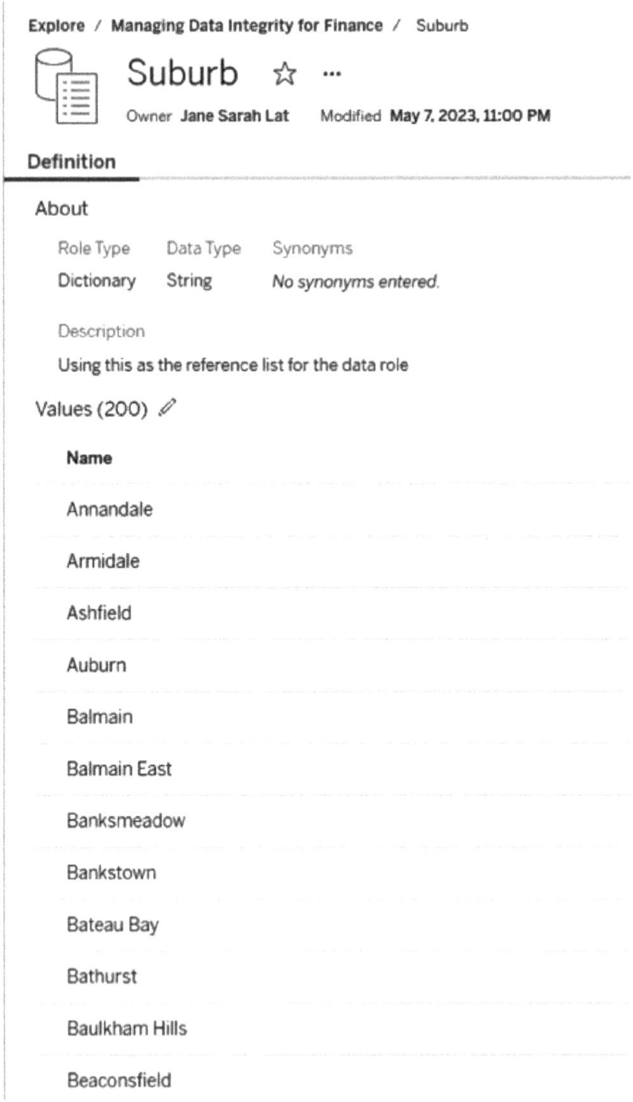
Explore / Managing Data Integrity for Finance / Suburb
Suburb
Owner Jane Sarah Lat
Modified May 7, 2023, 11:00 PM
Definition
About
Role Type
Dictionary
Data Type
String
Synonyms
No synonyms entered.
Description
Using this as the reference list for the data role
Values (200)
Name
Annandale
Armidale
Ashfield
Auburn
Balmain
Balmain East
Banksmeadow
Bankstown
Bateau Bay
Bathurst
Baulkham Hills
Beaconsfield

Figure 5.58 – Published data role in Tableau Cloud

At this point, you might be thinking, *"Why do we need to publish the list as a data role? Is this really necessary?"* Tableau Prep already has the **Data Role** functionality built in, which we will cover in the next steps. What we did was create a *custom list* against which to validate the data not available in the default settings.

Once we have confirmed that this has been published, go back to Tableau Prep and load the `Sales_Transactions.xlsx` file. The next steps will go through validating the suburbs in this file from the reference list we have created.

Loading the `Sales_Transactions.xlsx` file will add a sheet icon to the workflow. Next, click on the + sign beside it and select **Clean step**. In the *profile pane, data grid*, or *list view*, click on the **Abc** string icon beside **Suburb**, choose **Custom** under **Data Role**, and then select **Suburb**, as seen in *Figure 5.59*:

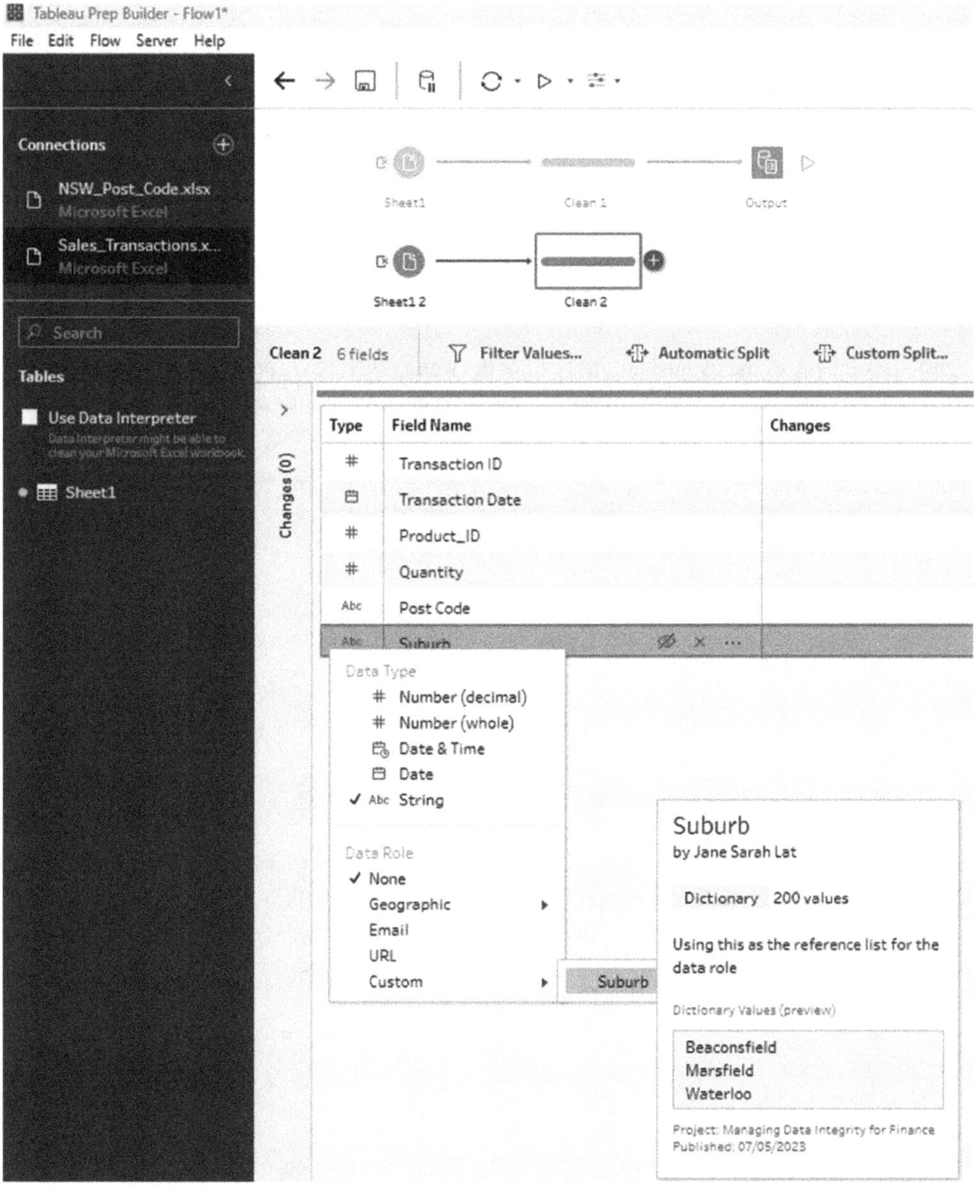

Figure 5.59 – Selecting the Suburb data role that has been created

As we mentioned earlier, there are data roles built into Tableau Prep to evaluate the data values with established patterns such as **Geographic**, **Email**, or **URL**. Since we published the **Suburb** list earlier, we can validate the values against our custom list.

The **Suburb** column will be validated against the reference list and will be highlighted by a red exclamation mark, as seen in *Figure 5.60*:

Figure 5.60 – Suburbs not found in the reference list are highlighted

If we right-click on any of the flagged items, we have the **Keep Only**, **Exclude**, **Edit Value**, and **Replace with Null** options, and under **Recommendations**, we have the options to update them as well, as shown in *Figure 5.61*:

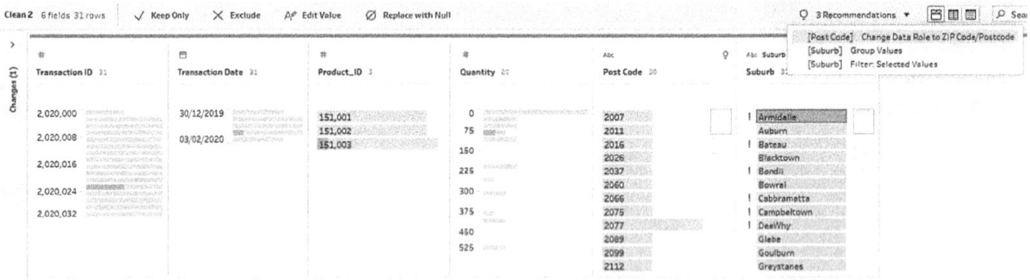

Figure 5.61 – Options to update the flagged items

If we select **[Suburb] Group Values**, a pop-up pane appears showing a preview for **Group Values** that will replace invalid values with matching values from the data role, or **Filter: Selected Values**, which will exclude rows with invalid values for the data role, as seen in *Figure 5.62*:

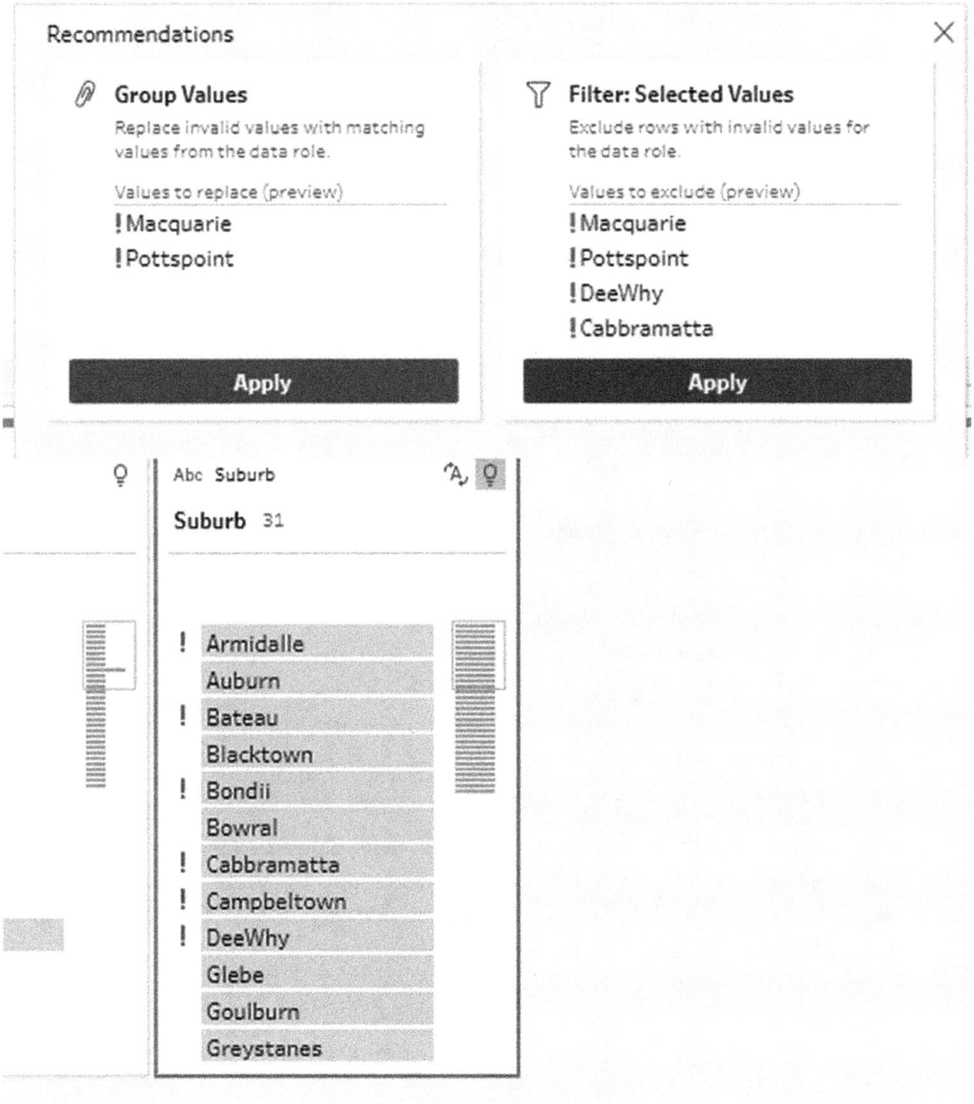

Figure 5.62 – Selecting Suburb group values

Let's select **Group Values** and click on **Apply**. This will run the workflow and update the values by **Pronunciation + Spelling**, which is the default, as seen in *Figure 5.63*:

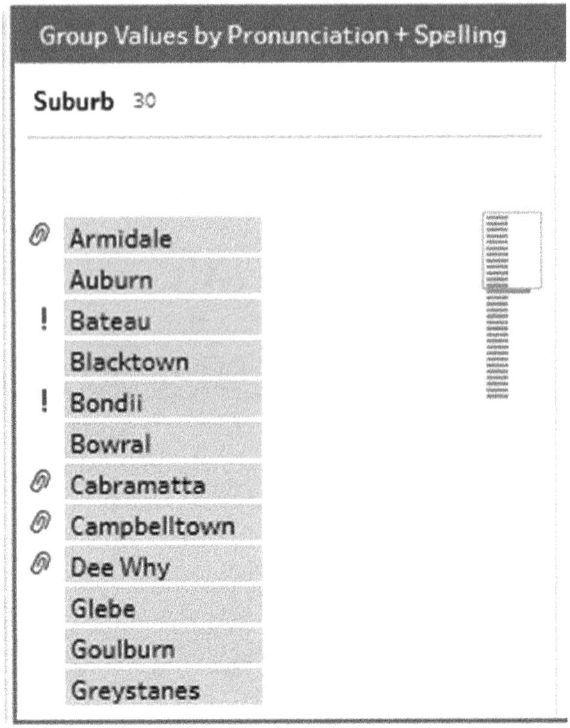

Figure 5.63 – Group values by Pronunciation + Spelling

We can see from the screenshot that suburbs, such as **Armidale**, **Cabramatta**, **Campbelltown**, and **Dee Why**, that have been updated have a paperclip beside them, while those that haven't, such as **Bateau** and **Bondii**, have a red exclamation point. The next few steps will cover filtering them and choosing between the **Edit** and **Replace with Null** options.

To do this, select the **...**, or ellipsis, icon beside **Suburb**. Under **Show Values**, select **Not valid**, as seen in *Figure 5.64*:

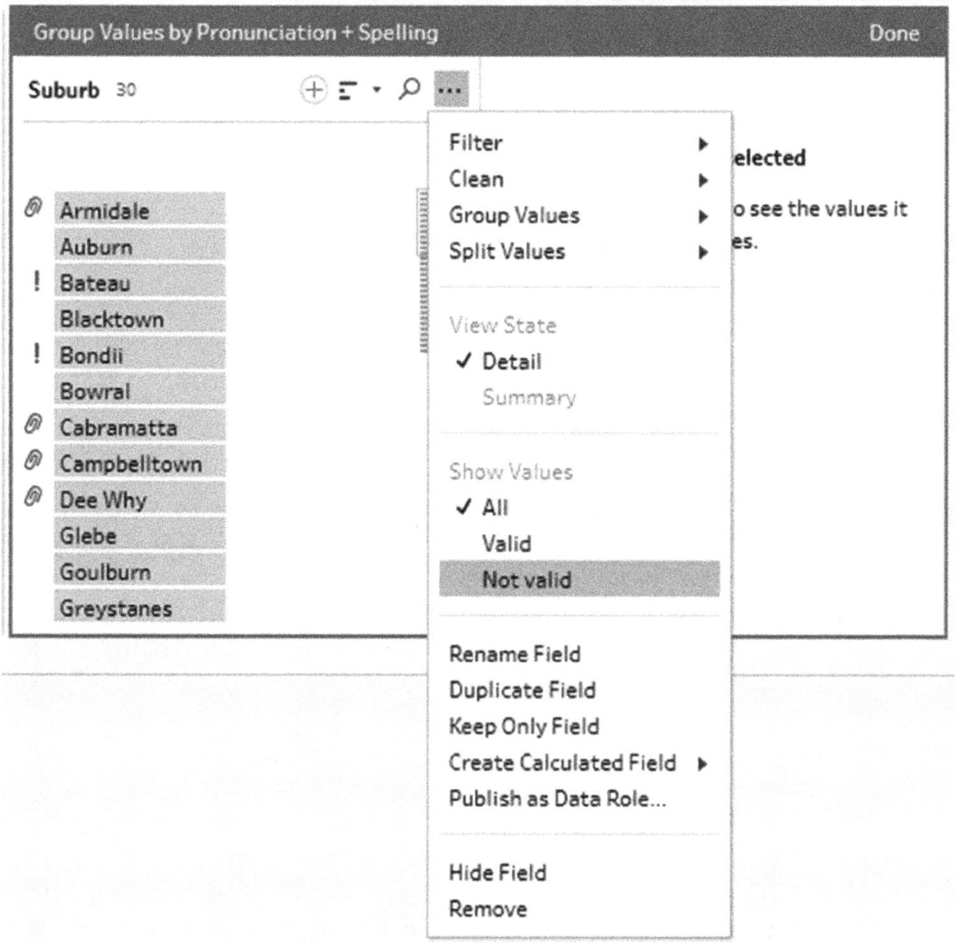

Figure 5.64 – Filtering the invalid items

This will filter the invalid items, as shown in *Figure 5.65*:

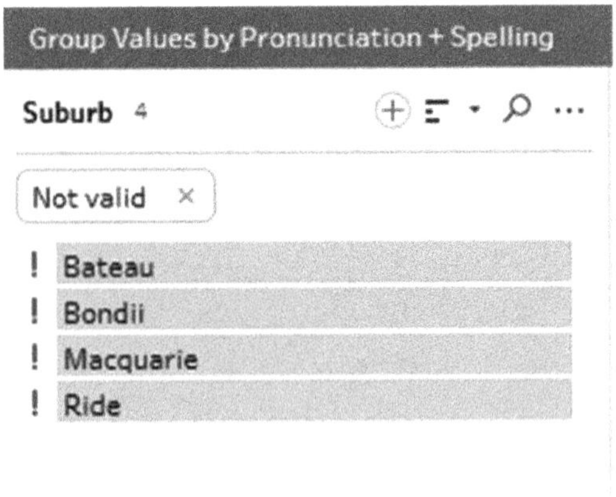

Figure 5.65 – Invalid data values are filtered

When we click on **Bateau**, the **Edit Value** and **Replace with Null** options appear, as shown in *Figure 5.66*:

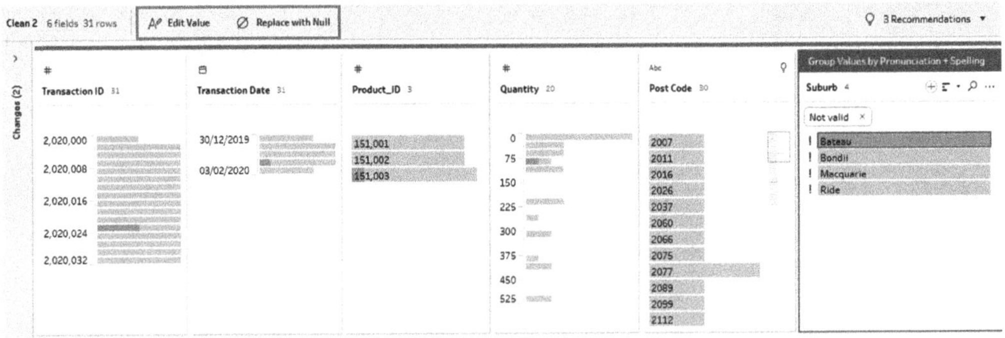

Figure 5.66 – Options to edit value or replace with null appear

Let's click on **Edit Value** and update **Bateau** to **Bateau Bay**, **Bondii** to **Bondi**, **Macquarie** to **Macquarie Park**, and **Ride** to **Ryde**. Once the edits are made, the items will disappear from the **Not valid** list. Let's remove this filter and select **All**, as seen in *Figure 5.67*:

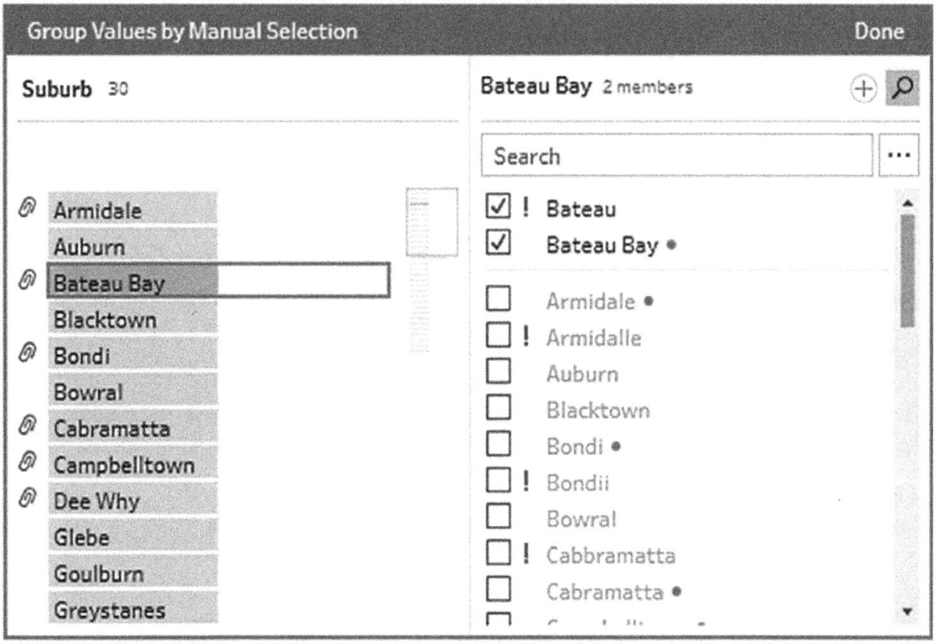

Figure 5.67 – Updated values of the suburbs after changes are made

We can see that the changes that we've made have been reflected and that all the suburbs in the list are valid! Having data roles to improve the consistency and validity of the data greatly enhances its quality and integrity. This feature has tons of applications, which can come in handy especially when working with large datasets.

Well done on completing the last topic for this chapter! We have covered different features available in Microsoft Power BI, Tableau Desktop, Tableau Prep, and Tableau Cloud, which facilitates data cleansing and preparation. If you are new to these tools, take the time to review what we covered, experiment, and learn more by checking out the resources listed in the *Further reading* section.

Summary

In this chapter, we discussed how to manage data integrity issues with BI tools. At the beginning, we learned how to ensure we have consistent data type formats in our working files. Then, we covered data profiling features such as column quality, column distribution, and column profiling. After that, we worked out how to cleanse the data. In addition to this, we learned how to identify data outliers as well as how to manage relationships in data models. Lastly, we went through how to deal with large financial datasets using data validation. We have explored really powerful techniques and concepts in this chapter. You should be feeling confident about what you have learned, knowing that you can use these techniques whenever you need to clean the data prior to analysis.

The topics in the next chapter will be pretty exciting! We will continue our journey with these BI tools and cover how to implement best practices!

Further reading

For additional information on the topics covered in this chapter, you may find the following resources helpful:

- *10 Best Practices for Successful Data Quality*: `https://www.talend.com/resources/data-quality-best-practices/`
- *Clean, transform, and load data in Power BI*: `https://learn.microsoft.com/en-us/training/modules/clean-data-power-bi/`
- *What is Power Query?*: `https://learn.microsoft.com/en-us/power-query/power-query-what-is-power-query`
- *Using the data profiling tools*: `https://learn.microsoft.com/en-us/power-query/data-profiling-tools`
- *Best practices when working with Power Query*: `https://learn.microsoft.com/en-us/power-query/best-practices`
- Tableau Prep—*Use Data Roles to Validate your Data*: `https://help.tableau.com/current/prep/en-us/prep_validate_data.htm`

6

Implementing Best Practices When Using Business Intelligence Tools

In the previous chapter, we learned how to use **business intelligence** (**BI**) tools to fix data integrity issues. We also covered the various data profiling features available and how to remove empty cells, remove duplicates, manage relationships in data models, identify data outliers, and deal with large financial datasets using data validation.

In this chapter, we will discuss the best practices when using **Power BI Desktop**, **Tableau**, and **Alteryx Designer** for data quality and integrity. By the end of this chapter, you will have a better understanding of how to leverage best practices when using these **BI** tools to ensure data integrity in finance.

We'll cover the following in this chapter:

- Handling confusing date convention formats
- Using data visualization to identify data outliers
- Managing orphaned records

By the end of this chapter, you will have a deeper understanding of what these BI tools can do. *Exciting!*

Technical requirements

This chapter is a continuation of our discussion from *Chapter 4, Understanding the Data Integrity Management Capabilities of Business Intelligence Tools*, and *Chapter 5, Using Business Intelligence Tools to Fix Data Integrity Issues*. Thus, we will be using the same tools and datasets that we used previously:

- **Power BI Desktop**: April 2023 or later (no licenses required)
- **Tableau Desktop**: 2023.1 or later (free trial version)
- **Tableau Prep Builder**: 2023.1.0 or later (free trial version)
- **Tableau Cloud**: (free trial version)
- **Alteryx Designer**: 2022.3 version or later (free trial version)

Our sample datasets are saved in the Packt **GitHub** repo: `https://github.com/PacktPublishing/Managing-Data-Integrity-for-Finance/tree/main/ch05`. *Chapters 5* and *6* both use the same datasets for the hands-on exercises.

> **Note**
> It is recommended that you read both of the previous chapters mentioned for better appreciation and understanding of this chapter. You may proceed once these have been read.

Handling confusing date convention formats

One of the most common data integrity issues encountered when dealing with date time values involves the inconsistent positioning of the month and date values in data entries and transactions. In some countries, `mm/dd/yyyy` is used for the date format. In other countries, `dd/mm/yyyy` is used. Of course, the number of days (that is, 01 to 31) exceeds the number of months (that is, 01 to 12). However, what if the record stored in the sheet or database is `03/06/1990`? If the assumed format is `mm/dd/yyyy`, then `03/06/1990` will be interpreted as `March 6, 1990`. On the other hand, if the assumed format is `dd/mm/yyyy`, then the same date will be interpreted as `June 3, 1990` instead.

Now, we have a data integrity issue when a single column involves *both* formats. There are a variety of reasons this could happen and one of the possible causes is if records from multiple data sources were merged into a single sheet or table without taking into account the assumed format of the **Date** data type. Once the data needs to be processed, if the date values are incorrectly interpreted (due to the confusion and inconsistency in the date format), the financial totals/aggregates would be affected since some formulas and reports are based on monthly totals.

> **Note**
>
> The solution for this would be to verify the format of the records based on the source. In addition to this, columns involving multiple formats require an additional layer of data integrity corrections so that only a single format is used in each column.

To ensure that the correct format is being used, checks need to be done when preparing the data prior to analysis. Let's go back to the example we loaded in *Chapter 5, Using Business Intelligence Tools to Fix Data Integrity Issues*, using the `Review Formatting.xlsx` file in **Tableau Desktop**.

Notice that the date format is all in numbers and assumptions can be made in terms of what they mean, as seen in *Figure 6.1*:

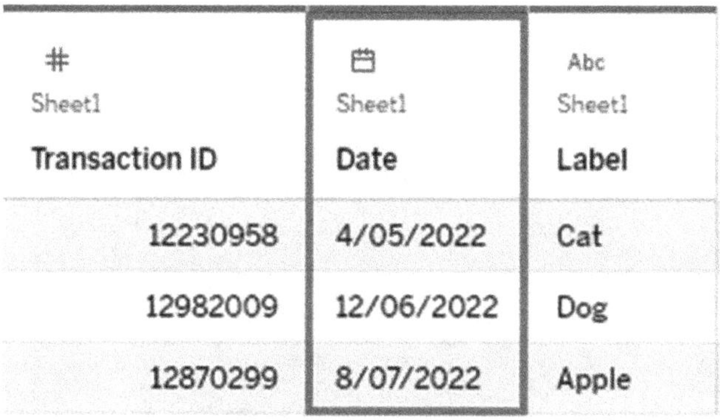
#
Sheet1
Transaction ID
Sheet1
Date
Abc
Sheet1
Label
12230958
4/05/2022
Cat
12982009
12/06/2022
Dog
12870299
8/07/2022
Apple

Figure 6.1 – Date format in numbers

Using and selecting a consistent format for the dates will assist in preventing confusion and mistakes. We can do this by going to the **Data** pane on the **Sheet1** page, clicking on the **Date** dropdown, selecting **Default Properties**, and choosing **Date Format...** as illustrated in *Figure 6.2*:

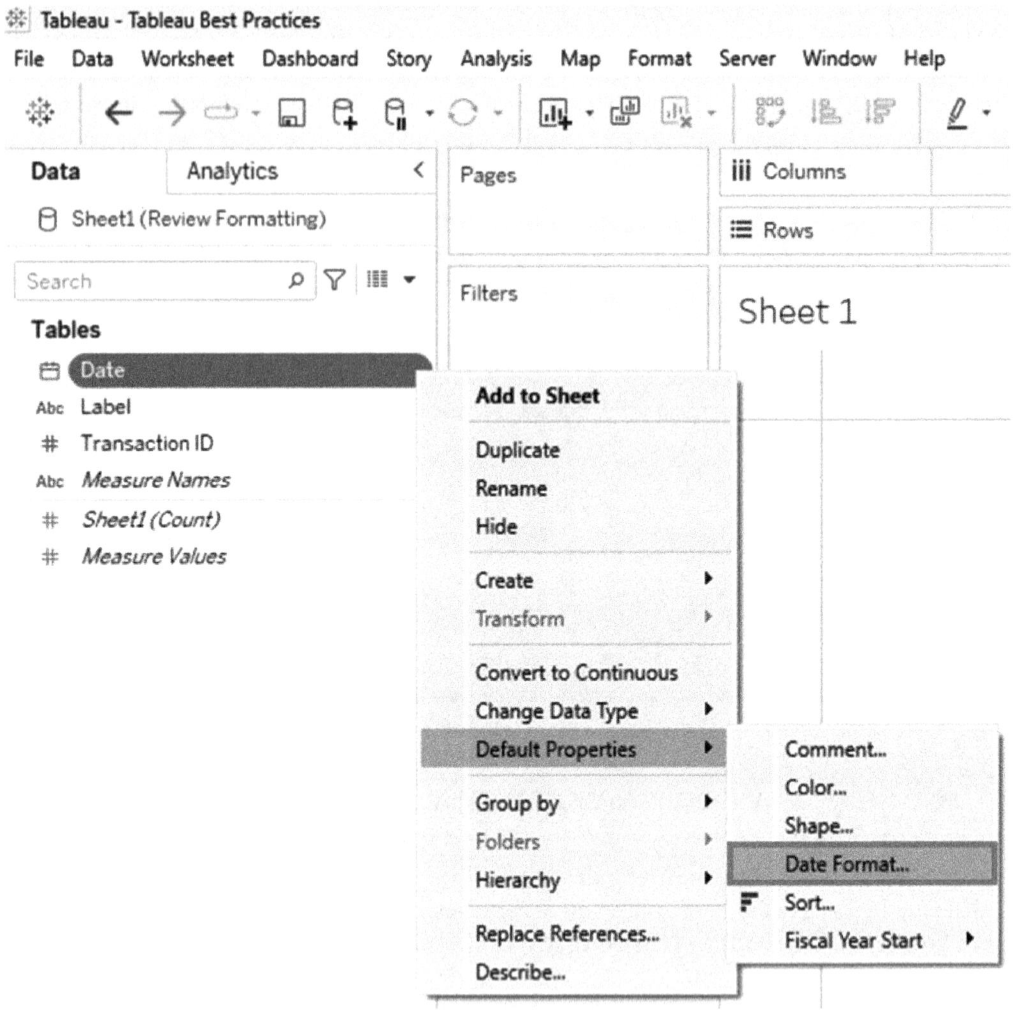

Figure 6.2 – Selecting the Date Format option

A pop-up window will appear to set the default date format. To avoid confusion and cater to international users, spelling it out, clearly showing the month name, as indicated in *Figure 6.3*, will address this risk.

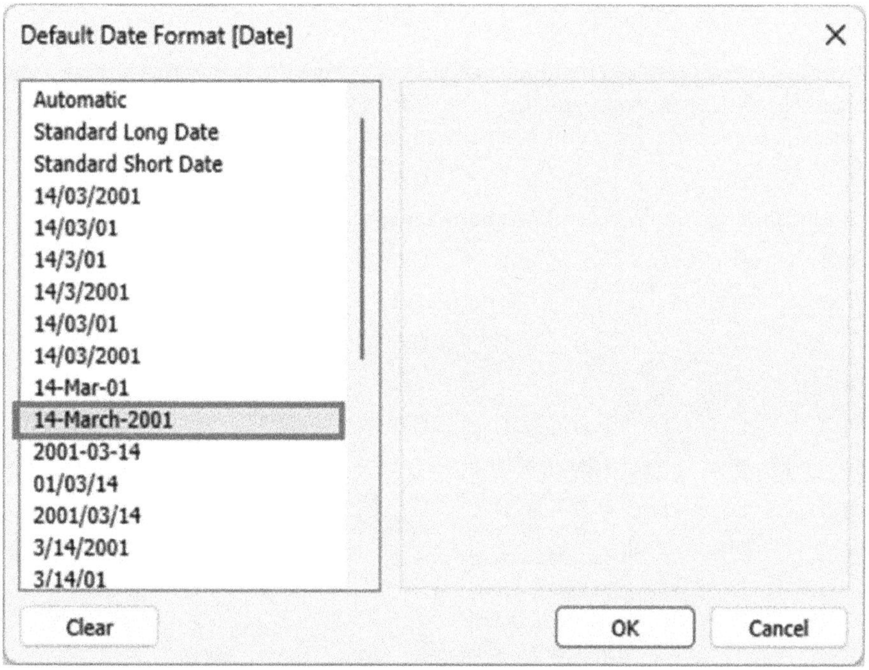

Figure 6.3 – Selecting the date format to avoid confusion

If you would like to choose another default format, feel free to do so as long as it is applied consistently and taken note of to avoid confusion.

When we go to the **Data Source** tab, we can see that the formatting we did has taken effect, as shown in *Figure 6.4*:

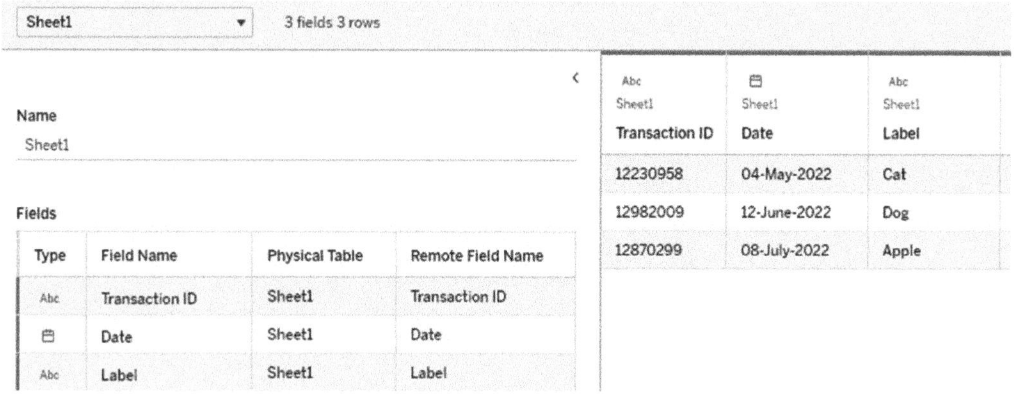

Figure 6.4 – The updated date format

This makes it easier to understand the dates, *don't you think so?*

Note

The date format being used is determined by the *locale* where the user is based. As we saw in the previous chapter, for Australia and the United Kingdom, the format being used is `dd/mm/yyyy` while for the United States and other countries, it is `mm/dd/yyyy`.

To update the settings, go to **File**, select **Workbook Locale**, and choose **More**.

Figure 6.5 – Setting the workbook locale for Tableau

A pop-up window will appear where the locale can be selected, as seen in *Figure 6.5*. Verifying the locale you are working in will avoid confusion as to the date format being used.

> **Important note**
> Ensuring that we are using the correct data convention when we are working on data is important. Otherwise, this could lead to erroneous analysis or distorted information affecting data integrity when we combine datasets from sources that come from different geographic regions.

Now that we have covered data type conventions, let's explore how we can use another key feature of business intelligence tools to improve the quality of our data.

Using data visualization to identify data outliers

Visualizations enable business professionals and companies to make sense of the numbers and deliver insights. They also make it easier to spot data outliers, as we will see in this section. Identifying outliers is important since they can significantly affect how you interpret the data and what actions you take. We can ask, *Is this data point correct?*, *Is there insight from this?*, or *Could this be a potentially fraudulent transaction?* In this section, we will visualize data outliers using Microsoft Power BI and Tableau through a **scatter chart** and a **histogram**.

Continuing our example from *Chapter 5, Using Business Intelligence Tools to Fix Data Integrity Issues*, about column distribution, let's further analyze the dataset for `2020_Transactions.xlsx` and review the sales quantity.

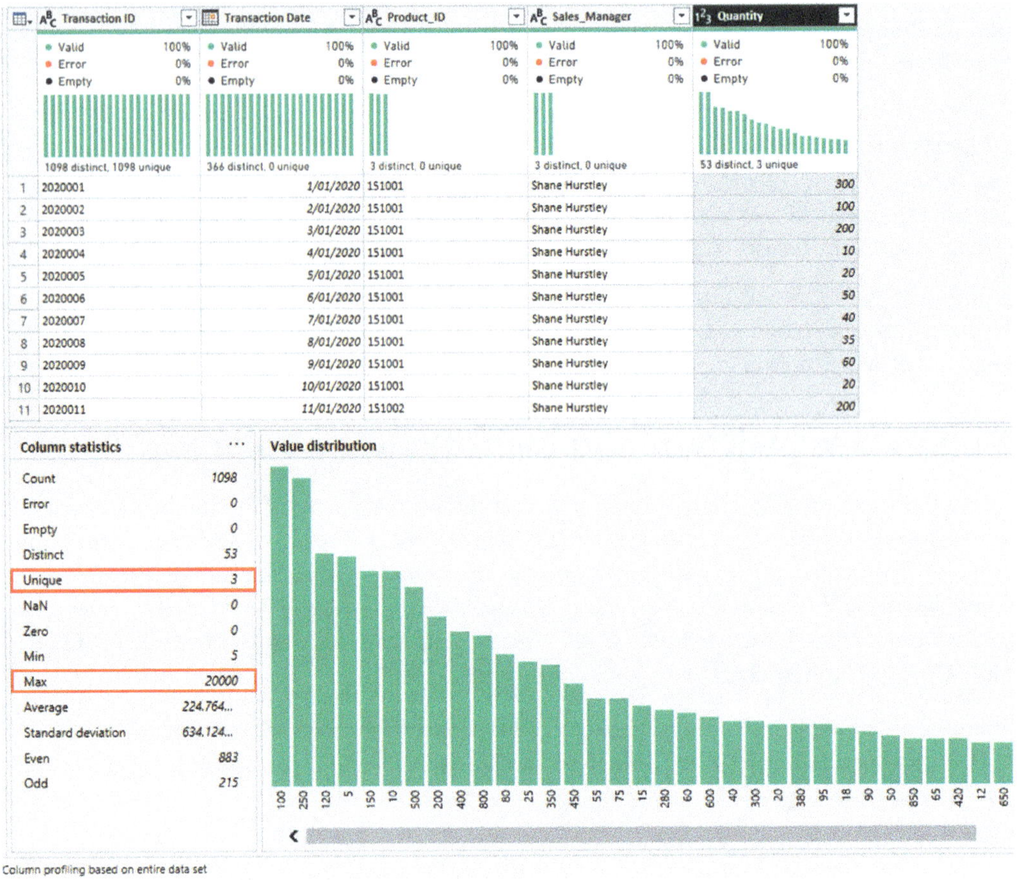

Figure 6.6 – Information about the column statistics and value distribution of the column

When we select the **Quantity** column, the **Column statistics** and **Value distribution** fields will appear, as seen in *Figure 6.6*.

> **Note**
>
> Ensure that the column profiling is based on the *entire* dataset so that it captures everything.

If we look at the bottom-left side for **Column statistics**, we can see, under the **Quantity** column, that we have three **Unique** values and that the **Max** quantity is 20,000.

As we mentioned at the beginning of this section, we will use data visualizations to help us identify the outliers. Click on **Close & Apply**, which will load the data in the model and lead you to the report canvas. We will create a visualization next.

Visualizing using a scatter chart

The Power BI visualizations are found under the **Visualizations** pane on the right side of the desktop app. Under **Build visual**, different types of charts and graphs can be created to make the data more easily understandable and presentable.

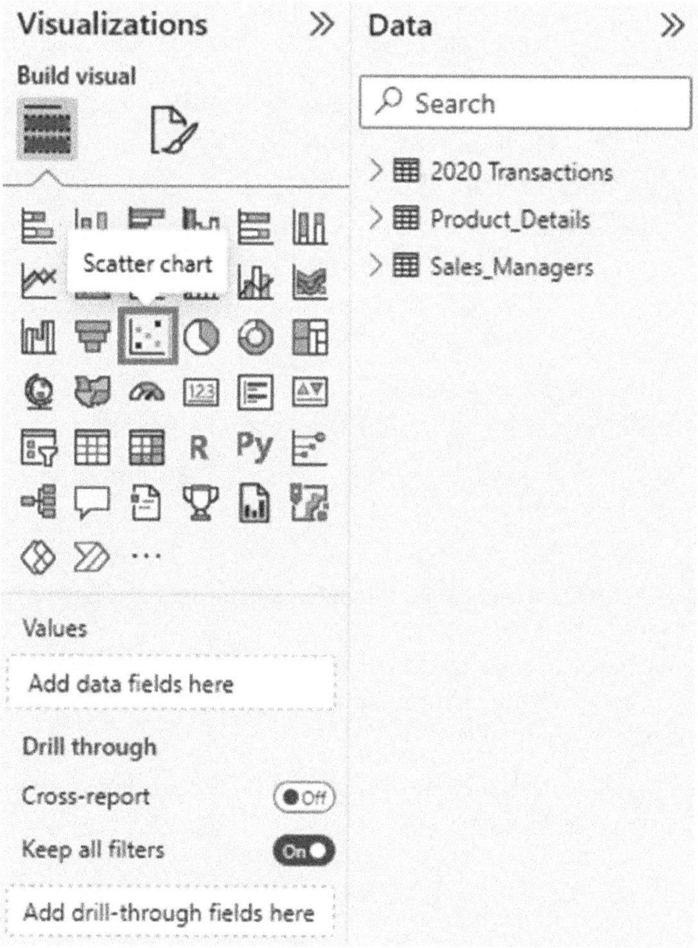

Figure 6.7 – Scatter chart in the Visualizations pane

First, let's visualize the data using the **scatter chart**, as highlighted in *Figure 6.7*.

> **Note**
>
> **Scatter plots/charts** allow us to visualize data and quickly see data points that do not fit the rest of the data.

When you click on the **Scatter chart** icon, it will create a blank template on the report canvas, as shown in *Figure 6.8*:

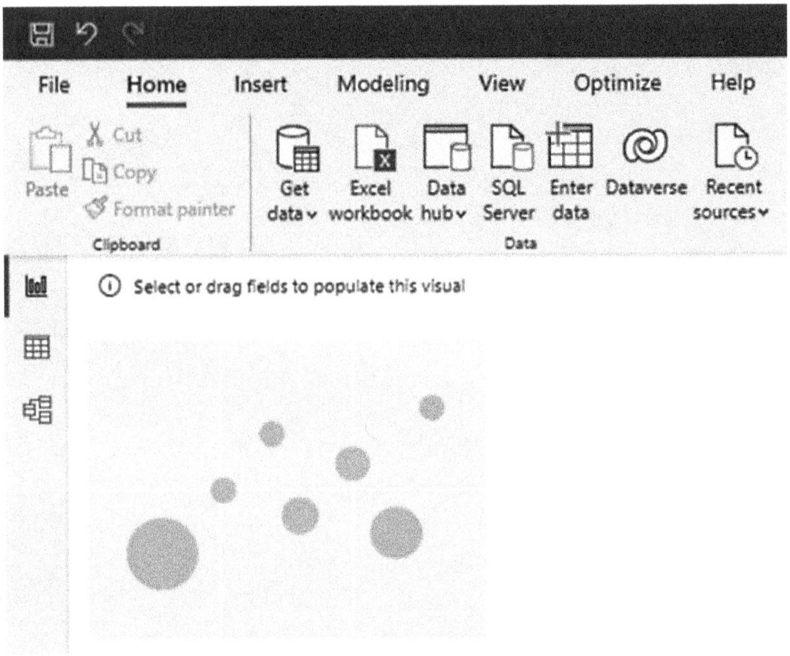

Figure 6.8 – Blank template for the scatter chart on the report canvas

We will next configure the values in the scatter chart to help us see how the *quantity* sold varies on a *monthly* basis. Being able to analyze a metric or **key performance indicator** (**KPI**) over a period of time helps in identifying potential outliers.

To do this, let's select **Month** in the **Data** pane and drag it under **X Axis**, then choose **Σ Quantity** and drag it under **Y Axis**, as seen in *Figure 6.9*:

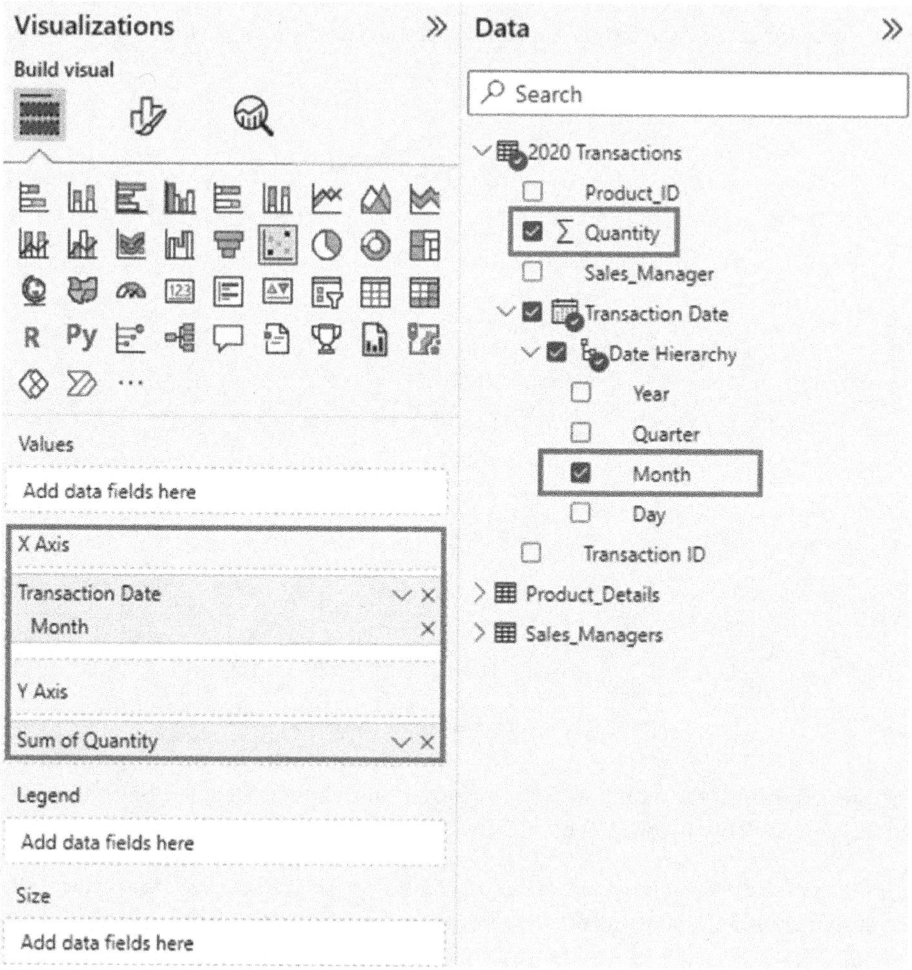

Figure 6.9 – Configuring the scatter chart

When Power BI Desktop identified **Transaction Date** correctly as dates, it created the **date hierarchies**, which enabled us to select **Month** for our analysis.

> **Note**
> To learn more about how to set up and use date tables in Power BI Desktop, check out `https://learn.microsoft.com/en-us/power-bi/transform-model/desktop-date-tables`.

Once we have dragged the fields to the correct axis, our scatter chart will reflect the sum of the quantity per month, as illustrated in *Figure 6.10*:

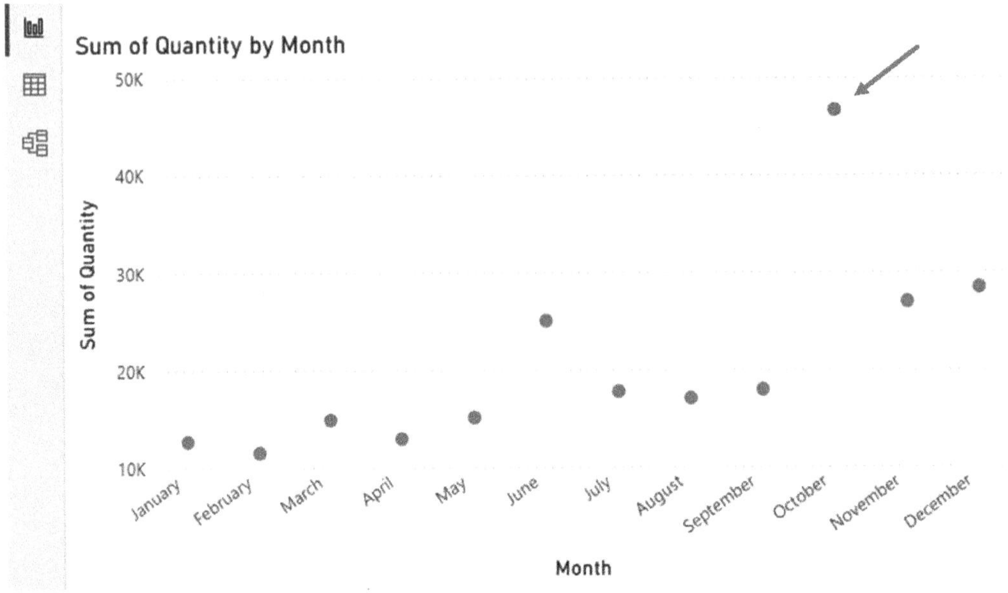

Figure 6.10 – Sum of quantity by month

From here, we can see that the month with the highest quantity sold is October. Given that we have identified this as an outlier, we can start asking the following questions:

- *Is this outlier due to potential errors in our data?* For this, we need to check the invoice billed to the customer or the supporting documentation to substantiate this information.
- *How does this compare with last year?* We can check whether this is because of seasonality in the products, which is causing the sales to fluctuate.
- *Was there a change in the demand for our products that caused the increase in a particular month compared with other months?* If so, this can be an opportunity to sell more of this product due to increased demand.

If we get confirmation that this data was input in error, and should be 200 instead, we need to go back to **Transform data** under the **Home** tab, as shown in *Figure 6.11* where we can edit the dataset. The next steps will cover how we can update and correct this.

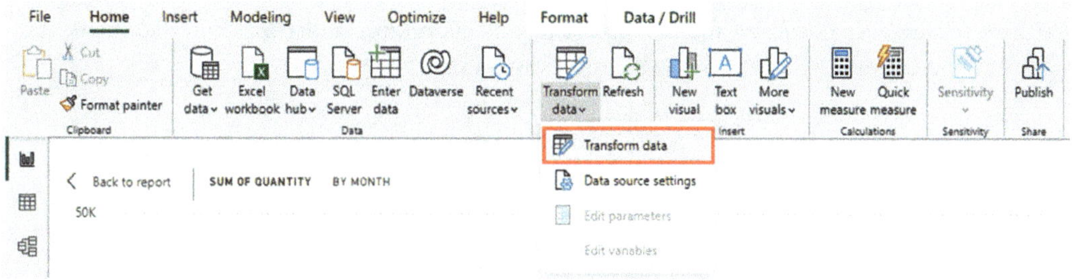

Figure 6.11 – Transform data under the Home tab

Once the 2020 transactions dataset has loaded, right-click on the **Quantity** column and choose **Replace Values...**, as seen in *Figure 6.12*.

> **Note**
>
> Choosing **Replace Values...** updates the data in Power BI but not in the source itself (such as in an SQL or Excel workbook). There are cases when the correct values need to be updated from the source so that the values are permanently fixed.

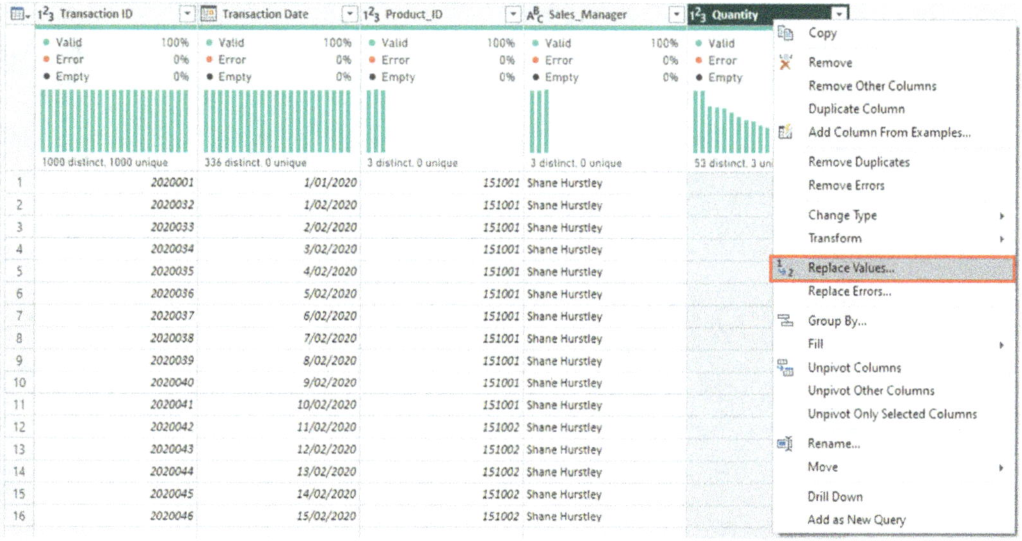

Figure 6.12 – Replace Values... in the Quantity column

A pop-up window will appear. Under **Value to Find**, let's put `20000`, which is the number we will replace, and under **Replace With**, let's put `200`, which is the correct quantity. Click on **OK**.

Now the value has been corrected and the **Max** value under **Column statistics** is now **850**, as seen in *Figure 6.13*, instead of 20,000, which was the previous amount.

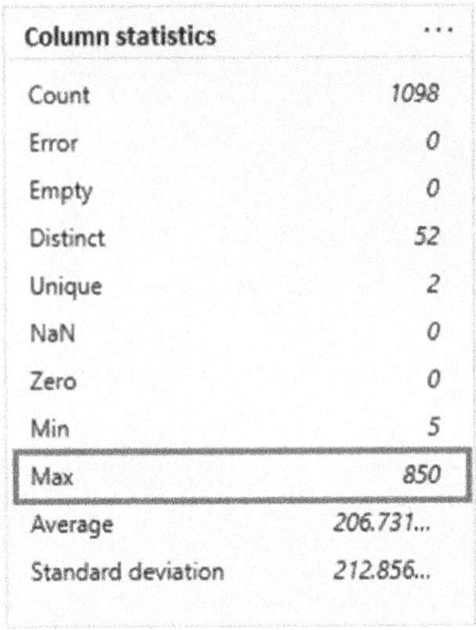
Column statistics
...
Count
1098
Error
0
Empty
0
Distinct
52
Unique
2
NaN
0
Zero
0
Min
5
Max
850
Average
206.731...
Standard deviation
212.856...

Figure 6.13 – Updated Column statistics showing Max value of 850

We can also try searching for 20,000 by clicking on the drop-down arrow beside **Quantity**. Since we have already replaced it, it will no longer appear in the search.

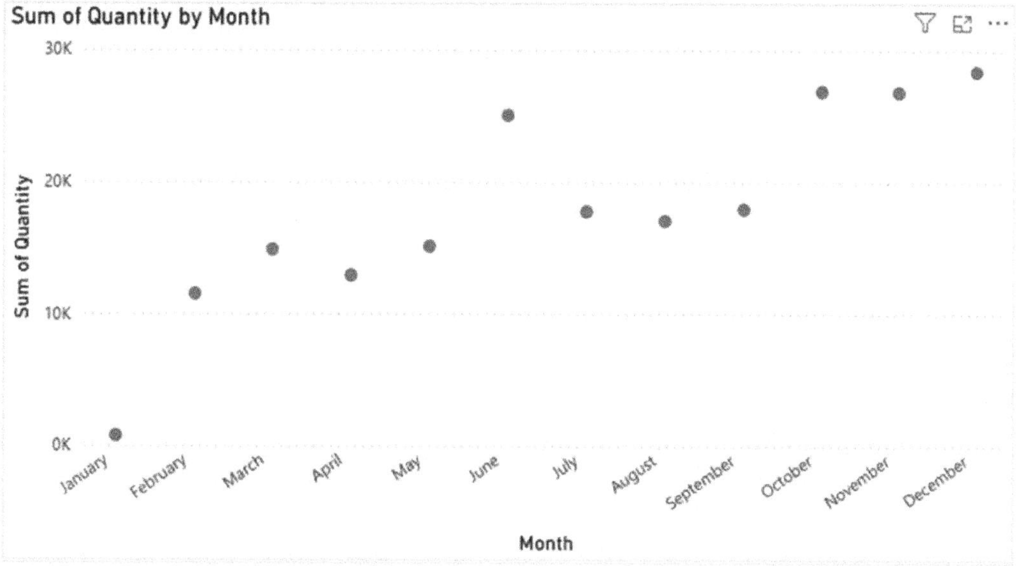

Figure 6.14 – Updated scatter chart after editing the data outlier

Click on **Close & Apply** to go back to the **Report View**. This will apply the changes to the scatter chart, as shown in *Figure 6.14*.

> **Note**
>
> To learn more about creating visuals to identify outliers in Power BI, check this link out: `https://learn.microsoft.com/en-us/training/modules/perform-analytics-power-bi/3-visuals`.

As we have learned from this section, visualizing data makes it easier to analyze the data and detect outliers. A scatter plot/chart is one of the visualizations we can use to do this. Another is by using a histogram, which we will discuss in the next section.

Visualizing using a histogram

In this section, we will visualize the same data using a **histogram** in Tableau Desktop. Histograms are used to display the frequency of data and group it into ranges or bins. It is also a great way to detect outliers, similar to a scatter chart.

Go back to the `2020_Transactions.xslx` file we loaded into Tableau Desktop in *Chapter 5, Using Business Intelligence Tools to Fix Data Integrity Issues*. We will be using this information for our histogram. Our discussion will be divided into three parts: *(1) creating the histogram in Tableau, (2) cleaning the data in Tableau Prep*, and *(3) updating the histogram*. Because we have already ensured that the data types are consistent in the previous chapter, we can jump right into the first part!

Creating the histogram

Our first step is to create the histogram to see whether there are any data points that are outside the normal range. In the bottom-left part of the screen, beside **Data Source**, click on **Sheet 1**.

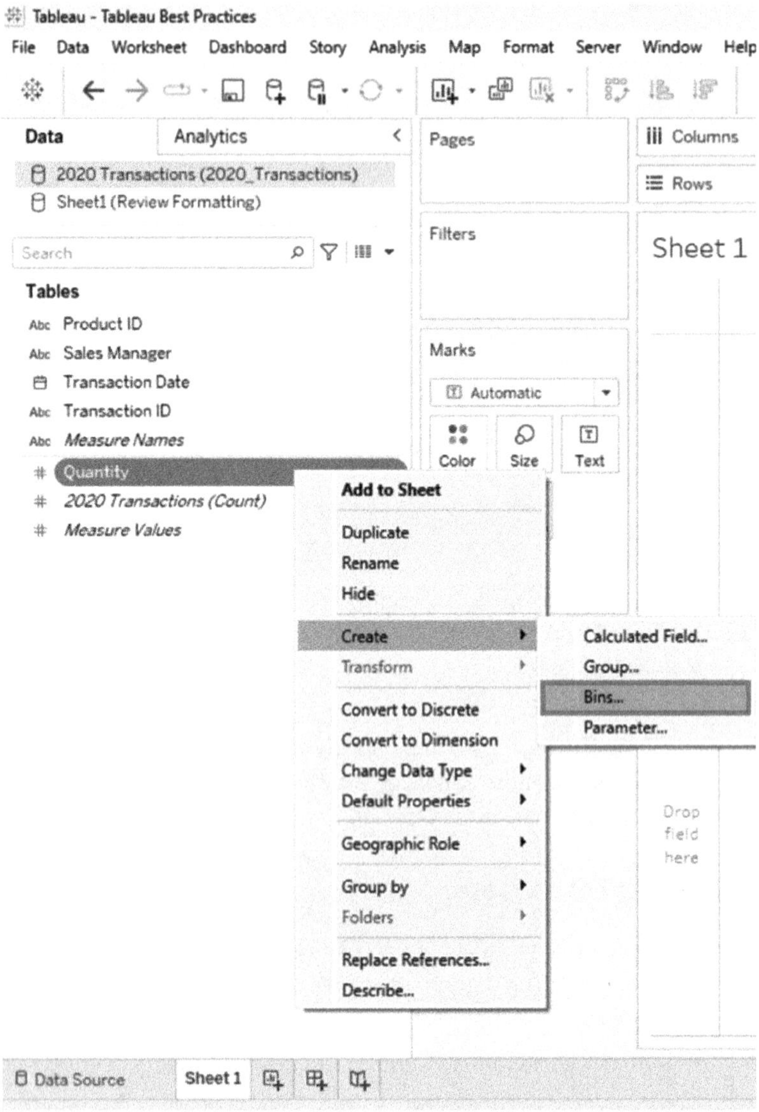

Figure 6.15 – Selecting Bins... under Quantity

Under **Measure Names**, click on the dropdown beside **Quantity**, select **Create**, and choose **Bins...**, as highlighted in *Figure 6.15*.

> **Note**
>
> Looking at the figure, you might be wondering why **Quantity** is colored *green* and the fields above are colored *blue*. This is because Tableau displays data based on whether the field is **discrete** (shown in *blue*) or **continuous** (depicted in *green*). If a measure or dimension is **discrete**, the values are limited or finite. In most cases, they will be used as headers, whereas if it is **continuous**, they are perceived as being infinite and are used to add axes to the visual.

Once this is done, a pop-up window will appear, as seen in *Figure 6.16*, showing a suggested bin size and the range of values in this measure:

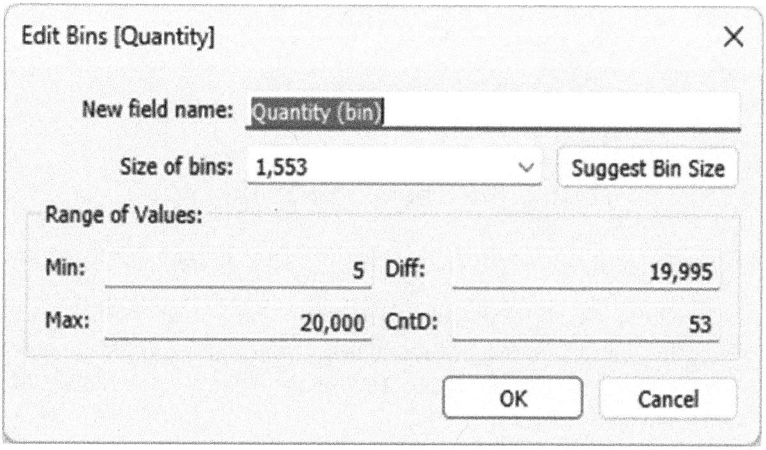

Figure 6.16 – Configuring the bins for the histogram

We can use the suggested bin size of 1,553 and click on **OK**. A new dimension will appear called **Quantity (bin)**, as shown in *Figure 6.17*:

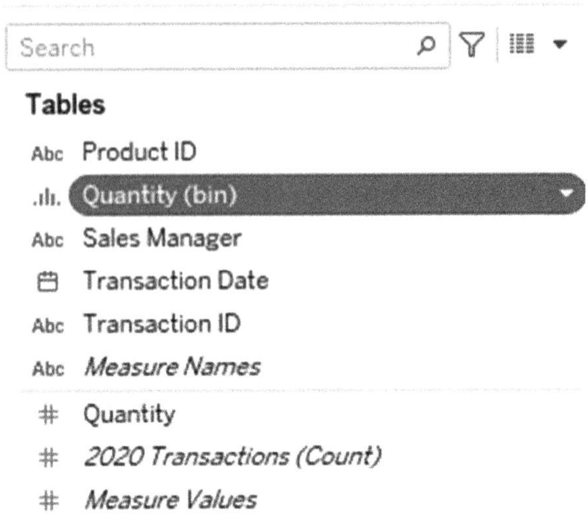

Figure 6.17 – New measure called Quantity (bin)

We will notice that the dimension created is colored blue, which indicates that it is discrete and finite.

We will now drag this to **Columns** and drag **Quantity** to **Rows**. Our histogram will be created with the bins on the *x*-axis and the quantity on the *y*-axis, as illustrated in *Figure 6.18*. Make sure that, for the rows, the measure being used is **Count**. To do this, click on the down arrow beside **SUM(Quantity)**, select **Measure(Sum)**, and choose **Count**.

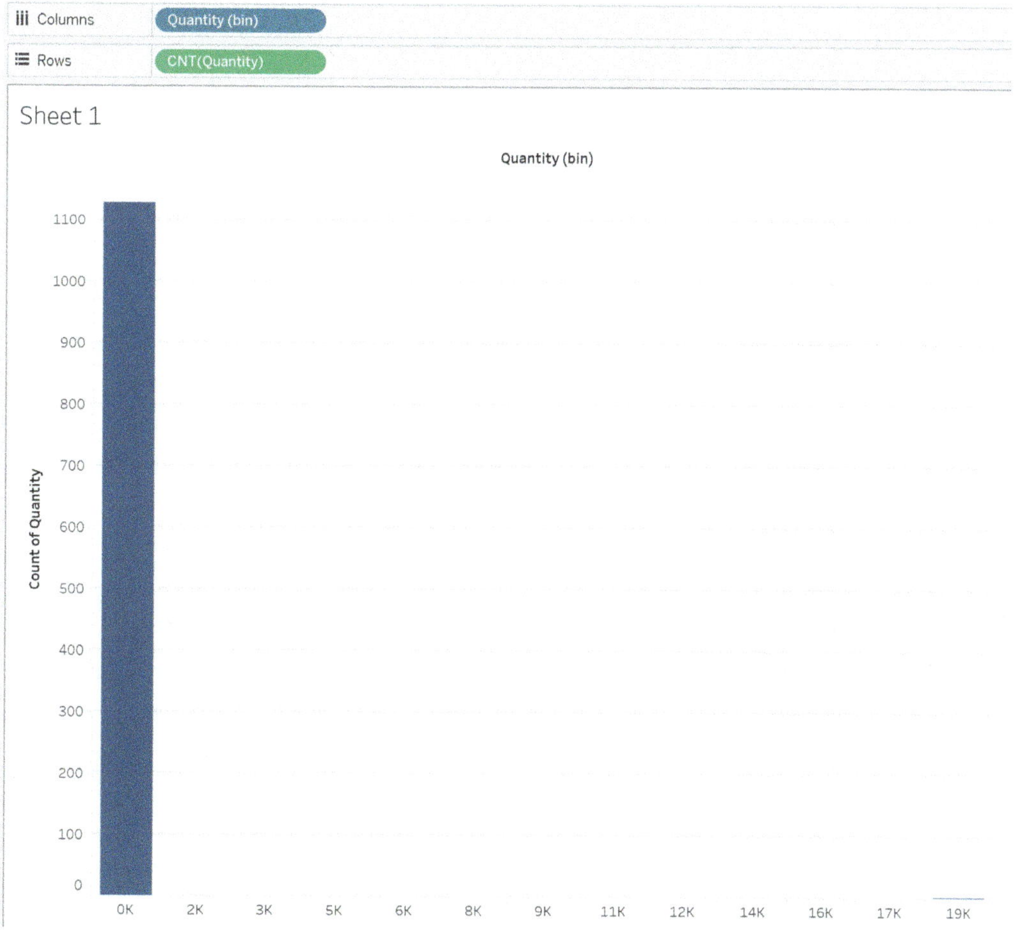

Figure 6.18 – Histogram showing the distribution of the quantity sold

We can gather from this image that the quantity sold per transaction is usually below 1,553, which is why they are under this bin, while there is another item on the right side of the chart. To view more information about the transactions in this bin, click on the bar and choose **View Data...**, as seen in *Figure 6.19*:

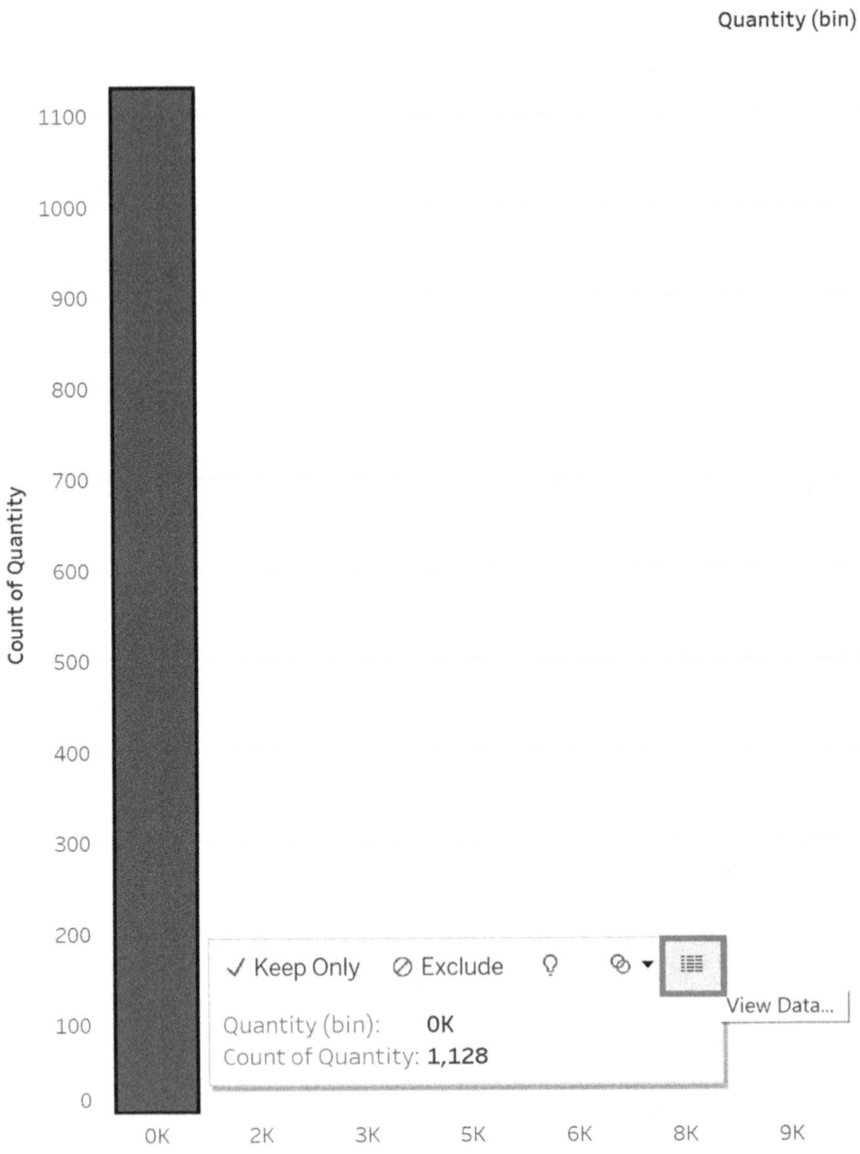

Figure 6.19 – Viewing data in this bin

A pop-up window will appear. Select **Full Data**, as seen in *Figure 6.20*:

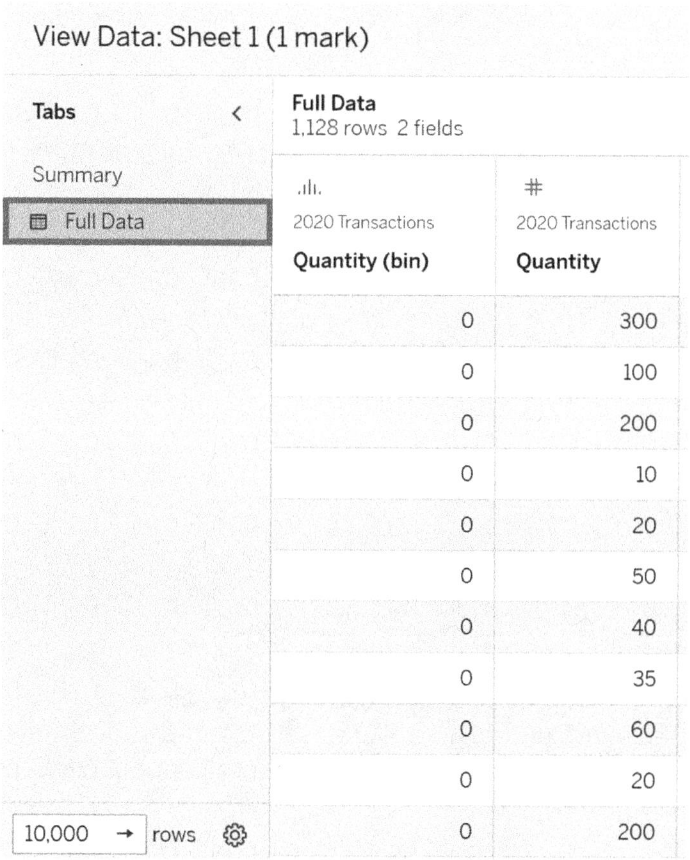
View Data: Sheet 1 (1 mark)
Tabs
Summary
Full Data
Full Data
1,128 rows 2 fields
2020 Transactions
Quantity (bin)
2020 Transactions
Quantity
0 300
0 100
0 200
0 10
0 20
0 50
0 40
0 35
0 60
0 20
0 200
10,000
rows

Figure 6.20 – Transactions under Full Data

This will list the transactions included under this bin. We can confirm from this information that our quantity sold per transaction does not exceed the first bin limit of 1,553.

Let's do the same for the other bin and view the data, as seen in *Figure 6.21*:

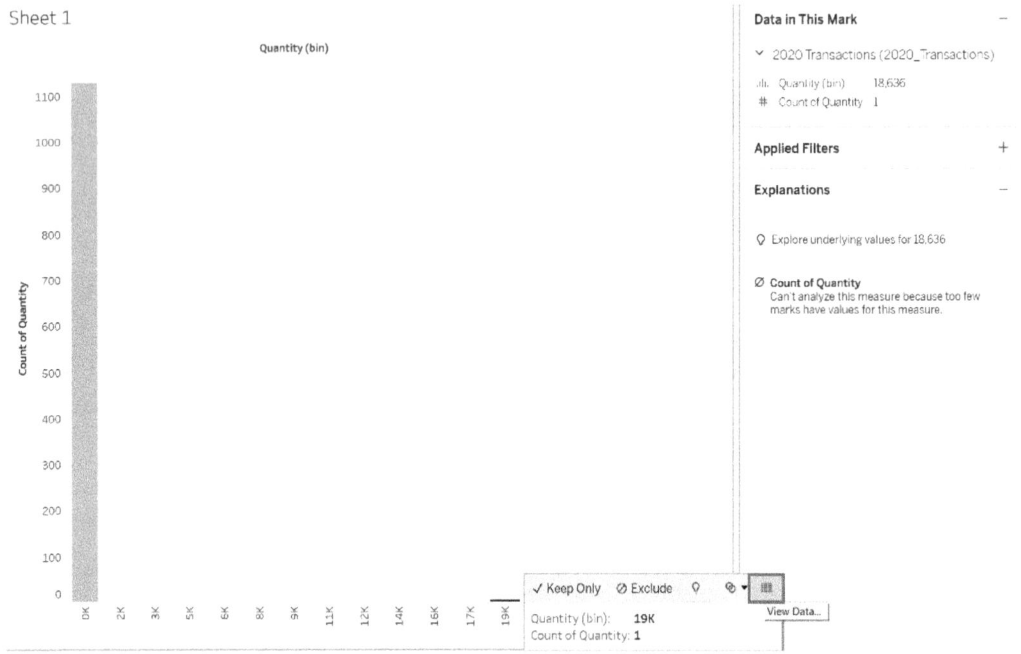

Figure 6.21 – Viewing data for the data outlier

When we select this, a pop-up window will appear, and under **Full Data**, we can see that there is only one transaction, as shown in *Figure 6.22*:

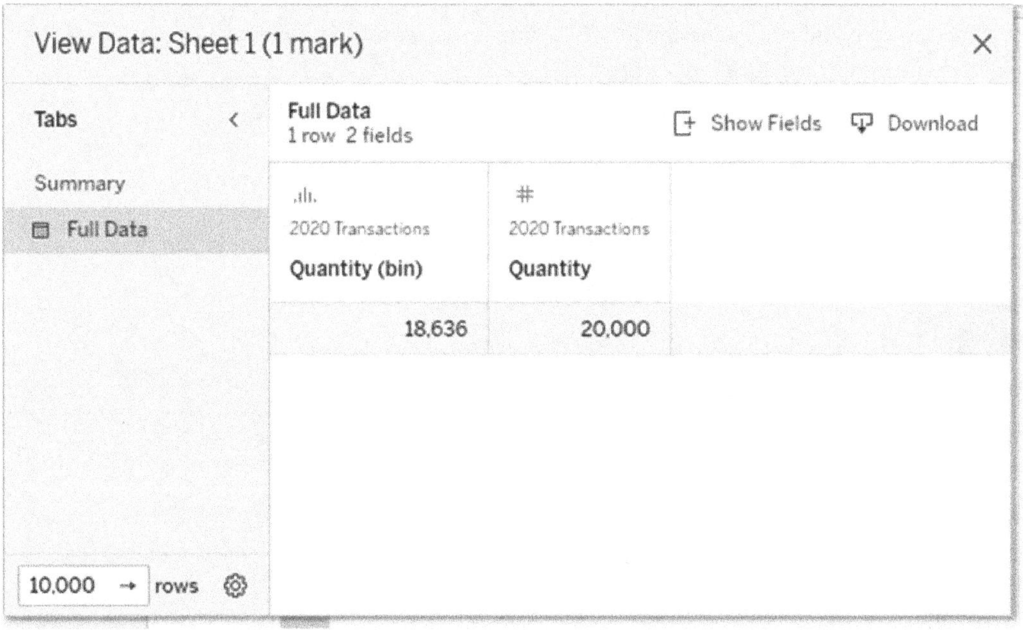

Figure 6.22 – Bin showing one transaction for the outlier

Similar to our questions when we were analyzing the scatter chart earlier, under *Visualizing using a scatter chart*, we can ask the following questions with regard to the outlier:

- *Is this outlier due to a potential error in our data?* For this, we need to check the invoice billed to the customer or the supporting documentation to substantiate this information.
- *How does this compare with last year?* If we have information for the previous years, did we have a similar transaction that reflects consistency year over year?
- *Was there a change in the demand for our products that caused this increase?* If so, this could be an opportunity to sell more of this product due to increased demand.

What if, after asking these questions to the Operations or Sales team, we found out that the transaction with 20,000 was done in error? *How do we delete this?* We will cover this in the next section.

Cleaning the data

In this part, we will be using Tableau Prep to clean our data and remove the outlier we identified in the previous section.

Open Tableau Prep and connect to the `2020_Transactions.xlsx` file. Once the information is loaded, our window will look like *Figure 6.23*:

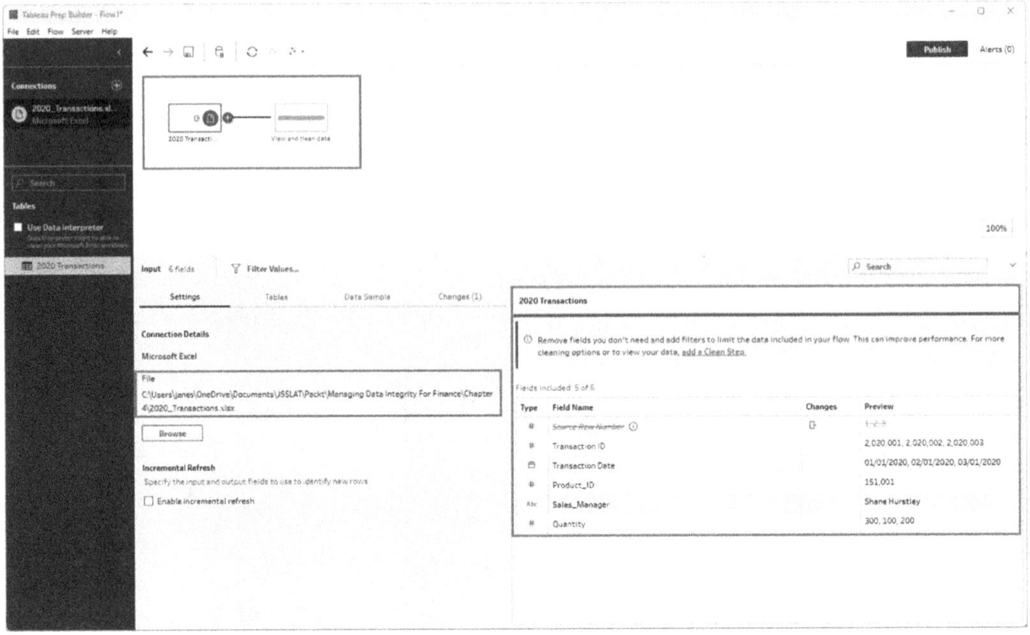

Figure 6.23 – Tableau Prep window after loading the data

A connection will be created where the changes we make will reflect in Tableau but not in the source file.

Next, let's update the type for **Transaction ID** and **Product_ID** from **Number (whole)** to **String**. Click on the # sign to view the options and select **String**. The types for the other fields are correct. Once the changes are made, it will look like *Figure 6.24*:

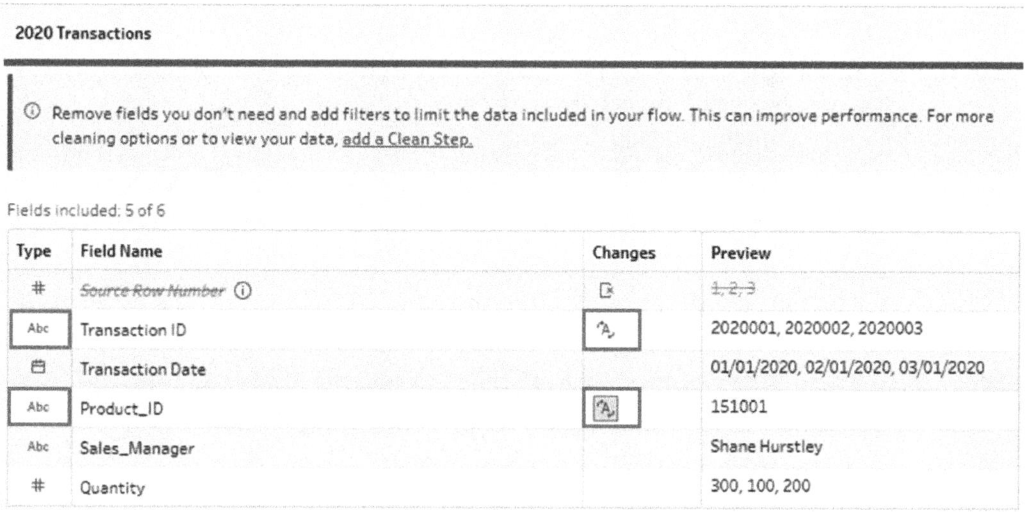

Figure 6.24 – Data type changes reflected for Transaction ID and Product_ID

A **Change Type** icon will appear under **Changes**, indicating that edits were made.

Next, let's click on the + sign beside the **2020 Transactions** icon and select **Clean Step**, as seen in *Figure 6.25*:

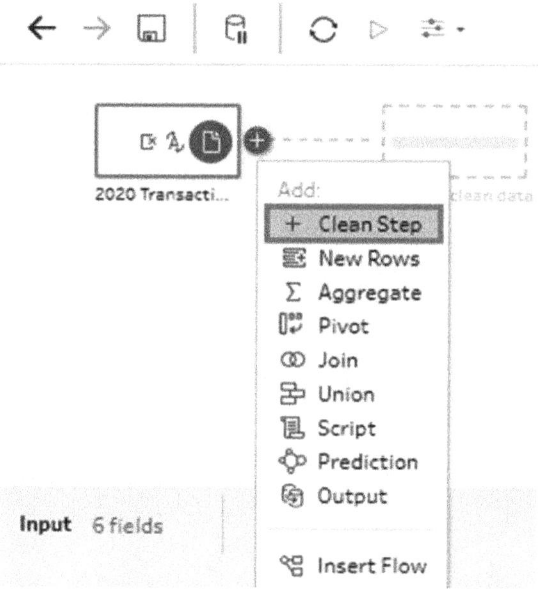

Figure 6.25 – Selecting Clean Step

This will add the **Clean Step** type in the workflow and show the bins. This step is important as it allows us to filter, exclude, and update the data types, and select data roles. We will be cleaning the data in this section so that we can update it for our visualization.

Select the last one with our data outlier. This will filter out the item we identified earlier, as shown in *Figure 6.26*:

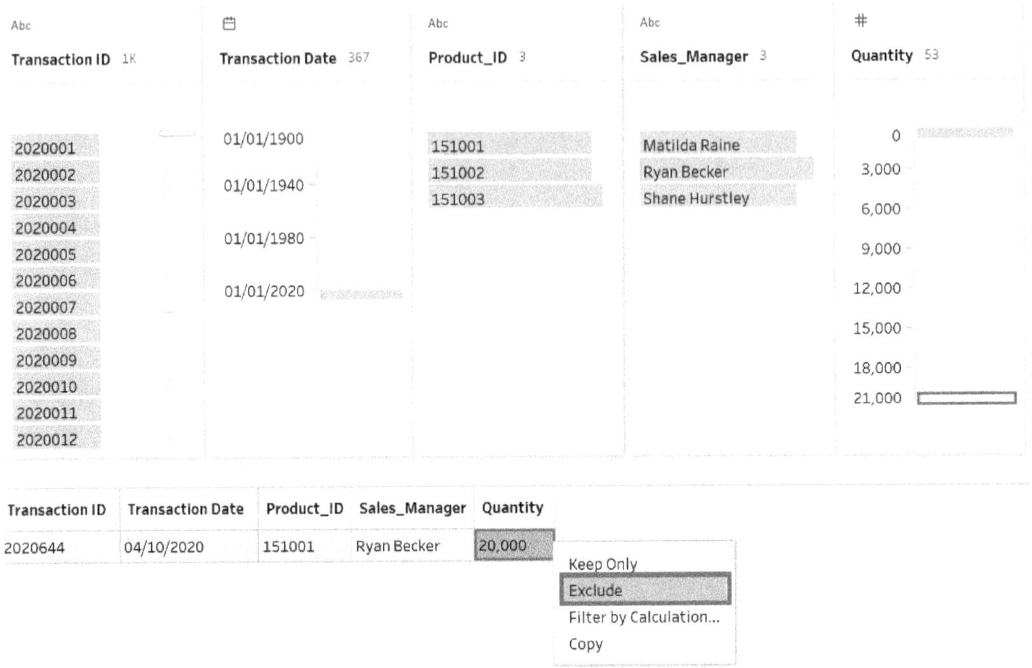

Figure 6.26 – Selecting the last bin and excluding it

Right-click on this item, as shown in the preceding figure, and select **Exclude** to remove the outlier.

If, later, you would like to undo this step, go to the **Changes** pane and click on the **X** mark to delete it, as seen in *Figure 6.27*:

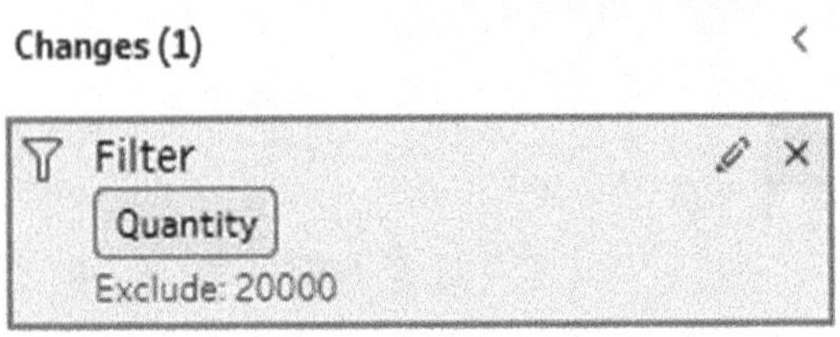

Figure 6.27 – Removing the modification made from the Changes pane

Now that we have cleaned the data, we will export it to Tableau Cloud to make it available to Tableau Desktop. At this point, you might be thinking *It would have been easier if we just deleted the 20,000 from the source data since it will flow to Tableau Desktop directly.* When we used Tableau Prep to make the changes, we created a workflow, which shows the changes that have been made. Directly changing the source file has its risks, and we are managing it through this tool. At the same time, publishing the output as a data source to Tableau Cloud makes the data available for other users who will use this information.

Let's add the step to create the output, as shown in *Figure 6.28*:

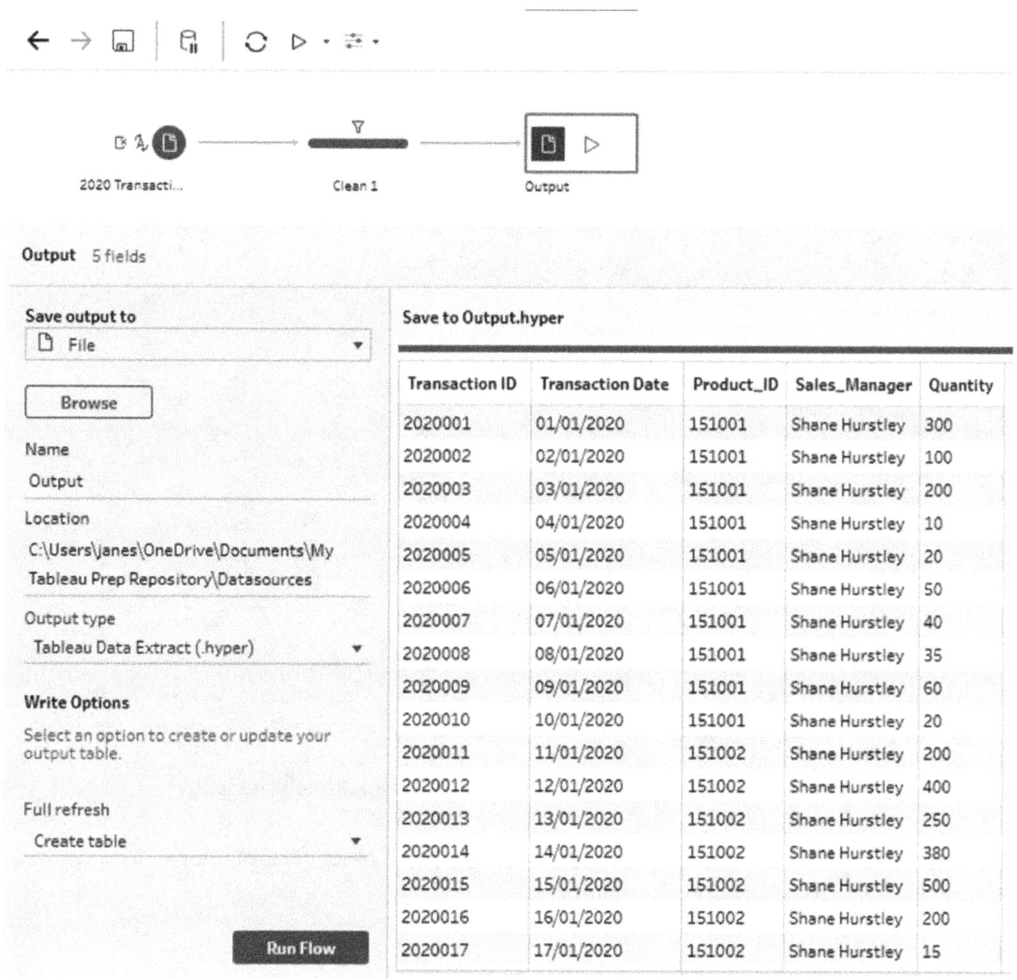

Figure 6.28 – Creating the output step in the workflow

For the next steps, we need to ensure that we are connected to the server to effectively change and configure our data source to be available to other users.

Under **Save output to**, let's select **Published data source**, and select the folder where you wish to save this, as seen in *Figure 6.29*:

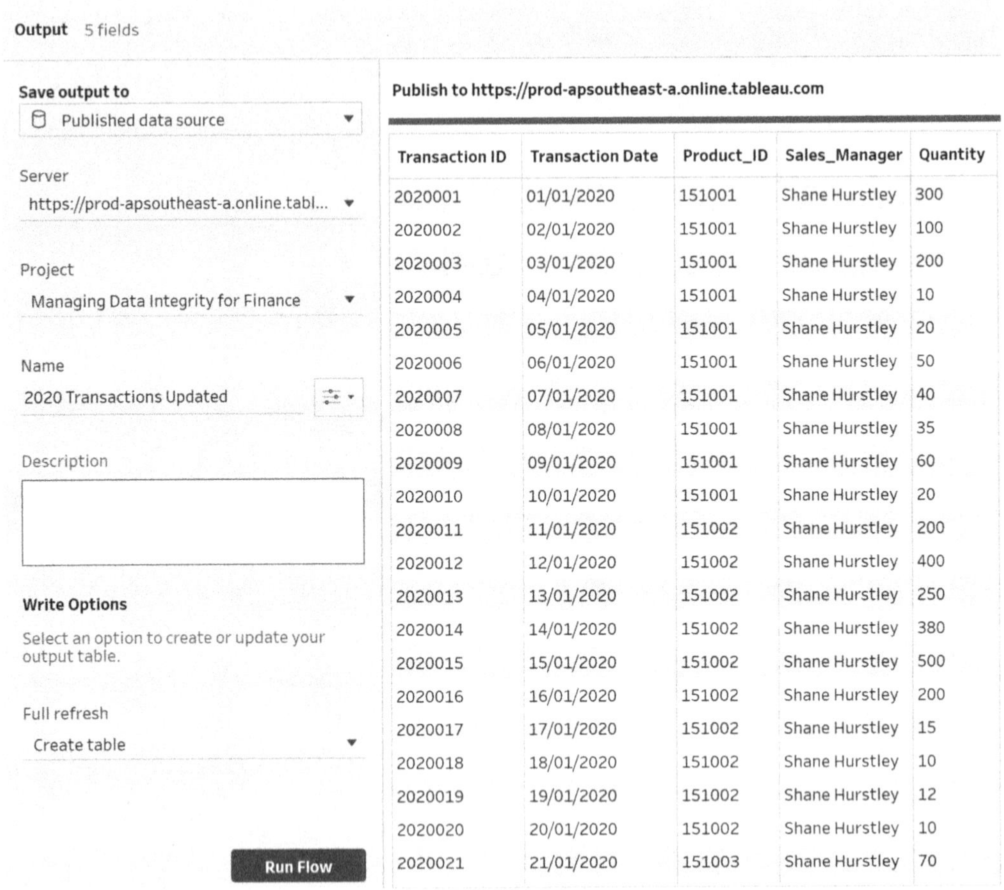

Transaction ID	Transaction Date	Product_ID	Sales_Manager	Quantity
2020001	01/01/2020	151001	Shane Hurstley	300
2020002	02/01/2020	151001	Shane Hurstley	100
2020003	03/01/2020	151001	Shane Hurstley	200
2020004	04/01/2020	151001	Shane Hurstley	10
2020005	05/01/2020	151001	Shane Hurstley	20
2020006	06/01/2020	151001	Shane Hurstley	50
2020007	07/01/2020	151001	Shane Hurstley	40
2020008	08/01/2020	151001	Shane Hurstley	35
2020009	09/01/2020	151001	Shane Hurstley	60
2020010	10/01/2020	151001	Shane Hurstley	20
2020011	11/01/2020	151002	Shane Hurstley	200
2020012	12/01/2020	151002	Shane Hurstley	400
2020013	13/01/2020	151002	Shane Hurstley	250
2020014	14/01/2020	151002	Shane Hurstley	380
2020015	15/01/2020	151002	Shane Hurstley	500
2020016	16/01/2020	151002	Shane Hurstley	200
2020017	17/01/2020	151002	Shane Hurstley	15
2020018	18/01/2020	151002	Shane Hurstley	10
2020019	19/01/2020	151002	Shane Hurstley	12
2020020	20/01/2020	151002	Shane Hurstley	10
2020021	21/01/2020	151003	Shane Hurstley	70

Figure 6.29 – Creating the Output file and saving to Published data source

Uploading a data source to Tableau Cloud, which is shared with other users of information, ensures that there is a single source of truth for your data.

After clicking on **Run Flow**, the file will be published and **Tableau Cloud** will open, as seen in *Figure 6.30*:

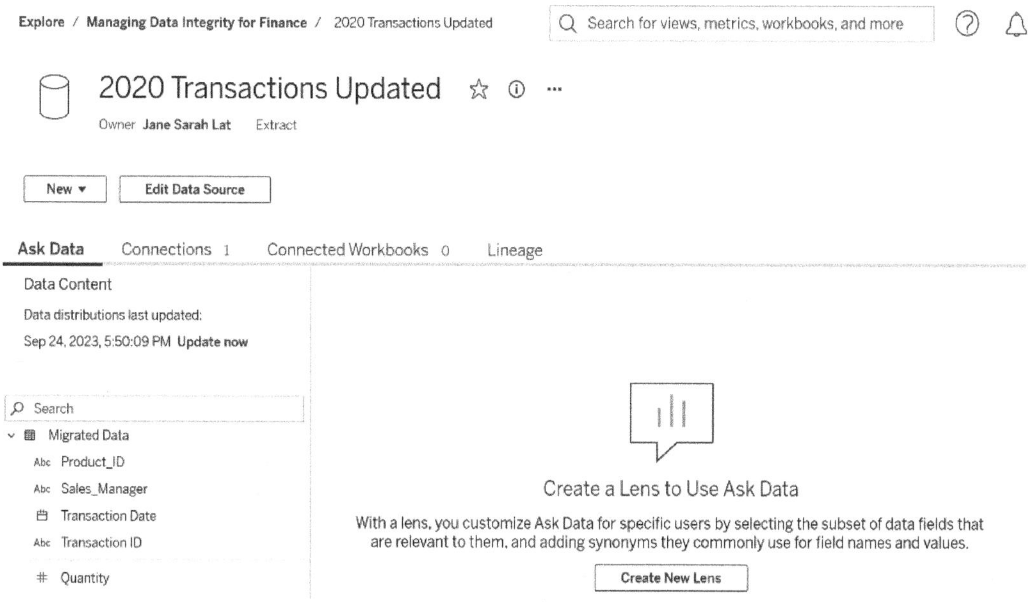

Figure 6.30 – Published in Tableau Cloud

Once the export is done, details about the data will be available, including **Connections** and **Lineage**, as seen in *Figure 6.31*:

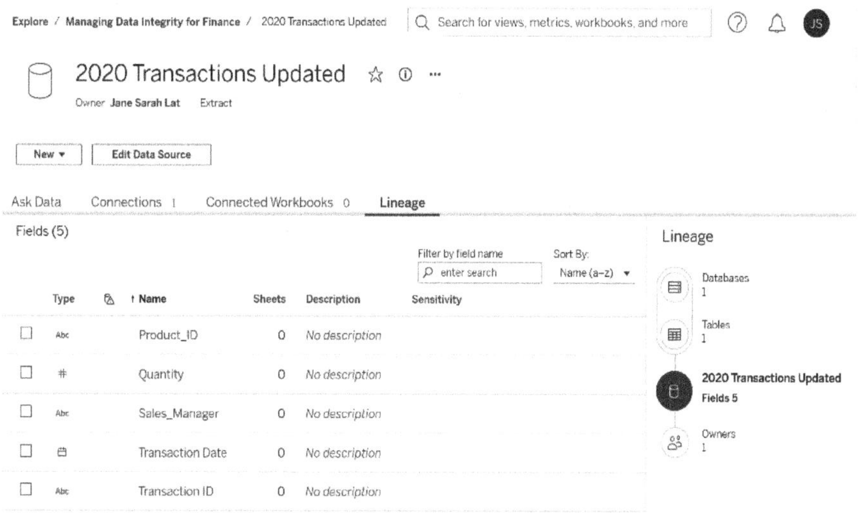

Figure 6.31 – Lineage available in Tableau Cloud

> **Note**
>
> To learn more about the lineage feature in Tableau Cloud, check out this link: `https://help.tableau.com/current/online/en-us/dm_lineage.htm`.

Now that the file has been published in Tableau Cloud, we can now use it to refresh the data in our histogram.

Updating the histogram

To make this change available in **Tableau Desktop**, going back to our working file from earlier, under **Data** click on **New Data Source**, as illustrated in *Figure 6.32*:

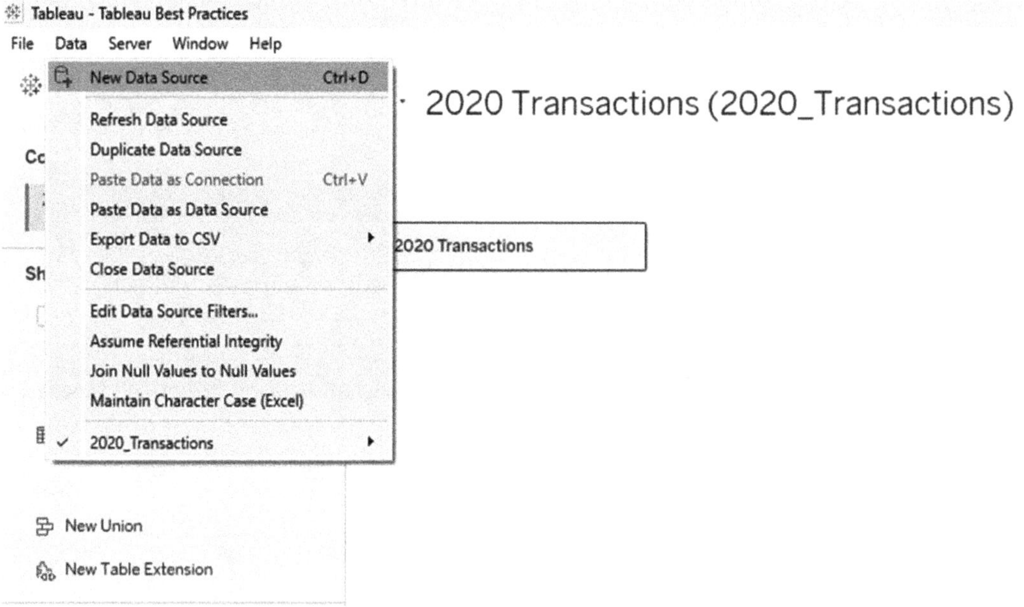

Figure 6.32 – Getting the data by adding a new data source

Under **Data**, select **New Data Source**, then select **Tableau Server**, and click on **Tableau Cloud** under **Quick Connect**. Once you have signed in, find the file we published earlier, as seen in *Figure 6.33*. Click on **Connect**.

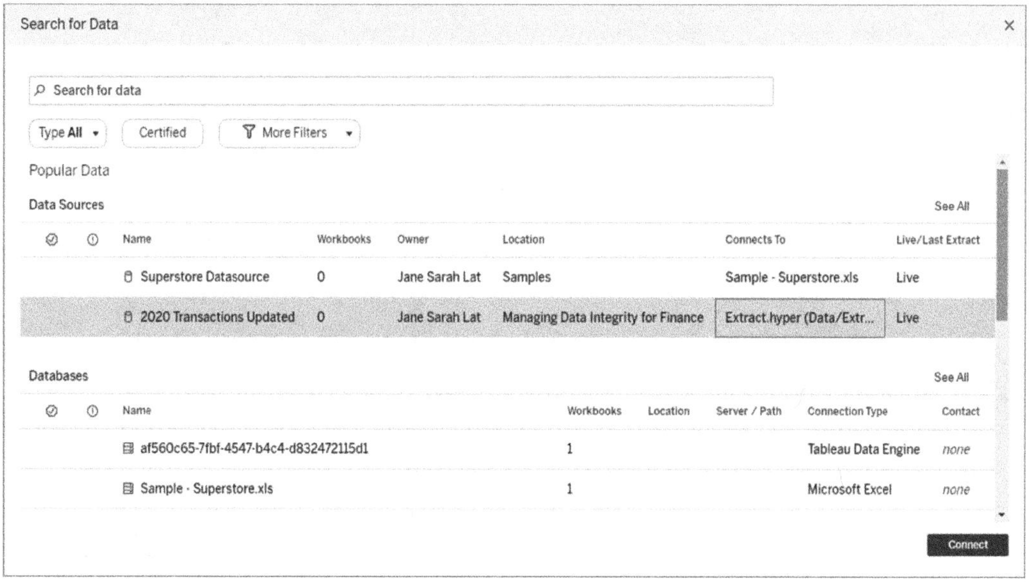

Figure 6.33 – Searching for the file published earlier

We can see the published data sources that we created or we have access to.

Once this information is loaded, we can see that the data source is now available under the **Data** tab as **2020 Transactions Updated**. Let's replace our data source for the visualization we created earlier. Of the three buttons beside the data source, click on **New Worksheet**, which will add **Sheet 2**. Next, let's right-click on **2020_Transactions** and select **Replace Data Source...**, as seen in *Figure 6.34*:

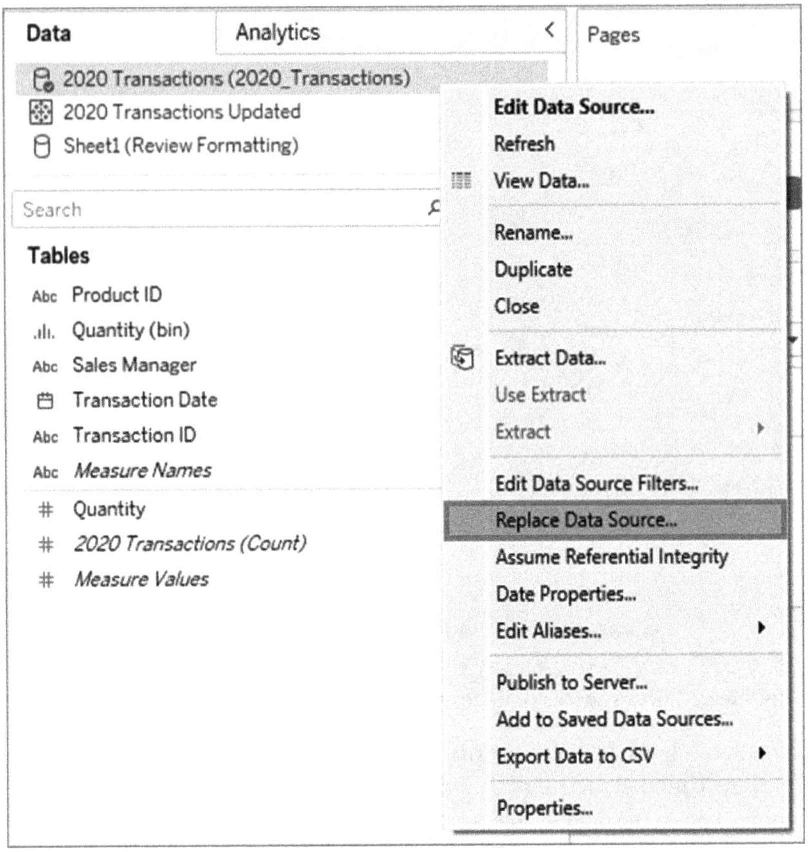

Figure 6.34 – Replacing the data source

A pop-up window will appear, as shown in *Figure 6.35*. For **Replacement**, let's select **2020 Transactions Updated**.

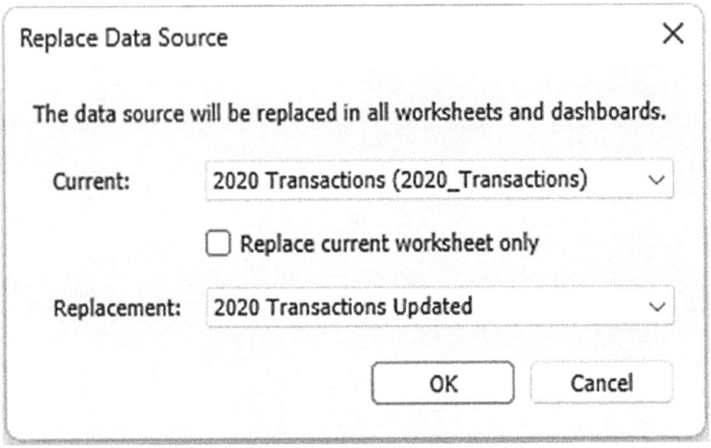

Figure 6.35 – Selecting the data source

Doing this step will allow us to keep the measure we created earlier—that is, **Quantity (bin)**, and we no longer have to re-work the steps to create it.

Once the data is refreshed, we will see that the outlier of 20,000 has disappeared, as shown in *Figure 6.36*:

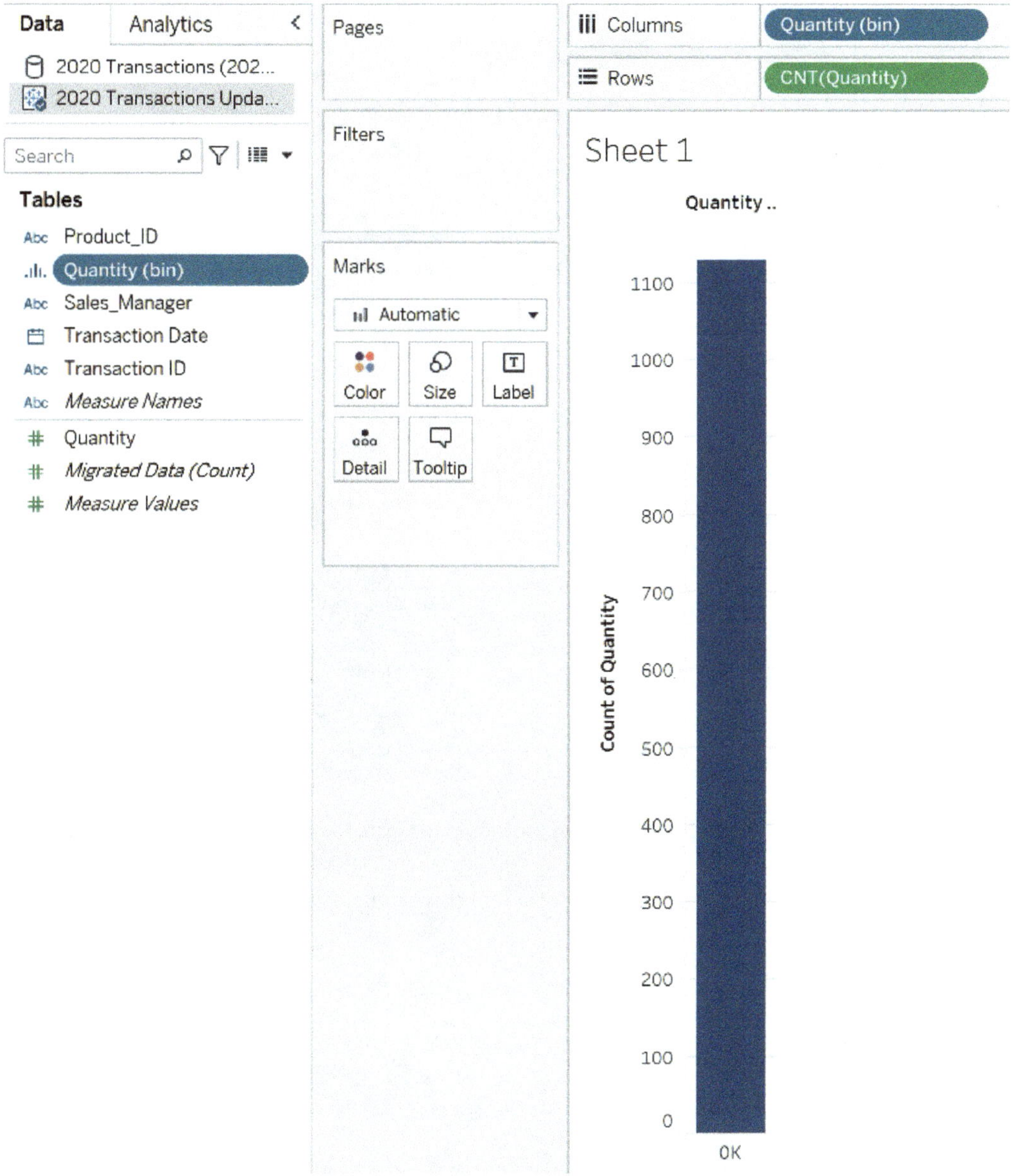

Figure 6.36 – Refreshing the histogram

If we want to dive deeper and update the bins for the histogram, we can hover over **Quantity (bin)** and select **Edit...**, as seen in *Figure 6.37*:

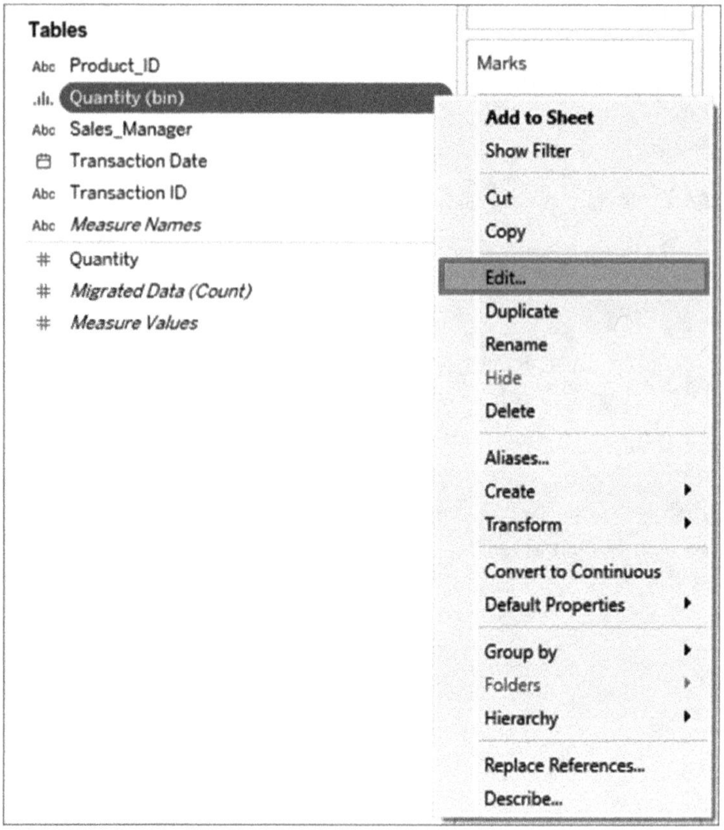

Figure 6.37 – Editing the bins in the histogram

We can click on **Suggest Bin Size** or input our own. For this example, let's use `100` as in *Figure 6.38*:

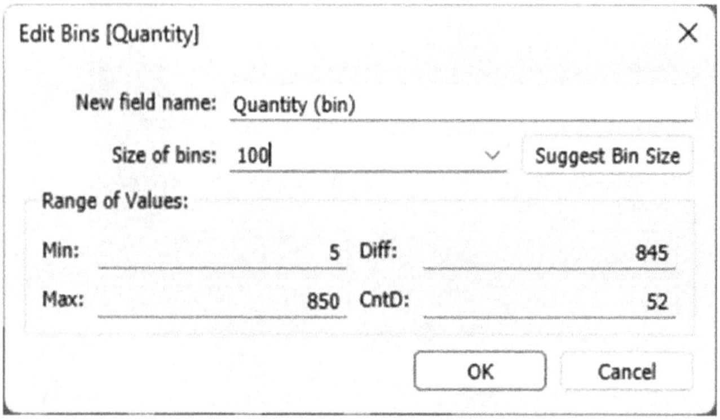

Figure 6.38 – Updating the bin size to 100

After we click on **OK**, our histogram will update. The histogram will be similar to what is shown in *Figure 6.39*:

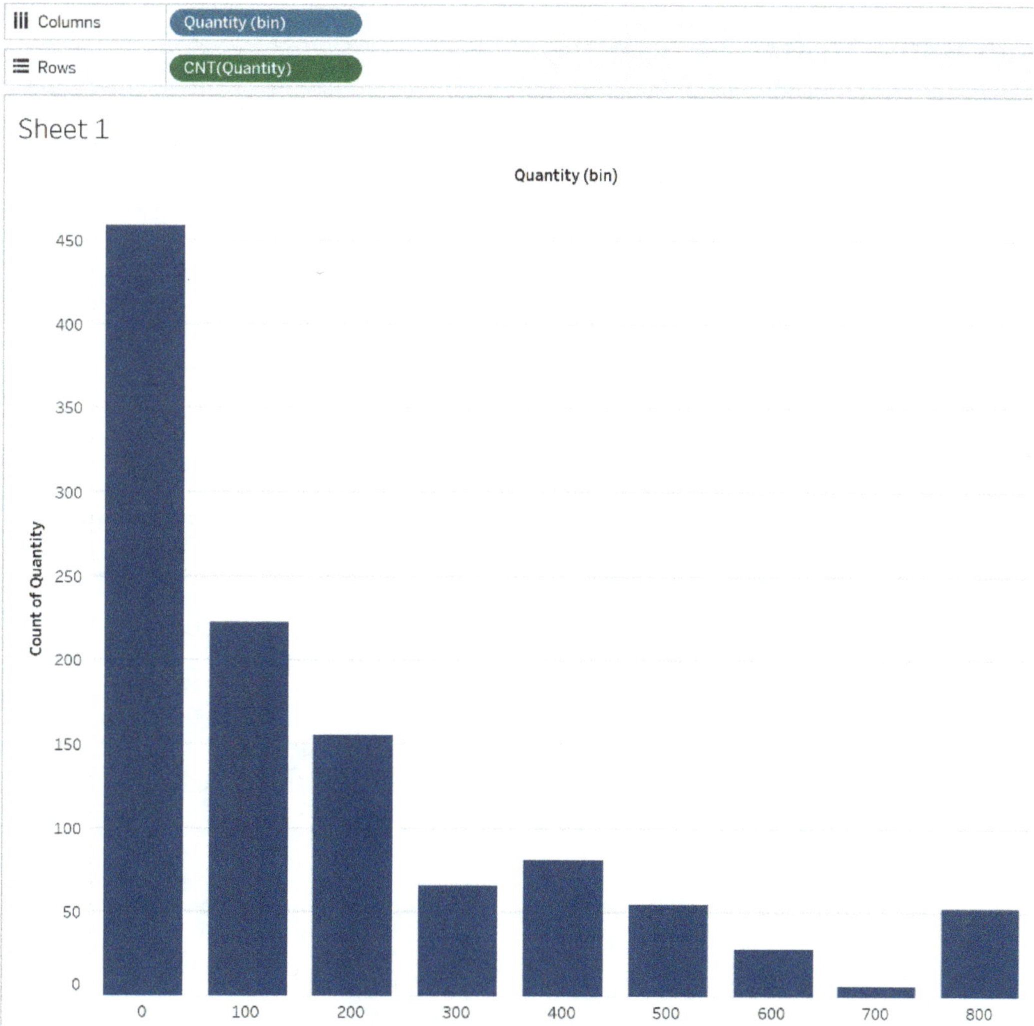

Figure 6.39 – Histogram updated after updating bin size to 100

We can see that, in terms of frequency, those between 0 and 99 units have the highest frequency, while those between 701 and 800 have the lowest.

We have just covered how to create a histogram and identify outliers in Tableau Desktop. We cleaned the information using Tableau Prep and uploaded the information to Tableau Cloud so that we could update the histogram we created. Now that we have visualized the data using the scatter chart and histogram, let's head on to the last section of this chapter.

What if, for example, one of the products in the **Product_Details** *table got deleted by accident?* This would lead to an issue called orphaned records, which we will discuss next.

Managing orphaned records

Orphaned records, as the name suggests, are records whose relationship to the parent record does not exist. If we delete `Product_ID 151003` for **Income protection insurance**, this means that the transactions for this product are not referencing any financial information contained in the **Product_Details** table.

In some cases, if raw financial data is provided and generated by a Dev team, and the Dev team does not perform **referential integrity checks**, issues may occur. Thus being able to detect orphaned records, especially when dealing with multiple records, as early as possible is critical.

The next steps will cover how to do this in Power BI.

Identifying orphaned records in Power BI

Let's go to **Transform data** and delete one of the product IDs. Select the **Income protection insurance** row and click on **Remove Rows** under the **Home** tab, as shown in *Figure 6.40*. Don't worry, we can undo this step later, under **APPLIED STEPS**.

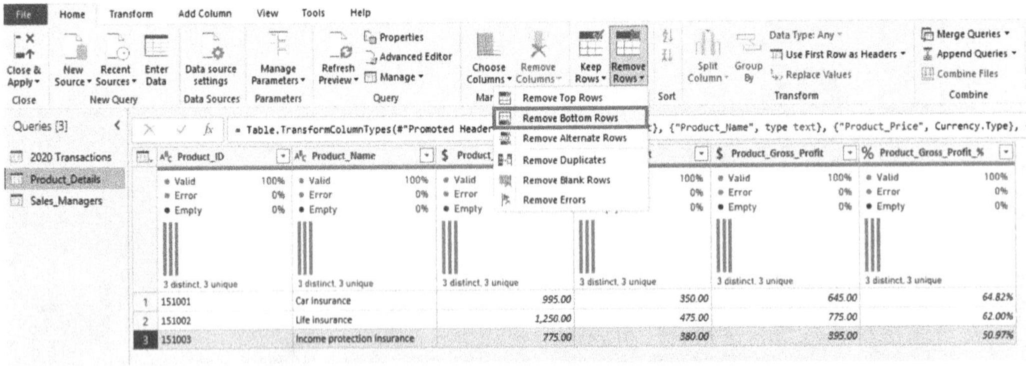

Figure 6.40 – Selecting Remove Bottom Rows under Remove Rows

A pop-up window will appear. Let's put `1` since **Income protection insurance** is at the bottom, as seen in *Figure 6.41*. Click on **OK**.

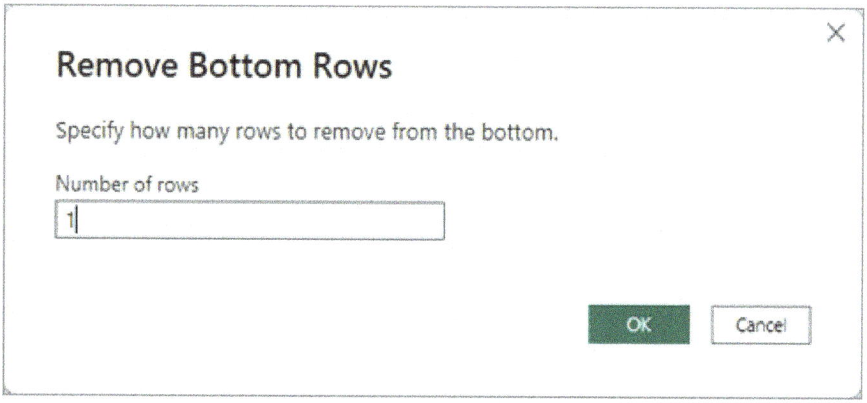

Figure 6.41 – Remove the bottom row

The updated table will look like *Figure 6.42*. The step we did has also been added under **APPLIED STEPS**.

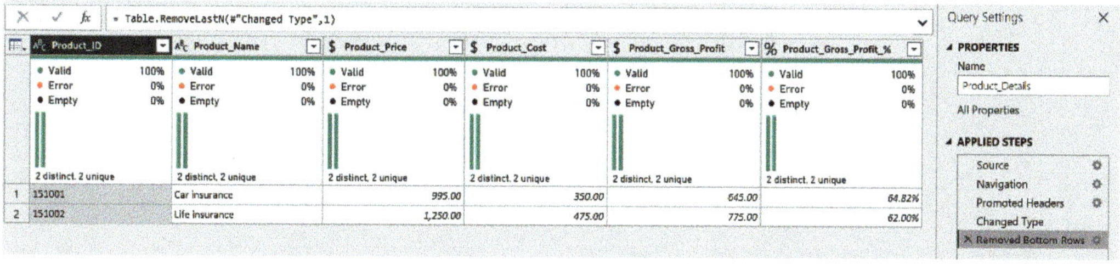

Figure 6.42 – Updated table after removing the bottom row

What if we weren't aware that an item was deleted from the table? How do we identify orphaned records?

Here are the steps to do this:

1. Under the **2020 Transactions** query, select **Merge Queries as New**, found under the **Home** tab, as shown in *Figure 6.43*:

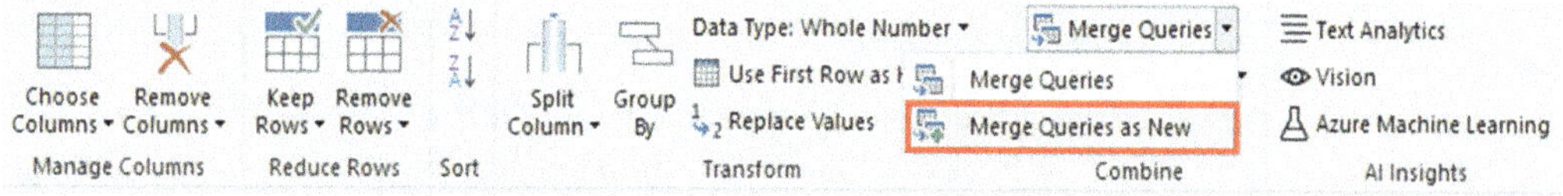

Figure 6.43 – Merge Queries as New under the Home tab

A pop-up window will appear, as seen in *Figure 6.44*:

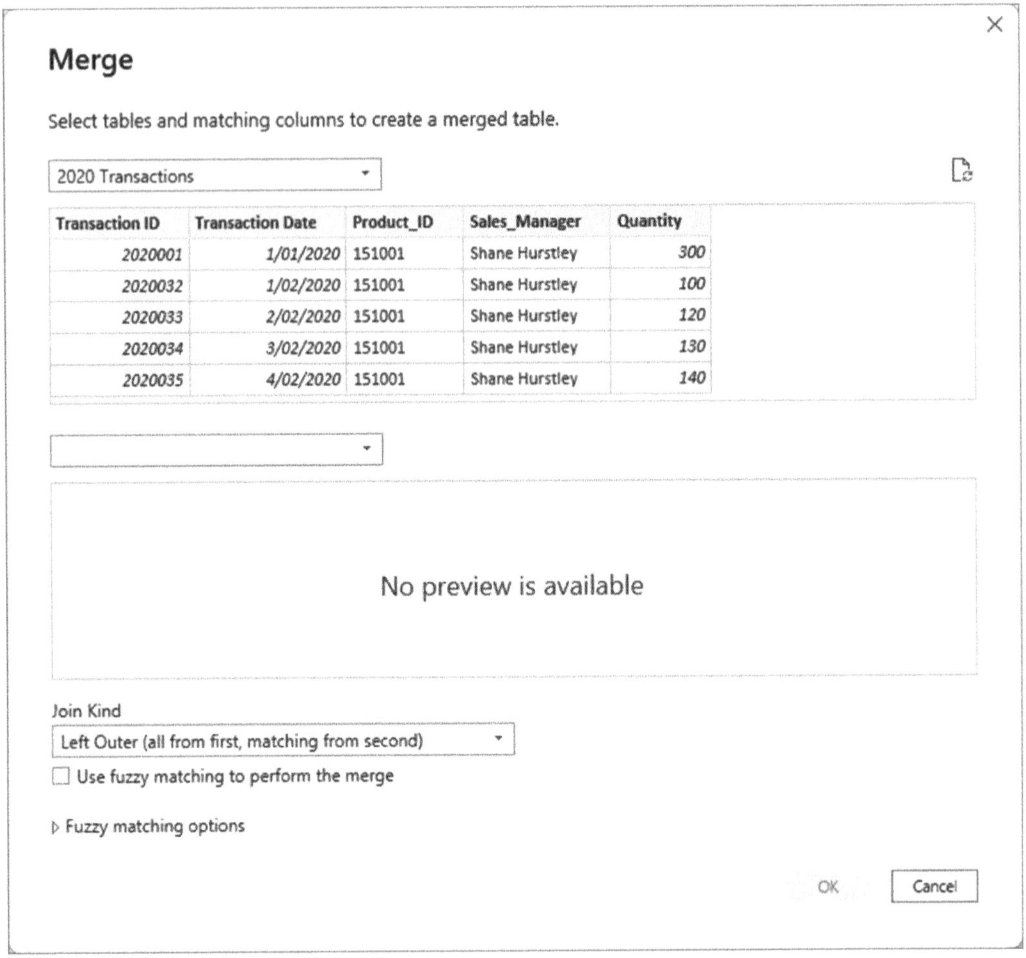

Figure 6.44 – Window to merge the tables

A preview of the underlying data is shown, making it easier to match the columns.

2. For the second table, let's select **Product_Details** and, under **Join Kind**, choose **Left Anti (rows only in first)**. Next, select the **Product_ID** column from both tables, which it will use for the join, as shown in *Figure 6.45*:

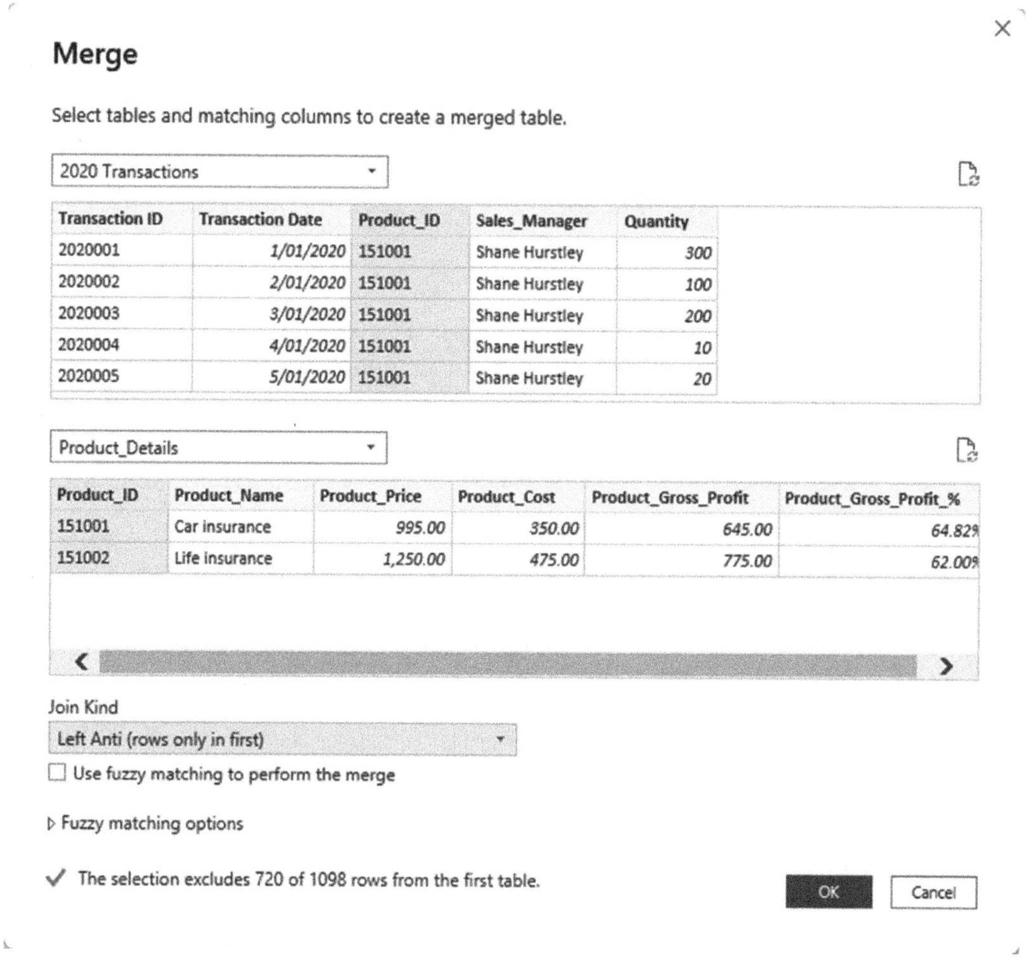

Figure 6.45 – Merging the two tables using the Left Anti join

After we select the two **Product_ID** columns in the tables, and select the join type, we get a message at the bottom: **The selection excludes 720 of 1098 rows from the first table**. This tells us that there are 378 rows of data that do not match product IDs `151001` and `151002`.

> **Note**
>
> A **left-anti join** operation is a type of join that returns the rows from the left table that do not have matching rows in the other table. This will return the rows from our **2020 Transactions** that are not found under **Product_Details**. To learn more about merging queries and different join operations, check out `https://learn.microsoft.com/en-us/power-query/merge-queries-overview`.

3. After we click on **OK**, a new query will appear named **Merge1**. Let's rename this as `Orphaned Records`. This will list all the records where **Product_ID** in the **2020 Transactions** file does not match with **Product_Details**, as illustrated in *Figure 6.46*:

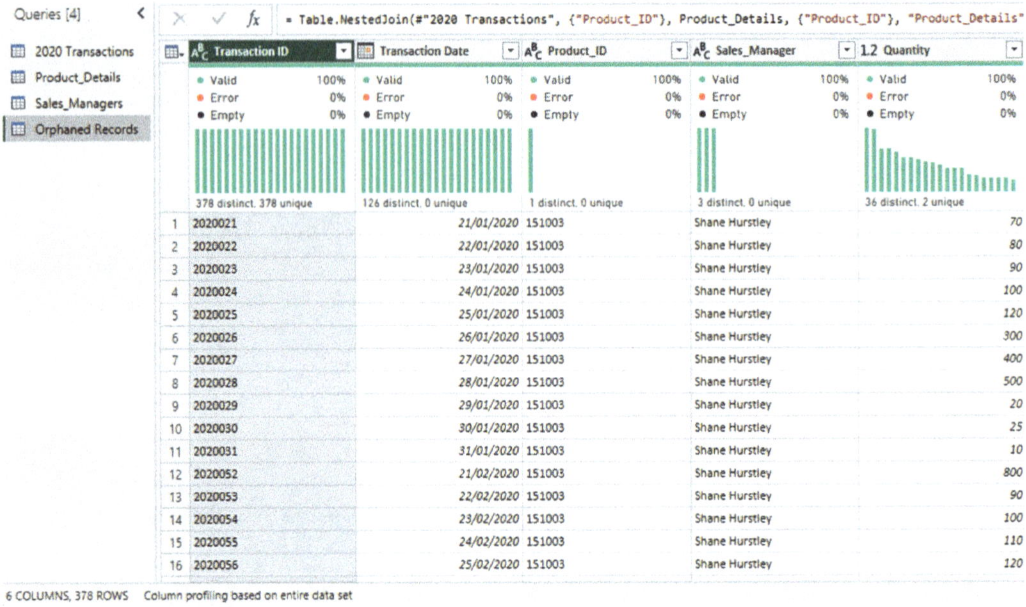

Figure 6.46 – List of orphaned records

We can see the 378 transactions for product `151003` that are tagged as orphaned.

> **Note**
>
> As we mentioned in the previous chapter, under the *Managing relationships in data models* section, ensuring that the relationships are well-defined facilitates this process and makes the results of the queries reliable.

The steps we discussed covered how to identify orphaned records in Microsoft Power BI. Now that we know how to do this, let's try doing this using another popular data analytics tool, called **Alteryx**.

Identifying orphaned records in Alteryx

We will use the same information from Power BI, and test how to do this in Alteryx. The edited Excel files that we will be loading have been updated to remove the duplicate values from the `2020_Transactions.xlsx` file and remove `Product_ID 151003` from the `Product_Details.xlsx` file.

Here are the steps to do this:

1. Open **Alteryx Designer**.
2. From the **In/Out** tab, drag the **Input Data** node to the canvas, as illustrated in *Figure 6.47*:

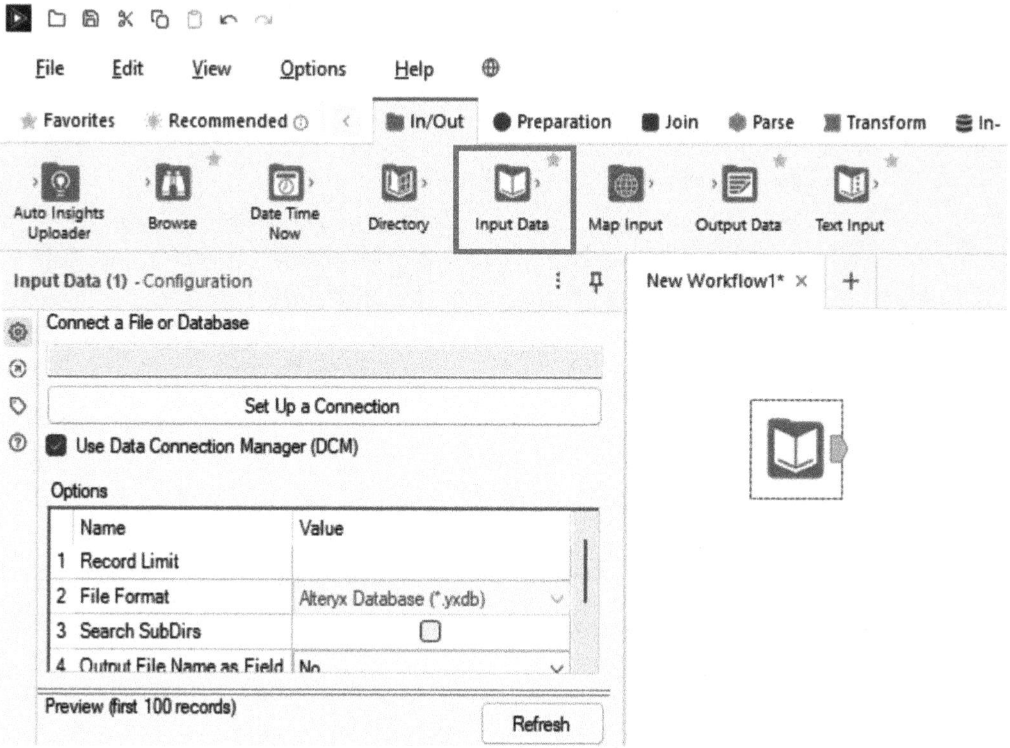

Figure 6.47 – Dragging the Input Data node to the canvas

If the **Input Data** node is available from the **Favorites** tab, you may also drag it from there.

3. Next, click on **Set Up a Connection** under **Connect a File or Database**.

4. The **Data connections** pop-up window will appear. In **Files**, we have the option to upload the file using either **Drag & drop** or **Select file**, as illustrated in *Figure 6.48*:

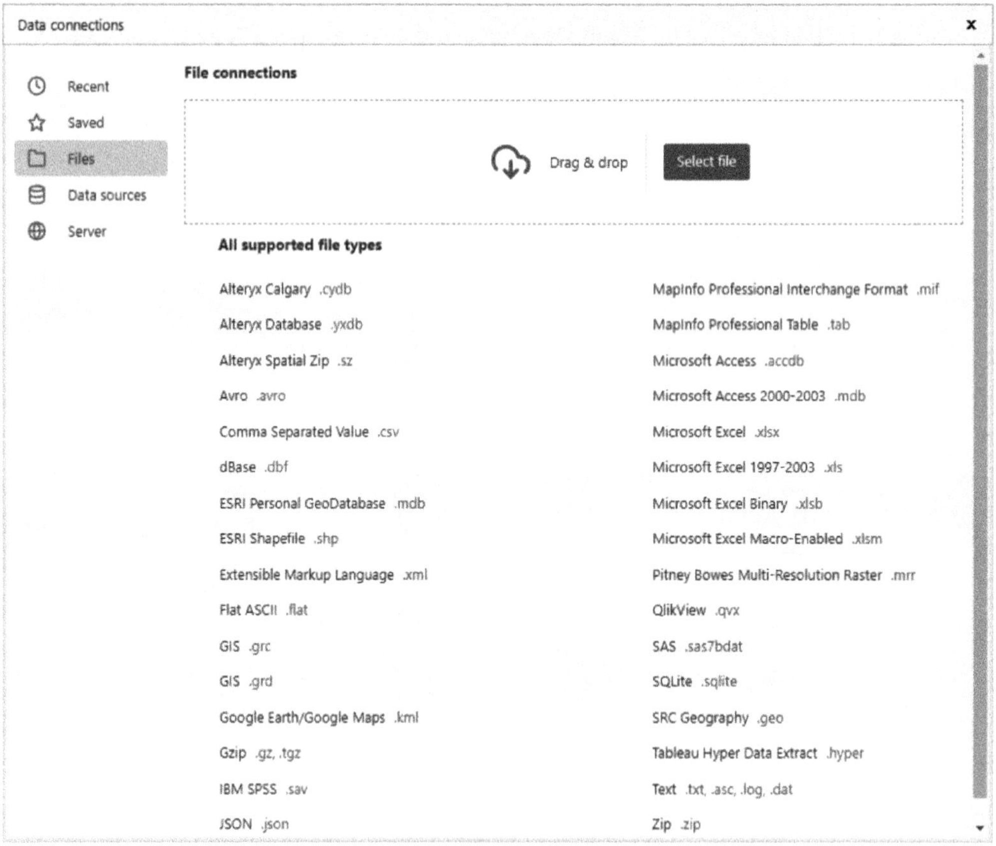

Figure 6.48 – Either drag and drop or select the file to be used

You will notice that connections can be created from different file types, data sources, and servers. Being able to combine data from various sources is an important feature of analytics tools.

5. Drag and drop the `2020_Transactions Edited.xlsx` file. A pop-up window will appear, as seen in *Figure 6.49*:

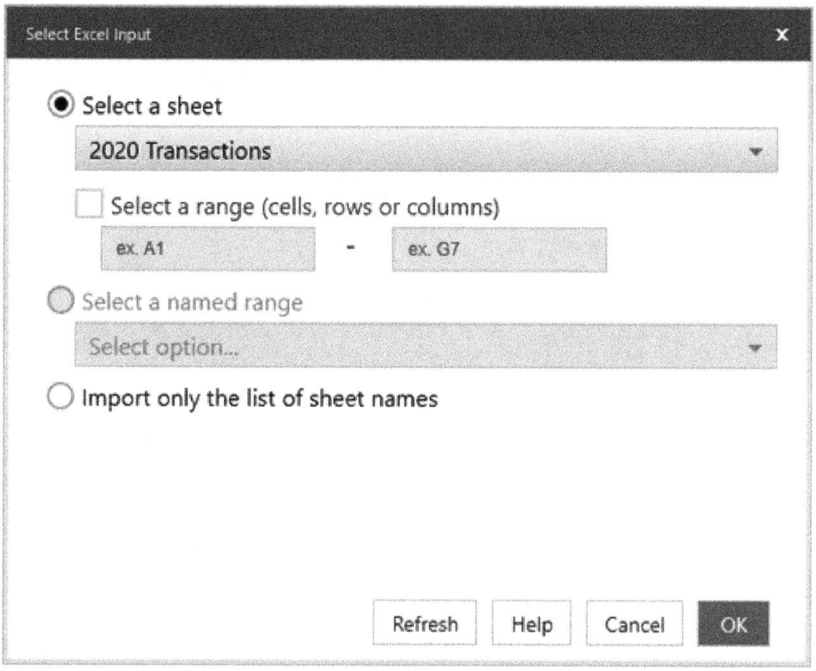

Figure 6.49 – Using the 2020_Transactions Edited.xlsx file for the input

This edited version of the file excludes the duplicate values that are in the unedited version. Use the default **Select a sheet** option with **2020 Transactions**, containing our dataset.

6. After we click on **OK**, the transactions from the file will be loaded, as seen in *Figure 6.50*:

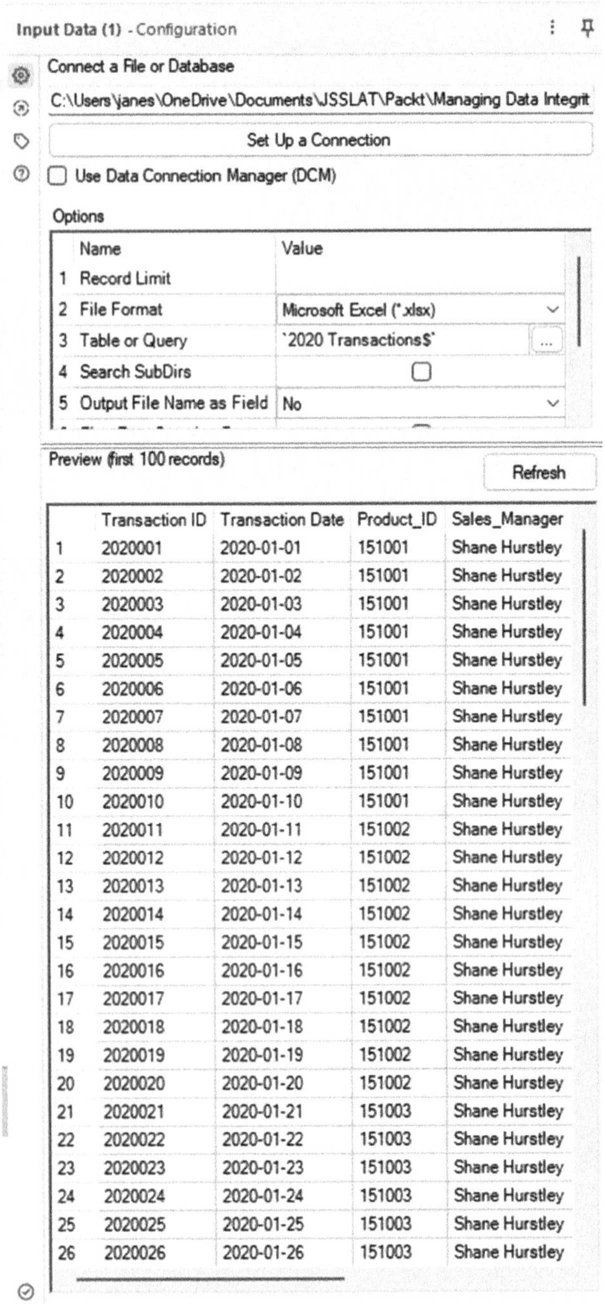

Figure 6.50 – Transaction records have been loaded

Now that we have loaded the first table containing all the 2020 transactions, let's add the second table for the product details, where we need to match the records to find the orphaned records.

7. Drag another **Input Data** node and click on **Set Up a Connection**.
8. This time, use the **Drag & drop** option for the `Product_Details Edited.xlsx` file. The pop-up window shown in *Figure 6.51* will appear.

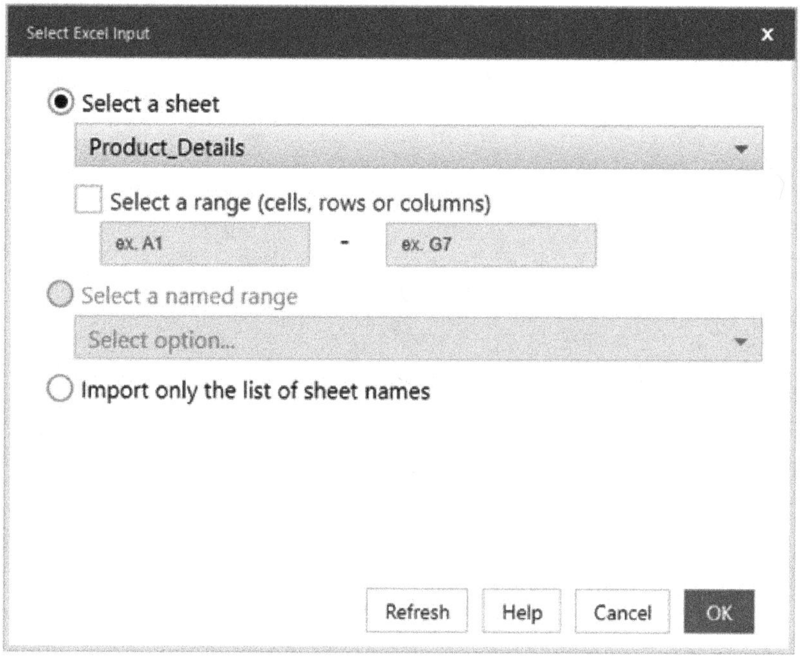

Figure 6.51 – Select Excel Input pop-up window

Since the settings already contain the correct dataset to load, click on **OK**.

The next steps involve joining two tables using a **left anti join** operation.

9. Under the **Join** tab, drag the **Join** node to the canvas. Our window will appear as shown in *Figure 6.52*:

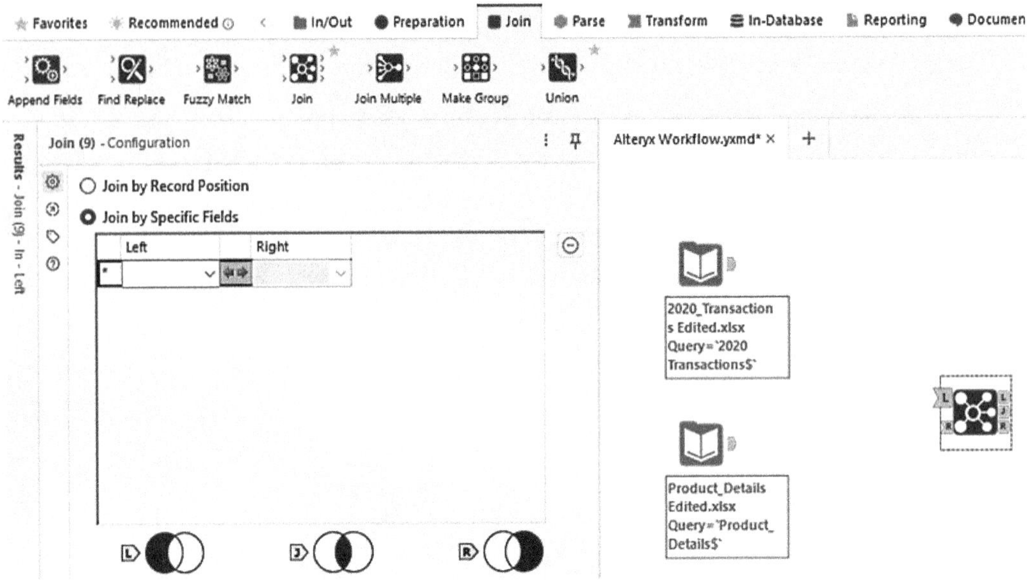

Figure 6.52 – After dragging the Join node to the canvas

You may place the nodes in any way you prefer. What is important is the flow of data from input to output.

10. Connect the **Input** nodes to the **Join** node by clicking on the green tip of the **Input** nodes and connecting them, as seen in *Figure 6.53*:

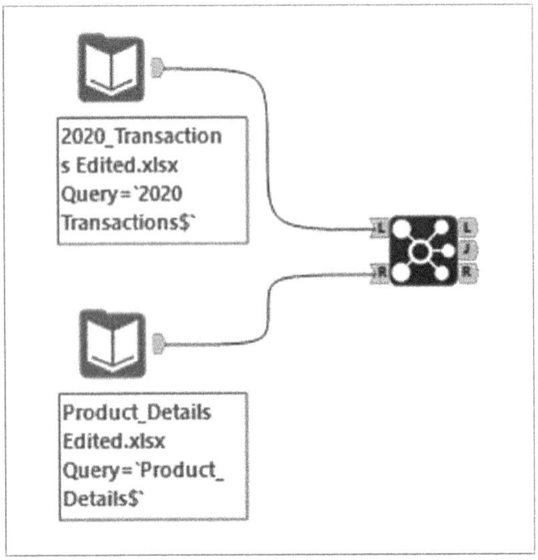

Figure 6.53 – Connecting the nodes

Once the input nodes are connected to the join node, you will be able to match the columns of the two files, which we will do in the next step.

11. Select **Product_ID** under both the **Left** and **Right** fields, as highlighted in *Figure 6.54*. This step will do the **left join** and will reflect the transactions with product IDs in both files.

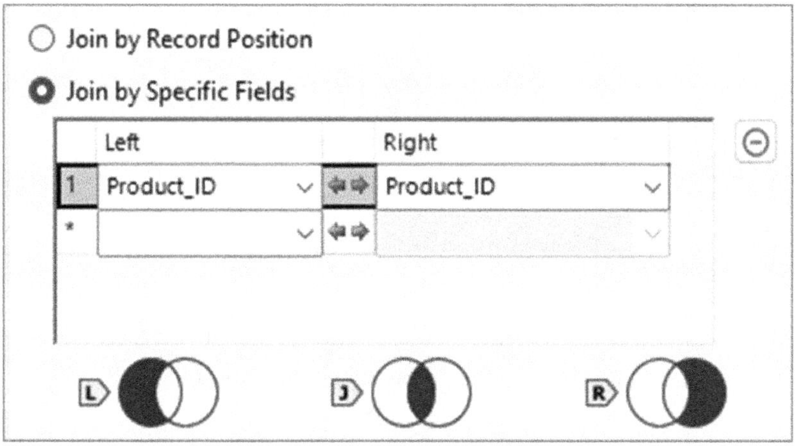

Figure 6.54 – Joining the inputs

After joining the tables, we can now export the output so that we can view the results.

12. Drag the **Output Data** node under the **In/Out** tab, as illustrated in *Figure 6.55*:

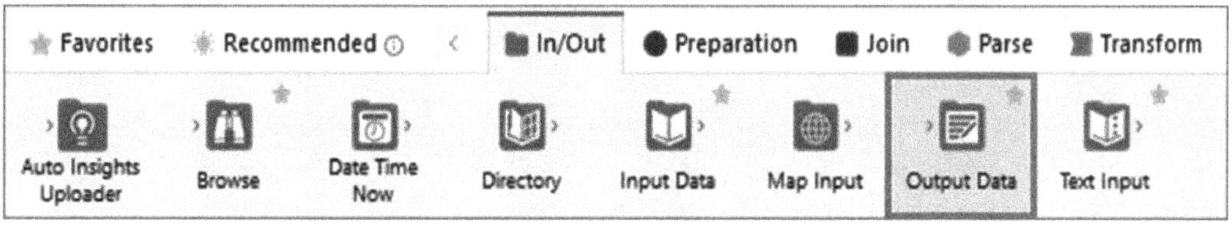

Figure 6.55 – The Output Data node under the In/Out tab

You may also drag this from the **Favorites** tab if it is available.

13. Dragging the **Output Data** node and connecting it to the **Join** node will reveal a message, as seen in *Figure 6.56*:

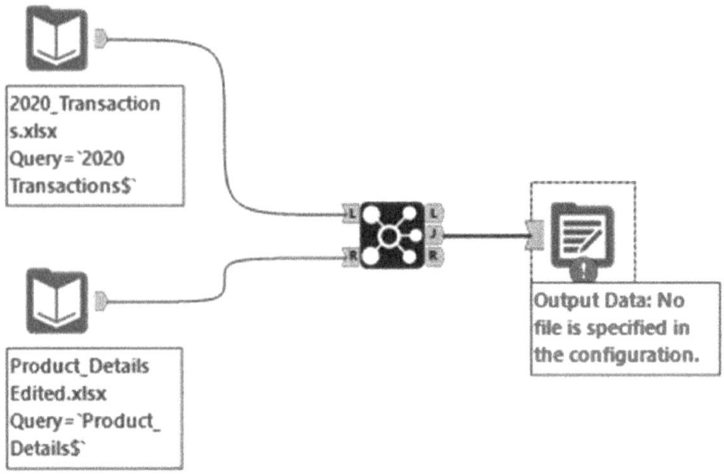

Figure 6.56 – Dragging the Output Data node to the workflow

This is because the output file where the results will flow has not been specified yet. We will do this in the next step.

14. Click on **Set Up a Connection**. Under **Files**, choose **Microsoft Excel**, as seen in *Figure 6.57*:

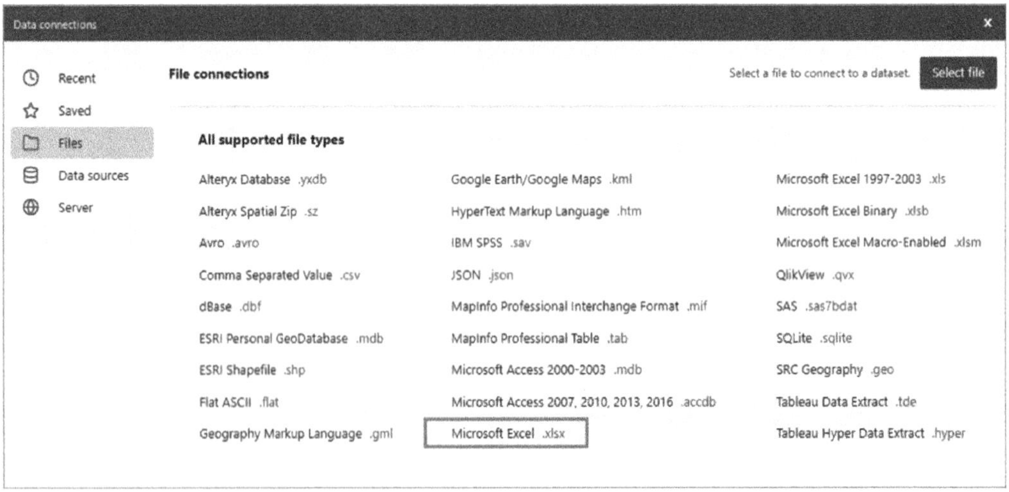

Figure 6.57 – Choosing Microsoft Excel in setting up a connection

15. Locate where you would like to save the file, as seen in *Figure 6.58*. For **File name**, use `Output Orphaned Records`.

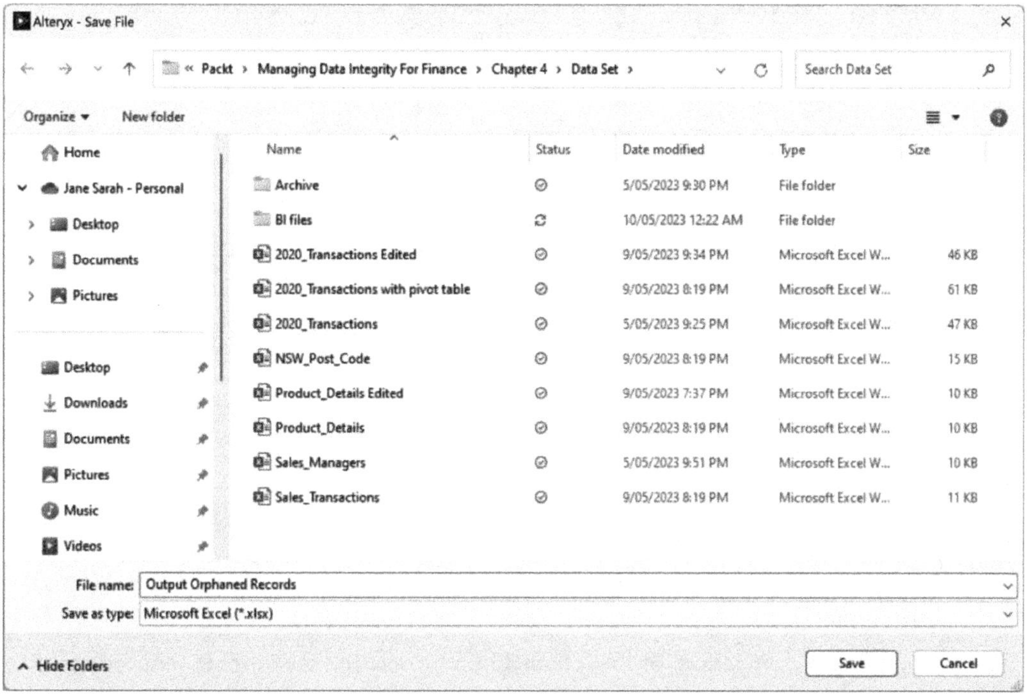

Figure 6.58 – Selecting the location where we will save our output

Click on **Save**.

16. A pop-up window will appear to specify the sheet, as seen in *Figure 6.59*:

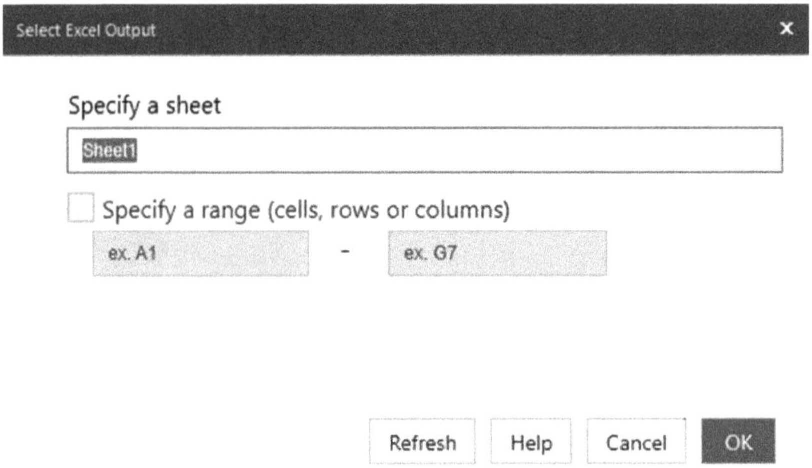

Figure 6.59 – Specifying the sheet for the output

Click on **OK**.

17. Under **Options**, which is found below **Set Up a Connection**, select **Microsoft Excel (*.xlsx)** for **File Format**, and **Overwrite Sheet or Range** for **Output Options**.
18. Let's update the connection for the **left anti join** by deleting the current connection and connecting the join node and the output node, as seen in *Figure 6.60*:

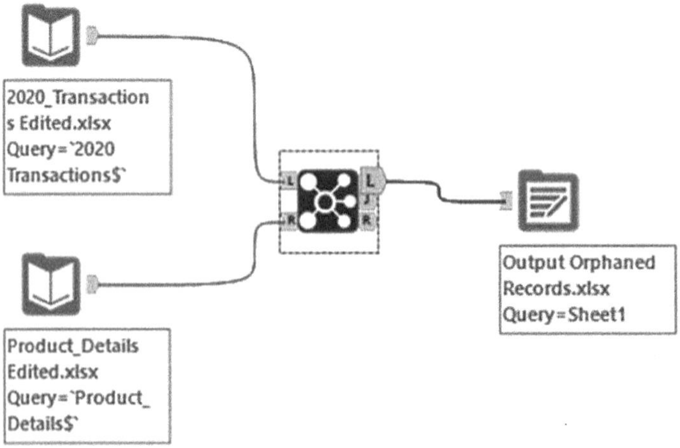

Figure 6.60 – Connecting the left anti join connector to the output file

> **Note**
>
> To learn more about the **join tool** and the different types of join in Alteryx Designer, check out this link: `https://help.alteryx.com/20231/designer/join-tool`.

19. Now that we have set up the steps, we can run the workflow. Under the **Options** tab, select **Run Workflow**, as seen in *Figure 6.61*:

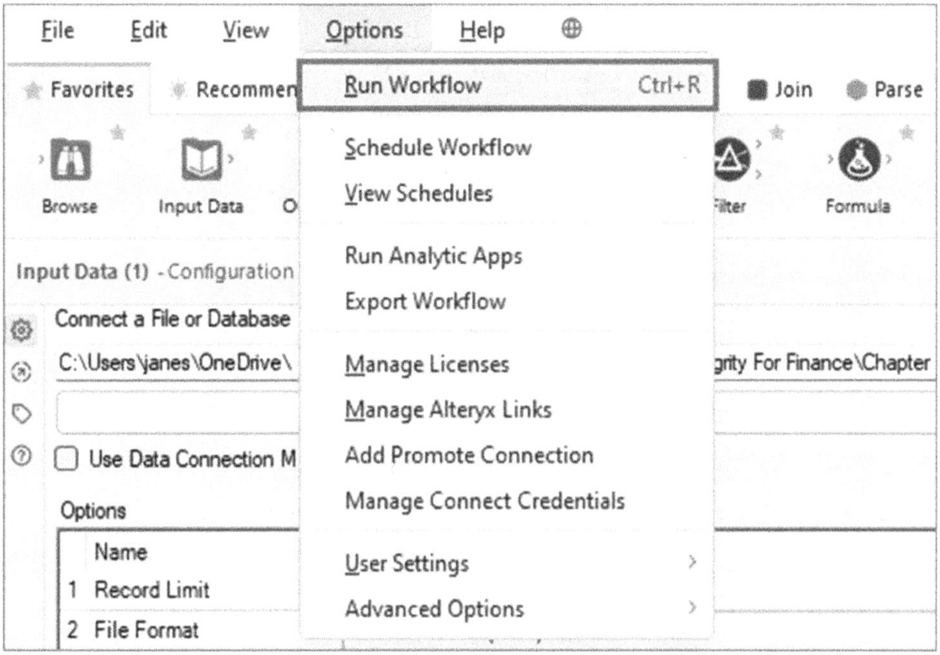

Figure 6.61 – Run Workflow

You can also use the **Run Workflow** button at the *upper-right side* of the **Workflow** pane.

20. Open the Excel file where the output is saved. This will list the orphaned records, as shown in *Figure 6.62*:

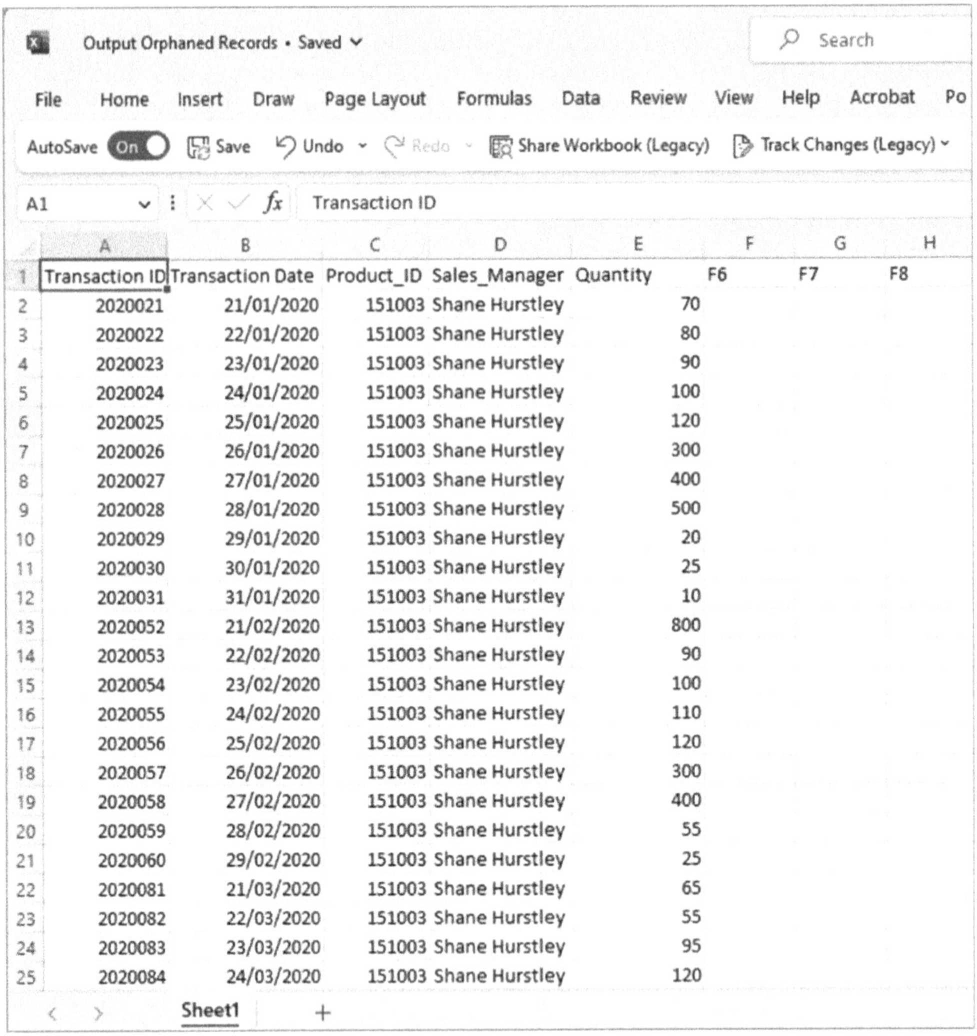

Transaction ID	Transaction Date	Product_ID	Sales_Manager	Quantity	F6	F7	F8
2020021	21/01/2020	151003	Shane Hurstley	70			
2020022	22/01/2020	151003	Shane Hurstley	80			
2020023	23/01/2020	151003	Shane Hurstley	90			
2020024	24/01/2020	151003	Shane Hurstley	100			
2020025	25/01/2020	151003	Shane Hurstley	120			
2020026	26/01/2020	151003	Shane Hurstley	300			
2020027	27/01/2020	151003	Shane Hurstley	400			
2020028	28/01/2020	151003	Shane Hurstley	500			
2020029	29/01/2020	151003	Shane Hurstley	20			
2020030	30/01/2020	151003	Shane Hurstley	25			
2020031	31/01/2020	151003	Shane Hurstley	10			
2020052	21/02/2020	151003	Shane Hurstley	800			
2020053	22/02/2020	151003	Shane Hurstley	90			
2020054	23/02/2020	151003	Shane Hurstley	100			
2020055	24/02/2020	151003	Shane Hurstley	110			
2020056	25/02/2020	151003	Shane Hurstley	120			
2020057	26/02/2020	151003	Shane Hurstley	300			
2020058	27/02/2020	151003	Shane Hurstley	400			
2020059	28/02/2020	151003	Shane Hurstley	55			
2020060	29/02/2020	151003	Shane Hurstley	25			
2020081	21/03/2020	151003	Shane Hurstley	65			
2020082	22/03/2020	151003	Shane Hurstley	55			
2020083	23/03/2020	151003	Shane Hurstley	95			
2020084	24/03/2020	151003	Shane Hurstley	120			

Figure 6.62 – Viewing the Excel output file

Another way to view this list without going to the Excel file is by clicking on the **Left** connector as shown in *Figure 6.63*, and this will display the orphaned records as well.

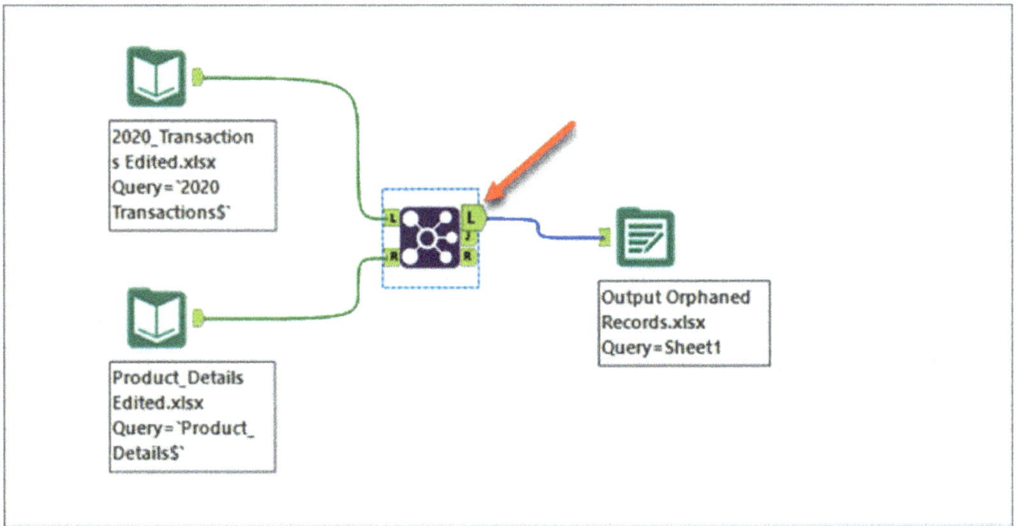

Results - Join (7) - Out - Left

8 of 8 Fields | Cell Viewer | 378 records displayed

Record	Transaction ID	Transaction Date	Product_ID	Sales_Manager	Quantity
1	2020021	2020-01-21	151003	Shane Hurstley	70
2	2020022	2020-01-22	151003	Shane Hurstley	80
3	2020023	2020-01-23	151003	Shane Hurstley	90
4	2020024	2020-01-24	151003	Shane Hurstley	100
5	2020025	2020-01-25	151003	Shane Hurstley	120
6	2020026	2020-01-26	151003	Shane Hurstley	300
7	2020027	2020-01-27	151003	Shane Hurstley	400
8	2020028	2020-01-28	151003	Shane Hurstley	500
9	2020029	2020-01-29	151003	Shane Hurstley	20
10	2020030	2020-01-30	151003	Shane Hurstley	25
11	2020031	2020-01-31	151003	Shane Hurstley	10
12	2020052	2020-02-21	151003	Shane Hurstley	800
13	2020053	2020-02-22	151003	Shane Hurstley	90
14	2020054	2020-02-23	151003	Shane Hurstley	100
15	2020055	2020-02-24	151003	Shane Hurstley	110
16	2020056	2020-02-25	151003	Shane Hurstley	120
17	2020057	2020-02-26	151003	Shane Hurstley	300
18	2020058	2020-02-27	151003	Shane Hurstley	400
19	2020059	2020-02-28	151003	Shane Hurstley	55
20	2020060	2020-02-29	151003	Shane Hurstley	25
21	2020081	2020-03-21	151003	Shane Hurstley	65

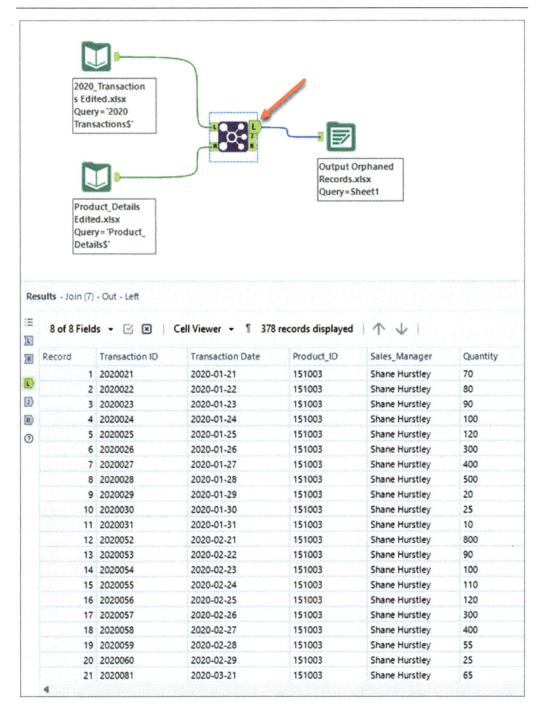

Figure 6.63 – Displaying orphaned records

Here, we can see from the details that 378 records are displayed, which is consistent with the list we got when we did this in Power BI.

When we encounter orphaned records, we first need to identify what caused the issue. Orphaned records are typically records that have lost their connection to other records in the database because the related record has been deleted or modified without updating the dependent record. Once the issue has been identified, there are a few approaches that can be taken to resolve this:

- **Delete the orphaned record**: If they are no longer needed, they can be removed from the database
- **Update the dependent records**: If the related records still exist but have been modified, the dependent records can be updated to reflect the changes
- **Reassign the relationship**: If the related record has been deleted, the dependent record can be updated to reference a different, but valid, related record

> **Important note**
>
> It is important to handle orphaned records with caution to avoid data loss or corruption. Seeking advice from a database administrator or experienced developer can be helpful in determining the best course of action for your specific situation.

Well done in getting to this point and completing the hands-on exercises! In this chapter, together with the previous two chapters, we discussed the various features and capabilities of various business intelligence tools to help you improve and enhance the quality and integrity of your data. There are a lot more things to uncover and learn from these tools, and I hope that this will motivate you to dive deeper and master these topics.

Summary

In this chapter, we discussed the *best practices* when using business intelligence tools such as **Microsoft Power BI Desktop**, **Tableau Desktop**, **Tableau Prep Builder**, and **Alteryx Designer**. We covered how to handle potentially confusing date convention formats by updating the format and checking the locale settings. Ensuring that date formats are consistent will help ensure that our analysis is accurate and reliable. Next, we used data visualization features such as the scatter chart in Power BI and the histogram in Tableau to identify data outliers. By working on these hands-on examples, I am sure that you have grown more confident in what you have learned. Lastly, we discussed how to find and manage orphaned records in both Power BI and Alteryx. Understanding various ways to address a problem is an important skill to develop.

Business intelligence tools are powerful tools to clean, transform, analyze, and visualize data. They can even be used to detect fraudulent transactions that affect financial report integrity. In the next chapter, we will discuss how financial reports are interpreted, how fraudulent transactions affect financial report integrity, and how to detect fraudulent transactions and anomalies.

Further reading

For additional information on the topics covered in this chapter, you may find the following resources helpful:

- Desai, Veeral, Fountaine, Tim, and Rowshankish, Kayvaun. *A Better Way to Put Your Data to Work*: `https://hbr.org/2022/07/a-better-way-to-put-your-data-to-work`
- *Strategic Finance Magazine Teaching the ETL Process*: `https://sfmagazine.com/articles/2022/august/teaching-the-etl-process/`
- *Visualization types in Power BI*: `https://learn.microsoft.com/en-us/power-bi/visuals/power-bi-visualization-types-for-reports-and-q-and-a`
- *What is Data Visualization? Definition, Examples, And Learning Resources*: `https://www.tableau.com/learn/articles/data-visualization`
- *Alteryx Join Tool*: `https://help.alteryx.com/20231/designer/join-tool`

7

Detecting Fraudulent Transactions Affecting Financial Report Integrity

In this chapter, we will delve into the crucial topic of detecting fraudulent transactions that have the potential to undermine the integrity of financial reports. Fraudulent transactions can have devastating consequences for businesses and stakeholders that would negatively impact trust and cause financial losses in the organization. We will explore various concepts, techniques, and solutions that can be implemented to identify and mitigate fraudulent transactions.

In this chapter, we will cover the following main topics:

- Understanding the major causes of fraud
- Common myths and misconceptions about financial fraud
- Interpreting financial reports
- Learning how fraudulent transactions affect overall financial report integrity
- Detecting and preventing fraudulent transactions and anomalies

By the end of the chapter, you will have a better understanding of how financial reports are interpreted and analyzed, and how to spot and stop fraud.

Technical requirements

This chapter builds on concepts introduced in *Chapter 1*, *Recognizing the Importance of Data Integrity in Finance*, under the *A quick tour of concepts relevant to data integrity management* section. You may revisit this part to better appreciate our discussion in this chapter.

At the same time, we will be using datasets from a fictional company for our hands-on exercise using **Microsoft Excel**. If you do not have Microsoft Excel, you may use **Google Sheets**, which is free with a Google account, instead. Our sample datasets are saved in the Packt **GitHub** repository, which can be accessed at `https://github.com/PacktPublishing/Managing-Data-Integrity-for-Finance/tree/main/ch07`. Save the file on your computer, as we will use it in the *Interpreting financial reports* section of this chapter. You may proceed once these are ready.

Understanding the major causes of fraud

Based on interviews conducted by a newspaper (specifics withheld for anonymity), the GST fraud that was promoted on TikTok was very simple to execute. All that the person needed to do was to apply for a business number, lodge the claim on the government website or app, and submit it to get the GST refund after a specified number of days. What made matters worse was that a number of social influencers on TikTok made people believe that it was okay, saying that it was a temporary loan.

The use of social media aggravated the situation and more than 50,000 people in that country took advantage of the weakness in the government agency's platform. As a result of these fraudulent claims, more than a billion US dollars were paid out (*converted using today's exchange rate*). The expectation was for people to submit a claim for their business expenses and be reimbursed for the allowable limit of the GST to help businesses with their cash flow. It started in late 2020 when banks noticed suspicious payments made to the accounts of people who were recipients of social security. In the middle of 2021, the fraud became more widespread and the banks flagged the *suspicious* payments to the reserve bank of the country. After the reserve bank met with the tax office in early 2022, it started to take action, and an operation to address the situation was undertaken. About **600 tax officers** were assigned to the case to review the claims and stop the fraudulent payments. Billions of dollars in false *claims* were prevented, and hundreds of millions of dollars in terms of *fines* and *penalties* were laid against the perpetrators in one of the *biggest tax frauds* in the history of the country.

Could this have been prevented or avoided much earlier? One way to identify these warning signs and potential vulnerabilities that indicate fraud is to understand the fraud triangle as illustrated in *Figure 7.1*. The **fraud triangle** is a concept developed by the American criminologist and sociologist Donald Cressey based on his research to aid in understanding the causes of fraud.

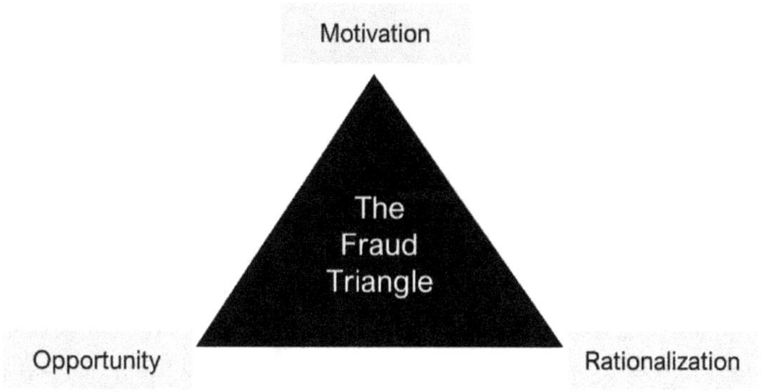

Figure 7.1 – The fraud triangle by Donald Cressey

Let's discuss the components of the **fraud triangle**:

- **Motivation** or **pressure**: This refers to the financial or personal circumstances that create a motive or incentive for individuals to commit fraud. This can include financial difficulties, excessive personal debt, addiction, or a desire for personal gain. When individuals face significant pressure, they may be more likely to engage in fraudulent activities to alleviate their situation.
- **Opportunity**: Opportunity refers to the conditions and circumstances that allow fraud to occur without being easily detected. Weak internal controls, lack of segregation of duties, inadequate supervision, and ineffective monitoring systems create opportunities for individuals to exploit and manipulate financial processes. When these opportunities exist, individuals with the motive may be tempted to engage in fraudulent acts.
- **Rationalization**: Rationalization is the process of individuals justifying their fraudulent behavior to themselves. They may convince themselves that they deserve the money, that their actions are temporary, or that they will repay what they have taken. Rationalization is often fueled by a perceived lack of alternatives or a belief that they can evade detection or punishment.

According to the fraud triangle, all three factors must exist for a person to commit fraud. Fraudulent conduct is much less likely to occur if any of the components are missing.

Note

Take, for example, an employee who is under *extreme* financial pressure given the rising cost of education for his/her three children. The employee feels resentful because he/she has not received a pay increase in the past year, due to the company's cost-cutting measures. There is motivation to engage in fraudulent activities and to rationalize that he/she deserves it. However, if the company has strong internal controls and the employee does not have the opportunity to exploit any control weakness, then this serves as a deterrent to commit fraud and decreases the likelihood that it will happen.

Coming back to our example earlier regarding the GST refund, there were people involved who were experiencing financial difficulty or receiving social security, which created the *motivation* to lodge fraudulent claims. At the same time, the fraud was promoted by influencers on social media, creating a kind of peer pressure where people saw that others were benefiting from it, which is why they decided to take advantage of it as well. This gave the people the motivation to engage in fraudulent activity. The weakness in the government process was exploited, which was based on self-assessment and an honor system. A person just needed to submit a business activity statement without attaching the receipts—*the receipts were only needed later on during an audit*. If the claim was not stopped, then the refund was paid in less than two weeks. It was this vulnerability in the controls that people took advantage of by claiming to have spent money to start a business and filing for a refund on the GST paid. There was no verification done to review the claim before paying out the refund, which gave them the *opportunity*.

Moreover, the social media influencers told people that it was a temporary loan, which made more than 50,000 people believe that it was okay to do. Given that it took a few years before arrests were made, there was a perceived low risk for people given the lack of consequences, and the individuals involved used this to *rationalize* that doing it was justified.

> **Note**
>
> *Warning signs* or *red flags* associated with the fraud triangle can serve as indicators that an individual or situation warrants further investigation. Going back to our example, the warning signs were payments made to individuals receiving social security, which the banks noticed, coupled with a significant spike in claims for GST refunds being processed by the government tax agency. Recognizing these warning signs can help organizations identify potential areas of vulnerability and take proactive measures to prevent and detect fraudulent activities.

Now that we have discussed the fraud triangle and why people commit fraud, we will now discuss some common myths and misconceptions. This will help us become more aware of the beliefs that could be potentially harmful if we are complacent.

Common myths and misconceptions about financial fraud

Understanding the myths and misconceptions surrounding financial fraud is critical for safeguarding assets and also for maintaining the integrity of financial reports. This section dives deep into common misconceptions and illustrates them with real-world examples and scenarios to give you a better understanding and awareness to counteract fraud effectively.

Myth 1—the impact of fraud is insignificant

The incorrect belief that financial fraud is immaterial or insignificant can lead to a complacent outlook toward financial monitoring and control. Such an attitude can set a bad starting point, allowing fraudulent activities to go unnoticed.

> **Note**
>
> For example, imagine yourself being a business owner who unfortunately overlooked minor discrepancies in the cash register only to discover months later that a significant sum had been embezzled by an employee over time! The accumulation of these small discrepancies would, of course, lead to a substantial loss that could severely impact your business's financial health.

Myth 2—fraud is very hard to detect

The misconception that fraud is hard to detect can cause negligence in financial governance, making organizations vulnerable to fraudulent activities. The truth is, with aggressive monitoring and the usage of modern data integrity management and monitoring tools, many fraudulent activities can be detected much earlier.

> **Note**
>
> Due to the absence of monitoring processes and tools, a hypothetical not-for-profit organization failed to notice irregularities in its financial statements for years, which allowed a bookkeeper to steal funds for a long period of time. Eventually, an external audit revealed the fraud. However, the organization already suffered financial and reputational damage, which illustrates the importance of robust internal controls and regular audits.

Myth 3—prosecution completely deters fraud

While prosecuting fraudsters is necessary, the belief that it considerably discourages fraud is a misconception. New fraud schemes constantly emerge, which emphasizes the need for proactive prevention measures. The evolving nature of fraudulent schemes demands a multifaceted approach to fraud prevention and deterrence. Despite high-profile prosecutions of fraud cases that we see in the news, numerous fraudulent schemes, such as asset misappropriation and scams, continue to plague individuals and businesses alike. These cases illustrate that prosecution alone is not a sufficient deterrent, and a proactive, systematic approach to fraud prevention is critical.

Myth 4—preventing fraud is only important for big institutions

The belief that fraud prevention is mainly for large institutions leaves small businesses vulnerable to fraud. Fraud prevention measures are essential for organizations of all sizes to safeguard their assets and ensure that the business continues to run properly.

> **Note**
>
> One example of a scam against small businesses is overpayments. The fraudster will pretend to be a buyer responding to an online or newspaper advertisement. After that, the scammer will pretend to send a payment via check or credit card that exceeds the agreed price. The scammer will then request for the victim to *return* the overpayment before that person realizes that it is a scam. This incident shows that businesses need to implement fraud prevention measures irrespective of size.

Myth 5—large companies are the common targets of fraud

The myth that fraudsters mainly target big corporations overlooks the vulnerability of small businesses and individuals. Fraudsters often exploit the lack of robust financial controls and oversights in smaller entities. Even a small family-run business can suffer from a significant financial loss due to inadequate financial controls. This example reiterates that fraud is not exclusive to large corporations and emphasizes the need to implement fraud prevention measures across all businesses of all sizes.

Now that we have discussed these myths and misconceptions, let's now discuss how financial reports are interpreted. This topic will help us better understand how fraudulent transactions affect a report's integrity and how we can detect these transactions and anomalies.

Interpreting financial reports

In *Chapter 1, Recognizing the Importance of Data Integrity in Finance*, we covered the most common types of financial statements: the **balance sheet**, **income statement**, and **cash flow statement**. In this section, we will build on these concepts and discuss how they are interpreted. I recommend going back to the basic concepts we discussed in that chapter to help familiarize yourselves with these topics further.

Financial statement analysis is a skill that business professionals and leaders need to equip themselves with. Understanding what these financial reports are and how to read them effectively will help you better understand what impacts a business's key drivers and how to make better decisions based on the data.

Here are the types of analysis that can be done to further understand the financial reports that we will cover in this chapter:

- Horizontal or trend analysis
- Vertical analysis
- Competitor and industry analysis
- Cash flow analysis

Horizontal or trend analysis

Horizontal analysis is a method used in financial statement analysis to assess the changes in financial data *over a specific period*, typically comparing the data from one period to another. It involves examining the line items of financial statements, such as the income statement or the balance sheet, and analyzing the changes in percentage or dollar amount between the periods.

> **Note**
>
> This analysis provides insights into the trends, growth rates, and overall performance of a company over time, which is why it is also called **trend analysis**.

Horizontal analysis can be performed for the different financial statements of the company. In this section, we will do a horizontal analysis of our hypothetical balance sheet for XYZ Company, as seen in *Figure 7.2*:

XYZ Company
Balance Sheet
As of December 31, 2022 and December 31, 2021 (in USD)

Assets		
Current Assets	**Dec 31, 2022**	**Dec 31, 2021**
Cash and cash equivalents	$ 53,174	$ 10,000
Accounts receivable	14,000	12,000
Inventory	12,500	18,000
Prepaid expense	2,500	2,000
Total current assets	**82,174**	**42,000**
Property, plant, and equipment - net		
Equipment	52,000	52,000
Less: accumulated depreciation	(9,750)	(3,250)
Land	60,000	60,000
Building	260,000	-
Less: accumulated depreciation	(3,900)	-
Property, plant, and equipment - net	**358,350**	**108,750**
Intangible assets - net		
Intangible assets	18,000	18,000
Less: accumulated amortization	(6,500)	(2,500)
Intangible assets - net	**11,500**	**15,500**
Total non-current assets	**369,850**	**124,250**
Total assets	**$ 452,024**	**$ 166,250**
Liabilities and Shareholders' Equity		
Current Liabilities		
Accounts payable	$ 28,012	$ 25,000
Accrued interest	3,900	-
Notes payable	15,000	15,000
Accrued expenses	4,476	6,000
Total current liabilities	**51,388**	**46,000**
Loans Payable	119,000	25,000
Long-term debt	**119,000**	**25,000**
Total liabilities	**170,388**	**71,000**
Shareholders' Equity		
Common stock	75,000	23,000
Additional paid-in capital	45,000	16,000
Retained earnings	161,636	56,250
Shareholders' Equity	**281,636**	**95,250**
Total liabilities and shareholders' equity	**$ 452,024**	**$ 166,250**

Figure 7.2 – Balance sheet example

By examining this balance sheet, we can get information about the *health* of the company. Here are some observations we can gather from this report (amounts are in USD):

- The reporting period ends on **December 31, 2022**, compared with a similar reporting period from the previous year ending on **December 31, 2021**
- The company's total assets for the current year are worth $452,024, which includes $82,174 worth of current assets and $369,850 worth of non-current assets
- The company's total liabilities are $170,388, which includes $51,388 worth of current liabilities and $119,000 worth of non-current liabilities made entirely of loans payable
- The company's shareholders' equity is $281,636, which includes $161,636 worth of retained earnings during this reporting period
- The total liabilities and shareholders' equity is $452,024, which equals the company's total assets

To understand the report further, we can perform a horizontal analysis on the balance sheet and gain a much deeper understanding of the numbers. The following list details the step-by-step procedure on how to do this:

1. **Obtain the comparative financial reports available**: Publicly listed companies in the United States have their financial reports available and published as required by the SEC. As a minimum, you need two periods available, but if you are able to get three or more years, the trends become much more visible because you can see the year-over-year changes. If information is available on a per-quarter basis, a quarter-over-quarter analysis can be done as well.

   For this example, we will use the hypothetical balance sheet information from *Figure 7.2*.

2. **Calculate the variance in terms of dollar value and percentage per line item**: In our example, we have information for our balance sheet items from December 31, 2022 and December 31, 2021. To get the variance in dollar value, we need to compare the difference for each line item for the two years. In this case, 2022 is our comparison year, while 2021 is our base year. Next, we calculate the percentage change by getting the variance, dividing it by the base year, and multiplying it by 100.

   Let's go back to our example and take **Cash and cash equivalents**, which is the first item on our balance sheet. We calculate the movement from 2021 to 2022 by getting the variance between these two years. In this case, **Cash and cash equivalents** increased from **$10,000** to **$53,174**, or by **$43,174**. Next, to get the percentage change, we divide **$43,174** by **$10,000** which is the amount for our base year. We multiply it by 100 to get 432%. *Figure 7.3* illustrates this step; the analysis is plotted on the right side of the financial data:

XYZ Company
Balance Sheet
As of December 31, 2022 and December 31, 2021 (in USD)

Assets	Dec 31, 2022	Dec 31, 2021	Analysis: Variance USD	Analysis: Variance %
Current Assets				
Cash and cash equivalents	$ 53,174	$ 10,000	43,174	432%
Accounts receivable	14,000	12,000		
Inventory	12,500	18,000		
Prepaid expense	2,500	2,000		
Total current assets	**82,174**	**42,000**		

Figure 7.3 – Calculating the variance in dollar value and percentage

Next, let's do this for all the line items, as seen in *Figure 7.4*:

XYZ Company
Balance Sheet
As of December 31, 2022 and December 31, 2021 (in USD)

Assets	Dec 31, 2022	Dec 31, 2021	Analysis: Variance USD	Analysis: Variance %
Current Assets				
Cash and cash equivalents	$ 53,174	$ 10,000	43,174	432%
Accounts receivable	14,000	12,000	2,000	17%
Inventory	12,500	18,000	(5,500)	(31%)
Prepaid expense	2,500	2,000	500	25%
Total current assets	**82,174**	**42,000**	**40,174**	**96%**
Property, plant, and equipment - net				
Equipment	52,000	52,000	-	-
Less: accumulated depreciation	(9,750)	(3,250)	(6,500)	200%
Land	60,000	60,000	-	-
Building	260,000	-	260,000	#DIV/0!
Less: accumulated depreciation	(3,900)	-	(3,900)	#DIV/0!
Property, plant, and equipment - net	**358,350**	**108,750**	**249,600**	**230%**
Intangible assets - net				
Intangible assets	18,000	18,000	-	-
Less: accumulated amortization	(6,500)	(2,500)	(4,000)	160%
Intangible assets - net	**11,500**	**15,500**	**(4,000)**	**(26%)**
Total non-current assets	**369,850**	**124,250**	**245,600**	**198%**
Total assets	**$ 452,024**	**$ 166,250**	**285,774**	**172%**
Liabilities and Shareholders' Equity			**Analysis**	
Current Liabilities				
Accounts payable	$ 28,012	$ 25,000	3,012	12%
Accrued interest	3,900	-	3,900	#DIV/0!
Notes payable	15,000	15,000	-	-
Accrued expenses	4,476	6,000	(1,524)	(25%)
Total current liabilities	**51,388**	**46,000**	**5,388**	**12%**
Loans Payable	119,000	25,000	94,000	376%
Long-term debt	**119,000**	**25,000**	**94,000**	**376%**
Total liabilities	**170,388**	**71,000**	**99,388**	**140%**
Shareholders' Equity				
Common stock	75,000	23,000	52,000	226%
Additional paid-in capital	45,000	16,000	29,000	181%
Retained earnings	161,636	56,250	105,386	187%
Shareholders' Equity	**281,636**	**95,250**	**186,386**	**196%**
Total liabilities and shareholders' equity	**$ 452,024**	**$ 166,250**	**285,774**	**172%**

Figure 7.4 – Performing horizontal analysis on the balance sheet

3. **Analyze the results**: Now that we have calculated the change between the two years, our next step is to check and analyze the movements per line item.

At this point, we can start asking questions such as the following:

- How much have my assets liabilities, and shareholders' equity changed in the last year?
- Which accounts are showing the most significant changes?
- Are they going up or down?
- Are these in line with my expectations and do they reflect the business transactions that occurred during the year?
- How do the changes in these accounts affect one another, and are they related to other financial statements available?

Here are some observations we can gather from examining the balance sheet figures and our calculations:

- **Current Assets**: Current assets increased significantly by $40,174, or 96%, driven largely by the increase in cash
- **Property, plant, and equipment—net**: Property, plant, and equipment increased by $249,600, or 230%, mainly due to the acquisition of the building at a cost of $260,000 in 2022
- **Long-term debt**: Long-term debt has increased by $94,000, or 376%, as a result of obtaining a loan
- **Shareholders' Equity**: Shareholders' equity has increased by a total of $186,386, or 196%, mainly due to retained earnings and the issuance of common stock in 2022

> **Note**
>
> You will notice that for the building and its related accumulated depreciation, we are getting **#DIV/0!** in our percentage calculation since we are dividing an amount by zero. This is useful in our analysis as we can see that there is something that has been added or is new to the data when comparing year over year.

Looking at these figures, we can dive deeper to see how the business transactions affect the financial accounts and how they could potentially impact the other financial statements:

- **Capital expenditure**: Given that the company acquired a building at a cost of $260,000 during the year, we can ask how it was financed. Looking at the changes in the other accounts, it looks like the company financed it largely by issuing long-term debt and issuance of stock, resulting in the significant increase noted for these accounts. These changes should be reflected in the **statement of cash flows** for the company.

The acquisition of the building should also affect our depreciation or the *process of allocating the building's cost over its expected useful life*. We should expect to see an increase in this account when we examine the statement of profit and loss for the company. We can also ask how many years we are expecting to use the building for and for how much we can sell it at the end of its useful life.

- **Cash reserves**: Our cash increased significantly by $43,174, or 432%, compared with the prior year. This creates a favorable impact on the company's *liquidity* and reflects the company's ability to pay its short-term debts.

  Cash is a critical account, with the goal of a business being not only to operate profitably but also *to generate cash from its operations*. Additional information about how a company generated its cash during the year is detailed further through the statement of cash flows. Moreover, additional analysis to measure key metrics can be done by calculating **liquidity** ratios, **working capital** ratios, and the **cash cycle**, which will be useful in understanding the business further.

- **Key financial ratios**: Financial ratios can be calculated from the balance sheet items to measure key ratios and evaluate a company's financial standing *as of a specific point in time*. In addition to the liquidity ratios and working capital ratios measured previously, other ratios such as **leverage** ratios and **solvency** ratios can be measured as well.

  Financial ratios can also be calculated by taking key figures from the other financial statements and assessing them with each other. For example, we can take the net income from the **statement of profit and loss** and use it to calculate the *return on assets* or *return on equity* based on the balance sheet. Doing this can give us a lot of insight into the financial performance of a company.

As we will cover in the next section, *Learning how fraudulent transactions affect overall financial report integrity*, companies can be under extreme pressure to meet financial targets and key ratios. This can lead to an increased motivation to commit financial statement fraud, which can be in the form of overstating assets or understating liabilities.

Performing horizontal analysis on the balance sheet has provided us with a lot of insight into the business year over year. Now that we have covered this, let's discuss how vertical analysis is done and how this analysis can help us gain deeper insights into the company's performance.

Vertical analysis

Vertical analysis is a technique used in financial statement analysis to evaluate the proportional representation of individual line items within a financial statement. It involves expressing each line item **as a percentage of a base figure**, typically the *total revenue* (in the case of an income statement) or the *total assets* (in the case of a balance sheet). By doing so, vertical analysis allows for a comprehensive understanding of the relative significance of each line item and its contribution to the overall financial picture of a company.

Let's take, for example, the income statement for our hypothetical company, as seen in *Figure 7.5*:

XYZ Company
Statement of Profit and Loss
For the Year Ended December 31, 2022 (in USD)

Comparative financial statement		
Gross Sales	**Dec 31, 2022**	**Dec 31, 2021**
Product A	$ 525,000	$ 475,000
Product B	85,000	85,000
Total Sales	**610,000**	**560,000**
Total Cost of Goods Sold		
Beginning Inventory	18,000	5,000
Purchases	230,000	200,000
Less: Ending Inventory	12,500	18,000
Total Cost of Goods Sold	**235,500**	**187,000**
Gross Profit	**374,500**	**373,000**
Expenses		
Franchise Fee	50,000	50,000
Insurance	15,000	5,000
Maintenance and Repairs	8,000	3,500
Office Supplies	5,000	3,000
Office Rent	25,000	26,750
Depreciation Expense	10,400	3,250
Amortization Expense	4,000	2,500
Utilities	16,750	8,000
Wages	30,000	30,000
Total Operating Expenses	**164,150**	**132,000**
Operating Income	**210,350**	**241,000**
Interest expense	3,900	-
Net Income Before Taxes	**206,450**	**241,000**
Taxes on Income	66,064	77,120
Net Income After Taxes	**$ 140,386**	**$ 163,880**

Figure 7.5 – Sample statement of profit and loss

This income statement provides information on how the company generated its income during the period covered in the report. Here are some findings we can glean from this report for the period ending **December 31, 2022**:

- The company had total sales of $610,000 coming from two main products
- The total cost of goods sold was $235,500 to realize this level of sales, leading to a gross profit of $374,500 for the year

- Total operating expenses of $164,150 were taken from the gross profit, leading to an operating income of $210,350
- After deducting $3,900 of interest expense, taxes on income of $66,064 have been calculated based on the net income before taxes, leading to a net income of $140,386 after taxes for the year

To understand the report further, we can perform vertical analysis on the income statement and gain a much deeper understanding of the numbers. The following list details the step-by-step procedures on how to do this:

1. **Obtain the comparative financial reports available**: As we covered in our discussion of horizontal analysis, public companies have their financial reports available and published as required by the SEC in the United States. Comparative reports for two reporting periods can be used in this analysis, but if you are able to get three or more years, it becomes easier to spot the trends and anomalies.

   In this example, we will use the hypothetical income statement in *Figure 7.5*.

2. **Calculate each line item as a percentage of a base figure in the report**: For the income statement, the *base figure* to be used is gross sales, and each line item will be stated as *a percentage of this key figure*. In our example, we have information from our income statement for the years ending December 31, 2022 and December 31, 2021. In this case, total sales will be our base figure, and then we divide each line item with this account.

   Going back to our example, we will take the gross sales of $610,000 and $560,000 for 2022 and 2021, respectively, and use them as our base figure, from which to calculate our percentages. In this case, we will divide the first line item, which is the gross sales from Product A in 2022 ($525,500), and divide it by the total sales ($610,000) to give us 86.1%. Let's do this for 2021 as well by dividing $475,000 by $560,000 to get 84.8%. *Figure 7.6* illustrates this step; the analysis is shown on the right side of the comparative income statement:

XYZ Company
Statement of Profit and Loss
For the Year Ended December 31, 2022 (in USD)

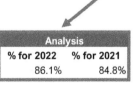

Comparative financial statement			Analysis	
Gross Sales	**Dec 31, 2022**	**Dec 31, 2021**	**% for 2022**	**% for 2021**
Product A	$ 525,000	$ 475,000	86.1%	84.8%
Product B	85,000	85,000		
Total Sales	**610,000**	**560,000**		

Figure 7.6 – Calculating each line item as a percentage of a base figure

3. The next step is to do this for all the line items, as shown in *Figure 7.7*:

XYZ Company
Statement of Profit and Loss
For the Year Ended December 31, 2022 (in USD)

Comparative financial statement				Analysis	
Gross Sales		**Dec 31, 2022**	**Dec 31, 2021**	**% for 2022**	**% for 2021**
Product A	$	525,000 $	475,000	86.1%	84.8%
Product B		85,000	85,000	13.9%	15.2%
Total Sales		**610,000**	**560,000**	**100.0%**	**100.0%**
Total Cost of Goods Sold					
Beginning Inventory		18,000	5,000	3.0%	0.9%
Purchases		230,000	200,000	37.7%	35.7%
Less: Ending Inventory		12,500	18,000	2.0%	3.2%
Total Cost of Goods Sold		**235,500**	**187,000**	**38.6%**	**33.4%**
Gross Profit		**374,500**	**373,000**	**61.4%**	**66.6%**
Expenses					
Franchise Fee		50,000	50,000	8.2%	8.9%
Insurance		15,000	5,000	2.5%	0.9%
Maintenance and Repairs		8,000	3,500	1.3%	0.6%
Office Supplies		5,000	3,000	0.8%	0.5%
Office Rent		25,000	26,750	4.1%	4.8%
Depreciation Expense		10,400	3,250	1.7%	0.6%
Amortization Expense		4,000	2,500	0.7%	0.4%
Utilities		16,750	8,000	2.7%	1.4%
Wages		30,000	30,000	4.9%	5.4%
Total Operating Expenses		**164,150**	**132,000**	**26.9%**	**23.6%**
Operating Income		**210,350**	**241,000**	**34.5%**	**43.0%**
Interest expense		3,900	-	0.6%	0.0%
Net Income Before Taxes		**206,450**	**241,000**	**33.8%**	**43.0%**
Taxes on Income		66,064	77,120	10.8%	13.8%
Net Income After Taxes	**$**	**140,386 $**	**163,880**	**23.0%**	**29.3%**

Figure 7.7 – Performing vertical analysis on the income statement

4. **Analyze the results**: Now that we have computed each line as a percentage of the total sales, our next step is to analyze and interpret how the items relate to each other. Reviewing them in this manner and seeing the income statement accounts as a percentage makes it easier to see the relative proportion of the numbers. This is the reason why vertical analysis is also called *common-size analysis*; it puts the financial results into context and makes it easier to compare financial performance across periods and even across industries.

At this point, we can start asking questions such as the following:

- Which product or service is contributing most to sales or revenues?
- Is the cost of production increasing or decreasing year over year?
- Did the gross profit margin increase or decrease year over year?
- Where am I seeing significant changes?
- Are these changes in line with expectations and reflecting the business transactions or other factors that occurred during the year?
- How do these changes affect one another, and how do they relate to the rest of the financial information that I have available?
- How do these margins compare with other companies in a similar industry? Are they selling similar products at a higher price or do they have lower costs of production?

Here are some observations we can gather from examining the income statement figures and calculations:

- **Sales**: The gross sales in 2022 for Product A are 86.1% of total sales compared to 13.9% for Product B. In terms of percentage, the company's total sales for Product A are slightly higher than in 2021 at 84.8%. Product B contributed a slightly lower percentage of sales, from 15.2% to 13.9%.
- **Cost of Goods Sold**: The total cost of goods sold increased as a percentage of total sales year over year from 33.4% in 2021 to 38.6% in 2022.
- **Gross Profit**: Gross profit has decreased from 66.6% in 2021 to 61.4% due to the increase in cost of goods sold.
- **Operating Expenses**: Total operating expenses as a percentage of total sales have increased from 23.6% in 2021 to 26.9% in 2022. Looking at the percentages, we can see that this is driven by the increase in insurance expense, depreciation expense, and utilities.
- **Taxes on Income**: We can see a decrease in taxes on income from 13.8% to 10.8% as a percentage of total sales. We are seeing a decrease because our total sales increased year over year. To get a better picture of this account and get more context, it can be compared with **Net Income Before Taxes**, as this is what the tax is based on.
- **Net Income Before and After Taxes**: Net income before taxes significantly decreased from 43.0% in 2021 to 33.8% in 2022. We can see the cumulative effect of the impact coming from the increase in the cost of goods sold and in total operating expenses year over year.

  Net income after taxes decreased as well, from 29.3% in 2022 to 23.0% in 2021. The net income percentage is an indicator of how profitable the business has been and how much profit is left after taking out all the expenses incurred during the year.

Examining these figures, we can go deeper and see how the business transactions affect the income statement report and how they interplay with the other financial statements. At the same time, we can use this to check whether there are business reasons for the change or potential anomalies in the information.

- **Cost of goods sold**: The cost of production increased year over year. We need to check what is causing this increase. Is this caused by an increase in the cost of the materials used in the production? What changed during the year that had an impact on the cost? Have we accounted for the ending inventory correctly?

  Alternatively, we can review the total sales and check whether we have recognized the sales in the proper period. We can see an increase in sales for Product A, but Product B has remained the same year over year at $85,000.

- **Operating expenses**: The operating expenses increased year over year. The income statement does not provide enough information as to whether the expense is fixed or variable. Given that the operating expense increased as a percentage of total sales, were there changes during the year that caused this to increase?

  We know from our analysis of the balance sheet that a building was acquired during the year. Could this be behind what is driving the increase in utilities, depreciation, and insurance expenses?

- **Net income**: Understanding the company's profitability is important. This answers an important question: *out of every dollar the company earns, how much of that covers the cost and how much generates profit?* Knowing this number is powerful, especially when you can compare it with the prior year or against competitors or other companies in the industry.

Competitor and industry analysis

Competitor analysis is a critical business practice that involves evaluating and understanding the strengths and weaknesses of rivals operating in the market. By gathering information about your competitor's strategies, products or services, pricing, and marketing tactics, you can gain valuable insights to help make better-informed business decisions.

At the same time, by measuring the financial ratios of a company's performance and comparing it with its competitors in the industry, a business can better understand how efficiently or profitably its competitors are operating, how they pay their obligations or liabilities, or how they finance their operations. Understanding this can provide some insight into where improvements can be made or highlight areas with irregularities.

To help with the analysis, we can ask questions to gain insights and make meaningful comparisons:

- How does our **current ratio** compare with our competitors'?
- What is the trend in our **quick ratio** compared to industry averages?
- How does our **gross profit margin** compare to our competitors'?

- Is our **net profit margin** higher or lower than industry averages?
- Are we more efficient in managing **accounts receivable** compared to our competitors?
- What is the **debt-to-equity ratio** of our competitors, and how does this compare to ours?
- How do our **financial leverage ratios** compare to our competitors?

In our hypothetical example, the net income after tax percentage is trending between 23% and 30%. We can compare this performance to competitors in our field and consider how our competitors are performing. *Is this the normal trend in the industry? If there is a significant gap, what could be causing it?*

Asking these questions can help evaluate and compare the business's financial performance against competitors, identify areas of strength and weakness, and detect potential errors. Moreover, by performing these types of analyses, we can gauge the reasonableness, dependability, and accuracy of the financial reports, which are founded on the integrity and quality of the data.

Cash flow analysis

In this section, we will analyze the statement of cash flows for a hypothetical company, as seen in *Figure 7.8*:

XYZ Company
Statement of Cash Flows
For the Year Ended December 31, 2022 (in USD)

Cash flows from operating activities	**Amount**
Net income	$ 140,386
Adjustments to reconcile net income to net cash provided by operating activities:	
Depreciation and amortization	14,400
Changes in current assets and liabilities:	
Increase in accounts receivable	(2,000)
Increase in prepaid expenses	(500)
Decrease in inventory	5,500
Increase in accounts payable	3,012
Increase in accrued interest	3,900
Decrease in accrued expenses	(1,524)
Net cash provided by operating activities	**163,174**
Cash flows from investing activities	
Capital expenditures	(260,000)
Net cash used from investing activities	**(260,000)**
Cash flows from financing activities	
Proceeds from issuance of long-term debt	94,000
Issuance of common stock	81,000
Dividends paid	(35,000)
Net cash provided by financing activities	**140,000**
Net increase in cash during the year	43,174
Cash at the beginning of the year	10,000
Cash at the end of the year	**$ 53,174**

Figure 7.8 – Statement of cash flows for a hypothetical company

As we can see from the report, cash flows come from the different activities done by the company:

- **Operating activities**: The cash inflows and outflows from operating activities relate to the generation and use of funds in normal, day-to-day business operations.
- **Investing activities**: The cash inflows and outflows from investing activities relate to the purchasing and selling of assets such as marketable securities, real estate, or intangible assets.
- **Financing activities**: Cash inflows and outflows from financing activities refer to transactions involving debt and equity.

Here are some observations that we can gather from examining the cash flow statement figures:

- **Cash flows from operating activities**: The statement of cash flows has been prepared using the **indirect method** where the cash flow calculation starts with the net income for the period. The net income is used as a *starting point* and adjusted with the transactions that would impact cash given that the income is calculated using the accrual method of accounting.

  From the net income of $140,386 for 2022, adjustments have been made for the depreciation and amortization, as well as the changes in current assets and liabilities to get the cash flow from operations of $163,174. Net income and cash flow from operations usually move in the same direction, though there are cases when that is not the case.

  Having a positive cash flow is a sign that the company is generating cash from its day-to-day operations.

- **Cash flows from investing activities**: We can see that the company paid $260,000 of capital expenditures in 2022 relating to the purchase of the building.
- **Cash flows from financing activities**: To finance the purchase of the building, the company issued long-term debt of $94,000 and common stock of $81,000. At the same time, it paid its shareholders dividends amounting to $35,000 during the year.
- **Net increase in cash**: The company significantly increased its cash from $10,000 to $53,174 in 2022. Having available cash is a good indicator of the company's ability to meet its financial obligations. However, an assessment of the reasonableness of the cash available should also be made, and an analysis of where to use the funds should be conducted to potentially pay off debt or invest back into the company.

Having discussed the different types of financial analysis available, we have set the foundation for the next section to see how the types of fraud affect overall financial report integrity.

Learning how fraudulent transactions affect overall financial report integrity

In this section, we will discuss fraudulent transactions and their damaging effects on the overall integrity of financial reports. Fraudulent transactions, characterized by deceit, manipulation, and misrepresentation, pose a significant threat to the credibility and accuracy of financial information.

There are governing bodies all over the world that are involved in fraud prevention to safeguard the interests of investors, uphold a fair and productive market, and aid in capital investments. Some of the major regulatory bodies in the world include the **Securities and Exchange Commission** (**SEC**) in the United States, the **Financial Conduct Authority** (**FCA**) in the United Kingdom, the **Financial Services Agency** (**FSA**) in Japan, and the **Australian Securities and Investments Commission** (**ASIC**) in Australia.

According to the SEC, the most common reasons for committing fraud are as follows:

- **Fulfilling earnings projections**: Being able to hit earnings targets is often linked to a company's financial stability and management's effectiveness, which stakeholders and investors highly regard. However, this *pressure* to achieve or exceed targets can tempt individuals and organizations to engage in fraud. By manipulating earnings, reports can show better financial performance to meet the expectations of investors.
- **Raising the value of the company's share price**: Boosting a company's stock value is often aimed at improving the market outlook and enriching shareholder value. However, this can lead to the *motivation* to tamper with financial reports or other behaviors that can lead to elevating stock prices, misleading investors, and creating a false sense of financial security.
- **Hiding the declining financial state of the company**: Hiding the deteriorating financial status of a business is a tactic employed to deceive investors and prevent the decline of the value of its shares. By doing so, companies can temporarily hide the true state of the company's financial health, giving a false impression of steadiness or growth. This can encompass a variety of techniques such as *inflating revenues*, *not recognizing liabilities*, or *capitalizing expenses*, which enhances the financial outlook of the business.
- **Enhancing the company's performance to secure upcoming investments or debt financing**: Engaging in fraudulent actions to boost the company's performance can temporarily portray an illusion of financial solidity and stability. Investors and creditors rely on financial statements to gain an understanding of the company's ability to meet its short-term and long-term liabilities and obligations. In addition to this, there are also agreements between lenders and borrowers wherein **financial covenants** are put in place to protect the lender. An example would be for the borrower to maintain *a good credit standing* or maintain a certain *debt-to-equity ratio*, which is the level of total debt the company has divided by its total equity.

- **Boosting management compensation**: By engaging in fraudulent behavior through enhancing the reports and performance of the business, management can improve the outlook of the business to exceed the financial targets and unlock performance-based bonuses and incentives. Moreover, management might engage in practices to hide the declining performance of the business to keep their jobs.

Fraud can come in different forms, and it is not always possible to eliminate the risk of fraud. In this section, we will discuss scenarios involving **fictitious revenues**, **improper capitalization of expenses**, and **misrepresentation of liabilities and debt**. Now that we have discussed common reasons why individuals and businesses engage in fraud, let's look into specific examples of how financial reports can be altered to improve the financial outlook.

Fictitious revenues

According to the study done by the **Committee of Sponsoring Organizations** (**COSO**) on *Fraudulent Financial Reporting: 1998–2007*, the primary methods employed in fraudulent activities often involved the improper recognition of revenue (61% of companies that committed fraud), followed by overstating assets or capitalizing expenses (51%).

One of the most well-known financial statement fraud cases in history is a scandal that was accomplished by artificially boosting revenues and capitalizing expenses by recording reported line cost expenses as assets. The company was experiencing a decline and was not generating revenue. The company presented itself as a business with significant growth potential with a target of double-digit growth. It also aimed to keep its reported line cost expenses at 42% of revenues.

In the *Report of Investigation*, it was found that significant revenue account adjustments were made after the quarter close in order to report that they had achieved the ambitious revenue growth targets set by the CEO and CFO.

During the investigation, they uncovered revenue discrepancies amounting to more than $958 million that were inaccurately recorded by the company from the first quarter of 1999 to the first quarter of 2002. In addition to this, their accounting advisors had identified an additional $1.107 billion in recorded revenue in this timeframe. This was questionable due to the circumstances surrounding the records and the insufficient evidence available.

Improper capitalization of expenses

Continuing our example of this scandal, the company improperly classified the reported line cost expenses, which were payments made to external firms for utilizing their telephone lines as assets. During the investigation, they uncovered about $3.506 billion in line costs improperly capitalized or recorded as assets from the first quarter of 2021 to the first quarter of 2022. In addition to this, they uncovered about $377 million in adjustments to reduce line costs, resulting in a total of $3.883 billion.

The improper entries were made to keep the reported line cost expenses at 42% of revenues, even though with the declining revenues, this percentage was actually much higher. The company responded by creating fictitious revenues and improperly capitalizing expenses to create the impression that it was growing and operating profitably.

> **Note**
>
> This malpractice not only jeopardized the company's reputation but also misled stakeholders, investors, and the general public about its financial health. Such manipulations in financial reporting can have severe legal repercussions and can lead to a loss of trust in the market.

Misrepresentation of liabilities and debt

Leverage ratios are critical indicators used by analysts to assess a company's financial risk and stability. Lowering leverage ratios is generally perceived as positive, as it suggests a decrease in the proportion of debt relative to equity. This reduction implies lower financial risk and a stronger ability to manage debt obligations.

Unfortunately, some organizations engage in questionable accounting practices aimed at artificially lowering their leverage ratios, giving a false impression of stability. One method employed was the utilization of a financial instrument known as **Repo 105**. By temporarily removing substantial amounts of debt from its balance sheet just before reporting periods, one company created the illusion of reduced debt and improved leverage ratios.

These deceptive practices misled investors and analysts, painting a rosier financial picture than reality. Stakeholders were led to believe that the company had effectively minimized its financial risks and was on a healthier trajectory. However, when the true extent of its financial troubles came to light, it shattered investor confidence, ultimately resulting in the firm's collapse and subsequent bankruptcy.

> **Note**
>
> This scandal serves as a reminder of the critical importance of rigorous and meticulous financial statement analysis. It underscores the need for transparency, integrity, and thorough scrutiny when evaluating a company's financial well-being. Instances of deceptive practices, such as those employed by this company, can mask underlying risks and have far-reaching consequences for investors and the overall stability of the financial system.

Now that we have covered how fraudulent transactions affect overall financial report integrity, we will now head to the last section of our chapter, about the different ways to spot and stop fraudulent transactions.

Detecting and preventing fraudulent transactions and anomalies

While the impact of fraudulent transactions on financial report integrity is significant, there are measures that organizations can take to mitigate such risks, which we will discuss in this section.

Tone at the top

The **tone at the top** significantly impacts the level of fraud risk within an organization. When leaders and top management demonstrate a strong commitment to ethical behavior and integrity, it sets the foundation for a *culture of honesty* and *transparency* throughout the organization. This influences employees' attitudes and behaviors and ultimately shapes the organization's overall approach to fraud prevention. A **positive** tone at the top sends a clear message that unethical conduct, including fraud, will not be tolerated. It establishes the expectation that employees are expected to adhere to high ethical standards in their work. This tone should be consistently communicated and reinforced through various means, such as formal policies, training programs, and leading by example.

Conversely, a **weak** or **ambiguous tone** at the top can increase fraud risk within an organization. If leaders do not emphasize the importance of ethical conduct or fail to address fraudulent behavior promptly and decisively, it creates an atmosphere where unethical actions may go unchecked. This lack of commitment to ethical behavior can lead to a higher likelihood of fraud occurring, as employees may feel less constrained by the organization's values and more inclined to engage in fraudulent activities.

> Note
>
> This was what happened in a company where the CEO generated the underlying pressure for fraud. According to the investigation, he insisted on achieving the outcomes he had promised, displaying a disregard for the procedures that were meant to prevent inaccurate reporting. Moreover, critical financial information was restricted to a select group of senior executives. Over time, an increasing number of employees became aware of certain aspects that were deemed inappropriate.

Implementing strong internal controls

Strong internal controls within an organization act as a **safeguard** and **barrier** against fraudulent transactions and illicit activities. At the core of these internal controls is the ability to monitor, detect, and prevent unauthorized or irregular transactions that could indicate possible fraudulent activities. This involves the implementation of various controls, such as the segregation of duties, which we discussed in *Chapter 2, Avoiding Common Data Integrity Issues and Challenges in Finance Teams*, wherein no single individual has sole control over all parts of a transaction. This ensures that an individual cannot initiate, approve, and reconcile a transaction, which reduces the opportunity for fraudulent activity.

In addition to this, implementing strong view controls where only authorized personnel can access sensitive financial information also safeguards the organization against internal and external threats.

> **Important note**
>
> **Auditing**, both *internal* and *external*, also plays a critical role in detecting and preventing fraudulent transactions. Regular audits review and scrutinize the authenticity and reasonability of the financial records of an organization, ensuring that discrepancies and irregularities are identified in a timely manner. Automated systems for monitoring transactions and analyzing patterns can also be highly effective in detecting potential fraud. For instance, if a system is programmed to recognize and flag unusual transactions or amounts, it can quickly bring potential issues to the attention of management for further investigation. In addition to this, a **whistleblower program**, which allows employees and other stakeholders to report suspected fraudulent activities confidentially, can also serve as a vital internal control mechanism, enabling the organization to address issues proactively.

The implementation of strong internal controls cultivates and promotes a culture of accountability and integrity within an organization. By ensuring that transactions are conducted transparently and in compliance with applicable laws and regulations, organizations can safeguard their assets and enhance their credibility and trustworthiness in the eyes of stakeholders. A company that invests in strong internal controls demonstrates a commitment to ethical practices and financial stewardship, which can contribute significantly to its long-term sustainability and success.

Management review

Management review plays a vital role in the proactive detection and prevention of fraud within an organization. By regularly reviewing financial data, management can identify any irregularities or suspicious patterns that might indicate fraudulent activities. They analyze the information by comparing it with historical data, industry benchmarks, and budgeted figures to flag potential red flags that need further investigation.

If management detects any indicators of potential fraud during the review process, they promptly investigate the matter. Internal investigations may be conducted, involving the internal audit function or engaging external experts when necessary. Taking immediate action to address red flags not only helps prevent further losses but also acts as a deterrent for potential fraudsters.

> **Note**
>
> Management review also extends to overseeing the organizational structure and ensuring that an appropriate **segregation of duties** is maintained. Ensuring that no single individual has control over all phases of a transaction is pivotal in mitigating the risk of fraud. For example, the person responsible for approving vendors should not be the same person responsible for processing payments. Management should also engage in reviewing employee behaviors and lifestyles for any red flags indicative of fraud, such as employees living beyond their means or exhibiting secretive behavior regarding their work. By maintaining a level of vigilance and actively involving themselves in various aspects of the organization, management not only aids in detecting fraudulent activities but also in creating an environment that is resilient to these threats to safeguard the organization's assets and reputation.

Ratio analysis

Ratio analysis, which involves comparing different financial metrics and indicators, can be a valuable tool for detecting potentially fraudulent transactions within an organization. Anomalies or sudden changes in financial ratios that cannot be explained by normal business operations or market conditions might signal fraudulent activities or financial misstatements. For example, if the *accounts receivable turnover ratio*, which is a measure of how effective the collection process of a company is, suddenly drops without a corresponding change in credit policy or market conditions, it might indicate issues such as revenue recognition fraud. Similarly, a significant discrepancy between the growth rates of net income and cash flows from operating activities may suggest that a company is manipulating its earnings. This is because these two financial metrics are expected to move together, and also because cash flow cannot easily be altered compared to net income.

> **Note**
>
> Specifically, *ratio analysis* can help auditors and financial analysts identify red flags or indicators of possible fraudulent activities by enabling them to scrutinize the consistency, reasonability, and trends of financial information over time. For example, analyzing *profitability ratios* such as the gross profit margin and comparing them with industry benchmarks and historical data can unveil inconsistencies that might be due to fraudulent activities. If the margin is higher than the industry standard, further analysis needs to be done to determine why.

To effectively utilize ratio analysis in fraud detection, it is important to establish a benchmark of normal operational or industry ratios to which the company's actual ratios can be compared. Making use of a combination of horizontal, vertical, and industry comparative analyses, organizations can gain insights into any unusual fluctuations or discrepancies in their financial data. Furthermore, integrating ratio analysis with other forensic accounting techniques, such as **Benford's law**, the **Beneish model**, and indirect methods of reconstructing income, enhances the effectiveness of fraud detection mechanisms, providing a comprehensive approach to safeguarding the organization against fraudulent transactions.

Therefore, ratio analysis, when systematically integrated into an organization's internal audit and control framework, becomes a critical tool in strengthening its defense against financial fraud.

Utilizing data analytics and machine learning in fraud detection

Data analysis and **machine learning** (*a subset of artificial intelligence*) play a very important role in detecting and preventing fraudulent transactions by enabling organizations to review, analyze, and investigate large amounts of transactional data to identify inconsistencies, anomalies, or patterns that might suggest fraudulent activities. Using various techniques and algorithms, organizations are now able to build *models* that can help predict and identify potential fraud. Here are a few examples:

- **Clustering algorithms** can help group transactions into different categories, and any transaction that does not conform to a predefined category might be flagged for further investigation.
- **Classification algorithms** can be trained on historical data to identify transactions that are likely to be fraudulent based on past patterns.
- **Anomaly detection** techniques help identify outliers or transactions that deviate significantly from established patterns or norms. For example, a sudden spike in transactions from a particular location or transactions of unusually high value could be automatically flagged for further review.

Machine learning models can be trained to continually learn from new data, thereby enhancing their ability to detect fraudulent activities over time. With these, organizations can instantly detect and flag suspicious transactions to mitigate potential losses.

> **Note**
>
> In addition to what has been discussed already, auditors and investigators can utilize **network analysis** to visualize relationships between different entities and transactions and go through large volumes of financial data to uncover hidden patterns and relationships that would help uncover complex fraud schemes involving multiple parties.

At this point, you should have more tricks up your sleeve for detecting fraudulent transactions that could affect the integrity of financial reports! Feel free to read this section as many times as needed to help you grasp the important concepts discussed in this chapter.

Summary

Detecting fraudulent transactions that affect financial report integrity is a critical challenge faced by organizations worldwide. In this chapter, we covered the **fraud triangle** to understand potential causes of fraud. Next, we talked about how financial reports are interpreted and discussed the different kinds of financial analysis that can be done. In the next part of the chapter, we discussed how fraudulent transactions affect overall financial report integrity. We explored the most common examples of financial statement fraud in the forms of **fictitious revenues**, **improper capitalization of expenses,** and **misrepresentation of liabilities and debt**. As we closed the chapter, we learned about the different ways to detect and prevent fraudulent transactions and anomalies. This chapter has given you the foundational skills and capabilities to understand financial reports and fraud detection.

In the next chapter, we will learn how to use database locking techniques for financial transaction integrity. We will learn how specific SQL and database techniques can prevent transaction data integrity issues.

Further reading

We have barely scratched the surface of this topic. For more information on what we covered in this chapter, feel free to check out the following resources:

- *Forensic Analytics and Management Accountants Report*: `https://asiapac.imanet.org/research-publications/statements-on-management-accounting/forensic-analytics-and-management-accountants?`
- *Committee of Sponsoring Organizations of the Treadway Commission (COSO) Internal Control – Integrated Framework*: `https://www.coso.org/guidance-on-ic`
- *Enron: The Smartest Guys in the Room*: `https://www.youtube.com/watch?v=_0vRuHn9MmI`
- *Speech by SEC Staff: Why Does Fraud Occur and What Can Deter or Prevent It*: `https://www.sec.gov/news/speech/2008/spch090908lar.htm`
- *PwC's Global Economic Crime and Fraud Survey 2022*: `https://www.pwc.com/gx/en/services/forensics/economic-crime-survey.html`

Part 3: Modern Strategies to Manage the Data Integrity of Finance Systems

In this part, you will learn about intermediate and advanced solutions, including managed cloud-based ledger databases, database locks, and artificial intelligence, to manage the integrity of financial data in systems and databases.

This part has the following chapters:

- *Chapter 8, Using Database Locking Techniques for Financial Transaction Integrity*
- *Chapter 9, Using Managed Ledger Databases for Finance Data Integrity*
- *Chapter 10, Using Artificial Intelligence for Finance Data Quality Management*

8

Using Database Locking Techniques for Financial Transaction Integrity

In *Chapter 1, Recognizing the Importance of Data Integrity in Finance*, we discussed how locking techniques such as **mutual exclusion locks** can help maintain the integrity of transactions and financial data. These locking techniques (as well as the database constraints discussed in *Chapter 2, Avoiding Common Data Integrity Issues and Challenges in Finance Teams*) help ensure that financial numbers and transaction values add up, even if simultaneous actions or operations are happening at the same time. In this chapter, we'll build on top of what we learned in the previous chapters and dive deeper into how **race conditions** can affect financial transaction integrity in databases and how these race conditions can be handled properly. This chapter will offer practical guidance on using specific SQL and database techniques to prevent transaction data integrity inconsistencies and issues.

Here are the topics that we will cover in this chapter:

- Getting started with SQL
- Learning how **race conditions** impact the transaction integrity of financial systems
- Reviewing how database locks prevent financial transaction integrity issues
- Guaranteeing transaction integrity with **database locks**
- Best practices when using database locks

By the end of this chapter, you will have a better understanding of how race conditions affect the data integrity of financial transactions and how database lock—in particular, row-level locks—address this risk. Without further ado, let's begin!

Technical requirements

Before we dive into our discussion, we must have the following in place:

- A web browser (to download the PostgreSQL installer)
- **PostgreSQL** version 15 or later (If you haven't installed this yet on your machine, don't worry—we will cover the step-by-step installation in this chapter)

The PostgreSQL queries are saved in the Packt **GitHub** repository for this book and can be accessed at `https://github.com/PacktPublishing/Managing-Data-Integrity-for-Finance/tree/main/ch08`.

Once these are ready, you may proceed with the next steps.

Getting started with SQL

In *Chapter 5, Using Business Intelligence Tools to Fix Data Integrity Issues*, we worked with spreadsheets to manage and organize data. **Spreadsheets** can be used to perform various calculations, data processing, and basic data storage operations. However, there are other ways to store and manage information, especially when the data grows in volume. For one, we can make use of **databases**, which are specialized systems designed to store, retrieve, and manage vast amounts of structured data. They offer a structured framework with clear linkages between data tables, facilitating more effective data management and querying.

Structured Query Language (**SQL**) is a programming language that's used to manage relational databases. Two of the most popular types of relational databases are MySQL and PostgreSQL. **MySQL**, which was developed by Oracle, is the most widely used relational database management system. In this chapter, we will be using **PostgreSQL**, which is a free, powerful, open source relational database that allows for the structured storage of data. It is also **ACID**-compliant, which ensures that transactions are handled consistently and dependably. We will cover the ACID qualities—that is, **atomicity**, **consistency**, **isolation**, and **durability**—in the next part of this chapter. We will see how SQL can be used to manage the integrity of the data at the transaction level.

In this section, we will cover how to install PostgreSQL's **pgAdmin4**, learn how to create a database and a table, and then insert data into the table. We will be using what we create in this section for our hands-on example later in this chapter to address **race conditions** and use **row-level locks**.

With this in mind, let's head on to the next step!

Installing PostgreSQL

Go to `https://www.postgresql.org/download/`, as shown in *Figure 8.1*, to download the program installer:

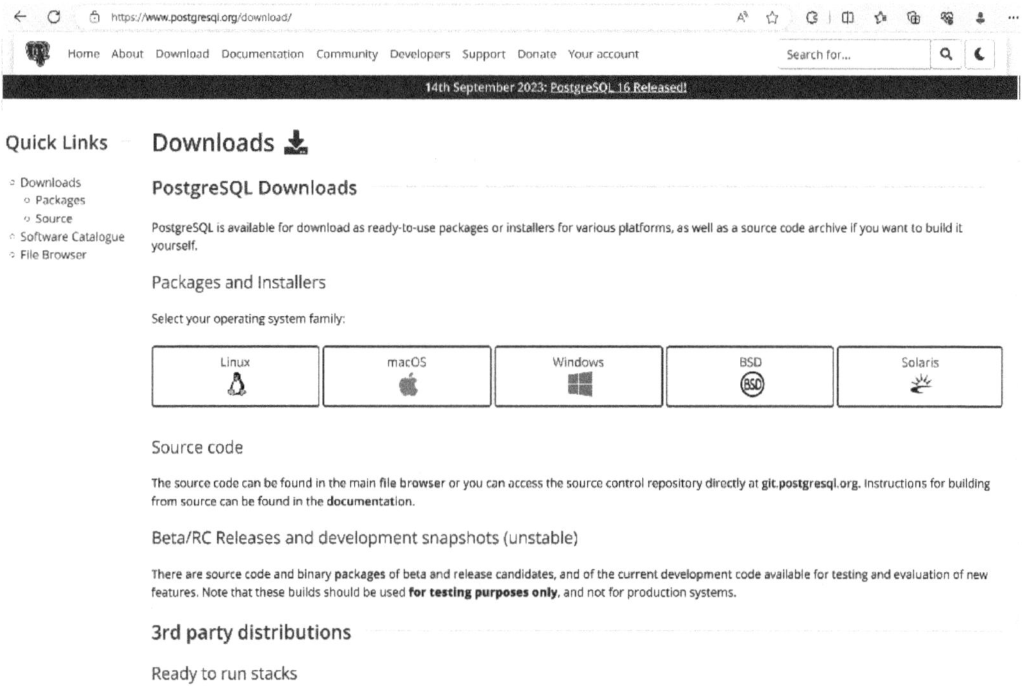

Figure 8.1 – Website to download PostgreSQL

Choose the operating system that you are working in. As I am using Windows, I will select the Windows installer. Once you are on the Windows installer website, click on **Download the installer**. This will take you to the EnterpriseDB website so that you can download the installer.

> **Important note**
>
> Please note that the installation instructions and steps outlined in this chapter may vary depending on your operating system, so ensure you follow the specific guidelines relevant to your system for a successful setup.

Select the latest PostgreSQL version available for your machine. Note that for Windows, the 64-bit platform is compatible with this application. Once you click on Windows x86-64 for the latest version, you will see the `postgresql-16.0-1-windows-x64.exe` file in your `Downloads` folder. Once it has finished downloading, double-click on it to start the installation process.

PostgreSQL Setup Wizard will appear.

Click on **Next** > to be taken to the **Installation Directory** field, as shown in *Figure 8.2*:

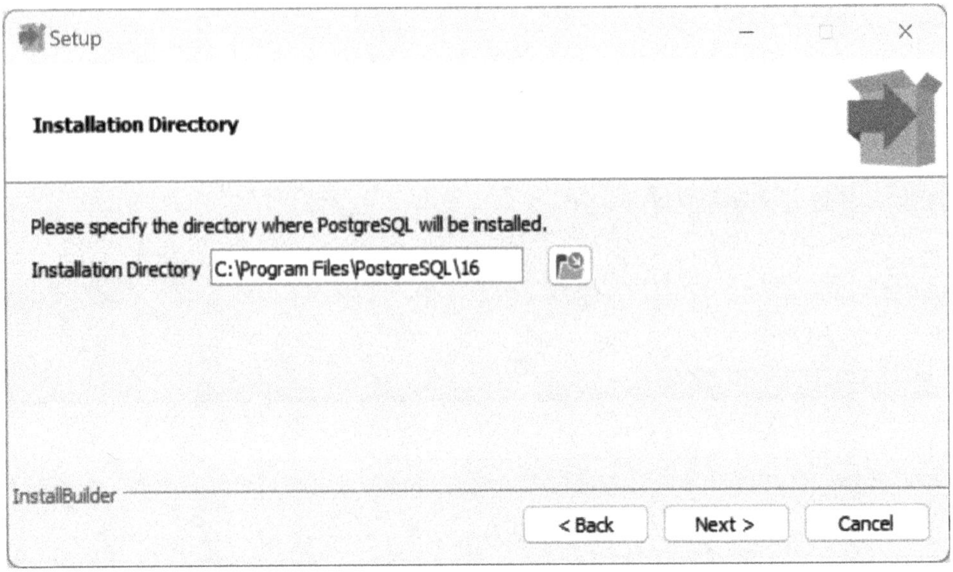

Figure 8.2 – Selecting the installation directory

Once here, you can install all the default selected components, as seen in *Figure 8.3*. Again, click on **Next** >:

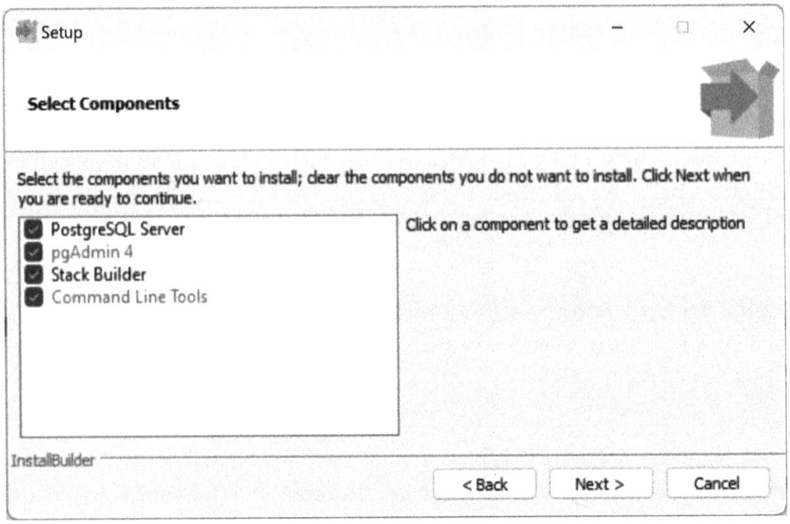

Figure 8.3 – Selecting the components to be installed

At this point, you'll be shown the directory where the data will be saved, as shown in *Figure 8.4*:

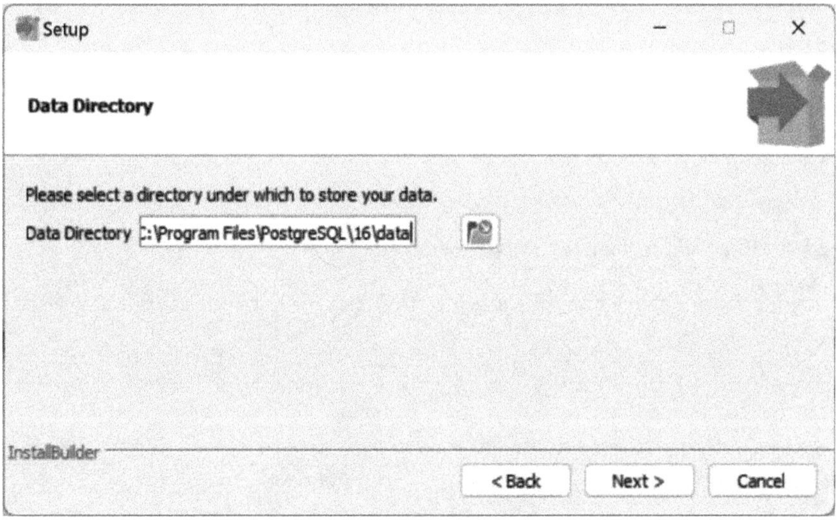

Figure 8.4 – Selecting the directory where data will be stored

Creating a password is the next step, as shown in *Figure 8.5*:

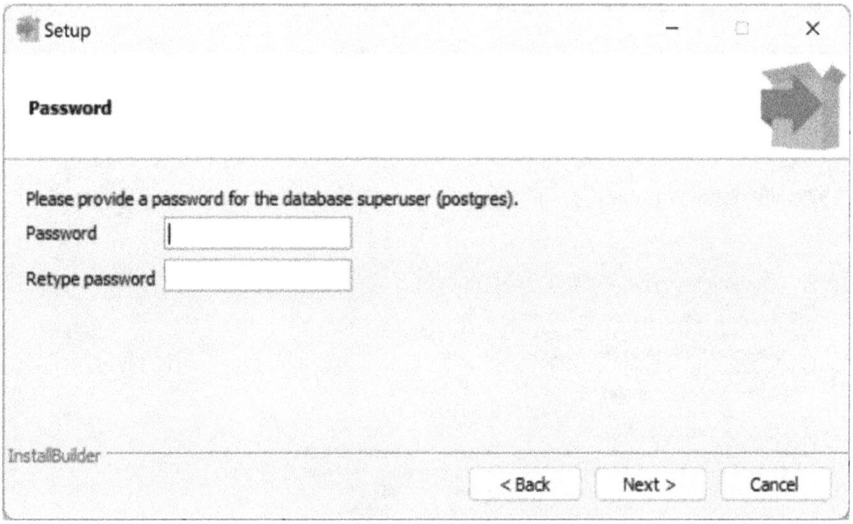

Figure 8.5 – Setting a password

> **Note**
>
> Let's use `postgres` as the password to make it easier to remember. Remember that this should not be used in production environments, but for this example, this should do the trick.

Once you have created your password, click on **Next** >. This will lead you to a page where you must enter a port number, as shown in *Figure 8.6*. You may use the default port provided.

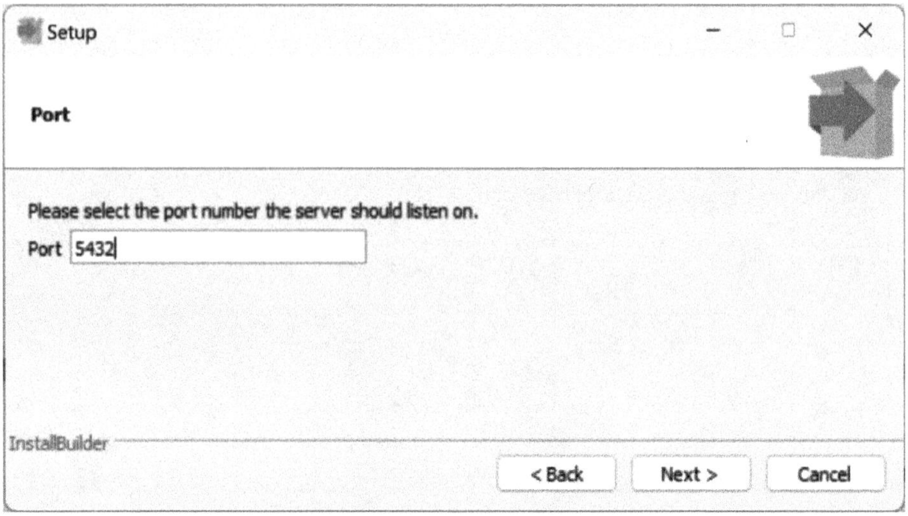

Figure 8.6 – Selecting a port number

You will be prompted with the locale for the new database cluster. Keep the default and click on **Next** >.

After clicking on **Next** >, the pre-installation summary will be shown, as seen in *Figure 8.7*:

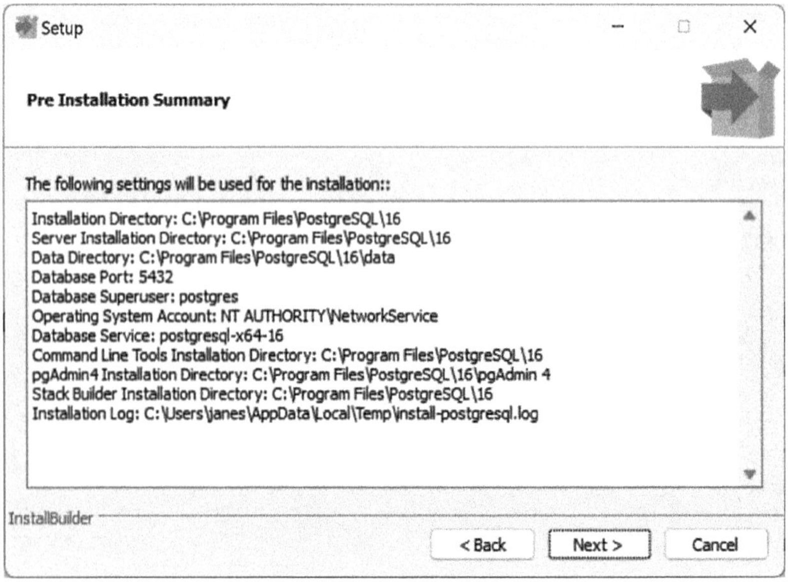

Figure 8.7 – Pre-installation summary

A message will appear showing that PostgreSQL is ready to be installed. Click on **Next** >.

Once the installation is complete, you'll be notified that the setup has finished, as illustrated in *Figure 8.8*:

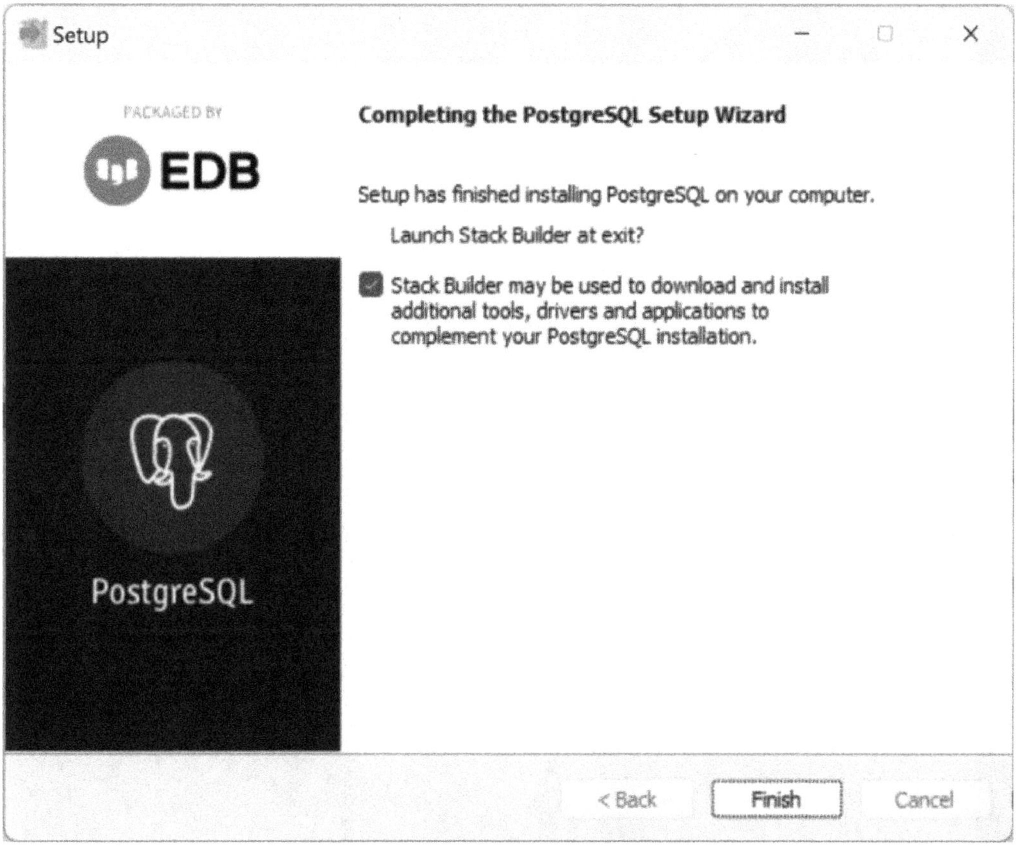

Figure 8.8 – Completing the PostgreSQL setup wizard

Uncheck the **Stack Builder** button since we do not need to install it right now. Then, click on **Finish**.

Next, we must launch pgAdmin 4 by typing it in the **Search** bar, as shown in *Figure 8.9*:

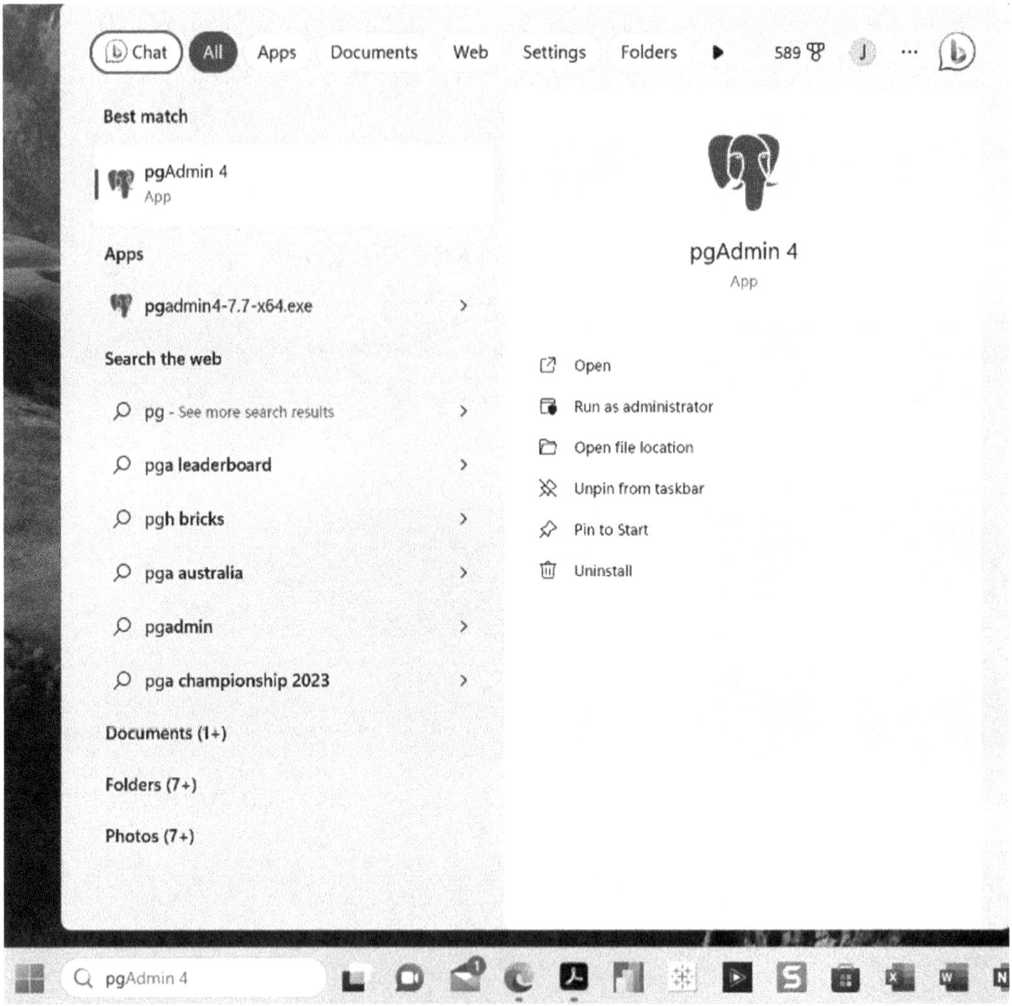

Figure 8.9 – Searching for pgAdmin 4

This was one of the components we installed earlier, as shown in *Figure 8.3*. pgAdmin 4 is the most popular open source graphical tool for managing, developing, and administering PostgreSQL. After clicking on the pgAdmin 4 icon, the tool will be launched, as shown in *Figure 8.10*:

Figure 8.10 – Starting pgAdmin 4

When the user interface launches, as seen in *Figure 8.11*, you'll be prompted to create a master password for pgAdmin:

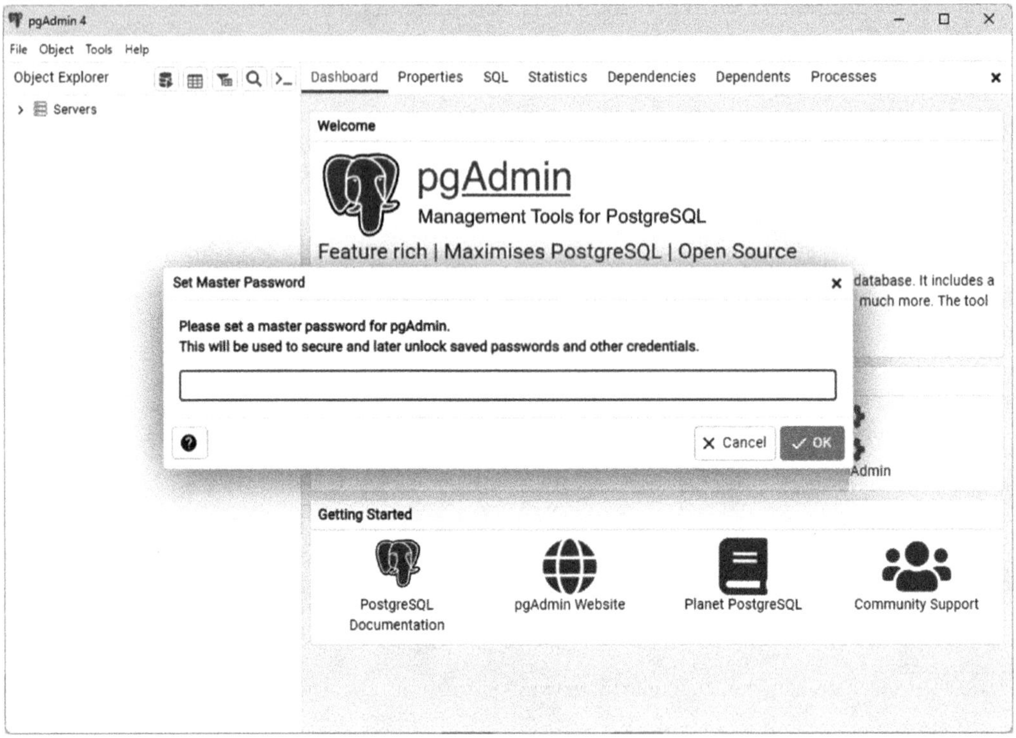

Figure 8.11 – Launching pgAdmin 4

Once you've done this, the user interface will appear, as shown in *Figure 8.12*:

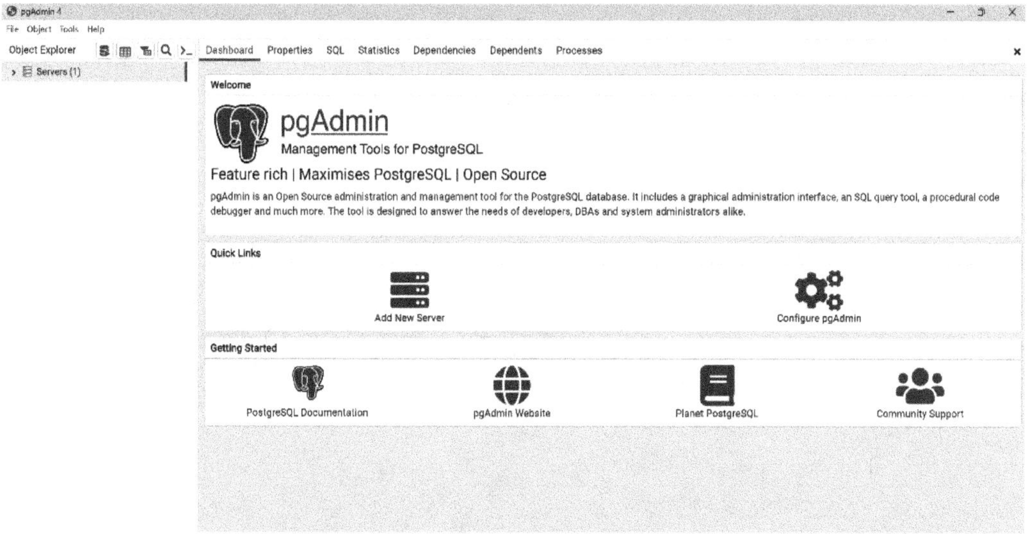

Figure 8.12 – Interface of pgAdmin 4

When you click on the button beside **Servers**, you will be prompted to enter the password, as shown in *Figure 8.13*:

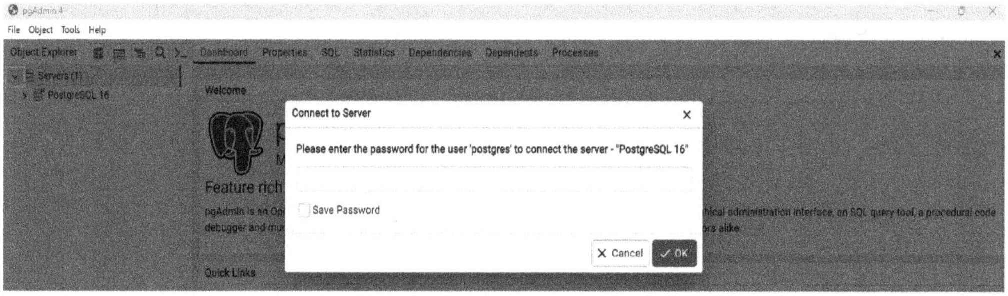

Figure 8.13 – Connecting to the server

Type in the password you created earlier (*Figure 8.5*), then click on **OK**.

A message stating **Server connected** will appear on the *lower right-hand side* of the window.

Once the setup is complete and a connection to the server has been established, our next step is to create a database.

Creating a database

Now that we have finished setting up the connection with the server, we can create a database where we can store and maintain the data in a structured format. In pgAdmin 4, on the left-hand side panel, right-click on **Databases**, choose **Create**, then click on **Database…**, as shown in *Figure 8.14*:

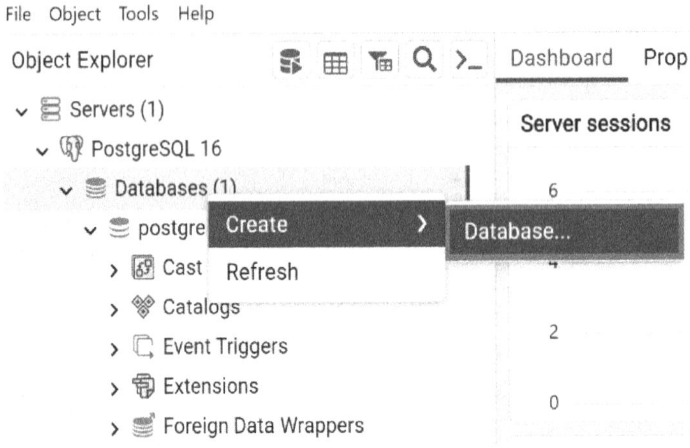

Figure 8.14 – Creating a new database

The **Create – Database** pop-up window will appear, as illustrated in *Figure 8.15*. We will call it `MyDatabase`:

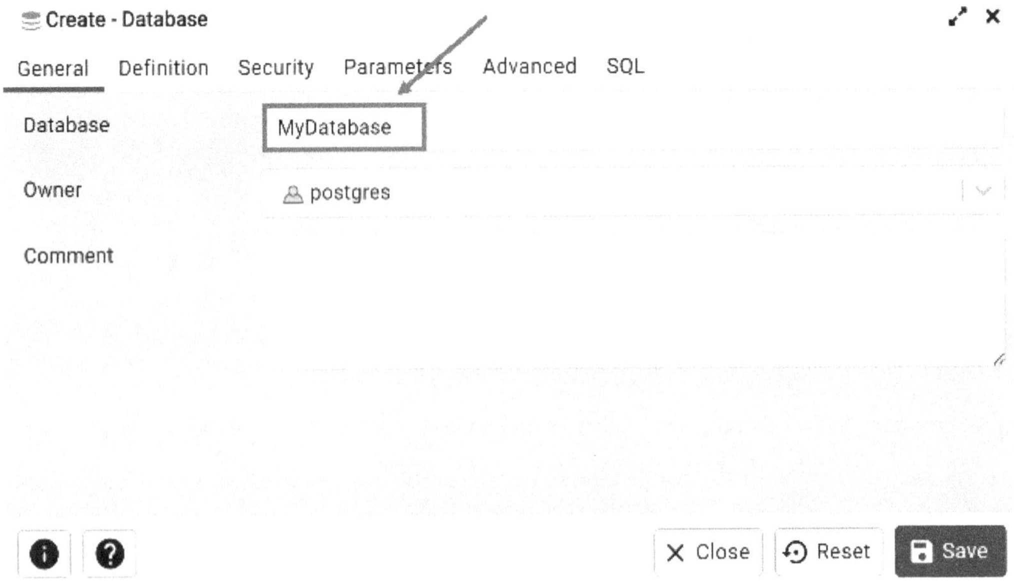

Figure 8.15 – Naming the database

MyDatabase will be created and shown in the **Object Explorer** panel, as seen in *Figure 8.16*:

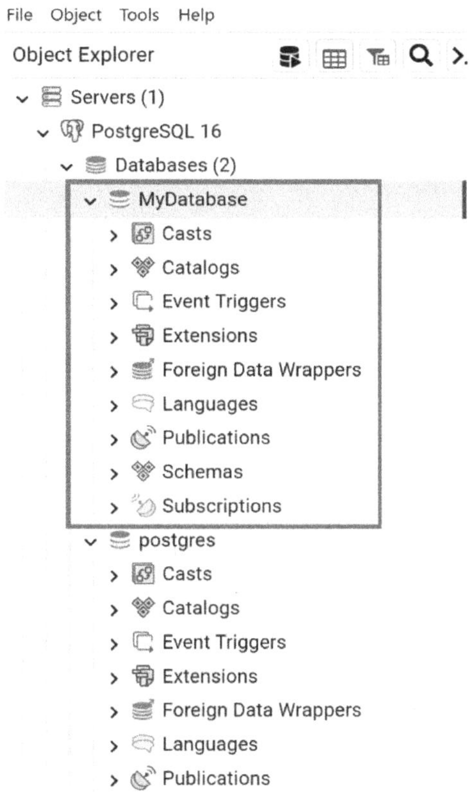

Figure 8.16 – Newly created database added to the Object Explorer panel

This panel contains the databases that are available on the server, as well as the details of the tables and columns that will be added. Now that we have created the database, we will create the table where we will input the information for our hands-on exercise.

Creating a table

A **table** is similar to a spreadsheet in that it contains the data in a structured format. Let's right-click on the new database we created, as seen in *Figure 8.17*, and select **Query Tool**:

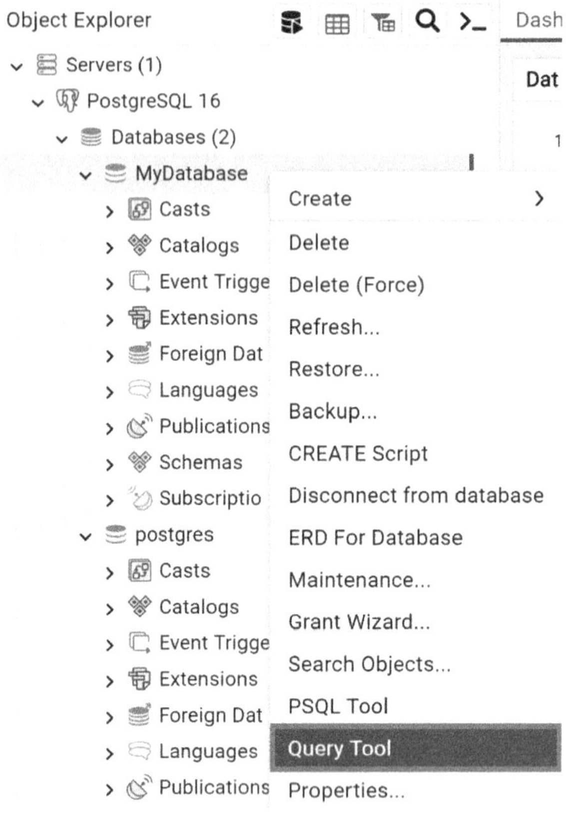

Figure 8.17 – Launching Query Tool

The **Query** pane will appear, as seen in *Figure 8.18*:

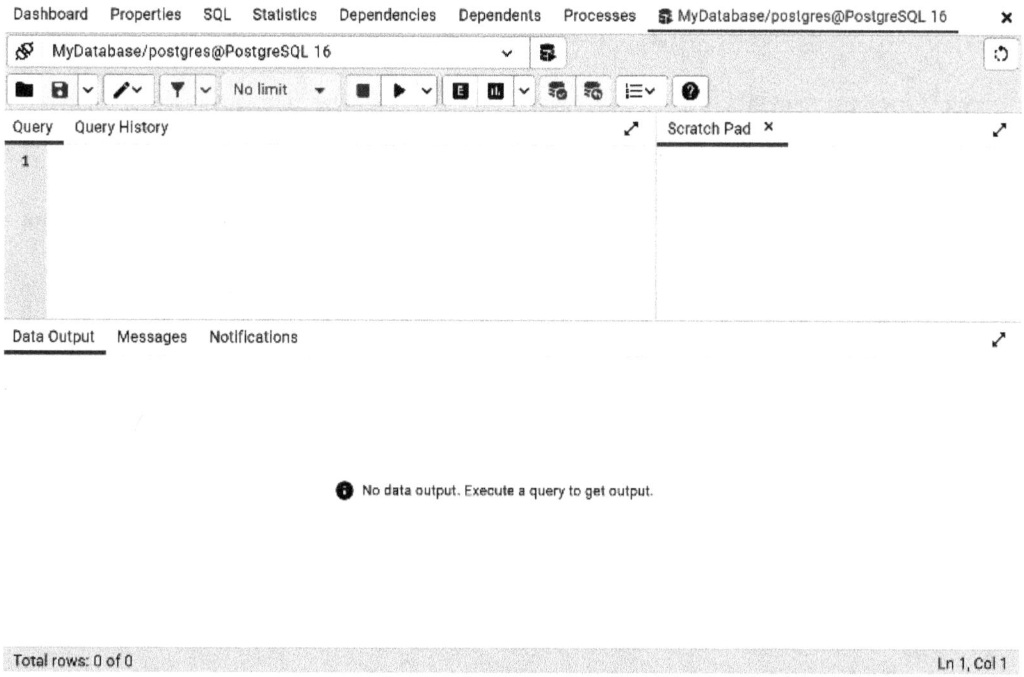

Figure 8.18 – The Query pane

This is where we will be running our **PostgreSQL** code to create the table.

We will create a table called `tickets` with four columns called `id`, `event_name`, `ticket_price`, and `is_booked`, as seen in *Figure 8.19*:

id	event_name	ticket_price	is_booked
1	Concert A	50.00	false
2	Concert B	75.00	false
3	Conference X	100.00	false

Figure 8.19 – Table containing ticket information

To do this, we will type the following PostgreSQL code in the **Query** box:

```
CREATE TABLE tickets(
    id SERIAL PRIMARY KEY,
    event_name VARCHAR(255) NOT NULL,
    ticket_price DECIMAL(10,2) NOT NULL,
```

```
    is_booked BOOLEAN NOT NULL DEFAULT FALSE
);
```

Let's review the purpose of each column:

- `id`: We will use the `SERIAL` type, which will automatically generate a unique value for each row. This will serve as the `PRIMARY KEY` value, making sure that each row has a unique identifier.
- `event_name`: We will use the `VARCHAR(255)` type, which means that it can store a variable-length string of up to 255 characters. It is designated as `NOT NULL`, which means that it cannot be empty and must always have a value.
- `ticket_price`: We will use the `DECIMAL(10,2)` type to represent a decimal with a precision of 10 digits and a scale of 2. It is designated as `NOT NULL`, which means that it cannot be empty to ensure that a valid ticket price is indicated.
- `is_booked`: We will use the `BOOLEAN` type to represent a true/false value. It is designated as `NOT NULL` with a `DEFAULT` value of `FALSE` to indicate whether a ticket is booked or not.

Next, click on the **Execute** button or press *F5* to execute this query. A message will be displayed stating that the table has been created, as seen in *Figure 8.20*:

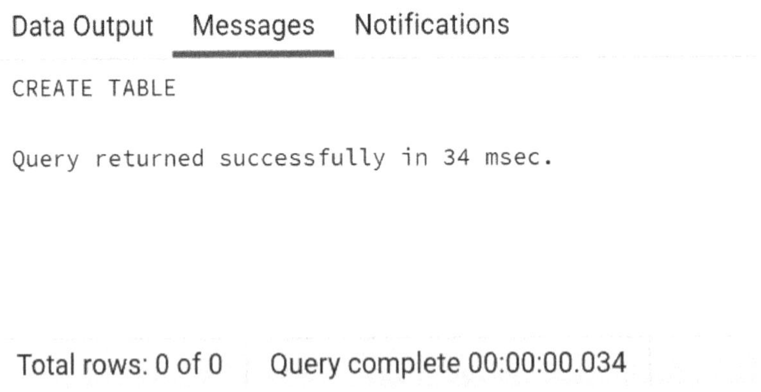
Data Output
Messages
Notifications
CREATE TABLE
Query returned successfully in 34 msec.
Total rows: 0 of 0
Query complete 00:00:00.034

Figure 8.20 – Table has been created

To check whether the proper columns have been created in the table, we can use `SELECT` to view them. But before that, clear the `CREATE TABLE` statement that we ran earlier.

Once this has been cleared, we must type the following code in the **Query** tab and run it:

```
SELECT * FROM tickets;
```

This will SELECT all the columns from the tickets table. The result will be shown in the **Data Output** tab, as seen in *Figure 8.21*:

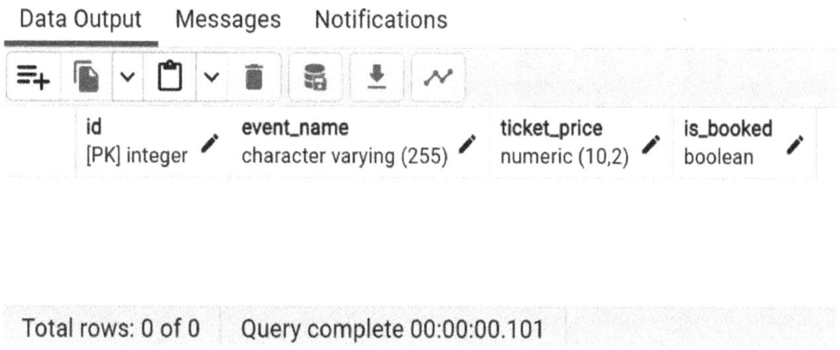
Data Output
Messages
Notifications
id
[PK] integer
event_name
character varying (255)
ticket_price
numeric (10,2)
is_booked
boolean
Total rows: 0 of 0
Query complete 00:00:00.101

Figure 8.21 – Displaying the columns that have been created

This confirms that our table has been created properly with the specified columns.

> **Note**
>
> We are using * to select all the columns since the information we are working with is small. In practice, it is better to specify which columns we wish to use, especially when working with large datasets.

Now that we have created the columns, the next step is to create some test data and add the ticket prices.

Inserting data into the table

Next, we will insert data into the columns so that we can simulate available tickets for the events. Make sure that you clear the statement you ran previously before adding the following code:

```
INSERT INTO tickets (event_name, ticket_price) VALUES
    ('Concert A', 50.00),
    ('Concert B', 75.00),
    ('Conference X', 100.00);
```

This will insert the given values into the event_name and ticket_price columns.

After typing this, click on **Execute**. You will get a message stating that the query has been returned successfully.

To view the table again, remove the previous INSERT statement and type this code:

```
SELECT * FROM tickets;
```

This will show the table with the updated information, as shown in *Figure 8.22*:

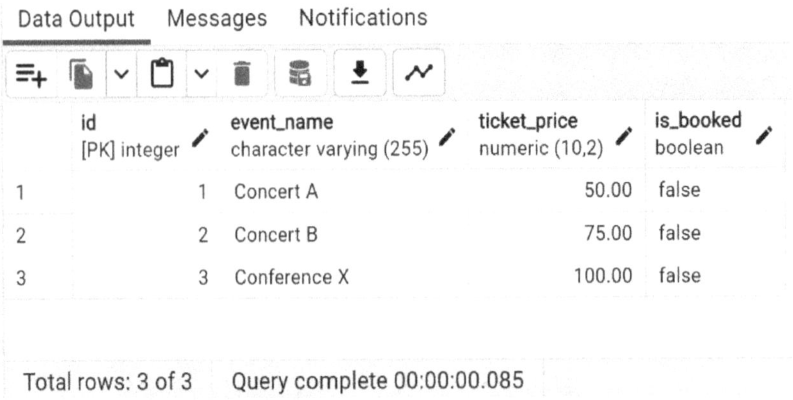
Data Output
Messages
Notifications
id
[PK] integer
event_name
character varying (255)
ticket_price
numeric (10,2)
is_booked
boolean
1 1 Concert A 50.00 false
2 2 Concert B 75.00 false
3 3 Conference X 100.00 false
Total rows: 3 of 3
Query complete 00:00:00.085

Figure 8.22 – Displaying the table after inputting values

Before we move on, let's save our newly created database by clicking on the diskette icon shown in *Figure 8.23* and naming it `MyDatabase`:

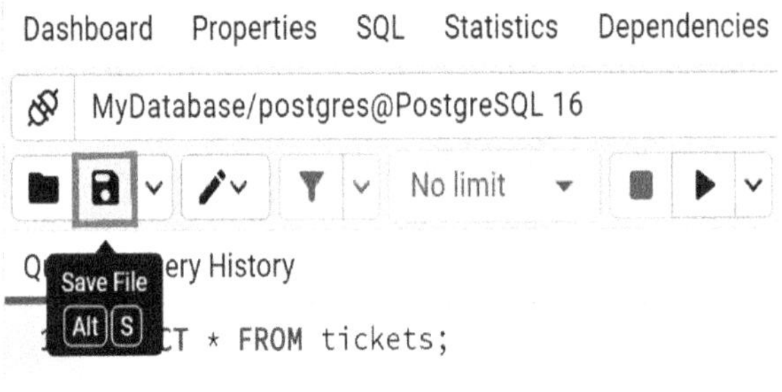
Dashboard
Properties
SQL
Statistics
Dependencies
MyDatabase/postgres@PostgreSQL 16
No limit
Save File
Alt S
ery History
T * FROM tickets;

Figure 8.23 – Saving the PostgreSQL database

When you click on this icon, a pop-up window will appear, prompting you to choose a location to save the file as well as to enter the filename. Once you've done this, a message will appear at the *lower right-hand* side of the window confirming that the file has been saved successfully (after completing the steps required). We will use this later when we are testing the row locks.

We have just covered how to install pgAdmin 4, how to create a database and a table, and how to insert data into the table. We will be using this table when we simulate the race conditions and the database row-level lock in the next few sections. What we've discussed here are the basic concepts when working with PostgreSQL. In the next section, we will dive deeper into another key concept—**ACID properties**—and how this relates to **race conditions**.

Learning how race conditions impact the transaction integrity of financial systems

Earlier in this chapter, we mentioned that PostgreSQL transactions have the ACID properties of atomicity, consistency, isolation, and durability. These qualities ensure that transactions are handled consistently and dependably. Let's take a moment to discuss these in detail:

- **Atomicity**: A database is said to be atomic when it needs the entire set of transactions to succeed for the changes to be reflected in the database. If one of the smaller operations fails, the *entire* operation will fail. But if all the tasks succeed, the entire operation will succeed and be reflected in the database.
- **Consistency**: A database is consistent when the data adheres to the rules and relationships established in the database. Only changes that keep the data in a valid state should be made during a transaction. If the transaction is successful, it changes the database's valid state to another. If this does not work, the database remains unchanged.
- **Isolation**: This refers to the practice of keeping each transaction independent of each other. The changes are not seen by others accessing the information until the changes are completed. By doing so, inconsistencies and errors in the data are prevented.
- **Durability**: This refers to the property of the database where once changes are saved after a successful transaction, the information is intact and will not be lost, even if it encounters a system crash or mishap.

Let's take, for example, an online banking transaction where customers perform transactions simultaneously. **Atomicity** guarantees that transfers from one bank account to another are either fully carried out, or if there is a problem, it is fully rolled back. After each transaction occurs, **consistency** makes sure that the account balances are correct. Because of **isolation**, concurrent transactions cannot interfere with each other. Finally, **durability** guarantees that even if the system crashes, the banking records are safe and remain in place.

Financial systems' databases can be accessed by multiple users simultaneously. If a user is only viewing the transaction, this is okay. However, if updates are being done simultaneously, there is a risk that the changes may not be reflected properly in the database. To ensure that data integrity is maintained for the database, these updates must be managed properly.

Processes can be executed sequentially or concurrently. **Sequential execution** carries out the actions one after the other in a specific order. Each activity in a sequential process needs to be finished before moving on to the next. On the other hand, **concurrent execution** entails running two or more processes at once and enables the tasks to overlap or be executed simultaneously. This is where the proper level of **isolation** between concurrent transactions is necessary. *Figure 8.24* illustrates the difference between the two:

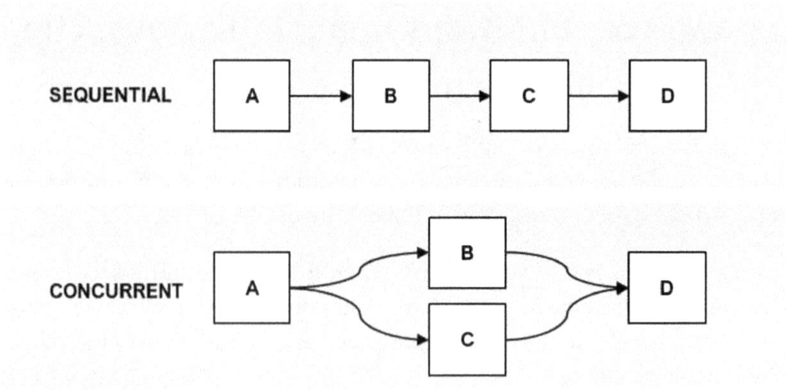

Figure 8.24 – Sequential versus concurrent execution

Data integrity issues *may* occur when two or more processes access a particular transaction and make updates simultaneously, which affects the outcome of the process. This scenario is what you call a **race condition**.

For example, let's say that two people, Person A and Person B, who don't know each other are looking at seats that are available in a movie theater online for a very popular movie, and they've found that there is only one ticket available. Both Person A and Person B check and try to book the same ticket *at the same time*. Booking the ticket would result in making the ticket unavailable; however, if the tickets are booked simultaneously, a **race condition** can occur, as illustrated in *Figure 8.25*:

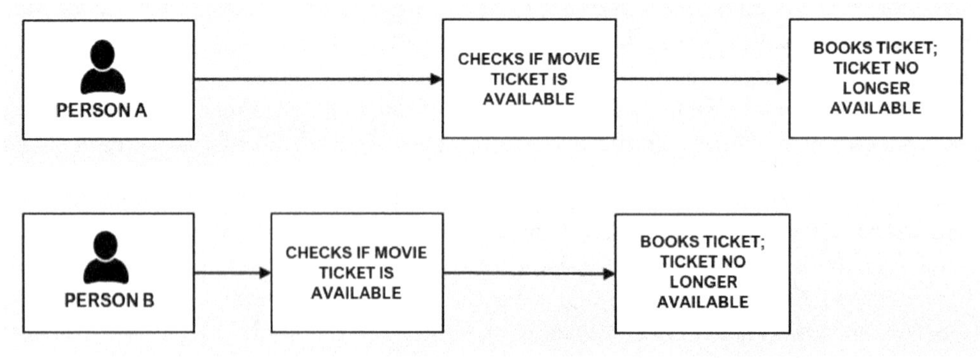

Figure 8.25 – Race condition in buying the last movie ticket

The outcome will be different if the booking happens sequentially, which will result in either Person A's or Person B's booking being rejected. Various controls can be used to address race condition problems in databases, which will control and handle multiple users' access to shared data.

> **Important note**
>
> While this *seems* unlikely to happen, imagine having *thousands* of transactions happening at the same time (for example, because of a sale at midnight)! These transactions may overwrite the values of the *same record* in the database, which will cause data integrity issues. These are a bit tricky to correct and resolve, especially when the transaction's operations or events are not logged separately.

One way to prevent race conditions from occurring is by using **database locks**. We'll see how that works in the next section.

Reviewing how database locks prevent financial transaction integrity issues

Database locks are essential for maintaining the integrity of financial transactions. They play a critical role in preventing conflicts and ensuring that concurrent access to data remains consistent. By controlling the simultaneous modification of shared resources, such as records or tables, locks ensure that transactions have exclusive access to the records they need (*and ensure that the numbers add up correctly!*). This helps maintain the accuracy and reliability of financial data by preventing data inconsistencies and conflicts.

Let's go back to the table we created earlier, as shown in *Figure 8.26*. For instance, we need to update the price of the ticket for **Conference X** and add `$10`. A price increase of `$10` is added depending on the demand:

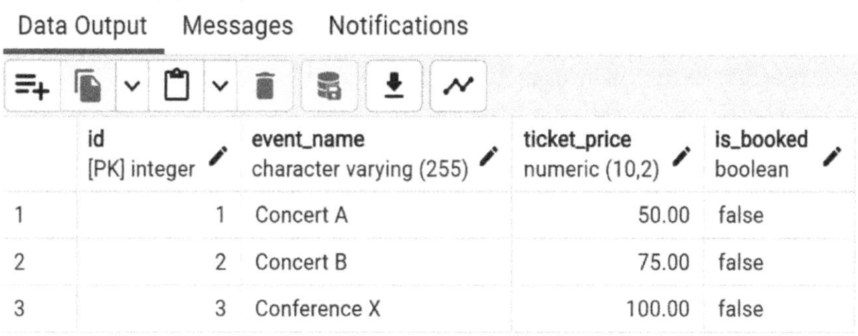

Data Output
Messages
Notifications

	id [PK] integer	event_name character varying (255)	ticket_price numeric (10,2)	is_booked boolean
1	1	Concert A	50.00	false
2	2	Concert B	75.00	false
3	3	Conference X	100.00	false

Figure 8.26 – Current ticket prices

If only one person is making the change to the database, there would be no problem. *However, what if two people were making the change at the same time?*

This is where the different types of **explicit locks** in PostgreSQL come in:

- **Table-level locks**: You can choose to lock the entire table so that others will be unable to make changes.
- **Row-level locks**: Instead of locking the entire table, you can lock the specific row that you are working on to prevent others from modifying it.
- **Page-level locks**: Databases often store data using fixed-size pages. Here, the lock is applied to the entire page and prevents others from working on it while you make changes.
- **Advisory locks**: This is a form of lock that allows you to coordinate operations among many transactions without enforcing strict locking constraints. They provide you more control over how locking is implemented and give different components of your program a method to communicate with one another.

> **Note**
>
> If you are using a different database, feel free to check what locking capabilities and options are available.

In this chapter, we will use **row-level locks** to address **race conditions** and cover a hands-on simulation of **race conditions** when two people try to update the ticket price for **Conference X** in our table in *Figure 8.26*. First, we will see what will happen if a **row-level lock** is *not* applied when transactions occur concurrently.

Steps for Person A:

A separate query window will be used to simulate the steps for each person. We will type all the code first, and run them simultaneously to mirror the race conditions:

1. Start the function definition by using the following block of code:

   ```
   CREATE OR REPLACE FUNCTION update_ticket_price1()
   RETURNS VOID AS $$
   DECLARE
       price1 DECIMAL(10,2);
   ```

   Here, we are declaring a variable to store the value of the ticket for Person A.

> **Note**
>
> Do not press *F5* or click on the *Execute/Refresh* button yet as our function definition is not complete at this stage.

2. Continuing from the previous step, add the following block of code to select the ticket price for **Conference X**:

```
BEGIN
    SELECT ticket_price INTO price1 FROM tickets
WHERE id = 3;
```

   Similar to the first step, do not run it yet.

3. Next, let's add the following line of code to simulate a delay of 30 seconds:

```
PERFORM pg_sleep(30);
```

> **Important note**
>
> You may be wondering, *Is it really necessary to add a 30-second delay?* For our hands-on purposes, we are placing a **sleep call** to simulate the race conditions. Keep in mind that in production, when `pg_sleep` is active, the session will be in a waiting state and might hold resources needed by others in a high-concurrency environment.

4. After the 30-second delay, let's proceed with incrementing the value of the price by `$10` by adding the following line of code:

```
price1 := price1 + 10;
```

5. Let's wrap up the function with the following block of code:

```
UPDATE tickets SET ticket_price = price1 WHERE id = 3;
END;
$$ LANGUAGE plpgsql;
```

   Here, we are updating the ticket price with the incremented value from the previous step.

At this point, our **Query** pane for Person A should look similar to what's shown in *Figure 8.27*:

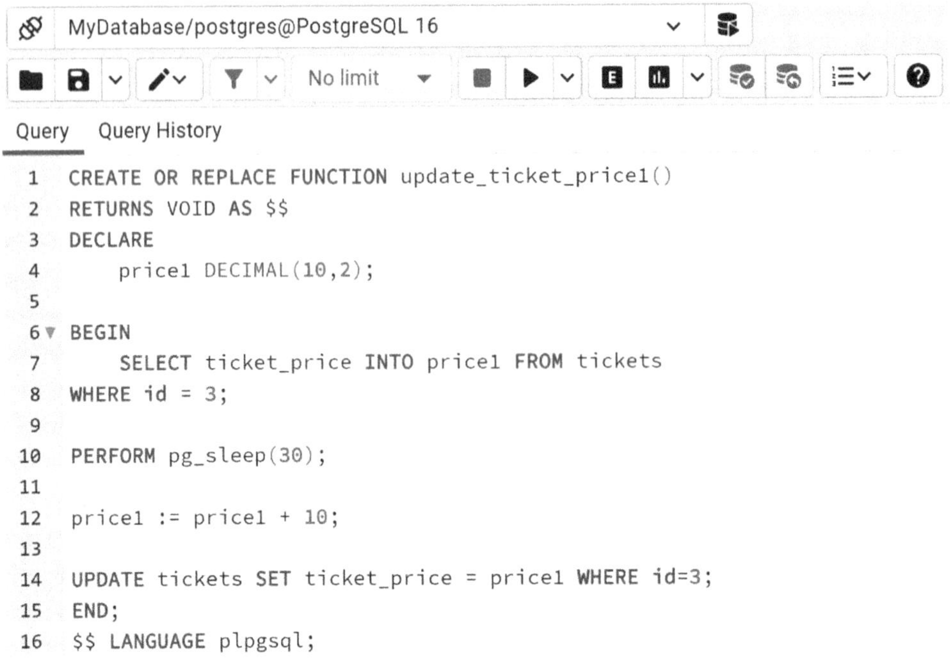
MyDatabase/postgres@PostgreSQL 16
No limit
Query
Query History
CREATE OR REPLACE FUNCTION update_ticket_price1()
RETURNS VOID AS $$
DECLARE
    price1 DECIMAL(10,2);
BEGIN
    SELECT ticket_price INTO price1 FROM tickets
WHERE id = 3;
PERFORM pg_sleep(30);
price1 := price1 + 10;
UPDATE tickets SET ticket_price = price1 WHERE id=3;
END;
$$ LANGUAGE plpgsql;

Figure 8.27 – Code in the Query pane for Person A

> **Note**
>
> The `$$ LANGUAGE plpgsql;` line tells the program that it is written in **PL/pgSQL language**, which enables more advanced logic compared to regular SQL. If you are interested in learning more about this, check out `https://www.postgresqltutorial.com/postgresql-plpgsql/introduction-to-postgresql-stored-procedures/`.

6. To trigger the function, we will need to add the following lines of code:

```
SELECT update_ticket_price1();
SELECT * FROM tickets;
```

   Its purpose is to execute the function and show us the updated ticket price for Person A.

Now that we have typed in the statements for Person A, we need to create another instance of the **Query** pane. This will be for Person B, and we will place it next to the first one.

Steps for Person B:

Here are the steps for adding a new **Query** pane where we will input the statements for Person B:

1. Right-click on `MyDatabase` and select **Query Tool**, similar to what was shown in *Figure 8.17*. This will add the **Query** pane, as shown in *Figure 8.28*:

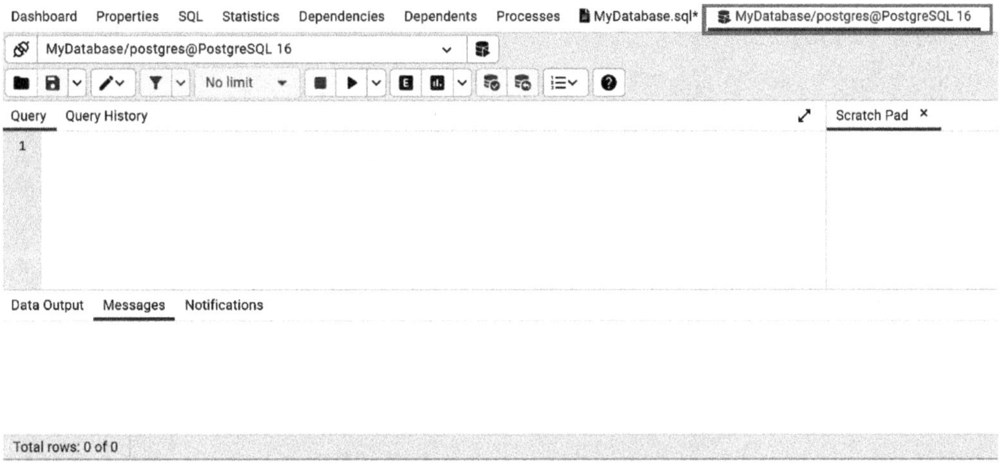

Figure 8.28 – Adding a Query pane for Person B

We want both our **Query** panes visible when we run the race condition. To address this, we will detach it.

2. Right-click on the newly added pane and click on **Detach panel**, as shown in *Figure 8.29*:

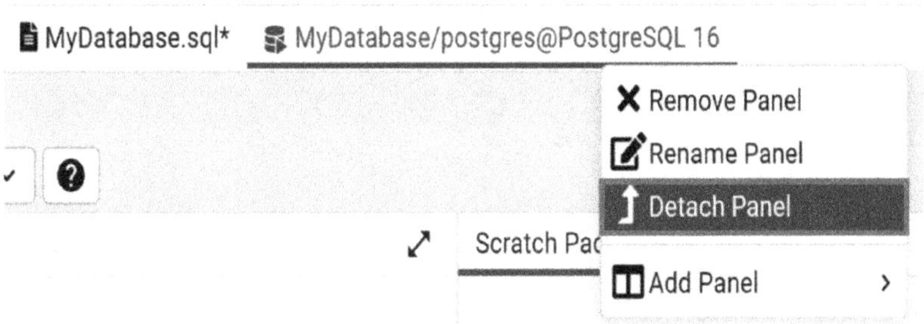

Figure 8.29 – Detaching the new Query pane

This will separate the pane and place it on top of the query for Person A. It will look like what's shown in *Figure 8.30*:

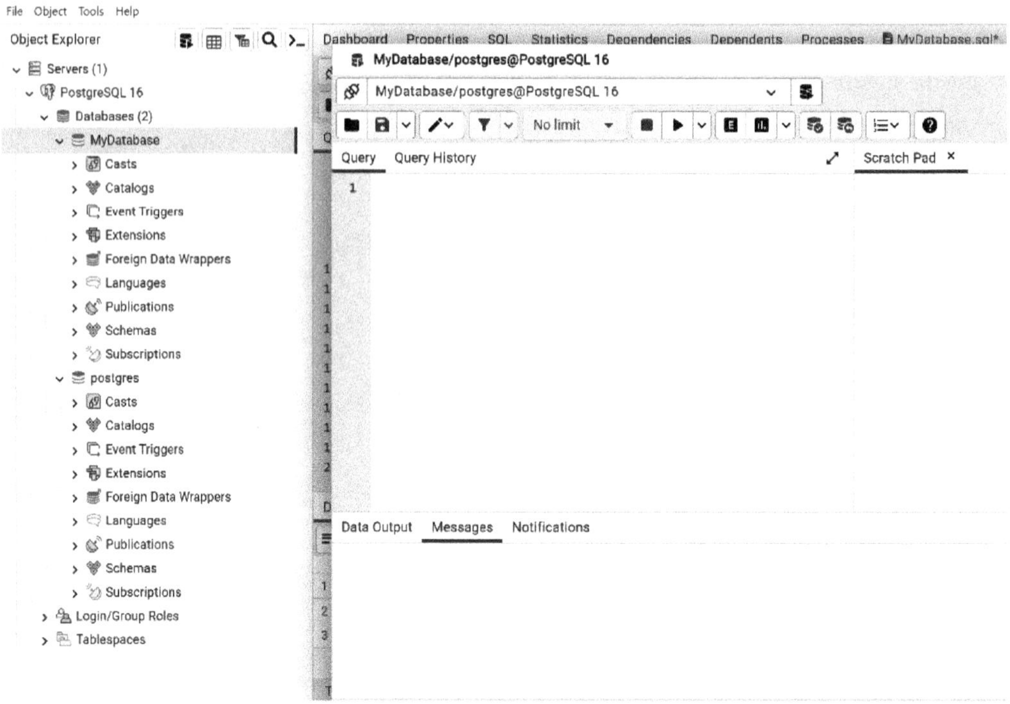

Figure 8.30 – What you'll see after the query pane has been detached

3. Next, we will drag the detached panels so that they align with each other. Move your cursor to the top part of the pane; when your cursor changes its shape so that it looks like four arrows pointing in opposite directions, drag it to the right. This can be seen in *Figure 8.31*:

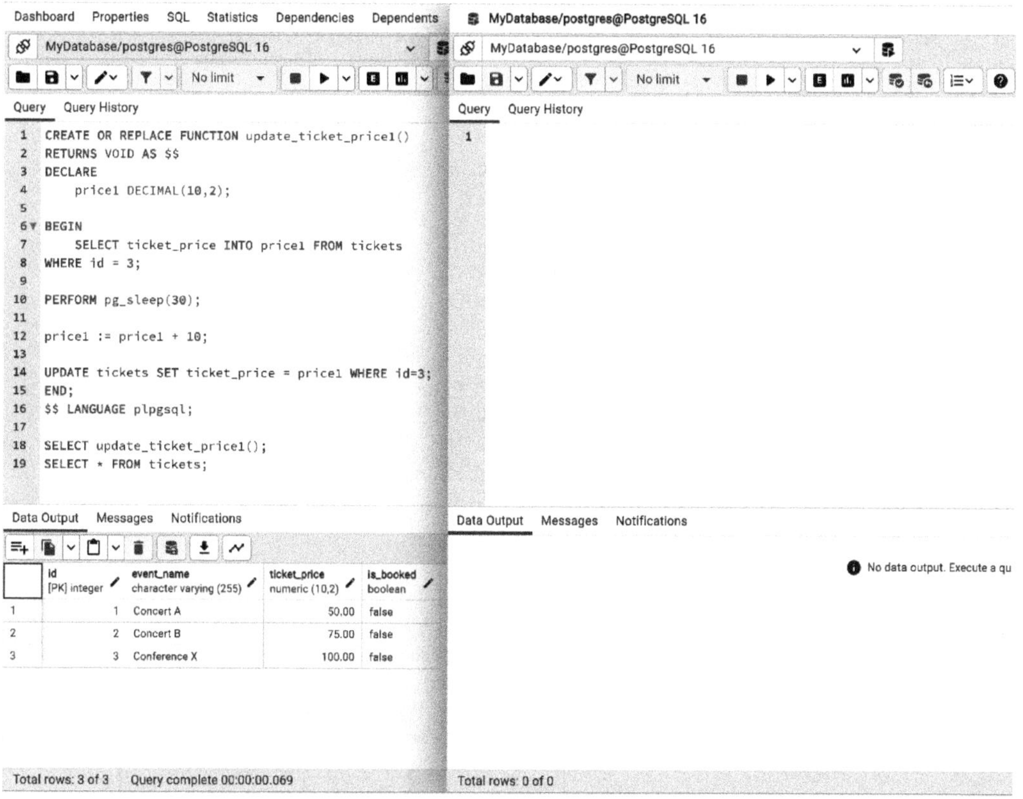

Figure 8.31 – Query panes side by side

You might be wondering, *Why do we need to do this?* As you can see, aligning the **Query** panes side by side makes them easier to work with. Ensure that you can see the entire **Data Output Panel** properly.

Now that this is ready, we can type in the code for Person B.

> **Note**
>
> If the **Query** pane becomes confusing, you can go back to your original layout by clicking on **File** at the *top-left* corner of the pgAdmin 4 window and selecting **Reset Layout**.

4. Enter the following statements to create a function that's similar to what we created for Person A, putting a sleep call for 30 seconds. This time, we will be adding `$15` to the price of **Conference X** compared to `$10` for Person B to make the example clearer:

```
CREATE OR REPLACE FUNCTION update_ticket_price2()
RETURNS VOID AS $$
```

```
DECLARE
    price2 DECIMAL(10,2);

BEGIN
    SELECT ticket_price INTO price2 FROM tickets
WHERE id = 3;

PERFORM pg_sleep(30);

price2 := price2 + 15;

UPDATE tickets SET ticket_price = price2 WHERE id = 3;
END;
$$ LANGUAGE plpgsql;

SELECT update_ticket_price2();
SELECT * FROM tickets;
```

5. *What happens when these occur simultaneously?* Let's find out by doing just that and executing one after the other. First, run the query for Person A, as shown in *Figure 8.32*:

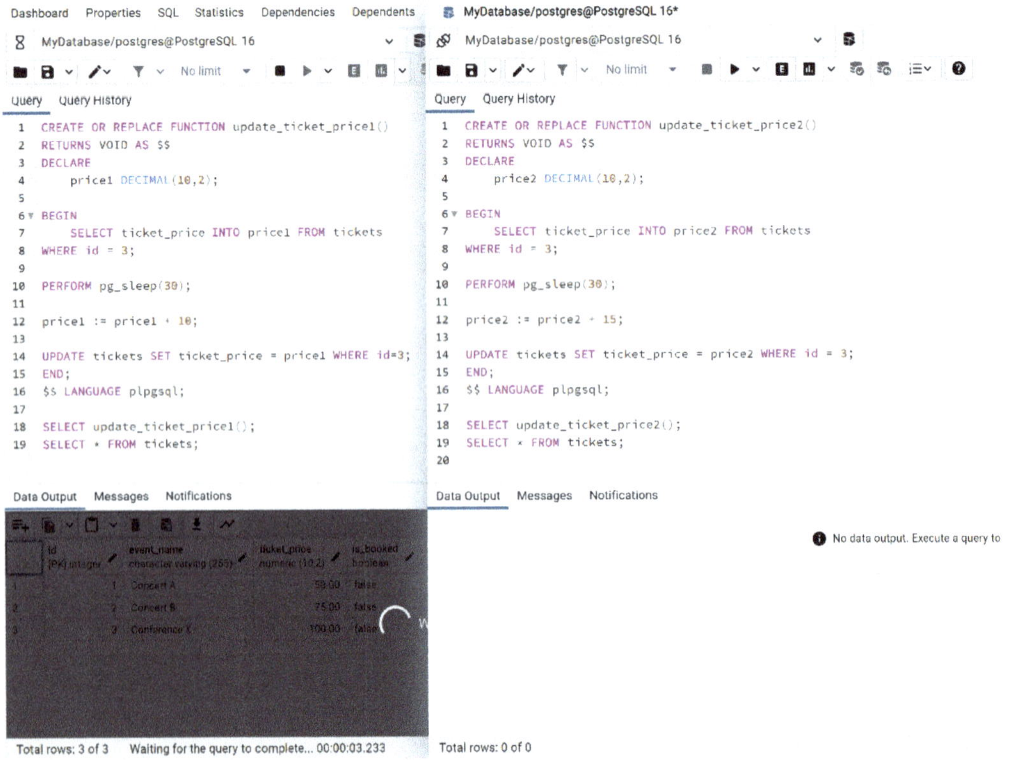

Figure 8.32 – Running the query for Person A

You will see that the **Data Output** panel for Person A has turned gray since it is currently running the query while the *30-second delay* is in effect. A message stating **Waiting for the query to complete** will be displayed.

6. Then, while it is running, click on the execute button for Person B. The queries should look like what's shown in *Figure 8.33*:

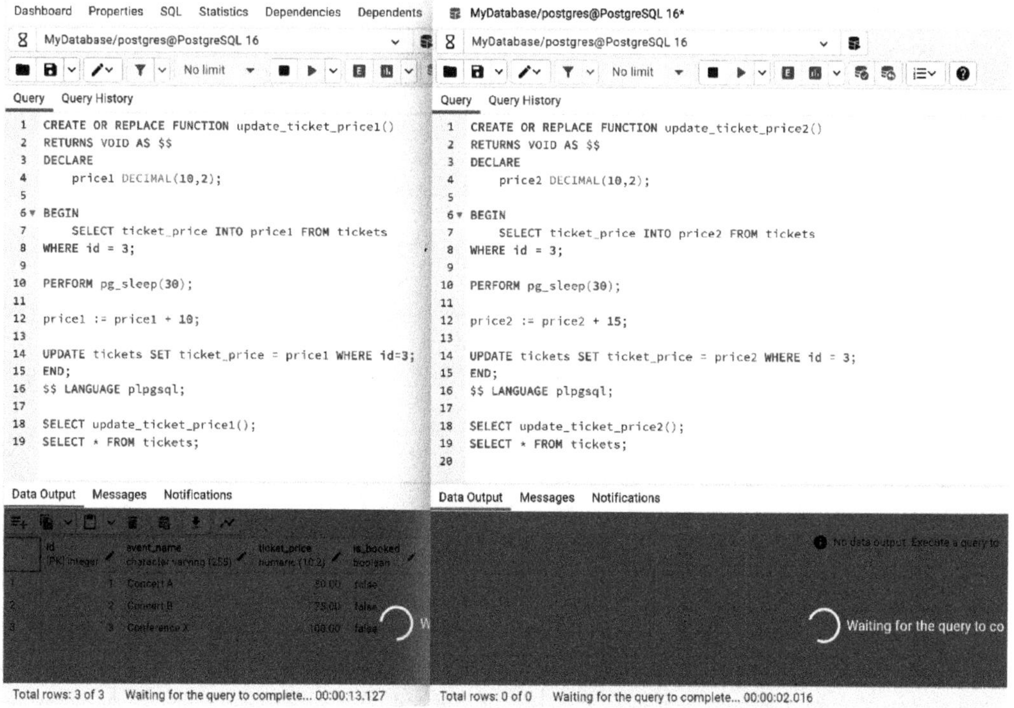

Figure 8.33 – Running queries for both Person A and B

The query for Person A, which was executed first, will be completed first, followed by Person B's query.

Once both have finished running, you will see the results, as shown in *Figure 8.34*:

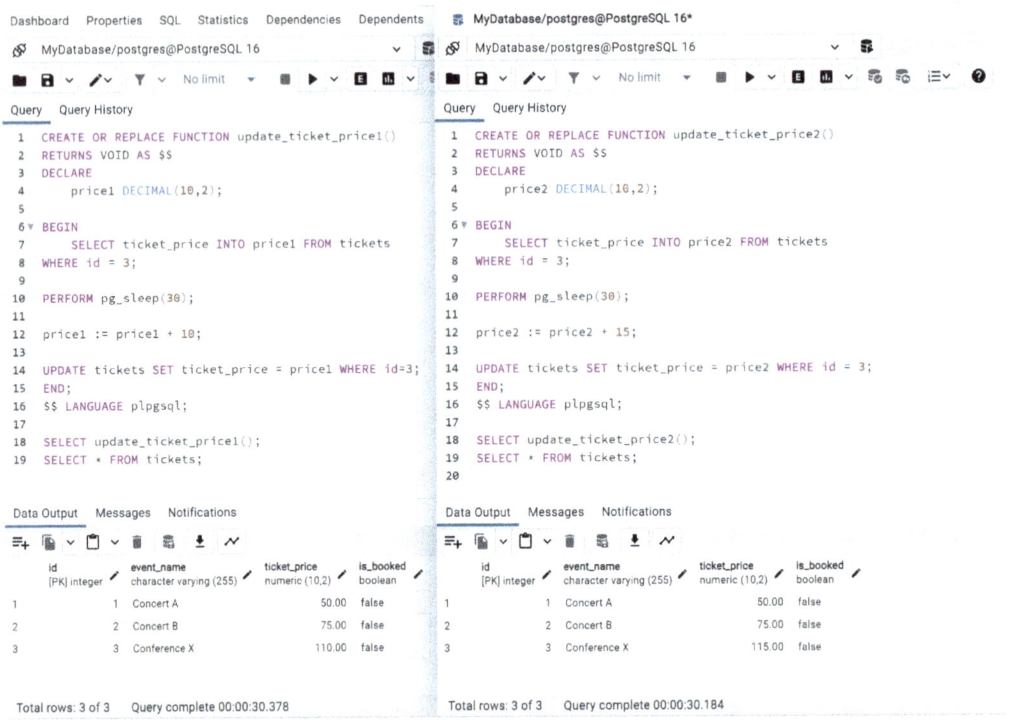

Figure 8.34 – The output after running the two queries simulating a race condition

As you can see, both changes were made to the initial `$100` we had from *Figure 8.26*. For Person A, the ticket price for **Conference X** is `$110`, which is the initial `$100` plus the `$10` increment. When Person B made the change, it did not take into account that someone was making an update and added the `$15` to the initial `$100` price. It looks like we *magically* lost `$10` because of a race condition. *Oh no!*

> **Important note**
>
> If you encounter an error message while working on this hands-on example, go back through the steps and make sure that the code has been entered accurately. I also placed the queries in the **GitHub** repository where you can access the code for easier reference: `https://github.com/PacktPublishing/Managing-Data-Integrity-for-Finance/tree/main/ch08`.

Because a **row-level lock** (*or an alternative locking technique*) has not been used in this example, the update has been made on the initial price, and the change did not take into account that another transaction was running at the same time. *Figure 8.35* illustrates this further:

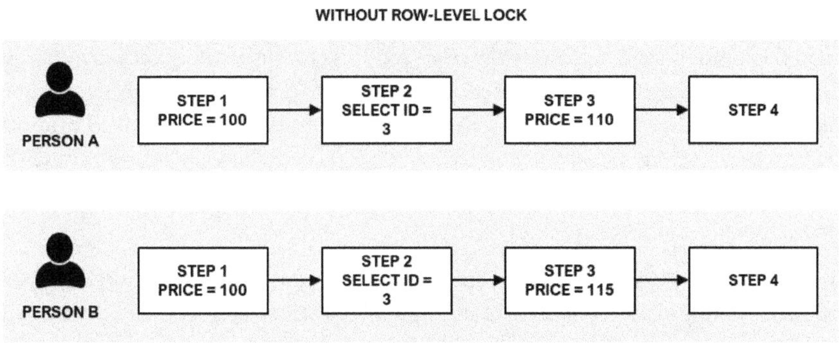
WITHOUT ROW-LEVEL LOCK
PERSON A
STEP 1 PRICE = 100
STEP 2 SELECT ID = 3
STEP 3 PRICE = 110
STEP 4
PERSON B
STEP 1 PRICE = 100
STEP 2 SELECT ID = 3
STEP 3 PRICE = 115
STEP 4

Figure 8.35 – Workflow without a row-level lock

7. Since this is not correct, let's set the ticket price for **Conference X** back to `$100` again. So that we do not have to delete the query, let's open another **Query** pane and type the following code:

```
UPDATE tickets SET ticket_price = 100 WHERE id = 3;
SELECT * FROM tickets;
```

Check whether the price has indeed been updated to `$100`.

This example shows how concurrent transactions can cause data integrity issues if proper **database locks** are not put in place. By using locks, we can ensure that the modifications that are made are reflected correctly in the database. In the next section, we will discuss how database locks—in particular, row-level locks—can address this situation.

Guaranteeing transaction integrity with database locks

Figure 8.36 illustrates how a **row-level lock** ensures that the transaction is completed first before the next one is run:

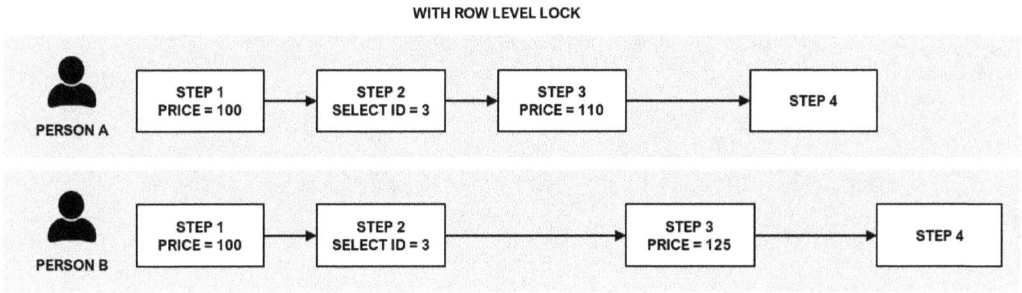
WITH ROW LEVEL LOCK
PERSON A
STEP 1 PRICE = 100
STEP 2 SELECT ID = 3
STEP 3 PRICE = 110
STEP 4
PERSON B
STEP 1 PRICE = 100
STEP 2 SELECT ID = 3
STEP 3 PRICE = 125
STEP 4

Figure 8.36 – Workflow with a row-level lock

Step 3 for Person A will add `$10` to the price, making it `$110`. Because a row-level lock has been applied, Person B will not be able to update the price for Ticket X *until the update operation of Person A has finished*. Then, once the change has been made for **Person A**, the update operation of **Person B** will proceed (after waiting in the queue), adding the `$15` to the correct revised price of `$110`, leading to `$125`. *Amazing, right?*

> **Note**
>
> Note that Person A and Person B have no idea that another concurrent operation is happening! Row-level locks simply ensure that even if multiple transactions are happening concurrently, the operations updating the same record would queue automatically and the numbers would still add up!

Here are the steps on how to do this in terms of our example:

1. Go back to the **Query** panes for Person A and B. We will use the `SELECT FOR UPDATE` statement when selecting the ticket price in lines *7* and *8*. For **Person A**, the code should look like this:

```
SELECT ticket_price INTO price1 FROM tickets WHERE id =3 FOR
UPDATE;
```

2. Add the `SELECT FOR UPDATE` statement for **Person B** as well. It should be like:

```
SELECT ticket_price INTO price2 FROM tickets WHERE id =3 FOR
UPDATE;
```

The **Query** panes will be similar to what's shown in *Figure 8.37*:

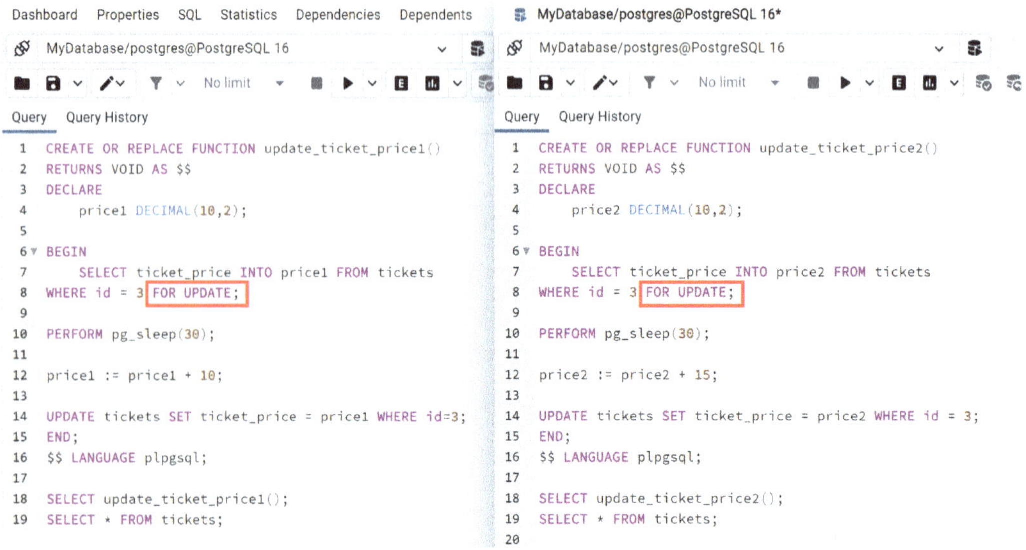

Figure 8.37 – Using SELECT FOR UPDATE statements to enable row-level locks

> **Note**
>
> Using the `SELECT FOR UPDATE` statement applies a row-level lock on that row and *waits for the previous instance to complete*, before going to the next.

3. Once we have updated the code for both Person A and Person B, execute them one after another, similar to what we did in *Steps 5* and *6* for Person B in the previous section. The query for Person A will finish first, *and when the row level lock has been released*, it will start executing the query for Person B.
4. Once the code has been run, the updated **Query** pane and results will be reflected, as shown in *Figure 8.38*:

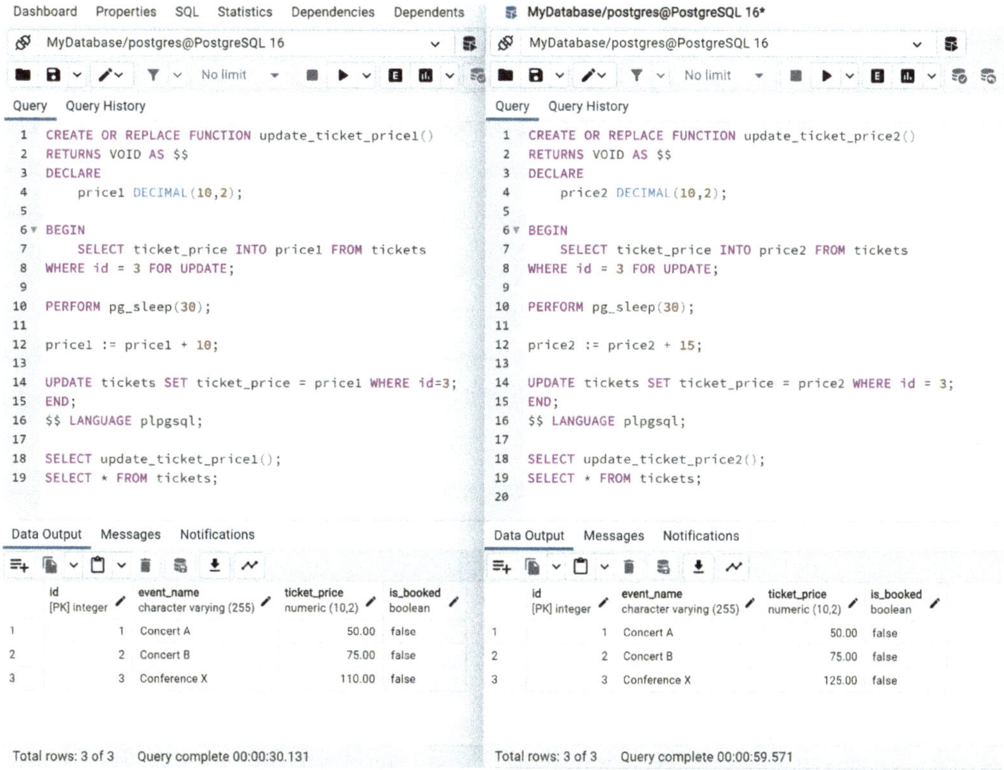

Figure 8.38 – The output after running the queries

As we can see, the ticket price of **Conference X** for Person A has been updated to `$110`. Then, the lock was released and enabled Person B to update it. Thus, `$15` was added to `$110` after Person A made the changes, instead of the initial `$100` we had in the table.

Applying a **row-level lock** is one of the many ways to ensure the data integrity of transactions. Now, let's review the best practices for using database locks.

Best practices when using database locks

When working with database locks, it is important to follow best practices to ensure smooth and efficient operations. Here are some best practices to keep in mind:

- **Use locks when they are needed**: Applying locks can affect performance, so only do it when it's absolutely required. Reduce the time that locks are in place. Locks should be applied as late as possible, and then released as soon as they are no longer required.
- **Use appropriate lock granularity**: Instead of locking entire tables or large sections, lock the specific rows or objects that need protection. This limits the scope of the lock and improves *concurrency*.
- **Understand transaction isolation levels**: The acquisition and release of locks are affected by various isolation levels. Learn about the many isolation levels that are available and select the best one for your application's concurrency and consistency requirements.
- **Avoid deadlocks**: The use of explicit locks, as discussed earlier in this chapter, increases the probability of **deadlocks** occurring. This is a situation where processes come to a stop waiting for a resource, which is locked in another process, to be released. Proper transaction management and application architecture must be put in place to prevent this from happening.
- **Investigate other options**: Using locks may not always be the most efficient solution. Consider alternative approaches that better suit the needs of the application, such as **optimistic concurrency control** or **application-level locking** if these are more appropriate.

Following these best practices will help you manage the locks in your database more effectively, ensuring that data integrity, concurrency, and performance are balanced.

Summary

In this chapter, we discussed how to get started with **PostgreSQL** by installing it, creating a database and a table, and then inserting data into the table. These are some of the basic concepts when working with databases, and by knowing these key concepts, you can build on them to create more ways to work with the data. Next, we discussed how **race conditions** affect transaction integrity for financial systems, and how **database locks** prevent financial transaction integrity issues. After that, we discussed how to guarantee transaction integrity with database locks, with the use of **row-level locks**. Lastly, we discussed the best practices when using database locks to ensure smooth and efficient operations. By understanding how database locks work, we can improve the data integrity and performance of our applications.

In the next chapter, we will discuss how to use **managed ledger databases**, specifically **Amazon Quantum Ledger Database** (**QLDB**), which is *a non-relational database*, for finance data integrity. Leading enterprises have started to utilize managed ledger databases to keep track of and manage sensitive financial data and transactions. *This is going to be an exciting topic!*

Further reading

To dive deeper into the topics we discussed in this chapter, feel free to explore these additional resources:

- *PostgreSQL documentation on explicit locking*:
  `https://www.postgresql.org/docs/current/explicit-locking.html`
- *Why use PostgreSQL?*:
  `https://www.postgresql.org/about/`
- *PostgreSQL Tutorial*:
  `https://www.postgresqltutorial.com/`

9

Using Managed Ledger Databases for Finance Data Integrity

In the previous chapter, we discussed how we can use the database-locking capabilities of **relational database management systems** (**RDBMSs**) to prevent data integrity issues in financial transactions. In this chapter, we will be shifting our focus a bit and discussing another type of database called ledger databases. Specifically, we'll use **Amazon Quantum Ledger Database** (**QLDB**), which is a *purpose-built* fully managed ledger database built by the cloud service provider **Amazon Web Services** (**AWS**). We will explore the core concepts of this database and learn how its unique set of features and capabilities can help maintain and manage the integrity of financial records and transactions. Of course, we'll dive deep into various hands-on solutions and examples to help us better understand how we can utilize the features of this database service for financial data integrity management.

The flow of our discussion will be as follows:

- Introduction to ledger databases
- Reviewing the internals of ledger databases
- Understanding how ledger databases prevent data integrity issues
- Exploring the best practices when using ledger databases

By the end of this chapter, you will have a deep understanding of the different components that make this database unique, and how it maintains the data integrity of financial transactions.

Technical requirements

Before we dive in, we must have the following in place:

- A web browser
- Any text editor (such as Notepad or Sublime Text) where we can store the specific values (for example, the *digest*) that will be used in the hands-on solutions in this chapter

The **PartiQL** queries (*a SQL-compatible query language used in QLDB and certain databases*) are saved in the official Packt **GitHub** repository and can be accessed from `https://github.com/PacktPublishing/Managing-Data-Integrity-for-Finance/tree/main/ch09`.

> **Note**
>
> In this chapter, we will be setting up a managed ledger database resource on AWS. If this is your first time using AWS, feel free to check out the following video to help you get started: `https://www.youtube.com/watch?v=a9__D53WsUs`.

Once these are ready, you may proceed.

Introduction to ledger databases

In the previous chapters of this book, we primarily made use of the capabilities of RDBMSs to help us solve various types of data integrity issues and challenges. While this type of database would be a good default option for most finance and technology professionals, other types of purpose-built databases can offer significant advantages in specific use cases. These purpose-built databases may include *NoSQL databases*, *graph databases*, *time-series databases*, and more, each designed to excel in handling particular data models and workloads. One such example that maintains an *immutable* and *verifiable* record of transactions over time is the **ledger database**. This type of database makes use of financial ledger concepts where each journal is appended only and cannot be altered once recorded. Because of these properties, companies from various industries that have strict requirements, which require transparency can make use of this type of database.

In this chapter, we will use Amazon QLDB, one of the managed database services on AWS. Since QLDB is a managed service, engineers can use the ledger database right away and they don't need to worry about the operational duties of maintaining, patching, and managing the server where the database application is running. What makes this database service unique is its capability to keep a **complete** and **cryptographically verifiable** history of the changes in the data.

Important note

Since Amazon QLDB provides a complete and cryptographically verifiable log of the transactions, it can be used in applications where tracking changes to the data over time is *critical*. For example, it can be applied in **banking** where an immutable record of financial transactions is necessary, especially given the audit and compliance requirements. Another application is in **vehicle registration** to track the life cycle of the vehicle, including changes in ownership. At the same time, it can be used in **supply chains** to manage the essential data required for production and share it with their partners in the network. There are so many applications for this incredible solution! To learn more about the different use cases, feel free to check out `https://aws.amazon.com/qldb/customers/`.

To understand this database service better, let us discuss some concepts you need to know about:

- **Hashing**: The ledger utilizes **SHA-256**, which stands for *secure hash algorithm 256-bit*. It is from the SHA-2 family, which is the successor of SHA-1, and is considered one of the stronger hash functions. SHA-256 is also used for verification by several **cryptocurrencies**, including **Bitcoin**. A high-level process of how the hashing function works can be seen in *Figure 9.1*:

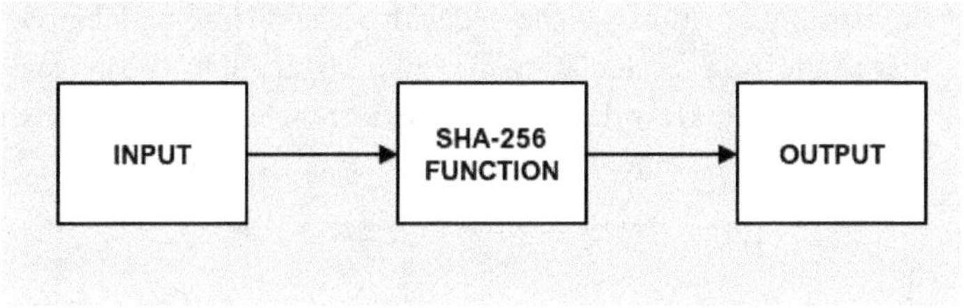

Figure 9.1 – The process of applying the SHA-256 function from input to output

What this means is that when a SHA-256 function is applied to an input, it will result in a hash output. This output is like the human fingerprint—*unique to a person as a product of one's genes and environment* that will not be the same even for identical twins. Moreover, if the input is changed just by *one letter*, the output will be completely different, as shown in *Figure 9.2*:

Input	Output (SHA-256 hash)
decade	59cd793c05f0e9e7ff8cd1700d0d641bce31d149feafa74954ee376739c034cb
decide	5589aa5863c2d85622d06d651add002416e5513afdbb455666cdde01bb3e257d

Figure 9.2 – SHA-256 example

This means that the hash values generated for two QLDB documents would be unique, even if they vary only by one digit.

Another important thing to note about SHA-256 is that the process is *one-way*—the input will always result in the same unique output hash, and the output value cannot be converted back (*in theory*) to its plain text input values through a reverse process.

- **Digest**: SHA-256 is used to create the digest, which is a cryptographic version of the ledger's complete history *at a specific point in time*. The digest is used to verify the integrity and reliability of the data. We will cover how to obtain the digest to verify the revisions and how it changes in the *Getting the digest* and *Obtaining the digest* sections later in this chapter.
- **Merkle tree**: This hashing function is combined with a Merkle tree-based model to address the inefficiencies that result from recalculating the full hash chain for the journal when working with large data structures. This is widely used in **blockchain** technology, where the Merkle tree provides an effective means of validating extensive datasets.

> **Note**
> To learn more about the Merkle tree, feel free to check out its Wikipedia page: `https://en.wikipedia.org/wiki/Merkle_tree`.

- **Proof**: The proof is comprised of the hash values needed to recompute the digest using a Merkle tree beginning with a specified block. This is generated by QLDB for a specified digest and document revision.
- **Block address**: The block address is one of the requirements needed in verifying the authenticity of a document. This allows users to identify and locate a block in the journal by making use of its two key components—the *strand ID* and the *sequence number*. Here, a strand refers to a partition of the journal.

We will cover how these concepts work more deeply in the *Understanding how ledger databases prevent data integrity issues* section.

Now that we know what Amazon QLDB is and discussed some of the fundamental concepts, let's start by creating an AWS account to dive deeper into the internals of this ledger database.

Creating an AWS account

To access AWS services, we need to have an AWS account. Creating an account is straightforward! To do this, navigate to the AWS website (`https://aws.amazon.com/`) and click on **Sign In to the Console**, as seen in *Figure 9.3*:

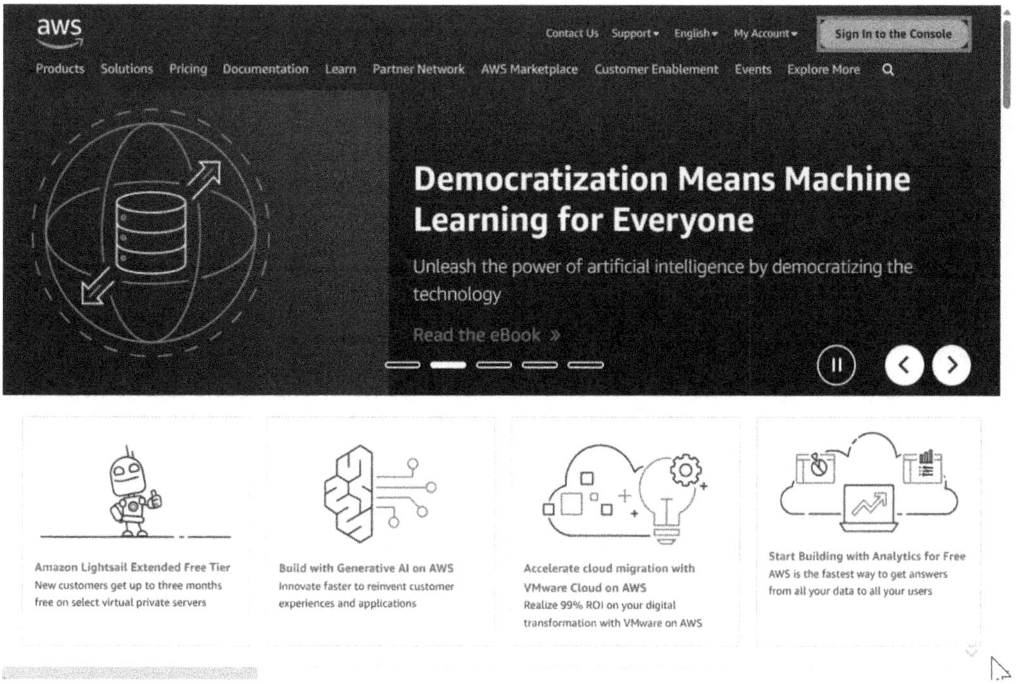

Figure 9.3 – Signing into the AWS website

If you are new to AWS, select **Create a new AWS account**, as illustrated in *Figure 9.4*, or sign in if you already have an account:

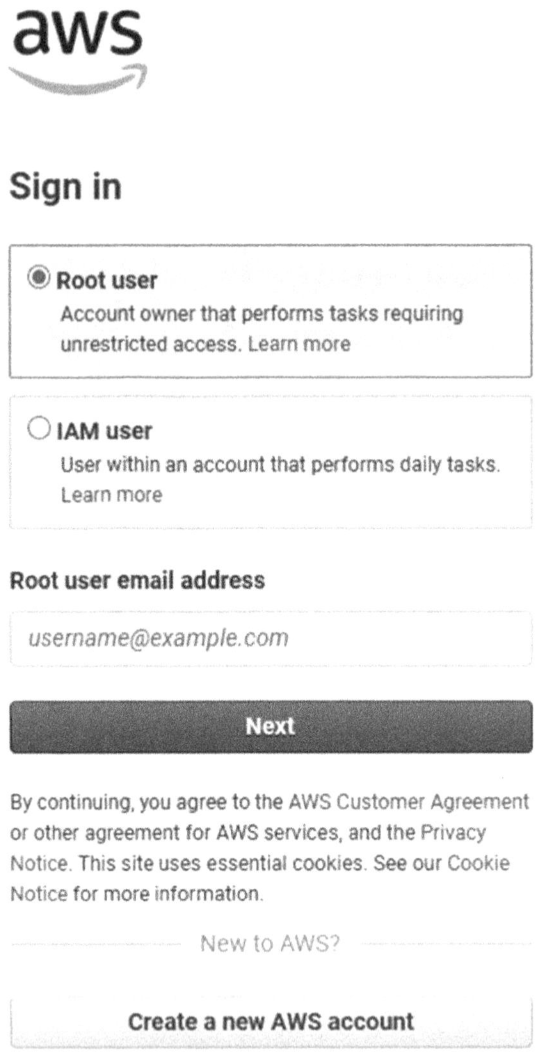

Figure 9.4 – Signing into AWS or creating a new AWS account

We will choose **Root user** for our hands-on exercises.

> **Note**
>
> We are selecting **Root user** in this instance. In practice, it is advisable to use **IAM user** with limited permissions for security purposes. However, for the hands-on exercise in this chapter, we should be fine with the root account.

Selecting **Create a new AWS account** will lead you to the sign-up page, as shown in *Figure 9.5*:

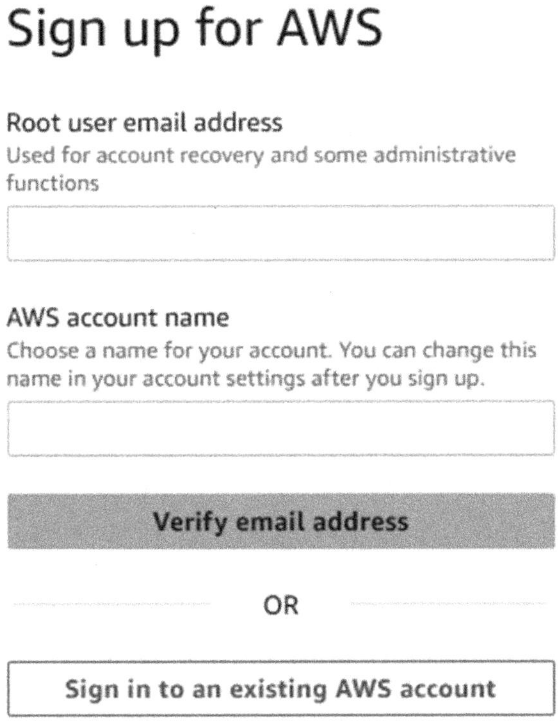
Sign up for AWS
Root user email address
Used for account recovery and some administrative functions
AWS account name
Choose a name for your account. You can change this name in your account settings after you sign up.
Verify email address
OR
Sign in to an existing AWS account

Figure 9.5 – Signing up for AWS

If you are creating a new AWS account, you need to enter your email address and create an AWS account name. You will be prompted to create a password, as well as provide your contact information and billing details, confirm your identity, and select a support plan. Let's select **Basic support – Free**, as seen in *Figure 9.6*:

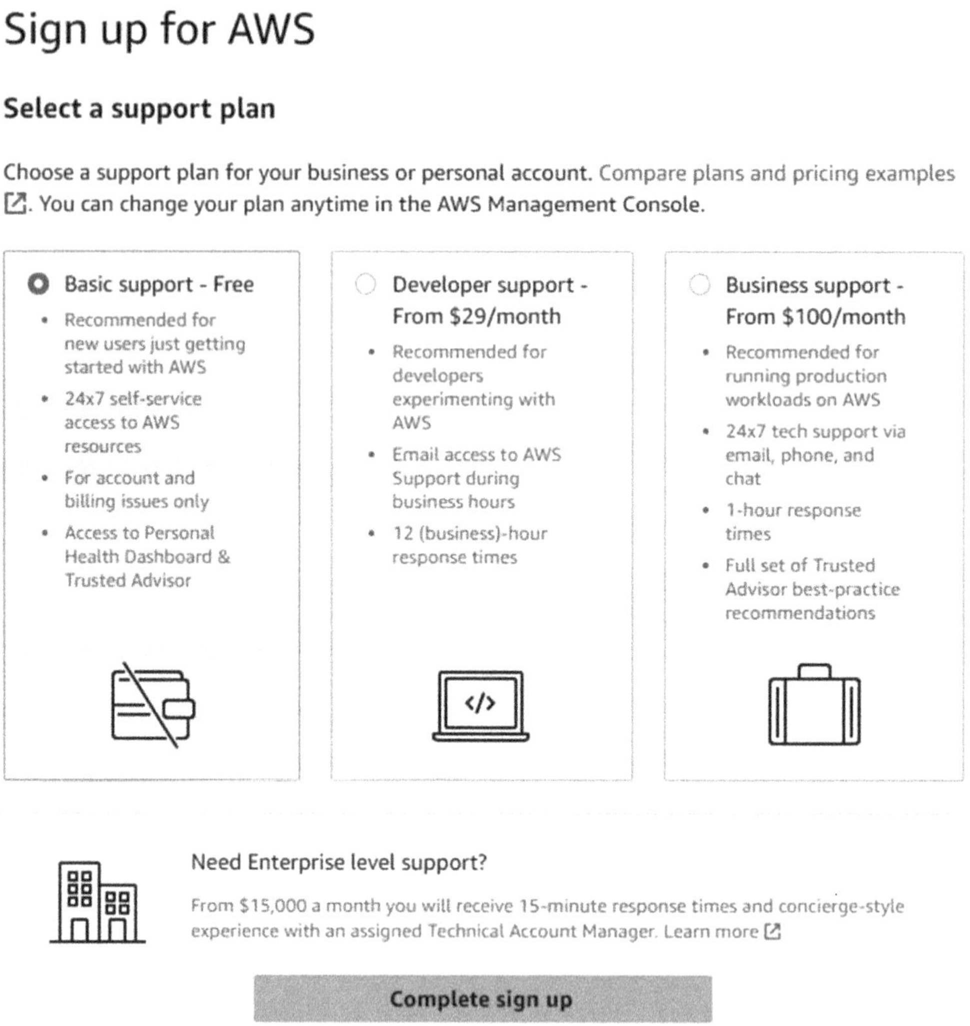
Sign up for AWS
Select a support plan
Choose a support plan for your business or personal account. Compare plans and pricing examples. You can change your plan anytime in the AWS Management Console.
Basic support - Free
Recommended for new users just getting started with AWS
24x7 self-service access to AWS resources
For account and billing issues only
Access to Personal Health Dashboard & Trusted Advisor
Developer support - From $29/month
Recommended for developers experimenting with AWS
Email access to AWS Support during business hours
12 (business)-hour response times
Business support - From $100/month
Recommended for running production workloads on AWS
24x7 tech support via email, phone, and chat
1-hour response times
Full set of Trusted Advisor best-practice recommendations
Need Enterprise level support?
From $15,000 a month you will receive 15-minute response times and concierge-style experience with an assigned Technical Account Manager. Learn more
Complete sign up

Figure 9.6 – Choosing a support plan

Then, click on **Complete sign up**.

Once you have done this, your account will be activated, and an email will be sent to your account to confirm this. When you receive the email, click on **Go to the AWS Management Console**. This will lead you back to the sign-in page, as shown in *Figure 9.4*. Type the email address you used while signing up and click on **Next**. On the next page, type in your password and click on **Sign in**, as illustrated in *Figure 9.7*:

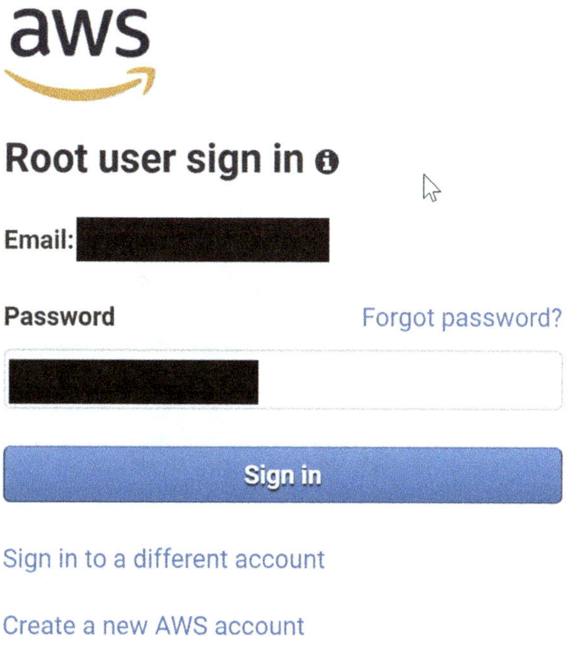

Figure 9.7 – Logging into the AWS Management Console

Once you have signed in, you will be taken to the **Console Home** page, as shown in *Figure 9.8*:

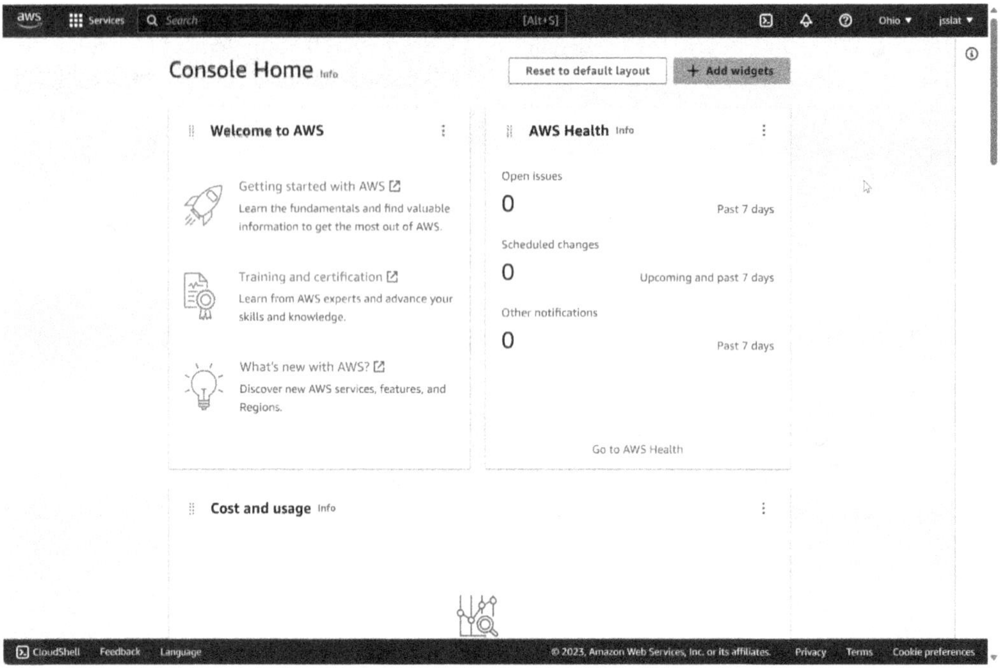

Figure 9.8 – Console Home

The **AWS Management Console** is the user interface where you can access and manage your AWS resources.

> **Note**
>
> You will also notice that in the *top-right* corner, the **availability zone** (**AZ**) defaults to **US East** (Ohio). You can select which AZ to use, but for now, let's keep the default. The ledger of Amazon QLDB is distributed over *various* AZs and has *multiple* copies per AZ. Since there is redundancy inside the region, this guarantees recovery in the unlikely event of an AZ failure.

Later in this chapter, we will export the journal data to an Amazon **Simple Storage Service** (**S3**) bucket, a storage service that can be used for storage, data backup, analytics, and auditing. But before that, we need to create the S3 bucket!

Creating an S3 bucket

Amazon S3 is an object storage solution that provides top-tier scalability, accessibility, and security. For us to export the journal later, we need to create a bucket first and then upload the journal to this bucket.

To create the S3 bucket, click on **Services** | **Storage** | **S3**, as shown in *Figure 9.9*:

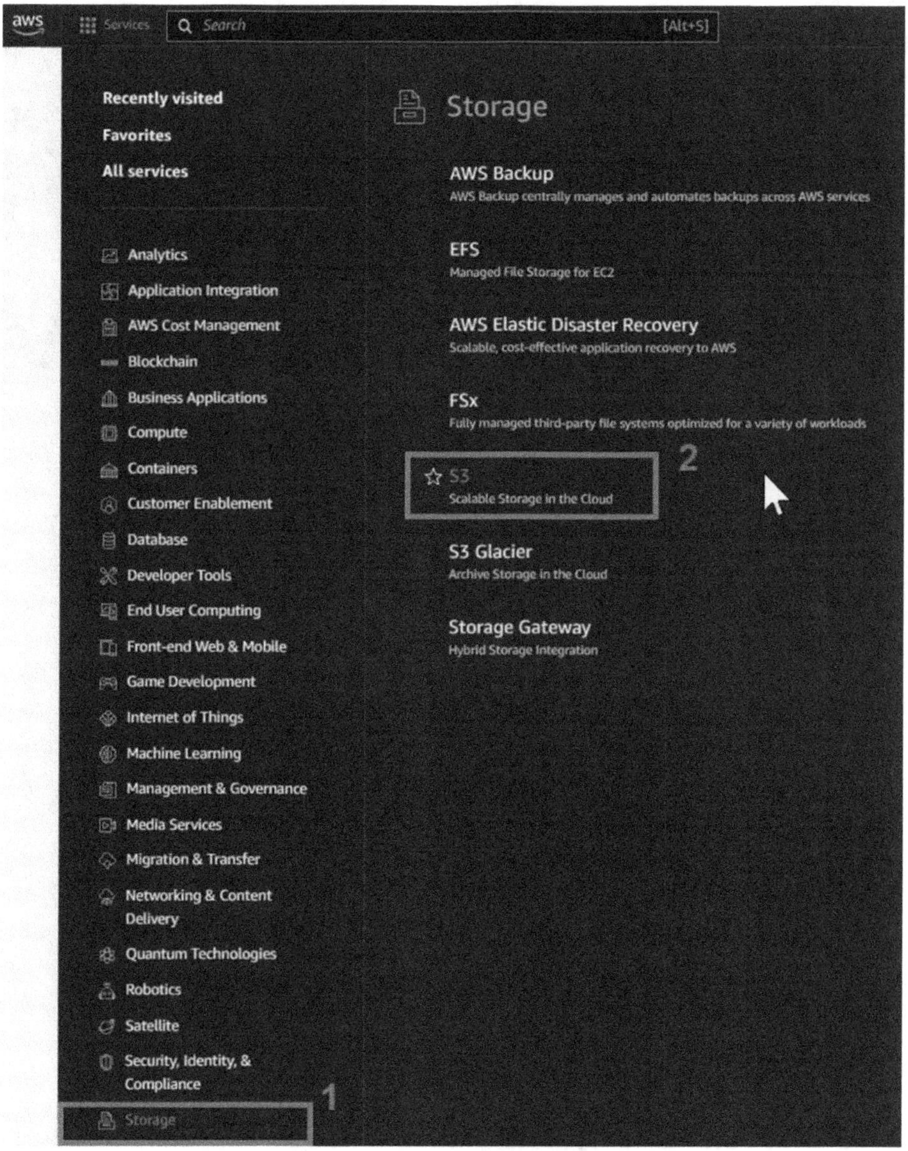

Figure 9.9 – Selecting Scalable Storage in the Cloud

Once the S3 console loads, open the navigation pane. This can be found at the *top-left* corner of the screen, below the AWS logo, as shown in *Figure 9.10*:

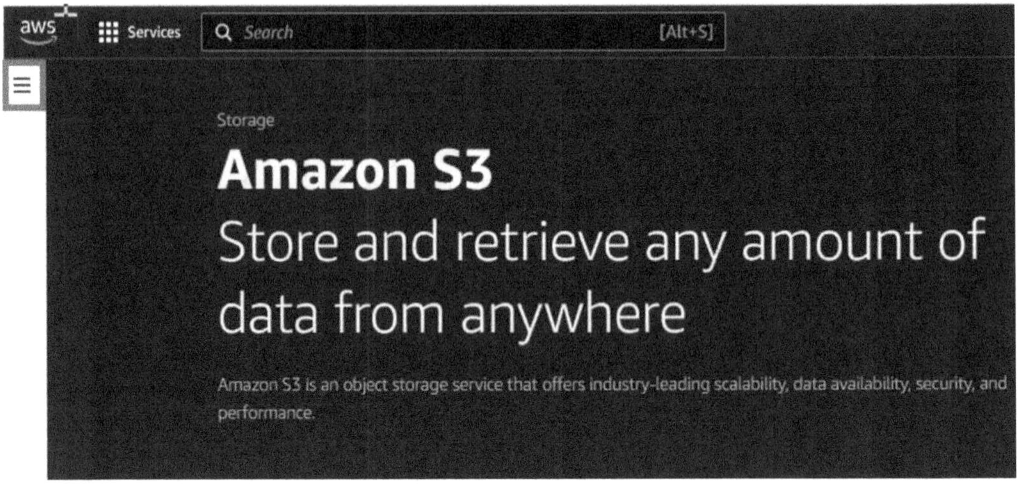

Figure 9.10 – Opening the navigation pane

When the navigation pane opens, select **Buckets**.

Next, click on **Create bucket**, as shown in *Figure 9.11*:

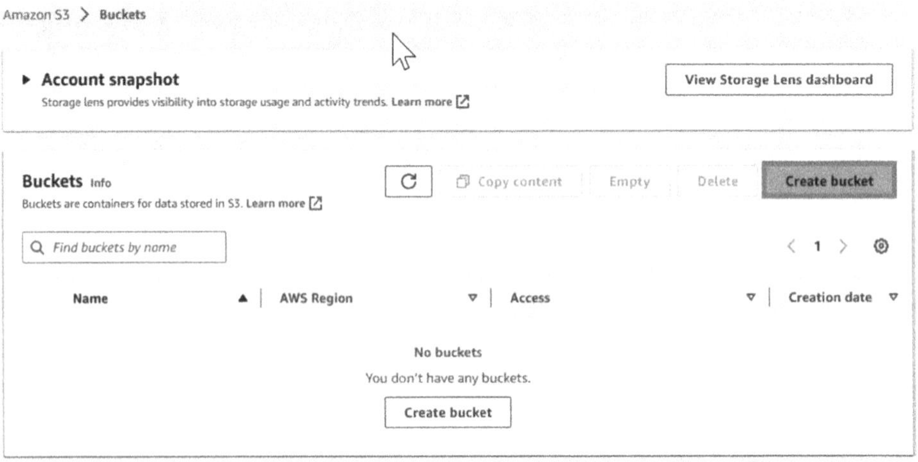

Figure 9.11 – Create bucket

This will lead you to a page containing details on how to configure the bucket, as illustrated in *Figure 9.12*. Make sure you provide a unique name to the bucket (for example, `my-qldb-export`; append a few random letters and numbers as well to ensure uniqueness):

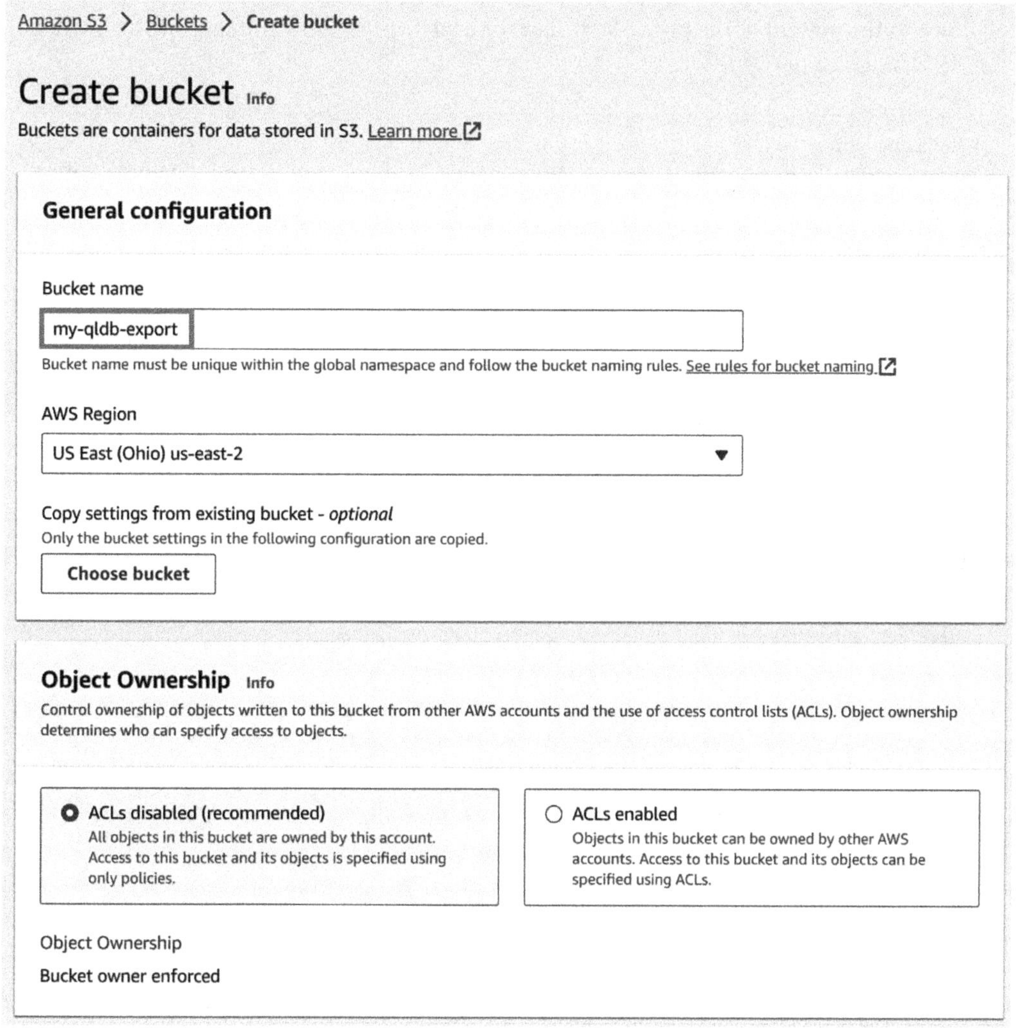

Figure 9.12 – Naming the bucket

> **Note**
>
> Remember that the bucket's name should be unique across *every AWS account* throughout all AWS regions. This means that no two customers can have the same bucket name. To learn about the bucket naming rules for S3, check out `https://docs.aws.amazon.com/AmazonS3/latest/userguide/bucketnamingrules.html`.

Scroll down to the bottom of the page. We will keep the default settings and then click on **Create bucket**, as highlighted in *Figure 9.13*:

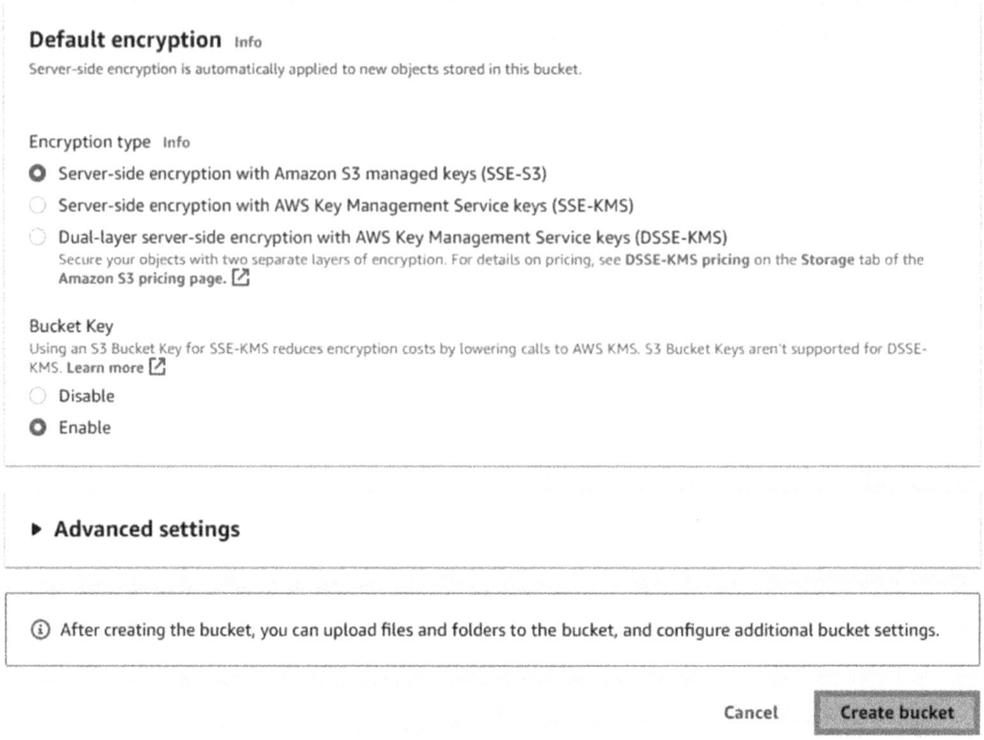

Default encryption Info
Server-side encryption is automatically applied to new objects stored in this bucket.
Encryption type Info
Server-side encryption with Amazon S3 managed keys (SSE-S3)
Server-side encryption with AWS Key Management Service keys (SSE-KMS)
Dual-layer server-side encryption with AWS Key Management Service keys (DSSE-KMS)
Secure your objects with two separate layers of encryption. For details on pricing, see DSSE-KMS pricing on the Storage tab of the Amazon S3 pricing page.
Bucket Key
Using an S3 Bucket Key for SSE-KMS reduces encryption costs by lowering calls to AWS KMS. S3 Bucket Keys aren't supported for DSSE-KMS. Learn more
Disable
Enable
Advanced settings
After creating the bucket, you can upload files and folders to the bucket, and configure additional bucket settings.
Cancel
Create bucket

Figure 9.13 – Finalizing the bucket creation process

Once this process of complete, a message stating that it has been successfully created will appear, as shown in *Figure 9.14*:

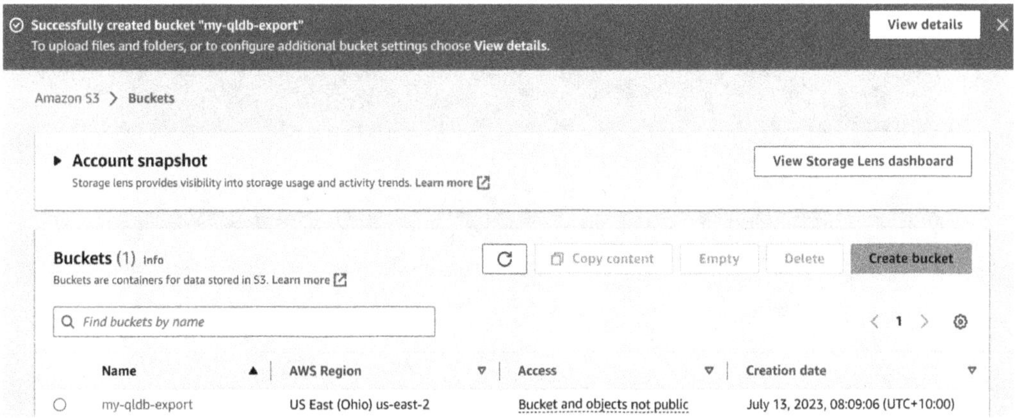

Figure 9.14 – Successfully creating the bucket

Now that we have created the S3 bucket, let's navigate to the QLDB console. We will come back to this S3 bucket page later once we have finished the relevant steps in QLDB.

The next section covers how to create a ledger in QLDB and add the records that we will work on to further illustrate the core concepts.

Creating the Amazon QLDB ledger

In the field of accounting and finance, a **ledger** contains *a record of all the financial transactions of the business*, thus providing transparency and auditability. Similarly, the ledger in Amazon QLDB keeps a comprehensive history of all the changes in the data and can be verified cryptographically. You can simply think of Amazon QLDB as a purpose-built database with additional capabilities and features.

In this section, we will discuss how to create the ledger that will store the table and queries.

Click on **Services** again. This time, select **Database** | **Amazon QLDB**, as shown in *Figure 9.15*:

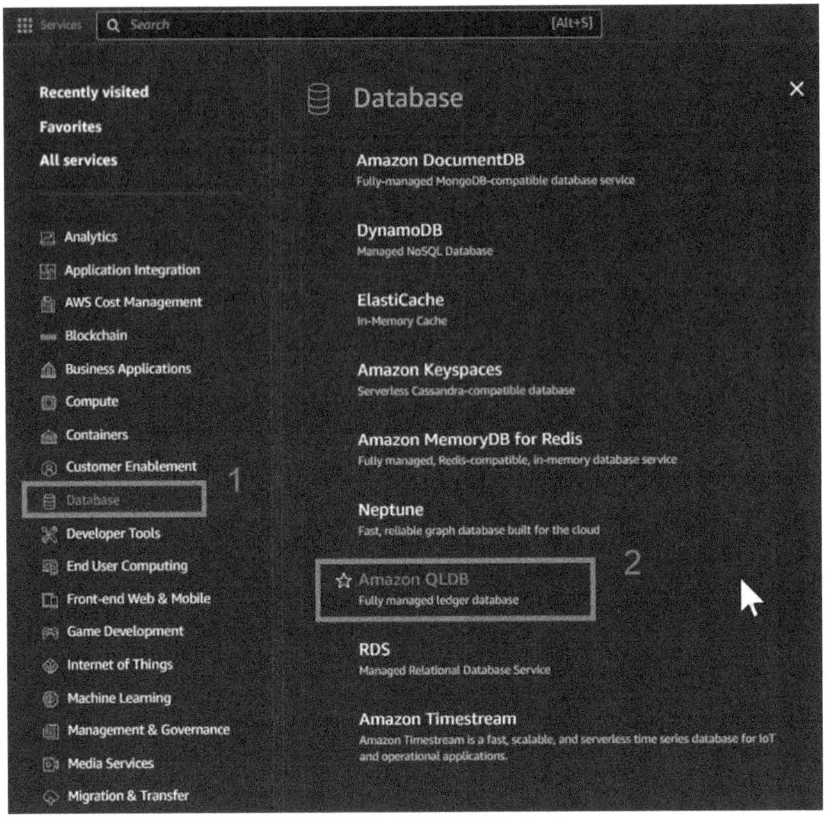

Figure 9.15 – Selecting Amazon QLDB

Once the Amazon QLDB page loads, click on **Create ledger**, as shown in *Figure 9.16*:

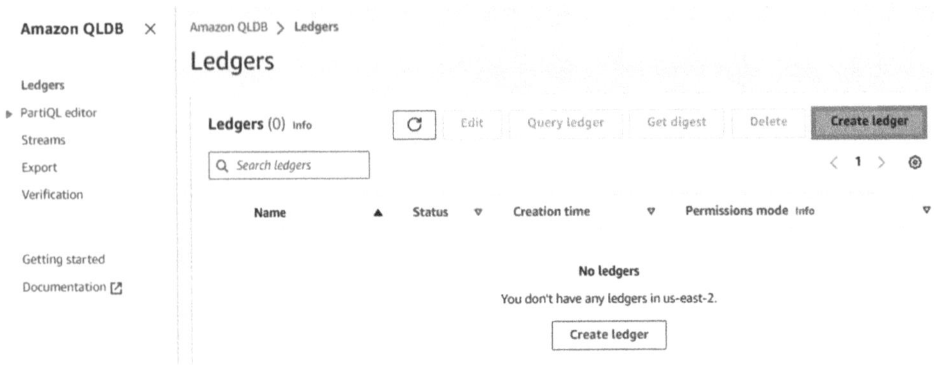

Figure 9.16 – Creating a ledger

Input the ledger's name. We will name it `myBanking`. Then, click on **Create ledger**:

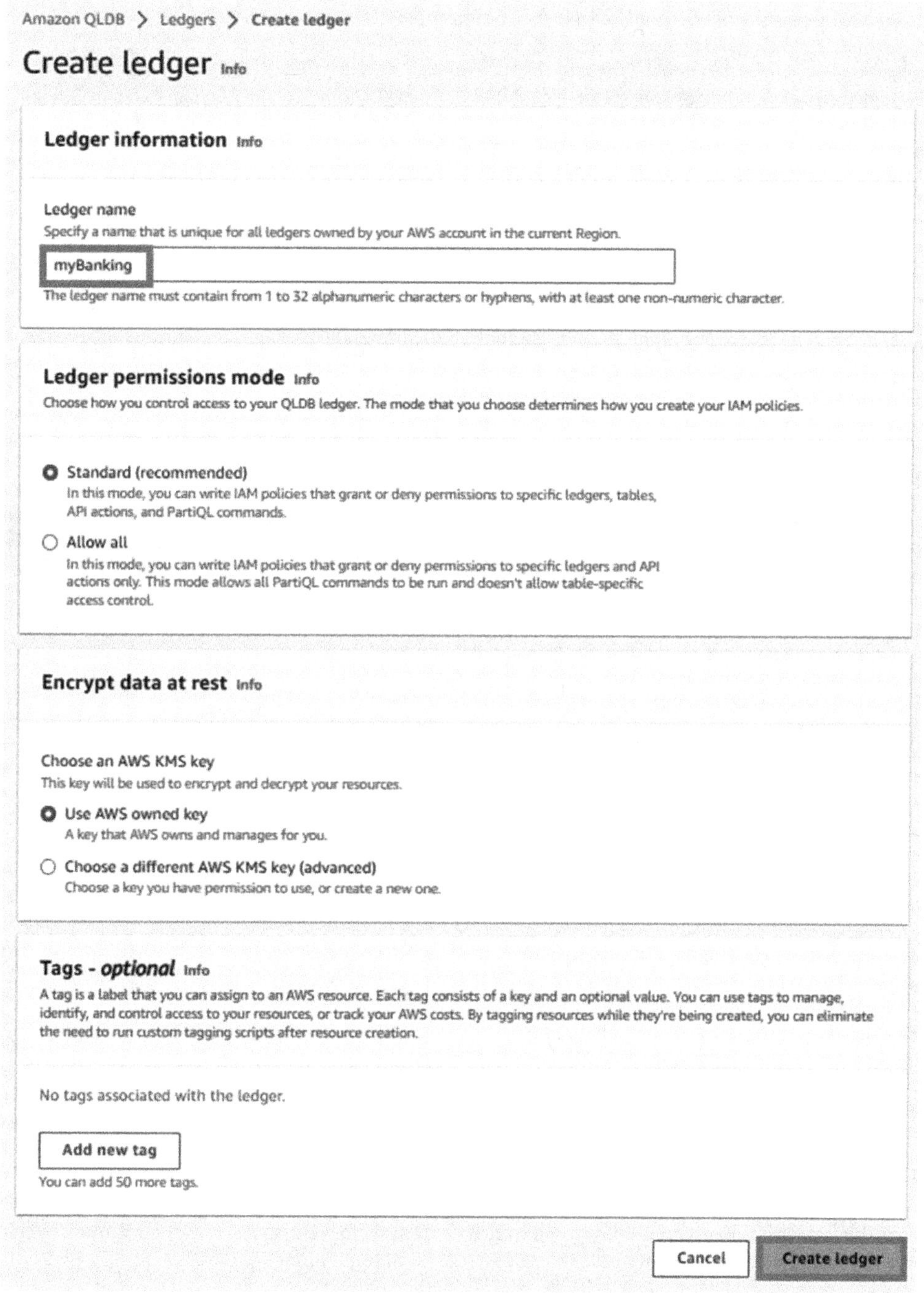
Amazon QLDB > Ledgers > Create ledger
Create ledger Info
Ledger information Info
Ledger name
Specify a name that is unique for all ledgers owned by your AWS account in the current Region.
myBanking
The ledger name must contain from 1 to 32 alphanumeric characters or hyphens, with at least one non-numeric character.
Ledger permissions mode Info
Choose how you control access to your QLDB ledger. The mode that you choose determines how you create your IAM policies.
Standard (recommended)
In this mode, you can write IAM policies that grant or deny permissions to specific ledgers, tables, API actions, and PartiQL commands.
Allow all
In this mode, you can write IAM policies that grant or deny permissions to specific ledgers and API actions only. This mode allows all PartiQL commands to be run and doesn't allow table-specific access control.
Encrypt data at rest Info
Choose an AWS KMS key
This key will be used to encrypt and decrypt your resources.
Use AWS owned key
A key that AWS owns and manages for you.
Choose a different AWS KMS key (advanced)
Choose a key you have permission to use, or create a new one.
Tags - optional Info
A tag is a label that you can assign to an AWS resource. Each tag consists of a key and an optional value. You can use tags to manage, identify, and control access to your resources, or track your AWS costs. By tagging resources while they're being created, you can eliminate the need to run custom tagging scripts after resource creation.
No tags associated with the ledger.
Add new tag
You can add 50 more tags.
Cancel
Create ledger

Figure 9.17 – Creating the ledger

We will keep the default settings for our hands-on example.

A message will pop up stating that the ledger is being created, as shown in *Figure 9.18*:

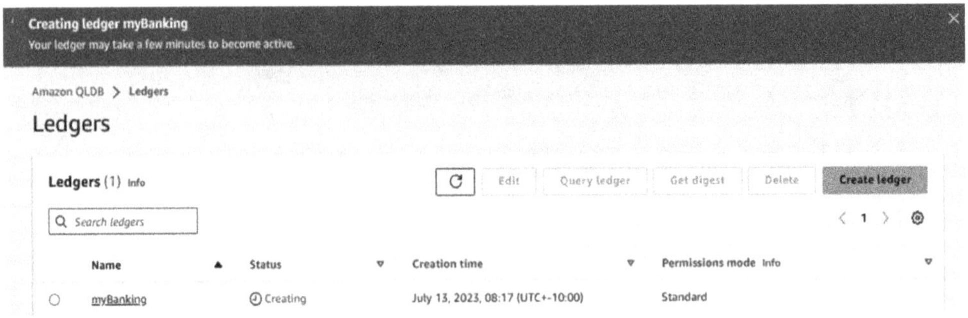

Figure 9.18 – The ledger is being created

A clock icon will appear under **Status**, which will change once the process is completed:

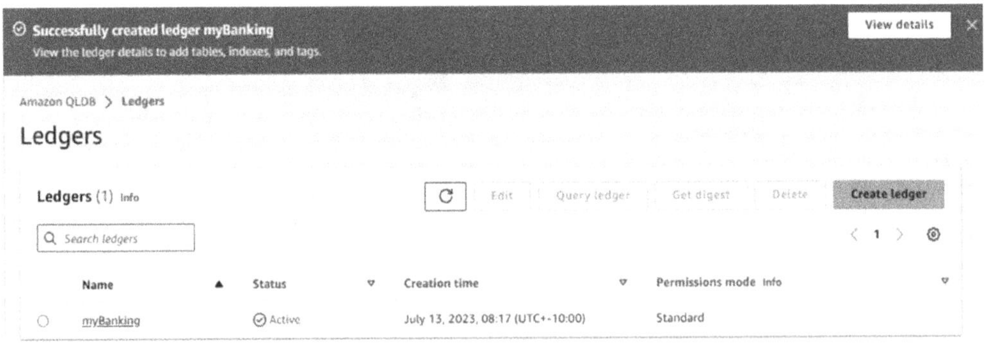

Figure 9.19 – The ledger has been created successfully

At this point, a message will appear stating that it has been completed and the status will now show as **Active**, as seen in *Figure 9.19*. That's all we needed to do to create the ledger resource! *Wasn't that easy?*

Now that we have created the S3 bucket and the QLDB ledger, in the next section, we will discuss fundamental concepts such as the *digest*, *table*, *PartiQL* editor, and *document* to set up our foundations for the verification process.

Reviewing the internals of ledger databases

Now that the ledger has been created, we will build on what we have discussed and continue covering more important concepts of QLDB. We will start by discussing the digest, creating a table, and inserting records into this table through queries.

Getting the digest

As we mentioned at the beginning of this chapter, a **digest** is a cryptographic version of your ledger's complete history *at a specific point in time*. This is one of the key components for the verification step, which we will discuss in the *Understanding how ledger databases prevent data integrity issues* section.

Continuing with our example, locate and click on the radio button beside **myBanking** to activate the **Edit**, **Query ledger**, **Get digest**, and **Delete** options. When we click on **Get digest**, it will generate the digest, as seen in *Figure 9.20*. This will contain the details that we will use later during the verification step:

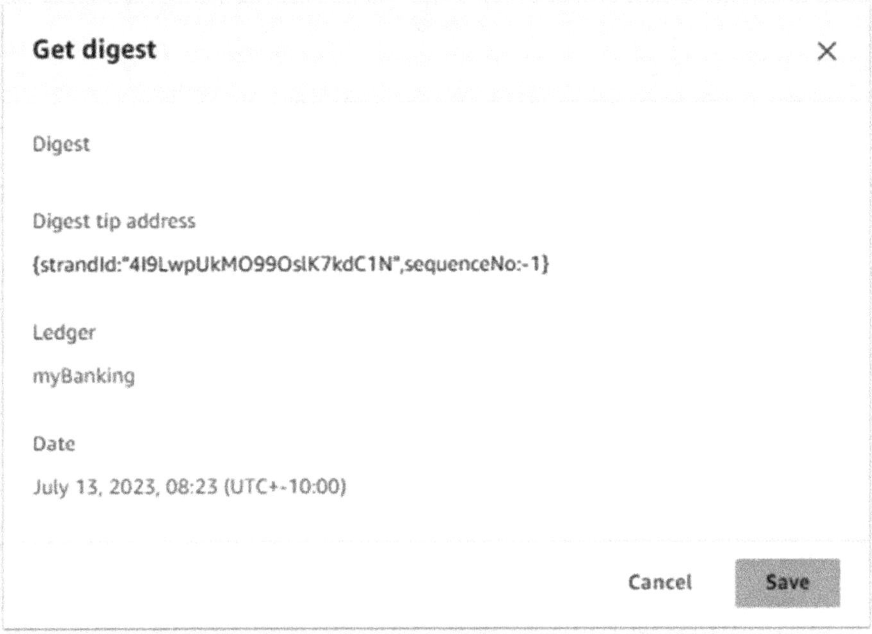

Figure 9.20 – The Get digest page

Click on **Cancel** for now. Let's go back and click on **myBanking** under **Name**. The next step is to create a table where we will input sample financial records.

Creating a table

We covered what a table is in *Chapter 8, Using Database Locking Techniques for Financial Transaction Integrity*. What makes a QLDB table different is that it does not enforce a rigid schema and allows for semi-structured data to be stored.

To create a table, click on **Create table**, as illustrated in *Figure 9.21*:

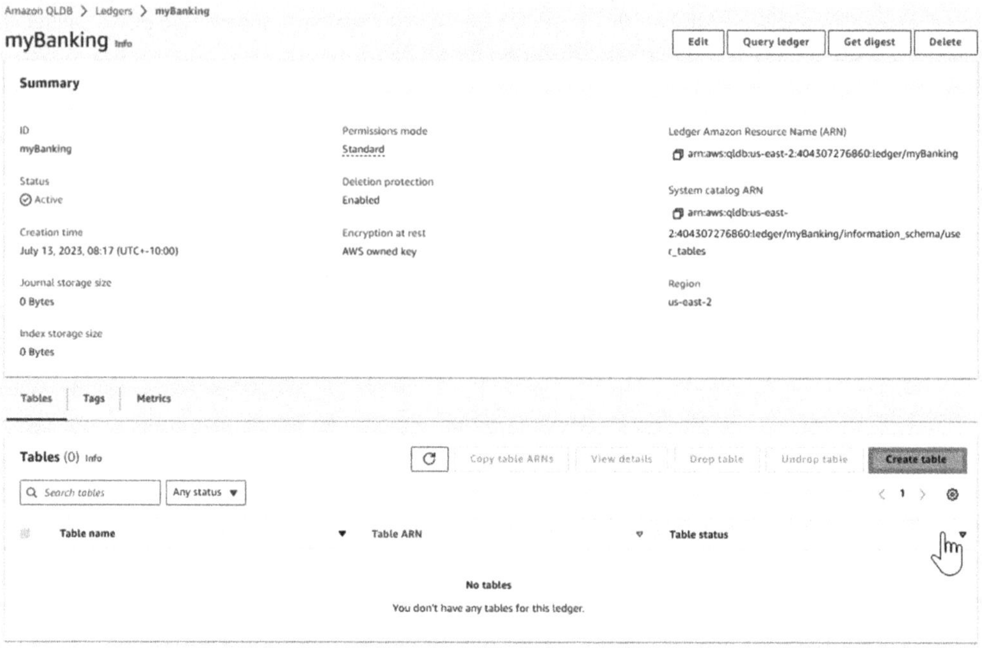

Figure 9.21 – Selecting the Create table option

This will take us to a window where we can name the table and create tags to manage the table resources. As shown in *Figure 9.22*, we will name the table `myCustomers` and then click on **Create table**:

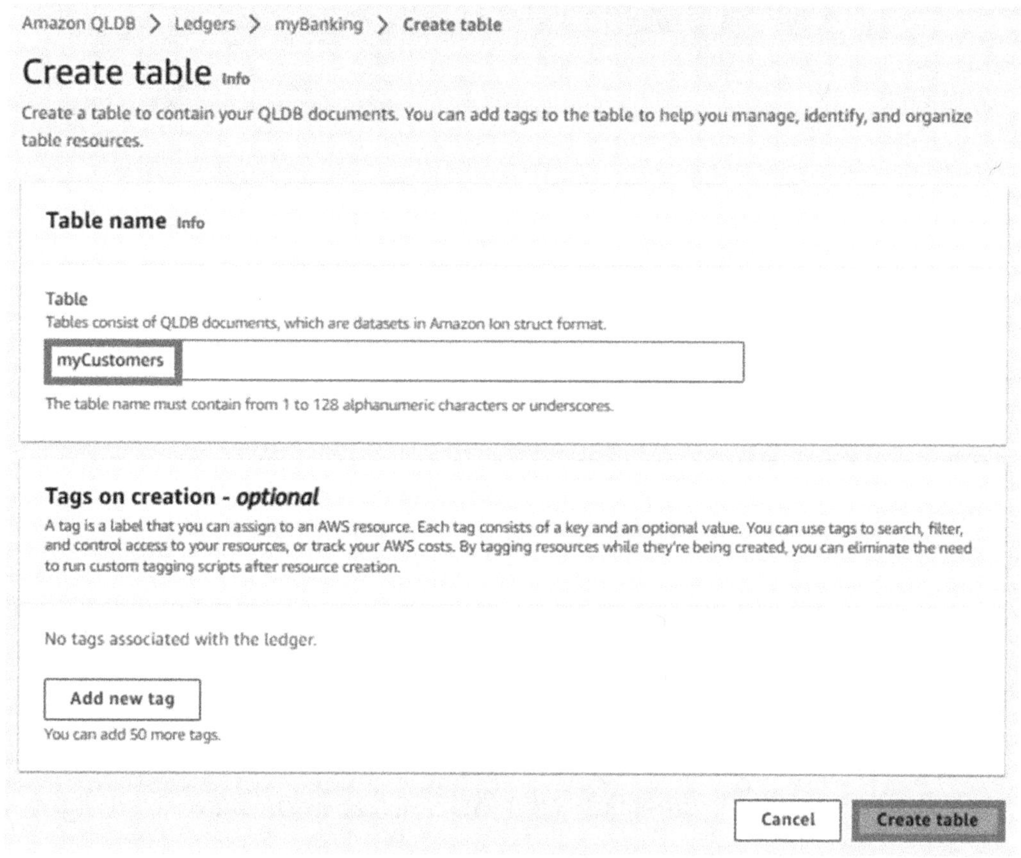
Amazon QLDB > Ledgers > myBanking > Create table
Create table Info
Create a table to contain your QLDB documents. You can add tags to the table to help you manage, identify, and organize table resources.
Table name Info
Table
Tables consist of QLDB documents, which are datasets in Amazon Ion struct format.
myCustomers
The table name must contain from 1 to 128 alphanumeric characters or underscores.
Tags on creation - optional
A tag is a label that you can assign to an AWS resource. Each tag consists of a key and an optional value. You can use tags to search, filter, and control access to your resources, or track your AWS costs. By tagging resources while they're being created, you can eliminate the need to run custom tagging scripts after resource creation.
No tags associated with the ledger.
Add new tag
You can add 50 more tags.
Cancel
Create table

Figure 9.22 – Configuring the table's details

The table is where the QLDB documents will be located.

A note will appear stating that the table has been successfully created. The table's status will also appear as **Active**, as shown in *Figure 9.23*:

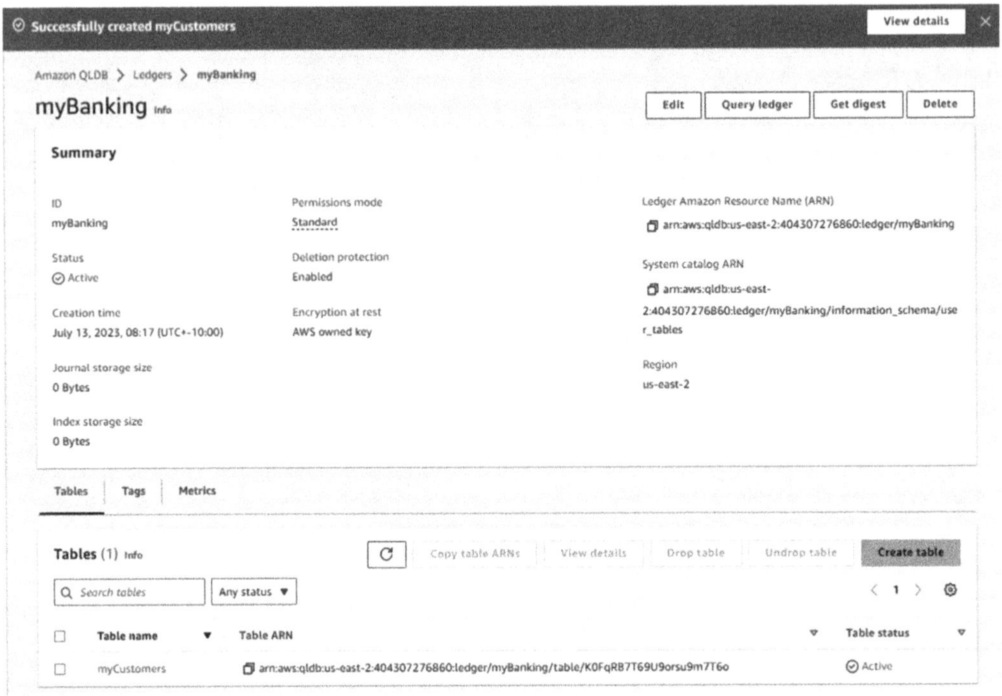

Figure 9.23 – Table created successfully

Now that we have created a table, we'll add details to it through the **PartiQL editor**.

Using the PartiQL editor

QLDB uses the **PartiQL** query language, which is a *SQL-compatible* language that enables efficient querying of data that supports semi-structured data.

> **Note**
>
> To learn more about the PartiQL query language, feel free to check out `https://aws.amazon.com/blogs/opensource/announcing-partiql-one-query-language-for-all-your-data/`.

To open the PartiQL editor, click on **myCustomers** under **Table name**; this will lead you to a page containing details about the table. In the *top-right* corner, click on **Query**, as shown in *Figure 9.24*:

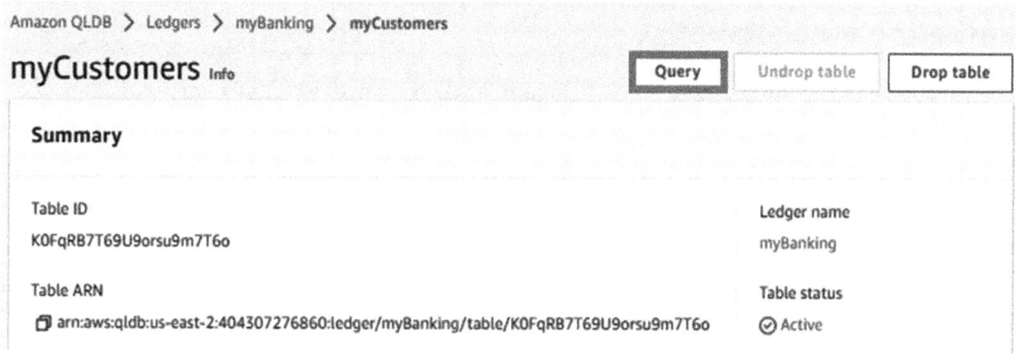

Figure 9.24 – Selecting Query to open the PartiQL editor

This will load the **PartiQL editor**, as seen in *Figure 9.25*:

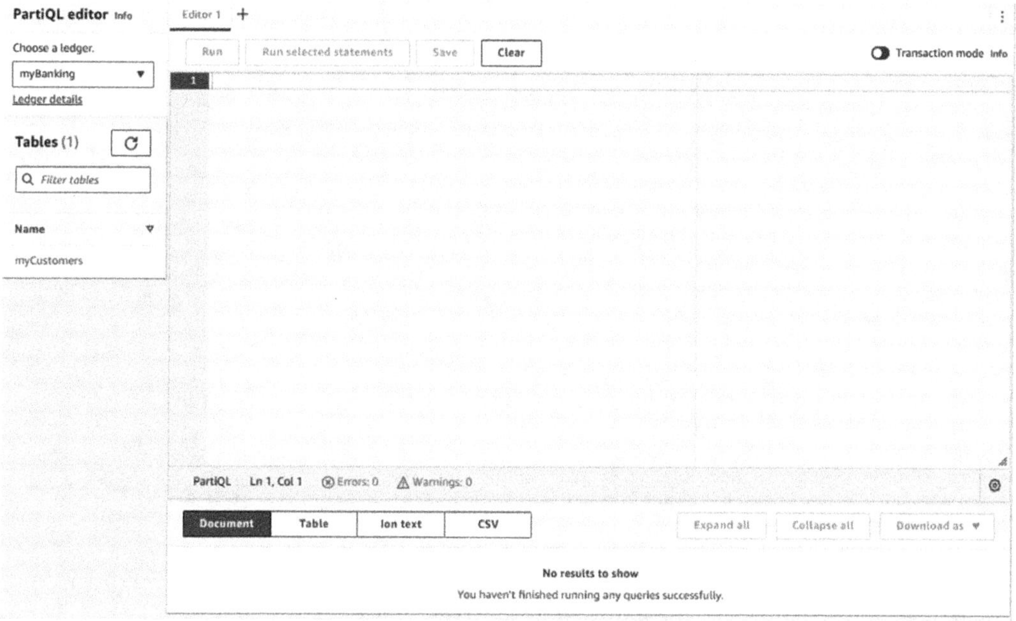

Figure 9.25 – The PartiQL editor

This is where we input our queries. Make sure that you have specified the correct ledger (under **Choose a ledger**). In our example, this is **myBanking**.

Now that we know where we can enter our queries, let's start inserting records into the table!

Generating a document

When we update the table or insert records, a **document ID** is created, which is a *unique identifier* for the data in the ledger framework. The document ID is important in maintaining the integrity of the document and enables its traceability. By using this unique identifier, as we will see in our hands-on example in this chapter, the document can be monitored and audited for any changes made.

Let's learn how to create a document using the PartiQL query language. Input the details of a customer named *John Ryan* into the editor and click on **Run**:

```
INSERT INTO "myCustomers" `{"CustomerName":"John Ryan",
"CustomerId":"S0001", "CustomerAddress": "55 Prairie, Lincoln Drive
20502", "Loans":{"Student":10000}}`;
```

Once the editor has completed the process, a message will appear, stating that it is complete, as illustrated in *Figure 9.26*:

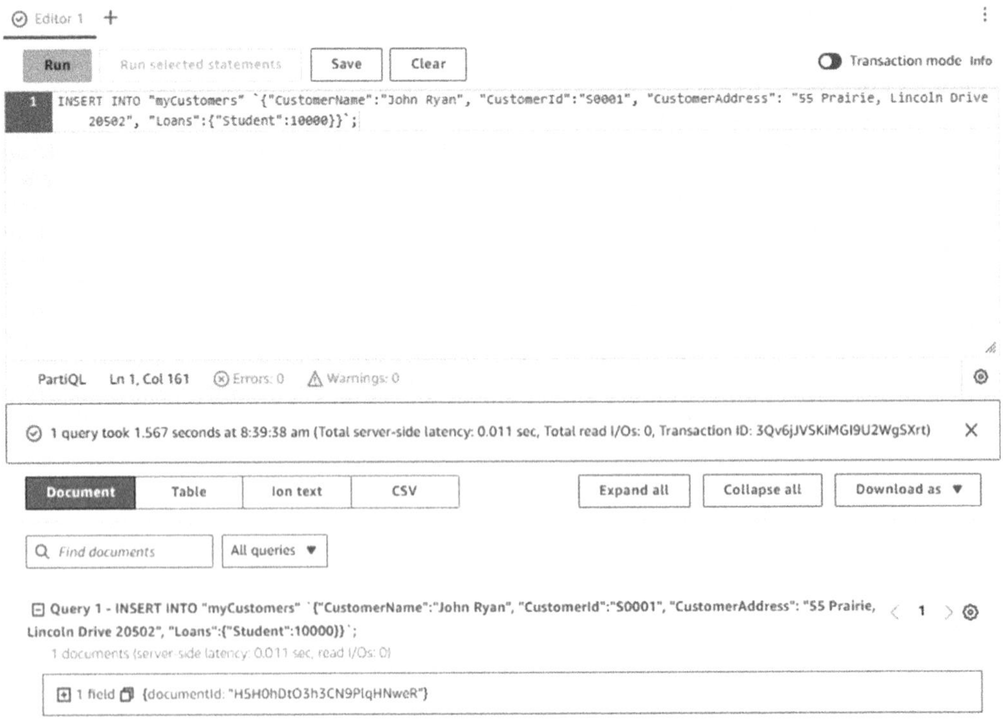

Figure 9.26 – Successfully inserting a record into the table

A document hash code will also be generated. Take note of this **document ID** since we will use this later during verification. Keep in mind that this specific ID may vary based on your hands-on exercise.

The next section will cover the *save* and *clear* functions in the editor.

Saving and retrieving a query

The PartiQL editor allows us to save queries and load them back into the editor later. This is particularly helpful when we want to save time and effort in creating queries. In this section, we will focus on how this function works.

Continuing with our example, click on **Save**, as highlighted in *Figure 9.27*, so that we can use this format as a reference later:

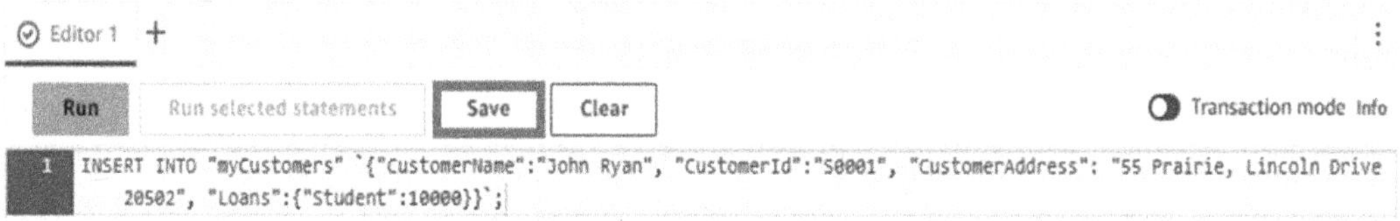

Figure 9.27 – The Save option

We will save this query as `Insert customers`, as shown in *Figure 9.28*:

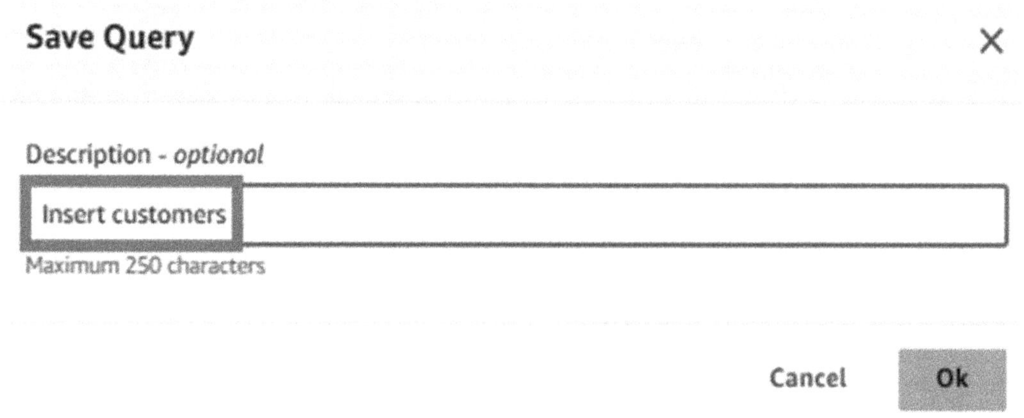

Figure 9.28 – Saving the query

Click on **Ok**.

Once saved, the query will go to **Saved queries**, as illustrated in *Figure 9.29*:

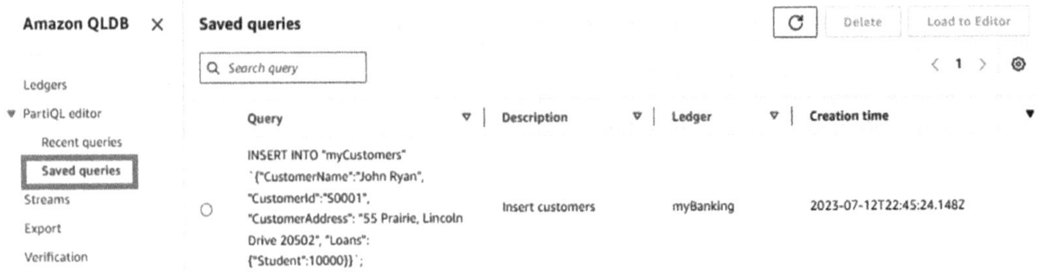

Figure 9.29 – Saved queries

It will also appear under **Recent queries**, as seen in *Figure 9.30*:

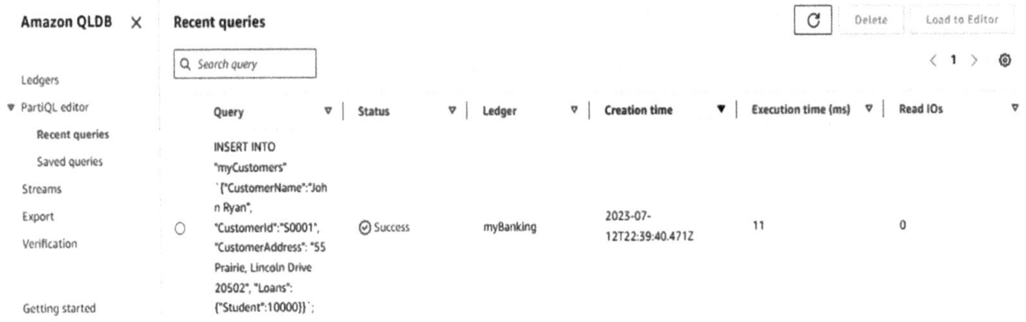

Figure 9.30 – Recent queries

Now that we have inserted a new record into the table, *how do we view it?*

Viewing the data in the table

This will be similar to the query we used in the previous chapter.

Let's clear the query, as shown in *Figure 9.31*:

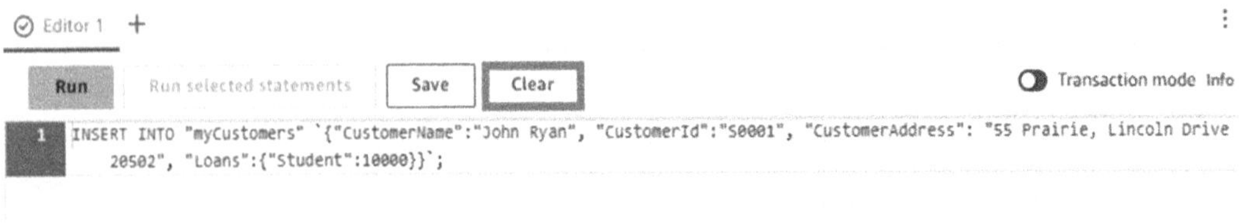

Figure 9.31 – Clearing the query

Now that we have cleared the query in the editor, let's insert the following SELECT statement and click on **Run**:

```
SELECT * FROM myCustomers;
```

Similar to what happened previously, a message stating that the query has run successfully will be displayed, as seen in *Figure 9.32*:

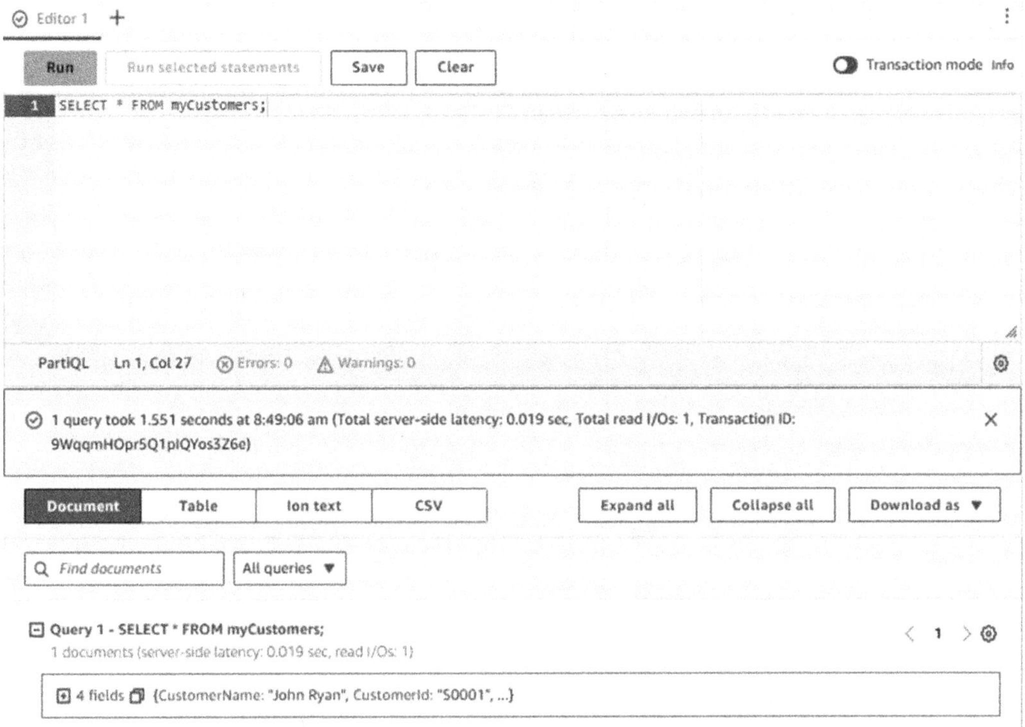

Figure 9.32 – Querying the record(s) from the table

Figure 9.33 shows that based on the code we typed in earlier, the editor has created the columns containing the customer details:

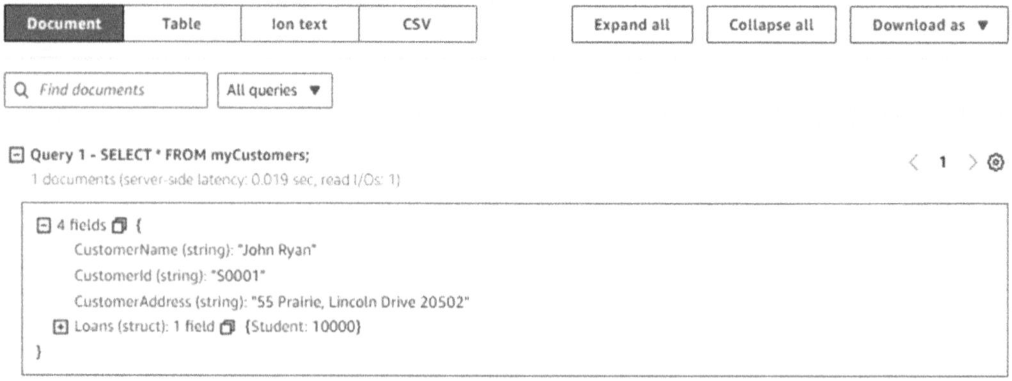

Figure 9.33 – Document view

To get the table view that provides a clearer layout of the data, click on **Table**, as illustrated in *Figure 9.34*:

Figure 9.34 – Table view

This view provides a clearer breakdown of the records that have been queried from the table.

Let's save this query again and name it `Select info`, as shown in *Figure 9.35*:

Figure 9.35 – Saving the query to select all records in the table

Click on **Ok**.

Now that we know how to insert records into the table, let's add some more.

Loading saved queries

Let's try loading the query that we saved back in the editor by adding some more records to the table. We will see that it makes the process easier. To do this, go to **Saved queries** and select the radio button beside **Insert customers**, as shown in *Figure 9.36*:

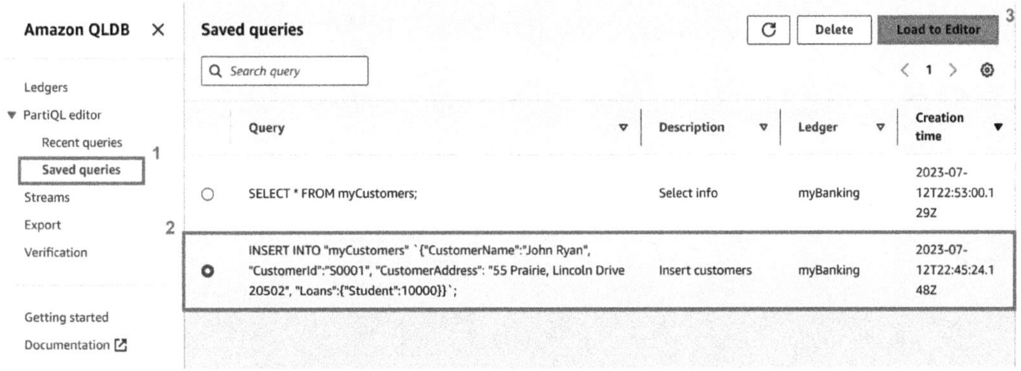

Figure 9.36 – Loading saved queries into the editor

Next, click on **Load to Editor**.

This will load the saved query in the editor, as seen in *Figure 9.37*:

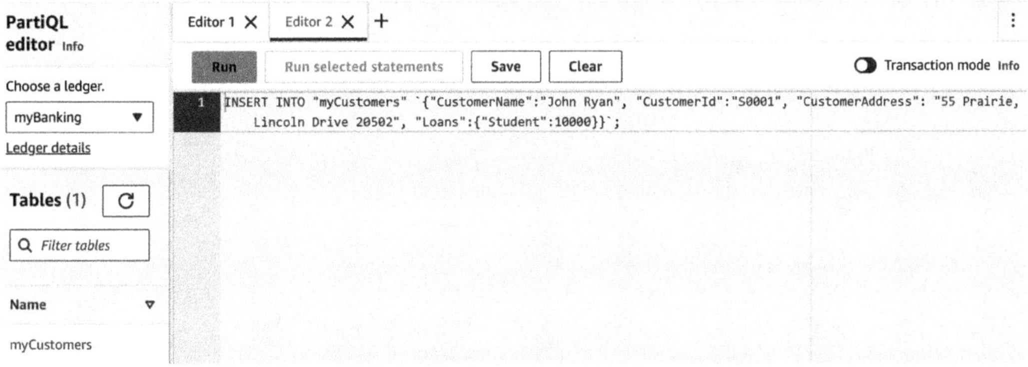

Figure 9.37 – Loaded query

We will use this as a template to insert new customer details.

Let's edit the query by adding the following:

```
INSERT INTO "myCustomers" `{"CustomerName":"Jack Kane",
"CustomerId":"S0002", "CustomerAddress": "77 Shawn St, Bradley Drive
20206", "Loans":{"Car":45000}}`;
INSERT INTO "myCustomers" `{"CustomerName":"Winnie Li",
"CustomerId":"S0003", "CustomerAddress": "86 Wonder Road, Sunrise
Drive 20238", "Loans":{"Home":350000}}`;
```

This will add the details of Jack Kane, who has a car loan, and Winnie Li, who has a home loan.

Next, locate and click on the **Run** button. A message stating that the query has been processed after a couple of seconds will appear, as shown in *Figure 9.38*:

Editor 1
Editor 2
Run
Run selected statements
Save
Clear
Transaction mode Info
1 INSERT INTO "myCustomers" `{"CustomerName":"Jack Kane", "CustomerId":"S0002", "CustomerAddress": "77 Shawn St, Bradley Drive 20206", "Loans":{"Car":45000}}`;
2 INSERT INTO "myCustomers" `{"CustomerName":"Winnie Li", "CustomerId":"S0003", "CustomerAddress": "86 Wonder Road, Sunrise Drive 20238", "Loans":{"Home":350000}}`;
PartiQL Ln 2, Col 163 Errors: 0 Warnings: 0
2 queries took 1.759 seconds at 7:21:46 am (Total server-side latency: 0.016 sec, Total read I/Os: 0, Transaction ID: DThymThl96iBlazLMvN90w)
Document
Table
Ion text
CSV
Expand all
Collapse all
Download as
Find documents
All queries
Query 1 - INSERT INTO "myCustomers" `{"CustomerName":"Jack Kane", "CustomerId":"S0002", "CustomerAddress": "77 Shawn St, Bradley Drive 20206", "Loans":{"Car":45000}}`;
1 documents (server-side latency: 0.011 sec, read I/Os: 0)
1 field {documentId: "L7SADm0c6lzltQXENHKQzw"}
Query 2 - INSERT INTO "myCustomers" `{"CustomerName":"Winnie Li", "CustomerId":"S0003", "CustomerAddress": "86 Wonder Road, Sunrise Drive 20238", "Loans":{"Home":350000}}`;
1 documents (server-side latency: 0.005 sec, read I/Os: 0)
1 field {documentId: "6LtwTICwO9bIlnXlhbYbnH"}

Figure 9.38 – Adding records to the table

We can also see that the unique document IDs for each record are also generated.

With the changes we've made here, *what does our table look like now?*

Nesting automatically

QLDB supports **nesting**, which is similar to putting data containers inside another container. This makes it simpler to understand the *context* of the data and minimizes the *risk* of inconsistencies. Leveraging this structure enables efficient data management, making querying the dataset more efficient, and enhances the data integrity. Let's see what nesting looks like when we look at our table.

Once again, let's go to our saved queries and load the query we saved earlier called **Select info**, then click on **Run**.

When we click on **Table**, we will see that nesting has automatically happened for the types of loans, as shown in *Figure 9.39*:

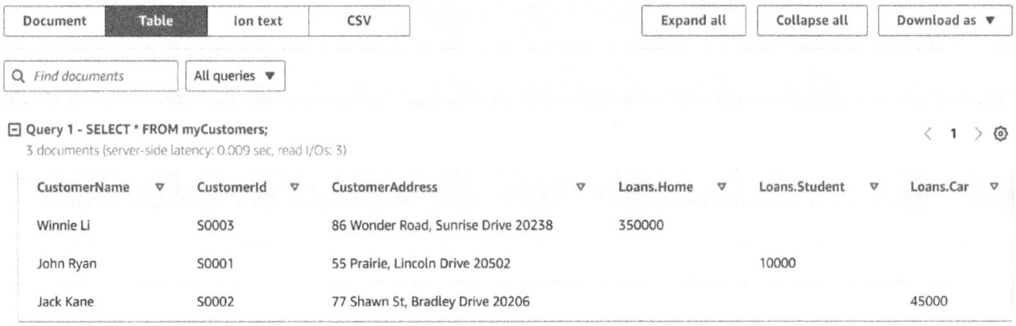

Figure 9.39 – Updated table with nesting

It has created a container for `Loans` and placed the different types of loans, making it easier to maintain and understand. This enhances the consistency and quality of the data.

Now that we have covered the fundamentals, let's discuss how the **verification** process works and dive deeper into the concepts.

Understanding how ledger databases prevent data integrity issues

In this section, we will discuss the steps and components to perform the various verification procedures. We will dive deep into the queries on how to do this, as well as discuss the *immutability* of the ledger by covering the built-in *history* function. By doing this, we will see how QLDB can maintain a *complete* record of the changes we have made and show how *cryptographic verification* is done. These features are what make this database unique and help maintain the integrity of the data.

> **Note**
>
> **Cryptographic verification** in QLDB is a method that ensures the integrity and authenticity of the data within the ledger. This is possible by utilizing *hash chaining* combined with a *Merkle tree-based model* to perform the verification. Because of this capability, the integrity of the ledger is maintained, making it well-suited for use where an accurate and reliable record of transactions is essential.

Now that we have covered some of the basics, let's discuss how verification works.

Verifying the document

If we click on **Verification** from the left panel, as seen in *Figure 9.40*, we will see that there are two prerequisites to do this. First, we need the **document ID** and **block address**, and second, we need the **digest**:

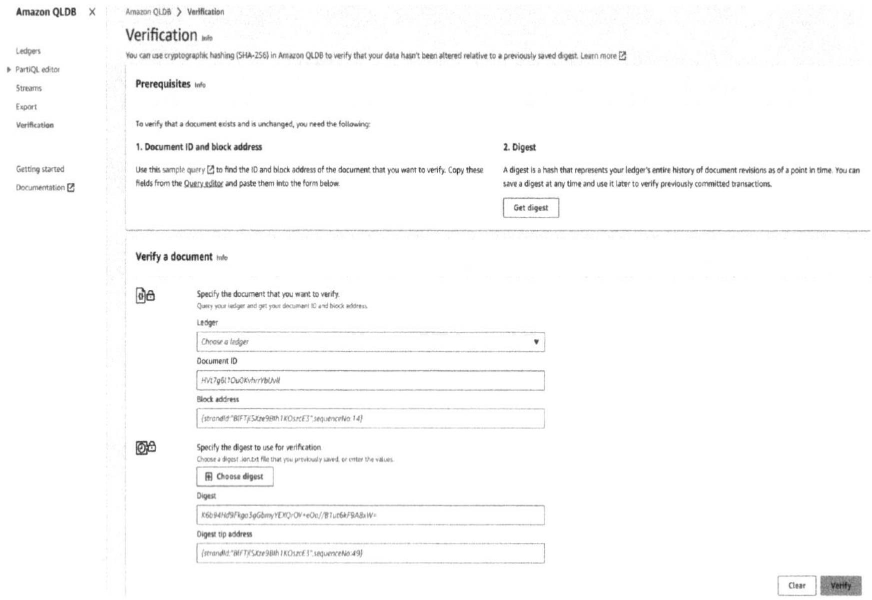

Figure 9.40 – The two prerequisites for verification

We will verify the record for the `H5H0hDtO3h3CN9PlqHNweR` document, which is for John Ryan, the first customer we placed on the table under the *Generating a document* subsection. Use the documentID that you got in this step as found in *Figure 9.26*.

Next, we need to get the *block address* for this customer to locate the block where the document is in the journal. To do this, we will input the following query in the editor and then click on **Run**:

```
SELECT m.metadata.CustomerId, m.blockAddress
FROM _ql_committed_myCustomers AS m
WHERE m.data.CustomerId = 'S0001'
```

This statement will select the related block address for the customer. When we run these statements, it will generate the block address.

Let's click on **Download as** | **Ion text**, as shown in *Figure 9.41*:

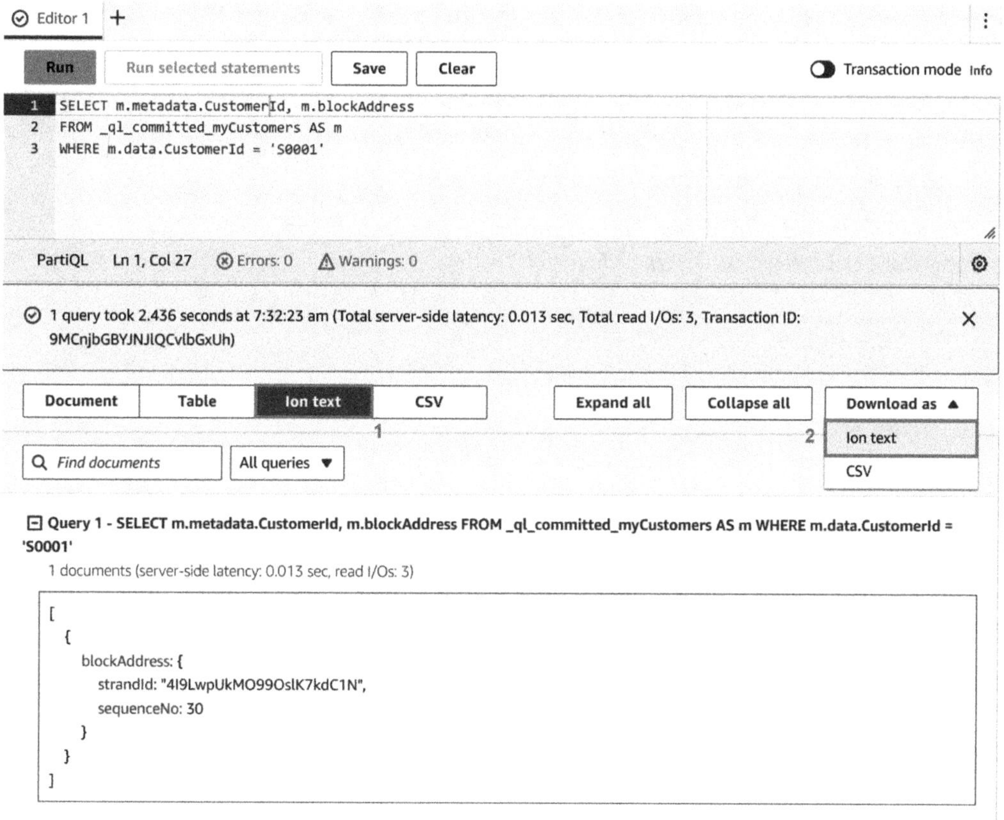

Figure 9.41 – Downloading the file as ion text

This will download the block address to the `Downloads` folder. Save this file as `Metadata_01` in a location on your computer. Note that the block address generated will differ based on your hands-on.

Now that we have the block address, let's get the digest.

Go back to **Ledgers**, click on the radio button next to **myBanking**, and then click on **Get digest**, as shown in *Figure 9.42*:

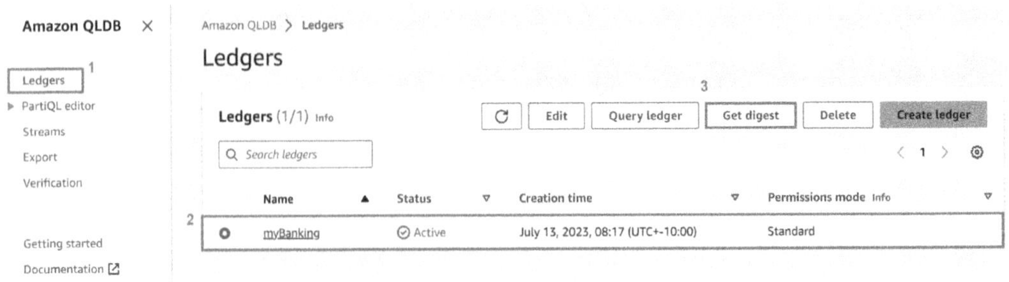

Figure 9.42 – Getting the digest

> **Note**
>
> This is the same step we performed earlier in *Figure 9.20*.

The digest will be generated, as shown in *Figure 9.43*:

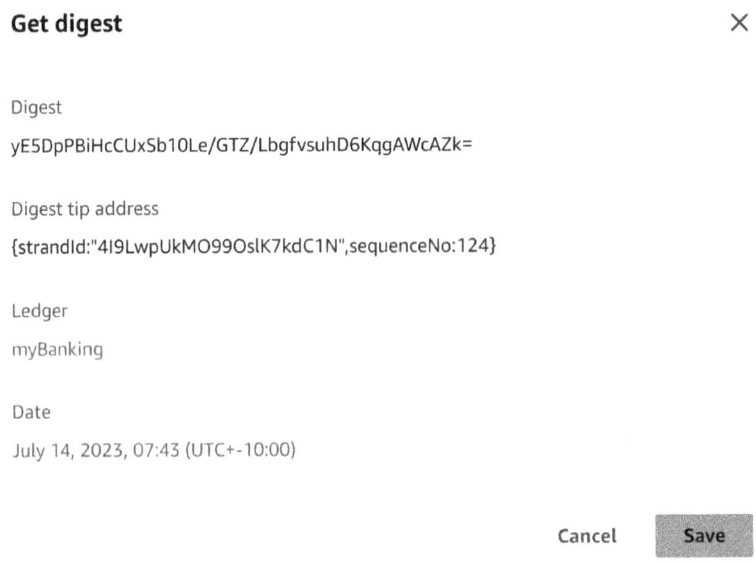

Figure 9.43 – Getting the details of the digest

When you save the file, it will go to the `Downloads` folder. Save this file as `Digest_01`, preferably in the same place where `Metadata_01` is. Note that the digest generated (similar to the block address) will differ based on your hands-on.

Now that we have everything we need, we can perform the verification step by getting the following:

- **Ledger**: Ensure that the correct ledger is selected. In our example, we are working on **myBanking**.
- **Document ID**: Get the document ID we generated earlier, which is `H5H0hDtO3h3CN9PlqHNweR`. The document ID is automatically created when inserting, updating, or deleting a document. If there is a need to retrieve the document ID, we can check this by viewing the metadata. We will discuss this in the *Working with history and data* section later in this chapter.
- **Block address**: Copy the block address that we got from *Figure 9.41*. This is saved in `Metadata_01`.
- **Digest**: Take the digest in `Digest_01`, which we obtained from *Figure 9.43*. This is what is inside the quotation marks.
- **Digest tip address**: We got this together with the digest. Ensure that the two *backslash* (\) characters are removed before verifying the document. Note that the sequence number for the digest is higher than the sequence number in the block address.

Once the form has been completed, as shown in *Figure 9.44*, click on **Verify**:

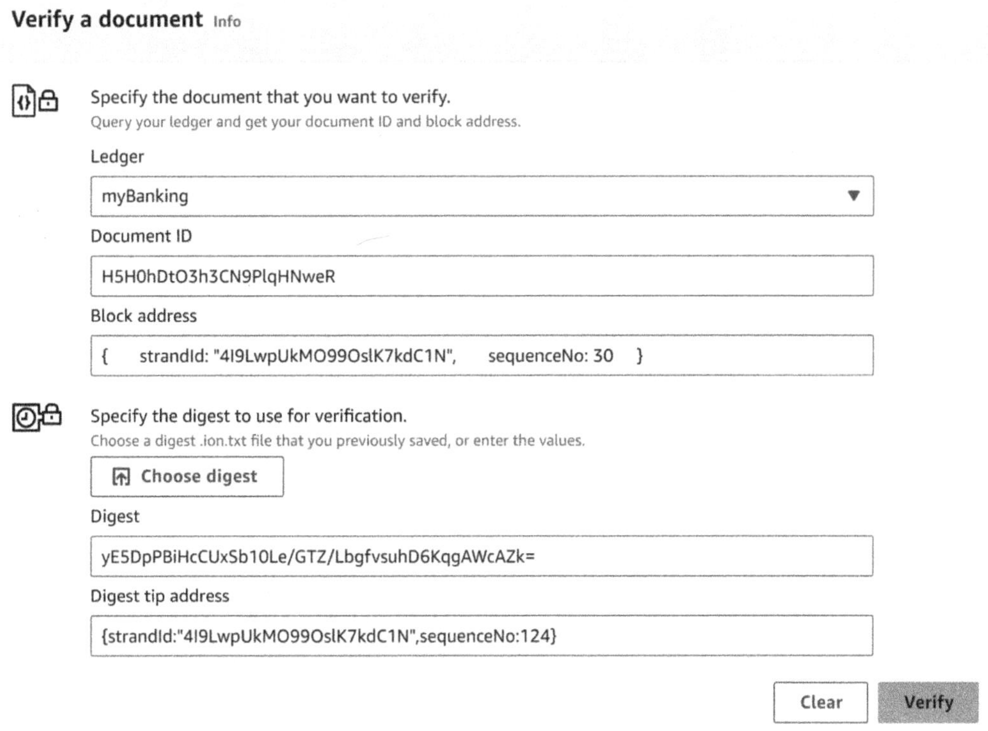
Verify a document Info
Specify the document that you want to verify.
Query your ledger and get your document ID and block address.
Ledger
myBanking
Document ID
H5H0hDtO3h3CN9PlqHNweR
Block address
{ strandId: "4I9LwpUkMO99OslK7kdC1N", sequenceNo: 30 }
Specify the digest to use for verification.
Choose a digest .ion.txt file that you previously saved, or enter the values.
Choose digest
Digest
yE5DpPBiHcCUxSb10Le/GTZ/LbgfvsuhD6KqgAWcAZk=
Digest tip address
{strandId:"4I9LwpUkMO99OslK7kdC1N",sequenceNo:124}
Clear
Verify

Figure 9.44 – Inputting the details for verification

The verification process will run, and then state that the document has been verified, as shown in *Figure 9.45*:

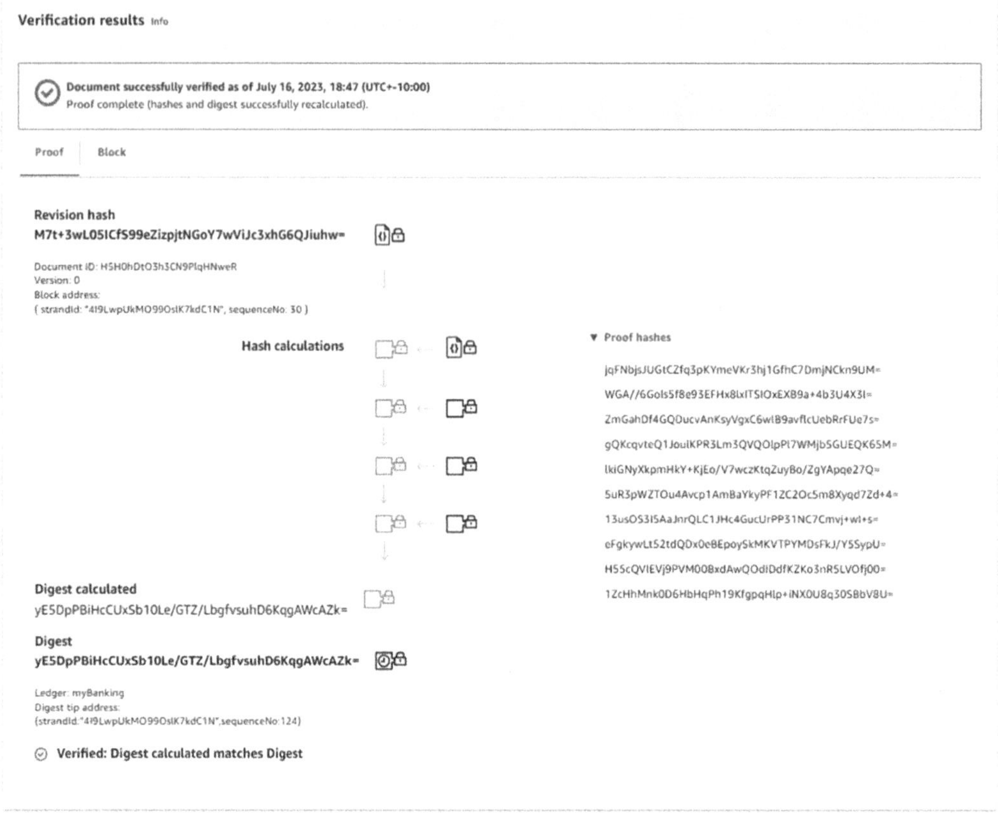

Figure 9.45 – Confirmation that the document has been successfully verified

The verification process involves *recalculating* the digest resulting from the series of hash calculations done for the revision. When this recalculation is the same as the digest that was calculated previously, the verification is successful.

Let's examine the image further. Underneath **Document ID**, we can see that the version is `0`. This means that this is the *initial* revision of the document, and every update to this document will reflect an incremented version number. The **proof hashes** on the **right** side of the image are the sequential list of hashes that are generated by QLDB; these are used to recompute the digest.

When you click on **Block**, additional details about the document will be shown, as seen in *Figure 9.46*:

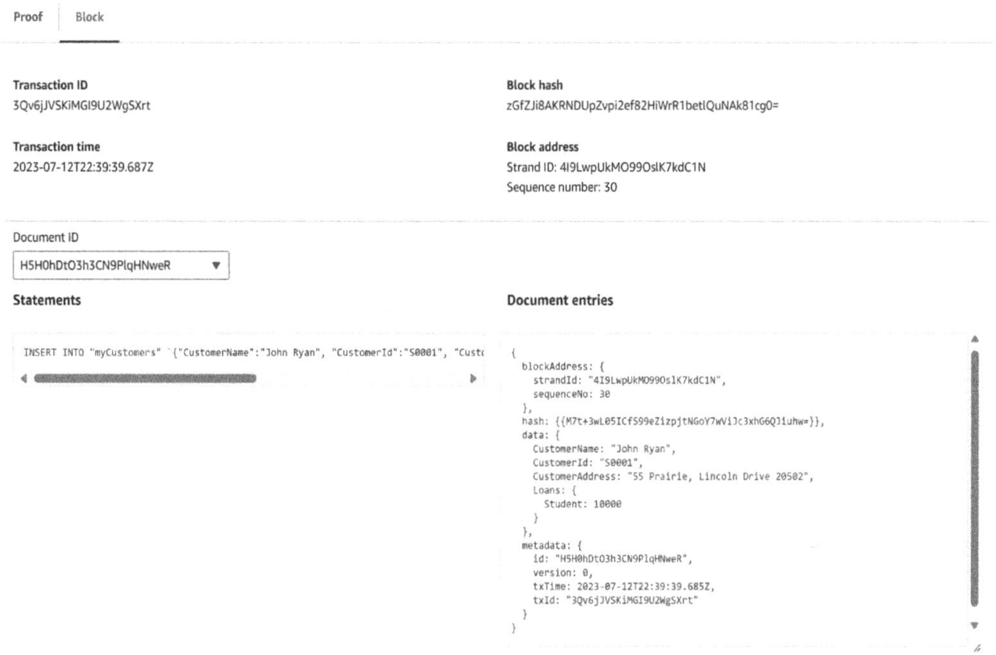

Figure 9.46 – Details when selecting Block

We can see that it provides the details regarding the document's **Statements** and **Document entries**. This matches what we did in *Figure 9.26*.

> **Note**
>
> Do not close this window—we will return to it later when we discuss *Obtaining the digest*.

Updating the transaction

Let's assume that John Ryan has taken out another loan, this time a USD 5,000 car loan. To do this, create a new instance of the PartiQL editor and input the following code by using the `UPDATE` statement:

```
UPDATE myCustomers AS m
SET m.Loans.Car = 5000
WHERE m.CustomerId = 'S0001';
```

After entering this, click on **Run**. The results are shown in *Figure 9.47*:

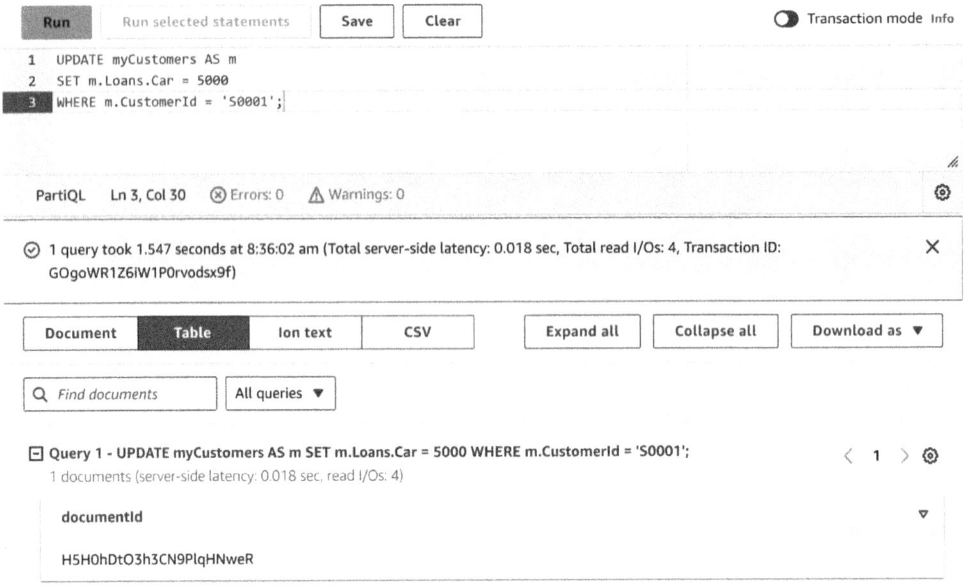

Figure 9.47 – Updating the customer record

We can see that the document ID remains unchanged. Next, let's run the `SELECT metadata` statement again, similar to how we got the results in *Figure 9.41*, to get the block address for this customer. The block address for this update is shown in *Figure 9.48*:

Figure 9.48 – Getting the document details after the update

Note that the **strand ID** for the block address remained the same, but the sequence number changed. Let's download this, as we did previously, and name it `Metadata_02`.

When we query the records from the table, we will see that the car loan has been updated for this customer, as shown in *Figure 9.49*:

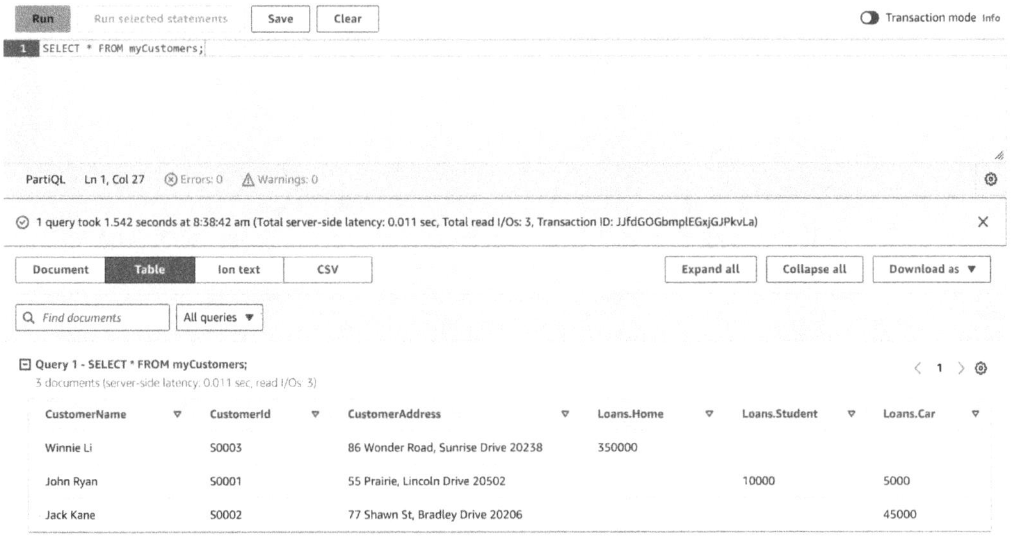

Figure 9.49 – Updated car loan for the customer

Earlier, we mentioned that the digest changes and reflects the history at a specific point in time. *Does this mean that we cannot use the digest we downloaded earlier?* We will answer this in the next section.

Obtaining the digest

Let's go back to the verification window we worked on earlier in *Figure 9.44*. Let's replace the block address with the details we saved to `Metadata_02`, which we got after we updated the car loan.

After we replace this and try to verify the document, we will get a message stating that **The sequence number of the block address must be less than or equal to the sequence number of the digest tip address**, as shown in *Figure 9.50*:

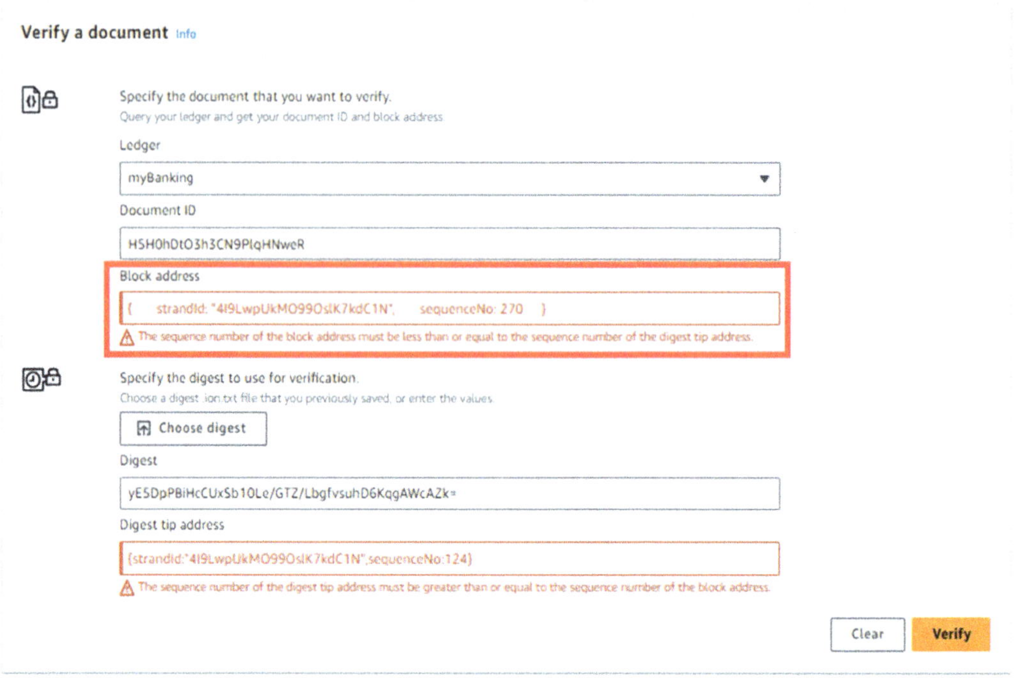

Figure 9.50 – Verifying the document by updating the block address only

If we use the block address after the update, without changing the *digest* and *digest tip address*, we will get an error message because the digest was *recalculated* using SHA-256 with a Merkle tree-based approach after the update. This is how a document is cryptographically verifiable. The digest serves as a *distinctive* marker to validate the integrity of the document revision *at a particular point in time* and covers the history of the data.

To get the correct digest, go back to **Ledgers**, as shown in *Figure 9.20*. The updated digest will look like what's shown in *Figure 9.51*. We will save this as `Digest_02`:

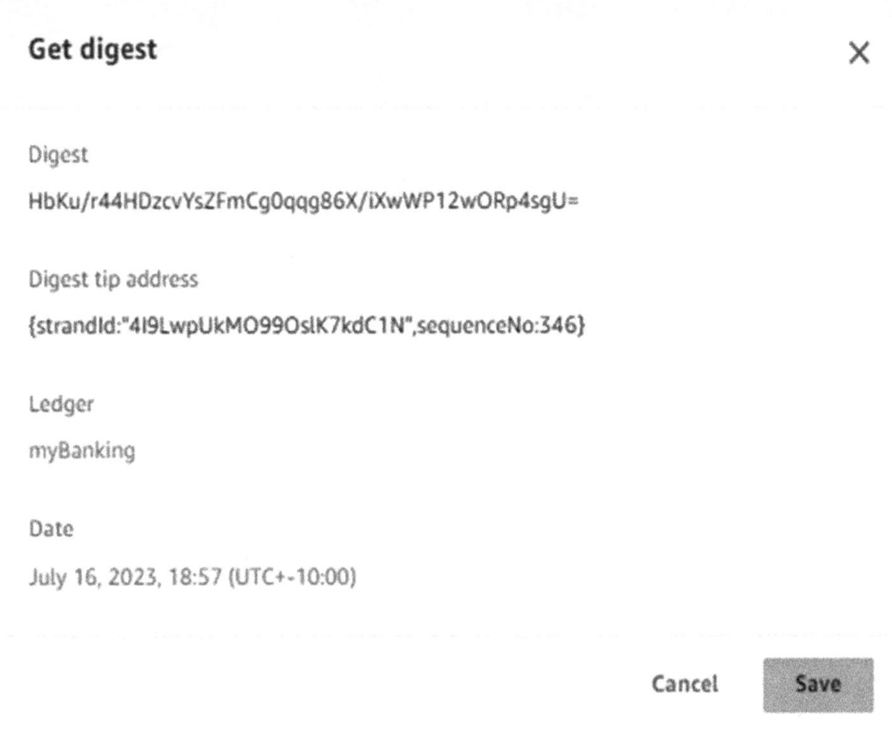

Figure 9.51 – Updated digest

Now that we have the updated one, we can verify the transaction again.

Verifying the results

Using these details, update the digest and digest tip address in the verification step, as illustrated in *Figure 9.52*:

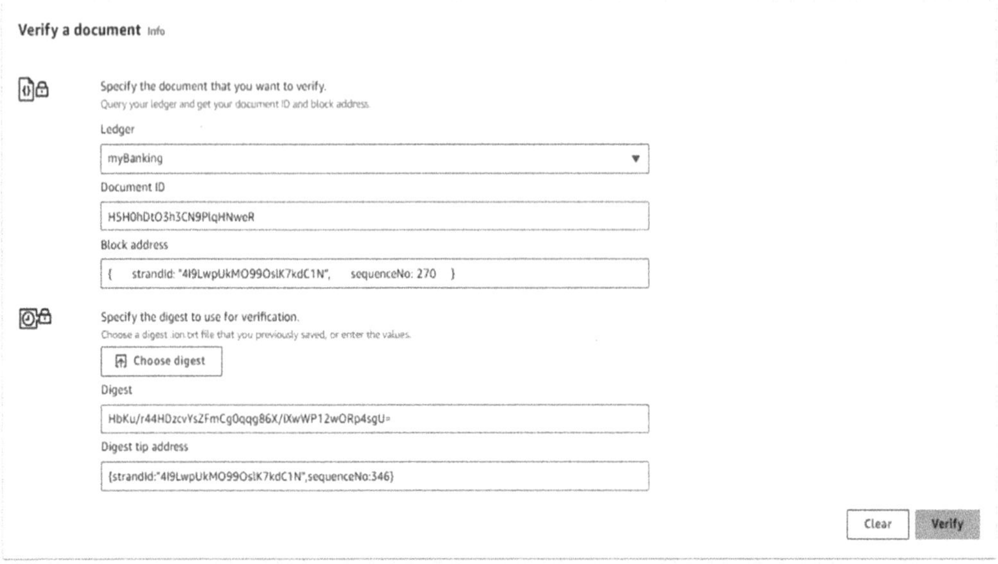

Figure 9.52 – After updating the digest and digest tip address

We can see that the unique combination has changed. Click on **Verify** to get the results shown in *Figure 9.53*:

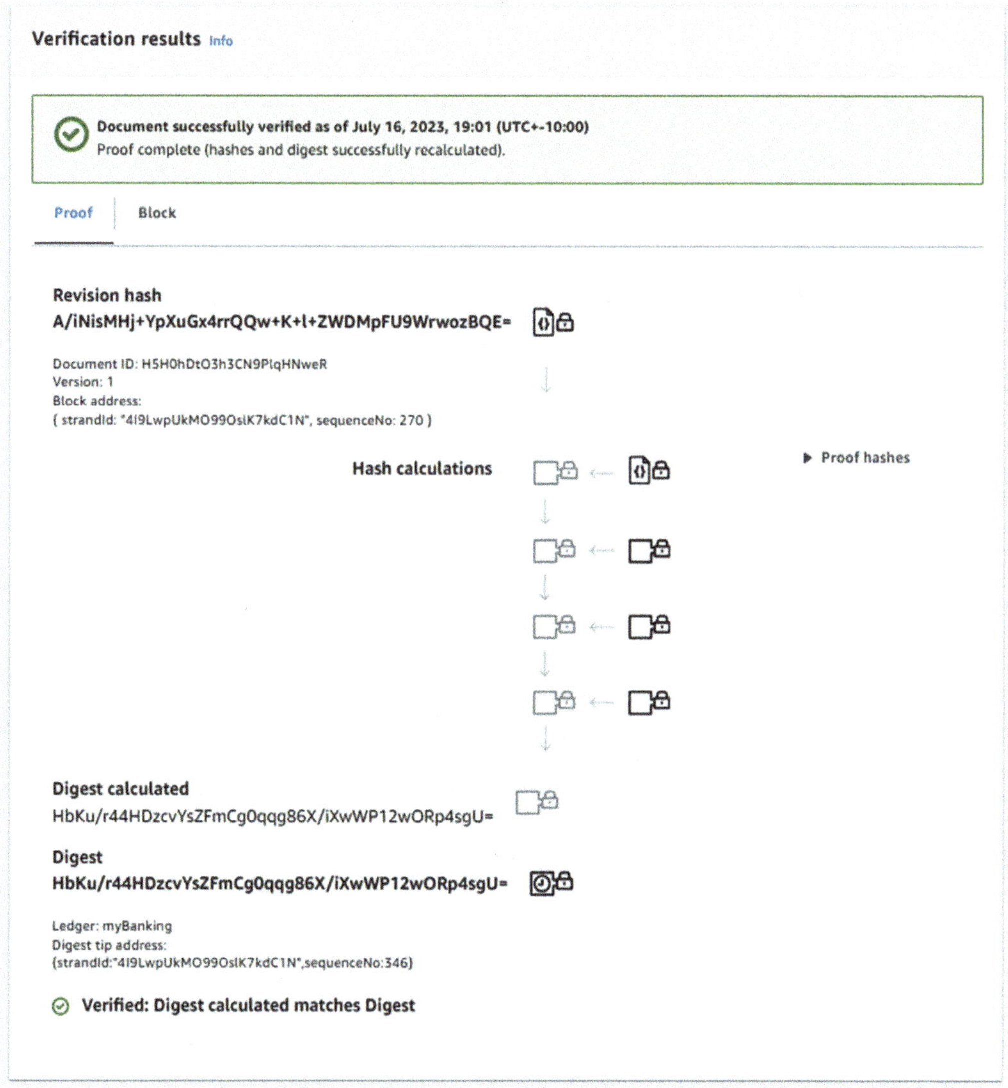

Figure 9.53 – Updated document verified

Notice that the version has been updated to `1` since this is the first revision of the document. The sequence for the digest tip address is also higher than the sequence in the block address.

Now, click on **Block**, as shown in *Figure 9.54*:

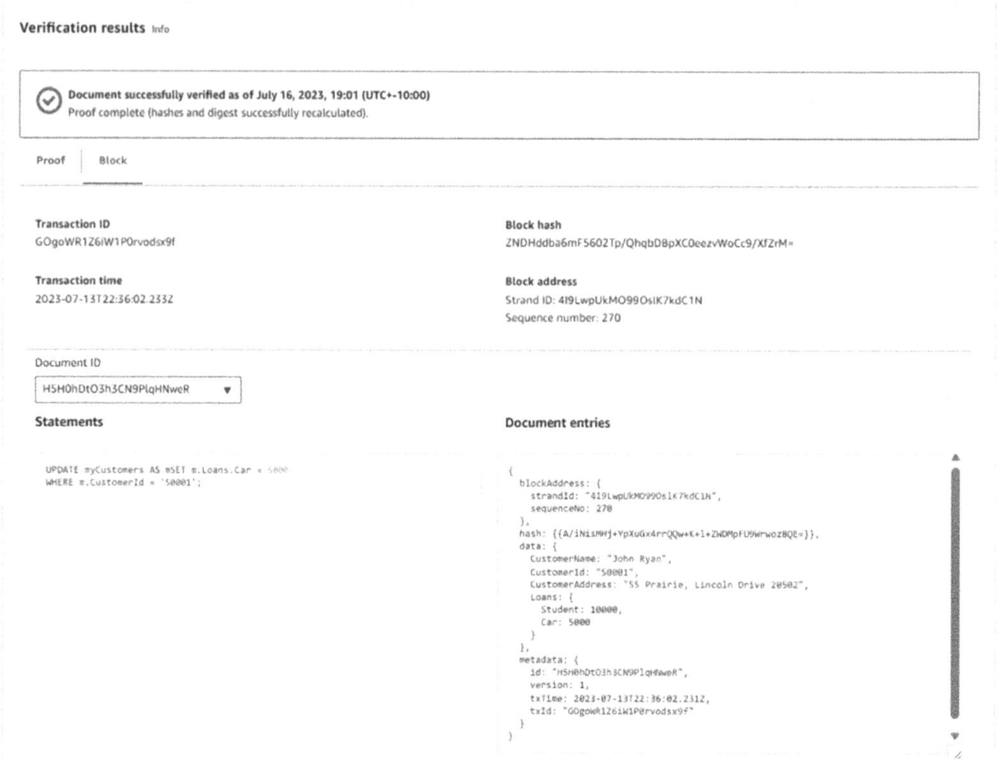

Figure 9.54 – Reviewing the block under Verification results

Under **Statements**, we can see the `UPDATE` statement we made when the customer took out the car loan for USD 5,000. Then, under **Document entries**, we can note see the **data** and **metadata**.

> **Note**
>
> We will discuss this in more detail in the *Working with history and data* section.

Now that we've covered how verification works, let's move on to another important characteristic of Amazon QLDB, which is the **immutability** of the ledger. *How do we test this?*

Deleting records from the ledger

Now, let's delete all the records from the table! In this section, we can note that even though we deleted the records in the table, we can still reconstruct the history of the changes made. *Awesome, right?*

Input the following DELETE statement in the editor and click on **Run**:

```
DELETE FROM myCustomers;
```

This will delete the records from the table and show the document ID(s), as shown in *Figure 9.55*:

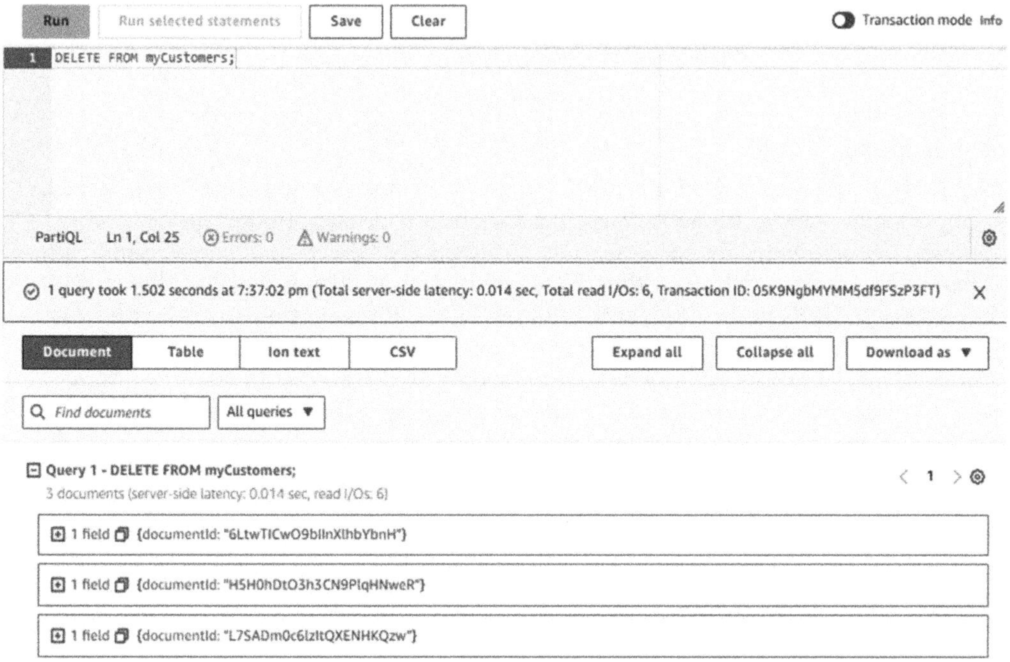

Figure 9.55 – Deleting the record(s) from the table

Notice that the document IDs that are shown are the same ones that were generated for the steps we completed in *Figure 9.26* and *Figure 9.38*.

When we run the statement we saved as **Select info** to get all the records from the table, it will return an empty result, as shown in *Figure 9.56*:

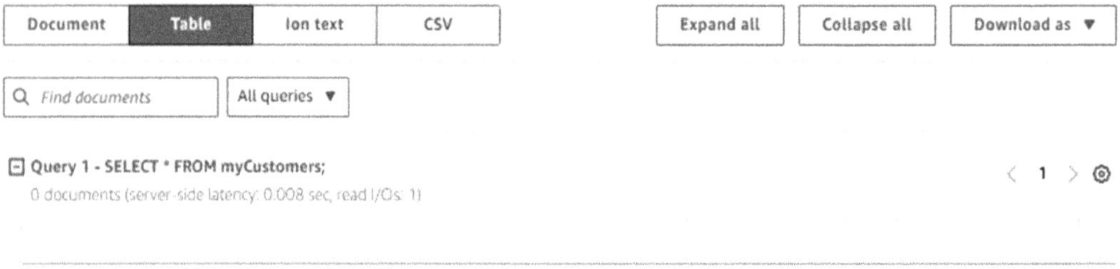

Figure 9.56 – No records loaded from the table

> **Important note**
>
> Using the `DELETE` statement only performs a logical deletion of the document. This is carried out by creating a new revision that marks the document as deleted. The only instance where this principle of immutability does not hold is through the process of **data redaction**. This is designed to comply with regulatory requirements such as the **General Data Protection Regulation** (**GDPR**) in the European Union, and the **California Consumer Privacy Act** (**CCPA**). To learn more about this, check out `https://docs.aws.amazon.com/qldb/latest/developerguide/working.redaction.html` and `https://docs.aws.amazon.com/qldb/latest/developerguide/what-is.overview.html`.

Though there are no records in the table, given that the ledger is immutable, we can still retrieve the history. We'll discuss this next.

Working with history and data

Amazon QLDB has a built-in *history* feature that allows us to view the complete records of the transactions.

To do this, we will modify our `SELECT` statement, like this:

```
SELECT * FROM history(myCustomers);
```

This statement will retrieve the historical data, as seen in *Figure 9.57*:

Figure 9.57 – Retrieving the historical data

Let's click on **Table** to see the query results better. The results are shown in *Figure 9.58*:

Figure 9.58 – Showing the history in table format

When we inspect the results, we will see that they reflect all the transactions we did. If we look at **John Ryan**, we will see that the initial input we did is reflected under block address sequence number `30`. Then, we updated the car loan, which is reflected under block address sequence number `270`. When we deleted the record from the table, it was reflected under block address sequence `447`.

If you would only like to see the data, replace `*` with `data` in the `SELECT` statement, as shown here:

```
SELECT data FROM history(myCustomers);
```

This will only show the data from the table, as reflected in *Figure 9.59*:

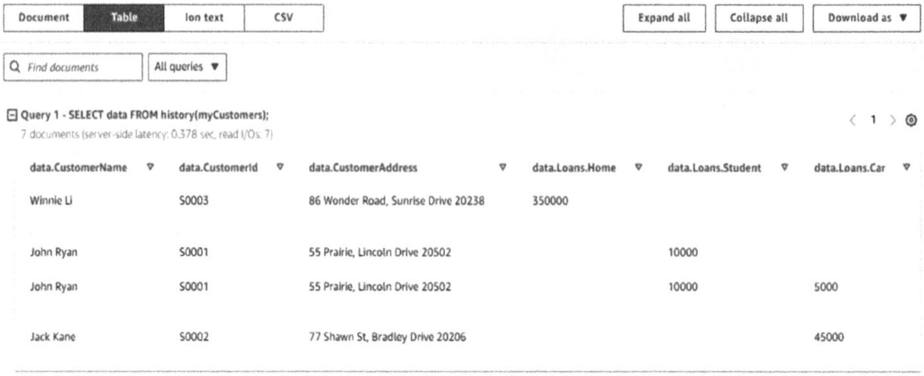

Figure 9.59 – Showing the data from the table history

Now that we have discussed the immutability of Amazon QLDB, let's assume that the records were deleted accidentally and insert the initial records again:

```
INSERT INTO "myCustomers" `{"CustomerName":"John Ryan",
"CustomerId":"S0001", "CustomerAddress": "55 Prairie, Lincoln Drive
20502", "Loans":{"Student":10000, "Car":5000}}`;
INSERT INTO "myCustomers" `{"CustomerName":"Jack Kane",
"CustomerId":"S0002", "CustomerAddress": "77 Shawn St, Bradley Drive
20206", "Loans":{"Car":45000}}`;
INSERT INTO "myCustomers" `{"CustomerName":"Winnie Li",
"CustomerId":"S0003", "CustomerAddress": "86 Wonder Road, Sunrise
Drive 20238", "Loans":{"Home":350000}}`;
```

When we run this query, the records will be updated and new document IDs will be created, as shown in *Figure 9.60*:

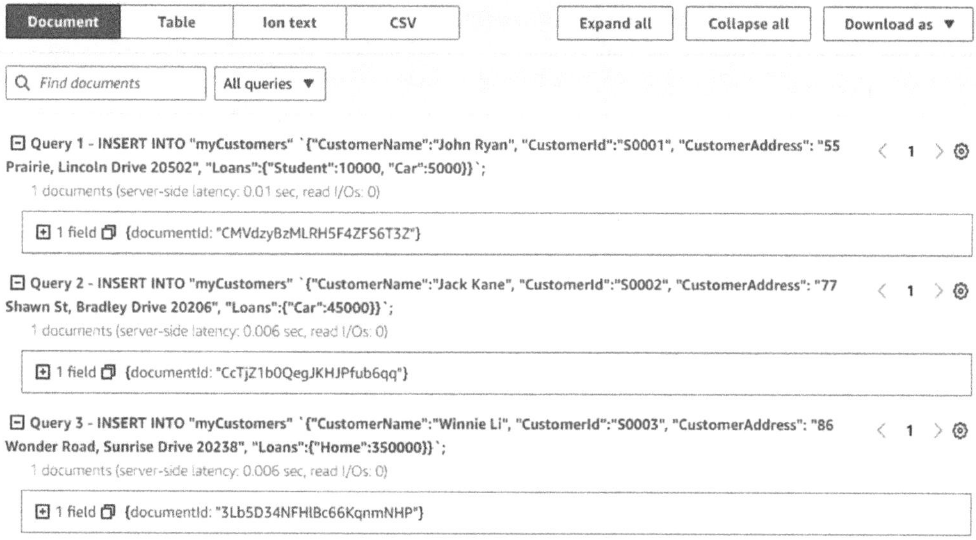
Document
Table
Ion text
CSV
Expand all
Collapse all
Download as ▼
Find documents
All queries ▼
Query 1 - INSERT INTO "myCustomers" `{"CustomerName":"John Ryan", "CustomerId":"S0001", "CustomerAddress": "55 Prairie, Lincoln Drive 20502", "Loans":{"Student":10000, "Car":5000}}`;
1 documents (server-side latency: 0.01 sec, read I/Os: 0)
1 field {documentId: "CMVdzyBzMLRH5F4ZFS6T3Z"}
Query 2 - INSERT INTO "myCustomers" `{"CustomerName":"Jack Kane", "CustomerId":"S0002", "CustomerAddress": "77 Shawn St, Bradley Drive 20206", "Loans":{"Car":45000}}`;
1 documents (server-side latency: 0.006 sec, read I/Os: 0)
1 field {documentId: "CcTjZ1b0QegJKHJPfub6qq"}
Query 3 - INSERT INTO "myCustomers" `{"CustomerName":"Winnie Li", "CustomerId":"S0003", "CustomerAddress": "86 Wonder Road, Sunrise Drive 20238", "Loans":{"Home":350000}}`;
1 documents (server-side latency: 0.006 sec, read I/Os: 0)
1 field {documentId: "3Lb5D34NFHlBc66KqnmNHP"}

Figure 9.60 – New document IDs generated

If we select all the records from the table, our table will reflect this, as if we had the original data before we deleted the records. However, if we select the data from the history, it will show the modifications that have been made, as shown in *Figure 9.61*:

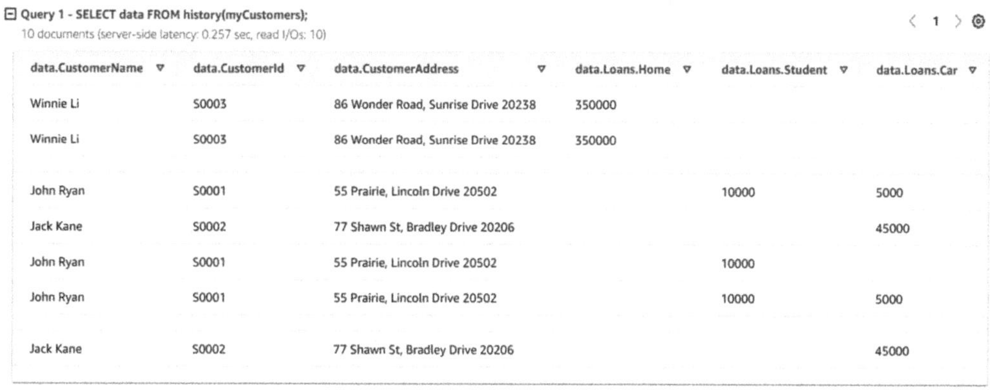
Query 1 - SELECT data FROM history(myCustomers);
10 documents (server-side latency: 0.257 sec, read I/Os: 10)

data.CustomerName	data.CustomerId	data.CustomerAddress	data.Loans.Home	data.Loans.Student	data.Loans.Car
Winnie Li	S0003	86 Wonder Road, Sunrise Drive 20238	350000		
Winnie Li	S0003	86 Wonder Road, Sunrise Drive 20238	350000		
John Ryan	S0001	55 Prairie, Lincoln Drive 20502		10000	5000
Jack Kane	S0002	77 Shawn St, Bradley Drive 20206			45000
John Ryan	S0001	55 Prairie, Lincoln Drive 20502		10000	
John Ryan	S0001	55 Prairie, Lincoln Drive 20502		10000	5000
Jack Kane	S0002	77 Shawn St, Bradley Drive 20206			45000

Figure 9.61 – Getting the data from the history

Moreover, if we get all the records from the history, we will see the modifications that were made to the document through its *metadata version number*, as shown in *Figure 9.62*:

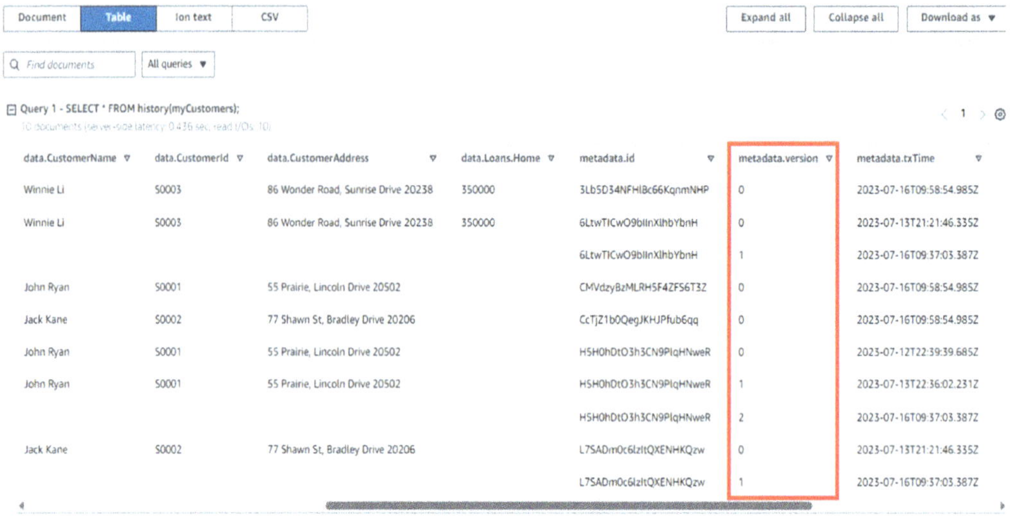
Document
Table
Ion text
CSV
Expand all
Collapse all
Download as
Find documents
All queries
Query 1 - SELECT * FROM history(myCustomers);
1

data.CustomerName	data.CustomerId	data.CustomerAddress	data.Loans.Home	metadata.id	metadata.version	metadata.txTime
Winnie Li	S0003	86 Wonder Road, Sunrise Drive 20238	350000	3Lb5D34NFHIBc66KqnmNHP	0	2023-07-16T09:58:54.985Z
Winnie Li	S0003	86 Wonder Road, Sunrise Drive 20238	350000	6LtwTICwO9bllnXlhbYbnH	0	2023-07-13T21:21:46.335Z
				6LtwTICwO9bllnXlhbYbnH	1	2023-07-16T09:37:03.387Z
John Ryan	S0001	55 Prairie, Lincoln Drive 20502		CMVdzyBzMLRH5F4ZFS6T3Z	0	2023-07-16T09:58:54.985Z
Jack Kane	S0002	77 Shawn St, Bradley Drive 20206		CcTjZ1b0QegJKHJPfub6qq	0	2023-07-16T09:58:54.985Z
John Ryan	S0001	55 Prairie, Lincoln Drive 20502		H5H0hDtO3h3CN9PlqHNweR	0	2023-07-12T22:39:39.685Z
John Ryan	S0001	55 Prairie, Lincoln Drive 20502		H5H0hDtO3h3CN9PlqHNweR	1	2023-07-13T22:36:02.231Z
				H5H0hDtO3h3CN9PlqHNweR	2	2023-07-16T09:37:03.387Z
Jack Kane	S0002	77 Shawn St, Bradley Drive 20206		L7SADm0c6lzltQXENHKQzw	0	2023-07-13T21:21:46.335Z
				L7SADm0c6lzltQXENHKQzw	1	2023-07-16T09:37:03.387Z

Figure 9.62 – Metadata version

Here, you will see that the initial revision of the document has a version of `0`, and even though changes have been made to the document, the document number remains the same, but the version is incremented with each revision. Let's take, for example, the customer John Ryan with **CustomerId** `S0001`. When we inserted his record in the table, the `H5H0hDtO3h3CN9PlqHNweR` document was generated with a version of `0`. After that, when he took a USD 5,000 car loan and we added this record, it was reflected under version `1`. Then, when we deleted the journal (or log), the version was reflected under `2`.

> **Note**
>
> You might be wondering, *Why was it that when we deleted John Ryan and added the record back, it generated a different document number with a version of 0?* This is because when we deleted `H5H0hDtO3h3CN9PlqHNweR`, that ended the life cycle of the document representing its final revision. Thus, no further revisions can be made to this document.

By using the built-in *history* function, we can see that the ledger is immutable and that the changes that are made are *append-only*. This provides visibility into the data's lineage and illustrates the completeness and verifiability of the revisions we made.

Through the revisions we made to the table and the verification steps we performed, we illustrated the immutability of the ledger. Since we can see the history of the changes and cryptographically verify the revisions made, the integrity of the data is maintained.

Now that we have finished making the necessary updates and modifications in QLDB, we can export this to the S3 bucket we created previously.

Exporting the journal

Exporting the journal enables various use cases and requirements such as data storage, analysis, and auditing. This feature enables organizations to move the ledger data safely to an external storage solution such as S3.

To do this, click on **Export** from the left panel. This will lead us to the page shown in *Figure 9.63*:

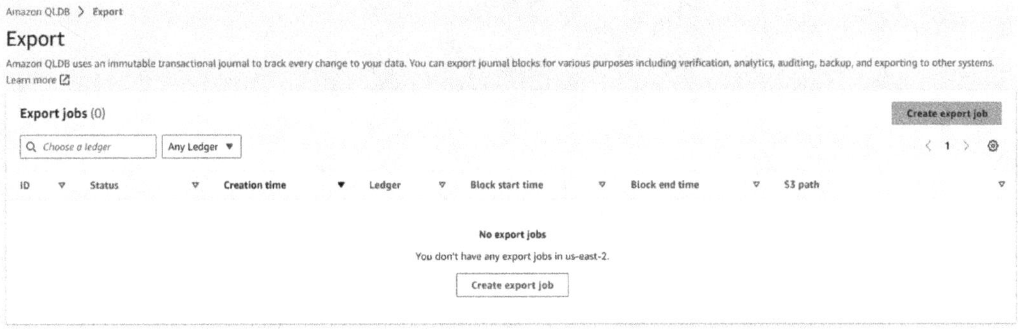

Figure 9.63 – Exporting the journal block

Click on **Create export job**.

Update the ledger by selecting **myBanking**, as well as the start date and time, as seen in *Figure 9.64*:

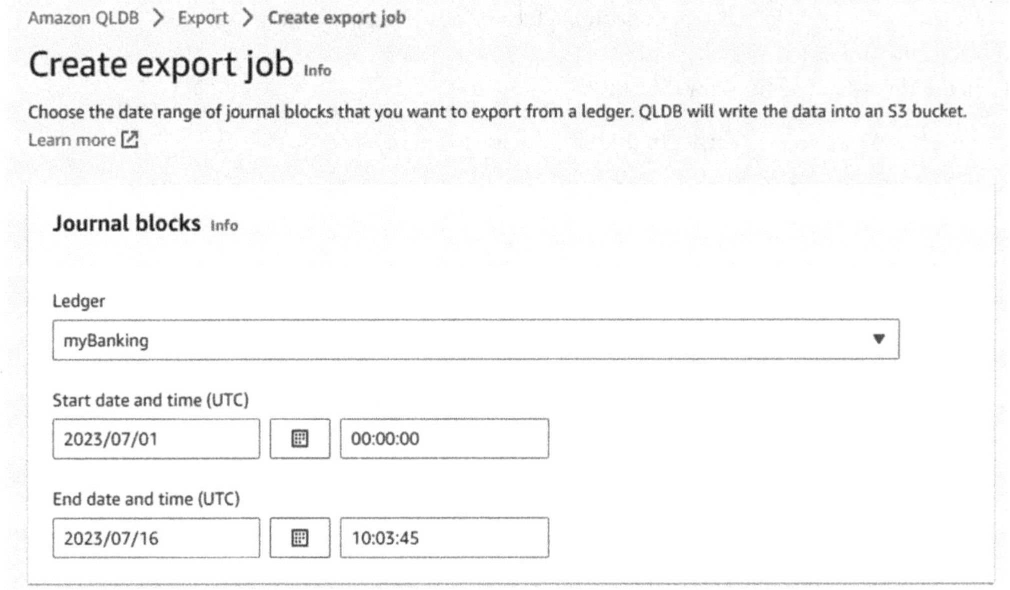

Figure 9.64 – Updating the export job details

End date and time (UTC) will be filled in automatically.

Next, click on **Browse S3** and find the bucket we created previously, as seen in *Figure 9.65*:

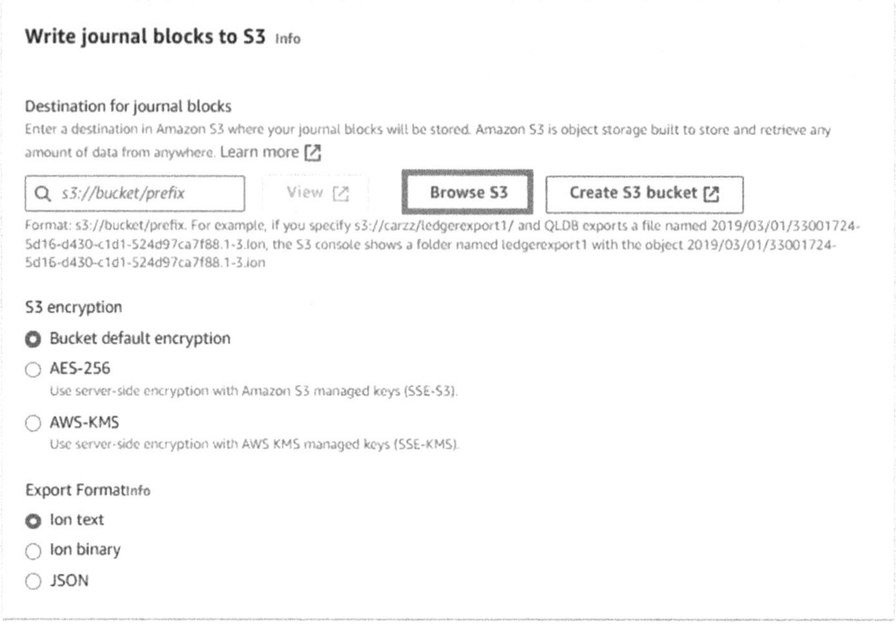

Figure 9.65 – Configuring the settings of the export job

We will use the default settings for the others.

Locate the bucket we created earlier in this chapter, as shown in *Figure 9.66*:

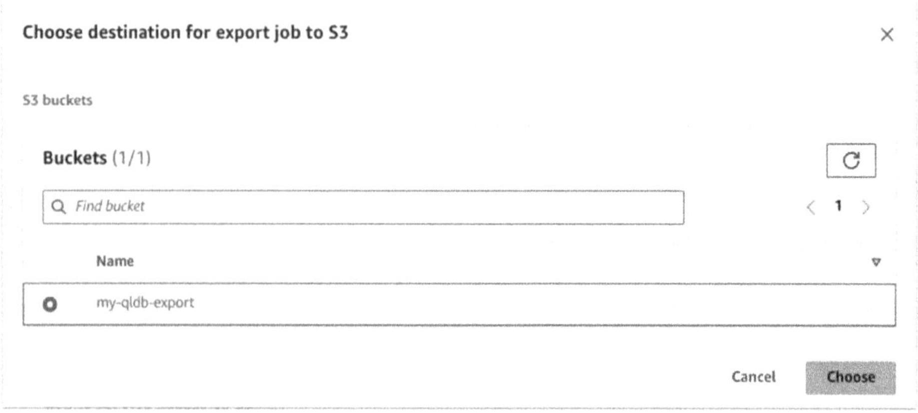

Figure 9.66 – Choosing the destination for the export job

Click on **Choose**.

This will update the bucket prefix and the bucket name, as highlighted in *Figure 9.67*:

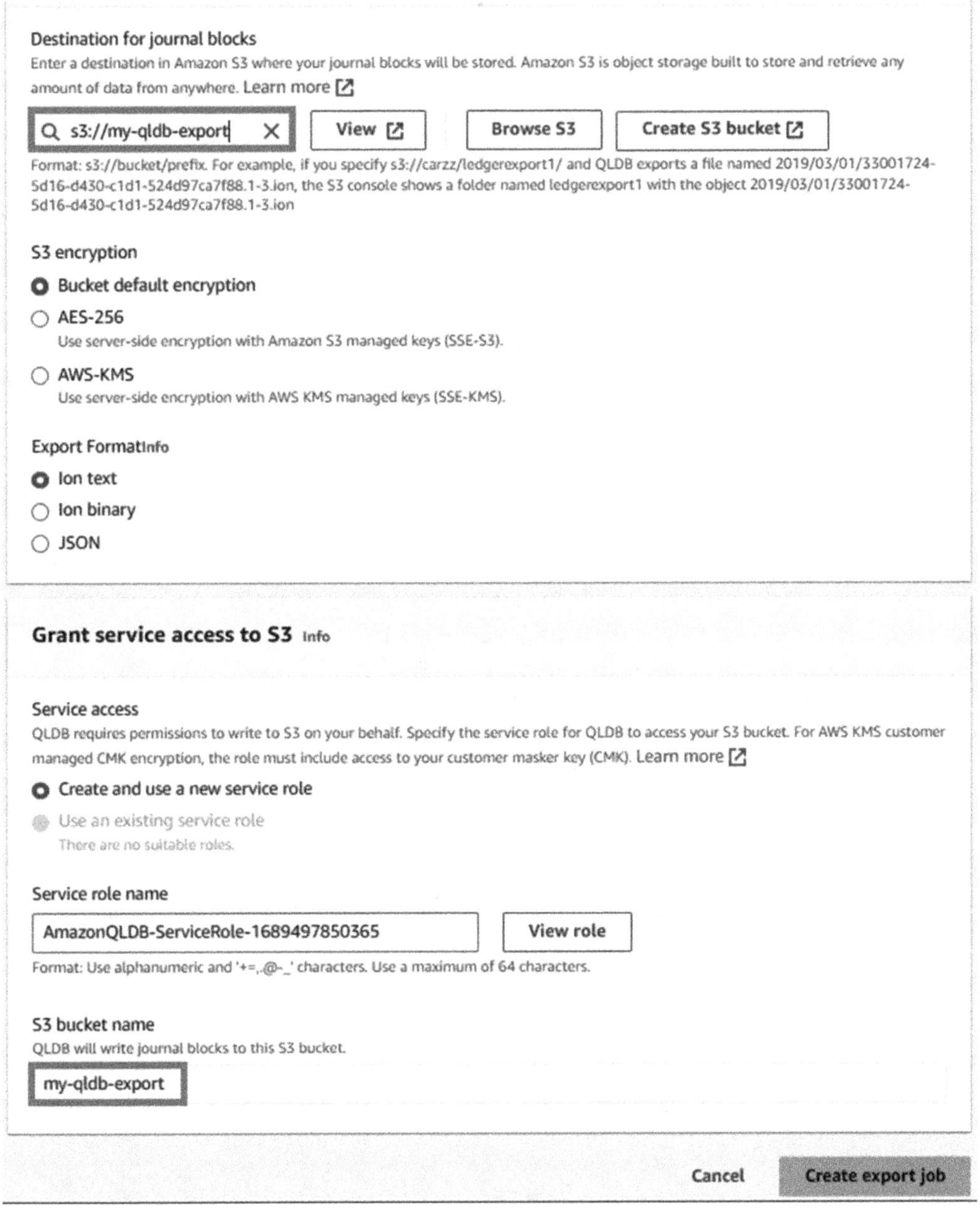

Figure 9.67 – S3 bucket details updated

After that, click on **Create export job**.

Once the data in QLDB has started exporting, a message will appear stating that it is in progress. Once this step is completed, we'll see that the journal blocks have been exported successfully, as shown in *Figure 9.68*:

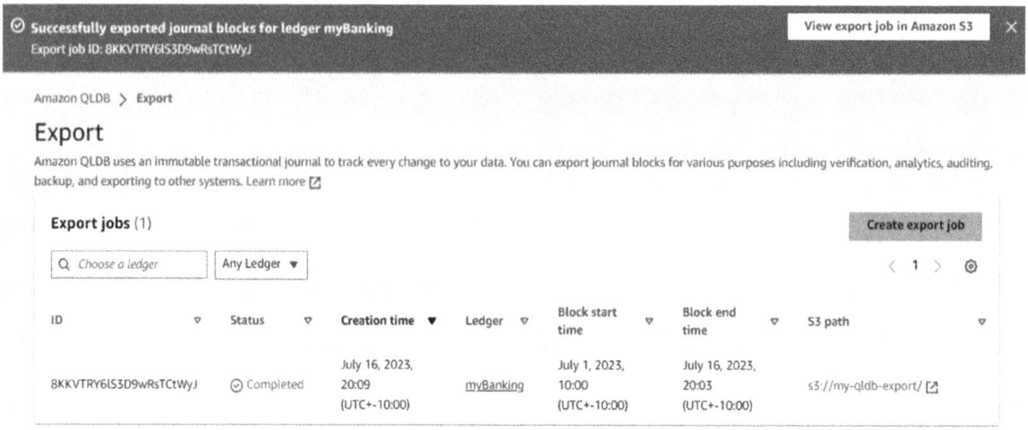

Figure 9.68 – Export completed

Clicking on **s3://my-qldb-export/** under the **S3 path** will lead us to the S3 bucket where our exported data is saved, as shown in *Figure 9.69*. Note that the name of your S3 bucket may be different (*depending on the name you used when creating the S3 bucket*):

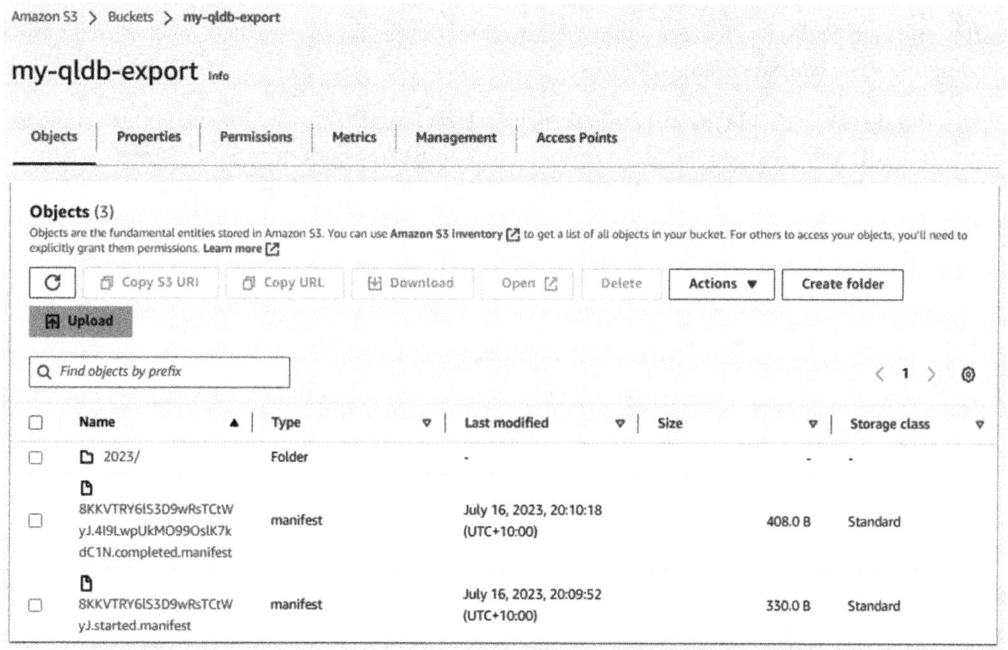

Figure 9.69 – S3 export

Exporting the journal data to S3 is a good step to ensure that our data is stored and can be retrieved at any time (*even if the ledger database resource gets deleted*).

Let's look at the data that's been exported by clicking through the **2023/** > **07** > **16** > **10** folders until we find the **ion** file, as shown in *Figure 9.70*:

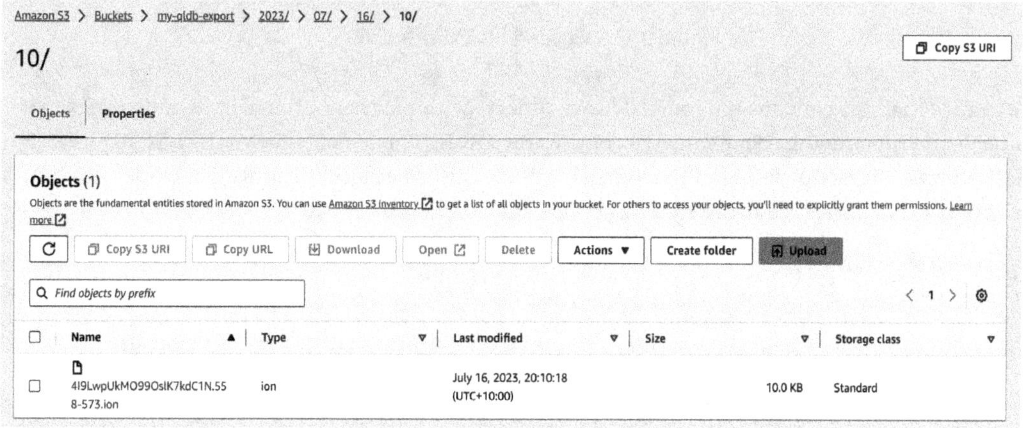

Figure 9.70 – Getting the exported ion file

Note that the path and set of folders will differ based on the results of your hands-on exercise and depending on when you exported the journal.

Next, tick the checkbox beside the ion file and click on **Download**. This will download the ion file to your `Downloads` folder. Open the file; it should look similar to what's shown in *Figure 9.71*:

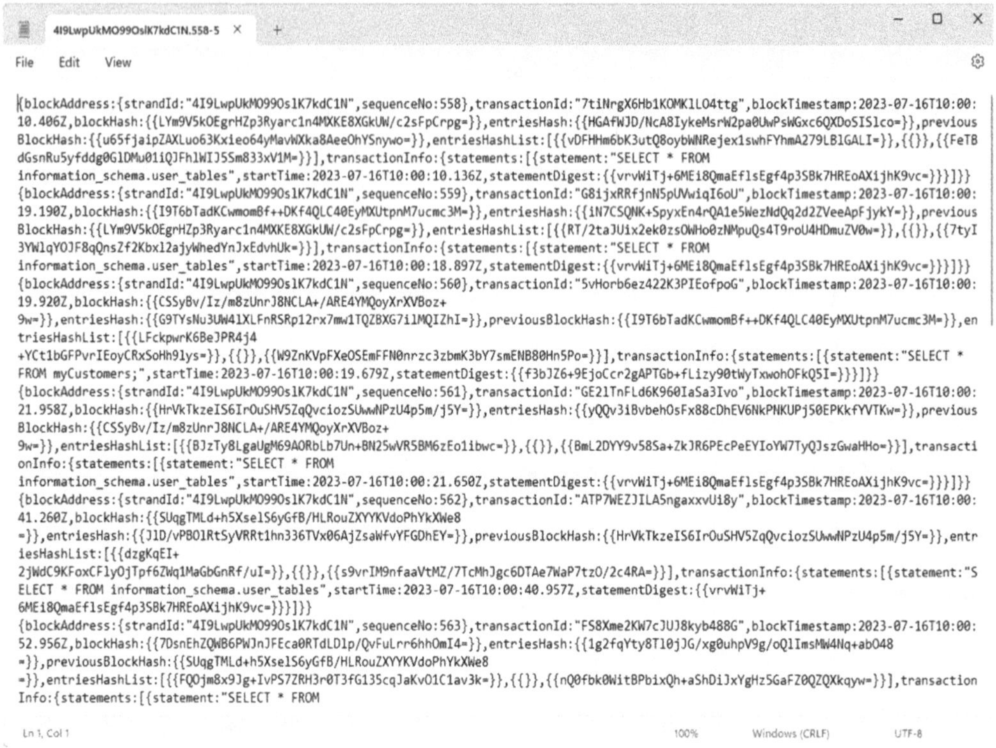

{blockAddress:{strandId:"4I9LwpUkMO990slK7kdC1N",sequenceNo:558},transactionId:"7tiNrgX6Hb1KOMKlLO4ttg",blockTimestamp:2023-07-16T10:00:10.406Z,blockHash:{{LYm9V5kOEgrHZp3Ryarc1n4MXKE8XGkUW/c2sFpCrpg=}},entriesHash:{{HGAfWJD/NcA8IykeMsrW2pa0UwPsWGxc6QXDoSISlco=}},previousBlockHash:{{u65fjaipZAXLuo63Kxieo64yMavWXka8AeeOhYSnywo=}},entriesHashList:[{{vDFHHm6bK3utQ8oybWNRejex1swhFYhmA279LBlGALI=}},{{}},{{FeTBdGsnRu5yfddg0GlDMu01iQJFhlWIJ5Sm833xV1M=}}],transactionInfo:{statements:[{statement:"SELECT * FROM information_schema.user_tables",startTime:2023-07-16T10:00:10.136Z,statementDigest:{{vrvWiTj+6MEi8QmaEflsEgf4p3SBk7HREoAXijhK9vc=}}}]}}
{blockAddress:{strandId:"4I9LwpUkMO990slK7kdC1N",sequenceNo:559},transactionId:"G8ijxRRfjnN5pUVwiqI6oU",blockTimestamp:2023-07-16T10:00:19.190Z,blockHash:{{I9T6bTadKCwmomBf++DKf4QLC40EyMXUtpnM7ucmc3M=}},entriesHash:{{iN7CSQNK+SpyxEn4rQA1e5WezNdQq2d2ZVeeApFjykY=}},previousBlockHash:{{LYm9V5kOEgrHZp3Ryarc1n4MXKE8XGkUW/c2sFpCrpg=}},entriesHashList:[{{RT/2taJUix2ek0zsOWHo0zNMpuQs4T9roU4HDmuZV0w=}},{{}},{{7tyI3YWlqYOJF8qQnsZf2Kbxl2ajyWhedYnJxEdvhUk=}}],transactionInfo:{statements:[{statement:"SELECT * FROM information_schema.user_tables",startTime:2023-07-16T10:00:18.897Z,statementDigest:{{vrvWiTj+6MEi8QmaEflsEgf4p3SBk7HREoAXijhK9vc=}}}]}}
{blockAddress:{strandId:"4I9LwpUkMO990slK7kdC1N",sequenceNo:560},transactionId:"5vHorb6ez422K3PIEofpoG",blockTimestamp:2023-07-16T10:00:19.920Z,blockHash:{{CSSyBv/Iz/m8zUnrJ8NCLA+/ARE4YMQoyXrXVBoz+9w=}},entriesHash:{{G9TYsNu3UW41XLFnRSRp12rx7mw1TQZBXG7ilMQIZhI=}},previousBlockHash:{{I9T6bTadKCwmomBf++DKf4QLC40EyMXUtpnM7ucmc3M=}},entriesHashList:[{{LFckpwrK6BeJPR4j4+YCt1bGFPvrIEoyCRxSoHh9lys=}},{{}},{{W9ZnKVpFXeOSEmFFN0nrzc3zbmK3bY7smENB80Hn5Po=}}],transactionInfo:{statements:[{statement:"SELECT * FROM myCustomers;",startTime:2023-07-16T10:00:19.679Z,statementDigest:{{f3bJZ6+9EjoCcr2gAPTGb+fLizy90tWyTxwohOFkQ5I=}}}]}}
{blockAddress:{strandId:"4I9LwpUkMO990slK7kdC1N",sequenceNo:561},transactionId:"GE21TnFLd6K960IaSa3Ivo",blockTimestamp:2023-07-16T10:00:21.958Z,blockHash:{{HrVkTkzeIS6IrOuSHV5ZqQvciozSUwwNPzU4p5m/j5Y=}},entriesHash:{{yQQv3iBvbehOsFx88cDhEV6NkPNKUPj50EPKkfYVTKw=}},previousBlockHash:{{CSSyBv/Iz/m8zUnrJ8NCLA+/ARE4YMQoyXrXVBoz+9w=}},entriesHashList:[{{BJzTy8LgaUgM69AORbLb7Un+BN25wVR5BM6zEo1ibwc=}},{{}},{{BmL2DYY9v58Sa+ZkJR6PEcPeEYIoYW7TyQJszGwaHHo=}}],transactionInfo:{statements:[{statement:"SELECT * FROM information_schema.user_tables",startTime:2023-07-16T10:00:21.650Z,statementDigest:{{vrvWiTj+6MEi8QmaEflsEgf4p3SBk7HREoAXijhK9vc=}}}]}}
{blockAddress:{strandId:"4I9LwpUkMO990slK7kdC1N",sequenceNo:562},transactionId:"ATP7WEZJILA5ngaxxvUi8y",blockTimestamp:2023-07-16T10:00:41.260Z,blockHash:{{SUqgTMLd+h5XselS6yGfB/HLRouZXYYKVdoPhYkXWe8=}},entriesHash:{{J1D/vPBOlRtSyVRRt1hn336TVx06AjZsaWfvYFGDhEY=}},previousBlockHash:{{HrVkTkzeIS6IrOuSHV5ZqQvciozSUwwNPzU4p5m/j5Y=}},entriesHashList:[{{dzgKqEI+2jWdC9KFoxCFlyOjTpf6ZWq1MaGbGnRf/uI=}},{{}},{{s9vrIM9nfaaVtMZ/7TcMhJgc6DTAe7WaP7tzO/2c4RA=}}],transactionInfo:{statements:[{statement:"SELECT * FROM information_schema.user_tables",startTime:2023-07-16T10:00:40.957Z,statementDigest:{{vrvWiTj+6MEi8QmaEflsEgf4p3SBk7HREoAXijhK9vc=}}}]}}
{blockAddress:{strandId:"4I9LwpUkMO990slK7kdC1N",sequenceNo:563},transactionId:"FS8Xme2KW7cJUJ8kyb488G",blockTimestamp:2023-07-16T10:00:52.956Z,blockHash:{{7DsnEhZQWB6PWJnJFEca0RTdLDlp/QvFuLrr6hhOmI4=}},entriesHash:{{1g2fqYty8Tl0jJG/xg0uhpV9g/oQlImsMW4Nq+ab048=}},previousBlockHash:{{SUqgTMLd+h5XselS6yGfB/HLRouZXYYKVdoPhYkXWe8=}},entriesHashList:[{{FQOjm8x9Jg+IvPS7ZRH3r0T3fG135cqJaKvO1C1av3k=}},{{}},{{nQ0fbk0WitBPbixQh+aShDiJxYgHz5GaFZ0QZQXkqyw=}}],transactionInfo:{statements:[{statement:"SELECT * FROM

Figure 9.71 – Viewing the exported file

We can see that this contains the **journal block objects** with the transaction details and entries that reflect the revisions to the document. Also, notice that `SELECT` statements such as `SELECT * FROM myCustomers;` are included in the journal export. This is because the journal includes not only the revisions but also all **committed** transactions, including *reads*.

Important note

Since Amazon QLDB provides a record of transactions that is complete and can be verified cryptographically, it can be used where the need to track changes to the data over time is important. Consider an **insurance company** that needs a platform containing the history of transactions that can be authenticated in case of a dispute. In this scenario, having an immutable log will make it faster to pinpoint the original transaction, as well as the events that have transpired, which will aid in a quick resolution. Another application is in **healthcare management**, where the privacy and integrity of the data are necessary. If there is a need to audit or reconcile the medical history of a patient, QLDB ensures that the healthcare provider has accurate and tamper-proof records that enhance patient care while maintaining compliance with regulatory standards. These are just a few applications of this ledger which provide solutions to data integrity challenges that companies face.

At this point, we have covered what ledger databases are, the key concepts relevant to data integrity, and how QLDB helps prevent data integrity issues. Now that we have discussed these, let's move on to the last step, which is *cleaning up* the resource(s) we created in this chapter.

Cleaning up

After working with cloud applications, we must clean up and remove the resources we set up. If we fail to do this promptly, this might lead to us paying unnecessary costs for cloud services that are not in use. In this section, we will focus on deleting the QLDB ledger database resource.

Here are the steps to do this:

1. Click on **Ledgers** and tick the radio button beside the `myBanking` ledger that we created. Next, click on **Delete**, as seen in *Figure 9.72*:

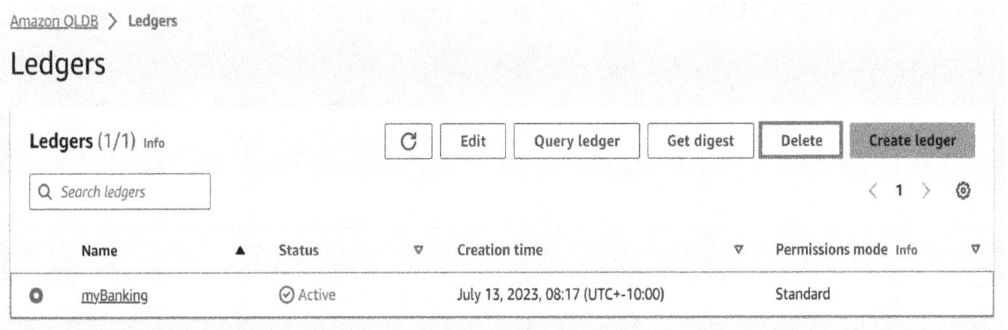

Figure 9.72 – Deleting the ledger

A pop-up message stating **myBanking may not be deleted while deletion protection is enabled** will appear, as shown in *Figure 9.73*:

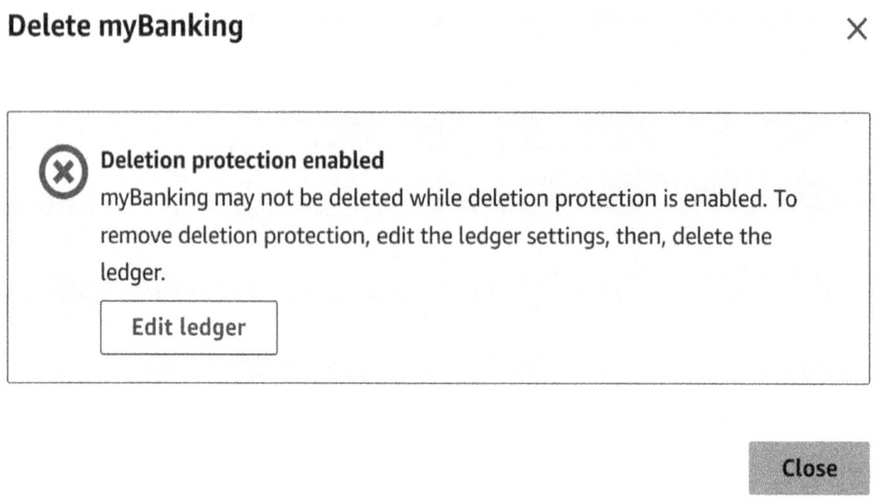

Figure 9.73 – Deletion protection enabled

2. Let's click on **Edit ledger**. We will now edit the permissions, as shown in *Figure 9.74*:

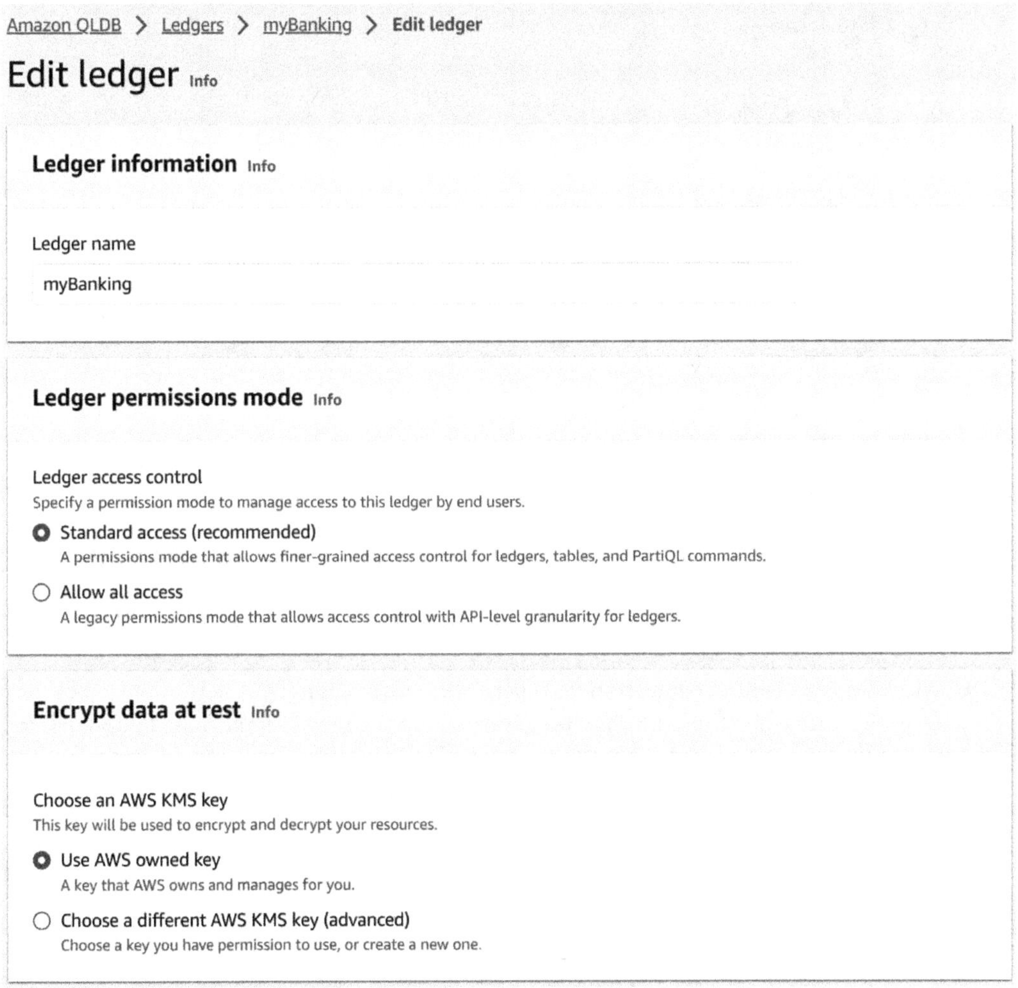
Amazon QLDB > Ledgers > myBanking > Edit ledger
Edit ledger Info
Ledger information Info
Ledger name
myBanking
Ledger permissions mode Info
Ledger access control
Specify a permission mode to manage access to this ledger by end users.
Standard access (recommended)
A permissions mode that allows finer-grained access control for ledgers, tables, and PartiQL commands.
Allow all access
A legacy permissions mode that allows access control with API-level granularity for ledgers.
Encrypt data at rest Info
Choose an AWS KMS key
This key will be used to encrypt and decrypt your resources.
Use AWS owned key
A key that AWS owns and manages for you.
Choose a different AWS KMS key (advanced)
Choose a key you have permission to use, or create a new one.

Figure 9.74 – Edit ledger

3. Scroll down to find the **Deletion protection** section, as shown in *Figure 9.75*:

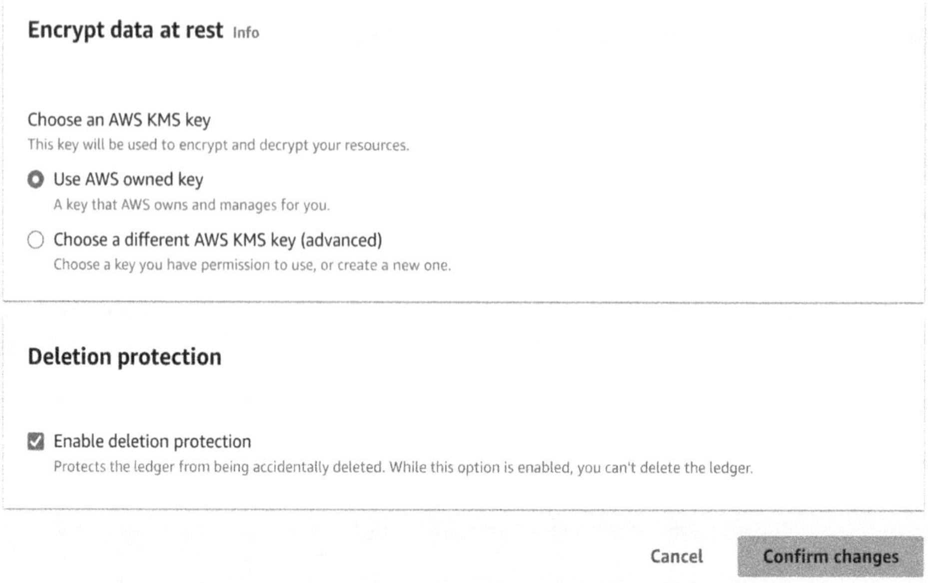

Figure 9.75 – Deletion protection

4. Uncheck **Enable deletion protection** and click on **Confirm changes**. A note at the top of the screen will indicate that the ledger has been updated successfully. Tick the radio button beside the ledger's name again and click on **Delete**. Then, a message stating **Deleting this ledger will permanently remove all of its data** will appear, as shown in *Figure 9.76*:

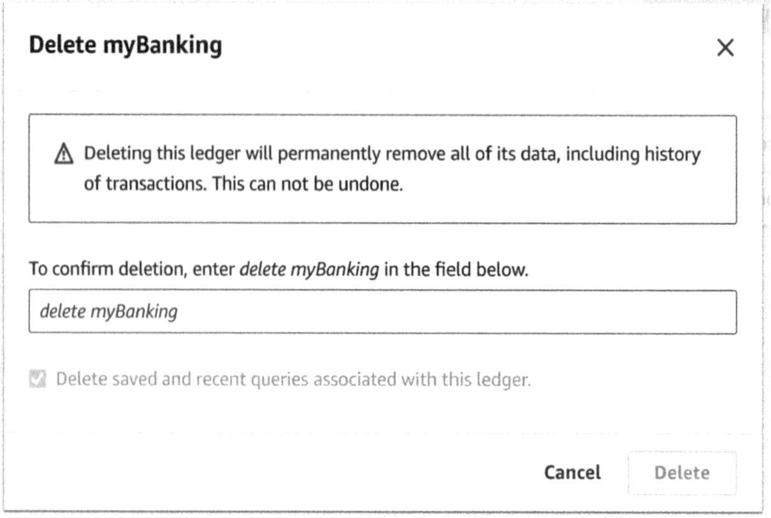

Figure 9.76 – Delete myBanking confirmation

5. Type `delete myBanking` to confirm this action and click on **Delete**. This will start the deletion process, which will take a couple of minutes. Once this is complete, a message stating that it has been deleted will appear, as shown in *Figure 9.77*:

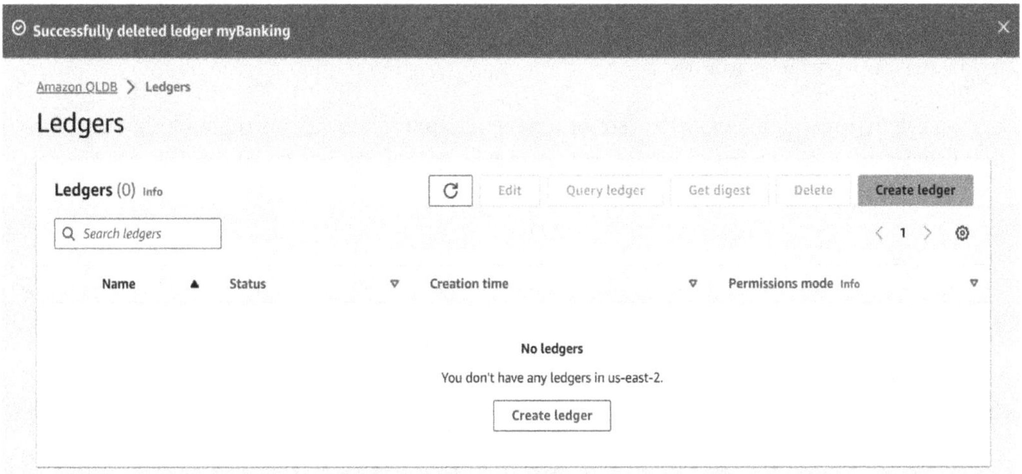

Figure 9.77 – The ledger has been deleted

With this, our cleanup process is complete, and this wraps up our hands-on exercises in QLDB!

> **Important note**
>
> Note that deleting the QLDB resource (that is, the ledger) does not automatically delete the resources in the S3 bucket. That said, make sure you review and delete all resources in the AWS account. For more information on AWS billing and cost management, feel free to check out `https://docs.aws.amazon.com/cost-management/latest/userguide/what-is-costmanagement.html`.

I hope that what we've discussed has enabled you to gain a deep understanding of the concepts that are unique to this database and where they can be used. In the next section, we will cover the best practices when using this database.

Exploring the best practices when using ledger databases

In this chapter, we covered a lot of important concepts on how QLDB retains a comprehensive and verifiable record of modifications made over time. This capability enhances the ledger's transparency and maintains its data integrity. In this section, we will look at the best practices when working with ledger databases. They are as follows:

- **Data structure**: Implement a data structure that fits your needs. Organize and design the tables in a way that makes it easy to search for and retrieve data efficiently.
- **Immutability**: Since QLDB is immutable and contains a verifiable history of all the changes, make use of this capability to maintain data integrity and traceability.
- **Querying**: There are some constraints concerning querying the data in QLDB. These must be taken into consideration when writing queries for optimal performance.
- **Cost management**: Make sure you have a good understanding of how QLDB pricing works, which includes *storage*, *input and output* (*I/O*), *read and write* requests, and *data transfer* costs.
- **Access controls**: Control who can access the data in the ledger by ensuring that the right level of permissions is put in place when reading or modifying the data. Make use of AWS **Identity and Access Management** (**IAM**) to manage this.

> Note
>
> Note that Amazon QLDB is just one of the ledger databases offered by cloud service providers such as AWS. That being said, it's important to check out the relevant best practices and techniques based on the service or solution being used.

Keep in mind that these best practices will vary on a case-by-case basis and will depend on the specific requirements you are working on. In the *Further reading* section, I have placed links to various Amazon QLDB topics so that you can go through the latest documentation.

Summary

In this chapter, we discussed how ledger databases can help us with data integrity management. In our hands-on examples, we specifically used Amazon QLDB, a fully managed ledger database available on AWS. We started by creating an AWS account and then creating an S3 bucket where our journal data from QLDB would be exported. After that, we created the QLDB ledger resource and covered the basic concepts such as getting the *digest*, the *PartiQL editor*, how to create a table, and inserting data into the table. Then, we covered how verification is done in QLDB, and why being *immutable* and *cryptographically verifiable* are crucial in preventing data integrity issues. We also covered how to work with the built-in *history* function and data even though they have been deleted. Lastly, we covered the best practices when using ledger databases, particularly for QLDB. Now that you are equipped with a solid understanding of these concepts, you know how the use of this type of database can enforce data integrity in your finance systems.

The next chapter is our last! In the last chapter of this book, we will discuss a very interesting topic—using **artificial intelligence** for finance data quality management. It's a must-read!

Further reading

To dive deeper into the topics we discussed in this chapter, feel free to explore these additional resources:

- *What is Amazon QLDB?*: `https://docs.aws.amazon.com/qldb/latest/developerguide/what-is.html`
- *From relational to ledger*: `https://docs.aws.amazon.com/qldb/latest/developerguide/what-is.relational-ledger.html`
- *Amazon QLDB glossary*: `https://docs.aws.amazon.com/qldb/latest/developerguide/qldb-glossary.html`
- *Data verification in Amazon QLDB*: `https://docs.aws.amazon.com/qldb/latest/developerguide/verification.html`
- *Querying revision history*: `https://docs.aws.amazon.com/qldb/latest/developerguide/working.history.html`
- *Optimizing query performance*: `https://docs.aws.amazon.com/qldb/latest/developerguide/working.optimize.html`
- *Amazon Quantum Ledger Database (QLDB) pricing*: `https://aws.amazon.com/qldb/pricing/`

10

Using Artificial Intelligence for Finance Data Quality Management

Congratulations! You've made it to the last chapter of this book! In this chapter, we will be covering **artificial intelligence** (**AI**) and how various AI-powered solutions and techniques can address data integrity issues. Consider a scenario where a large dataset containing sales transactions has missing or incorrect details. Instead of fixing these data integrity issues manually, we will explore how we can use AI to automatically identify these discrepancies, suggest potential changes, and even perform necessary corrections. *Exciting, right?*

That said, these are the topics that we will cover:

- Introduction to AI
- Applications of AI in finance
- Detecting anomalies in financial transaction data
- Handling missing financial reporting data with AI
- Best practices when using AI for data integrity management

By the end of this chapter, you will have a better understanding of what AI-powered solutions can do and how these can help accelerate various data quality management processes.

Technical requirements

The first two hands-on examples in this chapter utilize datasets we used in *Chapter 5, Using Business Intelligence Tools to Fix Data Integrity Issues*, and *Chapter 6, Implementing Best Practices When Using Business Intelligence Tools*. For a greater appreciation of our hands-on examples, it is recommended that you read these chapters. If not, it is still okay to jump right into it. The other requirements are as follows:

- **A ChatGPT Plus account**: Sign up and upgrade to the **Plus** version at `https://chat.openai.com/auth/login`
- **Microsoft Excel** (2016 version or later)

The datasets have been saved on **GitHub**. You can access them by going to `https://github.com/PacktPublishing/Managing-Data-Integrity-for-Finance/tree/main/ch10`.

> **Note**
>
> Once you are done with the hands-on examples in this chapter, feel free to downgrade your subscription and go back to the *free* version.

Introduction to AI

Remember the image shown in *Figure 10.1* from *Chapter 1, Recognizing the Importance of Data Integrity in Finance*? You might be surprised that this image is AI-generated!

Figure 10.1 – The wolf hidden among the sheep

Here, the wolf hidden among the sheep symbolizes the subtle yet potentially catastrophic effects of data integrity issues. If you were to upload this image to an AI-powered solution such as ChatGPT, you would be amazed that it would be able to flag an anomaly in the uploaded image:

```
The image you've uploaded seems to depict a field teeming with sheep.
However, upon closer inspection, there is a notable anomaly: amidst
the sheep, there is a wolf. The wolf stands out because of its
distinct appearance, which contrasts with the sheep. This inclusion of
a wolf in a flock of sheep could be an intentional choice for a visual
puzzle or to create a humorous effect, as wolves are predators of
sheep and not typically seen mingling peacefully among them.
```

As you can see, developments in the realm of AI have grown significantly in recent years. This has allowed computers to mimic human intelligence and process information, create solutions, analyze data, optimize processes, and even generate new data. To understand how powerful AI-powered solutions are, let's briefly discuss the different concepts of **AI**, **machine learning** (**ML**), **deep learning** (**DL**), and **generative AI**:

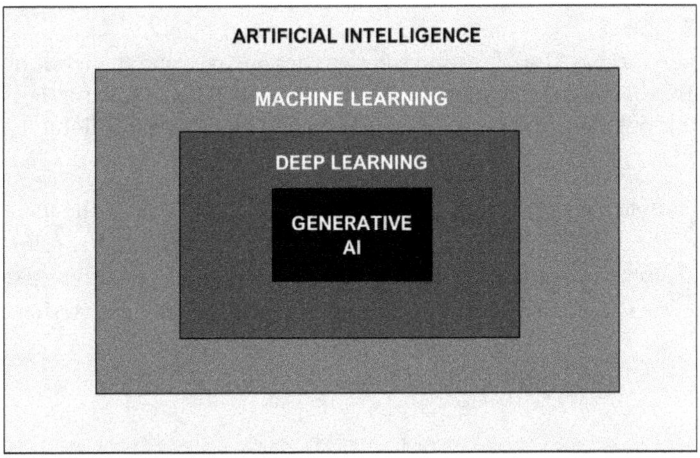

Figure 10.2 – Connection between AI, ML, DL, and generative AI

Figure 10.2 provides a high-level illustration of how these concepts are interrelated:

- **AI**: This encompasses a wide range of technologies to design machines capable of performing tasks that can replicate a human's ability such as *learning* and *problem-solving*. AI can do this by making use of mathematical and logical processes to mirror the way humans can absorb new data and formulate decisions.
- **ML**: This is a *subset* of AI that allows machines to learn unsupervised, see patterns, and make decisions with little human intervention. The ML model becomes more sophisticated as it trains on more data and can improve its performance based on the data it analyzes.

- **DL**: This is a *subset* of ML that makes use of complex algorithms and architectures such as **neural networks**, which mimic (*to some extent*) the connections of the human brain arranged in interconnected layers. It can process large amounts of data and understand the different attributes related to it. For example, once a DL model knows what an object looks like, it can recognize this object in a different image.
- **Generative AI**: This is a type of AI that makes use of DL techniques and capabilities to *generate* new content such as text, music, and images. It makes use of complex architectures, large amounts of training data, and natural language processing for content creation.

In this chapter, our hands-on solutions will focus primarily on using a generative AI solution called **ChatGPT** for solving various data integrity issues. What makes this tool very useful and powerful is that this solution can understand **natural language**. Here, you can enter prompts similar to how you interact with a fellow human being, and it will provide a response for you. We can type a prompt (that is, *an input text or question*) in the chat and it will provide us with an answer.

> **Important note**
>
> Note that there are various AI services and solutions designed to cater to diverse use cases and requirements! That being said, you must be aware that ChatGPT is just *one* of the AI tools and solutions available out there, similar to **Google Bard** and **Microsoft Copilot**.

Let's begin with a simple hands-on example. On the *top left-hand* side of the main screen of the ChatGPT interface, select **GPT-4** or the *latest* version available for **Plus** users. You will see that the features for DALL-E, web browsing, and data analysis are now combined in this version, without us having to switch between them, which is an improvement from the previous versions:

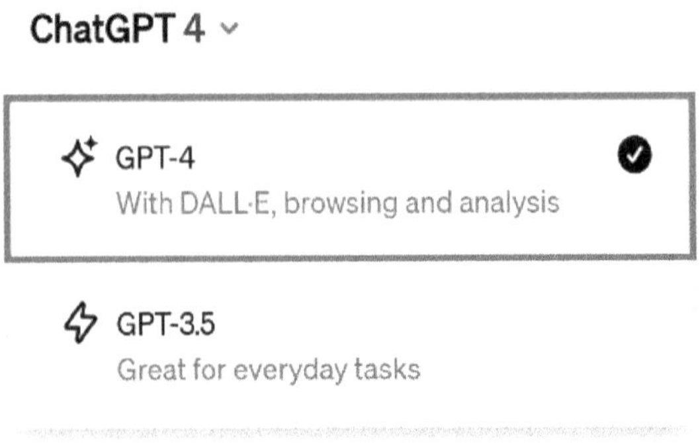

Figure 10.3 – Selecting GPT-4

Once this is enabled, you will notice that a *paper clip* sign that enables you to attach files has appeared in the chat box, as shown in *Figure 10.4*:

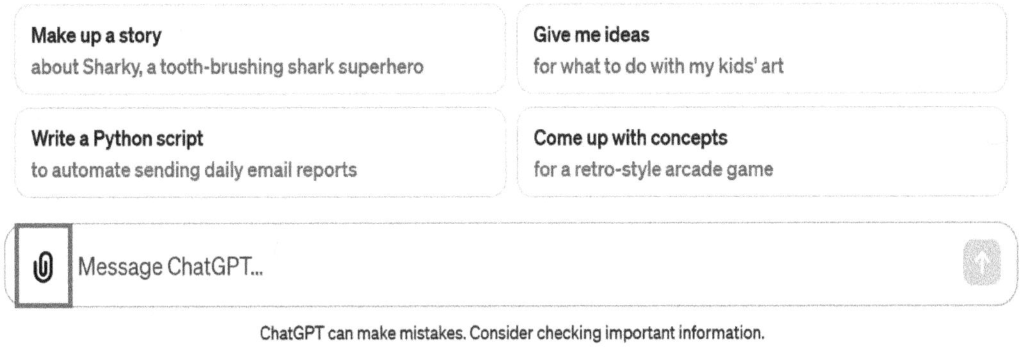

Figure 10.4 – Attaching files in the chat box

We will make use of this capability to upload files in our hands-on examples, starting in the *Detecting anomalies in financial transaction data* section of this chapter.

> **Important note**
>
> Note that in *Figure 10.4*, there is a note saying that "*ChatGPT can make mistakes. Consider checking important information.*" The results that are generated by the model can sometimes contain errors or inaccurate information; these are called **hallucinations**. This happens for a variety of reasons, such as the type of data it has been trained on, limited context that the user has provided, or limitations in the model that prevent it from accurately understanding the information.

For now, let's try asking how we can use ChatGPT for data integrity by searching the internet using the following prompt:

```
Search the internet and answer how can I use ChatGPT for data
integrity?
```

After pressing the *Enter* key, it will start generating a response, similar to what's shown in *Figure 10.5*:

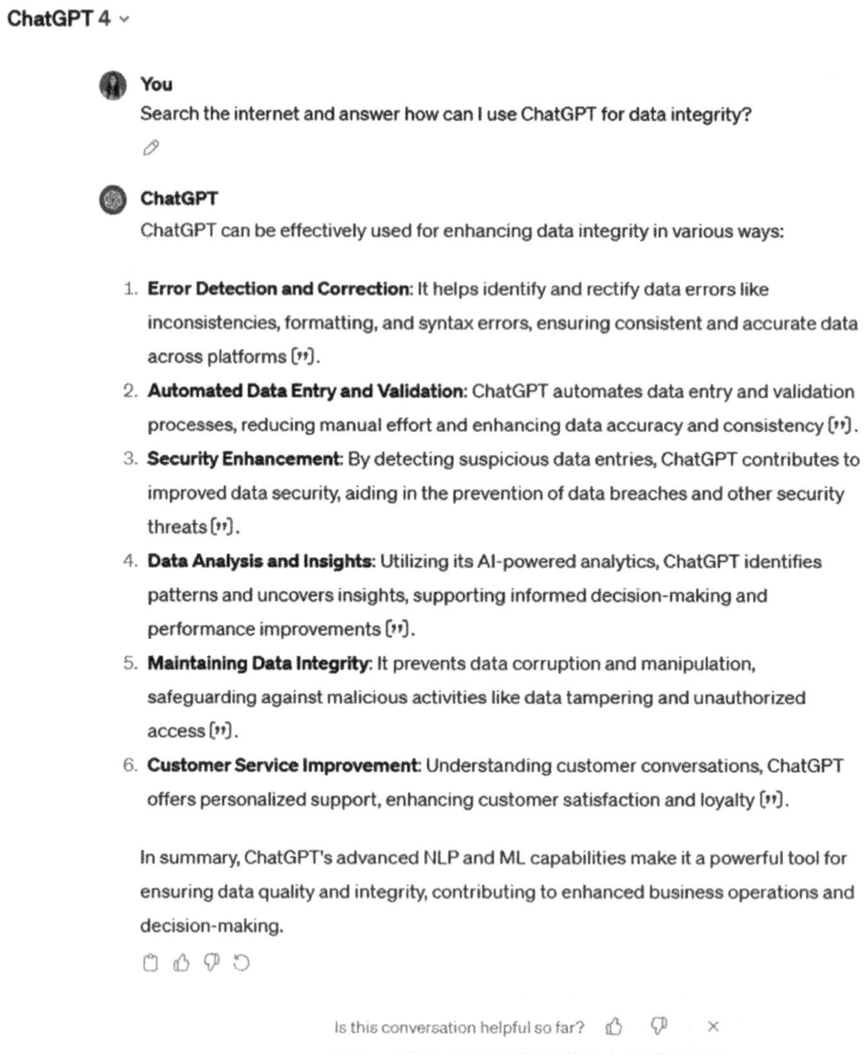
ChatGPT 4
You
Search the internet and answer how can I use ChatGPT for data integrity?
ChatGPT
ChatGPT can be effectively used for enhancing data integrity in various ways:
1. Error Detection and Correction: It helps identify and rectify data errors like inconsistencies, formatting, and syntax errors, ensuring consistent and accurate data across platforms [”].
2. Automated Data Entry and Validation: ChatGPT automates data entry and validation processes, reducing manual effort and enhancing data accuracy and consistency [”].
3. Security Enhancement: By detecting suspicious data entries, ChatGPT contributes to improved data security, aiding in the prevention of data breaches and other security threats [”].
4. Data Analysis and Insights: Utilizing its AI-powered analytics, ChatGPT identifies patterns and uncovers insights, supporting informed decision-making and performance improvements [”].
5. Maintaining Data Integrity: It prevents data corruption and manipulation, safeguarding against malicious activities like data tampering and unauthorized access [”].
6. Customer Service Improvement: Understanding customer conversations, ChatGPT offers personalized support, enhancing customer satisfaction and loyalty [”].
In summary, ChatGPT's advanced NLP and ML capabilities make it a powerful tool for ensuring data quality and integrity, contributing to enhanced business operations and decision-making.
Is this conversation helpful so far?

Figure 10.5 – How ChatGPT can be used for data integrity

As we can see, it searched the internet and gave us different ways on how it can be used for data integrity. We will be testing specifically for error detection and correction, data validation, and data analysis in this chapter.

> **Note**
>
> Note that you may get a different set of results and responses from ChatGPT.

If you click on **Explore** on the *top left-hand* side of the screen, a section called **My GPTs** will appear, as shown in *Figure 10.6*. Here, you can make your own version of a ChatGPT chatbot to fit a particular task or subject, as well as access the GPTs that OpenAI has developed:

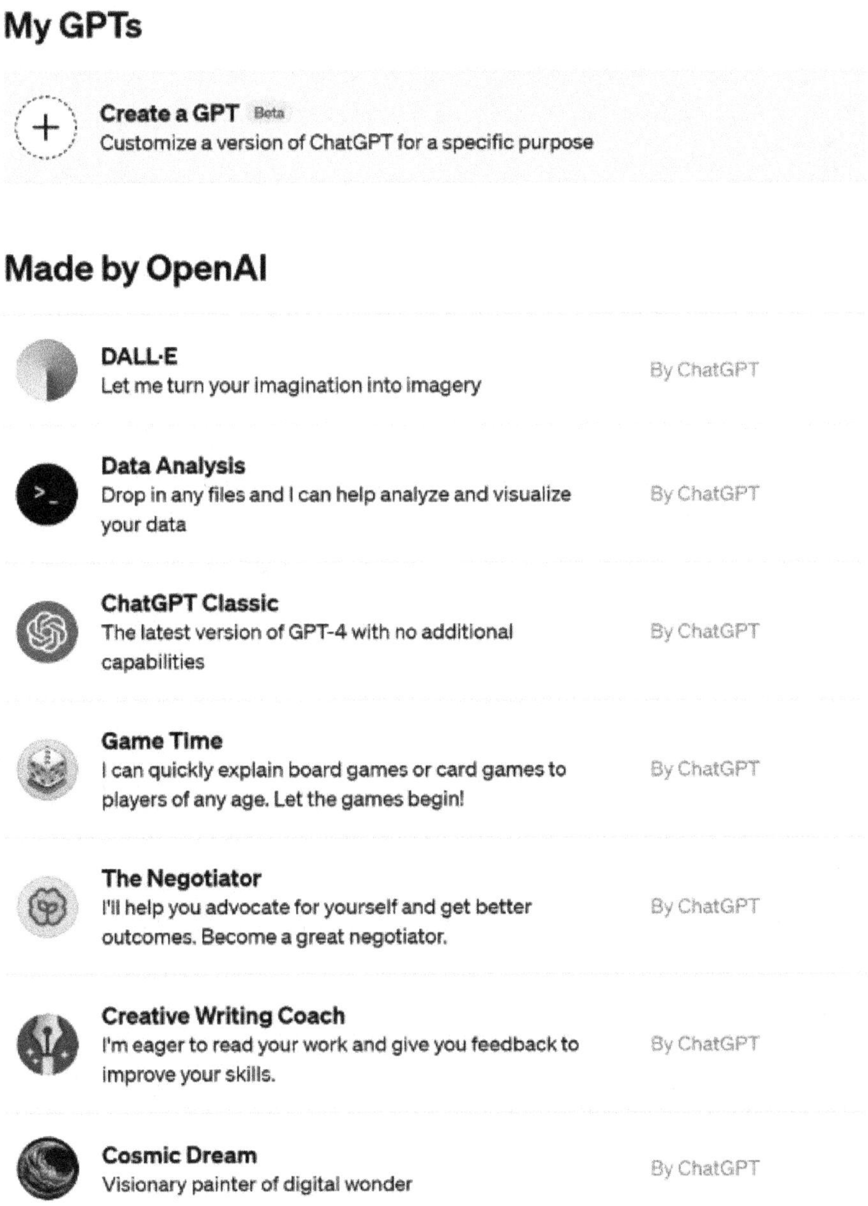
My GPTs
Create a GPT Beta
Customize a version of ChatGPT for a specific purpose
Made by OpenAI
DALL·E
Let me turn your imagination into imagery
By ChatGPT
Data Analysis
Drop in any files and I can help analyze and visualize your data
By ChatGPT
ChatGPT Classic
The latest version of GPT-4 with no additional capabilities
By ChatGPT
Game Time
I can quickly explain board games or card games to players of any age. Let the games begin!
By ChatGPT
The Negotiator
I'll help you advocate for yourself and get better outcomes. Become a great negotiator.
By ChatGPT
Creative Writing Coach
I'm eager to read your work and give you feedback to improve your skills.
By ChatGPT
Cosmic Dream
Visionary painter of digital wonder
By ChatGPT

Figure 10.6 – The My GPTs section

OpenAI's **GPTs** should not be confused with the technical term **generative pre-trained transformers** (**GPTs**). As shown in *Figure 10.6*, GPTs allow anyone to create their own versions of ChatGPT for specific use cases without having to write code, while the term GPT covers various models that make use of the transformer architecture for different tasks, such as translating languages and generating text, among others. For more information on the custom versions of ChatGPT, check out `https://openai.com/blog/introducing-gpts`.

As the focus of our discussion is on analyzing the data and checking its integrity, let's click on **Data Analysis**.

> **Note**
>
> At the time of writing, these features are available to paying subscribers. If you are unable to see the GPTs made by OpenAI, similar to what is shown in *Figure 10.6*, feel free to use the following link to access the **Data Analysis** GPT: `https://chat.openai.com/g/g-HMNcP6w7d-data-analysis`.

Next, we'll discuss what the applications of AI are before we dive into our hands-on examples. We will cover three examples under *Detecting anomalies in financial transaction data* and *Handling missing financial reporting data with AI* so that you can become more familiar with it.

Applications of AI in finance

The scope of AI for finance is expanding rapidly, thus enabling the automation of processes, assisting professionals in becoming more efficient at their jobs, as well as creating potential solutions to solve problems. That being said, here are some of the applications in finance in general:

- **Outlier detection**: AI helps in understanding the normal transactions to identify any anomalies.
- **Credit scoring**: ML models can process large datasets and use the patterns learned to predict creditworthiness and the ability to repay loans more accurately.
- **Report generation**: With AI, you can automate the creation of reports and contracts. One particular example is **Alteryx AiDIN**, which can be used to generate **magic documents** and help you create your first draft automatically so that it can be sent to key business partners.
- **Missing data identification**: As AI processes data efficiently, it can find missing and incomplete data in your datasets. This is helpful during analysis since missing data can impact the accuracy and dependability of your reports.
- **Data creation**: It can also create additional data based on the existing information it has.
- **Data validation**: This ensures that the data in a dataset is correct and meets the criteria being set. We will cover this in more detail in our first hands-on example in the next section.

The applications of AI listed here are not exhaustive and many more practical applications are being used by organizations globally. We will cover some of these through our hands-on examples in this chapter. We'll start with our first example, where we will use ChatGPT to search for irregularities in the data.

Detecting anomalies in financial transaction data

In this example, we will work on the datasets we used in the *Dealing with large financial datasets using data validation* section in *Chapter 5, Using Business Intelligence Tools to Fix Data Integrity Issues*. We will test whether we can validate the data against another table containing the correct values. The steps are as follows:

1. Create a new chat using the **Data Analysis** GPT, as illustrated in *Figure 10.7*:

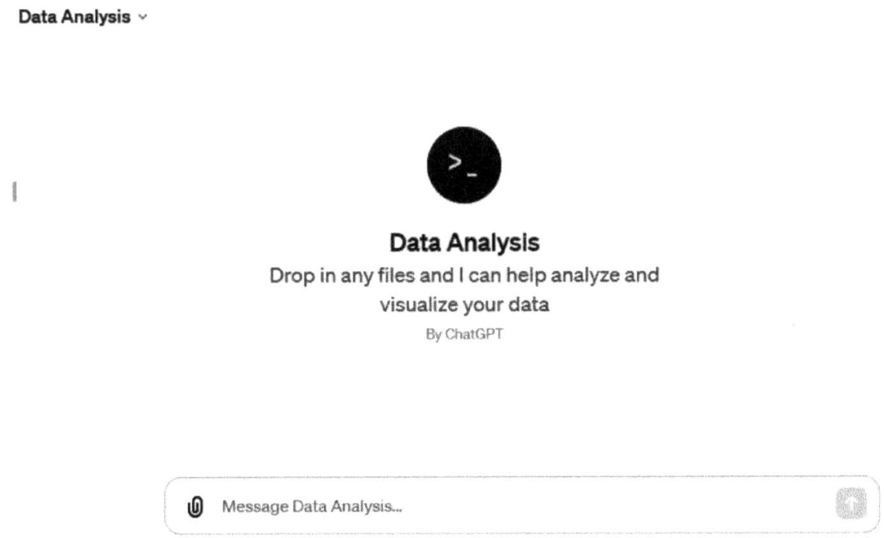
Data Analysis
Data Analysis
Drop in any files and I can help analyze and visualize your data
By ChatGPT
Message Data Analysis...

Figure 10.7 – Using the Data Analysis GPT

To access the **Data Analysis** GPT, click on **Explore** in the sidebar and select **Data Analysis** from the list of GPTs available. If you can't see the GPTs, feel free to use the following link to access this: `https://chat.openai.com/g/g-HMNcP6w7d-data-analysis`.

> **Note**
>
> You may also search for `chatgpt data analysis gpt` via Google Search; you should find the GPT in the list of results. Alternatively, you may use **GPT-4** as it has the **Advanced Data Analysis** feature included. Note that you might get a different set of results or answers from ChatGPT if you use GPT-4 instead of the **Data Analysis** GPT.

2. Click on the *paper clip* sign to upload the `Sales_Transactions.xlsx` and `NSW_Post_Code.xlsx` files. Do not press *Enter* yet.

   Type the following prompt inside the text bar then press the *Enter* key to submit it together with the two files:

```
Please examine the contents of these two files and provide
information as to their data structure and type of data that
they contain.
```

   The result should yield a response similar to what's shown in *Figure 10.8*:

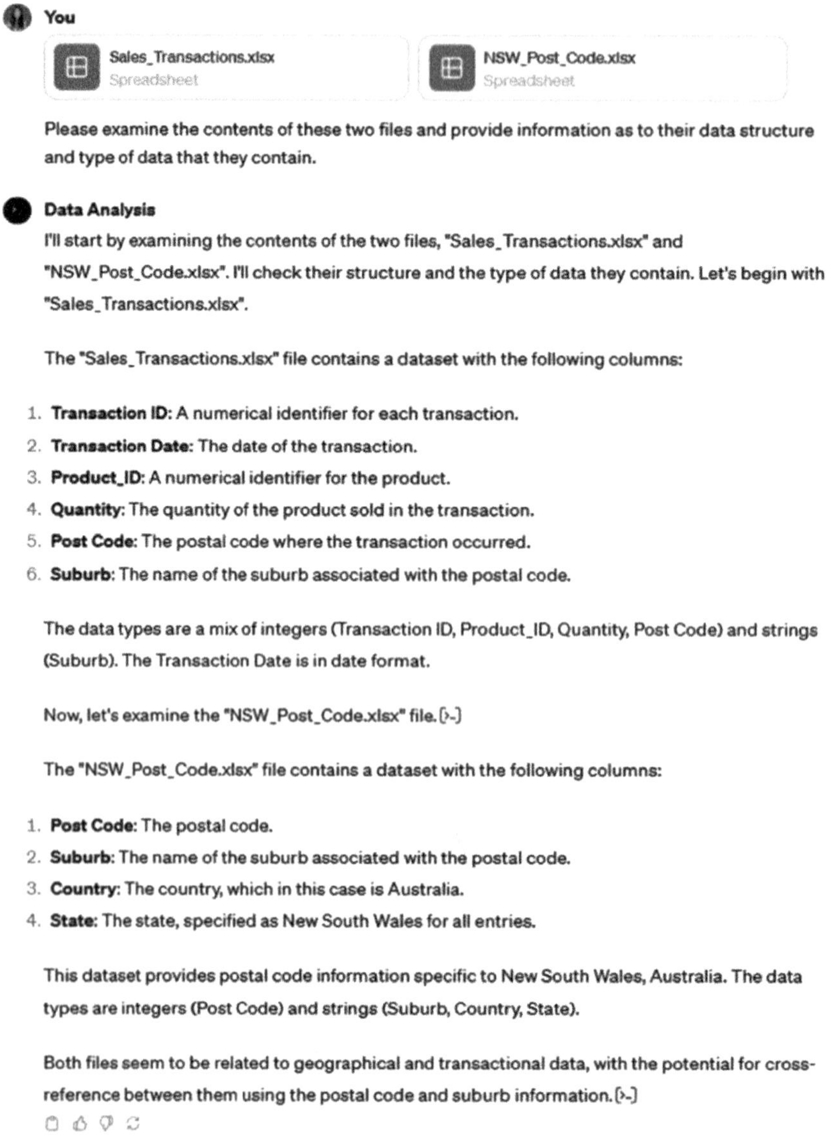
You
Sales_Transactions.xlsx
Spreadsheet
NSW_Post_Code.xlsx
Spreadsheet
Please examine the contents of these two files and provide information as to their data structure and type of data that they contain.
Data Analysis
I'll start by examining the contents of the two files, "Sales_Transactions.xlsx" and "NSW_Post_Code.xlsx". I'll check their structure and the type of data they contain. Let's begin with "Sales_Transactions.xlsx".
The "Sales_Transactions.xlsx" file contains a dataset with the following columns:
1. Transaction ID: A numerical identifier for each transaction.
2. Transaction Date: The date of the transaction.
3. Product_ID: A numerical identifier for the product.
4. Quantity: The quantity of the product sold in the transaction.
5. Post Code: The postal code where the transaction occurred.
6. Suburb: The name of the suburb associated with the postal code.
The data types are a mix of integers (Transaction ID, Product_ID, Quantity, Post Code) and strings (Suburb). The Transaction Date is in date format.
Now, let's examine the "NSW_Post_Code.xlsx" file.
The "NSW_Post_Code.xlsx" file contains a dataset with the following columns:
1. Post Code: The postal code.
2. Suburb: The name of the suburb associated with the postal code.
3. Country: The country, which in this case is Australia.
4. State: The state, specified as New South Wales for all entries.
This dataset provides postal code information specific to New South Wales, Australia. The data types are integers (Post Code) and strings (Suburb, Country, State).
Both files seem to be related to geographical and transactional data, with the potential for cross-reference between them using the postal code and suburb information.

Figure 10.8 – Results of the initial analysis

ChatGPT will analyze what is inside the files and give you additional information about what kind of data it contains.

Assume that, for this example, the `Sales_Transactions.xlsx` file contains data that has been collected from the customer transactions and that the `NSW_Post_Code.xlsx` file is an internal file that is considered as the main list. Since the `Sales_Transactions.xlsx` file is taken from customers, there may be errors in the data. If we need to analyze the sales based on the geographic location of the customers, *which is the suburb*, we might encounter errors if the data is not cleaned.

3. To help us validate the data, we need to compare the suburbs in the two files by entering the following prompt:

```
Please validate the Suburb column in the Sales_Transactions.xlsx
file to the NSW_Post_Code.xlsx file. Please identify any suburbs
that have mismatches using this column between the two files.
```

As shown in *Figure 10.9*, it reviewed the transactions and listed the suburbs that are inconsistent with the main list:

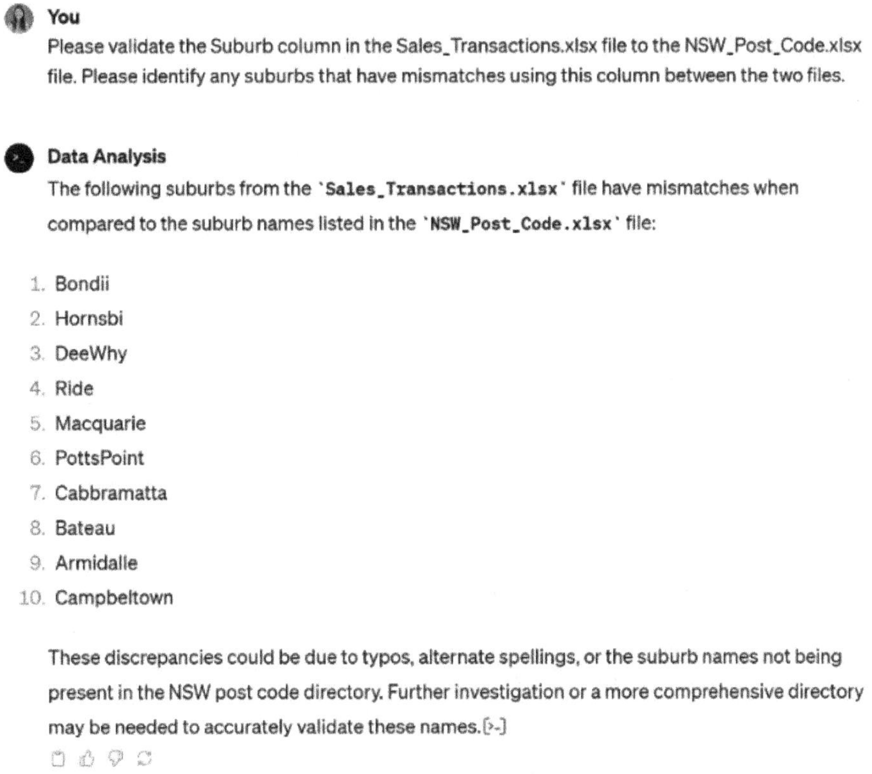
You

Please validate the Suburb column in the Sales_Transactions.xlsx file to the NSW_Post_Code.xlsx file. Please identify any suburbs that have mismatches using this column between the two files.

Data Analysis

The following suburbs from the `Sales_Transactions.xlsx` file have mismatches when compared to the suburb names listed in the `NSW_Post_Code.xlsx` file:

1. Bondii
2. Hornsbi
3. DeeWhy
4. Ride
5. Macquarie
6. PottsPoint
7. Cabbramatta
8. Bateau
9. Armidalle
10. Campbeltown

These discrepancies could be due to typos, alternate spellings, or the suburb names not being present in the NSW post code directory. Further investigation or a more comprehensive directory may be needed to accurately validate these names.[>-]

Figure 10.9 – Validating the misspelled suburbs

4. Now that we have identified the suburbs that are inconsistent with the `NSW_Post_Code.xlsx` file, we need to check what the correct names are. Type the following in the chat:

```
For these mismatched suburbs, find the closest match based on
the NSW_Post_Code.xlsx file based on similarity of spelling.
Please list them in a table format for review prior to any
updates.
```

This will map the **Suburb** column between these two files and proceed to update the incorrect data, as shown in *Figure 10.10*:

You

For these mismatched suburbs, find the closest match based on the NSW_Post_Code.xlsx file based on similarity of spelling. Please list them in a table format for review prior to any updates.

Data Analysis

Here's a table showing the closest matches based on similarity of spelling for the mismatched suburbs from the `Sales_Transactions.xlsx` file, compared to the `NSW_Post_Code.xlsx` file:

Mismatched Suburb	Closest Match
Bondii	Bondi
Hornsbi	Hornsby
DeeWhy	Dee Why
Ride	Ryde
Macquarie	Port Macquarie
PottsPoint	Potts Point
Cabbramatta	Cabramatta
Bateau	Bateau Bay
Armidalle	Armidale
Campbeltown	Campbelltown

These closest matches have been determined based on the similarity of spelling, using a threshold that prioritizes a higher degree of similarity. Before making any updates, it's advisable to review these matches to ensure they align with the intended data correction.

Figure 10.10 – Mapping the misspelled suburbs

As we can see, it has correctly identified the closest match for the items.

> **Note**
>
> If ChatGPT notes that there are suburbs that it cannot match, type `Lower the similarity threshold slightly and check for the best possible match again.` This should address this issue.

5. We are now ready to update the mismatched suburbs. In the chat, type the following:

```
Please update the mismatched suburbs in the Sales_Transactions.
xlsx file based on the closest match. Kindly show the
transactions in table format when completed.
```

This will give us the results shown in *Figure 10.11*:

You

Please update the mismatched suburbs in the Sales_Transactions.xlsx file based on the closest match. Kindly show the transactions in table format when completed.

Data Analysis

The mismatched suburbs in the `Sales_Transactions.xlsx` file have been updated based on the closest match from the `NSW_Post_Code.xlsx` file. Here are the first few updated transactions for review:

Transaction ID	Transaction Date	Product_ID	Quantity	Post Code	Suburb
2020001	2020-01-01	151001	300	2026	Bondi
2020002	2020-01-02	151001	100	2077	Hornsby
2020003	2020-01-03	151001	200	2099	Dee Why
2020004	2020-01-04	151001	10	2112	Ryde
2020005	2020-01-05	151001	20	2113	Port Macquarie

These changes reflect the corrected suburb names in the dataset. If this is satisfactory, I can save the updated file for you to download. [>-]

Figure 10.11 – Showing the transaction details after correcting the suburbs

> **Note**
>
> You might be wondering why we did not use the **Post Code** column to validate the suburbs. This is because, as we can see from the `NSW_Post_Code.xlsx` file, the post code is not unique to a particular suburb. For example, 2030 could be for Vaucluse or Dover Heights.

6. Now that we have reviewed and updated the datasets, we can download the data:

```
Please export the updated Sales_Transactions.xlsx file
reflecting the changes made.
```

The results will look something like what's shown in *Figure 10.12*:

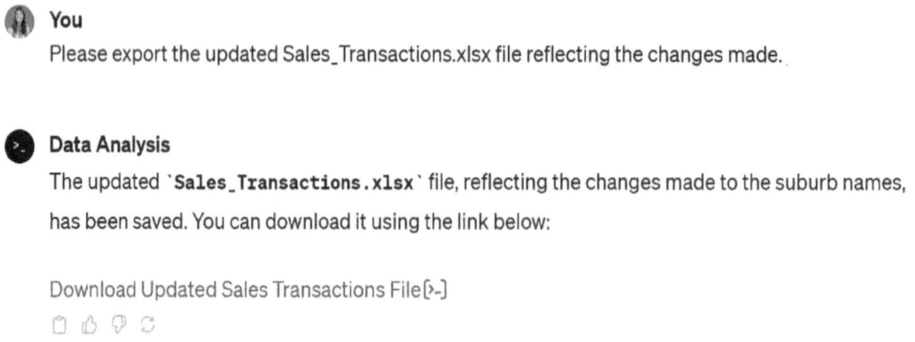
You
Please export the updated Sales_Transactions.xlsx file reflecting the changes made.
Data Analysis
The updated `Sales_Transactions.xlsx` file, reflecting the changes made to the suburb names, has been saved. You can download it using the link below:
Download Updated Sales Transactions File

Figure 10.12 – Exporting the corrected dataset

When you click on **Download Updated Sales Transactions File**, the file will go to your **Downloads** folder. With that, the file has been cleaned and is ready to be used for further analysis or reporting.

With these simple steps, we let ChatGPT perform **data validation** and simplified what we did in **Tableau** using simple prompts. Feel free to revisit our discussion in *Chapter 5, Using Business Intelligence Tools to Fix Data Integrity Issues*, under the *Dealing with large financial datasets using data validation* section.

> **Note**
>
> Note that the output, once generated and exported, needs to be validated manually as a potential result of hallucinations and misinformation.

Now that we are done with our first hands-on example, let's work on another one!

In the next example, we will use again the datasets from in *Chapter 5, Using Business Intelligence Tools to Fix Data Integrity Issues*. This will make us appreciate how efficient ChatGPT is in identifying duplicates, data outliers, and inconsistencies, and how we can utilize this tool to clean the data for us. We will also let it create a **histogram** and a **scatter chart**, similar to what we did in previous chapters. Let's go through the steps:

1. Create a new chat using the **Data Analysis** GPT, as we did in *Figure 10.7*. If this option is not available for you, feel free to use the **Advanced Data Analysis** feature (using **GPT-4**), as seen in *Figure 10.13*:

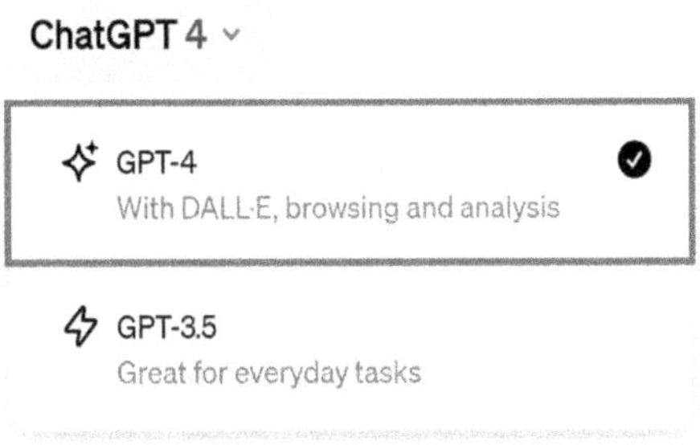

Figure 10.13 – Using GPT-4

Again, note that you might get a different set of results or answers from ChatGPT if you use **GPT-4** instead of the **Data Analysis** GPT.

2. Click on the *paper clip* icon to upload the `2020_Transactions.xlsx` file. Do not press *Enter* yet since we will include the following prompt:

```
Please analyze what this file contains and provide information
as to the data structure and type of data it has.
```

After inputting this, press *Enter*.

ChatGPT will analyze the file and confirm once it has completed the analysis. The resulting output will look similar to what's shown in *Figure 10.14*:

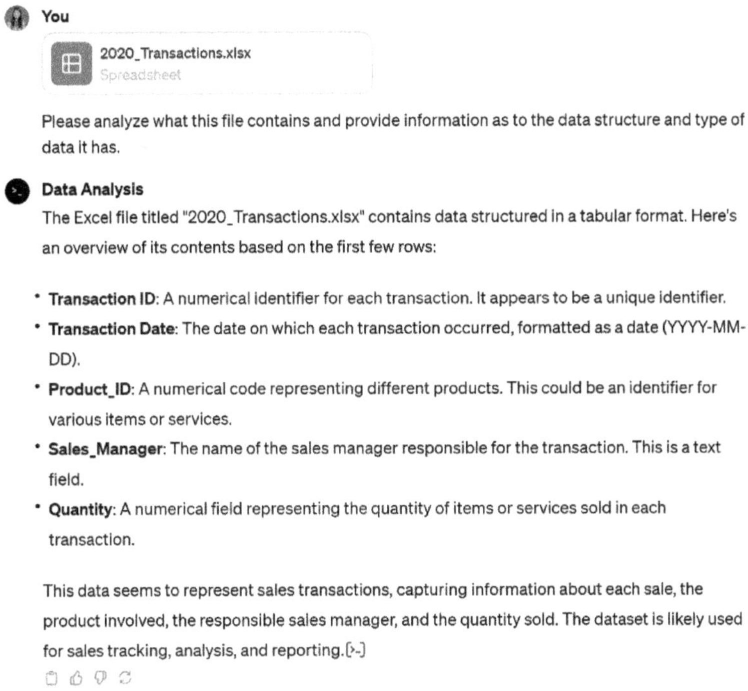

Figure 10.14 – Loading the 2020_Transactions.xlsx file for analysis

It will provide an overview of the data and the columns in the file, as well as a description of each of the columns.

3. Next, let's get a preview of the data in the file. Type the following in the chat:

```
Give me a preview of the data in the file.
```

It will show the results, list the columns, and provide a preview of the rows, as shown in *Figure 10.15*:

You

Give me a preview of the data in the file.

Data Analysis

Here is an extended preview of the data from the file "2020_Transactions.xlsx", displaying the first 10 rows:

Transaction ID	Transaction Date	Product_ID	Sales_Manager	Quantity
2020001	2020-01-01	151001	Shane Hurstley	300
2020002	2020-01-02	151001	Shane Hurstley	100
2020003	2020-01-03	151001	Shane Hurstley	200
2020004	2020-01-04	151001	Shane Hurstley	10
2020005	2020-01-05	151001	Shane Hurstley	20
2020006	2020-01-06	151001	Shane Hurstley	50
2020007	2020-01-07	151001	Shane Hurstley	40
2020008	2020-01-08	151001	Shane Hurstley	35
2020009	2020-01-09	151001	Shane Hurstley	60
2020010	2020-01-10	151001	Shane Hurstley	20

This table shows the transactions recorded over the first ten days of 2020. Each row represents a distinct transaction, including details like the date, product ID, sales manager involved, and the quantity sold. [>-]

Figure 10.15 – Preview of the transactions in the 2020_Transactions.xlsx file

Having a preview of the data in the file helps us examine what it contains and adds more detail, in addition to the description provided in the previous step.

4. Let's start performing specific analysis on the data. Type the following in the chat:

```
Please provide the basic statistics such as the number of
transactions in the file, as well as the number of unique and
distinct transactions for each column.
```

Then, press *Enter*. It will start generating a response, similar to what's shown in *Figure 10.16*:

You

Please provide the basic statistics such as the number of transactions in the file, as well as the number of unique and distinct transactions for each column.

Data Analysis

Certainly! Here are the basic statistics for the dataset in the "2020_Transactions.xlsx" file:

- **Total Transactions**: There are 1,129 transactions recorded in the file.
- **Unique Transactions Per Column**:
  - **Transaction ID**: 1,098 unique transaction IDs. This suggests that some transaction IDs may be repeated.
  - **Transaction Date**: 367 unique dates, which is more than the number of days in a year, indicating either an error or that the dates span multiple years.
  - **Product_ID**: 3 unique product IDs, indicating a small variety of products in the transactions.
  - **Sales_Manager**: 3 unique sales managers, suggesting a small sales team.
  - **Quantity**: 53 unique quantity values, showing a variety of transaction sizes.

These statistics give an overview of the diversity and distribution of the transactions recorded in the file, including the number of distinct values in each category.

Figure 10.16 – Steps to analyze the data

Our goal for this step is to analyze each of the columns to get a more thorough understanding of the data, as well as identify any potential irregularities or inconsistencies. As we can see from the results, it has provided details about each of the columns and called out possible errors under the `Transaction ID` and `Transaction Date` columns. We will review these in the next steps.

> **Important note**
>
> Make sure you review and check the results returned by AI-powered tools such as ChatGPT since these tools may hallucinate and return incorrect results.

Comparing this with our hands-on example in *Chapter 5, Using Business Intelligence Tools to Fix Data Integrity Issues*, the analysis was done in less than a minute compared to the multiple steps we did on loading the Excel file to **Microsoft Power BI** using **Get Data** and loading them into the **Power Query Editor**.

5. The next step is to check for duplicates under the `Transaction ID` column. Based on the results from the previous step, there are a total of 1,129 transactions in the file, but only 1,098 are unique. To do this, type the following in the chat:

```
Please check the Transaction ID column and identify if there are
any transactions that are repeated.
```

The transactions will be reviewed to check for any duplicates and will generate results similar to what's shown in *Figure 10.17*:

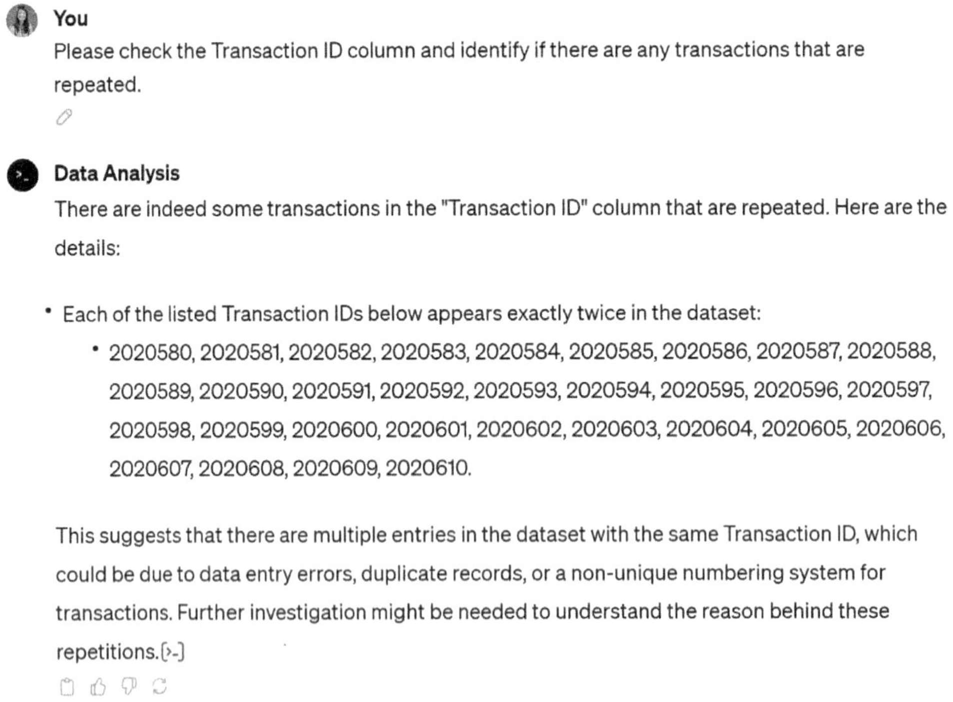
You
Please check the Transaction ID column and identify if there are any transactions that are repeated.
Data Analysis
There are indeed some transactions in the "Transaction ID" column that are repeated. Here are the details:
• Each of the listed Transaction IDs below appears exactly twice in the dataset:
• 2020580, 2020581, 2020582, 2020583, 2020584, 2020585, 2020586, 2020587, 2020588, 2020589, 2020590, 2020591, 2020592, 2020593, 2020594, 2020595, 2020596, 2020597, 2020598, 2020599, 2020600, 2020601, 2020602, 2020603, 2020604, 2020605, 2020606, 2020607, 2020608, 2020609, 2020610.
This suggests that there are multiple entries in the dataset with the same Transaction ID, which could be due to data entry errors, duplicate records, or a non-unique numbering system for transactions. Further investigation might be needed to understand the reason behind these repetitions.[>-]

Figure 10.17 – Reviewing the Transaction ID column

Going back to our discussion in *Chapter 5, Using Business Intelligence Tools to Fix Data Integrity Issues*, upon reviewing the **column statistics**, we found that there were duplicate entries in our data, which showed the count of *distinct* and *unique* entries.

As we can see, the results are aligned with the previous chapter's findings, where the duplicates have been identified.

> **Note**
>
> When we look at the end of the chat response, we will notice a [>_] icon, which is colored *blue*. If we hover our cursor over it, we will see that this will provide additional information about what ChatGPT has done and enable **View analysis**.

Click on the **View analysis** icon to further check the result. *Figure 10.18* shows the transaction IDs that have been repeated:

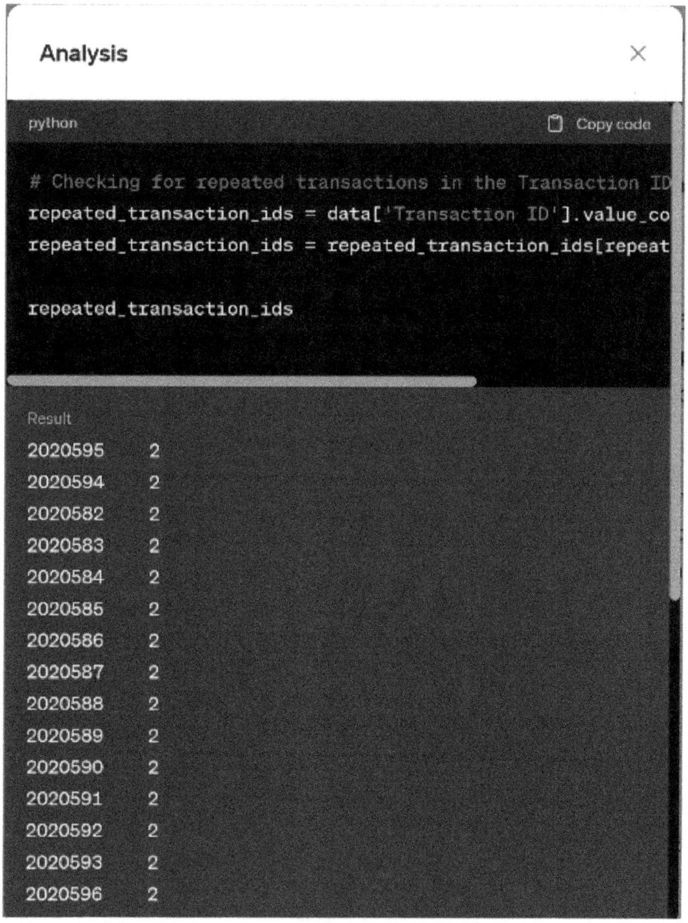

Figure 10.18 – Clicking on the View analysis icon

Checking this provides us with more detail about the analysis being done in the background.

> **Important note**
>
> Make sure you review and check the results returned by AI-powered tools such as ChatGPT since these tools may hallucinate and return incorrect results.

6. To check whether it has correctly identified the anomalies, type the following in the chat:

```
Can you show the duplicate rows in the dataset?
```

Then, press *Enter*. The results should look something similar to what's shown in *Figure 10.19*:

You

Can you show the duplicate rows in the dataset?

Data Analysis

Here are the duplicate rows in the dataset, sorted by the Transaction ID:

Transaction ID	Transaction Date	Product_ID	Sales_Manager	Quantity
2020580	2020-08-01	151001	Ryan Becker	250
2020580	2020-08-01	151001	Ryan Becker	250
2020581	2020-08-02	151001	Ryan Becker	44
2020581	2020-08-02	151001	Ryan Becker	44
2020582	2020-08-03	151001	Ryan Becker	55
...	...	...	...	...
2020609	2020-08-30	151003	Ryan Becker	25
2020609	2020-08-30	151003	Ryan Becker	25
2020610	2020-08-31	151003	Ryan Becker	10
2020610	2020-08-31	151003	Ryan Becker	10

(Only a portion of the table is shown here for brevity.)

There are 62 rows in total that are duplicated, each pair having the same Transaction ID, Date, Product_ID, Sales_Manager, and Quantity. These duplicate entries suggest either data entry errors or a systemic issue in recording transactions. [>-]

Figure 10.19 – Listing the duplicate rows in the dataset

ChatGPT has listed some of the duplicate rows; notice that the details for the identified transactions are similar. Also, note that the response from ChatGPT may be different, so it is important to double-check the results to ensure that this is accurate.

7. Our next step is to remove the duplicate rows. However, before we do that, let's quickly go to Excel and create a *pivot table* to review whether the items that have been identified are correct. As shown in *Figure 10.20*, 31 transactions have been duplicated, leading to a total of 62 rows:

Row Labels	Count of Transaction ID
2020578	1
2020579	1
2020580	2
2020581	2
2020582	2
2020583	2
2020584	2
2020585	2
2020586	2
2020587	2
2020588	2
2020589	2
2020590	2
2020591	2
2020592	2
2020593	2
2020594	2
2020595	2
2020596	2
2020597	2
2020598	2
2020599	2
2020600	2
2020601	2
2020602	2
2020603	2
2020604	2
2020605	2
2020606	2
2020607	2
2020608	2
2020609	2
2020610	2
2020611	1
2020612	1

Figure 10.20 – Identifying the duplicate transactions using a pivot table in Excel

Note that the details in the pivot table are aligned with *Figure 10.17*.

> **Important note**
>
> Make sure you review and check the results returned by AI-powered tools such as ChatGPT since these tools may hallucinate and return incorrect results.

8. Since we have confirmed that this is correct, let's go back to the chat and enter the following:

```
Please remove the duplicate rows identified then provide the
total distinct and unique transactions for the Transaction ID
column.
```

Once this is complete, ChatGPT will confirm that it has been cleaned, as shown in *Figure 10.21*:

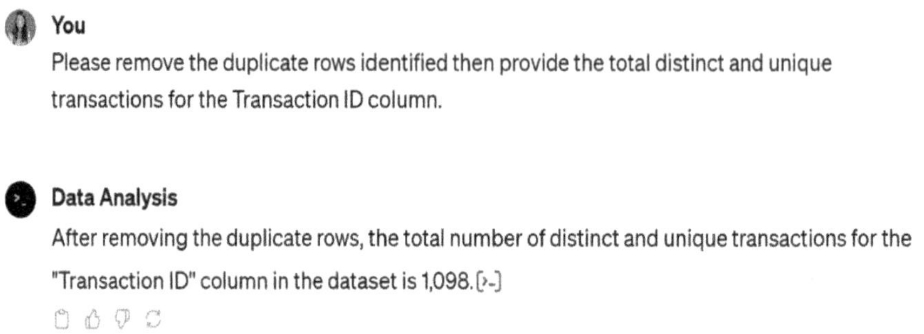
You
Please remove the duplicate rows identified then provide the total distinct and unique transactions for the Transaction ID column.
Data Analysis
After removing the duplicate rows, the total number of distinct and unique transactions for the "Transaction ID" column in the dataset is 1,098.

Figure 10.21 – Removing the duplicates from the dataset

We allowed ChatGPT to remove the duplicates for us.

9. Now that this is complete, let's continue with the next step, which is checking the *date consistency*. The transactions in the file are for 2020; based on *Figure 10.16*, there could be dates outside this year.

In the chat, type the following prompt:

```
Please provide the details of the transaction or transactions
that do not have a date in the year 2020.
```

ChatGPT will generate the result shown in *Figure 10.22*:

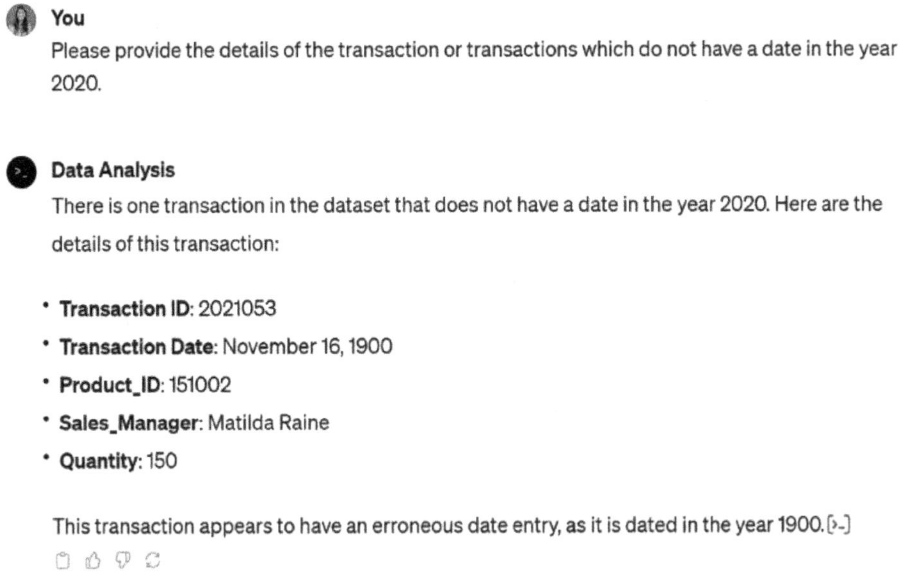
You
Please provide the details of the transaction or transactions which do not have a date in the year 2020.
Data Analysis
There is one transaction in the dataset that does not have a date in the year 2020. Here are the details of this transaction:
Transaction ID: 2021053
Transaction Date: November 16, 1900
Product_ID: 151002
Sales_Manager: Matilda Raine
Quantity: 150
This transaction appears to have an erroneous date entry, as it is dated in the year 1900.

Figure 10.22 – Identifying the transaction with date inconsistency

As we can see, it has correctly identified **Transaction ID: 2021053**, whose year is **1900**. This is consistent with our findings in the *Identifying data outliers* section in *Chapter 5*, *Using Business Intelligence Tools to Fix Data Integrity Issues*. Since the transactions are for 2020, we will update this field.

> **Note**
>
> If ChatGPT has given a different reply, feel free to modify the prompt and type in what it needs to do—for example, `Can you check the dataset for transactions that do not have a date in the year 2020? Can you show me the details?` By formulating prompts more thoughtfully, you will be able to guide the output generated by ChatGPT toward the objective you are after, resulting in a more accurate and valuable response.

10. To correct the year, type the following in the chat:

```
Please update the year to 2020 for the Transaction Date and show
the updated fields for this transaction.
```

This will proceed to update the transaction and return the results, as shown in *Figure 10.23*:

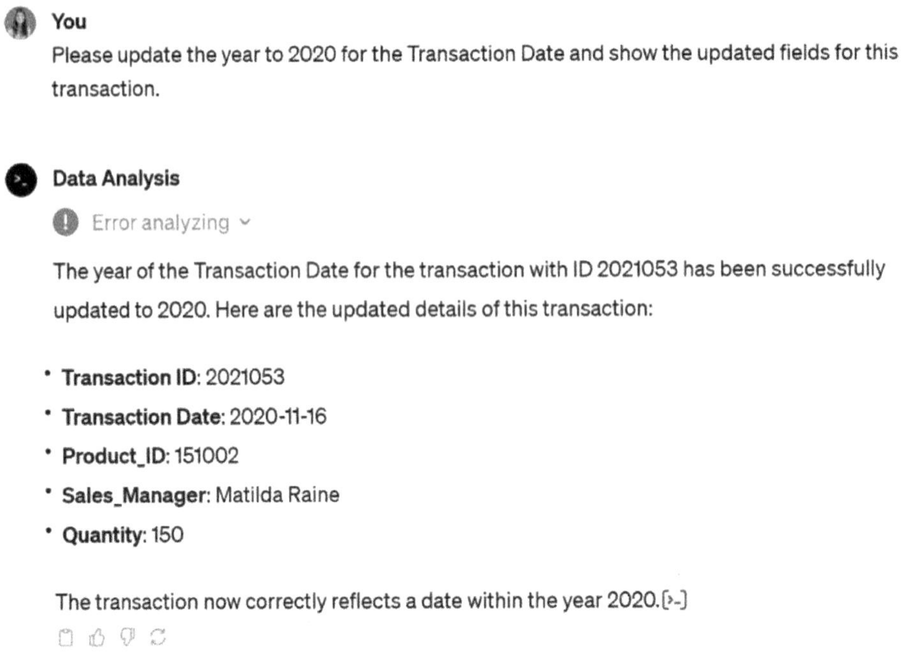
You
Please update the year to 2020 for the Transaction Date and show the updated fields for this transaction.
Data Analysis
Error analyzing
The year of the Transaction Date for the transaction with ID 2021053 has been successfully updated to 2020. Here are the updated details of this transaction:
Transaction ID: 2021053
Transaction Date: 2020-11-16
Product_ID: 151002
Sales_Manager: Matilda Raine
Quantity: 150
The transaction now correctly reflects a date within the year 2020.

Figure 10.23 – Correcting the date field for the transaction

Returning with the updated details allows us to ensure that the change is made correctly.

> **Note**
> Using AI-powered tools such as ChatGPT can pose *risks* associated with data integrity. A review of the results needs to be made given that AI models can hallucinate and return incorrect answers. At the same time, the training data used in developing these models may contain *biases*, which can be reflected in the responses. Thus, proper care needs to be exercised when making use of these models for data cleansing and analysis.

11. Now that we have reviewed the **Date** field, let's check the `Product_ID` and `Sales_Manager` columns. Based on the results from *Figure 10.16*, there were no indications of irregularities, but let's check anyway. Type the following in the chat:

```
Review the Product_ID and Sales_Manager columns to see if there
are any unusual values.
```

The results will look like what's shown in *Figure 10.24*:

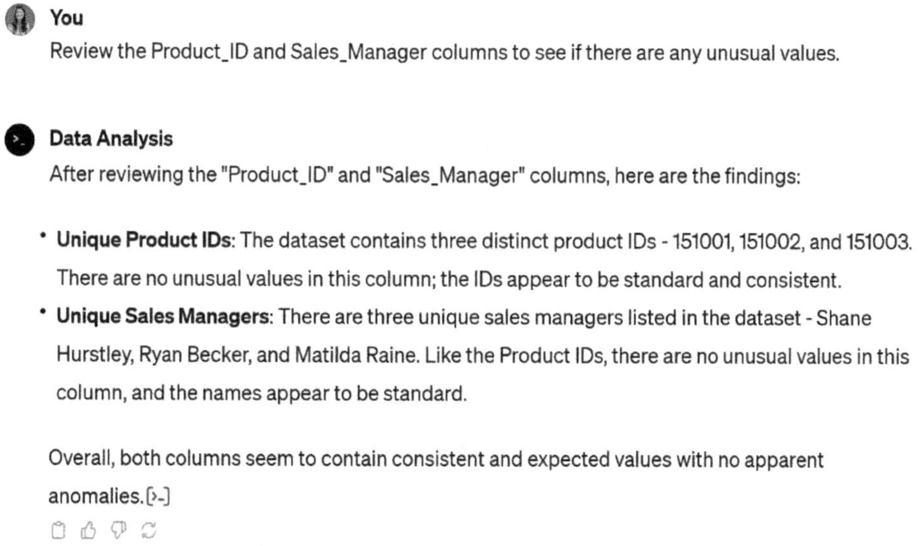
You
Review the Product_ID and Sales_Manager columns to see if there are any unusual values.
Data Analysis
After reviewing the "Product_ID" and "Sales_Manager" columns, here are the findings:
• **Unique Product IDs**: The dataset contains three distinct product IDs - 151001, 151002, and 151003. There are no unusual values in this column; the IDs appear to be standard and consistent.
• **Unique Sales Managers**: There are three unique sales managers listed in the dataset - Shane Hurstley, Ryan Becker, and Matilda Raine. Like the Product IDs, there are no unusual values in this column, and the names appear to be standard.
Overall, both columns seem to contain consistent and expected values with no apparent anomalies.

Figure 10.24 – Reviewing the Product_ID and Sales_Manager columns

We can see from the results that the details in these two columns are unique.

12. Given that there are no inconsistencies or unusual transactions for the `Product_ID` and `Sales_Manager` columns, let's move to the last step, which is reviewing the `Quantity` column. Type the following in the chat:

```
Provide the details of the top 10 transactions with the highest
quantities.
```

The results will be similar to what is shown in *Figure 10.25*:

You

Provide the details of the top 10 transactions with the highest quantities.

Data Analysis

Certainly, let's focus on the top 10 transactions with the highest quantities. I will provide you with the details for these transactions, including the transaction ID, date, product ID, sales manager, and the quantity involved. Let's retrieve this information.

Here are the details of the top 10 transactions with the highest quantities in the dataset:

Transaction ID	Transaction Date	Product_ID	Sales_Manager	Quantity
2020644	2020-10-04	151001	Ryan Becker	20,000
2020693	2020-11-22	151003	Ryan Becker	850
2020327	2020-11-22	151003	Shane Hurstley	850
2020235	2020-08-22	151003	Shane Hurstley	850
2021089	2020-12-22	151003	Matilda Raine	850
2021028	2020-10-22	151003	Matilda Raine	850
2020357	2020-12-22	151003	Shane Hurstley	850
2021059	2020-11-22	151003	Matilda Raine	850
2020967	2020-08-22	151003	Matilda Raine	850
2020662	2020-10-22	151003	Ryan Becker	850

The transaction with the highest quantity is transaction ID 2020644, with a quantity of 20,000 units. The remaining transactions in this top 10 list each have a quantity of 850 units. [>-]

Figure 10.25 – Listing the top 10 transactions based on quantity

When a quantity is highly unusual, this could *potentially* be an error or something that needs to be investigated further. Let's assume that in this scenario, during your investigation, you found that there was a manual error during the input of this transaction, and instead of `20,000`, the quantity should only be `200`.

13. Let's have this item updated by entering the following:

```
For Transaction ID 2020644, update the Quantity to 200 and show
the updated details.
```

The output will be as follows:

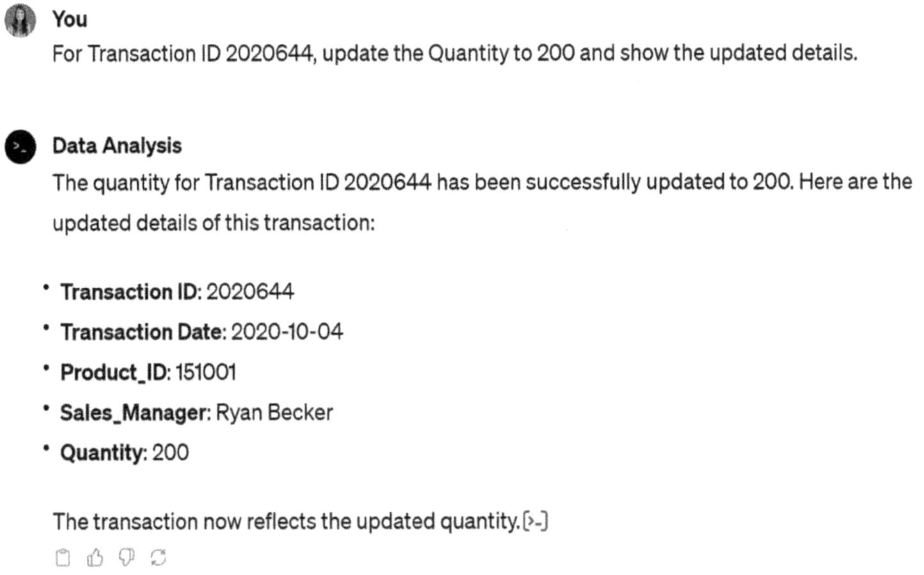
You
For Transaction ID 2020644, update the Quantity to 200 and show the updated details.
Data Analysis
The quantity for Transaction ID 2020644 has been successfully updated to 200. Here are the updated details of this transaction:
Transaction ID: 2020644
Transaction Date: 2020-10-04
Product_ID: 151001
Sales_Manager: Ryan Becker
Quantity: 200
The transaction now reflects the updated quantity.

Figure 10.26 – Correcting the quantity for the transaction

So far, we have performed the necessary steps to review the data and correct the errors to prepare for further analysis.

14. Now that we have cleaned the data, we can export the file to Excel by typing the following:

```
Export the cleaned data to an Excel file.
```

Once you press *Enter*, the file will be exported and you'll be given a link, as illustrated in *Figure 10.27*:

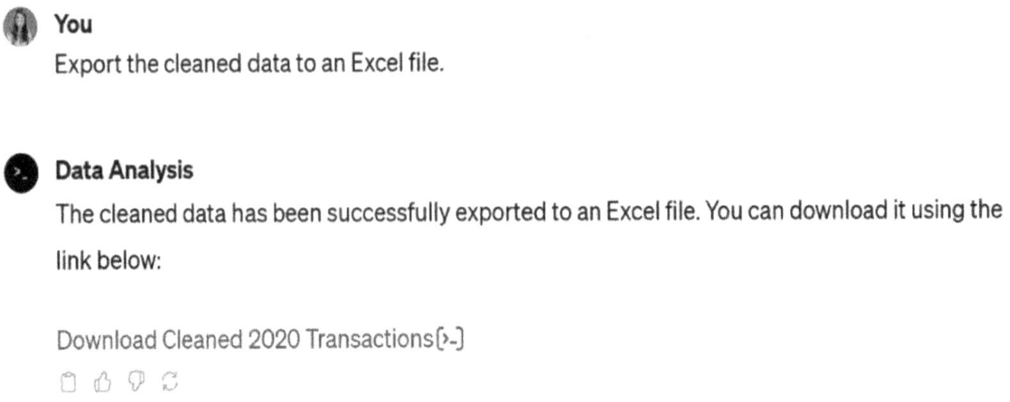
You
Export the cleaned data to an Excel file.
Data Analysis
The cleaned data has been successfully exported to an Excel file. You can download it using the link below:
Download Cleaned 2020 Transactions

Figure 10.27 – Exporting the cleaned dataset

When you click on the link, it will automatically go to your `Downloads` folder. Ensure that you download the file since you may need to upload the cleaned data in case ChatGPT is not able to retain the information from previous steps.

> **Important note**
>
> Make sure you review and check the results returned by AI-powered tools such as ChatGPT since these tools may hallucinate and return incorrect results.

ChatGPT can also create graphs and charts to help us understand the data better. In the next few steps, we will work on generating the **scatter chart** and **histogram** visualizations, similar to what we did in *Chapter 5, Using Business Intelligence Tools to Fix Data Integrity Issues*, and *Chapter 6, Implementing Best Practices When Using Business Intelligence Tools*.

15. We'll start by creating a scatter chart to show a graphical representation of the relationship between the volume of transactions (`Quantity`) and the period (`Months`). Type the following into the chat:

```
Using the original dataset uploaded, create a scatter chart with
sum of quantity on the Y-axis and the months on the X-axis.
```

ChatGPT will start generating the scatter chart based on our prompt, as shown in *Figure 10.28*:

You

Using the original dataset uploaded, create a scatter chart with sum of quantity on the Y-axis and the months on the X-axis.

Data Analysis

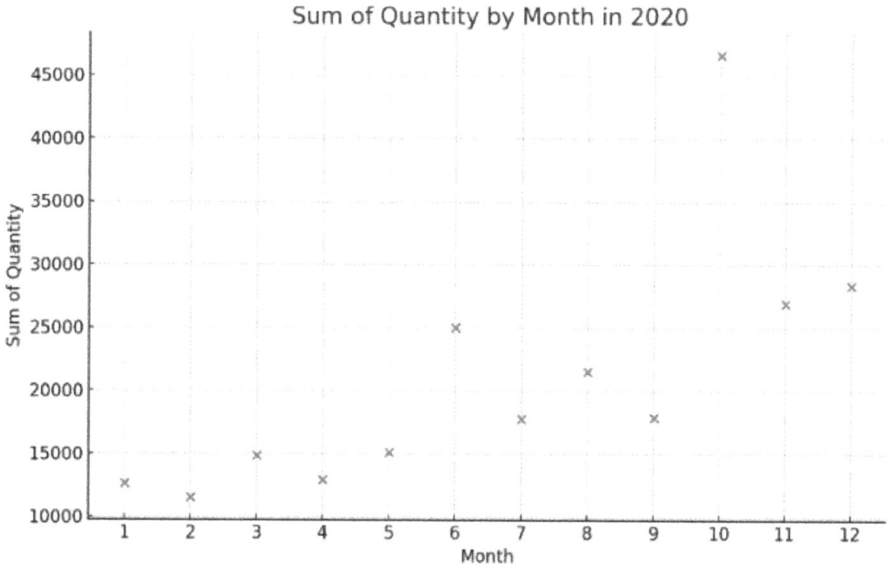

Here is the scatter chart representing the sum of quantities for each month in 2020:

- The X-axis represents each month of the year 2020, numbered from 1 (January) to 12 (December).
- The Y-axis shows the total sum of quantities for each month.

Each point on the scatter plot corresponds to a month, and its position indicates the total quantity of transactions for that particular month. This visualization provides a clear view of how the quantity of transactions varied month by month throughout the year 2020.

Figure 10.28 – Scatter chart using the original dataset

As we can see, it has created a scatter chart showing the total quantity of transactions per month and revealing data points that may be outside the normal range. This illustration is similar to what we did in *Chapter 6*, *Implementing Best Practices When Using Business Intelligence Tools*; this is shown again in *Figure 10.29*:

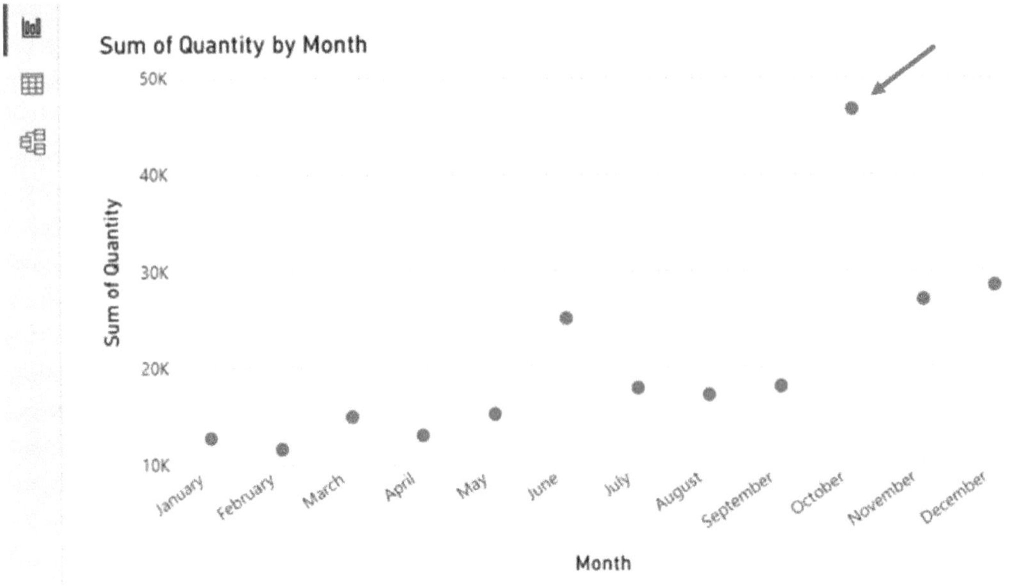

Figure 10.29 – A similar scatter chart from Chapter 6, Implementing Best Practices When Using Business Intelligence Tools

In the scatter chart we generated using ChatGPT, we can also see that the outlier we identified for October stands out.

> **Note**
>
> ChatGPT may provide a different set of answers. When this happens, consider modifying the prompt to ensure that the model provides a more accurate result.

16. How about we try asking it to create a histogram like what we did in **Tableau**? A histogram is a visual representation of the *frequency* of data points within specific ranges known as *bins*. Using a histogram makes it easier to understand how the values are distributed and assists in identifying potential outliers. To do this, let's type the following into the chat:

```
Using the original dataset, create a histogram using the
quantity column with bin size of 1,553.
```

It will create something like what's shown in *Figure 10.30*:

You

Using the original dataset, create a histogram using the quantity column with bin size of 1,553.

Data Analysis

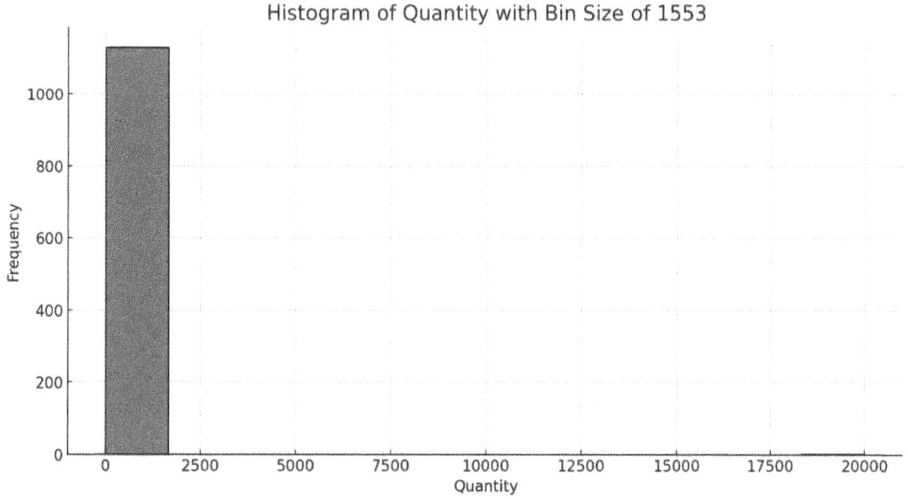

Here is the histogram based on the "Quantity" column from the original dataset, with a bin size of 1,553:

- The X-axis represents the quantity values.
- The Y-axis shows the frequency of each range of quantities.

Each bar in the histogram represents a range of quantities, and the height of the bar indicates how many transactions fall within that range. This visualization helps in understanding the distribution of quantities across the transactions in the dataset.

Figure 10.30 – Creating a histogram using the original dataset

From the histogram, we can see that the values are under the first bin and last bin, similar to what we generated in *Chapter 6, Implementing Best Practices When Using Business Intelligence Tools*. We will dive deeper into what this means in the next step.

> **Note**
>
> You might be wondering why we specifically used a bin size of `1,553` in the prompt. This is the bin size that was used to create the histogram in *Chapter 6*. Feel free to use a different one in creating the histogram. Our goal here is to see how the values in the `Quantity` column are distributed and to check whether there could be anything unusual to indicate anomalies in the data.

17. We need to get a bit more detail to know under which buckets our transactions are. Input the following prompt and then press *Enter*:

```
Under which buckets do our values fall? Include the number of
entries to understand the distribution.
```

The results will look like what's shown in *Figure 10.31*:

You

Under which buckets do our values fall? Include the number of entries to understand the distribution.

Data Analysis

Error analyzing

Here is the distribution of transaction quantities across different bins, with each bin having a size of 1,553:

Bin_Start	Bin_End	Count
0	1,552	1,128
1,553	3,105	0
3,106	4,658	0
4,659	6,211	0
6,212	7,764	0
7,765	9,317	0
9,318	10,870	0
10,871	12,423	0
12,424	13,976	0
13,977	15,529	0
15,530	17,082	0
17,083	18,635	0
18,636	20,188	1

From this table, it is evident that:

- A vast majority of the transactions (1,128 out of 1,129) involve quantities that fall within the first bin (0 to 1,552).
- Only one transaction falls in the highest bin (18,636 to 20,188), which corresponds to the transaction that had an unusually high quantity of 20,000 before it was corrected.
- All other bins between 1,553 and 18,635 have no transactions.

This distribution indicates that almost all transactions involved relatively small quantities, with just one notable exception. [>-]

Figure 10.31 – Understanding the frequency of values within each bin

From the explanation, we can see that most of the transactions are under the *first bin*, while one transaction is under the *last bin*, which is consistent with the histogram we generated. Given that one item has a quantity that is *higher than the usual range*, this can mean the presence of **outliers**.

> **Important note**
>
> If, during your session, you get an *error* message stating that there was an issue with the code execution or something similar, try **reloading the data** or **closing your browser** and opening it again. In addition to this, if you get a message that ChatGPT was *not able to retain* the information from previous interactions, **upload the files** related to the prompt. This should address this problem.

Since we previously corrected this transaction from `20,000` to `200`, let's ask ChatGPT to create another histogram using the cleaned data.

18. Type the following into the chat:

```
Using the cleaned data, create a histogram with a bin size of
100 based on the Quantity column.
```

The chart generated will be similar to:

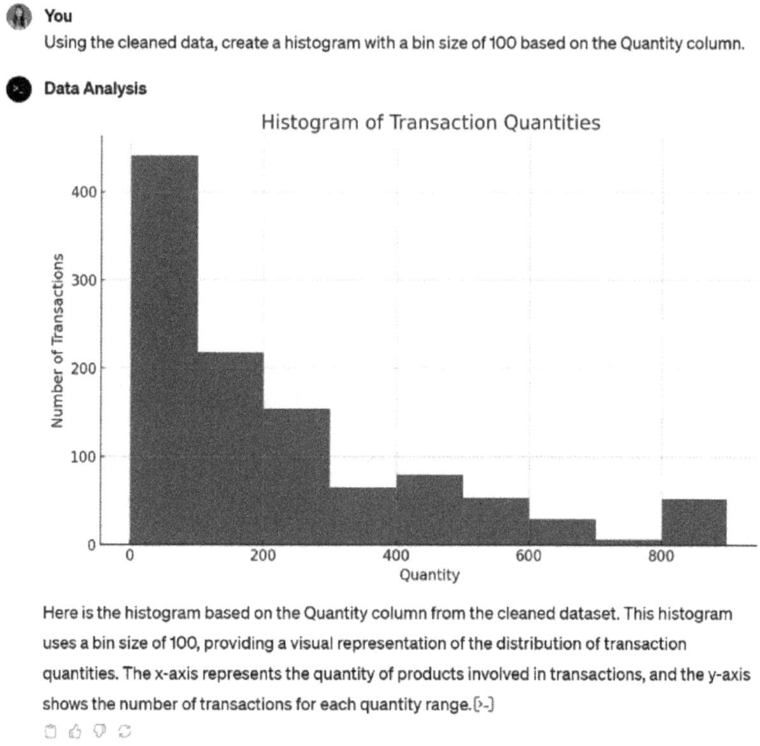
You
Using the cleaned data, create a histogram with a bin size of 100 based on the Quantity column.
Data Analysis
Histogram of Transaction Quantities
Number of Transactions
400
300
200
100
0
0
200
400
600
800
Quantity
Here is the histogram based on the Quantity column from the cleaned dataset. This histogram uses a bin size of 100, providing a visual representation of the distribution of transaction quantities. The x-axis represents the quantity of products involved in transactions, and the y-axis shows the number of transactions for each quantity range.

Figure 10.32 – Creating a histogram using the cleaned data

We created a similar visualization in Tableau in *Chapter 6*, *Implementing Best Practices When Using Business Intelligence Tools*. This has been reproduced in *Figure 10.33*:

Figure 10.33 – The histogram that was created in Tableau, as featured in Chapter 6

As we can see, we can use this tool to create visualizations that help us identify data outliers, detect anomalies, clean the data, and update the visualizations. Through this, we can enhance the integrity of the data. With the help of ChatGPT, we were able to replicate the steps we completed in previous chapters with the use of prompts and in a much more efficient manner.

You might be wondering, *What else can ChatGPT do? How about checking whether there are missing values in our data?* We will be discussing just that in the next section!

Handling missing financial reporting data with AI

In this section, we will use ChatGPT to help us understand what our sample Excel files contain and check for any outliers, missing values, and data inconsistencies. We will be using datasets created specifically for this section to get more appreciation for this tool's capabilities. The steps are as follows:

1. Create a new chat using the **Data Analysis** GPT, as shown in *Figure 10.34*. As an alternative, you may use the **Advanced Data Analysis** feature (using **GPT-4**), as shown in *Figure 10.13*:

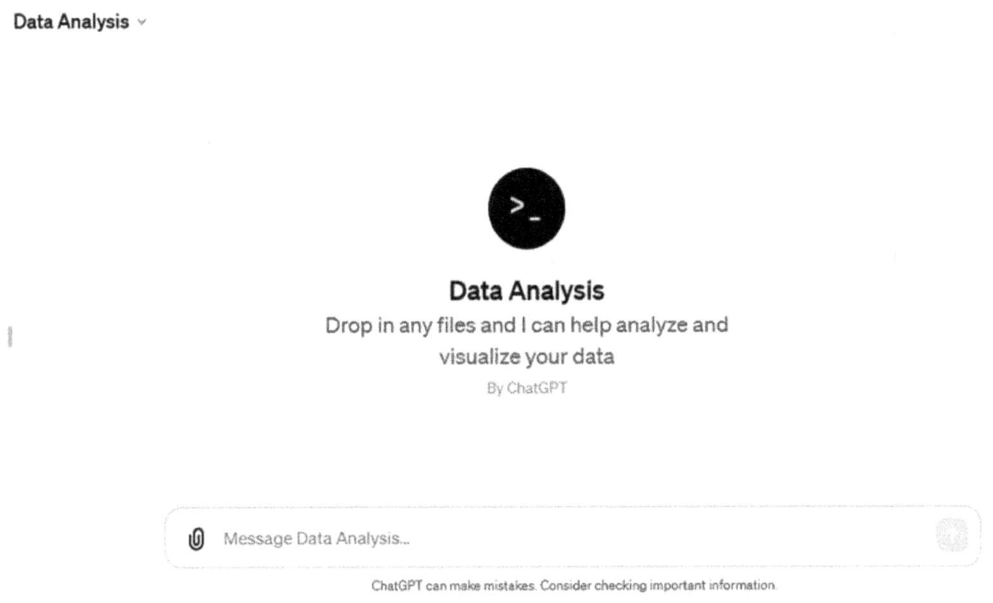
Data Analysis
Data Analysis
Drop in any files and I can help analyze and
visualize your data
By ChatGPT
Message Data Analysis...
ChatGPT can make mistakes. Consider checking important information.

Figure 10.34 – Using the Data Analysis GPT

> **Note**
> If you can't access the **Data Analysis** GPT from the **Explore** section in the sidebar, you may use this link: `https://chat.openai.com/g/g-HMNcP6w7d-data-analysis`.

2. Load the `2022 Transactions.xlsx`, `Products.xlsx`, and `Sales Price.xlsx` files and type this prompt:

```
Please examine the contents of these three files and provide
information as to their data structure and the type of data that
they contain.
```

The response will be something like what's shown in *Figure 10.35*:

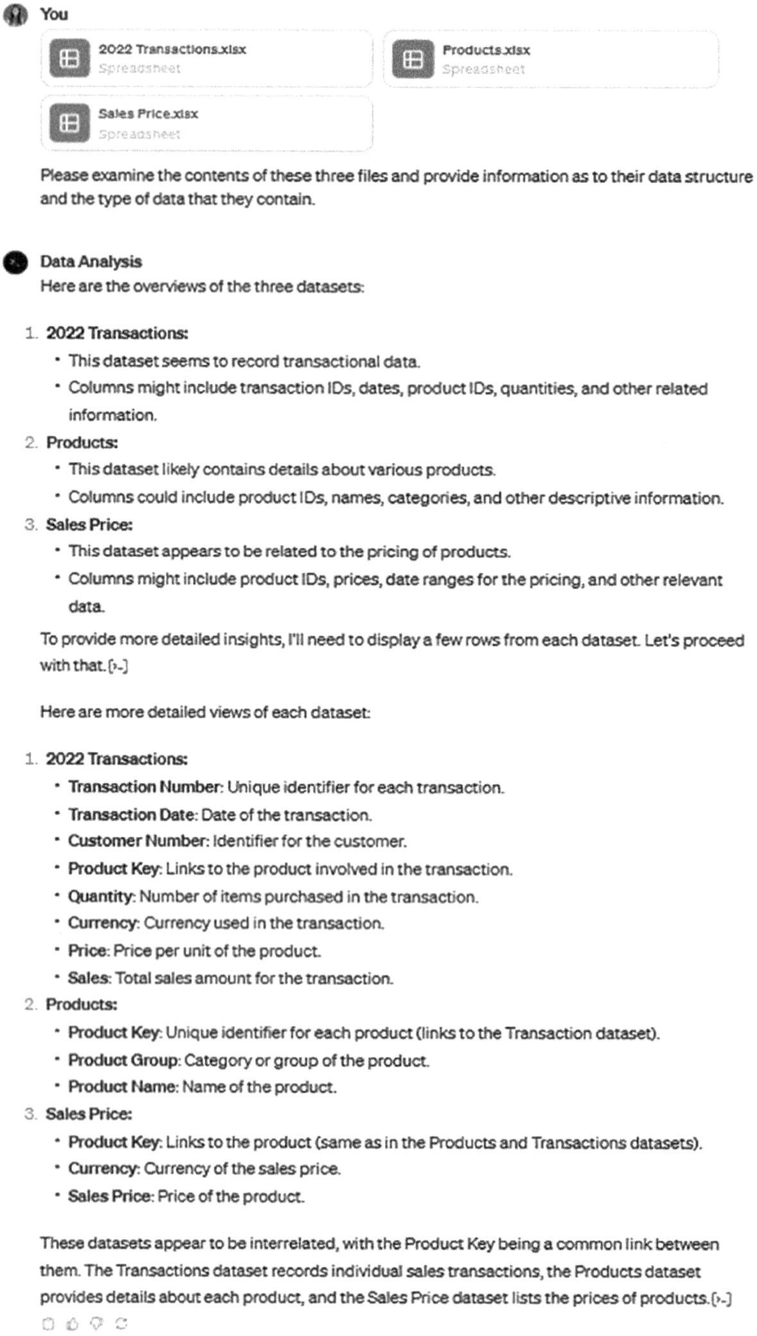

You

2022 Transactions.xlsx
Spreadsheet

Products.xlsx
Spreadsheet

Sales Price.xlsx
Spreadsheet

Please examine the contents of these three files and provide information as to their data structure and the type of data that they contain.

Data Analysis

Here are the overviews of the three datasets:

1. **2022 Transactions:**
   - This dataset seems to record transactional data.
   - Columns might include transaction IDs, dates, product IDs, quantities, and other related information.
2. **Products:**
   - This dataset likely contains details about various products.
   - Columns could include product IDs, names, categories, and other descriptive information.
3. **Sales Price:**
   - This dataset appears to be related to the pricing of products.
   - Columns might include product IDs, prices, date ranges for the pricing, and other relevant data.

To provide more detailed insights, I'll need to display a few rows from each dataset. Let's proceed with that. [>-]

Here are more detailed views of each dataset:

1. **2022 Transactions:**
   - **Transaction Number**: Unique identifier for each transaction.
   - **Transaction Date**: Date of the transaction.
   - **Customer Number**: Identifier for the customer.
   - **Product Key**: Links to the product involved in the transaction.
   - **Quantity**: Number of items purchased in the transaction.
   - **Currency**: Currency used in the transaction.
   - **Price**: Price per unit of the product.
   - **Sales**: Total sales amount for the transaction.
2. **Products:**
   - **Product Key**: Unique identifier for each product (links to the Transaction dataset).
   - **Product Group**: Category or group of the product.
   - **Product Name**: Name of the product.
3. **Sales Price:**
   - **Product Key**: Links to the product (same as in the Products and Transactions datasets).
   - **Currency**: Currency of the sales price.
   - **Sales Price**: Price of the product.

These datasets appear to be interrelated, with the Product Key being a common link between them. The Transactions dataset records individual sales transactions, the Products dataset provides details about each product, and the Sales Price dataset lists the prices of products. [>-]

Figure 10.35 – Loading the three Excel files for analysis

As we can see, ChatGPT has provided an overview of the files as well as a description of the columns for each of the files.

> **Note**
>
> If ChatGPT has given a different response, feel free to edit the prompt to something similar to `Can you examine and provide details on what data each of the files contain? Include the type of data and any notable characteristics observed.` Our intent here is to get an overall understanding of what kind of data is contained within these three files.

3. Next, let's start performing specific analysis on the files. First, we will work with the `2022 Transactions.xlsx` file and review whether there are any duplicate entries. Type this in the prompt:

```
For the 2022 Transactions.xlsx file, please check for possible
duplicate transactions using the Transaction Number.
```

The results will yield something similar to what's shown in *Figure 10.36*:

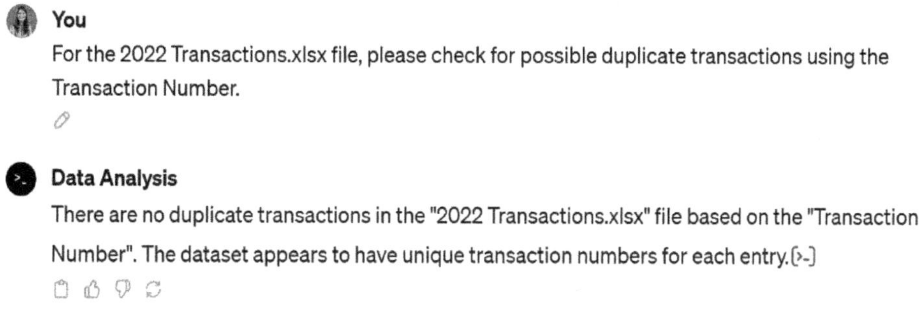
You
For the 2022 Transactions.xlsx file, please check for possible duplicate transactions using the Transaction Number.
Data Analysis
There are no duplicate transactions in the "2022 Transactions.xlsx" file based on the "Transaction Number". The dataset appears to have unique transaction numbers for each entry.

Figure 10.36 – Checking the file for duplicate transactions

> **Note**
>
> For this example, we are assuming that the `Transaction Number` value is a uniquely generated number based on the daily transactions of the company.

Great! Since there are no duplicate transactions, let's go to the next step!

4. Next, let's check whether there are any missing values in the data by inputting the following:

```
Can you check each of the columns in the 2022 Transactions.xlsx
file for any missing values?
```

ChatGPT will check the file and give us the results shown in *Figure 10.37*:

You

Can you check each of the columns in the 2022 Transactions.xlsx for any missing values?

Data Analysis

In the "2022 Transactions.xlsx" dataset, every column is complete except for the "Sales" column, which has 11 missing values. All other columns have no missing values.[>-]

Figure 10.37 – Checking for any missing values

5. Since ChatGPT has identified that there are missing values, we need to see what they are. Enter the following:

```
Can you please list the transactions with the missing values in
table format?
```

This will list the items, as shown in *Figure 10.38*:

You

Can you please list the transactions with the missing values in table format?

Data Analysis

Here are the transactions with missing values in the "Sales" column:

Transaction Number	Transaction Date	Customer Number	Product Key	Quantity	Currency	Price	Sales
32022080006	2022-08-06	10968025	10	15	USD	8.34	NaN
32022080007	2022-08-07	12860922	6	20	USD	3.25	NaN
32022080008	2022-08-07	10968025	6	25	USD	3.25	NaN
32022080009	2022-08-07	10968209	3	15	USD	3.84	NaN
32022080010	2022-08-07	12097272	3	6	USD	3.84	NaN
32022080011	2022-08-07	12609820	3	10	USD	3.84	NaN
32022080012	2022-08-08	12986902	3	15	USD	3.84	NaN
32022080013	2022-08-08	11098609	2	10	USD	1.92	NaN
32022080014	2022-08-08	11098609	2	5	USD	1.92	NaN
32022080015	2022-08-08	10968025	1	20	USD	2.56	NaN
32022080016	2022-08-08	12986902	5	5	USD	2.56	NaN

These transactions are missing the total sales amount, which is a critical piece of information for any transactional record.[>-]

Figure 10.38 – Missing values in the dataset

From the results, we can see that the values for the **Sales** column are missing; this is indicated with `NaN` (*Not a Number*). It is important to note that this is different from having a value of zero. What this suggests is that the cells are *empty* and do not contain any data. In certain cases, `NaN` is also used when the mathematical result is invalid, such as when a number is divided by *zero*. In this example, the column should have a value where **Sales** is calculated as **Price** multiplied by **Quantity**. In this case, we can ask it to calculate this column. We will do this in the next step.

6. In the chat, type the following:

```
Please calculate the Sales column by multiplying the Quantity
column with the Price column. Update the data and list the
transactions updated in table format.
```

Once we press *Enter*, ChatGPT will start creating the table. It will look something like what's shown in *Figure 10.39*:

You

Please calculate the Sales column by multiplying the Quantity column with the Price column.
Update the data and list the transactions updated in table format.

Data Analysis

Here are the updated transactions with the calculated "Sales" values:

Transaction Number	Transaction Date	Customer Number	Product Key	Quantity	Currency	Price	Sales
32022080006	2022-08-06	10968025	10	15	USD	8.34	125.10
32022080007	2022-08-07	12860922	6	20	USD	3.25	65.00
32022080008	2022-08-07	10968025	6	25	USD	3.25	81.25
32022080009	2022-08-07	10968209	3	15	USD	3.84	57.60
32022080010	2022-08-07	12097272	3	6	USD	3.84	23.04
32022080011	2022-08-07	12609820	3	10	USD	3.84	38.40
32022080012	2022-08-08	12986902	3	15	USD	3.84	57.60
32022080013	2022-08-08	11098609	2	10	USD	1.92	19.20
32022080014	2022-08-08	11098609	2	5	USD	1.92	9.60
32022080015	2022-08-08	10968025	1	20	USD	2.56	51.20
32022080016	2022-08-08	12986902	5	5	USD	2.56	12.80

These transactions now have their "Sales" values calculated and filled in.

Figure 10.39 – Updating the Sales column with missing values

As we can see, it can compute the missing values and update our data. Now that we have done that, the next steps will cover checking whether there are any outliers, missing data, or errors in the data, and using this tool to correct them.

7. In the chat, enter the following:

```
Please check the Quantity column in the 2022 Transactions.xlsx
file to see if there are any outliers.
```

It will start analyzing the file, giving us results resembling what's shown in *Figure 10.40*:

You

Please check the Quantity column in the 2022 Transactions.xlsx file to see if there are any outliers.

Data Analysis

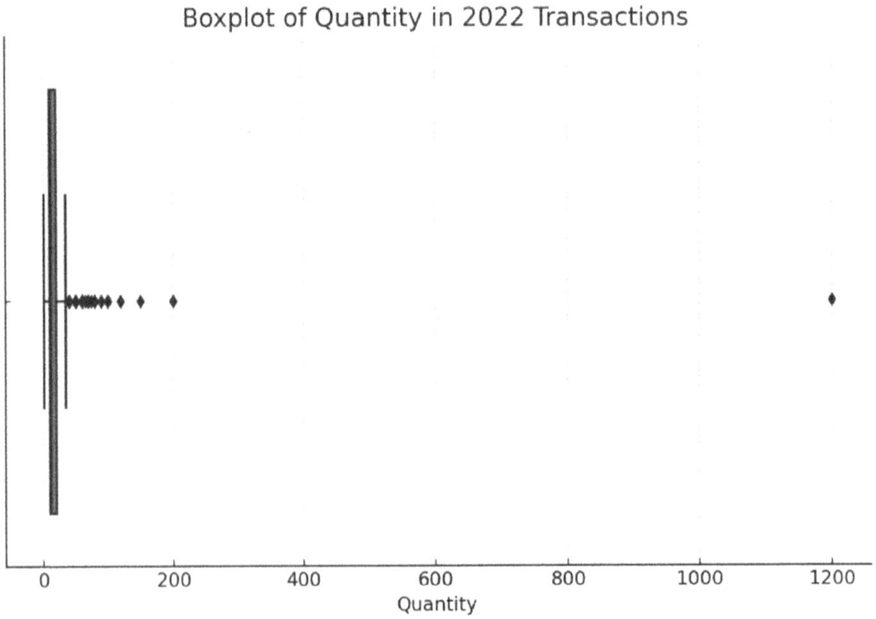

The boxplot of the "Quantity" column from the "2022 Transactions.xlsx" file indicates the presence of potential outliers. These outliers are represented by points that lie outside the interquartile range, as seen on the right side of the plot.

To further analyze these outliers, we can use statistical methods such as calculating the interquartile range and identifying values that lie outside a typical range (e.g., 1.5 times the interquartile range from the quartiles). Would you like me to perform this analysis?

Figure 10.40 – Checking for outliers in the dataset

It says in its response that there are transactions that are outside the normal range. What we can do next is check the ones with the biggest quantities.

8. Let's input the following in the chat:

```
Reviewing the Quantity column, please list in table format the
top 20 transactions with the highest quantities.
```

It will start creating a table, as shown in *Figure 10.41*:

You

Reviewing the Quantity column, please list in table format the top 20 transactions with the highest quantities.

Data Analysis

Here are the top 20 transactions with the highest quantities:

Transaction Number	Transaction Date	Customer Number	Product Key	Quantity	Currency	Price	Sales
22022110029	2022-11-12	12096820	2	1200	EUR	1.79	2148.0
22022030015	2022-03-05	16872096	2	200	EUR	1.79	358.0
22022100023	2022-10-15	12096820	6	200	EUR	2.99	598.0
12022080022	2022-08-11	16820921	3	150	AUD	5.99	898.5
22022070036	2022-07-25	12096825	3	120	EUR	3.59	430.8
22022100013	2022-10-10	12096825	6	120	EUR	2.99	358.8
22022080030	2022-08-16	13680921	1	100	EUR	2.39	239.0
12022120015	2022-12-08	12506900	2	100	AUD	2.99	299.0
12022100025	2022-10-15	15680920	6	100	AUD	4.99	499.0
32022100025	2022-10-15	12609820	1	100	USD	2.56	256.0
22022110026	2022-11-09	16872096	2	100	EUR	1.79	179.0
22022120015	2022-12-08	12930562	2	100	EUR	1.79	179.0
12022080005	2022-08-05	16920915	9	100	AUD	4.99	499.0
22022100025	2022-10-15	12930562	6	100	EUR	2.99	299.0
32022120015	2022-12-08	12860922	2	100	USD	1.92	192.0
22022070028	2022-07-16	12096820	6	90	EUR	2.99	269.1
22022060034	2022-06-25	13680921	3	90	EUR	3.59	323.1
22022010047	2022-01-30	11209860	6	90	EUR	2.99	269.1
22022080039	2022-08-20	12096827	6	80	EUR	2.99	239.2
22022090035	2022-09-24	12096827	6	80	EUR	2.99	239.2

These transactions represent the highest quantities sold in a single transaction for the year 2022.

Figure 10.41 – Showing the top 20 transactions

Next, we must check these items one by one, starting with the first one. We can view the invoices and match the details with what is in the report. For the first one, assume that you noted an error in the data and that instead of `1,200`, it should only be `120`.

9. To correct the data, we can input the change needed, and ChatGPT will update the data:

```
I reviewed the invoice for Transaction Number 22022110029. The
quantity should only be 120. Please update it and show me the
updated columns for this transaction.
```

It will start updating the information and provide results similar to what's shown in *Figure 10.42*:

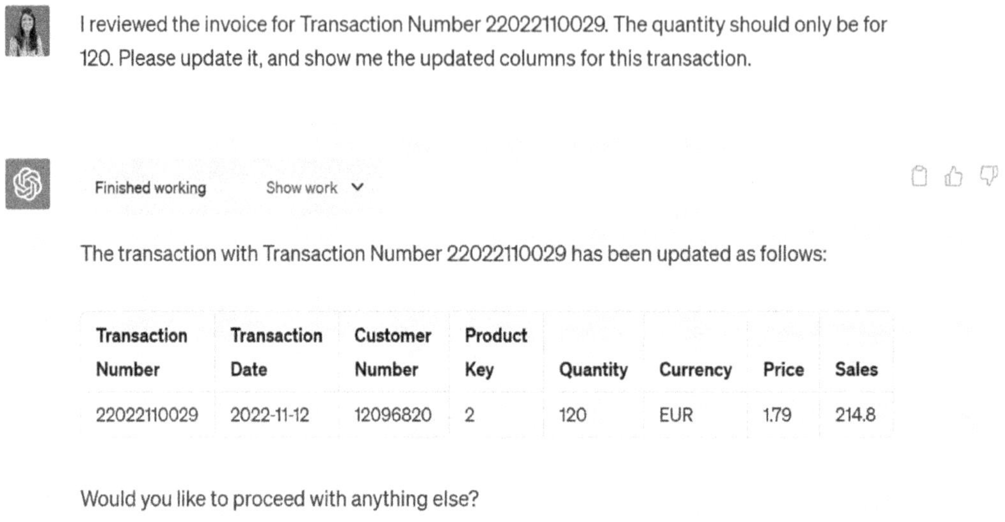

I reviewed the invoice for Transaction Number 22022110029. The quantity should only be for 120. Please update it, and show me the updated columns for this transaction.

Finished working Show work

The transaction with Transaction Number 22022110029 has been updated as follows:

Transaction Number	Transaction Date	Customer Number	Product Key	Quantity	Currency	Price	Sales
22022110029	2022-11-12	12096820	2	120	EUR	1.79	214.8

Would you like to proceed with anything else?

Figure 10.42 – Updating the Quantity column

In the previous steps, we reviewed the `2022 Transactions.xlsx` file. Next, we will match the prices and the products between the `Sales Price.xlsx` and `Products.xlsx` files.

10. Let's input the following in the chat:

```
Please review the Currency column and Price column in the 2022
Transactions.xlsx file with the Sales Price.xlsx file. If there
are any inconsistencies, please list them in table format and
add a column for the price difference.
```

This will provide us with the following findings:

You

Please review the Currency column and Price column in the 2022 Transactions.xlsx file with the Sales Price.xlsx file. If there are any inconsistencies, please list them in table format and add a column for the price difference.

Data Analysis

Error analyzing

It appears there was an issue with accessing the columns after merging the datasets. The column names might not have been aligned correctly. I will correct this and proceed to identify any inconsistencies between the "Currency" and "Price" columns in the "2022 Transactions.xlsx" file and the "Sales Price.xlsx" file. Let me retry that analysis.

Here are the transactions with inconsistencies between the transaction price and the sales price, along with the price difference:

Transaction Number	Transaction Date	Product Key	Currency	Transaction Price	Sales Price	Price Difference
32022110042	2022-11-25	6	USD	3.00	3.25	-0.25
32022110043	2022-11-26	6	USD	3.00	3.25	-0.25
32022110044	2022-11-27	6	USD	3.00	3.25	-0.25
32022110045	2022-11-28	1	USD	2.20	2.56	-0.36
32022110046	2022-11-29	2	USD	1.50	1.92	-0.42
32022110047	2022-11-30	3	USD	3.20	3.84	-0.64
32022110048	2022-11-30	5	USD	2.10	2.56	-0.46

These discrepancies indicate that the transaction prices for these specific transactions were lower than the expected sales prices listed in the "Sales Price.xlsx" file.

Figure 10.43 – Conducting the initial price review

From the results, we can see that it has identified seven transactions that have discrepancies.

11. Next, we can create a prompt to calculate how much the difference is in terms of sales:

```
Get the Quantity column for each of the transactions above and
use this to calculate the total price difference. List them in a
table format and include an overall total as well.
```

This will create a table, as shown in *Figure 10.44*, showing how much the difference is for each transaction:

You

Get the Quantity column for each of the transactions and use this to calculate the total price difference. List them in table format and include an overall total as well.

Data Analysis

Here are the transactions with their respective price discrepancies and the total price difference for each transaction, along with the overall total:

Transaction Number	Transaction Date	Product Key	Currency	Quantity	Price Difference	Total Price Difference
32022110042	2022-11-25	6	USD	10	-0.25	-2.5
32022110043	2022-11-26	6	USD	10	-0.25	-2.5
32022110044	2022-11-27	6	USD	10	-0.25	-2.5
32022110045	2022-11-28	1	USD	5	-0.36	-1.8
32022110046	2022-11-29	2	USD	20	-0.42	-8.4
32022110047	2022-11-30	3	USD	5	-0.64	-3.2
32022110048	2022-11-30	5	USD	5	-0.46	-2.3

Overall Total Price Difference:

- USD -23.20

This overall total indicates the cumulative impact of the price discrepancies across these transactions.[>-]

Figure 10.44 – Calculating the price variance

Assume that during your review with the sales manager, it was explained that the reason for the sales difference was the *sales discount* given to customers during *Thanksgiving*. You also *matched* it with the invoices. Thus, the records are correct and there is *no* need to update the sales price in the data.

At this point, we have checked both the quantity and price used in our sales transactions. We can now check the total sales or revenue for *each* product and ask ChatGPT to review whether all the products in the `Sales Transactions.xlsx` file are in the `Products.xlsx` file. We will cover this in the last part of this section.

12. Enter the following prompt:

```
Calculate the sales for each Product key in the 2022
Transactions.xlsx file and match it with the Products.xlsx file.
```

ChatGPT will analyze the two files and return something like what's shown in *Figure 10.45*:

You

Calculate the total sales for each Product Key in the 2022 Transactions.xlsx file and match it with the Products.xlsx file.

Data Analysis

Here are the total sales for each Product Key in the "2022 Transactions.xlsx" file, matched with the corresponding information from the "Products.xlsx" file:

Product Key	Total Sales	Product Group	Product Name
1	$9,787.15	Binders	Insert binder
2	$10,982.36	Binders	Ring binder
3	$23,023.52	Binders	Divider
4	$7,093.59	Boxes and storage	Archive box
5	$6,687.73	Boxes and storage	Document box
6	$32,355.34	Boxes and storage	Plastic box
7	$7,849.91	Boxes and storage	File storage
9	$6,475.81	Desk organizers	File rack
10	$16,170.17	Desk organizers	Desktop drawer

These figures represent the total sales amount for each product throughout the year 2022, providing a clear picture of the sales performance of each product.

Figure 10.45 – Checking the product key in the two files

ChatGPT states that there are nine products in total in the `Products.xlsx` file, including the total sales for each product key. However, we have not been specific enough in our initial prompt about what we want it to do. In this part, we want to ensure that there are no **orphaned records** or those *where the relationship with the parent records does not exist*. If we look at the results in *Figure 10.45*, we can see that there is no `Product Key 8`, which can indicate that this is *missing*.

> **Note**
>
> To learn more about what **orphaned records** are, refer to the *Managing orphaned records* section in *Chapter 6, Implementing Best Practices When Using Business Intelligence Tools.*

If we do not perform this check to identify these items, the risk would be that there could be potential missing data that we are not able to capture in our analysis. *What if we decided to get the total sales or revenue based on the* `Products.xlsx` *file and not match this with the total revenue based on the* `2022 Transactions.xlsx` *file?*

13. Next, let's input the following:

```
Can we make sure that all the products sold found in the 2022
Transactions.xlsx file are in the Products.xlsx file?
```

We'll receive the following output:

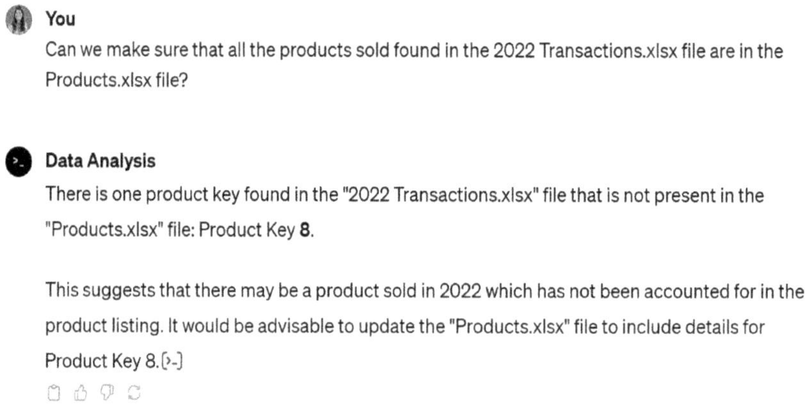
You
Can we make sure that all the products sold found in the 2022 Transactions.xlsx file are in the Products.xlsx file?
Data Analysis
There is one product key found in the "2022 Transactions.xlsx" file that is not present in the "Products.xlsx" file: Product Key 8.
This suggests that there may be a product sold in 2022 which has not been accounted for in the product listing. It would be advisable to update the "Products.xlsx" file to include details for Product Key 8.

Figure 10.46 – Product Key identified as not being in the 2022 Transactions.xlsx file

In the review, it found that there is one `Product Key` that is not in the `Products.xlsx` file. *What could have happened?* Perhaps it was deleted by mistake or removed accidentally. Assume that when you checked an earlier version of the `Products.xlsx` file, `Product Key 8` was there and it was for **Calculators**.

After, you gathered some more information by discussing it with the operations team and found that **Calculators** were removed and discontinued midway through the year as they were not selling as much. Given this information, you decided to have the latest `Products.xlsx` file updated.

14. Input the following into the chat:

```
Please update the Products.xlsx file with the details of Product
Key 8 to Calculator.
```

ChatGPT will proceed to update the file and provide you with a link to download it, as shown in *Figure 10.47*:

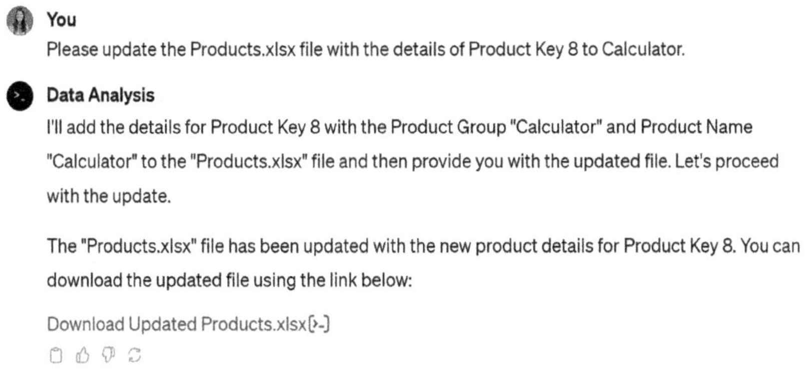
You
Please update the Products.xlsx file with the details of Product Key 8 to Calculator.
Data Analysis
I'll add the details for Product Key 8 with the Product Group "Calculator" and Product Name "Calculator" to the "Products.xlsx" file and then provide you with the updated file. Let's proceed with the update.
The "Products.xlsx" file has been updated with the new product details for Product Key 8. You can download the updated file using the link below:
Download Updated Products.xlsx

Figure 10.47 – Updating the additional product key in the dataset

Now that we have the updated products, we also need to get the updated `2022 Transactions.xlsx` file. Since we did not change anything in the `Sales Price.xlsx` file, we do not need to get an updated version.

15. Type the following into the chat:

```
Please export the updated 2022 Transactions.xlsx file which
reflects the changes we have made.
```

This will export the file and give you the download link, as shown in *Figure 10.48*:

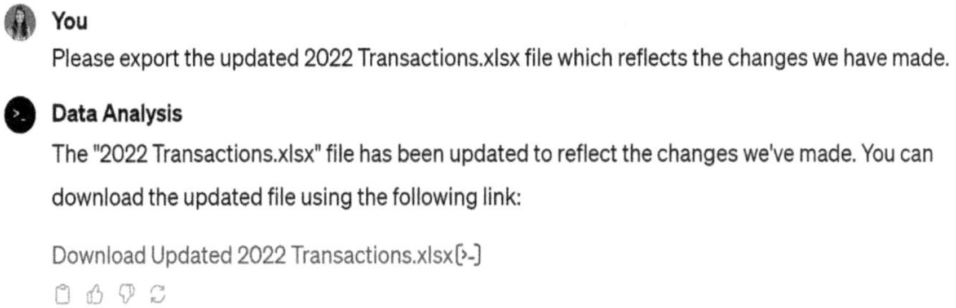
You
Please export the updated 2022 Transactions.xlsx file which reflects the changes we have made.
Data Analysis
The "2022 Transactions.xlsx" file has been updated to reflect the changes we've made. You can download the updated file using the following link:
Download Updated 2022 Transactions.xlsx

Figure 10.48 – Generating the updated 2022 Transactions.xlsx file

When you click on the links, the files will go to your `Downloads` folder.

> **Note**
>
> Make sure that you verify the results generated and the file downloaded to see whether the changes we made earlier have been reflected. This is to ensure accuracy given that AI tools may make mistakes.

That's it for our hands-on examples! I hope you now have a better grasp of how you can use this tool for data analysis and ensuring data integrity. Take some time to practice and familiarize yourself with this tool to get more comfortable using it every day!

With that, let's head to the last section of this chapter!

Best practices when using AI for data integrity management

Here are some of the best practices you can make use of when utilizing AI to improve the quality and integrity of your data:

- **Clearly state your goals**: Before you make use of an AI model, ensure that you are clear about what you want to accomplish. Knowing this will help guide you in your decisions in *selecting* the AI tool or *developing* the model to use for data cleansing, validation, governance, and compliance.
- **Create clear and effective prompts**: When using AI models, especially for generating content or answers to questions, it's essential to prepare prompts that are concise and specific to the desired outcome. This gives rise to the importance of **prompt engineering**, which is a *method of developing well-defined prompts* to help ensure that the AI or language model understands the context and your requirements to produce relevant and accurate results.

> Note
>
> **Creating well-structured prompts** is key to obtaining the desired output from an AI model. This is similar to talking to a friend, where the *depth* and *quality* of your questions determine the kind of conversation you will have. The more specific the details we provide and the more context we frame our questions with, the better and more meaningful the interaction will be.
>
> For example, when we ask ChatGPT to review a certain file, we can input vague prompts such as *Analyze these files.* or *Summarize the data in these files for me.* However, these prompts lack *clarity* and are *not specific* enough to indicate what type of analysis to perform, or what aspects of the data are important to the user. Using these prompts will most likely lead to output that is not aligned with the user's expectations, or analysis that does not provide value.
>
> Consider, on the other hand, this prompt: *Please examine the contents of these three Excel files and provide information as to their data structure and the type of data that they contain.* Here, we included specific details on the type of files and a clearer objective on what kind of analysis to perform. Through **effective prompt engineering**, we can generate responses that are more relevant and meaningful to our needs.

- **Maintain ethical standards**: When creating artificial or generated data, it is important to make sure the AI system adheres to ethical guidelines and legal requirements. Companies such as **OpenAI** and **Google** have implemented guardrails to ensure that their platforms are not misused to spread misinformation or to compromise the reliability of the data. Unethical prompts such as "*Generate a financial forecast that results in an overstated profit margin to attract investors.*" or "*Create fake sales data to bloat the revenue results.*" may lead to the AI refusing to comply with such requests, might flag the conversation for review because of mechanisms in place, or may lead to being banned from using the service.
- **Verify and test generated data**: Before using any data produced by AI, it is essential to put it through thorough validation checks before relying on the data it produces. The results that are generated can be very persuasive. However, given that hallucinations occur, verification steps need to be performed to minimize the risk of relying on incorrect information. In addition to this, you must be aware that the responses of these AI tools may change without warning. AI can make your work faster and more efficient. However, *AI tools and solutions are not immune to potential errors and mistakes*, which is why it is necessary to validate and check the results that are generated.
- **Review the data privacy policy guidelines**: Before utilizing AI tools, especially those with third-party subscriptions, it is best practice to review the *data privacy* guidelines. This is important since personal or confidential data might be used for other purposes or even shared with other companies. Understanding how the data is managed is critical for data privacy and integrity.

At this point, you should have a better understanding of what AI-powered solutions can do and how these can help accelerate various data quality management processes. At the same time, you have familiarized yourself with some of the relevant best practices when using AI for data integrity management.

Summary

In this final chapter, we discussed how we can utilize AI for data quality management. At the start, we covered what AI is as well as its applications in finance. After that, we worked on hands-on examples to detect **anomalies** in financial transactions using a generative AI solution called ChatGPT. We gained an appreciation of how we can use this tool to produce similar results as we did in previous chapters. Then, we dived deeper into how we can use this tool to find **missing data** entries and values in our transactions and correct them. Lastly, we discussed the **best practices** to make the most out of AI-powered tools and solutions for data integrity.

Congratulations on finishing this book! I hope you found this to be an incredible journey considering we've covered different practical solutions to address various data integrity issues and challenges. If there are areas or topics that are unfamiliar to you, feel free to go back and review them again. At the same time, I have included additional references under the *Further reading* section to help in understanding the topics better.

Further reading

For more information on the topics we covered, feel free to check out the following resources:

- *The economic potential of generative AI: The next productivity frontier*: `https://www.mckinsey.com/capabilities/mckinsey-digital/our-insights/the-economic-potential-of-generative-ai-the-next-productivity-frontier`
- *Gartner Experts Answer the Top Generative AI Questions for Your Enterprise*: `https://www.gartner.com/en/topics/generative-ai`
- *ChatGPT Code Interpreter: What It Is and How It Works*: `https://365datascience.com/trending/chatgpt-code-interpreter-what-it-is-and-how-it-works/`
- *Will ChatGPT Put Data Analysts Out of Work?*: `https://www.forbes.com/sites/bernardmarr/2023/02/07/will-chatgpt-put-data-analysts-out-of-work/?sh=76a468494030`
- *Embracing Generative AI: Opportunities and Risks for CFOs*: `https://www.forbes.com/sites/jackmccullough/2023/08/21/embracing-generative-ai-opportunities-and-risks-for-cfos/?sh=787b553057f7`
- *Introducing GPTs*: `https://openai.com/blog/introducing-gpts`
- *File uploads with GPTs and Advanced Data Analysis in ChatGPT*: `https://help.openai.com/en/articles/8555545-file-uploads-with-gpts-and-advanced-data-analysis-in-chatgpt`
- *Generative AI in the Finance Function of the Future*: `https://www.bcg.com/publications/2023/generative-ai-in-finance-and-accounting`

Index

A

B

H

I

J

K

L

M

S

T

U

V

W

X

Other Books You May Enjoy

If you enjoyed this book, you may be interested in these other books by Packt:

Driving Data Quality with Data Contracts

Andrew Jones

ISBN: 9781837635009

- Gain insights into the intricacies and shortcomings of today's data architectures
- Understand exactly how data contracts can solve prevalent data challenges
- Drive a fundamental transformation of your data culture by implementing data contracts
- Discover what goes into a data contract and why it's important
- Design a modern data architecture that leverages the power of data contracts
- Explore sample implementations to get practical knowledge of using data contracts
- Embrace best practices for the successful deployment of data contracts

Practical Data Quality

Robert Hawker

ISBN: 9781804610787

- Explore data quality and see how it fits within a data management programme
- Differentiate your organization from its peers through data quality improvement
- Create a business case and get support for your data quality initiative
- Find out how business strategy can be linked to processes, analytics, and data to derive only the most important data quality rules
- Monitor data through engaging, business-friendly data quality dashboards
- Integrate data quality into everyday business activities to help achieve goals
- Avoid common mistakes when implementing data quality practices

Packt is searching for authors like you

If you're interested in becoming an author for Packt, please visit `authors.packtpub.com` and apply today. We have worked with thousands of developers and tech professionals, just like you, to help them share their insight with the global tech community. You can make a general application, apply for a specific hot topic that we are recruiting an author for, or submit your own idea.

Share your thoughts

Now you've finished *Managing Data Integrity for Finance*, we'd love to hear your thoughts! If you purchased the book from Amazon, please click here to go straight to the Amazon review page for this book and share your feedback or leave a review on the site that you purchased it from.

Your review is important to us and the tech community and will help us make sure we're delivering excellent quality content.

Download a free PDF copy of this book

Thanks for purchasing this book!

Do you like to read on the go but are unable to carry your print books everywhere?

Is your eBook purchase not compatible with the device of your choice?

Don't worry, now with every Packt book you get a DRM-free PDF version of that book at no cost.

Read anywhere, any place, on any device. Search, copy, and paste code from your favorite technical books directly into your application.

The perks don't stop there, you can get exclusive access to discounts, newsletters, and great free content in your inbox daily

Follow these simple steps to get the benefits:

1. Scan the QR code or visit the link below

   `https://packt.link/free-ebook/9781837630141`

2. Submit your proof of purchase
3. That's it! We'll send your free PDF and other benefits to your email directly

www.ingramcontent.com/pod-product-compliance
Lightning Source LLC
LaVergne TN
LVHW080111070326
832902LV00015B/2516
* 9 7 8 1 8 3 7 6 3 0 1 4 1 *